Introduction to Humans in Engineered Systems

Roger Remington
Deborah Boehm-Davis
Charles Folk

WILEY

JOHN WILEY & SONS, INC.

Published by John Wiley & Sons, Inc., Hoboken, New Jersey
Published simultaneously in Canada

For general information about our other products and services, please contact our Customer Care Department within the United States at (800) 762-2974, outside the United States at (317) 572-3993 or fax (317) 572-4002.

Wiley publishes in a variety of print and electronic formats and by print-on-demand. Some material included with standard print versions of this book may not be included in e-books or in print-on-demand. If this book refers to media such as a CD or DVD that is not included in the version you purchased, you may download this material at http://booksupport.wiley.com. For more information about Wiley products, visit www.wiley.com.

Library of Congress Cataloging-in-Publication Data:

Remington, Roger W., 1947-
    Introduction to humans in engineered systems / Roger Remington, Charles L. Folk, Deborah Boehm-Davis.
      pages   cm
    Includes index.
    Includes bibliographical references.
    ISBN 978-0-470-54875-2 (hardback); ISBN 978-1-118-32995-5 (ebk); ISBN 978-1-118-33222-1 (ebk);
    ISBN 978-1-118-33271-9 (ebk); ISBN 978-1-118-39373-4 (ebk); ISBN 978-1-118-39375-8 (ebk);
    ISBN 978-1-118-39376-5 (ebk); ISBN 978-1-118-50762-9 (ebk)
      1. Human engineering.   I. Folk, Charles L.   II. Boehm-Davis, Deborah Ann.   III. Title.
    T59.7.R46   2013
    620.8'2—dc23
                                                                                          2012026243

Printed in the United States of America
10 9 8 7 6 5 4 3 2 1

*Dedicated to Karen Remington, Stuart Davis, and Valerie Greaud Folk
for all their love and support during this project, as always.*

Contents

Part III   The Human Element   101

10   Central Processing Limitations on Multitasking   181

11   Memory   210

Preface

Courses on human factors, human-system integration, engineering psychology, human-computer interaction, or applied psychology, though varying in specific content or approach, all share a common concern with the human as part of a system built by humans. The title of this book—*Introduction to Humans in Engineered Systems*—reflects that common link. Our core idea was to develop a program for the study of human-system integration based on the combination of a concept-oriented text with a flexible, interactive website. The book is designed to introduce major concepts and principles common across the various disciplines. As an integrating factor, the material is organized around the flow of information in control theoretic diagrams. A high-level treatment of control theory is a powerful way to link the various system elements, including the human, and to guide the analysis of real-world situations. The website (http://www.wiley.com/go/remington) provides a resource for pursuing topics in more depth. The website is conceived as a collection of exercises complete with the necessary programs to demonstrate concepts, case studies that provide a foundation for discussion, links to interesting demonstrations online, and material on topics not covered in detail in the text.

One of the underlying principles of control theory is that the behavior of human operators cannot be fully understood in terms of just mental and physical capabilities. It is necessary also to understand the goals the operator attempts to attain, the system being controlled (aircraft, car, computer), and the influence of the environment in which the system is embedded (including other people). The organization of the text reflects this focus on the human in context by treating four broad thematic areas.

Historical Perspective. This section is designed to prepare the reader for the material in later chapters by providing a fundamental understanding of the human as a component of a system. The concept of human-system integration is introduced with emphasis on systems-level thinking. A brief history chronicles the key role that usability has played in technological progress throughout human history, and documents how the increasing complexity of machinery and manufacturing has given rise to the modern study of human-system integration. Related disciplines (e.g., organizational psychology, engineering psychology) are discussed in terms of how they overlap with, or are different from, human-system integration.

The Environment. This goal of this section is to build awareness of the range of challenges posed by environments that characterize home and work. The key concepts introduced are adaptability and complexity. Because people are adaptable, the demands and incentives of the environment itself are strong determinants of behavior. Reliance on adaptability is seen in management approaches that emphasize a rule-governed, procedural, or incentive-based environment. Limits on adaptability are introduced through a discussion of environmental complexity and its role in human-system performance. Comparisons of fields such as medicine, transportation, and human-computer interaction provide examples of how different environments place different demands on human performance.

This section also introduces the kinds of quantitative techniques that characterize modern human-system analysis. This introduction will familiarize students with task analysis techniques, information theory, finite-state analysis, and signal-detection theory; and provide a brief introduction to human-system modeling. The key organizing concept introduced here, and used throughout the book, is control theory. Control theory is treated at a conceptual level to provide a framework for representing the flow of information in a way that highlights the interaction of all the components of the system. We introduce noise as a real factor in performance, and emphasize the contribution of feedback and lag as issues in human usability. Thus, this section is designed to provide the concepts and knowledge necessary to recognize the potential for user-related issues.

The Human Element. In the first two sections, the human is treated as an adaptable component of the entire system. This section introduces the student to the limits on that adaptability by characterizing human capabilities and limitations in information processing. The control theory framework is again used to represent the flow from perception to situation understanding, from situation understanding to action, and from action back to perception. The key points are not just that people have limited processing capacity, but that we are limited in particular ways which have implications when humans occupy decision-making roles in complex systems. Although all of the many aspects of human behavior are potentially relevant to human-system performance, this section focuses on key characteristics that strongly shape behavior in human-system interactions. To aid students in understanding the range of behavior, we distinguish the characteristics of human behavior associated with the *structural* properties of the human information-processing system (i.e., the visual and auditory sensory systems, the role of attention in mediating perception, and limits on multitasking) from those associated with the *contents* of the information-processing system (i.e., memory storage/retrieval and decision making/action selection). Structural factors in general determine the limits on how much information can be processed, whereas content factors determine how that information is used. We emphasize that this distinction is somewhat artificial, in that behavior is ultimately the joint product of these two. Nonetheless, it can be helpful to students in making sense of the large body of literature on human behavior.

Human-System Integration. Up to this point, students have been presented with a broad understanding of the discipline, knowledge of techniques for inquiring into system performance, and how the information-processing and decision characteristics of humans shape performance. In this final section, we present an analysis of an illustrative case history (the *Exxon Valdez* disaster) with the goal of showing how concepts and principles in the first three sections can be applied to the analysis of real-world situations, again within the context of a control theory framework. The key idea is that common intuition can be replaced by a structured approach to thinking about systems outcomes. Thus, this section examines how the environment, the human element, and the task to be performed come together to affect system performance. Operational constructs of situation awareness, workload, human error, and usability are discussed in terms of the underlying psychological principles developed in the first three sections.

The website (http://www.wiley.com/go/remington) complements the text and is structured around modules. Each module is structured into sections, as appropriate, including the goal of the module, description of the exercise, materials needed, instructions, readings for further information, and reference to the corresponding book section. Some modules contain questions and descriptions of case studies that can be used as the basis for discussion. Others contain interactive exercises that either demonstrate phenomena (e.g., control order) or provide opportunities for students to further explore material described in the book (e.g., task analysis). Links to demonstrations available on the web that illustrate basic psychological phenomena are also provided. Finally, some modules focus on material not covered in depth in the text (e.g., anthropometry). The website is designed to grow over time to include additional modules and materials; we also intend to update the modules to keep the material fresh. For example, we anticipate that as new technologies (for example, the iPhone) are introduced, articles and examples of them will be incorporated into the site. The instructor can tailor these modules to meet various pedagogical goals. Some of the modules will be suitable for undergraduates at the junior or senior level, others more suitable for graduate courses. Instructors also can select web modules as desired to focus on topics as they see fit. Thus, engineering departments may choose modules associated with finite-state modeling of systems, whereas human factors courses may focus on the task analysis modules, and engineering psychology classes may omit both and instead add extra modules on auditory processing. We hope that instructors who adopt the book will contact us with suggestions for new topics that they would like to see covered.

As with any project, this one consumed a great deal of time and effort. We thank those who helped us along the way, including Shayne Loft, Beth Lyall, Jennifer McKneely, and Hal Pashler, who read the book and provided us with many suggestions for improvements (although they should not be faulted for any remaining inaccuracies); and Rebecca Davis, who helped us with reference checking and indexing, as well as editorial feedback. We thank David Kidd, Brian Taylor, and Nicole Werner, who developed the initial ideas and structure for the exercises included in our website. We also thank our (very) patient spouses, Karen Remington, Stuart Davis, and Valerie Folk, who gave us the space we needed to produce the program we desired. Without their support, this project would not have been possible.

Roger Remington, Deborah Boehm-Davis,
Charles Folk

Part I

Historical Perspective

On 19 April 1770, James Cook, captain of HMS *Endeavor*, made the first direct recorded observations of the indigenous peoples of Australia, commonly referred to as aboriginals. They were of the Greagl tribe, whose territory was the area around what is today Sydney in southeastern Australia. The Greagl were but one of thousands of small groups of hunter-gatherers scattered across the continent. To the European sailors, the aboriginals seemed desperately primitive. For the most part they were naked, bathed in the grease of a native marsupial (the Australian possum) to protect them from the swarming flies and mosquitoes. They built no impressive shelters, nor did they appear to have permanent settlements. The sailors had previously encountered primitive natives in Patagonia along the banks of the Straits of Magellan. Yet the aboriginals seemed to lack even the accoutrements of these primitive natives. Despite this, the aboriginals showed a high degree of social organization, had a remarkable knowledge of the flora and fauna of their territory, possessed an impressive array of hand tools for hunting and fire sticks for keeping fires lit, and were skilled at acquiring ochre and other minerals for painting. As many Europeans would discover to their dismay, their spears could strike with deadly accuracy, and they were skilled in the use of spear throwers. European explorers and settlers were also to discover new tools, as for example, the boomerang and didgeridoo. Everywhere the explorers of the great age of discovery ventured and found people, they found sophisticated tools adapted to the needs of the local people and to which the people owed their existence.

Humans, it seems, are natural engineers. Evolution has imbued us with the capacity and compulsion to sculpt the environment in ways that not only enhance our ability to survive, but also just make the task of living "easier." Think about it: from the time we wake in the morning until we go to sleep at night, we are surrounded by a world of our own devising, an engineered environment. Alarm clocks wake us; refrigerators keep our food cold; stoves and microwave ovens heat our food; clothes keep us warm; automobiles or trains or busses take us to work, where we communicate and create using telephones, computers, and (the newest of creations) small handheld devices that instantly put us in contact with even the most remote places in the world. The companies and institutions in which we work are themselves engineered environments. The rigid hierarchy of one company shares with the free-flowing egalitarianism of its competitor the fact that each was created to fulfill a specific vision, to achieve a goal. On a larger scale, our society, though much more complex and difficult to manage, is itself a product of our own engineering. Laws are made with the express intent of achieving some societal outcome. Even customs are often vestiges of explicit solutions whose ancestry may or may not be traceable.

It appears that we were engineers from the very beginning. Using mitochondrial DNA (mtDNA) passed from mother to offspring, geneticists trace a common female ancestor of all living homo sapiens, "Eve," to around 200,000 years ago (Cann, Stoneking, & Wilson, 1987; Penny, Steel, Waddell, & Hendy, 1995). Similar analyses of the male Y chromosome yield a roughly comparable date (Cavalli-Sforza & Feldman, 2003; Mitchell & Hammer, 1996). Yet, archeologists have found flaked stone tools for cutting and hewing, made with considerable skill, dating from about 2.5–2.6 million years ago (Dominguez-Rodrigo, Rayne Pickering, Semaw, & Rogers, 2005; Sileshi, 2000). Not only are we engineers, we are descended from engineers. Indeed, it is not too speculative to suggest that our prowess as engineers facilitated our success as a species. There was a shift in climate around the Pliocene-Pleistocene boundary roughly 2.5–1.8 million years ago in which grasslands took over from dense forest, exposing our ancestors to new and dangerous challenges (Bobe, Behrensmeyer, & Chapman, 2002; DeMenocal, 2004; Reed, 1997). This created something of an evolutionary bottleneck: of the many proto-humans who existed at the time, only a few thousand emerged to give rise to the *Homo sapiens* of today. It may well have been our ability to engineer our societies and our tools that made it possible to survive.

It is true that many animals also engineer tools and alter their environment. Birds build nests, beavers build dams and lodges, termites and bees build hives, and crows have been observed to use rocks dropped from above to break shells. What makes us different is not just that we do more tool-making or more environmental modification (damage if you are of one ideological persuasion). More so than any other species, we humans seem to come equipped with characteristics particularly adapted to engineering.

For example, one important skill for engineers is the ability to build on previous successes. This skill requires being able to observe and learn from the behavior of others. In turn, learning from others includes formal instruction—another engineered system, devised for a purpose—but also informal learning, which occurs by mimicking the behavior of other members of a society. Studies have shown that children will observe an adult or an older child and repeat the actions they observe. In an experiment run on Australian and African children (Nielsen & Tomaselli, 2010), the children observe an adult going through an elaborate series of steps to open a rather odd-looking box. When presented with the box to open, the vast majority of children mimic the actions they have seen. The interesting outcome is that children above the age of four tend to mimic even when they know an easier way to open the box. Children under four years of age tend to use the simpler method they know to get the box open.

This kind of mimicry is not characteristic of even our closest kin, the great apes. It appears that as human children develop, they reach a stage of social maturity where it becomes important to pattern their behavior after that of other members of the group. The importance of this patterning is not simply that it builds social acceptance and cultural identity, but that it provides a natural mechanism for the transmission of skills, one of which would be the design and manufacture of tools. By observation, then, without overt instruction, children learn to manipulate the world in ways like others of their group do. In this example, we see the foundation for the accumulation of skill and knowledge, and for its transmission from one generation to another.

So, it is abundantly clear that humans are uniquely equipped to engineer their environments. Indeed, we live in a world full of overlapping engineered systems of which we all are a part. But how "good" are these systems? To what extent do they achieve their intended goals? How efficiently, reliably, and safely do they do so? One could argue that systems engineering simply follows a kind of natural selection process, with better systems "surviving" in such a way that there is always movement toward better and better (i.e., more efficient and reliable) systems. The development of tools is certainly one example of this kind of process.

In the past seventy years or so, this process has been accelerated by applying the tools of science to the evaluation and development of engineered systems (see, e.g., (Fitts, 1958). Driven by wartime increases in the technological complexity of the "tools of war," as well as their often-puzzling failures, psychologists and engineers began to systematically study the kinds of factors that influence the success and failure of human–machine systems in general. What has become clear from this study of "human engineering" is that understanding such systems requires a careful analysis of the environment, the human participant, and their interaction.

This book addresses the central conceptual issues associated with each of these three facets of human engineering. It is not meant to be an exhaustive compendium of the relevant research in these areas. Rather, it is meant to introduce students to the main concepts, assumptions, and approaches that have emerged in the study of human engineering. More detailed study of particular issues is available in the accompanying online modules. The book is organized into four sections. Part I provides historical context for the modern study of human-engineered systems, and also gives an overview of some of the real-world settings in which human engineering has been successfully applied. Most of the examples are drawn from aviation domains. In part this is because of the intense and long-standing concern over human error and safety in commercial aviation, as well as performance in military aviation. It is also because aviation environments demand much of the human operators, be they pilots, air traffic controllers, or maintenance workers. Where possible, we include examples from medicine, computer science, and driving. It must be noted, however, that the systematic study of human behavior is a much more recent development in those domains than in aviation. Part II focuses on the nature of environments, how they differ, what creates complexity, and techniques for modeling those environments. Part III focuses on the nature of humans, and their capabilities and limitations. We constrain our treatment of the vast literature on human behavior by shaping the discussion around characteristics that determine which of the many sensory events are perceived, how we construct meaning from sensory input, and how we select an action from many possible actions. Finally, Part IV addresses how the structure and content of the human information-processing system influences the capabilities and limitations of human performance, and shows how these characteristics interact with the nature of environments to affect human error and system safety.

REFERENCES

Bobe, R., Behrensmeyer, A. K., & Chapman, R. E. (2002). Faunal change, environmental variability and late Pliocene hominid evolution. *Journal of Human Evolution, 42*(4), 475–497. doi:10.1006/jhev.2001.0535

Cann, R. L., Stoneking, M., & Wilson, A. C. (1987). Mitochondrial DNA and human evolution. *Nature, 325*(6099), 31–36. doi:10.1038/325031a0

Cavalli-Sforza, L. L., & Feldman, M. W. (2003). The application of molecular genetic approaches to the study of human evolution. *Nature Genetics, 33*, 266–275. doi:10.1038/ng1113

DeMenocal, P. B. (2004). African climate change and faunal evolution during the Pliocene-Pleistocene. *Earth and Planetary Science Letters, 220*(1–2), 3–24. doi:10.1016/S0012-821X(04)00003-2

Dominguez-Rodrigo, M., Rayne Pickering, T., Semaw, S., & Rogers, M. J. (2005). Cutmarked bones from Pliocene archaeological sites at Gona, Afar, Ethiopia: Implications for the function of the world's oldest stone tools. *Journal of Human Evolution, 48*(2), 109–121. doi:10.1016/j.jhevol.2004.09.004

Fitts, P. M. (1958). Engineering psychology. *Annual Review of Psychology, 9*, 267–294. doi:10.1146/annurev.ps.09.020158.001411

Mitchell, R. J., & Hammer, M. F. (1996). Human evolution and the Y chromosome. *Current Opinion in Genetics & Development, 6*(6), 737–742. doi:10.1016/S0959-437X(96)80029-3

Nielsen, M., & Tomaselli, K. (2010). Overimitation in Kalahari bushman and the origins of human cultural cognition. *Psychological Science, 21*, 729–736.

Penny, D., Steel, M., Waddell, P. J., & Hendy, M. D. (1995). Improved analyses of human mtDNA sequences support a recent African origin for *Homo sapiens. Molecular Biology and Evolution, 12*(5), 863–882.

Reed, K. E. (1997). Early hominid evolution and ecological change through the African Plio-Pleistocene. *Journal of Human Evolution, 32*(2–3), 289–322. doi:10.1006/jhev.1996.0106

Sileshi, S. (2000). The world's oldest stone artefacts from Gona, Ethiopia: Their implications for understanding stone technology and patterns of human evolution between 2.6–1.5 million years ago. *Journal of Archaeological Science, 27*(12), 1197–1214. doi:10.1006/jasc.1999.0592

1

Natural and Engineered Systems

As its title suggests, this book is concerned with how humans interact with engineered systems. This immediately raises questions as to what we mean by an engineered system, what other systems might exist, and how an engineered system differs from other systems. Can the natural environment be considered an engineered system with evolution (natural selection) as the design driver? If not, what characteristics distinguish evolution through natural selection from the sort of engineered systems that are the topics of this book? Where can we draw the boundary?

In our view, the difference between natural and engineered systems is a function of three factors:

1. Design for a purpose
2. Design for a certain class of users
3. Design against failure

PURPOSEFUL DESIGN

Engineered systems have a goal, a purpose lacking in natural design. The modern scientific view of evolution (i.e., natural design) holds that there is no goal either at the level of an individual organism, a species, or an ecosystem as a whole. Rather, evolution uses mutation to generate diversity and natural selection to eliminate variants that are less competitive. According to modern theory, the world we see around us is the result of billions of such experiments having been conducted over billions of years. The natural world exists as it does because it worked, not because someone wanted it to work that way.

Contrast this with any of the millions of tools we have engineered, each with a clear purpose. Razors are meant to cut hair, clothes to be worn, televisions to project pictures, and so on. Even a computer, a device with multiple purposes, is really a mega-tool used to run software for doing specific jobs. Compare the modern racing bicycle with a cheetah. Every feature of the racing bicycle has been carefully crafted for speed. Design teams developed specifications, prototypes were constructed, and through iterative testing and modification the final product emerged. Similarly, the features of a cheetah are also shaped by the need for speed. The difference is that whereas the bicycle was deliberately designed for the purpose of speed, ancestors of the modern cheetah who were slightly faster than other of their species were able to exploit a niche and eventually their own species. The cheetah wasn't designed with the goal of running fast; that ability evolved because it proved useful to run fast. Successive generations of selective pressure have given the cheetah the speed and body characteristics it now possesses; those cheetah ancestors that were poorer runners left fewer of their genes surviving into the next generation.

This sense of purpose doesn't end with tools or instruments. It also characterizes how we organize ourselves into working, military, and social units, as well as our financial systems and educational institutions. Our laws are intended to produce a social environment that meets the expectations of its people and government. For example, the strict hierarchies that characterize military command structures, the organization of businesses, and even some social structures are desirable when it is important to guarantee top-down control over individuals and smaller units. It is true that hierarchies are a natural way for humans to think about structures, and because of this, hierarchies could be seen as natural forms of social organization shaped by evolution. But that would be overstating the case. When the need arose for more rapid decision making in the business domain, hierarchies were abandoned and more flexible control structures adopted—most notably by high-technology start-up companies—to reduce delays in getting products to market and to take advantage of rapid advancements in technology. Similarly, in military domains where high reliability is essential (e.g., aircraft carrier operations), strict command structures are relaxed to improve the reliability of information transfer (Pfeiffer, 1989). Thus, the trend toward decentralization has been driven by a deliberate desire to reap the benefits of more egalitarian organizations. The fact that it is often difficult to achieve the desired social or institutional engineering results does not reflect a general lack of deliberate purpose. Rather, it emerges from trying to engineer a complex system, one in which there are many decision makers, each pursuing goals that may or may not be compatible with those of the lawmakers or each other.

In differentiating engineering from natural selection, we do not mean to say that every implication of an engineered system, whether a nuclear power plant, organization, or society, is completely determined at the outset. On the contrary, trial and error—largely through iteration in the design process—has been the dominant paradigm in engineering, whether in the development of the modern graphical user interface, organizational structure, or social policy. The point is that these iterations are driven specifically to achieve a clearly stated purpose (fly faster than the speed of sound, win the battle, give a competitive advantage). The process reflects this purpose-driven engineering. At each stage of design, teams of engineers evaluate all aspects of the prototype system with respect to its purpose. Only when the system meets a set of predetermined criteria, which have been derived from a statement of goals, will it be fielded.

USER-CENTERED DESIGN

The second factor, design for a certain class of users, points to another deep difference between engineered and natural systems. We build tools, engineer social systems, write music, and create art, all with the intent that our product will be used or appreciated by other people—not just as an audience but also as active users. The identification of the intended user is a critical step in engineering design. We even build special devices for animals. Some of the earliest tools include harnesses that make it possible for animals to pull carts and chariots. More recently, adaptive devices for disabled pets have become more common.

Perhaps it is counterintuitive, but nothing is more illustrative of user-centered design than the arts: music, painting, literature, theater, and the cinema. On the surface, watching a movie or viewing a painting may seem to be a passive activity, but that is only because we cannot directly see the mental state of the viewer. In truth, a movie or painting is successful only to the extent that the human user actively engages with it; that is, to the extent that it evokes some emotional or mental response in a viewer. It is perhaps easier to see how designing for human use plays a role in video games and virtual environments, where it is important to have displays and controllers that not only work well, but also allow the person to become immersed in the artificial world (see, e.g., Bystrom, Barfield, & Hendrix, 1999; Cunningham, Billock, & Tsou, 2001; Ellis, Kaiser, & Grunwald, 1993). In a broader sense, this is true for all engineered systems. Indeed, the fact that success depends on a fit with human physical and mental characteristics is central to this book. If one devises a spear that is too heavy to be thrown or a social system that is unresponsive to human needs, those systems will fail.

Although it is easy to understand the examples of how a spear that is too heavy, or a computer mouse that is too sensitive, represent a poor fit to human capabilities, it may be a bit counterintuitive, or even controversial, to maintain that successful social systems are "designed" around human characteristics. After all, societies seem somehow organic, more an accumulation of customs and laws than a planned enterprise. They seem more like the twisted, crowded alleyways of old, medieval towns than the stately promenades and grid layouts of planned cities. Yet, some insight into the role of human nature can be gleaned from examining the "utopian" societies that have been established from time to time.

According to some sources, some 3,000 experimental utopian societies have been documented in human history, the vast majority of which have been in the United States, predominately in two periods: the early 19th and middle 20th centuries (Oved, 1993; Sosis, 2000; Sosis & Bressler, 2003). Many of these attempts at ideal societies were based on religious principles. Indeed, the Puritan settlement of New England and the Quaker settlement of Pennsylvania were in the main attempts to establish communities that embodied their religious beliefs about what constituted a perfect society. In the early 19th century, several communal societies were established based on religious principles, including the Shaker community in New York; the Amana Colonies, the Zoar Colonies, and the Bishop Hill Colonies; and Harmony, to name just a few (Oved, 1993). Shortly thereafter, secular communal colonies began to spring up, many of them based on the theories of social philosophers such as Charles Fourier (brought to the United States by Albert Brisbane) and Robert Owen. A basic tenet of these utopian societies, whether religious or secular, was the abandonment, or sublimation, of the twin concepts of ownership and competition in favor of communal property and cooperation. Virtually all of these utopian attempts were abandoned within twenty or thirty years of their initial establishment (Oved, 1993; Sosis, 2000; Sosis & Bressler, 2003). The principal reasons had to do with internal discord arising from conflicts in the distribution of goods and disparities in the degree of perceived cooperative effort (see, e.g., Sosis & Bressler, 2003). As a species, we appear to be possessed of a complex mix of traits, some of which encourage us to adopt group identities and cooperation, while others foster individual gain and competition. These perfect societies failed, in part at least, because they explicitly and knowingly rejected the individual orientation basic to our nature.

Nevertheless, a few of these societies flourished for far longer than others, and some are still with us today. The Hutterites, originally a 16th-century German religious group that later settled in the United States, still live in small communal settlements (Peter, 1987; Wikipedia, 2009), as do the Amish and Mennonites (Smith, 1981). An analysis of 250 such ideal communities of the early 19th century attributes success to strong religious and cultural pressures both to participate in cooperative endeavors and to support others in the community through the distribution of goods and labor (Sosis & Bressler, 2003). It is interesting to contemplate these successful societies as experiments that provide insight into the characteristics of the human social constitution.

Which characteristics of the user community are important considerations depend, of course, on the purpose for which the device or system is constructed. The social tendencies of humans may matter in the founding of a society, or the development of interactive websites, but will be less critical to the design of a new mouse or pointing device, the success of which will depend more critically on characteristics of the human motor system. Regardless, all human-engineered systems, in the sense we mean here, share the property that they are intended for use by an external agent. Very few systems in the natural world have use by an external agent or organism as the principal design feature. Indeed, antelope are not designed to be food for lions. Quite the contrary: Evolution has equipped them with mechanisms to thwart predators. A few anatomical structures, such as sexual organs (genitalia) and the mammalian nipple, do seem to have evolved to be used by other members of the same species. Still, even in these cases, it could be argued that these are adaptations designed to increase the chance of passing on an individual's genes. Nonetheless, the fact that engineered systems are designed for specific users has an important implication: It means that the designer must understand the physical, mental, and emotional makeup of the user community. For example, it will not do to create a social structure that many will feel is unfair, just as people will not adopt computer software that is too difficult to use. Designing for others requires an understanding of how people perceive fairness. Likewise, it will not do to devise a tool that people find too effortful to use or too complicated to learn.

DESIGN AGAINST FAILURE

Natural selection succeeds by failure. That is, better fit individuals outperform less fit individuals. We do not mean to restrict this to the overly simplistic notion of 19th-century social Darwinism. There are many strategies to succeed in nature, and often-popular conceptions of conflict and competition omit the more important qualities of cooperation, friendship, intelligence, talent, and sociability. Nonetheless, the process of natural selection means that some organisms will fail. Mutation, the key to variability, is itself most often deleterious, leading to failure more often than to success. The difficult quest for food and mates also takes its toll.

In contrast, success by failure is not a particularly desirable approach to design for human-engineered devices, social systems, and entertainment. We do learn from failure, more perhaps than we learn from success. But, unlike natural selection, engineering design is often geared toward preventing failures, as they can incur substantial cost. Indeed, we have engineered laws that more often than not allow us compensation in the case of failure. Among other things, this makes failure very expensive for the designers. Then too, as our systems become more complex, with the lives of many people depending on their success, failure can become a tragedy. Thus, we cannot have aircraft design eventually succeed by having the poorer designs crash (though this occurred frequently in the very early history of powered flight). The same is true of cars, trains, medicine, and many other endeavors. As a result, aircraft designers spend years developing and testing all the systems that go into a new aircraft before that craft is actually produced. This is true of many industries. Failure is, we hope, confined to the design process.

Nonetheless, it is expensive to produce a complex device that is as free of defects as needed. The capital investment in research and development is a major expense for many companies. Not only is it expensive, but adequate testing also can add years to the development cycle. For example, in 2011 Boeing announced further delays in the development of its 787 Dreamliner, which has direct financial implications for the many airlines that have placed orders for these aircraft.

The process of designing and testing to eliminate failure is a rigorous engineering discipline. Not only does it include the physical and software systems, but it has also increasingly come to include the human response to the new system. The reason for this concern with the human operator is that as engineered systems have become increasingly complex, human behavior has remained much the same—and it will continue to be the same, at least for the near future. The role of the human in engineered systems has evolved with the access to vast amounts of data, linked communication systems, joint activity by several team members, and the requirement to make rapid analyses and decisions in increasingly complex environments, often with the lives of many at stake. Yet, evidence suggests that our brains are not that different from those of our ancestors in antiquity. The burden is on designers of modern information systems to understand the abilities and limitations of the human operator and to ensure that information presentation and control authority are predicated on these abilities and limitations.

The complicated logic of modern computerized devices can baffle even the most experienced users. When advanced automation was introduced into modern aircraft, there were numerous incidents in which the pilots made poor, sometimes disastrous, decisions based on a flawed or incomplete understanding of how the system worked. Add to this the fact that we now carry around with us cell phones, portable video players, and mp3 players that distract us rather than helping us fully attend to the world around us. The potential for cell-phone use to distract drivers has become a real issue, as evidenced by major rail accidents attributed to the train driver being distracted by texting or talking on a cell phone (Associated Press, 2008, 2009; National Transportation Safety Board, 2003, 2009, 2010, 2011).

How have we now reached a point where the devices that are supposed to make our lives better and easier actually make it more difficult? If we have been designing for ourselves for so long, you might think we had solved the problem. In part, this is because designers are only now beginning to come to a formal understanding of how people work. It has often been assumed that with practice people could adapt to whatever was required of them to use a device. We have reached a point where this is no longer true. To see how that has happened, it is useful to consider the historical roots of the practice of engineering for human use.

SUMMARY

This chapter described the differences between natural and engineered systems as a function of three factors. First of all, engineered systems have a goal or a purpose that is lacking in natural design. Second, designs are focused on users. We build tools, engineer social systems, write music, and create art all with the intent that our product will be used or appreciated by other people—not just as an audience but also as active users. Finally, unlike natural selection, engineering design is often geared toward preventing failures, not towards allowing systems to fail through natural selection.

REFERENCES

Associated Press. (2008). Commuter train engineer didn't hit brakes. Retrieved from www.msnbc.msn.com/id/26732536/ns/us_news-life/t/commuter-train-engineer-didnt-hit-brakes/#.Tp0F4k-Kzow

Associated Press. (2009). Train crash probe focuses on cell phones. Retrieved from www.msnbc.msn.com/id/29494331/ns/us_news-life/t/train-crash-probe-focuses-cell-phone-use/#.Tp0FR0-Kzow

Bystrom, K.-E., Barfield, W., & Hendrix, C. (1999). A conceptual model of the sense of presence in virtual environments. *Presence: Teleoperators and Virtual Environments*, 8(2), 241–244. doi:10.1162/105474699566107

Cunningham, D. W., Billock, V. A., & Tsou, B. H. (2001). Sensorimotor adaptation to violations of temporal contiguity. *Psychological Science*, 12(6), 532–535. doi:10.1111/1467-9280.d01-17

Ellis, S. R., Kaiser, M. K., & Grunwald, A. C. (1993). *Pictorial communication in virtual and real environments*. London, UK: Taylor and Francis.

National Transportation Safety Board. (2003). *Railroad Accident Report RAR-03-01: Collision of two Burlingon Northern Santa Fe freight trains near Clarendon, Texas, May 28, 2002* (No. RAR-03/01). Retrieved from www.ntsb.gov/investigations/summary/RAR0301.html.

National Transportation Safety Board. (2009). *Railroad Accident Report RAR-09-02: Collision between two Massachusetts Bay Transportation Authority Green Line trains, Newton, Massachusetts, May 28, 2008* (No. RAR-09-02). Retrieved from www.ntsb.gov/investigations/summary/RAR0902.html.

National Transportation Safety Board. (2010). *Railroad Accident Report RAR-10-01: Collision of Metrolink train 111 with Union Pacific train LOF65-12, Chatsworth, California, September 12, 2008* (No. RAR-10-01). Retrieved from www.ntsb.gov/investigations/summary/RAR1001.html.

National Transportation Safety Board. (2011). *Railroad Accident Brief RAB-11-06: Collision of two Massachusetts Bay Transit Authority light rail passenger trains, Boston, Massachusetts, May 28, 2009* (No. RAB 11-06). Retrieved from www.ntsb.gov/investigations/fulltext/RAB1106.html.

Oved, Y. (1993). *Two hundred years of American communes.* New Brunswick, NJ: Transaction Publishers.

Peter, K. A. (1987). *The dynamics of Hutterite society: An analytical approach.* Edmonton, Canada: University of Alberta Press.

Pfeiffer, J. (1989). The secret of life at the limits: Cogs become big wheels. *Smithsonian, 20,* 38–48.

Smith, C. H. (1981). *Smith's story of the Mennonites.* Newton, KS: Faith and Life Press.

Sosis, R. (2000). Religion and intragroup cooperation: Preliminary results of a comparative analysis of utopian communities. *Cross-Cultural Research, 34*(1), 70–87. doi:10.1177/106939710003400105

Sosis, R., & Bressler, E. R. (2003). Cooperation and commune longevity: A test of the costly signaling theory of religion. *Cross-Cultural Research, 37*(2), 211–239. doi:10.1177/1069397103037002003

Wikipedia. (2009). Hutterite. Retrieved April 17, 2012, from http://en.wikipedia.org/wiki/Hutterite.

2

Historical Roots

When we speak about designing for human use, it is useful to distinguish between peoples' physical and mental characteristics. As humans, we have physical and mental strengths, but also limitations. Tools will be useful only to the extent that they exploit our strengths and avoid or compensate for our weaknesses. Historically, it is easy to see the ways in which adaptation to physical constraints has influenced design. Seeing progress in mental adaptation is more difficult; however, we will give examples of such progress that may at first surprise you.

ENGINEERING FOR PHYSICAL LIMITATIONS

Engineering has long had the purpose of augmenting our abilities, of overcoming the physical limitations inherent in our makeup. We are not the strongest, fastest, or nimblest of creatures. Without the aid of tools we would be at a great disadvantage in hunting or gathering food, and would have to rely primarily on scavenging for our protein intake. Given our limitations of speed and strength, it is not surprising that for most of our existence, tools have been specialized for physical work: hunting, digging, chopping, and plowing, to name but a few. These same physical limitations that spur us to engineer also must be considered in the design of our tools. The history of engineering, then, is also a history of discovering what designs work for the people who must use them. For example, the size of our hands and fingers determines the size of objects we can grasp, or the distance we can span from fingertip to fingertip. Ancestors to modern humans understood this: even the earliest stone tools were manufactured to fit nicely in the hand, as shown in Figure 2.1. Swords, hammers, axes, needles, and all manner of tools have always been made to size: large enough for the task, small enough to be manipulated, and light enough to be used without undue strain. Here we examine the ways in which our physical limitations dictate the shape and size of our tools and give examples of ingenious methods of circumventing those limitations.

Size

A good example of our ingenuity at physical design is the engineering of musical instruments. Woodwind instruments, for example, are tubes with holes at precise intervals to give the notes of the Western diatonic scale. Figure 2.2 shows several examples of

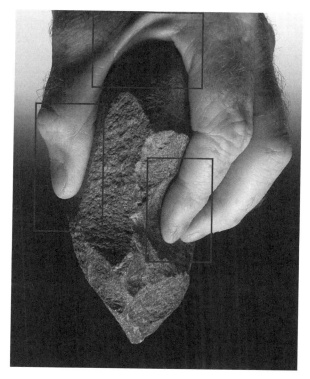

Figure 2.1 Early stone tools were adapted to fit the hand. *Source:* www.paleodirect.com (Paleo Direct, Inc.), by permission.

woodwind instruments, from a simple soprano recorder to a much larger bassoon. The length of the tube determines its fundamental pitch—for a given width, longer tubes produce lower pitches. Small woodwinds, such as fifes or flutes, have holes bored at precise places to emit the correct pitch when covered. This design is retained by the recorder, which consists of open holes that are closed by fitting the fingers over the bored openings. When you play a recorder, you quickly become aware that it is critical to close the holes completely so that no air escapes. This constraint makes it difficult to extend the open-hole design very far. The spacing of holes for a clarinet or oboe would be too far to allow most people to fully close the holes simply by covering them with their fingers. If you want to make a deep-sounding woodwind instrument, like a bassoon or baritone saxophone, the appropriate spacing between the holes will be too wide for a normal human hand to even reach the holes. The solution is an ingenious set of levers spaced perfectly for the average human hand, which close keys over the holes by twisting a cable running through a closed housing. In Figure 2.2, note the tubing on the smaller piccolo and larger bassoon compared to the open-holed recorder. The tubing is part of a mechanical valve system that allows the player to easily cover the holes on instruments too small or large otherwise. The next time

piccolo

recorder

oboe

bassoon   saxophone   flute   clarinet

Figure 2.2 Woodwind instruments. *Source:* www.learnersdictionary.com (Merriam-Webster's Learner's Dictionary © 2011, Inc.), by permission.

you look at a flute, clarinet, saxophone, or bassoon, note where the holes are compared to where the fingerings are that close those holes.

By the way, a similar principle is used in making brass instruments. You might recall seeing television ads in which Swiss mountaineers are playing extremely long horns that produce a deep, resonant sound, one that would carry a long distance to penetrate valleys and hills. The tips of these horns rest on the ground or a fixed support—not ideal for an orchestra or marching band. The same deep tone can be achieved by winding the long tube into a coil. When you see a sousaphone or French horn, you are looking at an instrument that is functionally identical to a long tube, just engineered in a way that supports use by people in a new environment.

Strength

The cultural desire to build large monumental structures appears to have a very long history. In addition to the familiar pyramids and temples of Egypt, Greece, and Rome, the very earliest cities along the Tigris and Euphrates Rivers in what are now portions of modern Syria, Turkey, Iraq, and Iran, and cities along the Jordan River in portions of modern Israel, Jordan, and Lebanon show signs of large-scale monument construction dating well past 5000 BCE. This was not confined to what is now referred to as the Middle East. Early cities in China along the Yangtze and Yellow River valleys (e.g, Xi'an) also show evidence of highly organized construction of monuments and temples, dating back past 2000 BCE. We do not fully understand the construction techniques of these early civilizations, but they all had to solve the problem of how to lift and transport stones and other building materials that were too heavy for even a team of people to lift. A familiar system for doing this is the common pulley, which is an arrangement of wheels over which a rope or cable passes. Like the lever, the pulley gains mechanical advantage by increasing the distance along which a force is applied. Examples from warfare abound, such as the trebuchet, in which a large rope is twisted taut by means of a pulley to throw a large boulder against a fortified castle wall. The crossbow employs a pulley crank system to "cock" the bow into a high-tension position, which would be impossible for people to achieve otherwise. In a sense, then, the wheel and pulley allow us to do things we would not otherwise be able to do; they improve the design of existing systems to increase the performance envelope of an individual. Of course, any application of these devices must contend with the final force that has to be applied by the human user. It took years of strength training, for example, for an archer to gain the shoulder and arm strength to be able to pull the English longbow. In fact, one of the reasons for the crossbow and the success of early muskets (dangerous and inefficient as they were) was the ability to achieve greater projectile force with less well trained soldiers.

Speed and Efficiency

Design has also been driven by the desire to increase the productive output of workers. The concern with speed has a long historical precedent—the chariot and horse-drawn carriage certainly sped travel—and often arose in a military context where getting the edge on the opponent required marching faster or simply being quicker with the sword. The commercial concern with speeding up factories to increase output with fewer or less-skilled workers really came into its own with the Industrial Revolution that started in the 18th century.

For instance, the 18th and 19th centuries saw great advances in textile production. Weaving involves interlacing threads to produce a piece of cloth. Wood-framed looms had been used for weaving since around 4000 BC, and are still used widely today. These are operated manually, using coordinated movements of the arms and feet. The modern power loom, which had its beginnings in the 18th-century design of Edmund Cartwright, removes the weaver from the intricate coordination of the various components. Instead, a bank of spindles intertwines the threads in a regular way; the weaver is replaced by a person who now tends the spindles and ensures the fault-free flow of thread into the machine. Fewer people can now do more work. Further, they do not take as long to train and can be replaced more easily. The many weavers who staffed the looms prior to introduction of the power loom were skilled laborers, trained in the intricate workings of their machines. Power looms had no requirement for such highly skilled workers.

The loom is one early example of *automation*: a machine replacing a role once filled by a human. Note how this is fundamentally different from the wheel, pulley, or crossbow. First, in those latter cases, the machine did not replace a human. Second, no one previously was able to do what wheels, levers, and pulleys made it possible to do. With automation, there is a very real change in the role of the person and of the relationship between a person and the technology. It more often than not allows fewer, less-skilled individuals to replace a more numerous and more highly trained workforce.

Automation has been an inexorable progression for the past two hundred years and has had great social and technological impact. The Industrial Revolution was made possible by new forms of automation. In turn, automation was spurred by the demand for increased individual productivity. In itself, competition to make more goods with fewer people who required less training became a spur to new forms of automation.

As it is characterized in modern times, automation has been seen as a potentially disruptive force, pushing many people out of work and in some cases replacing them with devices that may lead to errors. It is a complex story that will be told in more detail later. It should be noted here, in a section devoted to the history of engineering for human use, that automation has often been driven by a concern over the costs of *training* and of maintaining a highly skilled workforce as much as productivity per se.

In this sense, automation is not fundamentally different from other types of engineering advances. For example, it is often puzzling why firearms were so widely adopted when they were so unreliable in the beginning. A musket of the 16th or 17th century was no match for the English longbow that had served so well in the English victories over the French at Poitiers, Crecy, and Agincourt during the 100 Years War. So why did the English army abandon the highly successful longbow for the musket, a weapon that could not shoot as far, nor as straight, often broke, and took a long time to load between rounds? The answer in part is that it took only a few weeks to train a musketeer to stand his ground, reload, and fire in unison with other musketeers. It took most of a young man's adolescence to master the longbow; hence, English kings often mandated compulsory training. However, following the Black Death of the 14th century, there were, for many years, too few men even to work the fields, much less to train extensively for years in longbow use. As a result, the skill needed became impossible to obtain, creating opportunity for an alternative to the longbow even if not initially as effective.

History is full of instances in which progress follows the introduction of devices that are easier for the majority of people to use. The development of the car over the past century is a good example. Early cars were finicky beasts, requiring highly coordinated manipulation to start and then to shift gears. Reducing the physical dexterity needed to drive was important in bringing the automobile to a mass market. The introduction of the automatic transmission made driving accessible to a very large number of people who would otherwise not attempt or complete the training required.

The automobile provides another example of the way human performance has affected the development of technology and business. Perhaps the best-known success story of the 20th century is the Ford Motor Company. Henry Ford established the company and built the first affordable car in America, if not the world. What is less well appreciated is that this achievement depended on automation and a keen understanding of human capabilities.

Ford did not invent the car. However, he made two changes that had a huge impact on productivity. He designed a car that could be easily assembled from a fixed inventory of interchangeable parts (parts that can be used to construct more than a single product type, or are used in many places in the product). Up to that time, cars were virtually hand crafted. One person, or a small team, would make the parts and fit them together. The results were often elegant and expensive—the Ferraris of their day. Assembly from interchangeable parts allowed Ford to make better use of the assembly line.

Although Ford is often credited with inventing the assembly line, he did not do so. There is some evidence that Ransom Olds (of Oldsmobile fame) had increased the rate of production of his car by using a nonmoving line (Ament, 2005). Ford, however, was inspired by the assembly lines of local meat-packing companies (Ford & Crowther, 1922; Wikipedia, 2011). His important contribution to the assembly line was a series of fine adjustments—tinkering—to make efficient use of the physical behavior of his workmen (no women were allowed to work on the assembly line). One key to his assembly-line innovation was to use a system of belts and pulleys to move the assembly line. In doing so, he brought the work to the worker, freeing the worker from having to physically move. The moving belt also made it possible for him to implement an important principle of assembly-line production: "Use work slides or some other form of carrier so that when a workman completes his operation, he drops the part always in the same place—which place must always be the most convenient place to his hand—and if possible have gravity carry the part to the next workman for his operation" (Ford & Crowther, 1922, p. 80). According to Ford, the efficiency of the assembly line is made possible because there is a "reduction of the necessity for thought on the part of the worker and the reduction of his movements to a minimum. He does as nearly as possible only one thing with only one movement" (id.). If a single person must put on the fenders, install the seats, mount the engine, and do all the other myriad assembly tasks, he does not get much practice at each task, and is constantly switching jobs. Doing only one job for 10 to 12 hours a day takes advantage of psychological principles of cognitive and motor processing to facilitate the automation of the action (Logan, 1988; Schneider & Shiffrin, 1977; Shiffrin & Schneider, 1977).

So important is an understanding of human skill to manufacturing that a new science of *time-motion study* was established specifically to facilitate the development of efficient production procedures (Barnes, 1966; Gilbreth, 1910). In a classic time-motion analysis, an assembly task is broken down into its component parts, a process called *task analysis*. Individual actions, such as screwing on a wing nut, are then timed. These elementary component operations are then combined to estimate the time to make a larger subsection (e.g., the dashboard), continuing up to the whole item. From this concern with productivity and efficiency, a new discipline called *operations research* (Barnes, 1966; Shrader, 2006) emerged, with mathematical techniques for estimating schedules and procedures that ensure an efficient and productive system. Operations research encompasses all aspects of a system, both human and nonhuman players, with time-motion studies still conducted to provide baseline data for human performance. It is interesting to note that operations research, like time-motion studies, treats human behavior as a schedule of primitive operations. Task analysis breaks human activity down to some desirable level of primitive operations from which a schedule of behavior is constructed. Operations research applies mathematical techniques that in certain cases enable precise predictions of outcomes. Later in the book we will see that the idea of simplifying behavior into a schedule of primitive events is still a useful technique used in human-system modeling.

The formal discipline of operations research got its greatest boost from military logistics during World War II. In World War I, Germany had produced a school for military logistics that included precise timetables for rail transport and troop deployment, and also included how far soldiers could march in a day. The vast amount of materiel shipped to the front by the allies in World War II necessitated an even more impressive logistical effort. It was important to develop a schedule from estimated times for shipping, land transport, and available people that would ensure the timely delivery of materiel vital to the conduct of military operations. The rapid advances in aviation, coupled with the increased importance of the military fighter aircraft, led to some of the first careful studies of the human as a controller of a complex system. Whereas earlier development of displays and controls for aircraft had been largely trial-and-error efforts, aviation research laboratories began to carefully investigate human visual, motor, and vestibular phenomena to improve the performance of pilots and aircraft (see e.g., Roscoe, 1948; Fitts, 1958). More than any other technology of the past, the airplane—and later spacecraft—placed people in highly unusual environments for which human bodies were not naturally designed. It is not surprising that some of the earliest and most consistent efforts to understand humans in engineered systems have been in the aerospace domain. The response of the human body to rapid changes in acceleration—g-forces—led to the design of safety harnesses and ejection seats for modern jet aircraft that would reduce the chance of serious injury from the ejection itself. The modern pressurized flight suit is also a technological marvel, designed to solve another of the problems of high g. One of the problems with high g-forces is that they can lead to a rapid decline in blood reaching the brain. Aviation human factors engineers developed a suit that would automatically adjust pressure to keep blood from flowing to the lower extremities, thereby ensuring that blood would be pumped to the brain.

Despite all these adaptive technologies and all the research into protecting the crew of high-performance aircraft, it is still the case that the human body is the limiting factor in aircraft performance. We are now seeing the development of drone aircraft. Currently these are controlled by teleoperation, with the "pilot" located on the ground and linked to the aircraft controls. In the near future, however, many foresee intelligent agents (i.e., computers) controlling fighter aircraft and making many (if not all) of the decisions, allowing the aircraft to operate at the g-force limits of its avionic capabilities, rather than the limits of the human pilot. At present, researchers are investigating autonomous aircraft that "swarm" like bees or ants to replace human pilots for reconnaissance missions. Fully automated drones may replace teleoperated drones in the near future, leaving the human operators as monitors.

Aircraft use also spurred the development of another field concerned with fitting systems to the human body: *anthropometry*. Anthropometry is concerned with designing systems that place controls and displays where people can easily reach, see, and manipulate them. This may at first glance seem trivial, but it is far from it. Take the example of a fighter aircraft cockpit. Not only must pilots fit into the seats, but from there they must also be able to see the instruments and reach the controls for all of the systems. So, how big should the cockpit be? This turns out to be a complicated question, in part because height, reach, sitting height, eye height, and width all differ from one person to the next. The solution has been to choose an "average" person and place things such that some percentage of the population, usually all but the top and bottom

5 percent, can fit. These considerations must also address women, who are on average shorter than men, and who are also flying fighter aircraft.

This book does not deal in depth with engineering around physical constraints. This should not be taken as an indication that anthropometry is a solved problem or an unimportant issue. On the contrary, research dealing with physical adaptations is a vibrant and flourishing area of great importance to manufacturers, and to our health. The design of chairs and workstations has become a specialty. Because many of us sit at desks for long periods of time typing on computer keyboards, slight imperfections in the match between our physiology and the arrangement of the keyboard, the height of and support provided by the chair, the angle of the monitor—all issues central to anthropometry—can lead to painful and recurrent wrist, back, and shoulder pain. Repetitive stress injuries account for a high percentage of worker's compensation claims. Engineers are actively researching the effects of keyboard design, desk height, and other factors in workplace layout; designing new shapes for tools, such as new keyboards; and investigating how joints in the human body react when asked to be held still to support typing, writing, cooking, and various other activities. Much of the recent work is supported by advanced computer techniques for three-dimensional (3-D) modeling of movement.

ENGINEERING FOR HUMAN COGNITION

As the preceding discussion shows, it is relatively easy to find historical examples of devices that have allowed us to overcome our inherent physical limitations, or of adaptations that took advantage of our natural physical talents to improve performance. It is much harder to sift through history and find examples of adaptation to cognitive limitations of people. In part, this is because the vast majority of people throughout the course of human history have performed physical labor. From the shovel to the plow to the loom, these devices have placed minimal demands on a person's ability to reason or even to learn. Indeed, only a tiny fraction of people in the whole of human history have had professions that we would think of as "white collar," demanding intellectual prowess as their primary talent. Such cases would include merchants, scribes (or later clerks), priests and other religious figures, chroniclers, and a handful of other professions. This does not mean that intellectual gifts were valuable only to these people, just that it took a little longer for the specialized tools that were developed to augment human intellectual capacity to emerge. For the most part, in these early professions, pen and paper (or chalk and tablet) were the only physical tools needed. Looking closer, we see that it was not the physical tools that were relevant, but something new: the conceptual and symbolic way in which abstract concepts were represented. In general, it has been the new representation or manner of conceptualization that has brought about better matches between intellectual work and human cognition. We briefly mention three that may surprise you.

Writing

The first development is perhaps the most obvious: writing. The act of writing is the act of representing the real thing, or the stream of sounds we emit when talking, with a

IDEOGRAMS

Character	Sound	Meaning
上	shàng	up
下	xià	down
二	èr	two
三	sān	three

PICTOGRAMS

Character	Sound	Meaning
日	rì	sun
月	yuè	moon
木	mù	tree

RADICAL + PHONETIC COMBINATIONS

	Symbol	Sound	Meaning
Character	沖	chōng	flush
Radical	水	shˇui	water
Phonetic	中	zhōng	middle

Figure 2.3 Chinese character types.

symbolic thing. The symbolic thing is the written text, which represents objects or thoughts in a way that allows the reader to understand what the writer meant to communicate ("said"). Examples of different writing systems are shown in Figure 2.3. It is no accident that the earliest examples of writing are essentially *pictographs*, schematic depictions of real things like wheat or goats or jugs of olive oil. Once things are written on a tablet, you can take them anywhere and show them to anyone. You can easily subtract, add, or substitute. You can keep track of past transactions that may be lost to memory. Also, it becomes easier to think precisely in very large numbers because you can easily accumulate and work with larger and larger units once you can write. Writing was a great boon to thinking, long before poetry, polemics, or fiction. With the introduction of writing, we have an example of technology augmenting the cognitive capacity of those who can master it.

In pictographic systems, symbols stand for an object, a state of being (e.g., sadness), or an action. Pictographic systems began with pictograms, whose shape is similar to the object being represented (see Figure 2.3). However, pictograms cannot represent abstract concepts. To express abstract thought, pictograms were augmented with ideograms, which are characters whose form bears no direct relationship to the form of the object, but does convey the main idea. The ideograms in Figure 2.3, for example, use the ascending or descending line element to signify up or down, respectively. Still, the combination of pictograms and ideograms cannot fully capture the richness of language. Indeed, in pictographic systems such as Chinese, ideograms and pictograms make up a small percentage of characters. More common are combinations of a symbol with no necessary relationship to the form of the object (a radical) plus a symbol that acts as a phonetic element. In Figure 2.3, the Chinese character for flush, for example, contains a radical related to water and a phonetic symbol whose meaning is unrelated but whose pronunciation (zhong) is similar to flush (chong). Thus, systems that began using pictograms evolved to include ideograms and combinations of meaning and sound symbols to indicate a given word. The lasting success of Chinese is evidence of the ability of these element combinations to capture the full complexity of language and subtlety of meaning.

Ideographic scripts, in general, have the property that symbols used to represent a word bear no systematic relationship to the meaning or the sound. In Chinese, for example, the brush strokes used to denote "father" bear no relationship to the strokes used to represent "mother," "sister," "brother," or any other family members. Nor is there any systematic relationship between strokes and sound. This lack of correspondence between the sound of a word and its visual form when written produces memory and other cognitive demands to enable reading of an ideographic script. It means that one must learn a larger number of arbitrary correspondences between the written and spoken forms of a word. Knowing what a word sounds like is no help when trying to figure out what its symbol may mean—there is no way to sound it out. These languages also make it difficult to create indexes, as there is no natural ordering of words.

Another early historical class of writing systems used symbols to represent syllables. A *syllable* is the smallest possible pronounceable sound unit, usually incorporating one or two consonant sounds and a vowel. Examples of syllabic systems include ancient cuneiform; one of the earliest writing systems found in the Near East, Mycenaean Linear B script; and Cherokee, a Native American language. Like ideographic languages, the relationship between the written symbol and the syllable is arbitrary; similar sounds can have very different symbols and there is no systematic relationship between the form of the character and its sound.

The first scripts in which there is a correspondence between the form of the character and its sound is the phonemic alphabet. English and nearly all other languages use a phonetic alphabet as the basis for writing. In phonetic systems, each symbol represents a small sound unit, the *phoneme*. The vowels and consonants of the English alphabet are (almost) examples of the phonemes of English. The great advantage of phonemes is that a small number of them can combine in an essentially infinite way to create all the words needed in any language. Phonemes combine in orderly ways to represent the way words sound; therefore, unfamiliar words can be "sounded out" as a way of mapping written to spoken language. In turn, this orderly relationship minimizes the cognitive demands placed on the reader.

It should be noted that the phoneme is by far the most abstract of the three symbol systems. A phoneme neither represents a visible thing in the world, as primitive pictographs do, nor is it a pronounceable unit of speech, as is a syllable. In fact, the same written letter is pronounced slightly differently depending on the surrounding letters, so there is no guaranteed match to a sound as with the syllable. It was quite an achievement to realize that speech could be broken down into such small, abstract units.

The point to be drawn from these writing systems is that each is fully capable of expressing all the meanings conveyed by language. However, phoneme systems place far fewer demands on our memories and allow us to use a strategy of sounding out an unfamiliar word to see if indeed we would recognize it when spoken. Though our modern phonetic alphabet was derived from that first used extensively by the Phoenicians (hence the term *phonetic*), along the coast of what is today Israel, its origins are probably Egyptian. Nonetheless, once introduced it proved versatile and rapidly spread to Greece and later to India via the Middle East. Much of its appeal is due to the ease with which people can learn, use, and adapt the script. That is, its appeal is cognitive ease of use. The story of adoption of the phonetic alphabet is an example of an important principle of human-centered design: *people are more productive and system safety is increased when the burden on human memory is reduced.*

Number Systems

Another historical example of success based on reducing cognitive demands comes from mathematics. Most countries today use Arabic numerals as the basis of arithmetic and mathematics. The term reflects the fact that Europeans adopted this method of numbering from the Arabs sometime during the Middle Ages. Actually, the Arabs had imported the numbers and numbering system from India some time earlier, and their system included the use of zero, which was not part of European mathematics before then. The symbols in use today, then, are more properly referred to as Hindu-Arabic numerals. Prior to the adoption of Hindu-Arabic numerals, European mathematical notation was derived from that used in classical Rome. Most of us have studied Roman numerals in school and are accustomed to seeing them on clock faces, as release dates of movies, and after the names of kings or queens. The Roman system involves denoting numeric values by letters of the alphabet: L = 50, M = 1000, C = 100, and so on. Note that in this system there is no obvious mathematical relationship between L, M, or C. Keep in mind that to the Romans, there was no other representational system. They did not think in terms of 50, 100, and so forth, but in terms of their only notation system; that is, M, D, L, C, V, and I. Thus, to learn addition, subtraction, multiplication, or division, people needed to learn arbitrary correspondences. There are tables to memorize in which $X \times X = C$, $V + C = CV$, and so forth.

In comparison, the Hindu-Arabic system uses positional notation; when we write 54, we can easily see that this number represents the quantity $5 \times 10 + 4$, or alternatively 5 tens plus 4. Procedures for addition, subtraction, multiplication, and division, as with Roman numerals, are often learned through tables. Division is somewhat easier with Hindu-Arabic numerals, but both systems appear to support all the basic operations; indeed, in the Roman system addition could be quite simple. Why, then, did the Hindu-Arabic system spread so widely as to become virtually the sole representational system for modern mathematics? It could be because it is somewhat easier to represent large-magnitude numbers, but the Romans had also developed ways of annotating their numerals that made for compact representations of large magnitudes. Rather, it is because the Hindu-Arabic system represents numbers in a way that capture the underlying structure of magnitude. As a result, it leads to insights about more complex mathematical concepts. Consider that a million is written as 1,000,000, a hundred as 100. It is easily seen that the difference is in the number of zeros (a concept not explicitly represented by the ever-practical Romans). In Roman numerals, a million was written as M with a line above it, a hundred as C. The two letters reflect nothing about the underlying mathematical space that would call out the relationship between the two. Once attention is directed at the number of zeros, it is a small step to scientific notation: a million represented as 10^6. From this, logarithms and other mathematical transformations are more likely to be perceived. The success of Hindu-Arabic numerals over Roman for mathematics highlights another principle: *representational systems that allow people to perceive relationships easily lead to more productive and fruitful work than those that require difficult cognitive processing.*

It turns out that our success in solving problems depends critically on the way in which we represent the problem, a fact that must be considered when designing complex systems.

Point-and-Click Interfaces

The principle of reduced memory load has also contributed to the success of a more recent product: the modern point-and-click computer operating system. Prior to the release of the Lisa personal computer by Apple, standard operating systems were text based. For example, in Unix and DOS, showing a directory of files, opening, deleting, renaming, or viewing a file are a few of the many actions that were completed by typing specific commands into the command-line editor. The same was true of text editors. Deleting text, writing new text, and even scrolling through documents all required typing in appropriate commands. This meant that a user needed to memorize all the commands for the operating system, as well as those for applications. These memory demands have been greatly reduced by the modern systems of the Macintosh and Windows family. In those systems, people manipulate visible icons directly. The act of opening a file is consistently done with a double click of the mouse, and that action has also been incorporated into many individual applications. Such direct manipulation interfaces achieve their ease of use by a combination of reduced memory load and tangible eye-hand manipulation. This highlights another important ingredient in human-centered engineering: *people will be more productive and less error prone when perceptual support is provided for decisions and actions, and will find it easier to manipulate tangible or visible objects than specifying abstract symbolic constraints.*

These three examples illustrate that advances in manufacturing and science have come about by technological developments whose chief innovation was their better fit to human physical and mental composition. It is important to emphasize again that there is no inherent limit on the ability of ideographic languages to represent all the words and concepts in a language, or for Roman numerals to represent all the numbers in mathematics. The advantage of the phonetic alphabet and Hindu-Arabic numerals lies in their ability to be easily grasped and manipulated by people. They provide representational systems that reflect critical features of language and mathematics, which allow us to see the nature of each more clearly, fostering innovation. Historically, such human-centered developments came to be adopted because they worked—a kind of evolutionary survival of the fittest. We have already noted that in the modern era, too much is at stake to allow failure to remain the dominant mode for eliminating bad design. In fact, one of the central defining features of the modern field of human-system engineering is the explicit treatment of the human as a component of the larger engineered system and the focused study of human behavior in the domain of interest. We now turn our attention to the development of the modern field of human-systems engineering, or human factors, whose origins can be traced in large part to World War II.

THE MODERN ERA

Prior to WWII, the study of humans in engineered systems as a formal field of study did not exist. Designs were developed and modified only when problems arose. The modern QWERTY keyboard used on almost all computers is an example of this. The initial arrangement of keys on the typewriter developed by Sholes caused the keys to jam. Sholes and his colleagues worked to increase typing speed while reducing the likelihood of the keys jamming (Yasuoka & Yasuoka, n.d.). However, the keyboard was not designed to optimize touch typing. Indeed, touch typing was not envisioned by these early designers; rather, they envisioned people using two fingers to type. The fact that the key arrangement has endured, despite suggestions that other arrangements can produce faster touch typing (Liebowitz & Margolis, 1990), is testament to another widespread principle: *convention can often dictate design over performance.* Most people have been trained on one particular system, which raises a barrier to implementation of a successor that does not conform to the established way.

The modern post-WWII era has seen continued growth in the study of humans in engineered systems. The field of human-systems engineering, in which human cognitive and physical performance is the center of interest, arose in response to changes in society and technology. Society has become more *safety* conscious. Whereas in the past technologies in manufacturing were developed chiefly to improve productivity, our society has become more concerned with the safety of industries, workplaces, transportation, and manufactured goods in general. Safety concerns have led to an exploration of the nature of *human error* and designs to reduce its likelihood. Factors that promote human error, such as *fatigue*, lack of *situation awareness, inattention*, and *workload*, have become major topics of research and development. Concern with human error itself reflects the growing presence of digital computers in products such as clocks and refrigerators, and *automated systems*, in which complex computer algorithms now control trains, aircraft, and cars. As we will see later, the algorithms used by automated devices can cause problems for users because it has become increasingly difficult for users to gain a good mental model for understanding how the computer works. To understand how the complexity of modern systems has affected human use and led to a separate field devoted to the study of humans in engineered systems, we briefly discuss issues associated with a few modern technological domains.

Aviation

Two key technological developments of World War II drove the creation of the modern field known as human factors or ergonomics: fighter aircraft and the digital computer. At the outset of World War II, the warplane inventory of most countries consisted of relatively slow biplanes not that different from those of World War I. Some were adapted as fighters, others as relatively ineffective bombers. By the end of WWII, the first jet fighters appeared, flying at speeds four or five times that of the aircraft available at the beginning of the war. As we commented earlier, the demand for faster and more maneuverable aircraft subjected pilots to highly unusual g-forces, producing physical stress never before encountered. But there were also issues of basic aircraft control. To fly fast, it is important to reduce the drag produced by the surface of the wing, which is generally accomplished by shortening the wing and sweeping the wings backward. The cost of this is reduced stability at low speeds. Moreover, people soon realized that delays in an aircraft's response to control inputs led to instability and loss of control as pilots were tempted to overcorrect.

The Wright brothers were the first to recognize the importance of human control and devised a system that warped the wings. Controlling the airflow over the wings is inherently difficult to do with precision, and it proved challenging to achieve linkages that pilots could easily control. To illustrate the problem, consider how control of an aircraft is achieved. The pilot uses the stick (or yoke) to control pitch (whether the nose points up or down), and bank (whether the aircraft tilts left or right). The rudders control yaw (pointing the nose left or right). The throttle controls thrust, the power the engine produces. The actual movements of the aircraft are achieved by linking the rudder and stick to moveable surfaces on the tail and wings, respectively. Figure 2.4 illustrates the control loop involved in landing an aircraft. The pilot has the goal of landing the aircraft, which includes subgoals associated with aligning to the runway and maintaining the correct speed and descent rate. To align the aircraft, the pilot moves the stick to the left or right. This causes the ailerons on each wing to move in opposite directions (one up, the other down), increasing the lift on one wing while decreasing it on the other. The plane banks right or left, as determined by its dynamic characteristics. The pilot then perceives the effect of the control input (stick movement) and compares that to the intended outcome. The difference is an error, which the pilot then selects another action to correct.

After several decades of trial and error, the formal system of *control theory* systematized what was known about control from empirical observation and provided a rigorous mathematical foundation for understanding and solving many control problems. Essentially, control theory is a mathematical formalism that allows the relationship between a pilot's intent, the aircraft's behavior, and the feedback to the pilot to be related

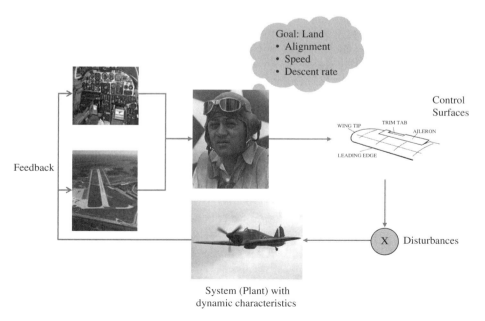

Figure 2.4 Simplified control loop for landing an aircraft.

systematically to the difficulty of controlling the aircraft. In fact, control theory relates the important elements needed to control any vehicle or any system whose state changes with time; thus, it is widely used to design automated systems. We will deal more with control theory in Chapter 6. Our interest in control theory is not primarily in its mathematical precision. Rather, we will take advantage of its clarity in highlighting important elements of human-system interaction across a wide range of systems.

The diagram in Figure 2.4 is a simplified depiction of the flow as used in control theory. The controller, in this case the pilot, has the *goal* of landing, which includes three more specific goals that the pilot is trying to maintain: alignment with the center of the runway, descent rate (change in altitude with time), and speed. In control theory, feedback (e.g., view of the outside, visual gauges, sound of the engine) is used to assess whether there is deviation from a goal. If so, there is a decision process that selects the appropriate corrective action. The action is transferred to the aircraft via a set of controls manipulated by the pilot. The aircraft has its own response to inputs, such as time delays and turn rates. The pilot monitors the effects of her action through feedback provided by the visual scene and by displays in the cockpit. The pilot is presumed to iteratively sample feedback to determine the magnitude of error between the current state and the goal, select the required action to reduce the error, and execute the action.

The pilot uses visual feedback to adjust the aircraft to correct for deviations from desired alignment, speed, and descent rate. Complications arise from excessive delays (lag) between control input and its effect (feedback), disturbances, nonlinear behavior of control surfaces, and inherent dynamics of the aircraft. The linkage between the controls the pilot manipulates and the control surfaces that affect the aircraft can be achieved purely mechanically, usually augmented by hydraulic systems much like the power steering in cars. On modern jet aircraft, however, mechanical connections are no longer the norm. Instead, in modern "fly-by-wire" aircraft, the pilot's movements are first sent to a computer where they are interpreted and turned into changes to the control surfaces.

There are many questions about the control loop that will be dealt with later. The point to emphasize here is the interrelatedness of the human, the system being controlled, and the environment in which that control occurs. The human pilot is responding to feedback, which is a combination of past inputs, the vehicle dynamics, and unforeseen factors in the environment. This interrelatedness is characteristic of virtually all human-system interaction. The demands of the aviation environment on the pilot's mental and physical capabilities largely spawned the field of human factors engineering to advance systematic design, measurement, training, and flying.

The Digital Computer

The second postwar development of great societal significance was the digital computer. We need not dwell on what it is or how it works, in part because computers have become such a staple in our lives that it is difficult to imagine life without one.

Interacting with a computer using a mouse illustrates the usefulness of understanding control theory. In using a computer mouse, the user has a goal, an error signal (distance from cursor to goal), and a set of control actions that can reduce the error. The mouse also has its own dynamics that will determine how the cursor responds to user inputs.

Try adjusting the "speed," or *gain*, in the control panel of your computer. Though strictly speaking this setting controls more than gain, for present purposes it can be treated as a gain control. The gain specifies how much the hand movement is amplified or attenuated. At high gain the cursor is very sensitive to the slightest movement, making it difficult to control precisely. At low gain it is very sluggish, moves slowly, and takes a larger hand movement to go the same distance. The point is that the control loop allows us to understand where in the process of control the mouse gain has its effect and how changes to it or other elements in the loop are likely to affect performance. Control theory is used in devices as different as the automated control of elevators and in understanding human control of automobiles. It is this general ability of control theory to represent a large range of human-system interactions that makes it suitable as an organizing principle.

Beyond questions of defining the ways in which we can provide input to the computer, why are they so difficult to use? Usability is of great concern to software developers, with consumer choices influenced by ease-of-use concerns. Indeed, when Google Maps appeared, there were already other mapping software packages in use. However, in contrast to most of the other applications, Google Maps allowed you to type an address into a single field rather than filling in separate fields for street, city, and state. Google Maps also offered a more intuitive way of navigating over the landscape by smoothly scrolling, rather than redrawing the page in the new location as a discrete update. The goal of creating more natural styles of human-computer interaction is seen as having great market potential.

The digital computer also plays a central role in automation. The vast majority of automatic control involves some kind of digital logic that interprets the input and decides what action to take. For example, when you push the button for an elevator, a computer determines when your request will be serviced with respect to all other requests; some elevator systems ask you to select your floor prior to boarding the elevator and instruct people which car to take to minimize stops for all passengers. Modern automobiles now have computers that monitor many aspects of engine behavior, including fuel consumption, fuel flow, and fault detection. Even the apparently analog speedometers are really receiving a digital signal from the car's computer, similar to many of the "analog" clocks that are actually controlled by digital chips.

Part of the problem in dealing with computers in automated systems is the nature of the logic itself. Science-fiction movies and television programs like to depict a cyborg such as Data as coldly logical with no "gray" areas. This stereotype has some truth to it, and can indeed cause problems when humans try to interact with computers. More to the point, digital logic has a number of unfortunate properties. First, it has a number of discrete states, called *modes*, in which the same input causes a different output. This can be a serious problem when an operator is mistaken about the current mode of the system. Consider the case of Air Inter Flight ITF148, which crashed on landing at Strasbourg, France, in 1992 (for details, see Aviation Safety Network, 2008). In setting the descent angle to −3.3 degrees, one of the crew typed −3.3 into the Flight Control Unit (FCU), the computerized automation module that programs flight path. The crew member did not notice that the FCU was in the "vertical speed" mode, not the expected "flight path angle" mode. As a result, he programmed a descent rate of 3300 ft/min, rather than the 800 ft/min it would have been in flight path angle mode. The Vosges Mountains near Strasbourg were shrouded in fog and the crew did not see them before impact. This is a tragic example of how a given input (in this case, the number −3.3) can have dramatically different results depending on the mode.

A second unfortunate property of digital logic systems is that they tend not to degrade gracefully, which is to say that even small errors can cause a complete (i.e., catastrophic) failure of the system. If you've done any simple computer programming, or even just entered a web address into a browser, you've probably experienced this problem, in that a small typographical error, such as typing a semicolon rather than a colon, can cause the program to simply stop or "hang." Contrast this with nondigital systems, in which a small error might produce less-than-optimal system performance but is unlikely to result in complete failure. Putting the wrong type of oil in your car might produce a rough-running engine and lower gas mileage, but it won't cause the car to stop.

A final problem with complex digital logic systems is the difficulty in anticipating how the machine will respond to inputs even when in the right mode. The computer does not have access to a powerful visual system, nor does it have the same computational limits on cognitive processing as a person does. As a rule, people are much better at *recognition-based* decisions and actions rather than deeply nested logical considerations. When we recognize a situation, we can almost "see" the solution. For computer automation, the same problem is solved by a series of complex equations that express the relationships among underlying factors. The problem is that human operators do not have access to the logic being used by the computer and hence are likely to get confused by the computer's behavior. When automation-induced aircraft errors began to receive serious attention in the 1980s, Wiener and Curry (1980) observed that crew members kept asking three questions of the automation over and over: what is it doing, why is it doing that, and what will it do next? The crew needs to know those answers to understand what is happening with their aircraft. That is, the answers are critical to maintaining *situation awareness*. Situation awareness is the understanding that allows people to reason and act effectively in context. In the Strasbourg example, the crew lacked awareness of the setting of the flight computer and the landing zone was obscured by fog: Both factors ultimately contributed to the accident. Noting the position of a single switch on a complicated device with many switches and knobs is a small thing. Yet, it is an example of how small errors can lead to major catastrophes when digital logic is involved.

In summary, devices continue to become more complex as they do more for us and do more of what we used to do ourselves. Now even consumer appliances—refrigerators and toasters—have computers in them that allow you to program them in intricate ways. Where once the study of humans in systems was restricted to military operations or space flight, it is now an important component of research and development across many disciplines. In the final section of this chapter we look at how fields concerned with human-system interaction are organized.

A FRACTURED FIELD

The study of humans in engineered systems is carried out in several related disciplines, within different departments of universities, in military labs, in industrial labs, by engineers, psychologists, by computer scientists, and by experts in their fields without specialized training. Despite this variability, all deal with the interrelatedness captured in the control loop, but approach the problems from somewhat different perspectives. We will give a short, though certainly not complete, history of the fields and how they relate to and differ from one another.

Human Factors/Ergonomics

Perhaps the oldest recognized and established field dealing with humans' interactions with engineered systems is *human factors/ergonomics*. Although some may believe that ergonomics focuses on issues surrounding physical constraints on performance, while human factors focuses on cognitive constraints, the reality is that human factors is a U.S.-centric term that is synonymous with ergonomics internationally. This field of endeavor began expanding as the post-WWII military research, primarily focused on aviation, pushed the boundaries of human physical and mental endurance. However, human factors/ergonomics research is not restricted to military systems; it makes significant contributions in domains ranging from simple consumer products to large, complex systems such as nuclear power plants.

The International Ergonomics Association defines "ergonomics (or human factors) [as] the scientific discipline concerned with the understanding of interactions among humans and other elements of a system, and the profession that applies theory, principles, data and methods to design in order to optimize human well-being and overall system performance" (International Ergonomics Association, 2011). Human factors/ergonomics is largely a generalist field, focused principally on the study of system performance within a specific domain. Because of its dual emphasis on human behavioral characteristics and design, it is most closely associated with programs in applied psychology, engineering psychology, or human factors engineering.

The tools and research methods used in human factors study vary considerably, but can be placed roughly on a continuum from basic to very applied. Basic research in psychology laboratories using artificial tasks seeks tight controls over stimuli and responses in order to discover fundamental properties of human information processing and motor behavior. For example, research on human memory has tried to discern how many different kinds of memories people have, what their storage capacities and decay rates are, and how they are used in daily life. Research on attention has been concerned with how people filter out irrelevant stimulation to focus on one out of several competing tasks or stimuli, and to determine how many things people can do at one time. The tasks used generally bear little resemblance to piloting, driving, surgery, or other target applications. Such laboratory research in engineering contexts seeks to discover fundamental properties of human behavior that generalize widely across domains, such as how joints function to allow people to lift objects or the best logic to use in designing a sophisticated system.

Some researchers have challenged the use of highly controlled laboratory experiments, questioning whether they provide characterizations of human behavior that are of direct use in understanding performance in complex, real domains. The idea that people adapt to the incentives and constraints they find in their environment is certainly not new. It was the cornerstone of behaviorism in the middle of the 20th century. Within the fields of human factors/ergonomics and experimental psychology there is widespread agreement that cognitive systems, memory, and perception have been shaped by the environment and that an understanding of how our perceptual, cognitive, and memory systems work can be informed by understanding the environmental demands to which they have adapted (see, e.g., Anderson & Schooler, 1991; Anderson et al., 2004). The debate is more about whether laboratory studies with artificial, well-controlled stimuli are indeed testing general properties of human information processing, as the science of psychology would claim, or whether it just tells us how people behave in those specific conditions—conditions that are seldom if ever present in the real world. A view that has been labeled *situated cognition* claims that understanding of human behavior outside of a given context is not achievable (Clancy, 1997). This is not just a debate over whether one can generalize from the laboratory to the real world. It is, at its core, a fundamental difference in how human behavior research is conducted.

At the other extreme, then, people attempt either to observe behavior in the real world or to observe users interacting with complex *human-in-the-loop simulations* that try to faithfully replicate the devices, practices, and context in which behavior will occur in the field. This work recognizes that focusing primarily on the human leaves out critical influences of the environment in which the human works, such as the social and corporate structure in which work is done. We often work in social contexts, sometimes in teams with other people, with goals reinforced by incentive structures of the organization. These conditions affect many of the minute-by-minute decisions we make on the job. Studying both human cognition and the systems within which the human operates gives us a more complete picture of how these decisions are arrived at and how actions are conditioned. Although this debate continues in academic circles, in practice, applied researchers and designers make use of scientific principles of human behavior in addition to detailed representations of the environments, activities, and devices specific to a given domain.

In between these two extremes, part-task simulations try to capture essential elements of the task in an attempt to provide both realism and tight control. For example, a part-task simulation of piloting may involve a set of dials that look a little like the altitude, airspeed, and heading dials in a cockpit and a task that has people responding as quickly as they can to deviations from normal. Thus, some aspects of the task setting are preserved, but the task itself and its dependent measure need not be of high fidelity.

Not surprisingly, given the philosophical perspective of researchers in human-systems engineering, research methods borrow from anthropology an emphasis on observation. Observations of people working with devices in the actual environment can be used for gathering preliminary information on whether a problem exists, evaluating a new system, and finding where concerns with organizational efficiency arise. People are observed in daily work behavior, with detailed records made of their movements, activities, discussions, and other aspects of the context.

Laboratory research consists chiefly of high-fidelity simulations of work environments. Whenever possible, experts are used in mock-ups that closely resemble the real work environment. The situated cognition view is especially attractive to engineers and computer scientists who are trying to develop systems that people will use in real-world scenarios. Because situated cognition rejects the notion of definable underlying properties of human behavior, these simulations are not meant to uncover fundamental properties of human cognition, but rather to guide designers in what will be effective in real applications.

Human factors practitioners also use a range of physiological measures, like heart rate, skin conductance, electroencephalograms, and others to assess the emotional state of the user. Which of the measurement methods is suitable depends on the purpose. Early in the design of a system, it will be useful to rapidly collect data on human performance presumed relevant to the future system. As development progresses, greater fidelity in simulation will enable designers to see what works in context. These issues are discussed in depth in the section on methodology (see Chapter 5).

Human-Computer Interaction

The development of computers as a consumer product led to a surge in research on the study of humans interacting with them in the early 1980s. Much of this research was directed at understanding how to present information in ways that people can easily use without excessive training, as well as on developing devices (like the mouse), interfaces to devices (such as menu systems), and software (like Google Maps) that are well adapted to human characteristics. Some research has also been aimed at finding methods that allow one to more easily evaluate how well a system is designed given known human processing limitations. Because the goal of research in human-computer interaction is often the evaluation of a new device—for example, a mouse controlled by the eyes, or a comparison of one version of a device to another—the human-computer research community has devoted considerable effort to improving techniques for measuring and predicting how users will perform with various interface styles (see, e.g., Card, Moran, & Newell, 1983; Gray & Boehm-Davis, 2000; John & Kieras, 1994; Pirolli & Card, 1999). Further, engineers and developers can make use of a wide variety of feedback, from the detailed data of full experiments to the comments of a few observers.

For many software companies, very useful data on their prototype designs can be obtained by *usability testing* in which people are asked to complete predefined tasks with the software. Subjective ratings are collected from the people, such as how well they liked the software and its ease of use. Objective measures are also collected, such as the number of errors that were made or how quickly the test users completed the tasks. Computer models that simulate people using the software are also used, and as we discuss later, can provide additional insights.

Human-Systems Integration

Most recently, the term *human-systems integration* has been used to refer to work being done by human factors/ergonomics practitioners. This label was developed by the Department of Defense, where human factors engineering forms one of eight core areas of study that the DoD feels are critical to the success of fielded military systems. Human systems integration is meant to be used in the design and acquisition phases of the product life cycle, and it "emphasizes human considerations as the top priority" (Naval Postgraduate School, 2011), focusing on manpower, personnel, training, system safety, personnel survivability, health hazards, and habitability in addition to human factors engineering.

The terminology has now been picked up by other groups. For example, the Committee on Human Factors, established through the National Academies in 1980, recently became a board and changed its name to the Board on Human-Systems Integration. They did this to focus attention on the systems approach taken to understanding how best to improve performance when people are working with devices. This board "provides new perspectives on theoretical and methodological issues concerning the relationship of individuals and organizations to technology and the environment, identifies critical issues in the design, test, evaluation, and use of new human-centered technologies, and advises sponsors on the research needed to expand the scientific and technical bases for designing technology to support the needs of its users. The Board also provides a formal and regular forum for sponsors to talk with each other and with a knowledgeable body of experts" (National Academy of Sciences, 2011).

SUMMARY

The history of devices, tools, machines, and systems of representation shows that advances have often come from designs that are better fit to human physical and mental capabilities. The modern era, roughly post-WWII, has seen the development of aircraft, spacecraft, and digital computers that have put people in unusual environments and presented them with tools that are inherently difficult to understand and work with. New systems of inquiry—human factors/ergonomics, human-computer interaction, and human-systems integration—have emerged as formal fields of study whose goal is to ensure that engineered systems are designed for people to use. Where once people were expected to adapt to the machine, now machines are expected to be adapted to humans.

REFERENCES

Ament, P. (2005). Assembly line history—Invention of the assembly line. *The Great Idea Finder*. Retrieved from www.ideafinder.com/history/inventions/assbline.htm

Anderson, J. R., Bothell, D., Byrne, M. D., Douglass, S., Lebiere, C., & Qin, Y. (2004). An integrated theory of the mind. *Psychological Review, 111*, 1036–1060. doi:10.1037/0033-295X.111.4.1036

Anderson, J. R., & Schooler, L. J. (1991). Reflections of the environment in memory. *Psychological Science, 2*(6), 396–408. doi:10.1111/j.1467-9280.1991.tb00174.x

Aviation Safety Network. (2008, January 11). ASN aircraft accident Airbus A320-111 F-GGED Strasbourg-Entzheim Airport (SXB). Retrieved from http://aviation-safety.net/database/record.php?id=19920120-0

Barnes, R. M. (1966). *Motion and time study: Design and measurement of work.* New York, NY: John Wiley & Sons.

Card, S. K., Moran, T. P., & Newell, A. (1983). *The psychology of human-computer interaction*. Hillsdale, N.J: L. Erlbaum.

Clancy, W. (1997). *Situated cognition: On human knowledge and computer representation*. New York, NY: Cambridge University Press.

Fitts, P. M. (1958). Engineering psychology. *Annual Review of Psychology*, *9*, 267–294. doi:10.1146/annurev.ps.09.020158.001411

Ford, H., & Crowther, S. (1922). *My life and work*. Garden City, NY: Garden City Publishing Co., Inc., http://books.google.com/books/about/My_life_and_work .html?id=4K82efXzn10C

Gilbreth, F. (1910). *Motion study: A method for increasing the efficiency of the workman*. New York, NY: van Nostrand.

Gray, W. D., & Boehm-Davis, D. A. (2000). Milliseconds matter: An introduction to microstrategies and to their use in describing and predicting interactive behavior. *Journal of Experimental Psychology-Applied*, *6*, 322–335.

International Ergonomics Association. (2011). Ergonomics. Retrieved from www.iea .cc/01_what/What%20is%20Ergonomics.html

John, B. E., & Kieras, D. (1994). *The GOMS family of analysis techniques: Tools for design and evaluation*. Pittsburgh, PA: Carnegie Mellon University.

Liebowitz, S. L., & Margolis, S. E. (1990). The fable of the keys. *Journal of Law and Economics*, *33*(1), 1–26.

Logan, G. D. (1988). Toward an instance theory of automatization. *Psychological Review*, *95*(4), 492–527. doi:10.1037/0033-295X.95.4.492

National Academy of Sciences. (2011). *Board on Human-Systems Integration*. Retrieved from http://www7.nationalacademies.org/dbasse/Board_on_Human-Systems_Integration.html

Naval Postgraduate School. (2011). Human systems integration. Retrieved April 17, 2012, from www.nps.edu/or/hsi/

Pirolli, P., & Card, S. (1999). Information foraging. *Psychological Review*, *106*, 643–675.

Roscoe, S. N. (1948). The effect of eliminating binocular and peripheral monocular visual cues upon airplane pilot performance in landing. *Journal of Applied Psychology*, *32*(6), 649.

Schneider, W., & Shiffrin, R. M. (1977). Controlled and automatic human information processing: I. Detection, search, and attention. *Psychological Review*, *84*(1), 1–66. doi:10.1037/0033-295X.84.1.1

Shiffrin, R. M., & Schneider, W. (1977). Controlled and automatic human information processing: II. Perceptual learning, automatic attending and a general theory. *Psychological Review*, *84*(2), 127–190. doi:10.1037/0033-295X.84.2.127

Shrader, C. R. (2006). History of operations research in the United States Army: Volume I 1942–1962. United States Army. Retrieved from www.history.army.mil/html/books/hist_op_research/index.html

Wiener, E. L., & Curry, R. (1980). Flight-deck automation: Promises and problems. *Ergonomics*, *23*(10), 995–1011. doi:10.1080/00140138008924809

Wikipedia. (2011). Assembly line. Retrieved October 25, 2011, from http://en.wikipedia.org/wiki/Assembly_line#CITEREFFord1922

Yasuoka, K., & Yasuoka, M. (n.d.). On the prehistory of QWERTY. *ZINBUN*, *42*, 161–174.

3

The Current Practice

Before we end our historical treatment and begin a technical analysis of environments, it is worth briefly describing a few of the many domains in which human-system specialists work. This is not meant to be an exhaustive study by any means. Rather, we have selected domains that illustrate some shared properties and concerns, but that involve different factors determining what people do and how the analysis of human behavior is integrated into actual work.

In any given domain, the human-system specialist is concerned with the application of technology and the usability of systems to maximize goals such as *safety*, *functionality*, *productivity*, or *market appeal*. A safe design is one that succeeds in minimizing the risk of human error, or mitigating the consequences of human error. A functional design is one that allows users to complete all of the tasks they would like to complete. A productive design allows the user to complete those tasks efficiently. Finally, a usable design is one that succeeds in being intuitive to use and is thereby easily learned, increasing its market appeal.

A design that maximizes functionality does not always also maximize usability. In fact, those goals are often in conflict. The violin, for example, is a wonderfully expressive instrument that, in the hands of a virtuoso, is capable of producing astounding music. It is functional in that it makes a broad range of timbre, speed, and scale available to the trained individual. Yet, it is not easy to use and takes many years of dedicated practice to master.

Experts often prefer devices that offer precise and efficient control of a variety of outputs once they have been mastered, even though they are more difficult to learn. In contrast, novices often prefer usable devices that produce a limited but acceptable range of outputs. In computer systems, for example, experts often prefer to use "hot" or "function" keys that must be memorized to execute tasks (such as opening or saving a file), whereas novices tend to prefer pull-down menus. In golf, professionals use clubs whose design affords precise control of the spin on the ball that can produce a desired trajectory and can be made to stop and even reverse upon landing. However, such clubs are notoriously unforgiving of small deviations from a perfect strike (much like a violin that squeals when the bow pressure is not precise). Novice golfers instead prefer clubs that limit the trajectory options but produce good outcomes even when the ball is struck poorly.

In most situations, some training will be required to use any device or perform any meaningful task. Human-system specialists are often involved in the design, execution, and evaluation of training.

These concerns are not separate, independent issues; rather, they interact with each other. Training and usability obviously have an effect on market appeal. In selecting a car, people often trade off factors associated with appearance (e.g., color and style) with ease of use (e.g., standard stick shift versus automatic transmission). However, the unique character of individual environments means that domains vary in the emphasis they place on each factor.

AEROSPACE

System design in commercial, military, and space flight domains tends to emphasize safety, as flight is an inherently dangerous activity. Despite this inherent danger, the 20th century became the era of mass commercial air travel. Millions of people across the globe fly each day with confidence that the aircraft, controlled by human pilots, will deliver them safely to their destination. The track record of safety, certainly for the developed countries, justifies this confidence. Airline accidents are major news when they occur, belying the fact that, per passenger mile flown, or time in travel, flying is the safest way to travel from one place to another that has ever been invented (Charette, 2011; Lowy, 2011; Takemoto & Jones, 2011).

It was not always so. In its early days, human flight was a risky business. Pilot training was absent or ad hoc, controls were makeshift, aircraft were flimsy, and navigation aids consisted of little more than observations of major terrain features. Aircraft routinely crashed, went off course, or just disappeared. No doubt much of this was due to mechanical failures, but human error has always been a significant contributor to accidents and mishaps. From the beginning, there has been a concern with reducing pilot error (see, e.g., Fitts, 1958; Roscoe, 1948).

In recent times, aviation research in human-system interaction has widened from the traditional investigations of "stick and rudder" handling qualities and visual displays that once dominated aviation human factors. Aeronautical engineers have a very good handle on how to design for human use in this regard. Nonetheless, interest still continues in the training of such skills. As the information load on the pilot continues to expand, designers are increasingly concerned with new display technologies that allow the pilot to better manage the information load. The widespread introduction of highly sophisticated automation had led to concerns about the management of these increasingly capable automated systems. The introduction of high levels of automation throughout the 1970s and 1980s changed the nature of piloting. Pilots who were accustomed to hands-on control of the aircraft were now being asked to program a computer that would fly the plane. Moreover, the computer now sat between their input and the control surfaces of the aircraft and would interpret their input, rather than just moving the control surfaces as directed. Pilots began losing awareness of what the aircraft was doing or what it would do. As a result, the long-time interest in displays, though still with us, has yielded ground to a growing interest in human interaction in teams that increasingly include automated devices as well as other humans.

The same concerns with safety of flight and human error have also been drivers of innovation in air traffic control. Before the September 11, 2001, attack in the United States, crowding in the airspace was reaching crisis proportions. Those attacks led to a dramatic decrease in air traffic, but passenger levels had largely recovered by 2005 and now exceed those before the attack (Bureau of Transportation Statistics, 2005, 2011). The problem for the air traffic controller is that the sky is now much more crowded, with more planes to route in the same amount of time to the same limited set of airports. Engineers and human-system specialists are now focused on how to design air traffic control operations for the near and long-term future. Human-system specialists are being included earlier in the design process, as concepts are being discussed. Previously, a human factors specialist might be asked either to fix up the displays so they looked good or to choose display symbols. Now, human-system specialists are being asked to comment on the possible human response to entirely new concepts of aircraft control and air traffic management. Although this is to be counted as a success story, it does place new and increased demands on those of us who study human behavior in engineered systems. We must come up with ways to extrapolate what we know about human behavior to environments that are still in the idea stage. The response has been a boost in the role of modeling and simulation to complement the standard empirical methods. In most cases, human-system specialists are being asked to provide evidence of safety, workload, and the likelihood of human error.

The Human-System Specialist in Aerospace

In the aerospace industry, human-system specialists work in close coordination with aerospace engineers at several points during the design of a new aircraft, new air traffic control suites, or new displays and controls. In a field as complex as aerospace, with such an overriding concern with safety, many years can elapse between the initial concept and its realization as an aircraft or new air traffic control equipment. New systems usually begin with a core concept that is developed to meet a set of requirements. For example, the military might specify that it wants an aircraft capable of a certain speed and maneuverability, with specific displays.

The example of the Boeing X-37 space plane (for more information, see Boeing, 2011; Parsch, 2009; Wikipedia, 2011a) provides a concrete example of how design works in aviation. A few years ago, there was intense interest in a commercially viable "space plane" that would take off like a normal plane but would fly into space, in a suborbital trajectory, and then return. With increasing globalization, there was growing pressure to shorten flight times between the major nations, and a possible market for new aircraft that could do so. The goal was to be able to fly from Los Angeles to Tokyo in a couple of hours. The space plane had to satisfy a large set of demands and constraints, from commercial feasibility to passenger comfort and safety. From these initial design objectives, a preliminary design concept emerged that defined the components of the system, along with those things that are well known and those areas where engineering research had to be done. Two of the key systems research efforts for the space plane were how to build an engine capable of transitioning from a jet to a rocket and, given the issues with reentry, how to design the cockpit of the plane to withstand the heat of reentry yet provide the pilot with good viewing conditions once in jet flight mode.

Once the preliminary design was agreed upon, separate teams began to work on the various subsystems that would constitute the plane, and conducted research on the difficult bits. Each independent subsystem produced prototypes of the various system components that were iteratively tested. In the next phase, the separate systems were integrated into a prototype vehicle. This progression is typical of aircraft design. A prototype usually goes through a series of iterative tests of increasing realism, undergoing modifications in response to each. Initial tests may be computer simulations that check all systems, or simulate the vehicle in different flight regimes. The human response to the flight controls and displays, as well as the development of procedures for operating the craft under all conditions, are both important components of this testing. Human-system specialists are actively engaged in devising test regimes and conducting tests that help develop the role of the pilot and the interaction of pilot and aircraft. For the X-37, these preflight phases lasted from acceptance of the initial concept in 1999 to the first flight test in 2006 (Wikipedia, 2011a). The X-37 development was transferred to the Air Force in 2004 and is currently undergoing continued flight tests, with two completed orbital flights.

We have already noted the involvement of human-system specialists in the testing of the prototype. In fact, human-system specialists are involved in most phases for systems that humans will be controlling, monitoring, or repairing. Displays and controls will be tested to ensure that they deliver the right information and match human perceptual and motor characteristics. Pilots and crew will be debriefed after testing to take verbal reports of their impressions of the system. Large-scale simulations will be conducted that test the system in field-like conditions. Human-system specialists will also serve on working groups to evaluate concepts and propose alternatives, or to fix problems. Finally, researchers will be involved in developing new displays or procedures that will enhance human capability. For example, in the space plane development cycle, psychologists and human factors researchers tested the viability of flying the plane without a windscreen, instead integrating the input from several cameras placed in the hull. The challenging questions related to how to fuse information from radar of different frequencies into a display that pilots could use. These concepts were not included in the final design, but provided valuable data. Indeed, the engineering process is littered with ideas that were either dead ends, failed to achieve performance levels, or were not commercially viable. Nonetheless, the research often provides the ideas for new concepts.

MEDICINE

Safety is also a major concern in medicine. According to some sources, medical error is the fifth leading cause of death in the United States (Medical News Today, 2007), with an estimated 98,000 deaths per year attributed to errors in hospitals (Institute of Medicine, 1999). Yet, systematic study of the human in medicine, and the application of human-system techniques to medicine, has emerged more recently than in aerospace or manufacturing. Like the aerospace domain, it arose from concerns about human error, but unlike aerospace there are fewer concerns with controls or usability. Human error in diagnosis, surgery, dosages, nursing care, prosthetics, and other practices are now being examined in the context of the environment in which they occur and the characteristics of human behavior in such environments. Many of the errors made by doctors and nurses have their roots in the hectic interrupt-driven intensive-care, emergency medical and surgical environments where decisions must be made quickly and where there are high demands on human memory and multitasking skills (Gaba, Howard, & Small, 1995; Grundgeiger et al., 2010; Santell, 2005).

For example, the airline industry has long used checklists to prevent errors of omission. A *checklist* is a written procedure that is followed like a script. In aviation, engineers try to anticipate all of the possible situations a pilot will likely face and provide a checklist to use in case one occurs. In this way, checklists greatly reduce the likelihood of a missed step or other erroneous execution of a procedure. They also free the pilot from having to know all responses to all situations in advance; when an emergency does happen, the pilot can focus on correcting it rather than trying to figure out what to do under intense time and emotional pressure. Physicians are now beginning to use checklists to prevent errors of this sort from happening in the medical domain (Hales, Terblanche, Fowler, & Sibbald, 2008).

The application of human-system technologies to medicine is not concerned solely with reducing error, but also with providing new treatments in specific cases. Devices are now being developed that offer enhanced productivity and usability to patients. Cutting-edge technologies for a variety of disabilities are now making their way into practice, with a growing research community involved in their continued refinement and development. For example, software tools are available that have been proven to help deaf individuals speak more clearly. Advanced prosthetic devices for amputees also have seen rapid progress in recent years. In the past, users had difficulty adapting to prosthetic limbs. They were heavy and required unnatural movements of unrelated muscles to move—a problematic situation especially for arms and hands, where dexterity is of paramount importance. Myoelectric arms are now available that use surface electrodes to detect electrical impulses from intact nerves that once controlled the missing limb. The user can give similar commands to move the prosthetic limb as would be given to move an intact limb. Research is under way to implant sensors under the skin that make direct contact with nerves to yield even more flexibility and control, as well as to give sensory tactile and proprioceptive feedback regarding the prosthetic limb.

New sensor arrays for the blind also have been an active area of research. It is even possible to use skin surfaces to represent the visual world (Kajimoto, Kanno, & Tachi, 2006; Kamel & Landay, 2002; Wall & Brewster, 2006). A high-resolution camera is used to project digital representations of a scene, including text, to a mechanical device that converts the digital image to a set of discrete pressure points on the skin surface. The mechanical pressure device can be connected to almost any skin surface, including the tongue, which is a good receptor for this input because it has many sensory nerve endings that give accurate feedback on tongue position and shape for speech. Surprisingly, blind individuals tested with these devices claim to have little trouble in converting the spatial pressure gradients on the tongue to visual images.

It is no longer a science-fiction fantasy to imagine improving or augmenting our inherent capabilities rather than simply bringing them closer to normal. The U.S. Defense Advanced Research Projects Agency (DARPA) and other branches of the military have been exploring ways to augment the cognitive capabilities of healthy young adults (see John, Kobus, Morrison, & Schmorrow, 2004).

The Human-System Specialist in Medicine

In the medical field, the human factors specialist tends to be loosely affiliated with the medical team and may serve as a consultant or independent researcher. In some cases, the human-system specialist will be trained in basic procedures and allowed to observe and record surgeries or to record doctors discussing possible diagnoses. A systematic involvement of human factors experts in medicine, as well as pharmaceutical research and development, has begun to emerge, but at present it is less extensive than in aerospace. In aerospace, aircraft companies and airlines employ human factors specialists directly. In medical domains, the specialists generally are employed by universities, and they conduct research and development as part of their academic careers.

In academia, there is an emerging specialty in such areas as emergency medical care, prosthetics, and aids for the disabled. One area of long-standing interest is in the reading of X-rays. This is far from an easy task: It takes years of practice as a radiologist to perfect this skill. Even then, errors are not as rare as desired. Fortunately, CT scans and MRIs provide much more accurate images of internal structures, taking much of the guesswork out of interpreting images. This is another lesson in the practice: Technology often advances at a faster pace than understanding. CT scans were developed and put into use long before technicians fully understood how to read and interpret X-rays. It is worth remembering that the problem of today is often eclipsed by the technology of tomorrow.

AUTOMOTIVE INDUSTRY

Car designers are concerned with both safety and comfort. Just as for aircraft, the design of displays and the quality of the feedback from controls such as brakes and steering is important. However, automobiles are consumer goods and as such must appeal to buyers. Thus, features that please drivers, making them more comfortable or making driving more convenient, are also important considerations. Knowing what sorts of features would attract a buyer to your car rather than a competitor's is part of the engineering mandate. Not that long ago, cruise control and power windows were expensive options available only on luxury models.

An emphasis on comfort does not mean that safety has been neglected. Since 1986, automobile safety regulations have required manufactures to install a taillight mounted high and in the center of the rear, more directly in the line of sight of the following driver (see Wikipedia, 2011b). This regulation is consistent with an analysis of human perception and attention (Malone, Kirkpatrick, Kohl, & Baker, n.d.). More recent models feature a rear camera that eases the problem of knowing where the back bumper is when backing up. There are also forward-looking radar devices in development that will alert you when you are in danger of a collision with the car in front, as well as infrared sensors with windscreen displays for night driving. An automatic braking system, activated when a collision is likely, is currently an option on high-end cars, and may soon become a standard feature. Automotive designers have been experimenting with "smart-car" concepts (see, e.g., Hancock & Verwey, 1997; Risto, Martens, & Wilschut, 2010; Stanton, Young, & McCaulder, 1997; van Waterschoot & van der Voort, 2009), including technologies in which the vehicle is monitored by sensors in the road, and fully or partly controlled by a computerized system that adjusts speed based on flow through the entire road grid. Still, until cars are driven completely automatically, there will be a concern for understanding how and why drivers err, and how they calculate the risks against the reward.

The Human-System Specialist in the Automotive Industry

As in the aerospace industry, most major automobile makers employ teams of human-system specialists in the design process to work side-by-side with automotive engineers. In part, they are involved in the design of new displays and features to attract consumers and increase safety. Because cars are sold worldwide, attention must be paid to the fact that each country has standards that define what features are mandatory. Human-system specialists will be responsible for ensuring that the car conforms to the standards of a given country with respect to visibility, mirrors, displays, steering, and other features that affect the driver and passengers.

COMPUTER INDUSTRY

Unlike the aerospace, medical, or automotive industries, the computer industry historically has had less concern with safety and more with ease of use and productivity. There is concern over the reliability of software and the dangers that errors could pose, but not so much with safe operation by the user. Instead, the success of the computer, and the reason the computer enjoys such a central role in modern society, can be largely attributed to a breakthrough in the usability of computers. Throughout the 1960s and well into the 1970s, computer use was prevalent only in scientific laboratories and business, where its capability for rapid computation was most appreciated. It was indeed a large electronic number cruncher. Early work by human-computer specialists was focused on the difficult problems of computer programming and software engineering in general. The digital logic of the computer proved a barrier to finding and fixing "bugs," or errors in the program.

When a mechanical system breaks, there is often a pattern of suspicious behavior—noises, errors—that tells the operator that something is wrong. There is also a kind of graceful degradation. In the digital computer, a single incorrect binary digit (a 1 or 0) can cause catastrophic failure at worst and puzzling behavior at best. As software programs became more complex, it became increasingly important to develop tools that programmers could use to help structure the code and to identify potential sources of errors.

By the 1970s, computer use was becoming increasingly widespread, with arguable increases in productivity and little progress in the way of usability. Home use of computers was confined to hobbyists who would solder their own circuits and were comfortable coding in long strings of 1s and 0s. High-level computer languages, such as FORTRAN and COBOL, were generally not usable on small home machines. A usability breakthrough was achieved in the 1960s and 1970s at Xerox PARC (Palo Alto Research Center). Researchers at PARC developed prototype systems that combined a mouse for pointing and input with a graphical user interface using icons and desk-like constructs, such as folders. Apple tried to market this in its Lisa system, but it was not until computer power increased enough to handle the heavy computational demands of the modern graphical, point-and-click interface that home computers took off. Software and hardware companies soon realized that usability was a key to success. Command-line interfaces, where users typed commands in a specified order, have been almost entirely replaced by the modern mouse-driven graphical user interface. As noted earlier, the phenomenal success of Google Maps, and later Google Earth, can in large part be attributed to its ease of use. Web-based map software had existed long before Google came to the table. Google, however, provided an easy way for people to scroll around a map, and this feature played an important part in garnering loyal fans.

The Human-System Specialist in Human-Computer Interfaces

In industry, IBM, Microsoft, and Apple have extensive research and development efforts. There is often close interchange between industry and academia. New versions of computers, such as the Apple and its associated iPad, iPhone, and iPod Touch devices, for example, make use of gestural interfaces where movement of multiple fingers can be used to indicate how the display should respond. Universities as well as industry have been actively involved in development and testing of these devices.

Even though there has been a systematic infusion of human-system specialists into industry, the types of work done differ considerably from those in aerospace, medical, or automotive industry. Safety is not a great concern for human-computer interfaces. Instead, new functionality and increased ease of use are the important drivers. Companies are in fierce competition, making time-to-market for new technologies very important. Thus, there are few large-scale usability experiments. Instead, testing consists of small, focused experiments conducted with a few subjects who give verbal feedback as well as performance data. In large industry laboratories, such as those at IBM, Microsoft, and Apple, more rigorous testing does occur, with data collected on time to complete prescribed tasks. In academia, empirical research is often complemented or augmented by the development of computer models that predict the time to perform standard tasks.

The importance of usability is not confined to its market appeal: It can determine the success or failure of expensive and critical infrastructure. For example, in 1996, the Federal Aviation Administration signed an agreement with Raytheon to develop a new workstation for air traffic controllers, named the Standard Terminal Automation Replacement System, or STARS for short. The FAA specifications for STARS were intended to provide a more flexible path for upgrades and lower maintenance costs than the existing terminals. In 1998, the air traffic controllers' union raised serious objections to the user interface of STARS. The union claimed that the FAA specifications failed to consider several important consequences of their choices for controllers. This led to a protracted dispute that was settled only by a redesign of STARS that included an additional 100,000 lines of computer code. This brought the cost up from the initial $940 million to a projected $4 billion. In the final analysis, the FAA agreed that it had erred originally in not seeking input from controllers and the controller union before specifying the design.

SUMMARY

This brief overview shows that demands of the environment in which a device is used will determine the relative emphasis placed on safety, productivity, usability, training, or market appeal. Although there is a shared set of basic principles that are widely accepted, the real innovations and detailed understanding depend on an in-depth understanding of the particulars in any domain. The many ways in which the domains place unique or special demands on people must also be addressed. We will now turn our attention to the classification and analysis of domains, emphasizing factors that affect behavior.

REFERENCES

Boeing. (2011). Boeing: X-37B orbital test vehicle. Retrieved from www.boeing.com/defense-space/ic/sis/x37b_otv/x37b_otv.html

Bureau of Transportation Statistics. (2005). *Airline travel since 9/11* (Special Reports and Issues Brief No. 13). Washington, DC: U.S. Department of Transportation. Retrieved from www.bts.gov/publications/special_reports_and_issue_briefs/number_13/html/entire.html

Bureau of Transportation Statistics. (2011, October 14). RITA/BTS/July 2011: Airline system traffic up 2.0 percent from July 2010 (BTS press release). Retrieved from www.bts.gov/press_releases/2011/bts051_11/html/bts051_11.html

Charette, R. (2011, September 6). How serious are the air safety concerns being raised in the press? *IEEE Spectrum.* Retrieved from http://spectrum.ieee.org/riskfactor/aerospace/aviation/how-serious-are-the-air-safety-concerns-being-raised

Fitts, P. M. (1958). Engineering psychology. *Annual Review of Psychology, 9,* 267–294. doi:10.1146/annurev.ps.09.020158.001411

Gaba, D. M., Howard, S. K., & Small, S. D. (1995). Situation awareness in anesthesiology. *Human Factors: The Journal of the Human Factors and Ergonomics Society, 37*(1), 20–31. doi:10.1518/001872095779049435

Grundgeiger, T., Sanderson, P. M., Orihuela, C. B., Thompson, A., MacDougall, H. G., Nunnink, L., & Venkatesh, B. (2010). Distractions and interruptions in the intensive care unit: A field observation and a simulator experiment. *Human Factors and Ergonomics Society Annual Meeting Proceedings, 54,* 835–839.

Hales, B., Terblanche, M., Fowler, R., & Sibbald, W. (2008). Development of medical checklists for improved quality of patient care. *International Journal of Quality Health Care, 20*(1), 22–30.

Hancock, P. A., & Verwey, W. B. (1997). Fatigue, workload and adaptive driver systems. *Accident Analysis & Prevention, 29*(4), 495–506.

Institute of Medicine. (1999). *To err is human: Building a safer health care system.* Washington, DC: National Academies Press.

John, M. S., Kobus, D. A., Morrison, J. G., & Schmorrow, D. (2004). Overview of the DARPA augmented cognition technical integration experiment. *International Journal of Human-Computer Interaction, 17*(2), 131–149.

Kajimoto, H., Kanno, Y., & Tachi, S. (2006). Forehead electro-tactile display for vision substitution. *Proceedings of the EuroHaptics* 2006, July 3–6, 2006. Paris, France, 75–79. http://lsc.univ-evry.fr/~eurohaptics/upload/cd/papers/f62.pdf.

Kamel, H. M., & Landay, J. A. (2002). Sketching images eyes-free: A grid-based dynamic drawing tool for the blind. Assets -02 Proceedings of the fifth international ACM conference on assistive technologies. New York, NY: ACM Press, 33–40, doi:10.1145/638249.638258.

Lowy, J. (2011, August 30). AP IMPACT: Automation in the air dulls pilot skill. Retrieved September 12, 2011, from www.google.com/hostednews/ap/article/ALeqM5gdmYSGPD7TdQa-QsiKHXDoTd_uaA?docId=a4e56bdd941949d9b5f711277b56bdf5

Malone, T. B., Kirkpatrick, M., Kohl, J. S., & Baker, C. (n.d.). *Field test evaluation of rearlighting systems* (NHTSA, U.S. Department of Transportation No. DOT-HS-5-01228). Alexandria, VA: Essex Corp.

Medical News Today. (2007, June 23). Medical error is the fifth-leading cause of death in the U.S. *Medical News Today*. Retrieved from www.medicalnewstoday.com/releases/75042.php

Parsch, A. (2009, November 23). Boeing X-37/X-40. Retrieved from www.designation-systems.net/dusrm/app4/x-37.html

Risto, M., Martens, M., & Wilschut, E. (2010). Introduction to the connected cruise control and related human factors considerations. In T. P. Alkim & T. Arentze (Eds.), 11th TRAIL Congress Connecting People – Integrating Expertise, November 23–24, 2010. Delft, The Netherlands. Delft: TRAIL (ISBN 978-90-5584-139-4).

Roscoe, S. N. (1948). The effect of eliminating binocular and peripheral monocular visual cues upon airplane pilot performance in landing. *Journal of Applied Psychology*, *32*(6), 649.

Santell, J. P. (2005). Medication errors: Experience of the United States Pharmacopeia (USP). *Joint Commission Journal on Quality and Patient Safety/Joint Commission Resources*, *31*(2), 114–119.

Stanton, N. A., Young, M., & McCaulder, B. (1997). Drive-by-wire: The case of driver workload and reclaiming control with adaptive cruise control. *Safety Science*, *27*(2–3), 149–159.

Takemoto, P., & Jones, T. (2011, July 6). Press release—FAA celebrates 75th anniversary of air traffic control. Retrieved from www.faa.gov/news/press_releases/news_story.cfm?newsId=12903&omniRss=press_releasesAoc&cid=102_P_R

van Waterschoot, B., & van der Voort, M. (2009). Implementing human factors within the design process of advanced driver assistance systems (ADAS). *Engineering Psychology and Cognitive Ergonomics*, *5639*, 461–470.

Wall, S., & Brewster, S. (2006). Feeling what you hear: Tactile feedback for navigation of audio graphs. In *Conference on Human Factors in Computing Systems*, April 22–27, 2006. Montréal, Québec, Canada, 1123–1132. New York, NJ:ACM Press, doi:10.1145/1124772.1124941

Wikipedia. (2011a, October 10). Boeing X-37. Retrieved October 31, 2011, from http://en.wikipedia.org/wiki/Boeing_X-37

Wikipedia. (2011b, October 22). Automotive lighting. Retrieved October 31, 2011, from http://en.wikipedia.org/wiki/Automotive_lighting

Part II

The Environment

At 4:00 A.M. on March 28, 1979, the polisher system within the secondary cooling system at the Three Mile Island nuclear power plant near Harrisburg, Pennsylvania, failed. Investigators believe that in the process of failing, the system leaked a small amount of water, which led to an incorrect indication that something was wrong with the secondary cooling system. This faulty indication led to a shutdown of the turbine and the engagement of emergency feedwater pumps, which are designed to cool down the secondary cooling system. Although the operator confirmed that the pumps were engaged, no one noticed that the pipes designed to carry the water to the cooling system were in the closed position. Thus, the water never made it to the secondary cooling system. Two indicators would have shown that the pipes were closed, but they were usually in an open position, so no one thought to check them. Further, one of the two indicators was obscured by a tag hanging from another switch located above the indicator. By the time the operators determined that the pipes were blocked, it was too late. The resulting rise in temperature and pressure led to the opening of the pilot-operated relief valve, which channels water into the system to reduce the heat and pressure. Unfortunately, the valve became stuck in the open position and continued to inject water into the system beyond when it should have stopped. Operators, who were aware that this had happened in the past, looked for an indication that the valve was actually closed. They mistook an indicator designed to show that the valve had received a *signal* to close as an indication that the valve had actually closed. "The operators could have been aware of none of these."

(Perrow, 1999, p. 22)

The study of humans in engineered systems is the study of people using tools to accomplish tasks within an environment. In the first chapter, we saw how concern for human use has been an essential driver of engineering since the first stone tools were produced. As the preceding case-study example illustrates, however, the cognitive complexity associated with our modern, sophisticated systems can lead to tools that are only incompletely understood. It is tempting to lay the blame on people: insufficient training, or lack of attention, for example. On closer inspection, it often turns out that the failure of the human operator can be traced to a failure to comprehend the complex, and often hidden, interactions among devices. The sophistication of modern systems requires a systematic study of humans in engineered systems. In Chapter 3, we saw how *human factors* research in aviation gained momentum during World War II. Aviation remains an important domain for human factors, but the study of humans in engineered systems has quickly spread to an ever-widening number of domains. In this section, we describe how the tools people use and the environments in which they work affect and help shape human behavior. Thus, we focus here on the external world, not specifically on the human operator.

It may seem odd to emphasize the impact of domains in a book whose focus is on the cognitive aspects of human behavior. In fact, an understanding of the nature of the environment, its characteristics, and its demands is essential to understanding the behavior of people (or of any organism, for that matter). In one sense, we are similar to one another because of a long process of evolution that has shaped us physically and mentally to survive: first on the grasslands, then in small communities, and now in large urban settings. As with all organisms, part of this adaptation is a behavioral repertoire that consists of habits, perceptions, and decision processes that have proven useful in that environment. The same forces that have shaped the convergent evolution of sharks and dolphins so that they have similar body configurations can also shape our behavior.

Adaptation also happens in the short term. To greater or lesser degrees, evolution has provided each species with the ability to learn so that its members can adapt in the short term to the specifics of their particular environments. We humans have a very flexible brain that can come up with wonderfully inventive ways to do, and get, what we want in a multitude of environments. To a first approximation, then, people will adapt their behavior to achieve their goals given the opportunities and constraints of the environment in which they operate. This principle was most eloquently stated by the Nobel Prize-winning computer scientist Herbert Simon (Simon, 1996), who wrote that:

> We watch an ant make his laborious way across a wind- and wave-molded beach. . . . Viewed as a geometric figure, the ant's path is irregular, complex, hard to describe. But its complexity is really a complexity in the surface of the beach, not a complexity in the ant. On that same beach another small creature with a home at the same place as the ant might well follow a very similar path.

If one were to examine the movements of the control stick, throttle, and pedals made by experienced fighter pilots, one would find a remarkable similarity for any given maneuver. Similarly, workers on an assembly line may hold a welding tool at different angles, but that angle is constrained, as they must achieve a secure joint between the two parts of the assembly within acceptable tolerances for alignment of the two parts. This is because only a small variation in input will be tolerated in achieving any particular maneuver. It is true that not all environments constrain our actions as severely as controlling a fighter aircraft or welding an assembly. We often have more freedom in how we satisfy those constraints to achieve our goal, but we are still very sensitive to incentives and constraints. Having said that, we frequently fail to fully adapt, and end up making errors or behaving inefficiently. This is commonly due to a mismatch between our natural behavioral tendencies, evolved over millennia in small groups foraging in savannah and forests, and the new demands of complex technologies and situations. We will treat these shortcomings in succeeding sections.

REFERENCES

Perrow, C. (1999). *Normal accidents: Living with high-risk technologies* (updated ed.). Princeton, NJ: Princeton University Press.

Simon, H. A. (1996). *The sciences of the artificial* (3rd ed.). Cambridge, MA: MIT Press.

4

The Varied Nature of Environments

The importance of the environment is well understood by human factors engineers and human-system engineers. The pyramid in Figure 4.1 (after Bisantz & Roth, 2008) depicts the relative contributions of the physical environment, the social and organizational structure, the technical system, the task situation, and practitioner characteristics. In this conceptualization, placing the details of human behavior at the apex indicates that they are less influential than environmental factors. Its point, in short, is to emphasize the influence of the environment on behavior, with the greatest influence coming from characteristics of the domain. Although this will not be true for all environments all the time, it highlights the central point that to understand humans in engineered systems, we must understand the nature of the environment in which they find themselves. Indeed, it is rare to find a human-system specialist who works across many domains. The typical human-system engineer, or human factors practitioner, specializes in one domain. In fact, many contributions have been made by human factors practitioners who began as domain practitioners—pilots, nuclear power plant operators, surgeons—and never received formal training in human behavior or psychology. The reason is that the details of the work environment matter quite a lot and it takes a long time to understand how they affect behavior. Although we do not necessarily agree with those who argue that an understanding of human cognition is not necessary (Hollnagel & Woods, 2005), we would agree that knowledge of general characteristics of human performance, though necessary, is not sufficient.

The goal of this section is thus to introduce you to the systematic analysis of domains. That environments differ is uncontroversial and obvious to everyone. No one would have a difficult time listing differences between a university professor writing a textbook in her office, a surgeon operating on a patient, a soccer player passing the ball to a teammate, a forensic analyst identifying fingerprints, a pilot flying an aircraft, or a customer service representative talking with a customer in a telephone call center. If you were to ask people to name differences, you would get a long list. What is not so obvious is how these differences shape or influence behavior. Given the importance of the environment, it is fair to say that even small things will matter. The question is whether there is a systematic taxonomy that divides domains in a way that provides insight into the behavior of humans in engineered systems. In this chapter, we discuss some underlying features that provide a basis for a qualitative distinction between environments from which behavioral consequences follow. We first distinguish between two fundamentally different types of

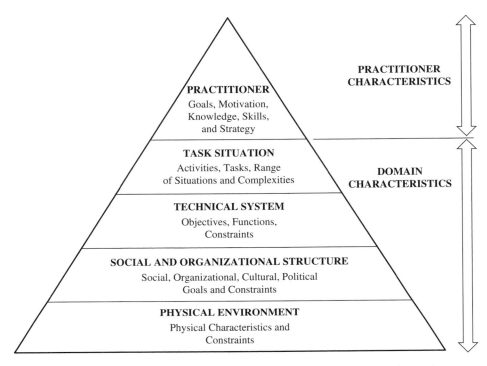

Figure 4.1 Schematic depiction of factors that affect human performance in complex environments. The importance is indicated by the level in the hierarchy (width), starting with the characteristics of the physical environment and ending with practitioner characteristics. *Source:* After Bisantz & Roth (2008).

domains, static and dynamic, each with its own unique set of problems. For each, we discuss the ways in which the workflow, demand for speed, presence and role of other people, and technology affect the human operator.

STATIC VS. DYNAMIC DOMAINS

If we compare the example of the professor writing a textbook to that of the soccer player, we can see a few differences that are indeed crucial. One is the extent to which the domain is *static* or *dynamic*. The key difference between static and dynamic domains is in how the external system behaves in response to user input and external factors. In *static domains*, the execution of an action causes a discrete change in state; further, no other agent or force in the environment causes additional changes in the activity. In *dynamic domains*, the execution of an action by the operator is filtered through a time-sensitive process involving lags, perturbations, noise, and complex systems dynamics. That is, the state of the system being controlled is constantly in flux, evolving in real time, determined by the actions of other individuals and other systems in the environment. Success in controlling a dynamic system depends on the operator taking into account all the physical factors impinging on the system at a given point in time, including noise, as well as the behavior of other agents, which can also affect how the system responds to any input. All of this must be done in real time, placing constraints on how long the operator can take to decide on a course of action.

Static domains are environments in which the system changes state only in response to a user input. Static domains are characterized by activities such as writing an article, watching television, reading, repairing a car or other device, human-computer interaction tasks (including some video games), and playing board games such as chess. Static domains in the workplace are not confined strictly to computer tasks, but also characterize jobs such as taking orders at fast-food restaurants, many other retail sales jobs, and auto mechanics. The common characteristic, as noted earlier, is that all of these activities are user-driven; the system waits for the user to make an input before making its response. Take writing an article as an example of a user-driven activity. As the writer continues to stare at the blank page, it becomes clear that nothing is going to change until she acts. This is a useful feature, in that the user has the ability to suspend the task, get up and leave, have lunch, watch a movie, get a good night's sleep, and return to the task the next day exactly where she left off. However, neither the ability to suspend the activity without penalty nor that fact that static activities can be easy to represent mathematically should be construed to mean that static activities are inherently easy. Writing is far from easy. Moreover, a sales clerk with a long line of customers will no doubt feel harried and stressed.

Dynamic environments are encountered in such activities as driving a car, directing traffic through an air traffic management system, or controlling a nuclear reactor. It is easy to see that the air traffic controller cannot simply stop all aircraft in his sector to figure out what to do, any more than a driver can stop monitoring the road to take a nap. Dynamic domains have the added complexity of the requirement to act in the moment, a requirement that curtails prolonged introspection and seldom allows consideration of the consequences of all possible actions. Take, for example, a soccer player. A soccer game is *dynamic* in that the state of the game is constantly in flux, evolving in real time, and determined by the actions of all players (as well as other factors such as wind, turf conditions, etc.). Even if the soccer player does nothing, the game will continue to evolve because all the other players in the game are making moves that constantly change the state of the game. No one is taking orderly turns waiting for another player to act. Because of this, a given action will be effective only for a small interval of time. It is this *sensitivity to time* that separates the static from the dynamic domain. Time per se is not changing the state of a dynamic system, but forces in motion acting on each other over time will. As a consequence, time matters, and opportunities for action come and go. Unlike the writer who can suspend the activity and walk away when the words don't come, the soccer player cannot suspend the game, but must quickly figure out what action to take in the moment.

It must be noted that no natural environment, or engineered one for that matter, is ever truly static. In truth, most domains have both static and dynamic aspects. Even while writing this chapter—a decidedly static task, as evidenced by the fact that leaving it for a day or two does not result in any new words on the page—the operations and processes inside the computer itself are dynamic. The computer's state changes somewhat independent of my input. There are moving parts (principally the hard drive) that wear with use. Chemical reactions, such as oxidation, are happening continually. Also, if one walks away, the operating system software is still active and will display a screen saver at some point in time. So, philosophically, it would be hard to defend the static case if we take it to that extreme. Likewise, even in games such as soccer there are discrete formations, such as penalty kicks or a throw-in, in which time matters less and players can formulate plays. However, as we will see, it is not generally useful to take the analysis to its philosophical extreme. For an understanding of human behavior in context, we can be content confining our interest to the principal drivers of goal-related activity that characterize each environment.

SOURCES OF DIFFICULTY IN STATIC ENVIRONMENTS

Most of the software systems people interact with while using a computer can be viewed as static. Yet, as evidenced by the continued difficulties people have using computers, static environments are not necessarily easy. Indeed, the computer is a good example of this because its response to inputs is very regular; it responds exactly the same way, assuming that it receives that information while in the same state. Therein lies a significant source of difficulty with static systems: uncertainty about the state of the system. Uncertainty can be confusion about which state the system is in, but most often uncertainty concerns which actions will lead to which outcomes given the system's particular state.

Modes

Static environments typically have multiple *modes*, meaning that actions will have different results depending on the state the system is set in (mode). A mode is a state of a system that will determine how it responds to inputs. Imagine, for example, the effect of hitting one of the function keys on the computer keyboard. Its effect will depend on which program is active at the time. The gearshift of a car is in fact a mode selector: the effect of stepping on the accelerator will depend on which gear is selected. Likewise, the result of pressing the "on" button on a universal remote will be determined by which device has been selected (e.g., the television vs. the DVR). A system with modes poses a particular problem, as it is necessary to stop and think about the state of the system before taking action. This adds complexity to the decision process, which in times of stress can lead to errors by human operators.

It may be surprising to learn that piloting a modern transport aircraft, such as a Boeing 747 or Airbus A320, involves many static, user-driven activities. Soon after the wheels leave the ground on takeoff, the pilot executes a program in the flight computer that she has programmed in advance. This program contains detailed instructions for flying the aircraft from point to point, including altitude and speed. Now, the flight domain is highly dynamic, so the pilot cannot go to sleep and expect nothing to change. Nonetheless, you might expect that the state of the flight computer itself will be user driven and not change unless the pilot makes a new input.

However, this is not necessarily the case. The flight computer is a complicated device that has multiple modes depending on whether the goal is to maintain a certain altitude, climb rate, and so forth. It also tracks the dynamic aspects of the domain and can respond to changes in altitude or other aircraft state, and can do so without telling the operator.

Pilots often express puzzlement at its behavior, leading to the well-known three questions (Wiener & Curry, 1980): What is it doing? Why is it doing that? What will it do next?

The crash of an Airbus A320 in Germany in 1988 serves as an example of how the modes in a modern aircraft can cause problems. Training on the A320 emphasized the protections its automation provided with respect to maintaining lift in all flight regimes. The flight controls simply would not allow the pilot to put the aircraft in a flight attitude that would risk stalling the aircraft. In the incident in Germany, the crew wanted to descend rapidly to the air show grounds. This first required that they disable one of the protections that would prevent them from descending steeply. Unfortunately, this caused the aircraft to revert to a mode in which other protections were disabled as well. As a result, the engines were not configured for rapid recovery (go-around), so when the throttle was applied to full power they were unable to generate the power needed to stop the descent.

Another example of the importance of mode in a human–machine system can be found in the Con Edison power failure in July 1977, which resulted in a 25-hour blackout in New York City. Severe weather had caused several of the substations feeding the city to fail. The operator at the central control center could have prevented the disaster by shutting down the power for portions of the city manually. To do so, the operator first had to put the system in the proper mode by turning a dial to the "Trip/reclose" position. Instead, under the pressure of the situation, the operator turned the dial to the "Frequency Control" position. Consequently, when he pressed the buttons to shut down a substation, nothing happened. The result was a 25-hour blackout that resulted in mayhem in the streets of New York City (Casey, 1998).

It is important to emphasize that the problem with modes is only partly a problem of human cognitive limitations. That is, modes simply make a system more complex. For example, if we were to take a device initially developed to control a television and then add to it the ability to control other devices, such as a digital video recorder or a stereo system, the new controller would require mode settings, reflecting the added complexity inherent in the environment.

Comprehension

Static environments can pose problems even in the absence of modes, or when modes per se are not the principal problem. In modern direct-manipulation computer interfaces, for example, the role of modes is greatly reduced by use of the mouse to select an item directly, and then select the required action from a series of menus that are continually displayed (see, e.g., Hutchins, Hollan, & Norman, 1985). Surfing the Web works similarly, with visible links directing the user to new information. Direct-manipulation interfaces reduce the number of modes the user must keep in mind by displaying a set of menus with the possible actions visible for inspection. Even when embedded in different software environments (e.g., a word processor vs. an email system), most modern interfaces provide visible menus the user can use to remind her of the possible actions. Overall, users find these direct-manipulation interfaces easier to use than the older systems with distinct modes that required textual input (Hutchins et al., 1985; Whiteside, Jones, Levy, & Wixon, 1985). However, the direct-manipulation interfaces themselves are not without problems (see Gentner & Nielsen, 1996; Hutchins et al., 1985; Lane, Napier, Peres, & Sandor, 2005). For example, the use of menus means that users must understand the terms used by the computer designer if they are to successfully complete the task. It may take time and practice before it becomes apparent which operations are available under the Edit menu as opposed to the File menu. The Web holds an even greater potential for difficulty, as the possible links are much larger than the possible menu items on a standard computer, and much less easily categorized. Ambiguity over the meaning of a link or menu item can greatly hamper the search for information (Pirolli & Card, 1999; Miller & Remington, 2004). Not only must designers pay close attention to the labels they use in menus and links, but users must also expect that even with well-designed interfaces it will be necessary to devote time and effort to understand the semantics of the interface or website.

SOURCES OF DIFFICULTY IN DYNAMIC ENVIRONMENTS

People working in dynamic environments also face uncertainty about which action to take and the state of the system. However, the added component of time creates a very different set of challenges. Many of the issues in dynamic environments are about when to act and when to expect *feedback*. In Chapter 6 we introduce *control theory* as a formal way of representing dynamic environments. Here we discuss some of the factors incorporated into the full control theoretical framework, which affect the ability of any agent to control any dynamic system. The factors enumerated in this section share a common theme: They all affect the expected response of the system to a control action compared to the actual feedback the operator receives after that action is taken.

Lag

Lag refers to the time between the input to a system and the response by the system. In general, we experience this as a lag between our action and its visible effect on the world. As a rule, the longer the lag, the more difficult it is for the operator to evaluate the feedback to decide on subsequent actions. In aircraft, a long lag between the movement of the control stick and the response of the aircraft gives rise to pilot-induced oscillations. Essentially, the pilot does not see the result of an action and decides prematurely to do more of the same. When the plane then begins to slew out of control in response to the added input, the pilot then rams it hard the other way. Because it doesn't respond immediately, he keeps the input in too long, and so on. You may have experienced a similar situation with unexpected slowdowns of email servers or social networking sites. When hitting "send" produces no discernible result, we tend to perform the same action multiple times, producing either multiple copies of the email or a system freeze. One could even speculate that governance has severe problems of lag. When laws are passed and policies put in place, it can be years before their true effects become apparent. Such long lags can make it very difficult to assign cause to whatever problems have been created: How are we to know whether this policy or that caused the current crisis? As we discuss in more detail later, humans also experience lags, as there is a noticeable lag between the presentation of a stimulus and the response to it. The point is that devices in general have time constants that determine how rapidly they respond to events in the world. Therefore, lag is an inescapable and complicating part of dealing with a dynamic system.

Plant Dynamics

Control theory also explicitly represents *how* the system responds to its inputs. People find it easier to deal with linear systems that have a short lag. A *linear system* is one whose output is a linear function of its input: If input of magnitude K produces output of magnitude Z, then an input of 2K will produce an output of 2Z. Figure 4.2(a) shows an example of how the output changes as a function of input for a system with linear control dynamics. A *nonlinear system* can have a multitude of different relationships between input and output, but it will not be guaranteed that if input K yields output Z then 2K will yield 2Z. A nonlinear system may behave linearly over certain ranges, but that will not be true across a wide range, or even for other well-defined ranges. Figure 4.2(b) shows the example of a nonlinear system whose output is a negatively accelerated function of its input. In such a system, if input K produces output Z, 2K < 2Z. In addition, small changes in input at low input levels will produce a larger change in output than the same change in input at high input levels. Negatively accelerated functions are found in systems with negative feedback, or where the output is constrained by physical limits such as the width of a pipe. Figure 4.2(c) shows a system whose output is a positively accelerated function of input. Here,

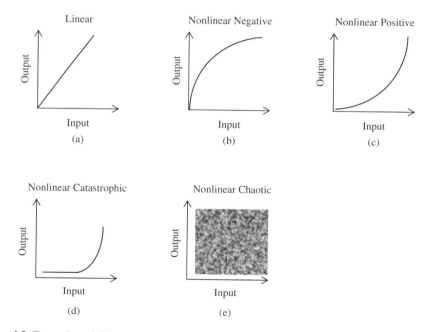

Figure 4.2 Examples of different control dynamics. (a) Linear dynamics: outputs proportional to inputs for levels of input. (b) Nonlinear negative dynamics: change in output decreases for same change in inputs at high input levels (characteristic of negative feedback). (c) Nonlinear positive dynamics: change in output increases for same change in inputs at high input levels (characteristic of positive feedback). (d) Nonlinear catastrophic dynamics: output stable but changes abruptly at some level of continuous input. (e) Nonlinear chaotic dynamics: output unpredictable with small changes in input.

2K > 2Z, and small changes in input at higher levels produce a greater change in output than the same input change at lower levels. Positively accelerated systems often contain positive feedback loops that amplify the input, as we often experience when we bring a microphone close to its speaker, producing a squeal that rapidly increases in loudness.

The final two systems in Figure 4.2 are not so common, but still deserve mention. Figure 4.2(d) shows the dynamics of a catastrophic system. In such a system, continuous changes in input over some range make no noticeable change in output until a boundary condition is reached, at which point the system abruptly takes on a different state. The classic example is the facial expression of a wolf or a dog. As the ears begin to flatten and the lips begin to curl up, the expression goes from one of happy, to puzzled, to fearful, and finally to angry. Similar "catastrophic" boundaries occur in the recognition of spoken speech. The difference between a "d" and a "t" is the time at which the vocal cords begin to vibrate. When we say "tug," for example, the vocal cords start to vibrate a few tens of milliseconds later than when we say "dug." The "t" is referred to as a voiceless phoneme, the "d" as a voiced phoneme. One of the difficulties English speakers have in learning French is that the French generally begin the voicing for both voiced and voiceless consonants earlier than do English speakers. However, we do not perceive continual changes in this voice onset time. If the time prior to voicing is varied by small amounts, our perception is not that the "t" becomes gradually more like the "d," but that at some point "t" simply changes to "d." Describing a system as catastrophic does not mean that it is inherently unstable. It means that continuous changes in an overt dimension (such as the position of the wolf's ears) signal discrete changes in the underlying state of the system (for example, going from puzzled to angry). In a sense, then, the boundaries between categories create regions where the same-magnitude change has a more dramatic, catastrophic, effect on the categorization.

Figure 4.2(e) shows a chaotic system in which the outputs are unpredictable from the input. The output is not random, in that there is a deterministic relationship between inputs and outputs. Rather, small changes in input can lead to very large changes in output. The inevitable error in input makes it impossible to know what the output will be. Most of the systems we engineer are not chaotic, or are chaotic only within specific boundary regions. It is interesting to speculate, however, to what degree our social and economic systems are chaotic. It certainly appears as though it is difficult to anticipate the outcome of legislation, social policy, or economic changes. Side effects often appear that were not anticipated beforehand.

In general, it is easy for people to control linear systems or systems with negatively accelerating input-output functions. To make this concrete, consider how the hot water knob of a shower would work with each of these control dynamics. Let's assume that you want to adjust the temperature of the water in your shower. If the system behaved as in Figure 4.2(a), you would only have to know how much you wanted to change it and the *gain* of the knob; that is, how much the temperature changes for any given displacement of the knob. You do not have to know the current setting of the knob. If an input of magnitude K (distance the knob is turned) yields a change in temperature of Z degrees, then to produce 2Z you would turn the knob 2K. Comparing Figure 4.2(b) with 4.2(c), it is clear that in a nonlinear system the distance the knob must be turned (K) to yield a desired change in temperature (Z) depends on the current position of the knob. In the negatively accelerated system of 4.2(b), the gain of the knob is greatest at low values, where the system is very sensitive to a small turn of the knob; this makes it easy to overcompensate and cause the water to get either too cold or too hot. The opposite is true of the positively accelerated system of 4.2(c). Its gain is greatest at high values. At low values it will take a larger displacement of the knob to get the water to its desired temperature.

The dynamic properties of a system include not only how its output varies as a function of its input, but also how its output varies as a function of time for any given input. We have already briefly introduced the concept of lag, defined as the time from taking an action to the feedback that informs the operator of the effect of that action. Lag is also a fundamental property of the dynamic response of a system. How the system behaves in time also determines its *stability*. A system is stable if it settles into a state corresponding to its commanded input over time. The signal that goes to a system is the sum of the control input from the operator plus disturbance caused by the environment (discussed in more detail later in this chapter). Loss of stability can occur if the external disturbance becomes large relative to the control input. Imagine, for example, if you set the temperature of your shower and several other users simultaneously begin using large amounts of cold water. Or, imagine trying to balance a pyramid-shaped object. If you set it on its base, it is very stable. However, if you try to balance it on its tip, the forces of gravity conspire with tiny errors in your control input to topple it almost immediately. This happens because when the pyramid is inverted, the large, heavy base makes it very sensitive to small deviations from perfect vertical. The systems in Figures 4.2(b–e) share this property, making them unstable in at least some region of input. In the positively accelerated system of Figure 4.2(c), for example, the gain of the system is very high for large inputs. In this region, small errors in the input coupled with external forces will make the system very hard to stabilize. Even with the control input held as steady as possible, the system will not settle into a stable state and will always be in danger of careening out of control. Unstable behavior of this kind is often associated with *positive-feedback* systems in which the output of the system is fed back into its inputs, creating a continuously amplified output. This is what leads to the screeching noise we hear when the microphone is moved too close to the speaker projecting its input. Stable behavior, by contrast, is typical of systems with *negative feedback*, in which the behavior of the system in time is *damped* so that it settles into a stable state. One way of damping a system is to compute the error between the commanded output and the actual output and feed this error signal back as input.

Most systems in the world, including the hot water control in the shower, are inherently nonlinear. At the extreme, there are chaotic systems such as the weather, which behave unpredictably over a long enough time scale. However, even simple systems, such as the pendulum, are nonlinear yet solvable. Nonlinear systems prove difficult for people to adapt to. An airplane makes a good illustration of a nonlinear system. The airplane flies because of lift produced by airflow over the wings, shown schematically in Figure 4.3. The top of the wing is curved just enough that the air flows smoothly over the surface. Diagram (a) shows airflow over a wing tilted upward with respect to the motion of the air (angle of attack). At a positive angle of attack, the curvature of the wing accelerates the air over the top of the wing's surface. Because the air flowing over the top of the wing must travel a greater distance due to the curvature, it must travel faster. This means the pressure will be greater on the bottom than the top. The dotted lines show how columns of

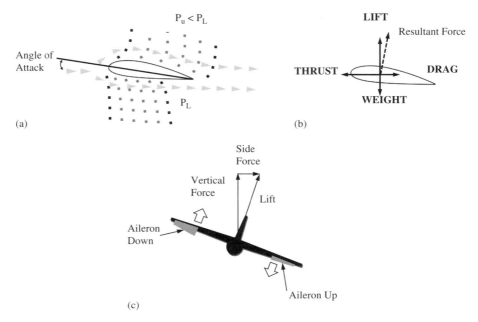

Figure 4.3 Nonlinear dynamics of aircraft control surfaces. Diagram (a) shows the accelerated airflow over a curved wing that generates lift. Other forces also act on the aircraft, as indicated in diagram (b). The pilot controls the aircraft by altering lift on the wings and other control surfaces (e.g., rudder). Controlling the aircraft is thus a matter of adjusting the pressure differentials to achieve the correct forces, a process that is inherently nonlinear.

air move faster over the top, with black dots indicating a column that started out aligned. The faster-moving air results in lower pressure above the wing (P_U) than below ($P_U < P_L$). This is the fundamental principle of *lift*. Modern aircraft turn by the use of ailerons that change the distance over the top of one of the wings. For example, for the aircraft to turn right, the left aileron is extended (the right may also be contracted) to create a greater surface area to flow across, increasing the difference in pressure between the top and bottom surfaces of the left wing. This causes greater lift in the left wing, and as the left wing rises the plane banks rightward (roll). The same principle is applied to the horizontal stabilizer on the rudder, which causes the nose to point up or down (pitch), and to vertical control surfaces on the rudder that point the nose left and right (yaw). The response of the aircraft to these changes in airflow is highly nonlinear, but can be described by complex fluid-flow equations (see Wikipedia, 2011, on Navier-Stokes equations).

Because people have a great deal of difficulty controlling a nonlinear system, one of the principal aims of engineers is to develop controls for aircraft, automobiles, nuclear power plants, and similar systems that change the control dynamics to approximate those of a linear system. It may sound magical to claim that one can simply change an inherently nonlinear system into a linear control system for the human. Indeed, it can be quite a complex and challenging problem. Nonetheless, it is easy to get a sense of how this is done by reconsidering our little temperature problem. In Figure 4.4(a) we have plotted the water temperature (output) as a function of knob position (input), assuming a nonlinear

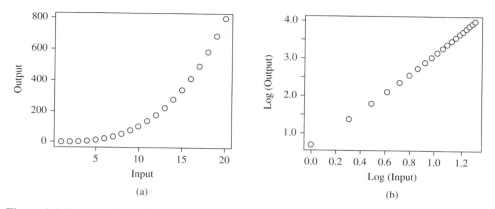

Figure 4.4 Nonlinear dynamics can often be transformed to nearly linear input-output relationships. Graph (a) shows the nonlinear input-output relationship defined by the equation of $y = x^3 + 4x^2$. Graph (b) shows the linear relationship obtained when the logarithm of the input is used to determine the logarithm of the output.

relationship. If instead we transform the axes so that the logarithm of the output is plotted as a function of the logarithm of the input, as in Figure 4.4(b), we once again have a predominately linear relationship. Thus, if we put a computer (or two) between the knob and the valve that controls the hot water flow, we can take distance turned as a desired input and compute the actual valve opening required to make it a nice simple linear system. This is in principle what engineers now do to make control of aircraft and automobiles much simpler and safer, though in a much more complex and rigorous way.

To fully appreciate how difficult systems can be for any operator, it is necessary to consider the combined effects of lag and nonlinear control dynamics. We will not go into detail here, as the full complexity would really be suitable for engineering courses. We can, however, provide a little intuitive insight. Consider the nonlinear hot water control in Figure 4.4. Normally, the water in the pipes is cool, and it takes a little time for the newly tapped hot water to begin to alter the temperature. If the knob has already been turned to where it is expected to yield a 30-degree (Celcius) shower, and the water doesn't heat in the time expected, the natural response is to turn it a bit more. Given that this is a positively accelerated nonlinear system, that little bit extra could result in a scalding-hot shower, as it would take a much less drastic turn to get the water very hot. The temporal uncertainty created by the lag interacting with the control dynamics creates extra problems for the controlling agent. With this example in mind, perhaps it is not surprising that government policy is so difficult to get right and always seems to have unintended consequences. Certainly the nonlinearity inherent in economics, plus the lag in response as people and institutions adapt to new regulations (input), make it very difficult at the outset to think through all the possible implications of policy.

Control Order

Another important property of any system one wants to control is what dynamic properties are being controlled—in short, its *control order*. The idea of control order is illustrated

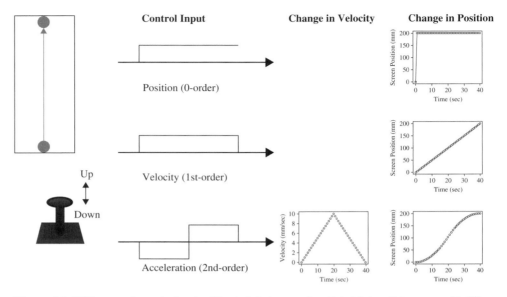

Figure 4.5 Differences in control order. The task is to use a joystick (pictured) to move a "ball" from the bottom to the top of the screen. The user makes a control input and observes a change in position of the ball over time. Zero-order (position) control: position of the ball is determined by position of the joystick. First-order (velocity) control: ball moves at constant speed determined by joystick position. Velocity must be returned to zero to stop the ball. Second-order (acceleration) control: ball moves first with increasing speed, then with decreasing speed. Both acceleration and velocity must be cancelled for the ball to come to rest.

in Figure 4.5, in which the task is to move an object (say, a blue ball) from a resting position on the bottom of a computer screen to a resting position at the top of the screen using a joystick. The joystick input could be configured to determine position, velocity, or acceleration. If the joystick controls the position of the ball directly, then the task is very simple. The position of the ball simply reflects the position of the joystick. This is the way a mouse works, for the most part. Of course, the problem is that when we want to make large movements, we must either move our hands a large distance, or repeatedly scroll the mouse to rotate its sensor. With the joystick, this is impossible, as the position is limited by the physical extent of the joystick. We can make this same physical extent cover more ground by increasing the gain, which is what determines the amount the ball moves for each little movement of the joystick. If we want the ball to cover more territory, then we must increase the gain so that small movements of the joystick make large changes in ball position. Of course, this will make it increasingly difficult to maintain a steady ball, as it increases the noise and amplifies the smallest tremor in our hands. When position is controlled directly, it is referred to as *zero-order control*.

Alternatively, the joystick could control the velocity of the ball. The distance the joystick was displaced would correspond to the speed of the ball in a particular direction. The gain now determines how much speed is imparted by unit displacement of the joystick: The higher the gain, the faster the ball moves for a given displacement. So, to move the ball to a location, the user would first input the speed, hold it there until just before it was on the target, and then move the joystick back to neutral to input a zero velocity. Unlike zero-order control, this is no longer similar to a natural pointing action. Instead, at the end the user's hand moves in the opposite direction to the target to cancel the velocity. This cancellation makes it necessary to estimate how long it will take to perceive and react. When velocity is controlled directly, it is referred to as *first-order control*. The term *first-order* refers to the relationship between velocity, which is the output of the control device, and position, which is the output of the system. According to the laws of motion, position is derived from velocity by a single integration operation: hence the name first-order. In zero-order control, the output of the control device is already positioned, so no integration is required: hence, zero-order.

To gain an intuitive sense of first-order control, consider using a typical DVD remote control to fast-forward through a recorded program. If you want to skip over some part of the program—say, the commercials in a recorded program—you can speed it up to 2x, 6x, 12x, or more. You are controlling the velocity, albeit in a discrete, digital way. The faster you go, the quicker you get through the parts that don't interest you. However, the cost is a greater timing error: At very high speeds you simply do not have enough time to recognize the beginning of the section you want and to depress the stop button without missing some content. This demonstrates the lag in your own perceptual-motor system.

People can become quite good at velocity control, and do even better when the control device is some combination of both zero-order and first-order control dynamics. If you experiment with your computer mouse, you will likely discover that the speed with which you move your hand affects the distance the ball will travel for the same physical displacement of the mouse. If you move the mouse quickly, the ball will travel further. Thus, both velocity and position are controlled, but by different attributes of the mouse movement.

As you might suspect, there is no theoretical bound to the control order of any device. However, for most practical purposes devices generally do not exceed *second-order control*, where the joystick controls the acceleration of the ball. With a second-order control device, the initial input determines the acceleration, which is integrated once to get velocity and again to get position. This is depicted in Figure 4.5. Controlling a second-order system can be tricky. To move the ball up, you would move the stick up to input the desired acceleration. For any fixed position of the acceleration control, the velocity of the ball would increase at a constant rate. Then the input would have to be exactly reversed to cancel out both the acceleration and the velocity. Figure 4.5 shows the case in which the input is maintained until exactly half the distance has been covered and then reversed and held constant while the ball decelerates to its resting position. As you might imagine, it can be difficult to get the ball to stop precisely where you intend. To do this you must accurately estimate the midpoint of the trajectory, reproduce the exact same displacement in the opposite direction, estimate the time to zero out the acceleration, and return the control to a neutral (zero) position. Moreover, the relationship of the position of the ball to the input is not so direct. Note that in Figure 4.5 the ball is traveling at the greatest velocity at the midpoint, amplifying any errors in estimating either the position or the perceptual-motor lags in your own system. It is no wonder, then, that when human control is involved, engineers try to design the control of systems to make them more closely approximate first-order control even when they are inherently second-order.

Perturbation and Noise

Thus far we have discussed factors inherent to the system, or plant, itself: lag, plant dynamics, and control order can all be calculated deterministically from the given equations of a particular aircraft, car, or other plant. However, there are influences external to the plant: perturbations and noise must also be considered as sources of difficulty in control. An aircraft is buffeted about by wind, a car vibrates according to irregularities in the road surface, the soccer ball bounces as determined by the grass surface. These are all examples of *perturbations* or external factors that affect the vehicle or plant in unpredictable ways from moment to moment. Imagine the task of positioning the ball in Figure 4.5 if noise were added to its position, velocity, or acceleration. It is perhaps easier to see the effects of these disturbances by imagining sailing a small boat on a fine, windy day. The rudder is set to steer a course that takes into account the underlying current, and the sails are set for the prevailing wind direction. If all goes according to plan, the dynamic state of the system should evolve such that you sail smoothly into the harbor for lunch. Indeed, if the day is calm, and you are an accomplished sailor, this will be the likely outcome. In contrast, should the day prove to be a bit more blustery, with swelling seas, the boat will not gracefully slide into the harbor, but rather will move first one way and then another, requiring constant supervision to correct the unwanted changes in direction caused by the sea perturbing the trajectory. If the swells are bad enough, it may even prove impossible to know whether your inputs are doing any good: The boat will appear controlled by the sea rather than its own rudder and sails. The rudder and sails provide one source of input to control the craft, but these are added to by the unpredictable sea swells. Essentially, your input is counting for only a proportion of the signal that determines the course of the boat. If you have ever been in a van or truck on the highway on a windy day, or a passenger in a plane landing in high winds, you will have a good sense of just how difficult it can be to control a vehicle in the face of strong perturbing forces.

The other source of unplanned variability and increased uncertainty is *noise*. Unlike perturbation, which reflects external factors acting to alter your control inputs, noise is an intrinsic property of all systems. You may intend to move the rudder of the boat a precise 30 degrees, but your actual motor output will be somewhere near that, not exactly 30 degrees, and slightly different each time. This is an example of motor noise in the controller agent itself. Such noise also exists in automated systems and mechanical systems, though it is often less than human motor noise. Noise is also present in the response of the vehicle to a given input. Two important sources of noise come from noise associated with feedback and decision noise associated with uncertainty in the evaluation of the situation and selection of the appropriate action.

Earlier we noted the importance of feedback for operating in a dynamic domain. Feedback is what allows the operator to correct errors in the controlled system. To stick with our sailing example, suppose the correct path for the boat is to steer toward a point of land and then turn into the marina inlet as the boat approaches that point. Let's say this is achieved by lining up the bow of the boat with a point on land. Every time the boat deviates to the left or right of that line, the operator (the skipper, in this case) must decide if a corrective input is required. If the boat is truly off course, then the rudder or sails must be shifted to correct the path. If it is just a momentary perturbation due to rough seas, perhaps it is best not to take action until more information about the path is available. Thus, there is noise associated with the actual perception of the boat's true path, which we call *perceptual noise*, as well as noise associated with the selection of the proper action (correct or stay the course), which we call *decision noise*. It is easy to see that if there is fog or the boat is a long distance from the shore, there will be increased perceptual noise, as it will be harder to perceive the actual alignment of the boat with the shore. If the boat is far away, there will be additional decision noise, but this will not be a problem, as the consequences of being a little off at that point are minimal and not worth worrying about. That is, the skipper can adopt a lenient criterion that holds course until a large deviation is noted. Fog is a different matter, as it affects steering close in. The uncertainty about the position of the land and perhaps of shoals, sandbars, or rocks that pose a real danger mean that the decision noise is now important, and a lenient criterion is no longer feasible.

INTERNAL VS. EXTERNAL PACING

Although control theory represents many of the factors that affect the difficulty operators have in selecting and evaluating their actions, it does not cover all such factors. One of the factors external to control theory that makes dynamic environments difficult is the pace of activity, which is often under the control of the environment, not the operator. We all have a natural pace to our actions: Some like it fast; others like it slow. Some people walk briskly, some amble. We are fortunate, perhaps, if we can determine the rate at which we work, but workplaces and daily life in general can vary quite a bit with respect to where activities originate and how much freedom we have to choose our pace of work. In *externally driven* environments, work arrives independent of the worker (server). If you are an office worker with a stack of forms to fill out, you may continue to receive them even though you no longer want more. A humorous example of this is the classic "I Love Lucy" episode in which Lucy works as an inspector on a conveyor belt in a chocolate candy factory. As the speed of the belt increases unexpectedly and uncontrollably, Lucy ends up putting candies in her hat, pockets, and mouth to try to control the flow. In contrast, in *internally driven* environments the worker determines the pace at which information arrives. A research scientist largely gets to choose when she will undertake her next experiment or paper and what its subject will be. A writer gets to determine what book to work on next. Of course, there is pressure to produce in both cases, which means that the choice is somewhat constrained over the long run, but on any given day, they can choose.

On the whole, most jobs are predominantly externally driven. For doctors, air traffic controllers, firefighters, bank tellers, supermarket cashiers, and most office workers, work shows up and they react. This has a consequence for planning analyses and measuring performance; that is, externally paced tasks naturally give rise to questions of productive capacity and can be analyzed accordingly. Thus, externally driven environments are often analyzed in terms of how much product an individual can produce per unit time. The question is often whether more police officers, firefighters, or chocolate factory workers are needed given the average wait time for services. In the case of police, for example, one might want to compute the average time it takes to respond to a distress call, or calculate how many additional police officers would be needed to achieve a certain response time.

However, workers may not be so interested in working at this maximal pace every day: They may desire a reasonable *workload* that keeps them busy, but not frantic. How can we get a handle on productivity to answer both the question of how to get more output from an organization and the question of how to measure how busy people are?

In contrast to externally driven domains, internally driven domains are generally evaluated by assessing quality. Academics, executives, writers, and possibly entertainers are more likely to be evaluated on the quality of the products they produce rather than by how quickly they produce them. There is an important caveat, though, as any real task has elements of both quality and quantity. For example, a faculty member may be judged on the quality of her scholarly articles. However, she may also be judged by the volume of quality articles produced. In air traffic control, there are periods in which the controller is typing information into a computer or dialing a phone, juxtaposed with episodes in which the controller is trying to redirect aircraft in real time. Finally, there are situations in which an environment that is typically internally paced can become externally paced, making the domain more demanding. Suppose that you had five seconds to respond to your opponent's move in chess. In fact, such time limits are often imposed in competitions to give the edge to the better player.

ERROR TOLERANCE

Another characteristic of environments that is critical to our understanding of the human–machine system is *error tolerance*. Our willingness to tolerate error differs across domains. Where the result of an error is merely inconvenience to the user, we are relatively tolerant of error. However, where the lives of people are jeopardized when failures or errors occur, we are less tolerant of error. A domain where error is not tolerated is commercial aviation. Millions of people across the globe fly each day with the assumption that the aircraft controlled by the human pilots flying them will deliver them safely to their destination. Because crashes have such a high fatality rate and they affect a large number of people, commercial air travel is possible only because people have confidence in its safety. The track record of safety, certainly for developed countries, justifies this confidence. Airline accidents are major news when they occur, belying the fact that per passenger mile flown, or time in travel, flying is by far the safest way to travel from one place to another that has ever been invented. It was not always so. In the early days, human flight was a risky business. Pilot training was absent or ad hoc, controls were makeshift, aircraft were flimsy, and navigation aids were little more than observations of major terrain features. Aircraft routinely crashed, went off course, or just disappeared. No doubt much of this was due to mechanical failures, but human error has always been a significant contributor to accidents and mishaps. Thus, as we discussed in Chapter 3, a persistent concern within the aviation human factors community has been the reduction of pilot error to achieve higher levels of safety.

This focus on safety is also seen in the medical domain. Because we trust our lives to doctors, and don't generally have the knowledge to do more than accept their expert judgments, it is critical to keep medical errors to a minimum. However, with less publicity attached to individual deaths as a result of medical error, there appears to be more tolerance for error in this domain. Despite precautions, medical error has been rated by some sources as the fifth leading cause of death in the United States (www.wrongdiagnosis.com).

An estimated 98,000 deaths per year are attributable to errors in hospitals (www.human factorsmd.com). These errors include medication errors (Santell, 2005) as well as wrong-site, wrong-person, or wrong-procedure events (Joint Commission on Accreditation of Healthcare Organizations, 2001). Here again, the primary focus of human factors research is on the reduction of human error in order to improve patient safety outcomes.

In other domains, such as the automotive industry, a focus on safety is combined with an eye toward user satisfaction. As with the medical domain, many fatalities occur as a result of automobile accidents. However, in this domain, the fatalities are less often a result of faulty design, and more likely a result of driver error or incapacitation. This too was not always so. Early cars did not have brake lights; this addition reduced the likelihood of rear-end collisions. Several years ago, traditional brake lights were supplemented by a taillight mounted high on the center of the rear, more directly in the line of sight of the following driver, which research had demonstrated would further reduce rear-end collisions (Malone, Kirkpatrick, Kohl, & Baker, n.d.). Now, automobiles are considered consumer goods and, as such, must appeal to buyers. Thus, features that drivers find pleasing—ones that make them more comfortable or make driving more convenient, such as cruise control and power windows—are important considerations, though they have little to do with safety.

Finally, in the area of human-computer interaction, where safety is not a concern, the focus of human factors research is on improving productivity, or effectiveness of the user. For example, a breakthrough was achieved in the 1960s and 1970s at Xerox PARC when researchers combined a mouse for pointing and input with a graphical user interface using icons and desk-like constructs, such as folders, as means of interacting with newly developed desktop computers.

SUMMARY

This chapter has examined the importance of considering the environment when trying to understand system performance. Static environments introduce issues associated with modes, that is, with understanding the state of the system. Dynamic environments add concerns about system lag, plant dynamics, control order, and perturbations such as noise. Some environments are paced internally, whereas others are paced externally; some can tolerate more error than others. All of these features play a role in how well a controller will perform within that environment.

REFERENCES

Bisantz, A. M., & Roth, E. (2008). Analysis of cognitive work. In D. A. Boehm-Davis (Ed.), *Reviews of human factors and ergonomics* (Vol. 3, pp. 1–45). Santa Monica, CA: Human Factors & Ergonomics Society.

Casey, S. M. (1998). *Set phasers on stun: And other true tales of design, technology, and human error.* Santa Barbara, CA: Aegean.

Gentner, D., & Nielsen, J. (1996). The anti-Mac interface. *Commun. ACM, 39*(8), 70–82. doi:10.1145/232014.232032

Hollnagel, E., & Woods, D. D. (2005). *Joint cognitive systems: Patterns in cognitive systems engineering.* Boca Raton, FL: CRC Press.

Hutchins, E., Hollan, J., & Norman, D. (1985). Direct manipulation interfaces. *Human-Computer Interaction, 1,* 311–338. doi:10.1207/s15327051hci0104_2

Joint Commission on Accreditation of Healthcare Organizations. (2001). A follow-up review of wrong site surgery. Retrieved from www.jointcommission.org/SentinelEvents/SentinelEventAlert/sea_24.htm

Lane, D. M., Napier, H. A., Peres, S. C., & Sandor, A. (2005). Hidden costs of graphical user interfaces: Failure to make the transition from menus and icon toolbars to keyboard shortcuts. *International Journal of Human-Computer Interaction, 18,* 133–144. doi:10.1207/s15327590ijhc1802_1

Malone, T. B., Kirkpatrick, M., Kohl, J. S., & Baker, C. (n.d.). *Field test evaluation of rearlighting systems* (NHTSA, U.S. Department of Transportation No. DOT-HS-5-01228). Alexandria, VA: Essex Corporation.

Miller, C. S., & Remington, R. W. (2004). Modeling information navigation: Implications for information architecture. *Human-Computer Interaction, 19,* 225–271.

Pirolli, P., & Card, S. (1999). Information foraging. *Psychological Review, 106,* 643–675.

Santell, J. P. (2005). Medication errors: Experience of the United States Pharmacopeia (USP). *Journal of Quality and Patient Safety, 31*(2), 114–119.

Whiteside, J., Jones, S., Levy, P. S., & Wixon, D. (1985). User performance with command, menu, and iconic interfaces. *Proceedings of the SIGCHI Conference on Human Factors in Computing Systems,* CHI '85 (pp. 185–191). New York, NY: ACM. doi:10.1145/317456.317490

Wiener, E. L., & Curry, R. (1980). Flight-deck automation: Promises and problems. *Ergonomics, 23*(10), 995–1011. doi:10.1080/00140138008924809

Wikipedia. (2011). Navier-Stokes equations. Retrieved October 29, 2011, from http://en.wikipedia.org/wiki/Navier%E2%80%93Stokes_equations

5

The Social Context

In Chapter 4 we introduced dimensions along which environments differ: static versus dynamic, internal versus external control of pacing, and tolerance for error. Another obvious difference in environments is the *social context* in which activities occur. For instance, the soccer player is a member of a team playing against another team. His actions must be coordinated with those of other team players to achieve the best outcome. He must also track and respond to the actions and perceived intent of the opposing players. In contrast, the writer may consult with editors, domain experts, friends, and others, but writing essentially is the act of a single person communicating with readers (with the possible exception of television sitcom writers, who do often write in teams).

Much could be said about human behavior in social situations. People often behave very differently in groups than they do individually, a topic we will deal with in more detail in subsequent chapters. Even there, however, our treatment will be limited. Indeed, the entire research field of *industrial-organizational psychology* is devoted to the study of people in teams and in large-scale organizations. Although organizational issues are important to the study of humans in engineered systems, they often center on motivational and personality matters, topics that go beyond the focus of this book. Indeed, there are significant differences in the level and method of analysis used in organizational psychology from that of the more traditional human factors, or human-system integration. Our interest in this chapter is not to treat the social context in its full complexity, but instead to highlight aspects of the social and organizational environment that characterize the challenges it poses for the human operator.

In terms of its effect in the environment, a key feature within the social context is group size, which has implications for communication and coordination requirements. The variety in group engagement and social structure can be illustrated by arranging some specific examples in order of group size, as has been done in Figures 5.1 and 5.2. On the *x*-axes in these figures, pictures of sample environments are arranged according to the number of people and the complexity of their interaction. On the far left is the example of a military sector analyst monitoring a radar screen for threat aircraft. This situation is not dissimilar in social context from that of a game player on a computer, an air traffic controller, or a writer, in that a critical part of the job is done as an independent observer. The output of this individual system is a function of the capacity of a single human information-processing system.

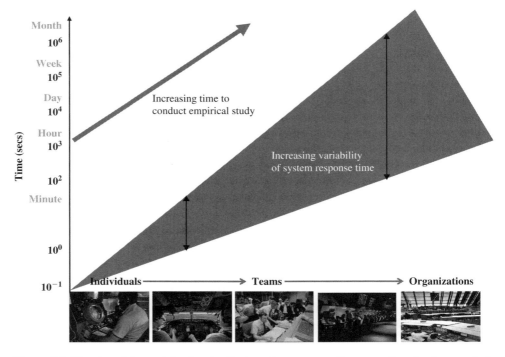

Figure 5.1 The size of the social network affects system response time as well as the time needed to conduct empirical tests of system functioning.

To the right of the radar controller is a picture of a two-person crew from a modern jet airliner. They act more directly as a team for critical tasks. For the landing or takeoff checklists, for example, the monitoring pilot (i.e., the pilot not flying) will read the checklist item from the manual and the pilot will perform the check and report. Thus, procedures establish separate roles and responsibilities for the pilot flying and the pilot not flying and in virtually all cases, there is close coordination between the two. In this system, the output is a function of the combined processing abilities of the small team, plus any additional communication overhead. Because all members need to complete their portion of the larger task, completion time will approximate the maximum time for an individual to complete, plus communication overhead. To the right of the cockpit example is a picture of one of the several small engineering teams that comprise the Launch Control Center at the Kennedy Space Center in Florida. Launch control is organized into teams of four or five people responsible for a specific subsystem of the vehicle (e.g., the space shuttle), such as fuel, navigation, computers, engines, and so on. Each of these teams is in contact with a much larger personnel force that interacts directly with vehicle systems..

To the right of the NASA Launch Control Center is a photo of one side of an air traffic control room. Each of the stations is responsible for traffic in a single portion of airspace, called a *sector*. Each sector control is staffed by two people: a radar controller, who is responsible for communicating with the aircraft in her sector and issuing appropriate flight

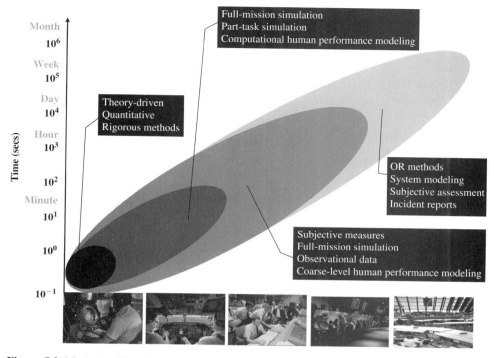

Figure 5.2 Methods of inquiry change as the scale of operations increases, becoming more qualitative, more subjective, and more focused on the system than the individual.

instructions (referred to as the *R-side*); and a support controller (referred to as the *D-side*), who is responsible for keeping track of upcoming traffic, arranging flight information, and assisting the radar controller in detecting and resolving conflicts. In this respect they are much like the pilot and monitoring pilot discussed earlier. The difference here is that the domain of interest is the entire airspace, which is controlled by the entire collection of sector controllers interacting in highly regulated ways. The coordinated activity of the ensemble of controllers determines how aircraft flow through the airspace and the capacity of the airspace in terms of number of aircraft. For a flight from Los Angeles to New York, for example, airport terminal controllers would ensure safe taxi and takeoff, then hand off the aircraft to departure control. Departure control, known as the Terminal Radar Control (TRACON), would coordinate routes for all inbound and outbound traffic before handing off to the first of a sequence of enroute control sectors. The series of enroute control centers would monitor the aircraft as it maintained its flight altitude and direction. Nearing the New York airport, the aircraft would once again transition into TRACON airspace for descent, then terminal control for landing. Because aircraft are handed off from one sector to the next, bottlenecks that occur in one sector affect all other sectors. Weather events also do not respect sector boundaries and thus require coordination across several sectors. For such a large-scale system, such as the airspace of the continental United States, the throughput, or number of aircraft per unit time, is determined by the entire network of joint radar D-side controllers.

The final photo is of the command structure that coordinates all the separate teams in the Launch Control Center at the Kennedy Space Center. In direct control is the NASA test director, who orchestrates the integration of all systems to keep the launch on schedule, or makes the decision to hold or abort. Final permission to launch is given by the launch director, who is in ultimate control of the ground team for launch. In this way the separate, highly interactive teams of four to five people are joined into a larger organization of quasi-independent teams that interact with each other chiefly through the NASA test director. Like the conductor of an orchestra the test director ensures the coordination necessary to launch. This environment represents a case in which group size has again increased dramatically. Nonetheless, Launch Control remains a tightly organized structure. In other large-scale domains individuals and small teams act quasi-independently. The benefit of this independence is an ability to flexibly respond to solve problems that require a more fluid flow of information. This is true, for example, of the modern large-scale command-and-control centers typical of military operations. The situation can change rapidly so that some level of autonomy must be given to small groups to make decisions on their own as the situation develops dynamically.

METHODOLOGICAL CONSEQUENCES OF GROUP SIZE

As we have seen, groups vary in size and organization. At one end we have the individual operator interacting with his or her piece of equipment: the elemental human-device team. The pilot and monitoring pilot, like the D-side and R-side controllers, constitute a small team. At the other end we have the large organizations, such as the NASA Launch Control Center or a modern military command-and-control organization, which can have several dozens of people interacting within formal and informational structures. As the size of the teams increases, several changes in the nature of the output of the team take place, for example, the time it takes to achieve a resolution to a problem and the variability of that time. There are also consequences for the researcher trying to study teams. As the team gets larger, the same precise measurements become harder and harder to collect and analyze. Different methodologies are employed with differing degrees of precision. Here we discuss a few of the important changes that occur as a function of group size.

Length/Variability of Response Times

In Figures 5.1 and 5.2, we have tried to give some indication of the implications of the scale of social interactions with respect to the study of such systems. Keep in mind that these figures are notional graphs that depict general trends, not established facts or data. What we have attempted to represent is the general notion that, as the size and complexity of social interaction increase, system response times tend both to increase and to become more variable. In part, this is an inevitable consequence of multiple subtasks, each of which must be completed to accomplish the overall goal. As Figure 5.1 shows, the time taken by a single human operator to make a simple decision and complete a response is on the order of a second or less, between 0.1 to 1 sec, or 10^{-1} to 10^{0} seconds. For a well-learned action sequence, such as opening a file on a computer, it would take between 1 and

10 seconds, or 10^0 to 10^1 sec. If, for example, we asked the radar operator shown in the leftmost photo for the altitude and speed of a specific aircraft, we would expect an answer in about 2 to 3 seconds. If it took much longer than that, we might ask again or begin to wonder if there was a problem. In contrast, if the NASA test director in Launch Control, shown in the rightmost photo, asked for the status of a problem being worked on by the propulsion team, she might be surprised if the answer came back in just a second. In fact, it might take several minutes, or in some cases days, to get an answer to the question posed.

In general, as the system gets larger, the average time to respond increases, as does the variability of response times. There is, of course, a logical explanation for the increase in response time, which is not necessarily rooted in the motivation or performance of individuals. The performance of an individual in isolation will not differ radically from that individual's performance within a group (with certain caveats that are discussed later). That is, human performance itself does not necessarily become slower or more variable when done in larger teams. It should not take any longer to press a key when one is part of a group than when one is working alone.

What does change is the nature of the questions that are typically asked with operations of different sizes. Because larger teams/organizations generally work on larger problems, the questions require querying several individuals. Further, the complexity of the task, not just the number of social interactions, determines completion times and variability. Large teams are the result of the need to complete complex tasks. As a result, more people will be involved in making decisions, leading to increased response times (Cooke et al., 2003; Cooke, Salas, Kiekel, & Bell, 2004; Foltz & Martin, 2009; Slaughter, Yu, & Koehly, 2009; see also Salas, Goodwin, & Burke, 2008). Further, group size affects the variability of the group's response time: As the size of the group increases, the *variability* in time taken will also increase. For individuals, the variability is generally on the order of a few seconds. However, for a large system, there may be times when getting the answer takes a few days.

Methods of Study and Analysis

The scale of the operation also dictates which methods of study and analysis are most feasible. When the focus is on the individual operator, rigorous experimental, quantitative methods can be used to produce very precise data on response time, errors, and the specific behaviors in which the operators engage. At this level, psychological theory can provide guidance, and in some cases competing theories can be tested. Such rigor is possible because the relatively fast response times and low variances make it feasible to conduct experiments that yield ample data for statistical analysis. Multiple conditions can be compared, for example, in part-task simulations, which preserve a few essential features of a real-world context, thus allowing a range of design options to be tested against a range of real-world concerns.

As the unit of study becomes the team or organizational response, involving increasingly more people, these rigorous quantitative approaches are supplanted by more qualitative, subjective methods. In many cases, it is quicker, easier, and more beneficial to rely on the subjective assessments of experts (Patterson, Roth, & Woods, 2010; Roth & Eggleston, 2010). For example, structured interview techniques can elicit a good understanding of why certain decisions were made, or what went wrong. It is also not uncommon for researchers to embed themselves in a complex environment for a prolonged period to collect observational data. In selected instances, empirical data will be collected in full-mission simulations. Such simulations attempt to faithfully replicate the real environment, and involve teams of highly trained individuals tested with realistic, challenging scenarios. Because these studies are so expensive and time-consuming, they are often limited to situations in which safety is critical or mission efficiency is essential.

The time required for testing and the importance of faithfully reproducing an environment are key considerations in the choice of study approach. If we want to conduct an empirical study to investigate changes to a radar display staffed by a single operator, then we can expect to collect responses every few seconds. In a few days we could test out a range of options. Because the variability is not terribly high, we can get very stable estimates of response time and accuracy that would give us statistical power. If, however, we wish to study the effect of changes in equipage for overall performance in the Launch Control Center depicted in the far right photo of Figures 5.1 and 5.2, we would face a much more formidable challenge. It might take several minutes to collect a single observation, meaning that we could not collect a very large number of observations without a very large-scale experiment. Given that the operations center has many more possible sources that influence the results, it would be necessary to collect a large amount of data to establish any score that was both well controlled and statistically reliable.

COMMUNICATION AND COORDINATION CONSEQUENCES OF GROUP SIZE

The scale of social and organizational units also has several consequences for communication and coordination. In general, the larger the unit, the greater the cost to coordinate its component activities. What do we mean by cost? A simple example will illustrate this. Suppose that each person can be viewed as having a fixed capacity of 5 units of work per interval of time. That is, if an individual works alone, she can do 5 units of work in that time period. If we add another person, the total work done will increase, but it will not double. Output will not double because there will be a cost to each individual related to coordinating their activities, without which the output would be duplicated or simply disorganized. For simplicity, let's just say that 1 unit of work for each must be devoted to coordination. Thus, whereas one person can do 5 units of work, two people can do 8 according to this simple system: 4 units each for work, 1 unit each for communication. Now, if a third person is added, each person is capable of 3 units of work, with 2 units allocated to communication, or a total of 9 units of work. Very little extra is gained by adding the third person. A fourth person actually results in a reduction of output according to this scheme, as 3 units go to communication and only 2 go toward work, for a total of 8 units. You may object that this is an unsophisticated treatment of the issue, and we would agree. It might well take less than one unit each for communication—or, conversely, the communication costs might go up exponentially with the number of people. Nonetheless, the example is accurate in essence. It relates to a well-known problem in the allocation of staffing: Adding more people may not only fail to solve the problem, but may also actually create additional problems (Cannon-Bowers, Salas, & Converse, 1993; Klein, 2000; Salas et al., 2008).

Notice that as the scale of operations is increased by adding more people, the layers of organization also increase. In the Launch Control Center, for instance, work is divided into vehicle subsystems, whereas for air traffic control the airspace is divided up into sectors. This makes sense, in that people must specialize because each person can do only so much work. This arrangement also has the property, important for our analysis, of reducing the communication overhead. Now each team consists of a small number of people. In the case of air traffic, the duo of an R-side and a D-side controller is the primary source of active coordination.

Other effects of increasing numbers and adding layers to an organization include limiting communications and increasing the rules regulating those communications. For example, coordination between air traffic control sectors is highly regulated and structured so that it places far fewer demands on the time of a given controller. The same is true of the NASA Launch Control Center or a military command and control center. In Launch Control, only one team member communicates to other teams through the NASA test director unless otherwise directed. As a result, unstructured, high-volume communication is limited to a few people working closely on a specific problem. Indeed, part of the art of organization is to build divisions where the interactions are naturally limited, reducing the demand for communication and coordination.

The principle of limiting communications in highly interactive teams to a few individuals appears to be reasonably widespread. In basketball, all five members of the team must have the presence of mind to know where all other team members are if they are to pass the ball effectively against a determined and quick defense. In soccer, where the team size is 11, there are effectively smaller subteams consisting of forwards, midfielders, and defenders. Examination of the distribution of passes from any one player would show that the nearby two or three other team members accounted for the majority of the exchanges.

In domains where the patterns of connectivity between individuals are unknown, we can gain insight into the structure and efficiency by using *network analysis*. Network analysis looks at the effect of the structure of interconnections on the time taken to achieve a goal, usually in terms of the path link or number of nodes that must be traversed. In the soccer example, the analysis might consist of the number of times the ball traverses the link between one player and another. If the hypothesis is that the team consists of smaller subteams of players grouped by vicinity, then the frequency with which the ball traverses a link should be a function of distance between positions.

Indeed, the effect of an organization's structure on communication can have widespread consequences for system performance. Figure 5.3 shows a typical hierarchical organizational structure, in this instance of sales representatives. Cynthia, June, and Bill report to a district manager, who in turn reports to a regional manager, who reports to the corporate headquarters. Authority flows from above, and information passes upward before passing laterally. The small black dots show that if Cynthia wants to cooperate with June, she must first gain approval to do so from District 1. The large gray circles show that if Barbara wants to coordinate with Tom in another region, approvals at all levels are required. In short, communication flows primarily upward and downward in the hierarchy, but not laterally. Thus, to get a message from one unit to another, it must travel up to the

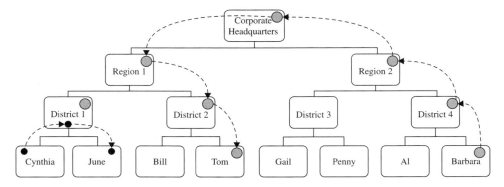

Figure 5.3 A hierarchical organization of sales representatives

nearest common node and then back down. You can see that such a structure does not facilitate rapid response. Instead, it ensures that all managers at higher nodes in the hierarchy are informed of decisions through top-down control over the flow of information from nodes lower in the structure, at the cost of increased response time and reduced flexibility.

In contrast, the network of Figure 5.4 represents a more horizontal organization in which entities at the same level can communicate and can take action. The dotted boxes signify that all entities within the box can freely communicate with each other and can authorize actions without clearance from higher levels. Now Cynthia and June can coordinate a sale without clearance from their district office. Likewise, Tom and Barbara can coordinate without all the upper levels being involved. This communication structure promotes rapid decisions that are sensitive to the situational conditions, by delegation of decision-making authority to those lower in the hierarchy. Earlier in this chapter, we discussed how important such flexibility is for dynamic environments in which the situation is fluid and rapidly changing. In the more horizontal structure of Figure 5.4, the average path length (number of

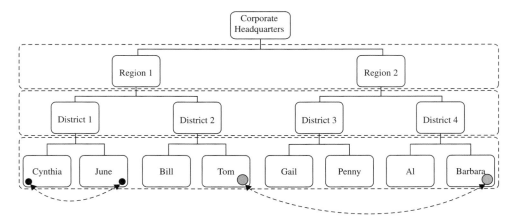

Figure 5.4 The same sales force depicted in Figure 5.3 with lateral communication and authority linkages

nodes) between any two people is less than in the hierarchical structure of Figure 5.1. Thus, when new information becomes available in one node, it can rapidly spread to all other nodes. The benefit of this lateral communication is a rapid response to changing events. The problem with this structure is that it is difficult for corporate managers to maintain control, as decisions are made and actions taken with only a few nodes involved. Because decision authority is vested in all nodes, there is no central node structure to approve or veto actions. District, regional, and corporate offices may not know what is going on in a timely fashion, and will find it hard to ensure that efforts are not duplicated and do not conflict. Duplication of effort or, worse, conflicting actions, (the "left hand" acts without coordinating with the "right hand") can create inefficiencies. In short, there is no perfect structure that works well in all circumstances.

In this discussion we have presented two extreme versions from which many hybrid structures can be crafted to suit the individual situation. In the past, most organizations were more or less strongly hierarchical. As competition mandated shorter times to market new products, companies had to adopt more flexible structures that allowed for faster internal communication to coordinate development. Even the military now embraces a much more flexible communication structure in which personnel on the ground at the scene have more decision-making authority. On the flip side, many small start-up companies embrace a fully egalitarian structure with open communication among all members. This helps to spread good ideas quickly, get feedback on possible courses of action, and promote group adhesion. However, as the company grows, this often becomes an unwieldy structure that limits growth.

Many small companies have failed to make the transition to medium size precisely because they failed to adopt more structured communications early enough. Once again, it is important to emphasize that we are not talking here about the behavior of people per se. That is, the problems of organization, communication, coordination, and structure are to a large extent inherent in the social situation and interaction between individuals in group settings. The tendency for people to behave in certain ways when in groups can have important effects on and consequences for the organizational structure. For example, people in hierarchical structures often feel disenfranchised, and consequently have low motivation, whereas people in egalitarian structures may become frustrated at perceived disorganization and frequent changes in direction. Nonetheless, many of the feelings that people have are to a large extent an outgrowth of the issues inherent in a given organizational structure.

SUMMARY

This chapter examined the role that social context plays in shaping the environment within which systems operate. Here, group size plays the most significant role in shaping the environment. The methodologies that can be used to understand performance will differ as a function of group size. Likewise, group size has a major impact on the amount and types of communications and coordination required to complete complex tasks.

The reader should note that we have not covered several important topics. Modern technology has made it possible to form teams that are not co-located. Not only is it possible to distribute work among the individual members of a team, but it is also possible to distribute the team members themselves. Such a distribution of people raises important issues as to the roles and influence of body language, facial expression, tone of voice, and other clues that we use, often intuitively, when working closely with others. The globalization of industry also means that teams now routinely consist of people from different cultures who may, again, not be co-located. If teams are to be effective, trust must be developed among people from vastly different cultures who, when dealing remotely, work using information transmission lines that may not allow one to see the full expressions of the other. The capability for remotely located teams consisting of diverse ethnic groups is very new, with little firm research as a foundation. It is an exciting area for future study.

REFERENCES

Cannon-Bowers, J. A., Salas, E., & Converse, S. (1993). Shared mental models in expert team decision making. In N. J. J. Castellan (Ed.), *Individual and group decision making* (pp. 221–246). Hillsdale, NJ: Lawrence Erlbaum Associates.

Cooke, N. J., Kiekel, P. A., Salas, E., Stout, R., Bowers, C., & Cannon-Bowers, J. (2003). Measuring team knowledge: A window to the cognitive underpinnings of team performance. *Group Dynamics: Theory, Research, and Practice*, 7(3), 179.

Cooke, N. J., Salas, E., Kiekel, P. A., & Bell, B. (2004). Advances in measuring team cognition. In E. Salas & S. M. Fiore (Eds.), *Team cognition: Understanding the factors that drive process and performance* (pp. 83–106). Washington, DC: American Psychological Association.

Foltz, P. W., & Martin, M. J. (2009). Automated communication analysis of teams. In E. Salas, G. F. Goodwin, & S. Burke (Eds.), *Team effectiveness in complex organizations: Cross-disciplinary perspectives and approaches* (pp. 411–432). New York, NY: Taylor and Francis.

Klein, G. (2000). Cognitive task analysis of teams. In J. M. Schraagen & S. F. Chipman (Eds.), *Cognitive task analysis*. Mahwah, NJ: Lawrence Erlbaum Associates.

Patterson, E. S., Roth, E. M., & Woods, D. D. (2010). Facets of complexity in situated work. In E. S. Patterson & J. Miller (Eds.), *Macrocognition metrics and scenarios: Design and evaluation for real-world teams* (pp. 203–219). Burlington, VT: Ashgate.

Roth, E. M., & Eggleston, R. G. (2010). Forging new evaluation paradigms: Beyond statistical generalization. In E. S. Patterson & J. Miller (Eds.), *Macrocognition metrics and scenarios: Design and evaluation for real-world teams* (pp. 203–219). Burlington, VT: Ashgate.

Salas, E., Goodwin, G. F., & Burke, C. S. (2008). *Team effectiveness in complex organizations: Cross-disciplinary perspectives and approaches*. New York, NY: Taylor and Francis.

Slaughter, A. J., Yu, J., & Koehly, L. M. (2009). Social network analysis: Understanding the role of context in small groups and organizations. In E. Salas, G. F. Goodwin, & S. Burke (Eds.), *Team effectiveness in complex organizations: Cross-disciplinary perspectives and approaches* (pp. 433–459). New York, NY: Taylor and Francis.

6

Analysis Techniques

In the previous chapters in this section, we discussed some of the ways in which environments differ and how those differences affect the human operator. Thus far, our discussion has been qualitative. In this chapter we provide insight into how researchers and engineers produce quantitative descriptions of environments. These quantitative descriptions are important, as they are often the basis for anticipating or predicting how the human operator will behave in some circumstance. Keep in mind that in this chapter we are not dealing directly with analytical techniques for representing human behavior. That will come in later chapters. Rather, we focus here on techniques for rigorous analysis of environments.

Human-system engineers analyze systems with a goal in mind. The goal is typically an improvement in safety, performance (e.g., productivity, efficiency), or both. These goals can be achieved in several ways. For example, performance might be improved by changing the allocation of functions (either between the controller and the machine or among personnel). It might also be improved by addressing personnel issues, such as identifying the characteristics of the operators who can best perform in the system or identifying the ideal number or organization of the staffing for a system. Finally, performance might be improved by the development of new training and procedures, or through redesign of the task or the interface.

The analyst's goal and the target of the intervention (e.g., function allocation vs. training) jointly determine how the specialist approaches the analysis of the environment or system and decides what information is important to derive from it. For example, if the interest is in describing what happens or happened, *descriptive* analyses might be conducted, such as a detailed ethnographic study detailing the activities that characterize the domain. Such an analysis would be conducted by inserting researchers into the field to get a flavor of the normal working environment. In other cases, interest may center on setting out proper procedures for operators to follow or investigating whether procedures were followed correctly. Such *normative* analyses are prescriptive, indicating responsibilities, duties, and what ought to be done.

In other cases, the specialist may be interested in characterizing the flow of behavior or the interrelation of the system tasks and activities. These questions are often approached using a *hierarchical decomposition* that divides the domain into a set of smaller discrete tasks as the starting point for a number of more *quantitative* analyses that can provide engineers with performance data. Hierarchical decomposition is one of the most frequently used ways of approaching a task analysis. The decomposition need not be strictly hierarchical, but can take the form of a network of states that can be used to answer questions about how long it will take to complete tasks, or what the workload will be for some selection of activities. Task decomposition is often used as a first step toward a *process model* that seeks to provide a functional representation of processes, which can lead directly to computational models. In this chapter we focus on some commonly used methods for analyzing environments.

MODELING STATIC ENVIRONMENTS: FINITE STATE REPRESENTATIONS

We are frequently interested in knowing how information flows when performing a set of actions in pursuit of a goal within an organization, or for a set of activities. Consider a simple example of using the Internet to find a specific piece of information, such as which capital city in the world is the smallest (as of 2010, Nuuk, Greenland). Suppose you are on a Web page where all the countries listed are categorized into large, medium, and small countries (but not capitals). That page contains 16 links for small countries, so you begin your search by clicking on the links to the small countries. From those locations you follow other links repeatedly until you find the smallest capital city. Each page can be considered a node in the space of all possible locations that can be reached from that state. Each link can be considered a transit from one state to the next, including the "Back" button that returns to the previous state. Given that the Internet has a few billion sites and deep interconnections, the space required to draw all the links and nodes present in the Internet would be impossibly huge.

Fortunately, we need not represent all the possible states of the Internet if we take a somewhat different approach. Consider the behavioral possibilities. A user selects a link, then determines if the information on the new page is the goal. If so, then she exits. If not, she evaluates the set of links. If none of them look like they will lead to the answer, she can press the "Back" button. Alternatively, she selects one of the links and begins the process again. This represents a routine, or procedure, that can be repeated. Figure 6.1 shows how this procedure can be represented as a *finite state-space diagram*; that is, a diagram containing a finite number of states and actions that transition between states. More information on finite-state diagrams and models can be found by searching the Web under those terms (for good places to begin, see Wikipedia, 2011d, 2011f).

The size of the state space representing the behavior is determined in part by the complexity of the domain and the specifics of its organization. For example, if the user is allowed to write in a search word that gives a large list of options, as Google does, then the size and composition of the state diagram will be different from our example above. Finite-state models are often used to represent the nature of the actions possible within a given domain. It is easy to see, for example, how this analysis could be generalized to using a computer, working on an assembly line, or being a checker in a supermarket.

The complexity of a given procedure in a finite-state model could be used to assess the difficulty of learning the routine, in that the number of states and number of conditions for transitioning between states must all be learned for good performance. In addition, for a finite-state model to adequately inform systems designers, the procedure must be accompanied

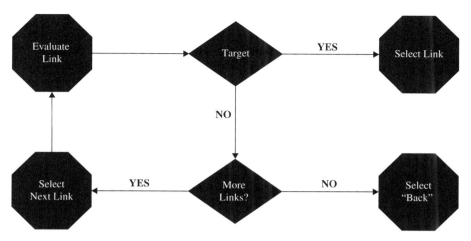

Figure 6.1 A simple finite-state model of searching through a list of linked Web pages, such as a menu or the World Wide Web. Each link is examined in turn to determine if it is close enough to the desired target to explore further. If so, it is selected. If not, the next link is selected and the process repeats. If no more links remain, the user is assumed to press the Back button and select a new link from the "parent" page.

by a representation of the environment. In our preceding Web search example, the time to find the smallest capital city will depend on the size and arrangement of the knowledge base being searched. This too can be represented as a state space. Virtually all static domains can be represented and analyzed using some type of state-space method and transforming them into an abstract representation can yield many insights. For example, it is now possible to mathematically compute the length of the path from one state to another (like the goal state). The length of the path can be used to indicate the time it will take to do a task, or task difficulty.

An abstract representation of the state space can clarify the difficulty for the user (human or otherwise—remember that this chapter is not about the human) in selecting a state that is likely to produce a good long-term outcome. The best move is not always the one that seems the best choice for that move, but rather the one that achieves a state that maximizes the likelihood of reaching a goal state while minimizing the chance of a bad outcome. Viewing domains in this way also highlights common elements between domains that superficially bear little resemblance to one another. For example, state-space analysis has been applied to chess, computer interaction, Web searching, database searching, programming the flight management system of a modern jetliner, tuning a radio station, and many other seemingly unrelated domains.

Finite-state modeling can also inform us of the time it takes to complete a set of actions. Given a finite set of states, and a set of operations that move from state to state, the time to get from any one state to another can be derived from durations assigned to the transition from one state to another and to the time to evaluate inputs for each state. Consider a finite-state model representing how a user of a Macintosh computer might open a document from a menu bar using the mouse. The current state of the mouse must be changed to the state where the mouse is over the File menu. When that has occurred (the mouse is over the menu title), clicking and holding the mouse button opens a submenu with a list of selections, which in turn will lead to other states. We can determine time to complete each of these activities (we will discuss how later). Lastly, the mouse is moved down and the Open command is clicked to complete the task. The finite-state model continues from there in the same fashion. Each action corresponds to a transition between states, and the times for each can be summed to yield an estimate of completion time for each subtask and the overall task. Timing estimates could be obtained in a similar way for alternate methods of opening a file, such as double-clicking the icon, or clicking-and-dragging the icon into another icon representing the application desired.

This example makes it easy to see, as discussed in Chapter 4, how a large number of states (modes), each mapping the same action to a different result, would be a problem for any kind of user: computer, robot, human, or otherwise. One way to visualize this issue is to consider something called a *state vector*. A state vector can be thought of as all the information that might be needed to determine which decision to make. In chess, for example, it might consist of the position of all the pieces for both players as well as assumptions about the opponent's likely responses. As the amount of information needed to select an action increases, so will the complexity of the problem. The state space can become very large when there are many states that are highly interconnected and where, from any given state, many subsequent states can be reached and more information is required to arrive at the best action. Even though a computer may do this flawlessly, the program describing its behavior would have to be much longer and include more special cases than a program that described a system with fewer or no modes.

Indeed, it is useful to keep this example in mind. Often we ascribe errors to the human or assume that limitations in processing capacity or unique failings of the human are responsible for usability problems, when in fact it would be a similar problem for the designer of a robot. A very famous characterization of the dependency of behavior on the environment comes from the Nobel laureate economist and behavioral scientist Herbert Simon: "We watch an ant make his laborious way across a wind- and wave-molded beach . . . . Viewed as a geometric figure, the ant's path is irregular, complex, hard to describe. But its complexity is really a complexity in the surface of the beach, not a complexity in the ant. On that same beach another small creature with a home at the same place as the ant might well follow a very similar path" (Simon, 1996, p. 51). In the remainder of this chapter we will pursue Simon's point and attempt to characterize the way the environment shapes behavior. In later chapters we will see how the behavior of the human operator is also affected by the nature of the way humans process information.

MODELING DYNAMIC ENVIRONMENTS

Dynamic environments are those that change state irrespective of control inputs from an operator—human or machine. As a consequence of the dependence on time, analyses of dynamic environments attempt to capture the flow of behavior. Because the initial impetus for dynamic models came from aeronautics and problems of aircraft control, it is not surprising that the focus has been on how an agent can control a vehicle to achieve a goal. A key property of dynamic environments is that they are inherently feedback driven. The operator assesses the situation, makes a decision on the spot, effects an action, and observes the result in order to begin the behavior loop all over again. It is this concern with control and sensitivity to feedback that dictates much of the way dynamic environments have been represented and understood. Here we shall touch briefly on two formal systems for representing inherent properties of environments that are true for and applicable to both artificial and human systems. The first, *control theory*, concerns the general problem of achieving the desired outcome and the factors that make it difficult to do so. The second, *signal detection theory*, describes the general problem of making an assessment of a situation and the factors affecting the difficulty of that assessment.

CONTROL THEORY

In Chapter 2, we presented a cartoon-like depiction showing the elements of a control loop for landing a plane, and introduced concepts of lag, plant dynamics, control order, perturbation, and noise. *Control theory* is a mathematical formulation for representing and predicting the behavior of an agent trying to control a system in the presence of noise and disturbance. The controller agent acts on the system and monitors the feedback to gauge the effect of that action and plan a new action. Our treatment of control theory will only introduce the major concepts. Much information regarding control theory can be found on the Web (e.g., Wikipedia, 2011a, 2011b; for a more mathematical approach, see Doyle, Francis, & Tannenbaum, 1992).

Let's begin with a very simple control loop. Imagine that you are attempting to set the time on your new digital clock. You have the controller (you), the controlled system (the clock), and the state of the world (the displayed time). To set the time, you need to push and hold a button on the top of the clock. When you do that, the time begins to increment, and you hold the button down until the clock displays the intended time. Even in such a simple controlled system, it is possible for error to occur. This error can come from a number of sources. Imagine first that the display changes by one minute for each push of the button. If you needed to add five minutes to the current time, you would push the button five times, presumably looking at the display after each update to ensure that the button push had its intended effect. If you are in a hurry, you might not wait for each update, and intend to push the button five times quickly and then confirm the intended time only at the end. In this case, you may miscount and push the button too many, or too few, times. Likewise, if the system is slow to respond, you might push the button five times, but not see the correct time displayed as quickly as you think it should be displayed. This might lead you to push the button an additional time, leading to a lag-induced error.

Imagine now that you push and hold the button down to increment the display, and that the longer you hold the button down, the more quickly the display increments. In this case, you will need to estimate how far off the current display is from the desired display and release the button soon enough that the display ends on your desired time. In this situation, there is likely to be error on your part in estimating the exact moment at which you should release the button. Even if you choose the correct moment, there may be a lag before your finger actually comes off the button, inducing lag on your part. In addition,

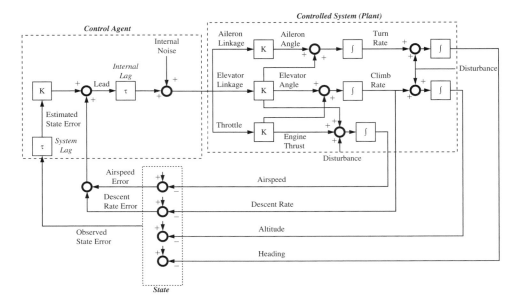

Figure 6.2 Simplified control loop for landing an aircraft. K = gain, ∫ = integration. Monitored state variables include airspeed, descent rate, altitude, and heading. The control agent used feedback of error from desired state to select an action. Evaluation of error should include lags in system response, and actions should include lags in internal response.

there may be noise in the system, either on the part of the control agent (you) or on the part of the controlled system (the clock) that leads to further error.

Now let's move to a more complex system. Figure 6.2 shows a more detailed conceptual treatment of the landing task that was shown in Chapter 2, Figure 2.4, with a more standard representation of the control loop. It must be emphasized that the model in Figure 6.2 is not intended to be a complete model of landing, nor even a correct model. The full details of landing are beyond the scope of this text, as are the mathematics that would be needed to make this a valid, correct model. Rather, our goal with this model is to introduce control theory at a conceptual level.

The control loop in Figure 6.2 has three major components: the controller agent, the controlled system (often referred to as the *plant*), and the state. These are indicated by the dotted rectangles. The plant, in this case the aircraft, consists not just of the physical parts, but also of the dynamics that will ultimately determine the feedback. The controller agent uses this feedback to select an action that will reduce the error between the desired and observed state variables. The assumption that the control agent's job is to reduce error is fundamental to classical control theory. Control of the plant is achieved through linkages to physical control devices. For our simplified aircraft, the devices of interest are the elevators, ailerons, and engine. The elevators function to pitch the nose of the aircraft up or down. The ailerons allow the aircraft to roll or bank by adjusting the lift independently on each wing. The engine produces thrust, which changes speed and, by changing the velocity of air over the wings, also affects the lift. To bank, the pilot sends a control signal to the elevators and aileron that causes a change in angular position of those surfaces. This changes the rotational acceleration of the aircraft, altering its bank angle. The turn rate of the aircraft is approximated by the integral of this acceleration over time. In turn, the integral of turn rate over time determines the heading. Altitude is determined similarly, from the joint settings of the elevators and engine, which are integrated over time to determine the climb or descent rate, then integrated again to determine altitude. A change in the thrust produced by the engine also changes the aircraft's acceleration, which is integrated to determine airspeed. As indicated, the elevators also affect airspeed: Given the same amount of thrust, pitching the nose down increases airspeed, and pitching it up decreases airspeed. The integration over time yields the four state variables for the simple controller of Figure 6.2 to monitor: airspeed, descent rate, altitude, and heading. At each instant, values of the observed variables are compared to the desired state values and an error score for each is computed. To keep the diagram readable, we do not show the error signal for each, but simply output an observed state error.

In a real control theory model, each box in Figure 6.2 would be associated with a mathematical expression that determined how the inputs would be transformed into outputs. These mathematical expressions allow one to compute control activity with precision by specifying the gain (K) of each element and how its output changes over time. In Figure 6.2, boxes labeled K replace this more complex function with a simple gain. Thus, aileron angle, for example, is assumed to be in proportion to the value specified by the linkage; changing the linkage instantaneously changes the angle. Though unrealistic, it will suffice for demonstration purposes. Other boxes are labeled with the integral sign, $\int$. This indicates that the output is determined by integrating the input over time. Circles in the model represent the combination of two or more outputs. Plus and minus signs indicate whether a given input is to be added or subtracted. The error signal is determined by subtracting the observed signal from the desired. All other combinations are additive.

The controller agent in Figure 6.2 is not meant to represent the human pilot depicted in Figure 2.4. As we will show in later chapters, this depiction is far too simple to capture much of the decision making of a human pilot. Instead, it is concerned primarily with the problem of estimation, which arises from time delays (lags) associated with its own internal time delays and those of the system. The box labeled "System lag" indicates that the controller must account for lags in the system response to its commanded inputs. If the controller commands a change in altitude, for example, it would change the thrust and horizontal elevator angle. Over time, this would change the climb rate, which again over time would change the altitude. Thus, the controller cannot immediately use the error between commanded and observed, but must allow the system time to adjust. Long lags increase the difficulty of control, as temporal estimation becomes less precise, and there is more time for the effects of external factors (disturbances) to accumulate. If the agent responds prematurely, the system will oscillate with increasing amplitude, ultimately becoming unstable.

To illustrate, consider an altitude change. If the controller does not estimate correctly how long it will take for the aircraft to respond and for its altitude to begin to change, the controller may assume that insufficient control actions were taken, and further increase the thrust and elevator angle. Very shortly, this will lead to a greater change in altitude than was originally desired. The same estimation problem will affect the attempt to correct the overshoot. If this continues, the system will begin to oscillate with ever-increasing amplitude. The control agent also needs to estimate the time taken to compute the maneuver. Given the errors in speed and descent rate, the control agent needs to adjust the amplitude of its output so that when the action is taken it will be appropriate for the state at that time. Problems of estimation are inevitable given the dynamics of real systems.

One of the strengths of control theory, or more generally in representing the environment as a behavioral loop, is the ability to see how environmental factors can make the control agent's job more difficult. Even with the highly simplified representation in Figure 6.2, it is clear that dynamic properties define how the controller must behave, as well as the kinds of difficulties imposed on the operator. This is a virtue of control theory that is often overlooked by human-system specialists: A human controller is constrained by the dynamics of the system in the same way as an automated controller. Control theory makes this clear by its detailed analysis of system dynamics. One of the significant engineering achievements of the last half of the 20th century was the development of optimal control theory, which characterized the human operator in control theoretic terms. We will say a bit more about this when we discuss the role of the human in complex systems.

Signal Detection Theory

The perception of feedback is critical to control in dynamic environments, as is the decision process that selects appropriate action. But, in a noisy environment, how should the control agent determine whether the observed error represents the true state of the world or just a momentary perturbation due to noise? In later chapters we will deal specifically with human decision making, but it is important to emphasize that these problems plague any agent trying to achieve a goal in a noisy environment. There is a quantitative characterization of decisions under noise that applies equally to human and automated agents, referred to as *signal detection theory*, or SDT for short. There are many good sources, including online sources, for learning more about SDT (e.g., Heeger, 2007; Wickens, 2001, Wikipedia, 2011c; for the classic work, see Green & Swets, 1966). SDT was developed to characterize how an *ideal observer* would behave given the information available and the noise. By ideal observer, we do not mean an observer who is always correct. Rather, it refers to a decision maker who weighs the likelihood of various outcomes with their associated costs in an optimal way.

What we mean by optimal here is that there is no other strategy that would result in better average decisions in the long run. For any given decision, a pure guess has some chance of doing better than a rational process. However, provided that the underlying process is not random, SDT provides a way of ensuring that one cannot do better in the long run. Like our treatment of control theory, we will avoid many of the mathematical details of SDT to concentrate on a conceptual understanding. The principal ideas are shown graphically in Figure 6.3. For now, let's assume that the problem is in deciding whether a target is present or absent. This is quite a common situation. In birdwatching, for example, it is often difficult to decide whether there is a bird in a distant tree or just some branch or twig. A quarterback in football must decide if the distance between the receiver and defender is large enough to chance a pass; a baggage screener at an airport must decide from an X-ray image whether the contents of a bag contain dangerous items. A key

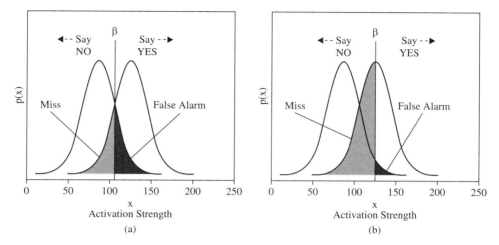

Figure 6.3 Illustration of the effect of activation strength, noise and signal distributions, and criterion on the decision to say that a target stimulus was present or absent. The abscissa plots the activation strength as a random variable. The ordinate plots the probability of a specific activation strength (on the abscissa) given the noise and signal distributions. The black region represents False Alarms (saying that a target was present when there was only noise). The gray region represents Misses (saying a target was not present when it was). When the distributions overlap, as they often do at threshold, the placement of the criterion determines the proportion of False Alarms and Misses.

characteristic of such decisions, especially for the quarterback and the baggage screener, is that it is important not to miss a real event (i.e. bird, threat) or to falsely assume that a real event is present when one is not. One can think of many similar situations.

In SDT, it is always assumed that decisions are made in the presence of noise. The interesting applications of SDT are those in which the signal is only marginally stronger than the noise; clearly, no analysis is needed when the target is easily determined. The noise is simply information in which the observer is not interested. Noise can arise from the environment, as in the case of camouflage, or from the detector itself, such as random fluctuations in a sensor. For the birdwatcher, leaves and branches constitute noise, while for the quarterback looking for a receiver, irrelevant nearby people—lineman, coaches, and other players—in his line of sight constitute noise. For simplicity, SDT can be decomposed into two component stages: an *observation* followed by a *decision* about that observation. SDT provides a rational way of deciding whether the target is present or absent for any given observation.

The *observation* is assumed to yield a value of activation strength (evidence), shown along the *x*-axis in Figure 6.3. This activation can refer to the voltage output of a receptor in a sensory device, as, for example, the output of a photodiode; or it can refer more abstractly to any form of evidence. By convention, the target (or *signal*, as it is referred to) produces more activation than does the noise. The presence of noise also means that the same external signal will not always produce exactly the same activation strength, but each will have a distribution of activation. This yields two distributions: a *noise* distribution (N) and a *signal* distribution (S). Values of the signal (S) and noise (N) distributions are assumed to be random variables of activation, x, each specified by a density function. The density function gives the probability that a specific activation value, x, would have occurred given S or N. These probability density functions are notated as p(x | N) and p(x | S), and refer to the probability that an observation yielding a value of x would occur by noise alone, or by signal alone, respectively. The problem tackled in the decision phase is to determine how likely it is that x came from S or N.

The *decision* phase outputs a binary, yes-or-no judgment indicating whether the detector concludes that a target has or has not occurred. To do this, the detector sets a *decision criterion*, ß, that defines a critical value of x. When the observation produces activation less then the critical value, the detector outputs a No; when the observation exceeds the critical value, the detector outputs Yes. The critical activation value, x_c, is derived from ß through the following relation: ß = p(x | S) / p(x | N). That is, ß is equal to the probability that you would observe x given that the signal is present divided by the probability that you would observe x given that the signal is not present. The detector is assumed to select ß to maximize performance. Figures 6.3 and 6.4 show ß placed in different locations relative to the two distributions. In graph (a) of these figures, ß divides the area under each of the two distributions equally. In graph (b) of these figures, ß creates a larger area under one of the two distributions.

Table 6.1 shows the four possible outcomes of a decision given two states of the world (signal present, signal absent) and two outcomes (say Yes, say No). A *Hit* occurs when the signal was present and the decision was Yes. A *Miss* occurs when the signal was present and the decision was No. A *Correct Rejection* occurs when the signal was not present and the decision was No. Finally, a *False Alarm* occurs when the signal was not present and the decision was Yes.

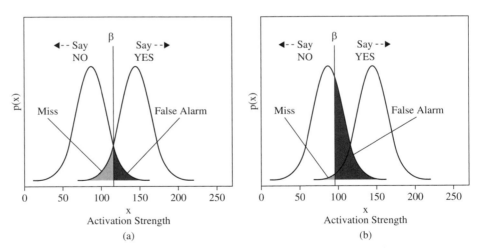

Figure 6.4 Illustration of an easy discrimination in signal detection theory. Overlap in signal and noise distributions is minimal, as the means are far apart relative to their variances. Note that placing the criterion (ß) midway between the means of the two distributions minimizes joint error (False Alarms and Misses). Moving the criterion to further reduce Misses, as shown in graph (b), produces a large increase in False Alarms for a small reduction in Misses.

Table 6.1 Decision outcomes as a function of state of the world

	STATE OF THE WORLD	
OUTCOMES	SIGNAL PRESENT	SIGNAL ABSENT
Say Yes	Hit	False Alarm
Say No	Miss	Correct Rejection

The shaded regions in Figure 6.3 show the associated portions of the density functions that correspond to the two types of errors that can occur: *Miss* and *False Alarm*. In Figure 6.3, the gray-shaded region shows the area under the signal distribution that is less than the criterion. The proportion of the distribution in that area gives the proportion of Misses. The black-shaded region shows the area under the noise distribution that exceeds the criterion. The proportion of the distribution in that area gives the proportion of False Alarms. Moving the criterion to the right of the intersection of the two distributions, as in graph (b) of Figure 6.3, will increase Misses (gray region), as a greater proportion of the signal distribution now falls to the left of the criterion. It will also reduce False Alarms (black region) by requiring higher activation strength to say Yes. That is, it reduces the proportion of noise observations that exceed the criterion.

The distance between the means of the signal and noise distributions will determine the exact proportion of Misses and False Alarms. In the case where the distributions are assumed to be normal with the same variance, the distance between the means determines how easy it is to discriminate signal from noise: a measure referred to as *d prime* (d′). Figure 6.4 shows a case in which d′ is increased. Note that the regions for False Alarms and Misses are a smaller proportion of the total distribution. Graph (b) of Figure 6.4 shows this case. In this instance, the detector takes more risk, and will say Yes with less activation strength.

To be concrete about this, let us assume that we are building a device to read the text on a computer screen as an aid to the blind. The visual input consists of white letters (and words) displayed on the darker background of the monitor (black would be best). The detector consists of an array of tiny photodiodes that span a region of text. Each diode records the value of the luminance of a very small patch of the screen. The lighter the patch, the more likely it is to be part of a letter. The size of the whole array is about the size of an individual letter. For each diode in the array, the *observation* consists of a single measurement of the luminance of a small patch of the screen. Its strength can be represented as a random variable, x, distributed around a mean value. When a single diode is positioned over the background, its reading will cluster around some low luminance value; when positioned over a letter, its reading will cluster around a larger value. In Figure 6.3, for example, the x-axis would represent the reading of a single diode; the y-axis would show the probability of that value given the signal and noise distributions. In the *decision* phase, our simple photodiode outputs whether its small patch contained signal or noise (this is the basic, no-frills model). In Figure 6.3, the mean of the noise distribution is 80, the mean of the signal 110. They have the same variance, 20. With no prior knowledge of the likelihood of a letter or background, and equal cost for False Alarms and Misses, the criterion would be set to the equivalence point of the two distributions to minimize both False Alarms and Misses. In this case, the setting p(x | S) / p(x | N) = 1 yields x$_c$ = 100.

Assume that our photodiode detector registered 105. It would say Yes, as that value exceeds the criterion of 100. It would not always be correct. The black region shows that sometimes noise alone produce values greater than 100. In our example, this could occur because of glare on a portion of the background, or because of imperfections in the medium (e.g., a poorly copied document). To compensate for these False Alarms, the detector could move the criterion higher, as in graph (b) of Figure 6.3. This might be a reasonable thing to do if the letters were large enough that it could afford to say No if only a part of the region contained the target. In this case, the cost of a miss is low since the other diodes would register a strong signal. Notice that in Figure 6.4, where the distributions are further apart (higher d′), our diode makes fewer Misses and False Alarms.

In general, what determines how the criterion should be set? As we have discussed, ß reflects the observer's decision bias, incorporating prior knowledge of the likelihood of a signal plus the relative weight assigned to Misses and False Alarms. Less evidence is needed if there is an *a priori* reason to believe that the signal is present, so a sample of lower strength or activation can be accepted as evidence of a signal than when prior information is absent. This is referred to as the *prior probability* of an event. In terms of our text-reader device, each letter is separated by black background. The probability that a letter will be present, then, increases with the number of No decisions, as they represent the spaces between letters. The criterion, ß, is also influenced by the *incentives*, expressed as the cost associated with a Miss or False Alarm. If there is a high cost to missing a signal but a low cost to a False Alarm, then the criterion, ß, should be lowered to avoid Misses, with the consequence of accepting a few more less-costly False Alarms. If our text device is reading an old, degraded piece of text, it may be better to increase the criterion, as Misses from individual photodiodes may be less damaging to interpretation than constant False Alarms.

The application of signal detection theory is not confined to the detection of physical or sensory events, but can be applied more broadly to a variety of decision problems. Consider, for example, when you are operating a vehicle, such as your car. You must be alert to whether the state of the car is within normal bounds or has developed a problem that would cause you to stop. Evidence for the state of the car can come from multiple sources—fuel and temperature gauges, for example—and also from the way the car handles on the road, and damps noises, bumps, or shudders. From this multisensory input you must decide if the car is behaving normally or not. We can consider the usual kinds of input to constitute the noise distribution. So, a small amount of bumpiness is to be expected, as are the array of common sounds the car makes when it accelerates, turns, or brakes. In other words, you have developed a sense of the noise distribution. Prior knowledge about the road you are driving on can also condition how you interpret deviations from normal. High values of the noise distribution (the normal behavior) can come from changes in driving conditions, such as the road surface; for example, more noise and bumpiness would be expected on a dirt road. With prior knowledge of these conditions, the criterion can be moved further to the tail of the distribution (more conservative) so that these are now attributed to noise, risking an increased rate of missed signals. The mathematical analysis of detecting deviations from normality can be a bit complicated, but the concept is nicely handled by signal detection theory. In our text-reader example, the reader is encouraged to develop the SDT analysis for the detector array as a whole.

Although signal detection theory does not explain the causes of accidents, it can be very helpful in structuring our thinking about what happens to cause them in general. In the early 1990s, there was an accident at the Dallas-Ft. Worth Airport in which a passenger airline landed without deploying its landing gear; the aircraft was destroyed, but there was no serious injury to passengers. There are many interesting facets of this particular case, but the main cause can be attributed to a failure to detect that the situation was not normal—that is, a Miss in signal detection terms. The captain and first officer were perplexed about why they could not bring their speed to within expected parameters; that is, they were simply going faster than they thought they should have been. They tried a number of things that should have lowered the speed, and though these measures had an effect, the speed continued at an elevated level. The captain decided that this was unusual but within normal bounds. That decision amounted to an acceptance that the high speed (the strong signal) came from the noise distribution rather than the signal distribution. In SDT terms, they had adopted a high criterion (conservative) for detecting that the aircraft was in an abnormal state. In fact, earlier the crew had become distracted while performing the prelanding checklist and had to pause it to do something else. When they returned to the checklist, they omitted a crucial step that would have lowered the landing gear (and reduced the speed). This reluctance to accept a non-normal state turns out to be a common problem among experienced operators in a wide range of contexts.

We have attempted only a rough outline of signal detection theory. Much more could be said about how d' is determined and how performance varies with changes to ß. Even with just this conceptual introduction, it should be clear that SDT is applicable to a wide range of problems. The idea that all human observations are made in the presence of noise and that decisions are always a trade-off between False Alarms and Misses is fundamental to all sorts of situations. When situations go out of control, the problem can often be attributed to a decision process that culminated in a decision not to act on evidence that was ambiguous—that is, a Miss.

Task Analysis

As we have shown, the environment is an important shaper of human behavior, and much useful information can be gained from understanding the incentives and demands placed on people by the environment, as well as the social contexts in which they act. Yet, this is not a complete understanding. Ultimately we interact with the environment by making decisions, taking actions, and accomplishing goals. In short, the understanding of humans in engineered systems must deal with *tasks*, the things that people are trying to accomplish. Task analysis (TA) is a well-established methodology for decomposing complex activities into understandable "chunks," and is widely employed by human factors practitioners, human-computer interaction research, and in human-system integration (Kirwan & Ainsworth, 1992; Usability Net, 2006). Task analysis can be seen as a way of taking complex relationships—systems and jobs—and breaking them down into progressively simpler elements—tasks and subtasks—that can then be used to understand performance.

We often speak broadly about professions or jobs, such as doing "police work." What we mean by that is a collection of much more specific tasks in which police officers often engage. In reality, no police officer does police work. Instead, she handcuffs a suspect, writes a situation report, or attends a briefing. Even at this level the analysis might be too coarse. Putting on handcuffs is a *procedure* involving many substeps, just as there are many sections to a police report. Our point is that there is a level of abstraction commonly used to describe what we think of as a task. A task is really just a collection of some activities, done in service of attaining a particular *goal*, that seems to cohere in a way that sets it apart from other tasks.

If this seems a little vague, that is because there is an inescapable vagueness about concepts like activities, tasks, and work. Ultimately an action will occur in the world that is observable to others, like clicking the handcuffs shut on the wrists of a suspect, or moving the pen across the paper on the report. However, it is not critical that we be so wedded to this concreteness. It is often more important to provide a useful level of abstract description that can help us to think about the complex environments in which we routinely work.

This points to the need to describe tasks at the appropriate level of analysis. In general, analysis levels range from the macro level to the micro level. At the macro level, concerns tend to focus on system-level issues, which means that they will focus on physical and behavioral attributes of the system and on issues of person-to-person communications. At the micro level, the focus tends to be at the motor-movement level, where the user is interacting with the system. At this level of analysis, cognitive attributes, such as the user's intention to execute a particular action, become important and therefore must be represented in the analysis. This level is where issues of perception, analysis, response times, and human error typically are considered.

For example, within the domain of human-computer interaction, macro-level concerns might revolve around whether the physical configuration of a networked set of workstations allows operators to collaborate to produce answers in a timely fashion. An adequate answer to this may be gained by measuring the average time it takes for each operator to complete her portion of the task plus the time required for the operators to coordinate with one another. The focus would be on the suitability of the software packages and network connectivity in supporting communication between operators. At the micro level, an analyst might be concerned with optimizing the interface for a single procedure and a given operator. This might entail, for example, recording the sequence of keystrokes needed to complete a specific task, like opening a file or searching a database. If the user must execute a different sequence of actions to complete each of these individual tasks, it will likely be difficult for the user to remember all of the alternative sequences and use the system effectively.

MEASURING COMPLEXITY USING INFORMATION THEORY

There is no doubt that some environments are more complex than others. For example, a nuclear power plant is a more complex environment overall than your kitchen. Further, we all intuitively recognize that some domains are easier at certain times than at other times. Operators would likely view a nuclear power plant with an alarm sounding as a more complex environment than that same plant when all is quiet and power is being generated as usual. Your kitchen may be viewed as a more complex environment when you are in the midst of preparing a meal that requires the heating and use of multiple appliances than when you are grabbing a prepackaged snack from the cupboard.

Finally, complexity is also a function of an interaction between the environment and the controller attempting to operate in that environment. That is, user expertise, or experience, can affect the perceived complexity of the environment. For example, an 11-year-old child will likely find the kitchen a more challenging environment than an adult. A trained and seasoned driver may find a crowded roadway less challenging than a less-experienced driver does.

However, scientists have struggled to find methods for measuring the inherent complexity in a domain or in using a device. The general field of complexity theory has wrestled with this question for many years. A number of suggested measures or algorithms have been suggested, but many are variants of *information theory*. Information theory attempts to describe the inherent uncertainty in a domain. To make this concrete, let's modify our previous Web example slightly so that you are now searching for a prize located on the page indicated by one of the 16 links. You have no other information, so all links are equally likely to lead to the prize. As in the game "20 Questions," you get to ask a series of yes/no questions about the location. The trick is to find the smallest number of questions to ask that will guarantee your getting the right answer every time. There are 16 possible locations, with no prior knowledge, so the probability that it is on any given page is

$$p(x) = 1/16$$

where x refers to a specific page and p(x) the probability that the prize is on that page. If you proceed by guessing individual locations, then each guess reduces your uncertainty by a small amount: 1/16, then 1/15, 1/14, and so forth. That is, each guess tells you whether or not it is behind that link, but says nothing about the remaining links. On average, this will take a little more than 8 guesses, though in some cases it can take as many as 16.

The key to the power of information theory is that you can reduce the number of guesses needed to arrive at the answer. Instead of asking about each particular location one by one, information theory says that you can query efficiently by separating the options in half and asking if the prize is reached by links 1–8 or 9–16. If the answer is 1–8, then you divide that in half, and continue in this manner until at the final choice there are only two options. If it is 9–16, you execute the same procedure on that half. Using this method will ensure that you will find the right location in 4 guesses. On any given trial you may find the correct location in fewer guesses, but if you follow this procedure then you will be sure to find it in no more than 4 guesses.

Following this logic, if you now consider a game in which there are 8 possible links, you will need at most 3 guesses. So, in a sense, the game with 16 locations is more complex than the game with 8 locations. The key factor behind the complexity of the game is uncertainty. In the 16-location game, there is simply more uncertainty about where the prize is than in the 8-location game. The intuitive explanation for why information theory provides a more efficient strategy than simply guessing a location is that each guess produces a greater reduction in uncertainty. Each guess eliminates half the remaining possibilities.

Notice that the number of guesses is related to the number of possibilities in a very orderly way. In fact, these are all powers of 2: $2^4 = 16$, and $2^3 = 8$. This power relationship can also be expressed in terms of logarithms to the base two: $\log_2(16) = 4$, $\log_2(8) = 3$. This suggests there might be some rigorous way to specify how the binary questions relate to uncertainty using powers of two. Information theory uses the relationship between the binary questions used to reach an answer and uncertainty using powers of two to compute a measure of uncertainty called *entropy*. In physics, entropy is associated with disorder, akin to the notion of uncertainty. The equation used by information theory to express the amount of entropy is

$$H[X] = -\Sigma p(x) \times \log_2(p(x)).$$

$H[X]$ is the entropy in binary digits, or *bits*, associated with X, where X denotes the entire space of possible states (locations, in the preceding example), x is a particular state (location), and $p(x)$ is the probability that the target is there (prize is on that page). We will not worry here about why the expression on the right is negative; just note that H will always be positive because the logarithm of a number from 0 to 1 is negative, and $p(x)$ is always between 0 and 1. H is not a function of X, but rather is a measure of the entropy in the space of all possible states of X. Conceptually, this equation can be understood by considering that the expression on the right can be roughly coded as the information provided by x, for any given x: denoted as $I(x)$. In our example, all links are equally likely to lead to the prize, so each carries the same information:

$$I(x) = -(1/16 \times \log_2(1/16)) = 1/16 \times 4 = 1/4$$

Summed across all 16 locations, the total entropy is 4, consistent with the uncertainty we saw earlier. Indeed, in cases involving different numbers of alternatives, entropy can be used interchangeably with uncertainty.

Why is the log multiplied by the $p(x)$? In the hidden prize example, a prize was hidden in one of 16 locations, and all possible locations were equally likely. However, that will not be generally true. Suppose, for example, that we bias the outcome so that the prize is behind link 5 40% of the time. In that case $p(x, x \neq 5) = (1-.4)/15 = .04$. Thus,

$$I(5) = -(.4 \times \log_2(.4)) = .4 \times 1.32 = .529$$

whereas for all other locations it is

$$I(x) = -(.04 \times \log_2(.04)) = .186$$

$$H(X) = .529 + 15 \times (.186) = 3.315$$

Knowing that the prize is more likely to appear in certain locations than others reduces the amount of entropy in the system. Thus far, we have discussed entropy as though it were completely determined by the alternatives in the environment. This is true, but incomplete in an important sense. Our knowledge of the domain determines the subjective entropy that guides our actions. In our example, if you didn't know of the bias in placing the prize, then you would act as though all locations were equally likely. Only over time would your behavior change as you learned the true distribution. Thus, learning modifies your subjective state of entropy to more closely match that of the environment. It also suggests that a key goal of design should be to reduce the subjective uncertainty. One way is to provide clues. If we label the links, we can provide some clue as to which links are likely to have the target and which are not. It turns out that link labels are an important source of information and that the proper selection of link labels can greatly decrease the uncertainty in the system.

Information theory is used extensively in software and hardware engineering, and in computer science. There, information theory is the basis for *coding theory*, which is used extensively in the design of compression algorithms. Compression is used widely to reliably transmit the maximum amount of information in the fewest bits. The idea is that information theory can be used to determine the minimum number of bits needed to guarantee a complete description of the environment. In the preceding case, 4 binary digits—*bits*—are sufficient to represent all possible placements of the prize. This means that one can relate the complexity of any domain to the number of bits needed to guarantee that all the information will be communicated. However, the picture is complicated by signal loss and noise during the transmission of information. Coding theory also helps to determine how much redundancy in the information sent will be required to guarantee a certain level of reliability. The need to build in redundancy to counteract signal loss and noise accounts for why systems typically cannot achieve theoretical minimum bit lengths.

MODELING THROUGHPUT USING QUEUING THEORY

We have already discussed how finite-state models can be used to estimate the time it takes to perform a set of operations. It turns out that a mathematical formalism, known as *queuing theory* (Gross, Shortle, Thompson, & Harris, 2008; Wagner, 1975; Wikipedia, 2011e), was developed to answer very similar questions. Initially, queuing theory helped with logistical planning for troop supply in World War II. When food or armaments are produced in large numbers, it becomes a complex problem to move them from the factories to the troops, who may be scattered in units across a wide front. Supplies could move by air, road, railway, ship, or even horse-drawn carts. Each segment of road and each ship or aircraft can be considered to have a certain capacity per unit time. That is, a road segment may be able to take at most 5 trucks per minute. Intersections would have a lower rate, say 2 per minute, as it is necessary to go more slowly and check for other vehicles. Once the network of roads, rails, ships, and aircraft are coded for capacity, it is possible to calculate the time needed to get equipment through using various routes.

The analysis itself can soon get very complex, but at its core it is simple. One assumes that a server (e.g., roadway intersection) receives input with a certain distribution (trucks arrive on average every 2 minutes, but with a bell-shaped function). That is, arrivals to a queue have a characteristic distribution over time. The idea behind queuing theory is shown in Figure 6.5.

Its central formula is quite simple:

$$\eta = \lambda\tau$$

In this equation, η is the average number of items in the queue, λ is the rate at which items arrive to the queue, and τ is the average time required for the server to complete one item.

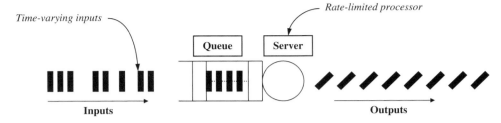

Arrival Rate(λ): mean # inputs per time (usually a Poisson distribution over time)
Server Delay(τ): mean time taken by server for each item
Queue Delay (ω): mean time spent waiting in queue
Queue Size(η): mean number of items in queue
Queue Policy: how items are taken from queue (e.g., first come first served, last in first out)

Mean # in Queue: $\eta = \lambda\tau$
Mean Queue Delay FIFO: $\omega = (\eta-1)\tau$

Figure 6.5 Elements of queuing theory. Events arrive to a processor (server) randomly with some density. The server takes a specified time to process each item. Which item is chosen to process next is set by a policy. The number of items in a queue, and their average wait time, can be calculated from the arrival rate, processing time, and queue policy.

A queue will have a policy that determines how items are selected from the queue. A common policy is *first in first out* (FIFO). A FIFO queue is what you likely experience when you call a company and get put on hold: Your call is taken in the order of arrival, meaning you must wait until all calls in front of you have been dealt with. It is also how one would analyze our road example using queuing theory. Computers and a few old hand calculators use what is called a *last in first out* (LIFO) policy. In a LIFO queue, the most recent item gets treated first, followed by each remaining item in reverse entry order. LIFO queues are useful if more recent information has a naturally higher priority. From the arrival rate, the processor rate, and queue policy, it is possible to compute the average waiting time, or queue length. In Figure 6.5 we show the average queue delay for a FIFO queue. It is somewhat more complicated to compute it for the LIFO queue.

Queuing theory becomes complex when it is necessary to compute the output of a network of servers with interconnections. Analysis using queuing theory can rapidly become impossible to handle mathematically, and is computationally very demanding because arrivals and server times are represented as distributions. It can easily be seen that the human operator can be considered a server just as any other component of a system could. The rate at which work arrives will determine how much remains to be done after a period of time.

Queuing theory is often used to determine how best to distribute work among a set of servers, each of which has a certain capacity for work. It is easy to see how it can be generalized to factories, doctor's offices, police units, customer service centers, and many other externally paced domains. A supermarket checkout register or a bank teller window are easy-to-understand examples. In those cases, each checker or teller (servers) works independently of the others and customers arrive every so often. If the goal is to make customers wait no more than a certain time, you can determine how many checkout clerks or bank tellers will be needed to achieve that given the rate at which customers arrive. If there are times of day when more customers arrive, it is easy to calculate how many checkers or tellers will be needed and schedule work shifts accordingly. For these purposes, it is simply a case of representing the human operator as a server with a fixed, limited capacity for doing things characterized by a time constant describing how long it takes to do a single unit of work.

For many situations, including checkout lines and bank lines, formal calculation is not really necessary. It is clear from history what are the busiest times, and easy to swap people in and out. There are, however, circumstances in which some components of the formal calculation are unknown. In airports, aircraft load and unload passengers at gates leased by the airlines, which must pay the airport for each gate they use. Each gate can be considered a server, as can a particular runway, and a single taxiway. With many flights coming in and going out, it becomes worth the time and effort, not to mention cost, to carefully analyze the number of servers and the restrictions on each server. It is possible to have a free (unoccupied) server that cannot be reached because aircraft have to access a particular taxiway (another server) that is very busy. Maybe now you can begin to appreciate how the arrangement of servers in a network can be crucial to productivity.

One of the assumptions made in queuing theory is that the server does not change any of its characteristics as a function of the rate of input. That is, it does the same things in the same way if items are arriving at a fast or slow pace; the only thing that varies is the size of the queue. Characterizing the human operator as an unchanging server may not adequately represent human behavior and learning, but we will return to this topic later.

SUMMARY

Improving system performance and/or safety is a key goal in human-system interactions. This chapter outlined a number of analysis techniques that can be used to describe systems that exist in both static and dynamic environments. We also talked about ways of measuring complexity in a system using information theory and modeling the throughput of a system using queuing theory. Further information on finite-state models, task analysis, signal detection theory, and information theory can be found by searching these terms and titles on the Internet.

REFERENCES

Doyle, J. C., Francis, B. A., & Tannenbaum, A. (1992). *Feedback control theory*. Macmillan Publishing. http://www.control.utoronto.ca/people/profs/francis/dft.html.

Green, D., & Swets, J. (1966). *Signal detection theory and psychophysics*. New York, NY, USA: Wiley.

Gross, D., Shortle, J. F., Thompson, J. M., & Harris, C. M. (2008). *Fundamentals of queueing theory* (4th ed.). Hoboken, NJ: John Wiley & Sons.

Heeger, D. (2007). Signal detection theory. Retrieved October 30, 2011, from http://www.cns.nyu.edu/~david/handouts/sdt/sdt.html

Kirwan, B., & Ainsworth, L. K. (1992). *A guide to task analysis*. Philadelphia, PA: Taylor and Francis.

Simon, H. A. (1996). The sciences of the artificial. Cambridge, MA: MIT Press.

Usability Net. (2006). UsabilityNet: Task analysis methods. Retrieved October 30, 2011, from http://www.usabilitynet.org/tools/taskanalysis.htm

Wagner, H. M. (1975). *Principles of operations research*. Englewood Cliffs, NJ: Prentice-Hall.

Wickens, T. D. (2001). *Elementary signal detection theory*. Oxford: Oxford University Press.

Wikipedia. (2011c). Control theory. Retrieved October 30, 2011, c from http://en.wikipedia.org/wiki/Control_theory

Wikipedia. (2011d). Control theory (sociology). Retrieved October 30, 2011, d from http://en.wikipedia.org/wiki/Control_theory_(sociology)

Wikipedia. (2011e). Detection theory. Retrieved October 30, 2011, e from http://en.wikipedia.org/wiki/Detection_theory

Wikipedia. (2011a). Finite-state machine. Retrieved October 30, 2011, a from http://en.wikipedia.org/wiki/Finite-state_machine

Wikipedia. (2011f). Queueing theory. Retrieved October 30, 2011, f from http://en.wikipedia.org/wiki/Queueing_theory

Wikipedia. (2011b). State diagram. Retrieved October 30, 2011, b from http://en.wikipedia.org/wiki/State_diagram

Part III

The Human Element

About 4:22 p.m., Pacific Daylight Time, on Friday, September 12, 2008, westbound Southern California Regional Rail Authority Metrolink train 111, consisting of one locomotive and three passenger cars, collided head-on with eastbound Union Pacific Railroad freight train LOF65–12 near Chatsworth, California. The Metrolink train derailed its locomotive and lead passenger car; the UP train derailed its 2 locomotives and 10 of its 17 cars. The force of the collision caused the locomotive of train 111 to telescope into the lead passenger coach by about 52 feet. The accident resulted in 25 fatalities, including the engineer of train 111. Emergency response agencies reported transporting 102 injured passengers to local hospitals. Damages were estimated to be in excess of $12 million.

The National Transportation Safety Board (2010) determined that the probable cause of the September 12, 2008, train collision was the failure of the Metrolink engineer to observe and appropriately respond to the red signal aspect at Control Point Topanga, because he was engaged in prohibited use of a wireless device—specifically text messaging—that distracted him from his duties. Contributing to the accident was the lack of a positive train control system that would have stopped the Metrolink train short of the red signal and thus prevented the collision.

"OKLAHOMA CITY — On his 15th birthday, Christopher Hill got his first cellphone. For his 16th, he was given a used red Ford Ranger pickup, a source of pride he washed every week. Mr. Hill, a diligent student with a reputation for helping neighbors, also took pride in his clean driving record. 'Not a speeding ticket, not a fender bender, nothing,' he said. Until last Sept. 3. Mr. Hill, then 20, left the parking lot of a Goodwill store where he had spotted a dresser he thought might interest a neighbor. He dialed her to pass along news of the find. Mr. Hill was so engrossed in the call that he ran a red light and didn't notice Linda Doyle's small sport utility vehicle until the last second. He hit her going 45 miles per hour. She was pronounced dead shortly after.

Later, a policeman asked Mr. Hill what color the light had been. 'I never saw it,' he answered."

(Richtel, 2009)

In Part I we provided an historical overview detailing the development of the field of human factors from a completely empirical basis to the formal study of humans in engineered systems that arose around the time of World War II. The formal field of study has two complementary aims: an understanding of the environment and its demands, and an understanding of human behavior with respect to those demands. In Part II we concentrated on a productive analysis of the demands of environments. The intent was to provide an understanding of how environments themselves can determine much of the complex behavior that we see. That is, the focus was on determining the extent to which the information requirements, tasks, uncertainty, and decision noise associated with a particular system affects performance. We saw that it would not be surprising to find that people are better at using a system with fewer arbitrary labels to be remembered, one that announced its state clearly, or used computer menus that reduced the uncertainty about which option to choose. However, the environment is not the only factor that influences performance when humans interact with engineered systems. Humans bring capabilities and limitations to the interaction. Thus, it is important in the analysis of humans in engineering systems to understand whether issues arise because of inherent system complexity or from an inter- action of the system with the particular kind of information processing that characterizes human cognition. It is to these human capabilities and limitations that we now turn.

As a general organizing principle, in Chapter 7 we introduce a distinction between capabilities and limitations arising from the *structural* properties of the cognitive system, and those arising from the way information *content* is stored and used. Accordingly, Chapters 8, 9, and 10 address the structural aspects of cognitive processing, including stages of information processing, capacity limitations, sensory systems, attention alloca- tion, and multitasking. Chapters 11 and 12 then address how the information is stored and retrieved in memory, and how it is manipulated to make decisions.

REFERENCES

National Transportation Safety Board. (2010). *Collision of Metrolink Train 111 with Union Pacific Train LOF65–12* (Accident Report No. RAR-10-01). Chatsworth, CA. Retrieved from www.ntsb.gov/doclib/reports/2010/RAR1001.pdf

Richtel, M. (2009, July 19). Drivers and legislators dismiss cellphone risks. *New York Times*. Retrieved from www.nytimes.com/2009/07/19/technology/19distracted.html

7

Determinants of Human Behavior

Although analysis of the environment is necessary to understand the human operator's contribution to system performance, it is not sufficient. Figure 7.1 shows that the behavior of human operators is a function not only of the environment and tasks, but also of the interactions of tasks and environments with the characteristics of human information processing and decision making. It is now time to turn our attention to the human characteristics that shape how we see the world and how we choose to act on the world. Only then will it be possible to begin to build a better understanding of why people behave as they do in engineered systems.

We need, however, to make a couple of general points about our treatment of human cognition, which arise from its inherent complexity and our growing but still limited understanding of how we process information and make decisions. First, it is not possible to catalogue all that is known about human cognition, or even all that could be relevant. Several major human factors compendia include chapters on visual processing, auditory processing, the motor system, decision making, speech perception, and more (Sanders & McCormick, 1993; Wickens & Hollands, 2000). These books are meant to give an in-depth treatment of a wide range of empirical phenomena with respect to central theoretical distinctions and practical applications. There are also several handbooks of human performance meant specifically for the designer or human factors analyst (Karwowski, 2006; Salvendy, 2006). These are meant to provide guidance on, for example, how to use color or how to size font. Though useful, they can only barely scratch the surface and to do so must give these facts without full context. In actuality, it is impossible to select only the relevant bits of human cognition to present. There is no well-defined subset of the panoply of phenomena that can in principle be said to cover the majority of circumstances. This must be acknowledged at the outset. What we try to do here is provide a set of central tenets that describe how experts think about human cognition, which can be reused from one context to the next. These tenets provide a basis for analysis when confronted with new problems or designs.

Secondly, the state of theory in psychology is not as well developed as in the "hard" sciences, such as physics or chemistry. The behavior of a human being is much more complex than that of an electron, even though it may not seem as strange. As a result, very few theories have wide acceptance, or the power to make accurate predictions in complex environments far from the simple laboratory tasks that provide the bulk of their support.

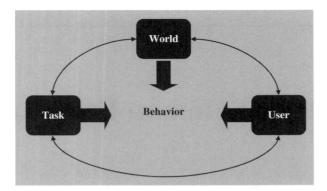

Figure 7.1 Behavior results from the interaction of the user, her goals, and the context (world) in which she is immersed.

Thus, we cannot simplify our treatment by discussing only one or two major theories. What we have chosen to do is to select concepts and principles that have solid empirical support from multiple well-controlled studies. In particular, we include those that will facilitate how to think about human capabilities and limitations in a range of contexts.

THE HUMAN FACTOR

One way to see the importance of understanding the way we process information, reason about the world, and make decisions is to first consider the task of controlling a device. Figure 7.2 provides a high-level flowchart of the information flow associated with a human operator in a system, similar to the informal control theoretic framework we introduced earlier. To control a system, let's say a car, the driver first needs to sample the external world. This would consist of the speedometer and other instruments as well as the roadway with other cars. This perceptual information must be interpreted in terms of the driver's goals. For example, the speedometer reading would have to be decoded into a meaningful number that reflected speed and then compared to the desired speed. Likewise, the perception of the roadway would reveal the distance behind the car in front, the position in the lane, and upcoming obstacles. If the assessed state deviates from a desired state, then a plan of action must be devised, predicted outcomes generated, and those outcomes assessed against the goals. Once the action is taken, the loop begins again with the assessed state compared to the expected outcome of the action.

Aside from labeling certain operations as "Perceptual Processing," "Cognitive Processing," and "Motor Processing," nothing in this diagram relates to how we as human drivers would do the task. As it stands, the diagram of Figure 7.2 could serve equally well as a high-level description of a robot driver. However, the robot and human drivers would satisfy the functional requirements of driving in ways particular to how they acquire information, reason about the nature of the world, and select actions that will achieve their goals. For example, engineers can build automated devices that fly aircraft, drive cars,

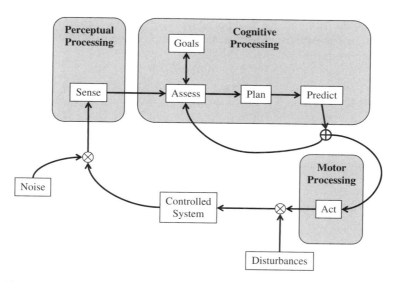

Figure 7.2 Depiction of information flow in terms of system control. The state of the controlled system is sensed and assessed against the goals of the context. This leads to a plan of action, the consequences of which are predicted. If the prediction conforms to the desired behavior, the action is taken; if not, the plan is further assessed and refined.

and control manufacturing plants. These devices can do as well as or better than a human in many respects. Indeed, in some well-defined domains, computerized decision-making models outperform even experts in the domain (e.g., Dawes, 1971). Still, human operators are needed in circumstances in which rapid and powerful perceptual processing is required. It is fair to say that modern automation is strong on the rational integration of multiple inputs, an area where we humans often fail, but weak on perceptual processing and relatively inflexible when faced with the need to be creative, a skill set at which humans excel. Automation meets the requirements in ways that differ significantly from those that humans use. As we discuss in Part IV, this can cause confusion for the human operator of a highly automated system. The point here is that, to understand how the human driver, pilot, plant engineer, or computer user approaches a task, and the problems that will arise, it is necessary to understand how human information processing provides both strengths and weaknesses that characterize the human operator—that make us uniquely human.

STRUCTURE AND CONTENT

As a starting point for discussion, and a general organizing principle, it is useful to distinguish between two broad classes of factors that influence behavior, which we describe as arising either from the structure or the contents of our minds. Factors associated with structure have to do with limitations in how much information we can process, in the details of our sensory systems, and in how our awareness of an event develops over a short interval of time after that event occurs. Factors associated with the contents of our minds have to do with how we manipulate knowledge, how we use what we know to shape our decisions, how biases influence our perception of the world, and how our beliefs shape the way we respond to events.

One way to understand the difference between structure and content is to consider a very old tension within cognitive psychology over what matters most: those cognitive events that occur in less than a quarter of a second, or those that take longer (say, several seconds) to occur? For most people it would be the latter. This is because our conscious experience is of the decisions we make, what knowledge we bring to bear on a problem that confronts us, or plans we make for the future. For example, in writing a work such as this book the author must be aware of the facts at hand and how those facts relate to the flow of ideas in the prose. This happens over several seconds or even minutes. When we do processing at this pace, we tend to be aware of the thoughts that precede our actions, particularly as we are often asked to justify our actions by our intentions, and criticized for failures that result from a faulty logical basis for action. This is also the time frame at which attitudes, biases, prejudice, and stereotyping are presumably detected. What links these things together is that they reflect the contents of our thinking. It is our manipulation of these contents, our recognition and possible inhibition of bias, our reasoning that occupies much of our self-reflection and our judgment of others. We all share the same ability for subjective mental experience and seemingly share the assumption that it plays a causal role in our behavior and that of others.

Less easily recognized is the role of structure. Our brains perform an amazing set of computations that allow us to perceive a seemingly unified world and that lead to the content described earlier. For example, while you may be aware of trying to learn French vocabulary through repetition, you are probably not aware of the complex associations that eventually lead to a memorized word, nor are you aware of exactly how you retrieve that word when you want to use it. What you are likely aware of is the intent to retrieve the word, not the process of retrieval itself.

Structure plays an important role in everything we do. As you no doubt learned in introductory courses, we do not perceive the world directly, but construct objects and events from patterns of activity in our sensory systems. This process goes through a number of stages with complicated feedback that is slowly being revealed by studies in cognitive psychology and neuroscience. It is the structure of the computational resources in this process that determines which things in the world get resolved first, how long it takes for information to accrue, the costs involved in manipulating the contents of one's mind, and ultimately the efficiency with which one interacts with the world. When we feel time pressure, it is often because we sense that the process will not keep pace with the events. Consider driving again. When first learning to drive, it seems like a horribly complex process because the underlying structure of your mind and brain is not adapted to the demands of driving. Things seem to happen too quickly and it is difficult to remember what to do and in what order to do them. With practice, the underlying structure adapts and driving now seems boring, so much so that we add talking on the cell phone to keep us occupied. Issues of attention, task management, workload, and proficiency are issues of structure.

This distinction between the study of structural properties of information processing and manipulation of content is apparent in the divergent tasks that people use and the formalisms they adopt to explain the results. Studies of structure often use briefly presented stimuli, threshold stimuli, or masked stimuli that challenge the observers' ability to see. This is because studies of structure are meant to uncover fundamental properties of information processing: what people are *able* to do, not what they *choose* to do. In contrast, studies of content are more often studies of how people manipulate information to reach a decision. Studies of content present people with situations and elicit verbal descriptions of their thoughts as they do the task, test their memories for aspects of what they have done, have them estimate how difficult a task was, or make reasoned judgments.

For the operator in a system trying to achieve some control goal, the distinction is not so apparent. Structure and content are continually interacting. Our biases, for example, can affect how efficient we are at processing and responding to certain information, showing that content can intrude on structure. Conversely, although we may be engaged in making a critical decision, a loud noise or quick movement may distract us, interrupting our train of thought. Structure has thus intruded on the manipulation of content. The knowledge we have to manipulate comes as a result of processing through the structure of our sensory and perceptual systems. As we shall see, the notion of selective attention plays a key role in mediating this interaction, tuning structure based on expectations, biases, beliefs, and state. Likewise, attention is also instrumental in altering the content, turning our decision mechanisms to new goals.

In the next two chapters of this section, we provide an overview of the structural properties of human information processing, moving from a discussion of sensory systems to deal with the issue of attention and fundamental computational limits in human cognition, and ending with a consideration of multitasking. Following this are chapters in which we provide an overview of issues of content, focusing on memory, the manipulation of knowledge and goals, and ending with a discussion of how decisions are arrived at and how they are biased. We will not discuss motor control issues in any depth, as this would require a more mathematical approach than is suitable for this book. However, we consider aspects of motor control in the discussion of structure and give special treatment to how output can influence the ways in which we organize our behavior. We also give a brief overview of language and perceptual-motor behavior, as these faculties play a key role in determining the success of human-system interaction.

LEVELS OF ANALYSIS

It is useful here to comment on the relationship of basic research to applications before proceeding to a treatment of human performance. Our understanding of human performance characteristics comes largely from laboratory studies of basic psychological processes. It is often the case that the level of analysis required for theory development in basic science is finer grained than what proves useful in practice. When testing theories, differences of a few milliseconds in critical conditions can be crucial, whereas in complex domains it is more common to analyze events that unfold over a few seconds or even minutes. Moreover, to achieve the required precision in testing theories, experiments are tightly controlled, with stimuli specially constructed for each experiment, and care taken to eliminate stimulation that could interfere. In contrast, behavior in complex domains rarely takes place under such tightly controlled circumstances.

Such differences in the conditions under which people perform in the laboratory compared to the typical workplace have made it difficult to apply theory to the real world. This difficulty has even led to a research methodology and philosophy, *Situated Cognition*, which denies that basic research has relevance to applications (Clancy, 1997; Hollnagel & Woods, 2005; Suchman, 1987). Proponents of Situated Cognition argue that experiments under rarefied laboratory conditions do not provide the general principles of human performance often touted by psychologists. Consequently, they criticize the "cognitivist" approach for its emphasis on the individual cognitive processes divorced from context. They argue instead that we can only find out about how people perform in the specific situations in which we study them. For example, suppose you wanted to measure the capacity of memory, and use this measure to determine whether air traffic controllers, or police dispatchers, or some other profession were in danger of exceeding memory capacity. Further, suppose that you chose to study memory by presenting people with made-up "words" that consisted of randomly chosen letters to study, and found that people could recall only on average four such strings. What implications would this have for how many real words people could recall, or computer commands, or complex instructions, or any of things we are routinely asked to hold in memory in other circumstances? Would the results of such an experiment say anything other than that with these random letter strings, under the conditions tested, people can recall on average four items? Even if the answer to this question were "yes", you would make the "cognitivist" error in presuming that this number would be crucial in characterizing human performance *in situ*. In practice, people would find a way around their limitations, or systems would evolve to compensate for shortcomings in memory. In air traffic control, for example, there is a limit on the number of aircraft allowed in a controller's sector of airspace at any time. In the office, people use sticky notes or other ways to support recall of important facts. So what good does it do to know that people can recall four nonsense strings?

This is an important debate, one that touches on the work of anyone who engages in applied or basic research, and one that affects a book such as this, where we must decide what basic science to present. It is not our intention with this book to attempt to resolve the debate, nor to convince you of the correctness of either side, nor even to offer an alternate compromise. In truth, the issue is one of generalization: discovering in what cases we can say that behavior in one circumstance will resemble behavior in another well enough that we can use it as a guide. Phrased this way, whether or not the basic science is useful depends on our goal. If we desire a detailed account of the actions of an individual in a specific context, then, for any sufficiently complex domain, it is probably beyond the current state of our science to provide sufficient detail to do so. However, if we want rough estimates of performance times and limits, then there are cases in which the basic science has proven useful.

Indeed, there is a growing demand for solid information on the nature of human perceptual, cognitive, and motor capabilities and limitations. This demand is coming from government and industry groups that are trying to develop increasingly sophisticated devices for displaying information to individuals and for characterizing the decision making of groups of people. This is driven in part by the cost involved in simulating new environments as faithfully as demanded by proponents of situated awareness. Over the past two decades, there has also been increasing interest in modelling human behavior in complex systems as a way to lower the cost of designing new information systems (Anderson & Lebiere, 1998; Kieras & Meyer, 1997; Laird, Newell, & Rosenbloom, 1987; Pew, 2008).

Imagine, for example, that you were tasked with designing and verifying the information displays and procedures for a military command and control center that consisted of hundreds of people, some of whom were in the same room while others were at distant locations. As a human-system engineer, you might be tasked specifically with ensuring that the tasks allocated to each individual (or team) and the information displays supporting those tasks would not overload an operator, and thus cause errors or delays in the timely flow of information through the system. Not only would it take a long time at significant cost to faithfully simulate this environment, but when the simulation was completed, it would be difficult to interpret the data from such a complex case. Instead, it would be useful, especially in early stages of design, to use estimates of human performance along with computer simulations of information flow to arrive at an initial design. Data on perceptual, cognitive, and motor processing times would allow estimates of how long it would take to complete specific tasks. Data on limits in memory or information processing could be used to give a rough idea of when a person is becoming overloaded (see Mitchell, 2009, for a good example of this approach).

It would be unwise, however, to base estimates on a single experiment, such as the memory experiment discussed earlier, or even on a few experiments. In the chapters that follow, therefore, we have included only those characteristics of human performance that have been supported by multiple findings often over many years. That is not to say that there is uniform agreement on all of them, or that none are controversial. Rather, the material presented has wide acceptance with much empirical support.

SUMMARY

Human characteristics shape how we see the world and how we act on the world. This chapter described how both the structure and contents of our minds influences these activities. The chapter also described the different levels at which behavior can be analyzed and how important it is to choose a level of analysis that is appropriate for the desired predictions about human behavior.

REFERENCES

Anderson, J. R., & Lebiere, C. (1998). *The atomic components of thought*. Mahwah, NJ: Lawrence Erlbaum Associates.

Clancy, W. (1997). *Situated cognition: On human knowledge and computer representation*. New York, NY: Cambridge University Press.

Dawes, R. M. (1971). A case study of graduate admissions: Applications of three principles of human decision-making. *American Psychologist, 26*, 180–188.

Hollnagel, E., & Woods, D. D. (2005). *Joint cognitive systems: Foundations of cognitive systems engineering*. Boca Raton, FL: CRC Press.

Karwowski, W. (2006). *International encyclopedia of ergonomics and human factors.* Boca Raton, FL: CRC Press.

Kieras, D. E., & Meyer, D. E. (1997). An overview of the EPIC architecture for cognition and performance with application to human-computer interaction. *Human-Computer Interaction, 12*(4), 391–438. doi:http://dx.doi.org/10.1207/s15327051hci1204_4

Laird, J. E., Newell, A., & Rosenbloom, P. S. (1987). SOAR: An architecture for general intelligence. *Artificial Intelligence, 33*(1), 1–64. doi:16/0004-3702(87)90050-6

Mitchell, D. K. (2009). *Workload analysis of the crew of the Abrams V2 SEP: Phase I baseline IMPRINT model* (ARL-TR-5028). Aberdeen, MD: U.S. Army Research Laboratory.

Pew, R. (2008). More than 50 years of history and accomplishments in human performance model development. *Human Factors, 50*(3), 489–496.

Salvendy, G. (2006). *Handbook of human factors and ergonomics.* Hoboken, NJ: John Wiley & Sons.

Sanders, M. S., & McCormick, E. J. (1993). *Human factors in engineering and design.* New York, NY: McGraw Hill.

Suchman, L. A. (1987). *Plans and situated actions: The problem of human-machine communication.* New York: Cambridge University Press.

Wickens, C. D., & Hollands, J. G. (2000). *Engineering psychology and human performance.* Upper Saddle River, NJ: Prentice Hall.

8

The Structure of Human Information Processing

As we noted earlier, the study of the structural aspects of human cognitive processing has been concerned with identifying how our awareness of the world develops rapidly over time. For example, when you walk into a new room to interview for a job, your sensory systems are flooded with sights, sounds, and temperature, and you quickly become aware of how you are oriented with respect to the surfaces of the room. Your body also adjusts automatically to any tilt of the floor, or even the relative angles of the walls. All of this occurs pretty much without your having to think about it. The good news about this is that it testifies to the power of our visual, auditory, tactile, and vestibular systems. They are able to do a tremendous amount of work without direction or conscious intervention from us, freeing us to think about the people who will be interviewing us. At the same time, because this is all happening beneath our awareness, it means that we do not necessarily have good insights into how we become aware of the world as we experience it.

The study of the structure of human cognition is the study of how it is that we go from the physical elements of the world that strike our sensory systems—light rays, sound pressure waves, chemical compounds, and so forth—to the sensory experiences of which we are aware—sights, sounds, smells, and so forth, and how those experiences in turn create a meaningful world that guides our decisions and actions. The structure of our information-processing systems determines our capacity for each of these, and also how and where that capacity is limited. It may help to understand what we mean by structure if you consider it akin to the operating system of a computer, like Windows or the Mac OSX. In a computer, the operating system and the hardware on which it operates make some kinds of computations more efficient than others, give priority to certain events over others, and define the elementary actions that can be executed. The analogy is not perfect, but illustrates our earlier claim that there is much going on below the surface of our awareness that has significant consequences for work, play, our daily lives, and our understanding of ourselves.

Our current understanding of how our perceptual and cognitive systems deliver the world we experience has been achieved over about 200 years of careful experimentation and theory. It is far from complete, but the broad outlines can be stated with some certainty, as can their implications for workplaces and daily life. Scientists who study the structure of human cognition have been concerned largely with how information flows in the system, with the characteristics of individual sensory systems, and with how those systems integrate information. In this chapter, we introduce you to the notion of information flow and describe broadly how human awareness develops.

To get some concrete idea of what we mean by *information flow* and of the kinds of issues that arise with respect to it, consider that you are a traffic engineer in charge of transportation in a large metropolitan area. In that job, a key issue would be the amount of time it takes to get from one place to another, as people will get quite angry if they can't get around efficiently. Travel time depends on several factors. If we restrict our concern here to cars on roadways, the most important factors would be the number of cars simultaneously trying to use certain roads; the carrying capacity of the roads; and bottlenecks in the system, such as traffic lights or construction, that greatly restrict the carrying capacity. Indeed, traffic engineers give a lot of consideration to relieving bottlenecks, as it doesn't do much good to build a major highway if that highway ends in a city street at a traffic light. This is one reason why many large cities build rings of highways encircling them. Even in those cases, however, the roads can become so congested that traffic is slowed because cars entering the roadway are competing with cars already on the roadway for limited space.

Considerations of bottlenecks, capacity, demand, and time to get from point A to point B (we will call this *throughput*) are not restricted to traffic flow (that was just our simple example), but are widespread, affecting disciplines as diverse as construction, telephone service, power grids, and computer circuits. There are whole branches of engineering and operations research devoted to its study. It is not surprising, then, that similar principles are at work in human cognitive processing. That is, the way the brain processes sensory input, makes decisions, and executes actions places limits on how much information we can successfully process per unit time (similar to the carrying capacity of the road system) and, importantly, restricts our ability to do two or more things at once (just as two cars cannot occupy the same roadway space).

Limits in our ability to do two or more things at once have recently made headlines with reports of automobile accidents attributed to the use of cell phones while driving, such as the tragic accident described in the preface to Part III. It has long been known that inattention, along with its subcategory distraction, are significant contributing factors in many automobile accidents. According to statistics for 2009 reported by the National Highway Transportation Safety Agency (NHTSA) on its website (National Highway Transportation Safety Agency, n.d.):

- 20 percent of injury crashes in 2009 involved reports of distracted driving.
- Of those killed in distracted-driving-related crashes, 995 involved reports of a cell phone as a distraction (18 percent of fatalities in distraction-related crashes).
- In 2009, 5,474 people were killed on U.S. roadways, and an estimated additional 448,000 were injured, in motor vehicle crashes that were reported to have involved distracted driving.
- The age group with the greatest proportion of distracted drivers was the under-20 age group—16 percent of all drivers younger than 20 involved in fatal crashes were reported to have been distracted while driving.
- Drivers who use hand-held devices are four times as likely to get into crashes serious enough to injure themselves.

- Using a cell phone while driving, whether it's hand-held or hands-free, delays a driver's reactions as much as having a blood alcohol concentration at the legal limit of 0.08 percent.

This last point is particularly germane to our discussion of the flow of information in human cognition. It is easy to see how taking one's eyes off the road to dial a phone number or send a text message could jeopardize safety. However, it came as a shock to many people that hands-free phones were no safer. How could that be? Psychologists who study human multitasking and are familiar with the structure of human cognitive processing were not surprised. Research over several decades has provided useful insights into the capacity and ability of humans to process information, all of which suggested that hands-free phones would indeed cause problems. Let's examine how our current understanding of human cognition leads us to such insights.

PROCESSING STAGES

At a broad level, we can characterize the flow of processing in the brain as proceeding from perception to cognition to motor output. That is, if we ask you to say the name of a letter presented on a computer monitor as fast as you can, the time it takes will be composed of the time it takes to complete a set of subprocesses. During perceptual processing, your visual system turns the pattern of light rays into a shape that can be recognized as a particular, known letter. Your cognitive system then attaches a name to this item from one of the 26 possible names. Finally, your motor system organizes the muscles of your face and tongue to say the selected name. This is a vast oversimplification of what actually happens. In particular, there are many more subprocesses than can be mentioned here, and their organization may not be as strictly serial as implied by the preceding description. For example, if a certain letter has been presented often, or you detect that it occurs after another letter, you could prepare for this expected letter. In that case, cognitive processing may prepare perceptual and motor operations in advance, prior to the completion of perceptual processing, or even prior to presentation of the stimulus. This is one of many examples proving that processing does not proceed only in a strictly "forward" direction, from percept to interpretation to action. Instead, expectations at cognitive and motor levels can affect the time it takes to complete lower-level processing through "backward" activation. Nonetheless, these considerations are secondary to our discussion of structure. A three-stage serial view has proven to be an extremely useful simplification, and will serve well as a framework for explaining the structure of information processing.

Figure 8.1 illustrates the three stages with some additional components. The major structural divisions are shown in the three columns labeled *Perception*, *Cognition*, and *Motor*. Perception refers to a set of operations that transforms physical stimulation from the external world into what roughly corresponds to the objects and events we experience. Perceptual processing includes the sensory processing unique to each modality—audition, vision, proprioception, vestibular, and so forth. It also includes operations referred to as *encoding* (not shown in Figure 8.1), which make contact with long-term memory, such that the output of perceptual processing is an object or a scene that is familiar or an indication of whether or not the object is recognizable. Encoding tells us that what we are seeing is

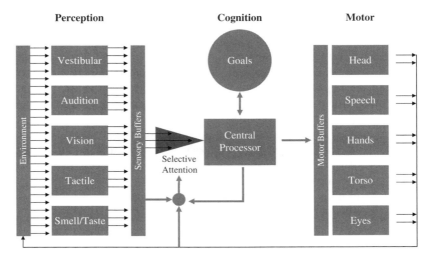

Figure 8.1 Flow of human information processing from sensory input to motor output. Each arrow represents a notional unit of information. Selective attention limits the amount of perceptual information input at any given time to cognition. A major function of cognitive processing is *action selection*, though that term should not be interpreted as a complete description of cognitive activity.

a face; it further tells us whether the face belongs to a friend or is unfamiliar. Likewise, when we see a common letter, its familiarity is conveyed through encoding, in contrast to a letter in a foreign script, which we do not recognize. Recognition is typically grouped with perceptual processing because both constitute a set of processes that occur habitually and automatically, and over which we have little or no control.

Motor processing refers to those mental operations needed to program and execute an action. Once you have decided on an action to take, the motor system must account for a number of variables before the right response can be executed. Ultimately, your intentions must be translated into precise contractions and relaxations of muscles, all in a highly coordinated manner. Consider the case in which you decide to reach for the coffee cup on your desk. A different motor program will have to be initiated depending on where on the desk the cup is, as different placements will require different activity from individual muscles. Even when reaching for the cup at the same location, the muscles activated will differ when you start from different initial hand and arm positions. In addition, the speed with which the cup is moved and its exact trajectory will depend on how full it is.

For the most part, as with perception and encoding, these adjustments are not something we think about. We walk down steps, over uneven ground, even on rocking boats with little difficulty. Some indication of the actual difficulties encountered by both perception and motor processing and their complexity comes from realizing that we have yet to build artificial vision or auditory systems that even remotely approach those of most mammals. Only in the past few years have we been able to build a robot that can walk and climb stairs on its own. We are still a long way from understanding how the human motor system works or duplicating it with any degree of fidelity. For example, very recent new discoveries point to a strong connection between perceptual and motor systems. An area in the brain called the parietal cortex has cells that fire in the presence of both stimuli and actions. In fact, part of the parietal cortex has been identified as a *mirror neuron* system in which there are neurons that fire both when we perform an action (like reaching for a cup) and when we see someone else perform the same action (Rizzolatti & Craighero, 2004). This suggests that we may understand the actions of others in terms of our ability to execute those actions ourselves. Further discoveries may point the way to new methods of training in sports and rehabilitation. We will treat the perceptual systems in more detail in later chapters of this section.

We now turn our attention to an expanded discussion of the middle piece—cognitive processing—and its practical implications. One final point must be made regarding Figure 7.2 and Figure 8.1 before continuing. Note that in Figure 7.2, all the components of the diagram are related directly to the control operation. Figure 7.2 describes the process of control as an engineer might see it. In contrast, the components of Figure 8.1 are meant to describe how all information is processed. They are not unique to any particular control action. Indeed, it is often necessary for the human factors specialist to translate the steps in an activity given in the task domain, as in Figure 7.2, into a set of corresponding operations within the psychological domain of Figure 8.1.

COGNITION AND ACTION

When discussing the three stages of information processing, we placed cognition between perception and motor processing. In the schematic of Figure 8.1, it sits between those two connected to the circle labelled "Goals" by a bidirectional arrow indicating a two-way exchange between Goals and the Central Processor. This placement was deliberate. Theories of human information processing view cognition as a range of specific mental operations responsible for selecting those actions in a particular context that best achieve immediate behavioral goals. Thus, it links perception and action systems with goals to effect goal-directed behavior. For example, a subject in a psychology experiment presented with a visual letter, such as *k*, may be asked to name the letter, or to push one of two keys to indicate whether it is a *k*, or an *n*, or to press keys to indicate whether it is in the first or last half of the English alphabet, upper versus lower case, and so forth. Likewise, if presented with a single digit between one and nine, participants could be asked to indicate whether it is odd or even, or greater or less than five. In all those cases the same perceptual object is treated differently depending on the immediate goals. For this linkage to be successful, cognition must maintain the goal state (e.g., "press left button if in the first half of the alphabet") and then control processing (e.g., identify letter versus determine whether the letter is in the first or last half of the alphabet) so that the decisions and the selected responses are consistent with behavioral goals.

We illustrate some of the operations of the Central Processor by considering a sample task shown in Figure 8.2. In this task, participants are required to say the words "high" or "low" when a tone is presented, depending on the pitch of the tone. If a visual letter is presented, they are required to press one key to indicate a *K*, and another to indicate an *L*. A stimulus is first encoded such that its strongly associated attributes are retrieved from

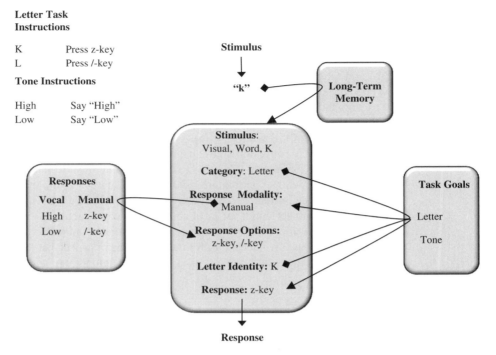

Figure 8.2 Example of goal-directed behavior in a choice response time task. Time flows downward. Task goals must be accessed to determine which of several responses to make.

memory. The example in Figure 8.2 indicates that perceptual processing produces a description of the stimulus as the visual letter *K*. The Central Processor then must determine both the modality and the identity of the stimulus to make the correct response. Task Goals specify that visual stimuli receive a manual key-press response. The Central Processor then retrieves the response keys and the Task Goals specify which key corresponds to the presented letter. In this case, the *z*-key is selected. Not shown is the further process of associating the *z*-key with the left finger. The sequence of events described here represents performance early in practice. With repetition, some of the subprocesses may merge into one. For example, it may not be necessary to separately determine the modality of the response as each stimulus comes to be strongly associated with a particular finger motion.

Within the structure of human information processing, the time taken to complete a task will be determined by the combined times for complete perceptual, cognitive, and motor processing. In almost all cases, however, the time to complete cognitive processing will account for most of the limitations on throughput, and will account for a greater percentage of time than will perceptual or motor processing. Of course, perceptual and motor processing times will vary with the complexity of the scene or the action, respectively. The range of variability in cognitive processing times across tasks is even greater. One way to see how this occurs is to consider one of the fundamental roles of cognitive processing: selecting a response.

COGNITION AND GOAL-DIRECTED BEHAVIOR

One way to think about cognition is to contrast it to perception. To a first approximation, perception consists of very powerful mental processes over which there is little if any control. Try as you might, you cannot easily change what your perceptual system will do. There are a few cases of reversible figures, such as the Necker cube, whose perception can be changed deliberately, as can the perception of some ambiguous pictures. Generally, however, you can change what you look at or listen to in the world, but not how your visual or auditory system produces its output. In the jargon of the day, perception is not, as a rule, cognitively penetrable. Visual illusions are a perfect illustration of this point. An illusion is a percept that is not an accurate depiction of the world. Yet, even if you know that, you cannot tell yourself not to see the illusion. Equally, the encoding of a set of lines into a letter is impenetrable as well; it is impossible not to see a *b* as a letter, barring of course brain injury that has damaged the ability to recognize letters. It is cognition that adds the flexibility we need to adapt our behavior to accomplish specific goals at a given time in a given circumstance. Although we cannot avoid seeing *b* as a letter, we can select to take very different actions on that letter depending on what we want to accomplish. Cognitive processing allows our goals to determine our actions.

We have given examples of how cognitive processing uses goals to select different responses to the same object when circumstances differ. This type of control is termed *executive control*, by reference to control from on top by executives in charge of a corporation. Though we have discussed executive control in terms of actions (response selection), it goes much deeper. Executive control over cognitive processing allows goals to determine much of what we look at or what we listen to. In short, executive control determines much of what we are aware. To illustrate, consider Figure 8.3, which is a graphic taken from Yarbus (1967). For the picture shown in the top left of Figure 8.3, the same participant produced distinct fixation and eye-movement patterns when told to report different information about the picture. That is, which portions of the picture were processed by perception and cognition depended on what the observer was looking for. This illustrates that our eyes do not necessarily go to the most salient or distinctive portions of pictures, but rather to those that contain the most relevant information with respect to a set of goals.

RESPONSE SELECTION

For simple tasks such as those described earlier, which constitute the bulk of experiments in cognitive psychology, the principal cognitive activity consists of response selection. *Response selection* refers to the act of assigning or associating one of several possible outcomes (e.g., pressing a designated key) to a particular stimulus. Psychological experiments often try to reduce cognitive processing to a simple stimulus-response mapping among a small set of response alternatives. Such a reduction in complexity is done in order to draw conclusions about the fundamental nature of human information processing; for example, the cost involved in selecting the simplest act. As we discuss later, though, response selection is much broader when considered in the context of activities that constitute much of our work or daily lives. Moreover, it is not the only cognitive activity of interest. Despite

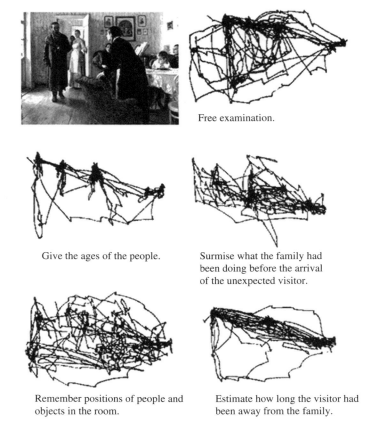

Free examination.

Give the ages of the people.

Surmise what the family had been doing before the arrival of the unexpected visitor.

Remember positions of people and objects in the room.

Estimate how long the visitor had been away from the family.

Figure 8.3 Eye tracking patterns for the picture in the upper left vary dramatically depending on the information the viewer is asked to glean. *Source:* After Yarbus (1967), adapted from http://en.wikipedia.org/wiki/File:Yarbus_The_Visitor.jpg.

these caveats, the act of selecting even a simple action from a set of alternatives in keeping with goals is the fundamental task of cognition. We illustrate this later by demonstrating how the study of simple stimulus-response tasks has yielded insights into the nature of human cognition with consequences for more complex tasks.

The Hick-Hyman Law

Response selection can be made more difficult in ways that have direct practical application. For example, the time required to make the correct response will generally rise as the number of alternative responses is increased. This relationship has been formalized as the Hick-Hyman Law which computes the estimated time to make a correct response as a function of number of possible alternative responses. Hick first observed that response times were linear with the logarithm of the number of alternatives (Hick, 1952). Hyman formulated this relationship in terms of information theory (Hyman, 1953).

$$H = \Sigma p_i \log_2 (1/p_i)$$

$$RT = a + bH$$

Recall from our earlier discussion of information theory that the first equation computes the information, or *entropy* (H), associated with a given action i, among n alternatives (i.e., $i = 1$ to n). In the second equation, RT refers to response time, H is the entropy measure from the first equation, and a and b are constants. The constant a reflects the time to perceive and respond to the stimulus. Note how the Hick-Hyman Law treats the difficulty of cognitive processing, and its related time, as independent of perceptual and motor processing times, which are reduced to a single constant. The constant b reflects the efficiency of cognitive processing. Conditions such as training or fatigue may alter how efficient cognitive processing is with respect to each bit of information.

The Hick-Hyman Law has been used extensively in human-computer interaction to predict or account for the time needed to select an action from a computer menu. For example, a study by Landauer and Nachbar (1985) examined the effect of number of menu options on the time to make a touch-screen selection. They tested both numbers and words and observed somewhat faster overall times with numbers. Regardless, reaction times were a linear function of the logarithm of the number of alternatives. Moreover, the effect of the efficiency constant, b, was evidenced by shallower slopes in last session compared to the first, which can be attributed to practice. Practice increases the processing speed for each bit of information. According to Information Theory, the amount of information is related to the entropy, which in turn is dependent on the probability of events. In the Hick-Hyman Law, the time taken for any set of alternatives depends on the entropy, which in turn depends on the relative probabilities of each event. In the Landauer and Nachbar study, all alternatives menu choices were equally likely; thus, the entropy at each level was maximal. This will not true in general. Instead, knowledge or expectations will alter the relative probabilities of a set of options.

The usefulness of the Hick-Hyman Law in estimating performance across a range of endeavors can be illustrated by a sporting example. In baseball, a batter must determine when to swing the bat and where the ball will be. He or she must consider the speed of the pitch (fast, slow) to time the swing correctly, as well as its horizontal location (inside, outside), vertical location (high, low), and curvature (level, dropping, curving left-right) to position the bat properly. In effect, the batter chooses from a set of alternative swings, including the choice not to swing. Likewise, pitchers have a set of pitches from which they can select that differ in speed, upward and downward movement, and placement. A Major League pitch averages between 80 and 90 miles per hour, covering the 60 feet 6 inches to home plate in less than half a second. The swing itself lasts about 250 msec. To initiate the swing in time to make solid contact with the ball just as it crosses the plate, a swing must be selected in about 250 msec or less.

Now, assume that a batter on a Major League team faces a range of pitchers. Some throw hard and can target specific locations, but have limited curvature and speed. Others

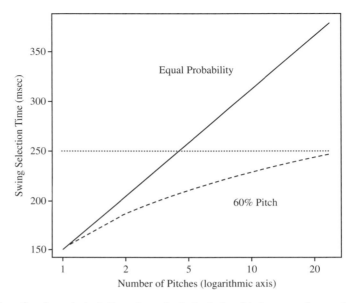

Figure 8.4 A notional graph depicting a hypothetical relationship between the number of pitches in a pitcher's repertoire and the time it will take a batter to select a particular swing. Solid line shows the linear relationship between response time (Swing Selection Time) and entropy (H) when all pitches are equally likely. The dashed line shows predicted swing selection time when the pitch can be predicted 60 percent of the time. The dotted line shows the estimated amount of time available to select the swing for a successful hit.

cannot throw as hard, but can make the ball curve. The best have a large number of pitches that vary all factors. How many pitches should a Major League pitcher master to be effective? One way to be good is to make it difficult for the batter to select the right swing in the 250 msec available. Figure 8.4 shows the Hick-Hyman Law applied to this problem, plotting the predicted time to select a swing as a function of the number of pitches. We have set the constants, *a* and *b*, to 150 msec and 50 msec, respectively, which is not an unreasonable assumption for a highly skilled person. The number of pitches is on a logarithmic axis so that it reflects the entropy (H) as the number of swing options increases. The solid line shows the prediction if the pitcher chooses randomly from the repertoire of pitches. According to this analysis, it only takes two bits of information—four different pitches—before the selection time begins to exceed the capacity of the human batter's swing selection time. So, if a pitcher can only throw a fastball, the best he can do is locate the pitch up, down, in, or out. Thus, the best strategy for this pure fastball thrower is to have a really fast fastball that reduces the selection time to below the 250-msec mark. A pure knuckle ball thrower can do better with only one pitch, as the location of a knuckleball pitch is more variable and less predictable. Alternatively, if a pitcher can throw two speeds (fastball and change-up) to all locations, the batter will have a much harder time. Note too that it doesn't take many pitches before the batter's task is predicted to be very difficult.

Fortunately for batters, few pitchers can throw that many different pitches accurately. Also, variations in location prove less problematic, as good batters can execute a late swing to foul the ball off. To illustrate the Hick-Hyman Law, we have simplified the situation considerably. Yet, there is another aspect of the law that also appears to have merit. We commented above that in many real world applications knowledge or context can alter the relative probability of a set of events. If a pitcher has a favorite pitch—one that he throws much more often than any other pitch—this reduces the uncertainty on any trial and, hence, the entropy in the swing selection. Alternatively, uncertainty will be reduced if the pitcher falls into a pattern in which his pitch selection becomes predicable. The Hick-Hyman Law predicts that this will make the batter's job easier. The dashed line in Figure 8.4 represents the prediction when the pitcher throws his favorite pitch 60 percent of the time. In that case, the average entropy in pitch selection will remain low. Hitters often "sit" on (wait for) a particular pitch if they detect any regular tendencies in a pitcher's selection.

Compatibility

Response selection can also be made more difficult by weakening or even reversing the natural relationship between the semantics of the stimulus and the required response. Conversely, it can be made easier by taking advantage of these natural relationships. This is called *stimulus-response compatibility*. For example, over time, experience in saying the word "red" after seeing the color red has resulted in a strong association between the word and the color. This is certainly true for the primary colors (red, green, yellow, blue). It is less true for color terms such as ochre, mauve, or chartreuse. Because we don't use those terms much, the connection with the colors is weaker, and there is less of a natural compatibility. When people are asked to rapidly name the primary colors, they do so quite well. However, if the responses are scrambled, so that participants say "red" to green and blue to "red," for example, response times will be much longer. This occurs because the scrambled word–color pairs engender a conflict between the word that is commonly associated with the color (which is now incorrect) and the word the responder is supposed to say. This is a well-known phenomenon in cognitive psychology called the Stroop effect (Stroop, 1935). Participants are asked to name the ink color in which words are printed. In the neutral case, the word "house" may be printed in red ink, for example, and the subject would say "red" as quickly as he or she could. In the compatible case, the word "red" occurs in red ink and participants are very fast and accurate in saying "red." In the incompatible case, however, when the word "green" is printed in red ink, participants are slow to say "red" to the ink color, and make more errors than in other conditions. A number of possible explanations for this have been given over the years, all of them acknowledging some form of conflict between the word string and the color, and an inability to fully ignore the word when naming the color. At present, the evidence suggests that this conflict occurs because both the word and the color activate the same response. The effect is reduced, though still present, when participants make a key press rather than speaking the word aloud. The effects of stimulus-response compatibility can also be seen in spatial tasks, where we are faster and more accurate in making responses that are compatible with the spatial layout. For example, responses made with a rightward movement, or even a right-finger key press, are faster for stimuli on the corresponding side (right) than the opposite.

These few examples are testament to the powerful and widespread effect of stimulus-response compatibility with practical consequences for daily life. A classic example of this

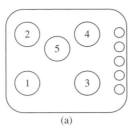 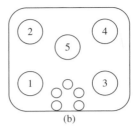

(a)   (b)

Figure 8.5 Diagram (a) shows the layout of the burners on the stove top of one of the authors (Remington) with the control knobs arranged vertically on the right. Numbers in parentheses indicate the burner controlled by each knob. Although the correspondence is regular, there is no perceptual cue to indicate the spatial correspondence. The layout in diagram (b) arranges the knobs in spatial correspondence to the burners. Note how it is no longer necessary to indicate which knob controls which burner.

is the layout of knobs and burners on kitchen ranges. Figure 8.5 shows the kitchen range of one of the authors (Remington). Here, knobs are arranged front to back on the right side of the range. The front knob controls the left front, the second knob the left rear, the third knob the right front, the fourth the right rear, the fifth the central hot plate. Even though this is a regular pattern, with a rule that can be learned, it is not a natural mapping, nor is it supported by any visual correspondence between the layout of the knobs and burners. A better layout would be to have the knobs arrayed with the same spatial relationship as the burners (Chapanis & Lindenbaum, 1959). The correspondence between burner and knob would be easily determined. As a general point, providing visual support for decisions improves human performance and system safety. When users can see the information, or get it easily by looking, it relieves them of having to learn a set of abstract relationships or relying on memory. As we see later, in busy situations memory can become overloaded, slowing the time to retrieve information and becoming more error prone.

Compatibility can be learned through repeated interaction, so that transferring from one device, or computer program, can be made more difficult if certain mappings are changed. The practical consequence of this for design is that adopting a common, uniform standard can facilitate performance. In the computer industry, operating systems and virtually all applications software have arrived at a common set of key mappings for saving files (Ctrl-S or Cmd-S on the Macintosh), cutting text (Ctrl-X), pasting text (Ctrl-V), and a few others. Another example of this is the current design of the typewriter and computer keyboard, referred to as the QWERTY keyboard for the first six letters on the top row. Inefficiencies include frequently used keys being mapped to an awkward finger (for example, the mapping of "e" to the middle finger), repeated letters being struck by the same hand, and a phenomenon known as *hurdling* in which a finger goes from top to bottom or bottom to top skipping the home (middle) row. This occurs, for example, when typing the word *minimum*. Other mappings of key positions to letters make better use of the natural dexterity of the hand, the best known of these being the Dvorak keyboard. However, despite the many advantages of this keyboard, acceptance has never been widespread, because skilled typists have learned strong associations between letters and key position. That is, through practice they have developed strong stimulus-response associations that make a redesign such as the Dvorak layout highly incompatible.

As we said earlier, cognitive processing is not limited to simple response selection acts, except if viewed very abstractly. Cognitive processing is essential to constructing a meaningful environment and to the shared communication of people's experience of the world. Language, whether spoken, written, or signed, is an integral part of our lives, allowing us to share knowledge and experiences. To understand language in any form, words or gestures must be integrated with the previous words and matched to concepts or to events in the external world. For example, if a friend says to you "look at Mary and John holding hands," the verbs and nouns of that sentence must be attached to their appropriate references and give you a picture that corresponds to the meaning of the utterance. It suggests also that Mary and John are present in your environment and that you should turn your head or eyes to look at them. These acts of comprehension, and the decision of whether or not to turn and look, all require cognition. We will have more to say about many of these mental processes when we discuss the contents of mind. The point to be made here is that the term *cognitive processing*, as currently used, covers most of what we do and certainly is involved in all but the most habitual actions.

THE NATURE OF CAPACITY LIMITATIONS

Returning for a moment to our traffic analogy, thus far we have only said that there is a road named *perception* that leads to a road named *cognition* that in turn leads to a road named *motor* processing. We have said nothing up till now about the capacity of those roads. Are these superhighways with many lanes meant to handle thousands of cars at any one time, or two-lane country roads meant to handle just a few dozen? Is the capacity of the roads fixed, or can it increase if needed? Do the roads go in only one direction, or can lanes be swapped around when necessary?

Research suggests that human information processing appears to be best described as a superhighway that abruptly becomes a one-lane road through a crowded city, then re-emerges as a superhighway. In addition, there appears to be a traffic director determining which lanes of the superhighway get to use the one-lane city street at any one time. What this translates to is a cognitive architecture in which high-capacity perceptual processing converges on a severely limited cognitive processor.

As it turns out, there are two major bottlenecks in the "traffic" flow of human information processing. The first places limits on the rate at which we can acquire information. This is more properly seen as a limit on the rate at which we can cognitively process information delivered by the sensory systems. Limits on information acquisition affect our awareness of the situation, and are of concern to engineers designing information displays. The second bottleneck places limits on how many separate, independent actions we can select at any one time. The latter places a limit on our ability to perform two or more tasks concurrently, with widespread consequences for safety.

In the next chapter, we consider how information is acquired and how its acquisition is limited. Following that, we investigate limitations in multitasking. These questions are important for human factors engineers, as it is often necessary to make design choices based on decisions of what to display and what not to display, how much information to present, in what format, and how to structure information in practice. Many of these considerations figure directly in calculations of workload with concerns for human error and safety. Human factors researchers are also guided by a desire to use technology efficiently to improve displays and controls to decrease the mental processing required of operators. Finally, these questions are of fundamental importance to an understanding of how our brains work, and as such have intrigued and vexed psychologists and cognitive scientists for many decades.

SUMMARY

This chapter described the overall structure of our information processing system. At a broad level, we characterize this processing as progressing from perception to cognition to action. We also suggest that behavior is driven by goals, by how we select responses, and by capacity limitations that arise during processing.

REFERENCES

Chapanis, A., & Lindenbaum, L. E. (1959). A reaction time study of four control-display linkages. *Human Factors*, *1*, 1–7.

Hick, W. E. (1952). On the rate of gain of information. *Quarterly Journal of Experimental Psychology*, *4*(1), 11–26. doi:10.1080/17470215208416600

Hyman, R. (1953). Stimulus information as a determinant of reaction time. *Journal of Experimental Psychology*, *45*(3), 188–196. doi:10.1037/h0056940

Landauer, T. K., & Nachbar, D. W. (1985). Selection from alphabetic and numeric menu trees using a touch screen: Breadth, depth, and width. *SIGCHI Bulletin*, *16*(4), 73–78. doi:10.1145/1165385.317470

National Highway Transportation Safety Agency. (n.d.). Statistics and facts about distracted driving. Retrieved from www.distraction.gov/stats-and-facts/index.html

Rizzolatti, G., & Craighero, L. (2004). The mirror neuron system. *Annual Review of Neuroscience*, *27*, 169–192.

Stroop, J. R. (1935). Studies of interference in serial verbal reactions. *Journal of Experimental Psychology*, *18*, 643–662.

Yarbus, A. (1967). *Eye movements and vision*. New York, NY: Plenum Press.

9

Acquiring Information

In Chapter 8, we identified two sources of capacity limitations in information: one dealing with the input of information, the other with determining meaning and constructing actions that achieve our behavioral goals. Here we deal with the first of these, how visual and auditory information comes to be perceived, and how only a small subset of that information comes to play a role in determining our actions.

From autos to nuclear power plants and points in between, we need information that comes in through our senses. Vision keeps us within our lane on the highway. Sonar operators recognize complex auditory patterns; musicians are trained to recognize intervals and have a repertoire of melodies they know. Cell phones use vibration and sound to signal an incoming call. Modern technology allows rings to be individualized so we can tell who is calling without looking. Aeronautical engineers incorporate a stick shaker on modern aircraft, which vibrates to alert pilots to an impending stall. Chemicals are added to natural gas to produce odor and color, which warn people of its presence (natural gas is odorless and colorless in its natural state). Note that across these examples, auditory, tactile, and olfactory information is principally for alerts. Only in the case of highly trained sonar operators and musicians is it the primary means of delivering content. Vision is our predominant modality and designers make extensive use of it for the delivery of basic content. Therefore, we cover vision in much more depth than audition, and omit coverage of other sensory modalities.

SENSORY PROCESSING

Vision

The fundamental unit of vision is the *photon*, a unit of light or electromagnetic radiation. Electromagnetic radiation is characterized by its frequency and wavelength, where *wavelength* refers to the distance between peaks of a regular oscillating waveform (or alternatively the troughs), and *frequency* to the number of peaks per unit time. Frequency (f) and wavelength (λ) are related by the following relationship:

$$f = c/\lambda, \text{ where c is the speed of light in a vacuum}$$

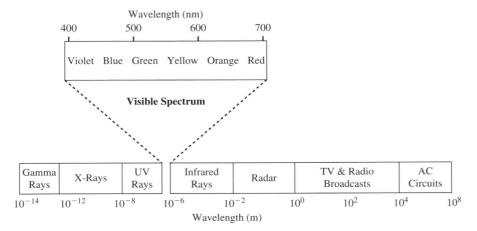

Figure 9.1 The visual system is sensitive to only a small fraction of the electromagnetic spectrum, consisting of the wavelengths of light between about 400–700 nm.

As shown in Figure 9.1, the eye sees only in the visible spectrum, which represents only a small portion of the full range of the electromagnetic spectrum. The wavelengths of light within the visible portion of the spectrum are seen as colors, ranging from violet in the short-wavelength portion (high frequency) to red in the long-wavelength portion.

In actuality, color processing is quite a bit more complex than that, as we shall see. Our perception of an object's properties, principally brightness and color, first depends on the interaction of light with surfaces in the environment. Factors relevant to this interaction are (1) the source illumination, (2) the reflectance of the surface, and (3) the reflectance of surrounding surfaces.

Illumination

What we see as color, or even objects, is determined by how the surfaces of an object reflect the light that strikes it. When light strikes a surface, all or a portion of the light can be transmitted through the surface, absorbed by the surface, or reflected back from the surface, as shown in diagram (a) of Figure 9.2. We refer to the light falling on a surface as *illumination*. There are more technical terms and measures that deal with the power per unit volume, but they need not concern us here. In this example, the reflectance is called *specular* because all of the light that is reflected is reflected back at the same angle at which it struck the surface. This property is characteristic of objects that produce glare when struck, such as mirrors or shiny surfaces. On most natural surfaces the reflected light is diffused, with only a portion reflected back along the angle of incidence. The rest scatters. Matte surfaces produce considerable scatter and thus do not produce much glare.

Reflectance of the Surface

An object's color depends, in part, on the wavelength of the light it reflects back. Each surface has a *reflectance*, which determines how much light is reflected back at a given

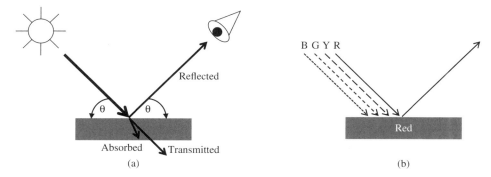

Figure 9.2 Illumination. Diagram (a) shows a case of pure specular reflection, in which the light is reflected back at the same angle at which it struck without scatter. The angle of incidence (θ) is the same as the angle of reflection. Diagram (b) shows how light at different wavelengths is absorbed or reflected. Blue (B), green (G), yellow (Y), and red (R) wavelengths strike a surface that reflects only wavelengths in the red portion of the spectrum. The surface will appear red under normal sunlight, as only red wavelengths will reach the eye.

wavelength. Diagram (b) of Figure 9.2 shows an idealized case in which an illumination source emits light at many wavelengths in the visible spectrum. We see the object as red because its surface reflects red wavelengths of light, while absorbing or transmitting other wavelengths. The amount of light reflected by the surface that reaches the eyes is referred to as *luminance*, measured as the amount of light per unit area, in candelas per square meter (cd/m^2) or footlamberts (fl: 1fl = 3.246 cd/m^2). Variations in luminance produce psychological changes in our perception of brightness. However, judgments of the brightness of an object are highly dependent on the surrounding context. The more light that an object absorbs relative to the objects around it, the darker it will appear; the more light it reflects relative to the objects around it, the brighter it will appear. Thus, the same object (identical luminance) will appear darker when against a light background, and lighter when against a dark background. Conversely, the perceived brightness of an object tends to remain constant even when viewed under different illumination conditions (i.e., different luminance). The fact that brightness judgments are not a function of absolute luminance reveals an important organizing principle of both lightness and color perception. Specifically, our perception of the brightness and color of an object is keyed not to absolute luminance or wavelength, but rather to the *reflectance function* of the object in its context, which remains constant under different illumination levels. This makes adaptive sense, given how often and quickly illumination conditions can change (as when the sun goes behind a cloud)!

However, one characteristic of a light source that can produce changes in perceived color is the spectral composition of the illumination. For example, a car is likely to appear to be a different color under fluorescent light than under sunlight. Sources of illumination differ not just in the amount of light they emit, but also in the spectral composition of the illumination, by which we mean the amount of light at different wavelengths. Figure 9.3 shows plots of the spectrum of sunlight in graph (a) and of a standard fluorescent light in graph (b). Graph (a) shows the power emitted by the sun at all wavelengths. The strong

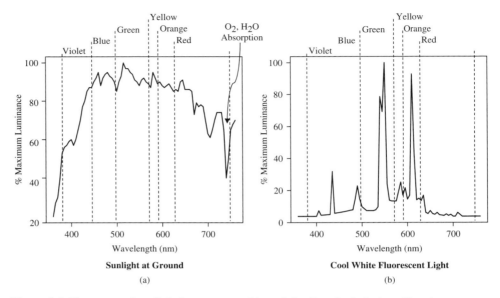

Figure 9.3 The power of sunlight is concentrated in and distributed relatively uniformly across the visible spectrum (Taylor & Kerr, 1941). Graph (a) shows the relative percentage of the spectral power of sunlight in the visible spectrum. Graph (b) shows the relative percentage of power in a cool white fluorescent lamp. Units are in percentage of total energy. The vertical dotted lines represent regions corresponding to the wavelengths of the specified colors. *Source:* Based on data from http://photoweb.gaugler.com/pw_tech/tech_index.html and data from http://en.wikipedia.org/wiki/Fluorescent_lamp.

peak in spectral power from 450–750 nm corresponds to the wavelengths in the visible spectrum. The eye has evolved to make use of the portion with the most radiant energy.

Sunlight has a moderately greater percentage of its illumination at or near 500 nm, but exhibits a continuous, though irregular, power spectrum over the entire range of the visible spectrum. In comparison, the spectrum of a fluorescent light, plotted in graph (b), is not continuous throughout the spectrum. Unlike sunlight, fluorescent sources emit discrete packets of energy in selective frequency ranges, indicated by the tall rectangular peaks. The practical significance of the power spectrum becomes clear when considering how illumination from different sources interacts with surfaces whose reflective properties differ. The broad spectrum of sunlight means that the luminance from surfaces that differ widely in the wavelengths of light they reflect (i.e., color), would contain ample energy at the reflected wavelength. In sunlight, hues in the 500–600 nm range, greens and yellows, will contain the most luminant energy. However, all wavelengths within the visible spectrum are emitted, so colors will be represented continuously across the spectrum. This is not true of the spectrum for fluorescent light. Not only will the large discrete peaks dominate, there are also portions of the spectrum with weak power. As a result, a car whose paint reflects only light from 600–700 nm will appear red under sunlight, but will appear much darker under fluorescent light of the same total illumination, as the energy in the fluorescent light is weak in that region, and the reflected light will have low luminance.

Reflectance of Surrounding Surfaces

The impact of the reflectance of surrounding surfaces can be seen in the atmosphere's effect on the spectrum of sunlight reaching terrestrial surfaces. The sky appears blue because the molecules in the atmosphere reflect short wavelengths (violet and blue) more than long wavelengths (red), so that violet and blue wavelengths are scattered. In the morning and evening, when the sun is low in the sky, the light must travel a greater distance through the atmosphere than when the sun is directly overhead. There is, thus, more loss of violet and blue, and the sun takes on a redder appearance.

The spectral properties of the illumination source and the surface reflectance are important determinants of both the color of objects and our sense of how bright objects are. Designers must be aware of the spectral properties that characterize the light sources and surfaces in a given environment to ensure that operators can detect, identify, and read the relevant displays under the range of lighting conditions they will encounter. However, we have yet to consider the other critical factor: how the human visual system processes the light rays reflecting off surfaces to render a world full of color and objects. After a brief discussion of the anatomy of the eye, we will then consider two aspects of vision that are important in understanding information processing in applied settings: the ability to resolve spatial detail and the perception of color.

Anatomy of the Eye

The eye is a device that produces an optical image of the pattern of light in the environment, and then converts that image into neural activity. The basic components of the imaging system are show in Figure 9.4, which shows the structure of the eye along with an enlarged diagram of a section of the retina. The amount of light entering the eye is determined by the *iris*, whose controlling muscles contract and dilate to produce changes in the diameter of the *pupil*. The *cornea* does most of the bending of light rays, with the *lens* providing the fine-tuning that results in an in-focus image on the surface at the back of the eye, known as the *retina*. When looking directly at an object, its image will be centered in an indented region of the retina knows as the *fovea*. The image produced by the cornea, pupil, and lens is converted into neural activity by virtue of light-sensitive neurons known as *photoreceptors*, which comprise the last of three layers of neurons that make up the retina (see Figure 9.4). There are two basic types of photoreceptors, *rods* and *cones*, which vary in their functional properties as well as distribution on the retina (both are discussed in later sections). Neural activity in the photoreceptors is transmitted and processed through layers of retinal neurons, consisting of *bipolar* cells, *amacrine* cells, *horizontal* cells, *ganglion* cells, and others. The interaction of cells in nearby retinal regions helps to sharpen the resolution of the image. The output fibers of the ganglion cells make up the *optic nerve*, which exits the eye at an area of the retina known as the *optic disc*. The optic nerve then sends the signals from the retina to the visual processing areas of the brain for further processing.

Although the optical characteristics of the eye are capable of delivering a sharply focused image to the retina, the transformation of that image into a representation of the external world is subject to the characteristics and limitations of the human sensory and perceptual systems. One example of a fundamental limitation in this transformation process that is of particular applied importance is the precision with which the system

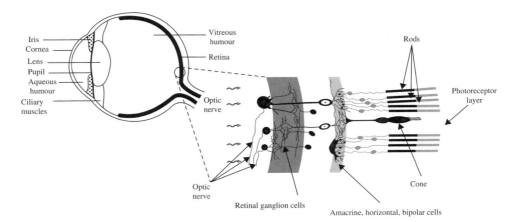

Figure 9.4 The basic components of the eye. Light rays are bent by the cornea, and then enter the eye through the pupil, whose diameter is determined by muscles controlling the iris. The lens produces a focused image on the back of the retina, where photoreceptors transform the light into neural activity which is then processed through layers of neurons and passed on to the visual areas of the brain by way of the optic nerve. *Source:* http://en.wikipedia.org/wiki/File:Fig_retine.png, based on public domain materials.

is able to code fine changes in the spatial distribution of luminance, which is known as *visual acuity*.

Visual Acuity

Visual acuity refers to the ability to precisely resolve the edges of objects. It is this precision that allows us to make fine discriminations between small letters, for example, or to determine the boundary between two objects. A very common test of visual acuity is the Snellen Eye Chart, shown in Figure 9.5. Most readers will be familiar with having to read progressively smaller text on the chart (with one eye covered) when getting a physical examination or a driver's license. This tests practical limits on one's visual acuity by measuring the ability to discern the tiny features that distinguish one letter from another.

As useful as the Snellen chart is for estimating a person's visual acuity, it is not precise enough to accurately measure the fundamental limits of the visual system's ability to process fine detail. For that, researchers use gratings, similar to those in Figure 9.6. A grating is simply an alternating sequence of darker and lighter bars. Figure 9.6 depicts two square wave gratings, with abrupt edges between the dark and light bars. The two gratings differ in how many bars are in the figure as well as in contrast.

In determining the fundamental limits on visual acuity, researchers measure the contrast threshold as a function of spatial frequency, which produces the contrast sensitivity function. *Contrast* is the difference in the intensity of the luminance between the light and dark bars. Formally, contrast is equal to the difference between the maximum and minimum luminance divided by their sum:

$$(L_{max} - L_{min})/(L_{max} + L_{min})$$

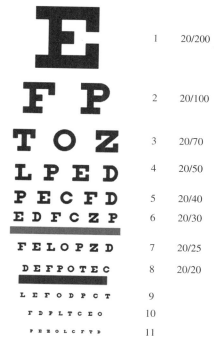

1	20/200
2	20/100
3	20/70
4	20/50
5	20/40
6	20/30
7	20/25
8	20/20
9	
10	
11	

Figure 9.5 The Snellen Eye Chart is commonly used for assessing visual acuity. *Source:* Dahl, 2008, based on public domain materials.

The *contrast threshold* is measured by determining the minimum contrast between dark and light bars needed to recognize them as individual bars. *Contrast sensitivity* is inversely related to threshold in that lower thresholds indicate high sensitivity to detecting that level of contrast, whereas high thresholds reflect low sensitivity. To understand how contrast sensitivity and contrast threshold relate to acuity, we first introduce the notion of spatial frequency.

Below each grating in Figure 9.6 we present a graph of the luminance profile for that grating (not an accurate rendering). The grating in diagram (a) is of higher contrast than the one in diagram (b), as its intensity difference between the light and dark bars (A) is greater. *Spatial frequency* refers to the number of cycles of the grating per unit distance in the visual field. For example, let's assume that each of the gratings in Figure 9.6 is presented over a 40-cm-wide region of a computer display. The grating in diagram (a) completes 4 cycles in 40 cm, or one cycle every 10 cm, which is its wavelength. Because there are 100 cm per meter, its spatial frequency will be 10 cycles/meter. The grating in diagram (b) completes 8 cycles in the same 40 cm. Its wavelength is 5 cm and its frequency is 20 cycles/meter.

The 40-cm-wide region will look quite different if your nose is against the computer screen than if you are standing in the hallway looking at it from some distance. For a general characterization of the limits on visual acuity, we need a measure that can be

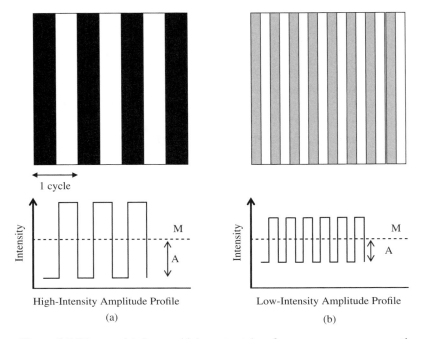

Figure 9.6 Diagram (a) shows a high-contrast, low-frequency square wave grating. Diagram (b) shows a low-contrast, high-frequency square wave grating. Corresponding amplitude profiles are shown below each grating. Square wave gratings are constructed by summing the odd harmonics of a sine wave grating.

applied to every viewing distance. Computing the visual angle subtended by objects in the environment provides such a general measure because it is proportional to the size of the image on the retina of the eye.

To understand visual angle, consider the diagram in Figure 9.7, in which we have rotated our low-contrast, high-frequency grating to see how its dimensions are processed by the eye. Light from the image in the world (or on the computer screen) passes through the lens of the eye to create a corresponding image of the object on the retina. (The image is upside down, but that doesn't matter.) From the geometry of intersecting lines, the size of R is determined by the visual angle V, and the distance from the lens to the retinal surface, Y. As the object comes closer, the angle V increases, as does the size of the *retinal image* (R). Likewise, as the object gets further away, the angle V decreases, as does the size of the retinal image. Because all of the cycles of the grating fit within the retinal image, changing the size of R changes the spatial frequencies present in the object. As the object moves further away, the same number of cycles now covers a smaller retinal area, increasing its spatial frequency with respect to the retinal image. Figure 9.7 shows the formula for calculating visual angle, with S as the width of the grating and D as the distance from the grating to the eye. The dotted line bisects angle V and line S, creating two right triangles, each with angle V/2. The $\tan(V/2) = (S/2)D$. Thus, $V/2 = \arctan(S/2D)$ and $V = 2 \arctan(S/2D)$.

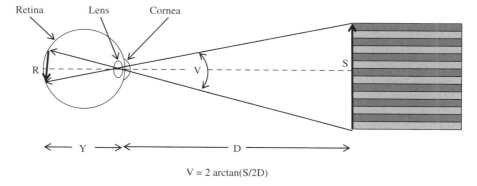

$$V = 2 \arctan(S/2D)$$

Figure 9.7 Computation of visual angle. S denotes the size of the object, D the distance of the object from the lens, Y the distance from the lens to the retina, and V the angle subtended by S. R is the image of S projected on the retina.

Plotting contrast sensitivity as a function of spatial frequency yields a *contrast sensitivity function*, examples of which are shown in Figure 9.8a and b. The plot in Figure 9.8a shows that contrast sensitivity increases as mean illumination is increased. Note that the higher curves correspond to higher illumination levels. The top curve reveals that maximum contrast sensitivity is high until around 10 cycles per degree, after which it drops sharply. Note also how the shape of the curve varies with illumination level. When illumination is very low, only low spatial frequencies are detected at all. As illumination increases, a broader range of spatial frequencies becomes detectable. The contrast sensitivity function places strong limits on the size of font for reading text or gauges at varying levels of illumination. Figure 9.8a explains why older folks who are farsighted (presbyopic) can read if they turn up the lights. In short, acuity is better under high levels of illumination.

The contrast sensitivity function almost entirely determines our ability to see fine detail. An important practical correlate of this is that the ease with which we can make out words and letters in text depends almost entirely on the luminance contrast between the print and the background, and not, for example, on color differences. Sometimes people will build websites with blue text on a black background, or yellow on white, thinking that the strong color contrast will make the characters distinct. This does not work well, as it is difficult (for reasons we discuss later) to achieve a high luminance contrast with blue on black, or yellow on white. A rough demonstration of this is shown in Figure 9.9, where we present grayscale transformations of yellow text on white, blue text on black, and red text on green. Removing the color simulates the luminance contrast available to the visual system in extracting the high spatial frequency information from letters printed in color.

Acuity and Retinal Eccentricity

Another factor that must be considered in design is that our acuity is best in the region where we are focused, but falls off rapidly on either side of the fixated region. The region of high acuity is called the *fovea*, which is situated at the center of the retina. The fovea

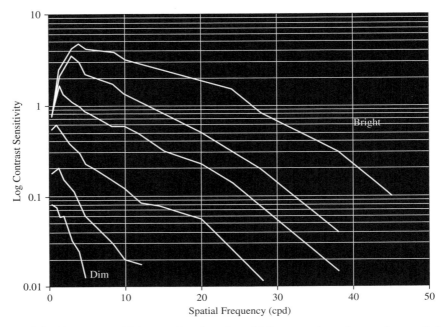

Figure 9.8a Contrast sensitivity as a function of spatial frequency in cycles per degree of visual angle (cpd). Contrast sensitivity is the inverse of threshold. The higher the contrast sensitivity, the lower the contrast needed for threshold perception of a luminance difference. This panel shows the effect of differences in mean field luminance on a 525-nm grating. Sensitivity increases with increasing luminance. *Source:* Adapted from Van Nes & Bouman, 1967.

comprises a circular area of roughly 1 degree of visual angle around the fixation point of our eyes. Returning to Figure 9.8b, the graph shows how the contrast sensitivity function increases as the grating is moved toward the fovea, and decreases as it is moved away. The principal reason for the fall-off in acuity has to do with the number and distribution of the two different photoreceptors in the eye, rods and cones. When light enters the eye through the pupil, it is focused by the lens onto the retina, a surface comprised of receptors sensitive to various wavelengths of light. The rods are most sensitive to light at low luminance levels. As luminance rises, the response of the rods quickly saturates and they can no longer distinguish objects, with a resulting loss of acuity. In contrast, the cones are not as sensitive to light at low luminance levels as the rods, but are able to tolerate much higher levels before saturating. Visual acuity across the retina corresponds closely to the distribution of cones (Palmer, 1999). Cones are packed very tightly in the fovea and their density falls off sharply with distance from the fovea. Rods, however, are abundant in the periphery but absent from the fovea. Acuity is high in a small region surrounding the fovea where cones are densely packed. Acuity falls off dramatically outside that area, in rough proportion to the fall-off in cone density.

A correlate of the distribution of rods and cones is that the same area of retinal stimulation in the periphery activates fewer neurons in visual cortex than does more foveal

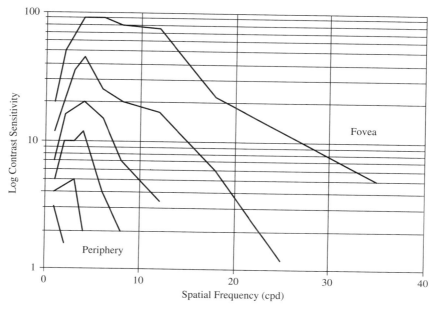

Figure 9.8b The effect of retinal eccentricity. Sensitivity increases nearer the fovea. Contrast sensitivity also varies as a function of grating type (square wave, sinusoid) and flicker rate. *Source:* Adapted from Rovamo, Virsu, & Näsänen, 1978.

stimulation. The contrast sensitivity function means that the periphery of the retina retains sensitivity to low spatial frequencies. This suggests that it should be possible to compensate for the fall-off in acuity with retinal eccentricity by decreasing the spatial frequency content of the image. We can both decrease the spatial frequency content of an object and

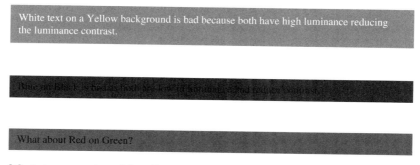

Figure 9.9 A demonstration of the effect of luminance contrast on reading. The top bar is a grey-scale image showing the luminance contrast produced by yellow text on a white background. It reads, "White text on a Yellow background is bad because both have high luminance, reducing the luminance contrast." The middle bar is a similar grey-scale image that reads, "Blue on Black is bad as both are low in luminance and reduce contrast." The bottom bar reads, "What about Red on Green?" Red on green is difficult because of the way color is processed.

offset the decreased neural activity by increasing the size of stimuli in the periphery. The larger retinal image will recruit more cortical neurons (see Daniel & Whitteridge, 1961). Figure 9.10 demonstrates this using what is referred to as an Anstis Array (Anstis, 1974), named for its creator, the psychologist Stuart Anstis. The size of each letter is adjusted so that each letter in the Anstis Array produces equal activity in the visual cortex. The size of letters in the periphery is scaled (magnified) to compensate for greater cortical representation near the center of the fovea, referred to as the *cortical magnification factor*. Maintaining strict fixation on the central dot, you can confirm by inspection that each letter can be clearly seen.

Adaptation

Rods and cones differ in another way that has practical consequences. You have no doubt noticed that when you enter a darkened room after being in bright sunlight, it takes a little while before you begin to see well. More precisely, contrast sensitivity increases (threshold decreases) the longer you are in the dark. This process is called *dark adaptation*. Figure 9.11 plots contrast threshold (*y*-axis) as a function of the number of minutes in the dark. The curve indicated by the solid line was the function observed experimentally. It is not smooth, but has a kink in it. This kink occurs because the curve actually reflects differences between rods and cones in their luminance sensitivities and adaptation levels. The dashed line for "Rod Adaptation" shows that rod thresholds increase in high luminance (sensitivity decreases). This is due largely to photopigment sensitivity and saturation. Cones, in contrast, lose some sensitivity under high illumination conditions. When entering a darkened room, both cones and rods begin to gain sensitivity as they adapt to the dark. Cone adaptation levels out at a point higher than that for rods. Cones never achieve the sensitivity of rods in low-light environments. Rods continue to gain sensitivity for up to 30 minutes before reaching their peak; thus, rods are our primary determinants of visual acuity in the dark. This means that under high light conditions, cones drive vision, whereas under low light, rods drive vision.

Figure 9.10 An Anstis Array. All letters should be equally visible while fixating on the center dot. The Anstis Array demonstrates that equating the cortical representation of objects compensates for decreases in acuity with retinal eccentricity. *Source*: http://psy2.ucsd.edu/~sanstis/Stuart_Anstis/ Peripheral_Acuity.html, reprinted with permission from Stuart Anstis.

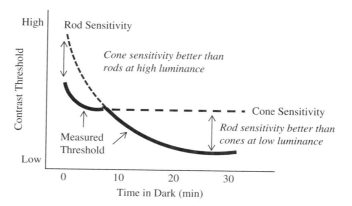

Figure 9.11 The adaptation function, measured as the contrast threshold (left vertical axis) as a function of time in the dark. Rod threshold is greater than cone threshold when light-adapted. Cones adapt more rapidly to the dark than do rods, but sensitivity levels off early.

Likewise, when you emerge from a dark room into bright sunlight, your rods and cones will take time to adapt to the new intensity. In their dark-adapted state they are too sensitive to light, causing the bright sunlight to make the scene appear washed out. This suggests that we can never see fine detail (high spatial frequencies) while dark-adapted. However, there is a solution. The bridge of a Navy ship at night is lit with red light; astronomers also use red light for reading and recording sightings. Why? In both cases, it is necessary to remain dark-adapted while remaining able to observe items that require acuity. Night observation (low luminance) is best using rod vision, because of the high sensitivity of rods in the dark-adapted state, as shown in Figure 9.11. Rods are insensitive to red wavelengths. Thus, using red light will not cause rods to lose their level of dark adaptation. However, cones are sensitive to red, so we can use the red light for higher-acuity vision.

Saccadic Eye Movements

The fall in acuity with retinal eccentricity has another important consequence. We can read (Rayner, 1998), monitor instrument readouts (Carbonell, Ward, & Senders, 1968; Senders, 1964), recognize faces, appreciate a painting (Yarbus, 1967), play sports (Hayhoe & Rothkopf, 2011), or engage in any activity that requires high acuity only by shifting our gaze to bring the fovea onto the object of interest. There are two separate eye-movement control systems that achieve this. The *pursuit* eye-movement system moves the eye smoothly to keep the fovea fixated on objects that move at slow to moderate speeds, less than about 30 deg/sec. Specialized neural circuitry for these movements allow us to track objects moving in the visual field that we wish to attend to without having to deliberately move our eyes. Smooth pursuit is specialized for tracking and cannot be used for acquiring visual information.

To voluntarily move the eyes, we use *saccadic* eye movements; that is, we fixate on portions of the visual world in rapid succession. Surprisingly, it turns out that the continuous, seamless world we perceive is actually constructed from small discrete "snapshots." We saw evidence of this in the eye-fixation patterns from viewing pictures, depicted in Figure 8.3. Each fixation brings high-acuity vision to a region of about 1° in diameter, roughly the width of the thumb at arm's length. Further, saccades are not made to contiguous regions of space. That is, we do not perceive a line by making a series of fixations that sample the line continuously along its length. Rather, we saccade to corners, ends, edges, and other informative parts of the scene. Figure 8.3 reveals discontinuities in the fixations. The long lines indicate successive fixations on quite separate parts of the picture. All the fixations in Figure 8.3 are saccades. Voluntary saccades occur routinely when searching for something, such as your car in the parking lot or a friend at the airport. They are also integral to activities such as reading, where there is evidence that they are closely coupled to the state of processing of each word in a sentence (Rayner & Pollatsek, 1987; Reichle, Rayner, & Pollatsek, 1999, 2004; Remington, Wu, & Pashler, 2011). We also saccade involuntarily, or at least without deliberate intent, to objects undergoing abrupt motion or to the sudden appearance of a salient stimulus.

The frequency with which we make saccades varies with the task, as does the exact pattern of fixations that results. When looking at a picture, reading text, or searching the computer desktop, we fixate items for about 250–400 msec before moving on to the next item, or at a rate of 3–4 saccades/sec. The duration of a fixation depends on the difficulty of the cognitive processing of the fixated material. Saccades made in response to an arbitrary signal—for example, a tone or the word "left" or "right"—take on the order of 300–400 msec to initiate, referred to as *saccade latency*. For saccades in response to arbitrary signals, latency will depend on the time taken to decode the signal.

Saccade latencies to stimuli that suddenly appear are on the order of 180–240 msec. The shortest saccade latencies occur when the fixated item vanishes just prior to the onset of the saccade target. These "express saccades" have latencies of around 70–100 msec. One explanation for the short latency of express saccades is that one step in making a saccade is disengaging from the currently fixated item (Posner, 1980). Removing the object at fixation eliminates the need to perform that step. When the saccade either falls short of or overshoots its target, a corrective saccade will be made, with latencies of 70–90 msec or less.

Corrective saccades pose an intriguing problem. Not much information processing can be done in just 70–90 msec. How does the saccade system determine that it needs a correction? It turns out that undershoots and overshoots are characteristic of a type of movement called *ballistic*. Ballistic movements, once begun, run to completion without further guidance. Another related term for this is *open-loop control*. Imagine throwing a ball. At some point in the process, you can no longer stop your hand and arm, or even alter their motion. At that point the motion becomes ballistic; it will execute the program it has with no further correction.

The same is true of the saccade. To illustrate, consider the following experiment based on a study by Ray, Schall, and Murthy (2004; see also Becker & Jürgens, 1979; Findlay & Harris, 1984). We present a target to the right or left of a fixation point to which participants make a saccade. On some trials, a second target appears after a variable delay. When this happens, the saccade to the first target must be cancelled, and a saccade made instead to the second target. If the delay between the two targets is less than 150 msec, participants redirect the saccade to the second target, albeit with an increase in latency. For delays of 150 msec or more, the saccade initially goes to the first target, followed by a corrective saccade to the second. This suggests two distinct phases in saccade programming. The initial phase allows cancellation of ongoing programming and a redirection of the saccade. The second phase is similar to the throwing example. Once this phase has begun, the programmed movement must be completed.

So what about the corrective saccades? It looks as though the saccade system can overlap the programming of successive saccades. In the two-target example, if the second target simply indicates the location of a following saccade, then participants will most often make a correct sequence to two saccades. However, the latency of the second saccade is reduced if the second target occurs prior to the onset of the first saccade. This suggests that the second saccade is being programmed in parallel with the first.

Another characteristic of ballistic movements is that the velocity of the movement is proportional to the distance moved. For distances of 60° or less, saccade velocity is a linear function of distance, referred to as the *saccade main sequence* (Zuber, Stark, & Cook, 1965). Peak saccade velocities approach 1,000 deg/sec. This means that the movement itself is very short, usually in the 30–50 msec range. It is marked by rapid acceleration, followed by an equally rapid deceleration.

Temporal Vision

The contrast sensitivity function describes how the visual system responds to spatial variations in light patterns. It also responds to variations in luminance over time. This was easily demonstrated until flat-screen televisions began to dominate the market. The older cathode-ray-tube televisions would illuminate the back of the tube at a frequency of 60 Hz. If you looked straight at the screen it would appear steady. However, if you looked from the side so that the screen was visible only in the periphery of your retina, you could see a definite flickering. This occurs because the flicker rate of 60 Hz is beyond *flicker fusion* threshold for cones, but not for rods. Flicker fusion refers to the rate of temporal alternation of light and dark patches at which you can no longer detect the flickering. For foveal (cone) vision, the critical flicker fusion rate is about 60 Hz, or 17 msec per frame. Fluorescent lights actually flicker about 120 times per second, but we perceive them as steady because this rate is well beyond the fusion threshold.

Flicker fusion plays a role in motion pictures. In a standard motion picture, the frame rate is 24 frames/sec. This happens to be the rate at which good motion is perceived. However, it is well below the critical flicker fusion threshold. This means that any variation in luminance from frame to frame will be easily perceived, resulting in a flickering picture. The rather ingenious solution hit upon to solve this was to keep the frame rate at 24 per second, but present each frame 3 times. This creates a flicker rate of 72 Hz, well above the 60-Hz fusion threshold.

Masking and Crowding

One final point regarding visual processing must be mentioned, as it has practical significance for information display. The perception of visual information can be impaired when presented in close temporal and spatial proximity to other objects. We have already discussed the elevated thresholds that occur with reduced contrast, as might happen if we are trying to spot an object in fog or haze. There, the contrast difference can be at or below threshold. Objects whose contrast thresholds are well above threshold can also be camouflaged by blending in with the surroundings, a fact exploited by predators and prey alike. Visual stimuli can also be *masked* by stimuli that precede or follow them at very short temporal intervals. For example, in *metacontrast masking*, detection of a briefly presented (50 msec or less) stimulus will be impaired when followed 50–150 msec later by flanking stimuli (Breitmeyer, 1978). Metacontrast masking reveals how magnocellular (transient) and parvocellular (sustained) channels interact in visual processing, but the critical spatio-temporal conditions for it occur rarely in daily life.

It is more common to encounter visual stimuli surrounded or flanked by other visual stimuli. In text, for example, letters are placed close together. In graphs or other information displays, this is often done to display as much as possible. Such practices can lead to *visual crowding*, in which the contours of surrounding objects interfere with the perception of another object. Visual crowding has been reported for a wide range of stimuli, including letter recognition (Bouma, 1970; Toet & Levi, 1992), orientation discrimination (Andriessen & Bouma, 1976), and face recognition (Louie, Bressler, & Whitney, 2007; Martelli, Majaj, & Pelli, 2005), to name but a few. Figure 9.12 illustrates the effect of crowding. Inspection of the figure reveals how crowding interferes primarily with peripheral vision. In the fovea, interference occurs only when flankers are within a four- to six-foot arc (Flom, Weymouth, & Kahneman, 1963; Toet & Levi, 1992), or not at all (Strasburger, Harvey, & Rentschler, 1991). Crowding is one factor contributing to the inability to process more than a few letters surrounding the fixated letter in a word. As more visual information displays make use of monitors, the possibility of placing as much information as possible on the scarce screen real estate becomes attractive. Not only could this produce crowding, it can also make finding information difficult, as we note later in this chapter.

The What and Where of Vision
Thus far we have discussed aspects of vision that determine our ability to recognize objects and discriminate them from other objects. That is, how the visual system determines "what" is present. The *what* system coexists with another, possibly earlier, *where* system. The where system provides information about the existence and location of objects in the visual world. Such information is critical to our ability to orient toward sources of information. We *orient* to objects and events in the world by turning the head and body toward them, and making a saccade to fixate on them. Similarly, the where system is critical when reaching to grab an object. The what and where systems comprise two partially independent pathways in the visual system. The where system receives input from a special class of retinal neurons, called *transient*, or *magnocellular* neurons. Transient neurons fire to sudden (transient) changes in luminance, but exhibit no response to the continued presence of the object. This is exactly what would be expected of a system designed to alert an animal to changes in the environment. In contrast, sustained, or parvocellular, neurons show no response to rapid changes. Instead, they respond to stimuli whose presence persists. The parvocellular (sustained) system extracts the fine detail and color we have been discussing. The magnocellular (transient) system transmits the existence and location of objects to guide attention, saccadic eye movements, and reaching actions.

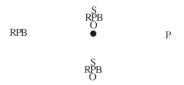

Figure 9.12 Examples of visual crowding. In each letter grouping, try to read the single letter, or the letter in the middle, while maintaining fixation on the small black dot. Note how flanking letters increase difficulty in the periphery, but not near the fovea.

Summary

In summary, the human visual system is sensitive to a limited range of wavelengths within the electromagnetic spectrum. Vision is further limited by the ability of rods and cones to resolve fine detail under various illumination conditions. This defines the contrast sensitivity function, which varies as a function of retinal eccentricity. These inherent limits in resolution make it necessary to sample the world in small snapshots, or fixations, by means of saccadic eye movements. We now turn the processes involved in the perception of color.

Color Vision

Earlier we commented that color was determined by the spectrum of the illumination and the reflective properties of the surface. This is true to a point. Ultimately, the color that we see, the kinds of color discriminations we can make, and defects in color vision, result from the specific way the human visual system processes the reflected luminance off surfaces. Color processing begins at the retina, where rods and cones respond to light of varying wavelengths. There are three different types of cone receptors, each with a unique function relating the amount of light absorbed to the wavelength. Figure 9.13 shows the relative spectral sensitivity of the three cone types, along with that of the rods. It is more common today to label these cone types as long (L), middle (M), and short (S), corresponding with the portion of the spectrum to which they are most sensitive. However, we will use the older designation of red (R), green (G), and blue (B) for L, M, and S respectively. The spectral sensitivity functions for the R and G cones overlap considerably. The peak sensitivity for R at 564 nm corresponds roughly to a greenish yellow. However, the R cones are much more sensitive to light in the 560–650 nm range, corresponding to red, whereas the G cones are more sensitive to light in the 400–550 nm region, corresponding to green. The B cones respond strongly to light at the short wavelengths corresponding to blue. The functions in Figure 9.13 plot the relative sensitivity for each, not the absolute sensitivity. In fact, B cones are much less sensitive to light than are R and G.

The visual system uses the activation of the three cones and rods to compute color and luminance in separate, independent channels. The luminance channel sums the input of all activations, though B contributes little. The color channel achieves a color by mixing the output of a Red-Green and a Blue-Yellow opponent system. The R-G opponent system computes the difference in activation of R and G cones. In effect, red and green cancel, as the output of the system will be zero if activation of R and G cones is equal. The

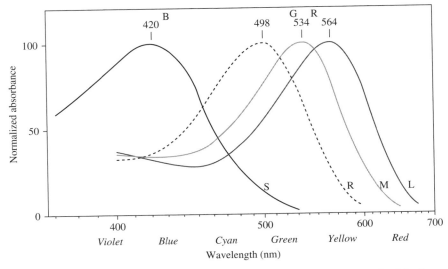

Figure 9.13 Spectral sensitivity functions for three cone types and rods. The peak of the L cone is the primary cone type for responses to red (R). The M cones correspond roughly to green (G), and the S cones are specialized for the short wavelengths of blue (B). The rod response is also shown. Values on the y-axis reflect the relative sensitivity with respect to the peak sensitivity, not the absolute sensitivity. *Source:* Adapted from Bowmaker & Dartnall, 1980.

B-Y system works similarly. It computes yellow (Y) by summing R and G activation, and then outputs the difference between this activation and that of B cones. This is why it is possible to have a bluish-green, or a yellow-red, for example, but not a bluish-yellow or a greenish-red. The general outline of the opponent color system was described by Hurvich and Jameson (1957). Evidence for the opponent processes was later supported by the discovery that neurons tuned to red were inhibited by green, and those tuned to green were inhibited by red, and similarly tuned B-Y cells (De Valois, 1965; De Valois, Abramov, & Jacobs, 1966). Figure 9.14 diagrams a very simplified version of the process.

CIE Color Space

Long before the working of the opponent systems was understood, the International Commission on Illumination (Commission Internationale de l'Eclairage, or CIE) first standardized a system for representing color based on empirical investigations. In these investigations, observers adjusted the luminance of each of three wavelengths (red, green, and blue monochromatic light sources) in a color mixture to match a given test patch of a single, known wavelength. This procedure makes use of the fact that a color associated with a pure wavelength of light can be reproduced by a combination of three other wavelengths, depending on the wavelengths chosen. These combinations are referred to as *metamers*. The resulting CIE color space (CIE, 1931) is shown in Figure 9.15. The data for this were compiled from a number of sources using different red, green, and blue primaries. Here we present the basic idea. The graph expresses every color in terms of a combination of two primary colors, X (horizontal axis) and Y (vertical). X corresponds

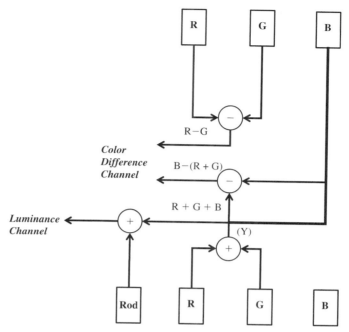

Figure 9.14 A simplified version of color and luminance processing. Activation is summed in the luminance channel. Red (R) and green (G) cones provide most of the activation. R and G are summed to get yellow (Y). Color difference channels compute the difference of R and G separately from the difference between R and Y (R + G). *Source:* After Hurvich & Jameson (1957).

roughly to red, Y roughly to green. The third variable needed to fully represent the color is the luminance (L), not shown. The bounded region that resembles a tongue or horseshoe is a chromaticity plot, and represents all the colors the human eye can perceive. The edges of the space indicate the wavelength of the color matched by the corresponding values on the vertical and horizontal axes under experimental conditions. In this rendering, the darker regions correspond to reds and blues, which do not contain much luminance. Note that the diagram defines the colors possible given some primaries, not the actual colors the user will experience. That depends on other factors.

The edges of the large bounded region represent the *hue*, or color value (chromaticity) of the wavelength. Colors around the edges are fully *saturated*. Saturation measures the amount of white in the color. For example, the same hue corresponding to red when fully saturated will appear pink as the saturation is reduced. Continued reduction of saturation leads to a whitish gray. The dot inside the horseshoe represents a white with equal power in all three wavelengths.

One of the useful aspects of the CIE representation is all the colors that lie on a straight line connecting any two wavelengths can be produced by mixtures of those two wavelengths. Likewise, any three wavelengths connected by straight lines can reproduce all the colors within the triangle formed. Color in print or on television remains

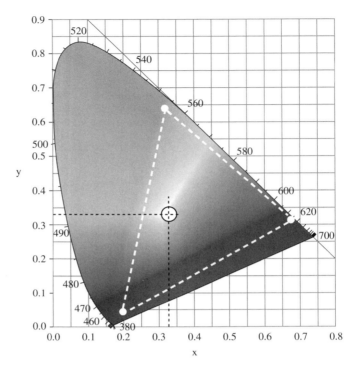

Figure 9.15 CIE XY chromaticity diagram. The central circle represents the point of achromatic white, which equates to equal amounts of all three primaries (X = Y = 1/3). The triangle shows the colors possible given three common primaries for color television. *Source:* Adapted from public domain image at http://en.wikipedia.org/wiki/File:CIExy1931.png.

predominately based on three-color system, though print and television use different primary wavelengths. The diagram of Figure 9.15 shows a triangular region marked by dashed lines within the horseshoe. This region represents the space formed by the three colors in a common cathode-ray-tube color television. When added together in various proportions, the three primaries can reproduce all the colors within this triangle. Note how much smaller this space is compared to the full CIE space. That means that the three colors used to present television pictures can capture only a fraction of the colors available to the human eye. In fact, no matter which three wavelengths are chosen, they will be insufficient to fully reproduce the bounded region. Modern flat-panel televisions based on liquid crystal or plasma technology produce colors differently from each other, and differently from the older cathode-ray-tube televisions. Yet, they still use predominately three colors. When it is claimed that computer graphics cards can reproduce millions of colors, it means that more of the colors within their respective triangular regions can be represented. Colors outside that region remain unattainable. More modern techniques include a fourth color, which can in principle come much closer to fully reproducing the colors in the CIE color space.

The Uses of Color

We commented earlier that color contrast did not produce the same sharply resolved corners and edges as did luminance contrast. Color is not as useful as luminance contrast for transmitting shape information. Color is, however, very good at separating objects. Even though it is difficult to read red on green, it is easy to separate green words and red words. If each word alternated between green and red, there would no problem reading only the green or only the red words. In general, color is a very effective way to segment a scene into regions. Thus, a unique color distinct from its background can be very effective in drawing attention to an object, as we shall see in the next section.

Because color makes a striking impact on the observer, it is tempting to assign numerous distinct colors to create visual "categories." For example, computer operating systems offer the option of labeling files and assigning a unique color to each. The goal is to facilitate finding the object or to use the color to recall the name or some other fact. We shall see later that the effectiveness of color in calling attention to an object diminishes as more colors are present. Moreover, it is prudent to limit the use of colors to recall category labels (e.g., red = danger, blue = friend). While the color may be distinctive, recalling an arbitrary label associated with it places a demand on memory. Generally, more than three to four such labels will begin to burden rather than help the operator.

Audition

As we noted earlier, auditory input is used principally to alert and communicate in most applications. Occasionally, alerts will contain information about the nature of the alert. Cell phones can be set to ring with different music or tones to signal different callers. Email systems can be programmed to chime differently depending on the urgency of the incoming email. As noted earlier with regard to using color to indicate category, we are limited in how many unique tones we can keep track of. The limits have more to do with memory than with auditory processing, as the range of sounds we can discriminate is much larger than the number of arbitrary sound "labels" we can remember.

When we hear a sound, we are hearing variations in air pressure waves. This is true whether the sound is a horn honking on the street, a concert we are attending, or music we are listening to over headphones. In the preceding discussion of visual acuity, we introduced the notion of spatial frequency, or variation in luminance over space. The concept is the same for sound, except that sound unfolds in time, not space. The wavelength of an acoustic pressure wave, therefore, is measured in units of time, usually seconds. For sounds, a wavelength is the time between the peaks of maximum pressure, or alternatively between the troughs of minimal pressure. The greater the number of wavelengths per unit time, the higher the frequency.

The fundamental properties of a sound are its *pitch*, *loudness*, and *timbre*. *Pitch* refers to the frequency of the pressure in cycles per second, or Hertz (Hz). As with spatial frequency, pitch has an inverse relationship with wavelength; that is, longer wavelengths have a lower pitch while shorter wavelengths have a higher pitch. The loudness of the sound is a function of the amplitude of the pressure wave, which itself is a function of the pressure difference of the peaks and troughs. *Timbre* refers to the character of the sounds we hear; it is what distinguishes a clarinet from a flute or a car horn.

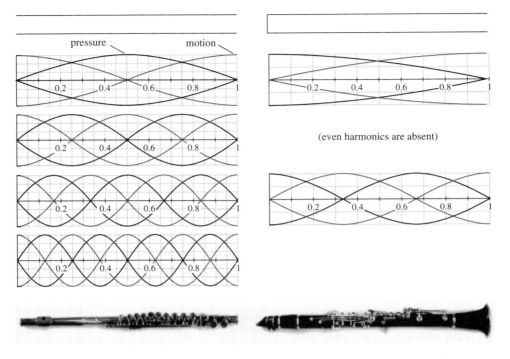

Figure 9.16 The relationship of airflow and pressure inside an open tube (flute) and a tube open only at one end (clarinet). Sound is reflected from the ends of the tube. At the open end the pressure is equivalent to the external pressure, but not at the closed end. *Source:* Reprinted with permission from Joe Wolfe (Wolfe, n.d.), www.phys.unsw.edu.au/jw/flutes.v.clarinets.html.

What we hear as a sound complete with pitch, loudness, and timbre is often the result of a pressure wave passed through a resonant chamber. When a clarinet player plays a note, she pushes air through a series of reeds, causing them to vibrate. These vibrations vary with the force of the air and the looseness of the lips, and can become quite complex. At the same time, she can hold down keys on the clarinet that close or open holes along the instrument. The key pattern determines the length of the closed tube. In turn, the length of the closed tube determines the pitch and timbre of the sound. The pressure wave travelling down the tube is reflected at both ends. The longer the tube, the greater the time it takes for this reflection, and hence the longer the wavelength. The lowest pitch is produced by the longest length and all holes closed.

The length of the tube also determines the *harmonics*. This can be seen from Figure 9.16, which shows how a moving column of air relates to pitch in tubes that are open (flute) and closed at one end (clarinet). Differences between the behavior of the closed and open tubes, as shown, produces much of the distinct character of the clarinet as opposed to the flute. The point to make, however, is that as the pressure wave is reflected back and forth in the tube, it gives rise to a series of waves at increasing frequency (shorter wavelength). The lowest pitch, corresponding to one complete cycle, is termed the *fundamental;* it is determined by the longest wavelength within the tube. The additional, higher-frequency waves are harmonics. The harmonics produced by an ideal tube are all whole-number multiples of the fundamental. This gives rise to a complex waveform. Thus, the sound we hear from a clarinet, flute, organ, or even a car horn, are composed of a fundamental, harmonics, and additional nonharmonic frequencies.

The tube can be considered a resonant chamber. Depending on its length, width, and shape, it will amplify some harmonics and attenuate others. The result is sound with different timbres, which we identify as unique sounds. The waves in Figure 9.16 are referred to as *standing waves*. They also occur in stringed instruments. There, the length of the string determines the fundamental and overtones. Those are then transmitted to a resonant cavity—the body of the guitar, cello, or violin—which amplifies some while attenuating others. Speech is produced in an analogous way. Air forced up from the lungs causes the vocal cords (larynx) to vibrate, again producing a complex pressure wave. The tightness of the vocal cords, unlike the reeds in a clarinet, can be increased or decreased, which will influence the pitch of sound. This pressure wave from the vocal chords is then transmitted to the resonant cavity of the mouth. The shape and position of the tongue, the size of the mouth, and a few other details determine the sound that emerges.

This brief discussion captures the essence of sound production, but requires embellishment to make certain concepts clear. To understand our perception of pitch, loudness, and timbre, it is first necessary to understand how complex waveforms are created. The fundamental unit of sound is the familiar sine wave, an example of which is shown in the top panel of Figure 9.17. Fourier analysis tells us that any complex sound can be represented as a sequence of summed sine waves. For example, the square wave and triangle wave in Figure 9.17 are created by combining the odd harmonics of a sine wave. The difference in shape is due to the weight given to each odd harmonic. The triangle wave weights higher harmonics much less than does the square wave. The sawtooth wave, shown in the bottom of the figure, is more complex. It contains both even and odd harmonics of the sine wave. The sawtooth wave is useful in simulating many musical instruments, as it contains a large number of frequencies.

The Human Auditory System

Mechanisms in the ear convert sound pressure waves into patterns of neural activation. A schematic of the ear and its internal structures is shown in Figure 9.18. The outer ear, or pinna, corresponds to the portion we can easily see—the ear lobe and rounded protruding structure. The outer ear collects and funnels pressure waves into the middle ear, amplifying them in the process. That is why losing the outer portion of the ear will reduce one's hearing even though all the other mechanisms are intact. Pressure waves travelling down the *auditory canal* cause vibrations of the *tympanic membrane*, or eardrum. The eardrum combines with the three small bones of the middle ear—the *malleus* (or hammer), *incus* (or anvil), and *stapes* (or stirrup)—to transform the variations in air pressure into mechanical vibrations that produce movement in the fluid contained within the cochlea. The fluid movement causes bending of the thin hairs along the basilar membrane within the cochlea. The bending of the hairs produces neural activity that we eventually perceive as sound. Figure 9.18 also shows that different frequencies tend to excite specific regions of the basilar

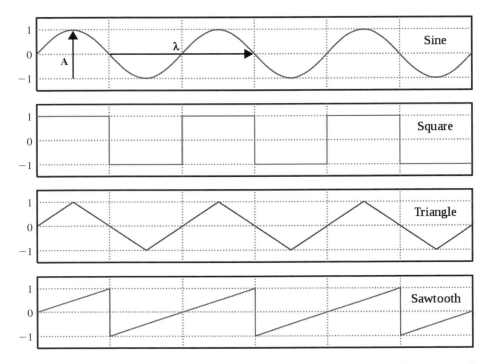

Figure 9.17 Four different kinds of waveforms. The square, triangle, and sawtooth waves can all be constructed by a weighted sum of the harmonics of sine waves. For example, both the square wave and the triangle wave contain only the odd harmonics of the fundamental sine wave. For the sine wave we note its amplitude (A), and wavelength (λ). *Source:* After public domain graphic from Wikimedia (Omegatron, 2006).

membrane. The basilar membrane is a coiled structure that decreases in width and stiffness from its base to its apex. Low-pitched tones cause greatest activation in the larger portion, near the base, whereas high-pitched tones selectively activate narrower portions near the end. It turns out that for a complex sound, the response of the basilar membrane can be predicted from the response of the component sine waves. Thus, position along the basilar membrane provides important information about pitch, although there is also evidence that low-frequency sounds tend to be coded in terms of the rate or timing of neural firing patterns (Fearn, Cartel, & Wolfe, 1999).

Auditory Perception

The objective measure of the amplitude of a sound is the decibel, dB, which measures the ratio of the relative power difference of two sources. When using the amplitude of a pressure wave, decibel level is expressed as:

$$dB = 20 \log (A_1/A_0)$$

where A_0 is the reference amplitude. Audible pressures span a range of 10 million units. Using the logarithm is convenient given this large range of differences. On a logarithmic

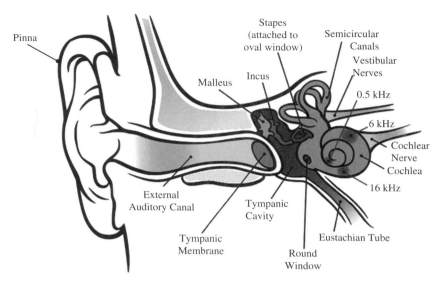

Figure 9.18 The structures of the ear. *Source:* From public domain materials of Chittka & Brockmann, 2005 at http://en.wikipedia.org/wiki/File:Anatomy_of_the_Human_Ear.svg.

scale, each unit is a power of 10 greater than the previous one, meaning that a decibel level of 3 has 10 times the amplitude difference as 2, 100 times as much as 1. Decibel levels above 100 dB become painful. Speech in the absence of background noise is around 40 dB, trains nearby may be 100 dB, and a rock concert as much as 120 dB. Keep in mind that the power falls off as the square of distance. The psychological, or perceived, measure of the loudness of a tone is a *phon*, which by convention is set so that 1 phon equates to 1 dB sound pressure level at a frequency of 1 kHz.

One of the common ways of assessing loudness perception is to present a tone at a predetermined amplitude and ask observers to adjust a reference tone so that it is equal in perceived loudness (see, e.g., Robinson & Dadson, 1956). Summary results of several investigations are shown in the equal loudness contours in Figure 9.19. Each line reflects the sound pressure level at the tested frequency on the *x*-axis required to match the perceived loudness of a 1000-Hz tone at a specified loudness (phon). The *x*-axis is in logarithmic units, with each vertical line corresponding to 10 Hz. The lowest curve, labelled Threshold, can be considered to define the limits of human hearing as it tests the ability to adjust the decibel level of a tone to match a threshold-level tone. It corresponds, roughly, to the contrast threshold function described earlier for vision.

Three key points emerge from Figure 9.19. First, the ear is most sensitive in the 2–5 kHz range for all loudness levels. Second, the range of hearing runs from around 20 Hz to 20 kHz. Below 20 Hz, we have limited perception of sound, although at high dB levels we can feel the vibrations produced by the sound. Third, there is a steep rise in threshold and perceived loudness for low frequencies. This is important in music recording. It means

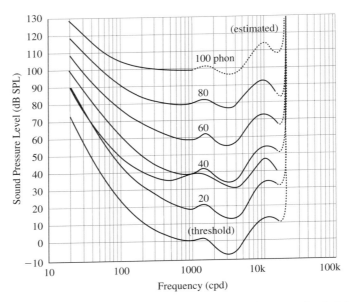

Figure 9.19 Equal loudness contours. Each line reflects the sound pressure level at the tested frequency (*x*-axis) required to match the perceived loudness of a 1000-Hz tone at a specified loudness (phon). The ear is most sensitive in the 2–5 kHz range. *Source:* From Lindosland, 2009, public domain.

that the mid range from 2–5 kHz is naturally the most dominant portion of the spectrum. Thus, the loudness control of many stereo receivers compensates for this by boosting lower frequencies.

Pitch, Masking, and Critical Bands
As discussed earlier, the pitch of a sound is measured in terms of frequency, or Hz. Our ability to discriminate two pure tones from each other on the basis of pitch varies as a function of several factors, including frequency, decibel level, duration of the tone, and whether the tone has an abrupt onset or is smoothly ramped in intensity. However, as a general rule, for frequencies greater than 500 Hz, an approximately 3 percent difference in frequency is needed to produce a noticeably different pitch. This means that the absolute pitch difference needed to discriminate two tones increases with frequency (Fletcher, 1940).

We noted earlier that pitch is encoded in part by the place along the basilar membrane. In fact, the place-coded response of the basilar membrane creates a set of frequency-centered bands, called *critical bands* (Fletcher, 1940). Essentially, a given region of the basilar membrane will respond to several frequencies, though most actively to one. Fletcher (1940) carefully studied the elevation in thresholds for detecting the presence of a pure tone in the presence of *white noise*, which contains all frequencies at equal amplitude. It sounds like a hissing sound that would be produced by saying "shhh." He filtered the noise to create a mask at different frequencies, and different bandwidth or spread. He observed that masking

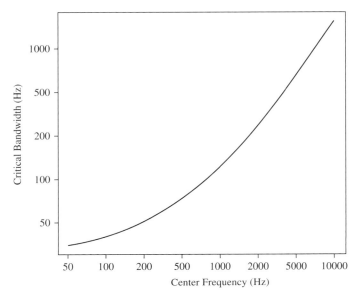

Figure 9.20 Approximate bandwidth (equivalent rectangular bandwidth) of the critical band as a function of frequency. The plot illustrates how the bandwidth increases with frequency. Critical bands describe the frequency tuning in the auditory system and determine the amount of interference (masking) that will occur if two tones are presented. *Source*: Adapted from Fletcher, H. (1940), Rev Mod Phys 12, 47–65.

noise within a certain region of frequency around the target tone elevated the decibel levels needed to detect the tone. This elevation in detection threshold is referred to as *masking*. The region in which masking was observed was denoted as the critical band. By varying the width of the masking noise, he was able to deduce the bandwidth of the critical band—or how wide the critical bands are. This is shown schematically in Figure 9.20, which uses the equal rectangular bandwidth approximation to the critical bandwidth in (Moore, 1983). When two pure tones fall within a critical bandwidth, they will not be heard as two distinct pure tones; rather, the effect will be heard as a fluttering, beating, or fuzziness. Figure 9.21 illustrates how the masking noise raises the threshold of detection for target tones.

Auditory Localization
The auditory system resolves the position of an object in space with respect to the head by detecting small differences in the time of arrival of sounds to each ear. As Figure 9.22 shows, sound on the side of a sound source, such as a speaker, must travel further to reach the ear on the opposite side than the one on the same side. This means that it arrives at the opposite ear later, causing what is referred to as an *interaural time difference (ITD)*. The maximum ITD occurs when the source is at 90°, directly across from one ear, which creates an ITD of around 650–700 msec. As the source moves toward the front or rear, the ITD decreases and reaches zero when in front or back. That is why it is difficult to tell if a stationary sound is coming from the front or the back. The auditory system also uses the

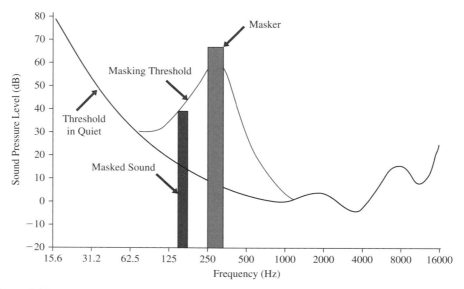

Figure 9.21 The effect of masking noise raising the threshold of detection of a target sound. *Source:* Public domain, http://en.wikipedia.org/wiki/File:Audio_Mask_Graph.png.

intensity difference to infer the source of the sound. From Figure 9.22, it can be seen that to reach the opposite ear, much of the sound travels through the head. The head transmits low-frequency sounds well but attenuates higher-frequency sounds, and this attenuation increases with frequency. In the range of 3–5 kHz, which encompasses speech, the head causes about a 6 dB attenuation. Roughly speaking, below about 600 Hz the auditory system primarily uses the interaural time difference, whereas above 1600 Hz it relies primarily on intensity differences.

Auditory-Visual Cross-Modal Interactions

Both visual and auditory information are telling us something about the world, what is happening and when it happens. At some point, then, the information coming from the eyes and ears must be integrated, or at least brought into correspondence, to give us a clear picture of events (Driver & Spence, 2000). This combining of auditory and visual inputs occurs quite early in the brain. Information from the magnocellular (transient) visual channels combines with auditory input in a midbrain structure called the superior colliculus. The superior colliculus plays an important role in guiding our attention and eye movements. Not surprisingly, then, there are interactions between visual and auditory inputs that affect where we perceive events coming from and when those events happen.

With respect to spatial location, the visual system is superior to the auditory system in its ability to precisely locate objects in space. The retina and early visual cortex are in fact organized in terms of the spatial position of the activation. As we have just seen, the auditory system uses time and intensity differences to compute location, which are

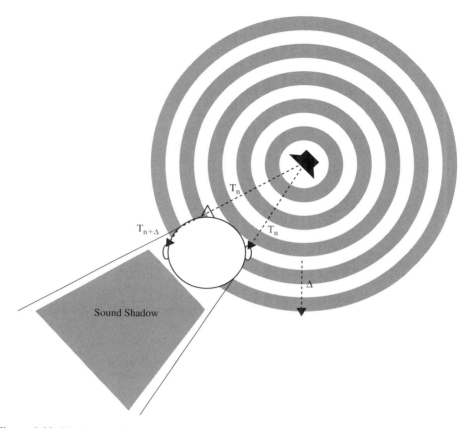

Figure 9.22 The interaural time difference. The sound arrives at the observer's right ear at T_n, at the left ear at T_{n+D}. In this case $D = 2l$. The head also attenuates the sound, especially at high frequencies, creating a sound shadow.

inherently more error prone. Thus, when the visual system integrates auditory and visual input as to the location of a sound, it relies more heavily on the visual input. The effect of this is to allow us to easily attribute the ventriloquist's voice to the dummy. The dummy's mouth is not even making the subtle alterations of lips that would correspond to what is being said. It is just that the good ventriloquist makes sure that his or her lips are making only tiny movements compared to the dummy. You can easily see that even if you are sitting in the front row of a theater, the dummy and ventriloquist are only a few inches apart. The ITD for speech coming from the dummy would not be detectably different from that for the ventriloquist's speech. Hence, our perceptual system attributes the sound to the object whose visually observed behavior corresponds most closely to the input. *Visual dominance* is often used to describe the preference given the visual over the auditory input in deciding the location of events. As you might suspect, visual dominance is greatest when the locations of two objects are close and diminishes as the distance is increased (Bermant & Welch, 1976; Jack & Thurlow, 1973; Witkin, Wapner, & Leventhal, 1952). As a general rule, perceptual judgments can be biased when the error is large relative to the actual mean difference. In signal detection terms (see earlier discussion), the visual input can be seen to bias auditory perception of localization (see Driver & Spence, 2000), which would alter the perception of closely spaced events without causing distant events to appear to come from the same location. The authors have not located any research showing whether a competing visual input would bias the location judgment of a distant auditory signal.

In a similar vein, it should be noted that pitch is naturally perceived in terms of "high" and "low." Elevation is also computed by the time and intensity differences used to compute the spatial position of an auditory signal, providing independent information as to a sound's elevation with reference to our own position in the world. Thus, there is a potential conflict in the interpretation of auditory sounds as signifying high and low. However, the experience of elevation due to pitch differs from that due to the source of the sound. To our knowledge, there is no evidence that visual dominance in spatial resolution of sounds extends to the perception of a pitch's tone, despite the apparent spatial character of the sound.

Visual dominance can extend to the discrimination of sounds as well as their relative locations. We are all familiar with the ability of some deaf people to read lips. It turns out that to some degree, we all read lips. That is, we are much better at understanding speech when we can see the speaker's lips than when we have only the auditory input. Sumby and Pollack (1954) tested the ability to discriminate spoken words in noise. They observed that under all noise conditions, speech intelligibility improved when listeners could see the speaker's lips. McGurk and MacDonald (1976; see also Massaro, 1987) had children and adults listen to a stream of consonant-vowel syllables (e.g., da, ta, ga, ka) at the same time they watched a speaker mouth either the same or a different syllable. Without the visual input, identification of the syllables was nearly perfect. However, when the visual input was incongruent with the auditory input, listeners made numerous errors. The visual input was biasing the perception of even clear speech.

Although the visual system dominates when resolving the spatial location of competing inputs, the auditory system appears to dominate in judgments of relative timing. The auditory system is better at judging the relative order of presentation for two tones presented close together in time (5–80 msec) than is the visual system in judging the relative onset of two light sources (Kanabus, Szelag, Rojek, & Poppel, 2002). It has long been known that intervals of less than 2 seconds are more accurately estimated when the inputs are auditory than when they are visual (e.g., Goodfellow, 1934; Grondin & Rousseau, 1991). People are also better at reproducing auditory than visual rhythmic patterns (Gault & Goodfellow, 1938), and more accurate at tapping a finger in synchrony (Bartlett & Bartlett, 1959). More direct evidence for the dominance of audition over vision comes from studies showing that an observer's judgment of the duration of a light is influenced by the duration of a simultaneously presented tone (Goldstone, Boardman, & Lhamon, 1959; Walker & Scott, 1981). A similar auditory bias is found when observers tap out temporal intervals (Repp & Penel, 2002).

Sensory Processing Summary

We have discussed the limits of auditory perception and noted characteristics of auditory and visual interaction. The limits on vision and audition provide the first level of filtering that occurs throughout information processing. By *filtering* we refer to a reduction in the amount of information transmitted. The contrast thresholds and wavelength sensitivity functions in vision, along with the thresholds for auditory perception, indicate that much is happening that our sensory systems do not transmit to us. We are reminded of this whenever we use a dog whistle, which emits tones at frequencies well above those perceptible by the human auditory system but are powerful signals for dogs. We are also aware that dogs, and indeed most animals, have a vastly superior sense of smell. Sharks have a set of electro-mechanical receptors that alert them to nearby prey. Homing pigeons have been hypothesized to have magnetic receptors in the brain that allow them to orient accurately in space. Thus, our sensory systems do not provide a complete picture of the world. However, the information loss due to sensory processing pales in comparison to that due to attention.

ATTENTION

It is hard to overstate the role of attention in determining our perception of the world. Our awareness of our environment is constituted primarily of those things to which we are attending or have attended. The capacity, control, and allocation of attention all figure prominently in what and how much of our sensory input we are able to use. Attention appears to be the primary limiting factor in determining what gets through sensory processing and continues on to central processing. Nevertheless, the extent of and our capability for processing of unattended items are perennial and fascinating subjects of research, as well as pertinent design considerations.

Selective Attention

In the Anstis Array of Figure 9.10, all the letters are equally perceptible, regardless of retinal eccentricity. The use of the cortical magnification function has overcome the sensory limits imposed by the differences in sensitivity of the fovea and periphery of the retina. But, if you remain tightly fixated on the center dot you will notice that you cannot simultaneously identify all the letters. Instead, keeping your eyes tightly fixated, you will note that if you attend to one letter, the attended letter, and perhaps one or two others, can be identified, but no more. When you shift attention to a different letter (keeping the eyes fixated), that letter becomes clear. In short, it is necessary to shift attention in turn to the letters of the display to identify them. This cannot be a sensory limitation, but must arise from some other part of the information-processing system.

In Figure 8.1, we designated the limiting factor as *selective attention*, placing it between the output of sensory processing and central processing. The location of attention in Figure 8.1 reflects the fact that our sensory systems transmit much more information per unit time than our cognitive systems can process. Selective attention plays the crucial role of allowing us to choose which information the cognitive processor will busy itself with, and, hence, which events will guide our selection of actions. How do we know this? The Anstis Array gives some indication of how perceptual information can be filtered (we use this term synonymously with *selected*). However, there are more revealing demonstrations of this.

The Cocktail Party Phenomenon and Echoic Memory

One early demonstration of an excess of sensory information, and the limited capacity of attention, is what has been called the "cocktail party phenomenon" (Cherry, 1953; Moray, 1959). We are all familiar with the experience of being at a gathering where several nearby groups are engaged in separate conversations. If we want, we can tune into any one of them and follow the speakers as they talk. However, we cannot simultaneously tune to two or more. We can swap from one to another, but cannot get all the various conversational threads at once. This cannot be due to limitations on our ability to hear, as we can stay in the same place and just tune from one to the other. Careful experimentation has in large part confirmed these observations.

In dichotic listening experiments, different speech sounds (words or syllables) are input to each ear simultaneously. If two conversations are presented, one to each ear, listeners can follow one or the other, but they show very substantial deficits in responding to questions about the conversations when trying to monitor both, or about the unattended conversation. If separate words or syllables are presented to each ear simultaneously, listeners can monitor one ear successfully, but cannot report the items presented to the other ear, and again show substantial deficits if they try to monitor both (Cherry, 1953). It is important to note that while people can only identify the words and syllables, or follow conversations, for the ear to which they attend, they are nonetheless aware that there is input on those other channels (Treisman, 1964; Treisman & Gelade, 1980), and they can report some features of what is going to the unattended ear. For example, listeners can report whether the voice in the other ear was male or female (Cherry, 1953). This is an important finding. It means even when not attended to, information is there, and it does get through.

It also means that the process of attending is not one simply of restricting the information that the sensory system can handle. That is, the limitation is not on the sensory system, but on or in some later process. People also have no trouble following a conversation that moves from one ear to the other (Treisman, 1964). Again, this means that the filtering of the messages must be happening after sensory processing, based on the content. Otherwise, when the message shifted to the other ear, it would not be heard. The conclusion from these studies is that the auditory system is providing more information than is possible for our cognitive systems to process.

The ability to follow a conversation that flows from one ear to another raises the question of how long the raw auditory information lasts. That is, if participants are monitoring one ear and switch to follow the message stream on the other ear, then the auditory information must last at least long enough to switch ears and pick up the message where it left off. It turns out that experiments generally support the notion of a sensory buffer that holds information for a short time before being overwritten by new input. In audition, this is called *echoic memory*, and is presumed to last on the order of a second or two (Darwin, Turvey, & Crowder, 1972).

As a sensory buffer, echoic memory is presumed to hold information in a state akin to a raw auditory signal, unprocessed with respect to content. One familiar demonstration of echoic memory comes from situations in daily life where you may be attending to one source (the television perhaps) at the same time someone asks you a question. We have just discussed how it is not possible to simultaneously monitor two conversations. Yet, often it happens that if you stop monitoring the television quickly enough, you will suddenly "hear" the question that was asked. Echoic memory has kept the auditory signal around long enough for it to be retrieved and comprehended.

Iconic Memory in Vision

A similar conclusion emerges from studies of visual perception. Sperling conducted seminal experiments in which he presented a matrix consisting of rows and columns filled with letters (Sperling, 1960). The letters were projected onto a screen using a tachistoscope, a device that allows very precise timing of visual stimuli. Matrices were either 3 x 3 or 3 x 4 and were presented very briefly, for approximately 50 milliseconds. In the whole-report condition, people were simply asked to recall the position and identity of as many letters as they could. Typical recall accuracy was between 3 and 5 items, or approximately 35 percent. In the partial-report condition, an auditory tone was presented at varying times after the matrix was erased. The pitch of the tone (high, medium, low) indicated which row (first, second, or third, respectively) the subject was to report. Because the target row was not known beforehand, the subject's response had to be based on a representation of the entire matrix.

The cue could be seen as an instruction to sample a portion of the entire contents. If the whole-report limit of 4–5 reflects the total information available from perception, then it should also be the results of totalling over all the individual samples. This was not the case. When the cue occurred just after the matrix was erased, participants were able to recall almost all the letters of any given row, overall approximately 75 percent of the entire display. The limitation in recalling visual information was not due to a limit on perception, but to a limit on later processes that selected items from a visual representation. This representation reflects a visual sensory buffer, called *iconic memory*, which holds the results of visual processing in an unprocessed, image-like form, much like echoic memory in audition retains an auditory image.

A key difference between the two is that items in iconic memory decay much faster than items in echoic memory. This makes sense when you consider that speech, music, and auditory events in general unfold over time, making it advantageous to have a longer-lasting sensory buffer. Moreover, speech processing relies heavily on more than just the instantaneous analysis of the sound. It often incorporates prior and subsequent context, further emphasizing the utility of a buffer that retains sounds for some length of time. Estimates of the duration of an echoic memory store range from 250–2000 msec.

The duration of iconic memory depends on a number of very specific lighting and presentation conditions, but generally the ability to report letters decreases rapidly over the first 250 msec. Aside from the specialization for spatial over temporal information, this short duration of iconic memory makes sense considering the massive amount of information in the visual image, which would be costly to maintain for long periods of time.

Resource and Data Limits

In our earlier mention of attention, we emphasized its importance by claiming that our awareness of the world is constituted primarily of those things to which we are attending or have attended. This is not to say that only attended information is processed. After all, when driving a car, our attention may be tuned to the road, the radio, or the passenger with whom we are talking. At the same time, we might notice a slight irregularity in the road, the sound of the engine, a smell, or subtle changes in the response of the car to inputs. It is clear, then, that some information is getting in that is not being actively attended.

To say that attention determines our awareness raises the natural question of whether subliminal stimuli, of which we show no awareness, influence our behavior. Research on this topic has fascinated psychologists. It has led to the practical suggestion that subliminal ads may induce us to buy more popcorn at theaters, or increase our desire for a specific brand of soft drink, all of which and more have been much discussed in the popular media. The jury is still out on the question of whether subliminal ads do actually bias us to feel hungry or thirsty or purchase the desired products. Nonetheless, many published reports in peer-reviewed scientific journals show short-lived (transient) effects of stimuli presented so briefly that we cannot say for certain that we saw anything. In particular, evidence shows that we can be "primed" to respond to certain words or pictures by preceding them with briefly presented words whose identity participants cannot report, or whose presence they cannot reliably detect (e.g., Draine & Greenwald, 1998).

The most convincing demonstrations of the effect of subliminal stimuli come from studies of what is called *masked priming*. In a masked priming study, a rapid series of visual events is presented to the observer. The observer is asked to determine whether a letter string in capital letters is a word (e.g., FROG) or a non-word (e.g., FRUG, GFRU). A trial begins with a pre-mask typically consisting of punctuation marks (e.g., %&#$) at each of the letter locations. Next, a prime word in lowercase is presented which is either related or not related to the following word (e.g., frog, cram). The prime is presented very briefly, from 10–50 msec depending on the nature of the task. Participants usually cannot reliably report whether or not the prime has occurred. Despite this, response time to indicate whether a target is a word is faster when preceded by the same word in lowercase, or by a related word (Forster & Davis, 1984; Neely, 1991). Similar studies have been done using briefly masked pictures (Bar & Biederman, 1998) and with words and pictures (Ferrand, Grainger, & Segui, 1994; Grainger & Dell'Acqua, 1999; Wagner, Desmond, Demb, Glover, & Gabrieli, 1997).

In considering what these results mean, it is important to note that in the case of subliminal stimuli, the presentation is too brief to fully encode the stimulus. The masks that immediately follow their brief presentation either stop or interfere with the cognitive processing of the prime. Thus, processing is *data limited*. The presentation has been too brief to allow full processing. What the facilitation of response times for matching primes shows is that even the brief presentation was sufficient to activate some semantic information, but not to make the person fully aware of the stimulus. No matter how much people try, they cannot fully overcome data limitations.

The nature of attentional limits is fundamentally different from the data limitation seen in masked priming, or even the data limits of sensory processing. Selective attention

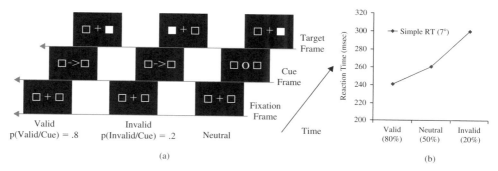

Figure 9.23 Spatial attention. A cue is presented pointing left or right to indicate the probable location of the target. The arrow cue is 80 percent Valid, 20 percent Invalid. The task is simply to press a key whenever either box is illuminated. Graph (b) compared reaction times for Valid and Invalid cues with those of a Neutral cue. Compared to a Neutral cue, Valid cues facilitate reaction time, Invalid cues inhibit reaction time.

is a resource that can be allocated to one event, object, or location. It represents a choice that the information-processing system has made as to which of the many sensory events should be given access to cognition.

Isn't it the case, by definition, that a stimulus you are not aware of is *unattended*, even if *data limited*? The answer, surprisingly, is "Not necessarily." A stimulus, such as a letter presented at one location on a computer monitor, is unattended when attention is directed toward or occupied with another object, such as a different letter at a different location on the screen (as in our Anstis Array example). Broadly speaking, in vision, a stimulus will be attended if either it, or its location, is attended. This can be demonstrated with the very simple experiment shown in Figure 9.23, a variant of that first performed by Posner and replicated many times since (Folk, Remington, & Johnston, 1992; Posner, Nissen, & Ogden, 1978; Posner, 1980; Posner, Snyder, & Davidson, 1980; Shulman, Remington, & McLean, 1979). In the simplest case, a trial consists of three frames presented in a fixed order: a *Fixation Frame* followed by a *Cue Frame* followed by a *Target Frame*, as can be seen in diagram (a) of the figure for each of the three conditions. The task for the subject is simply to press a single key (e.g., the space bar) when the interior of one of the boxes in the Target (third) Frame is illuminated, regardless of which box is lit. The Fixation (first) Frame consists of the two possible target locations (boxes) flanking a central cross, as shown in the bottom frame for each condition. Participants are instructed to maintain eye fixation on the cross throughout the trial. There are two possible cues in the Cue Frame, as shown in the middle frame for each of the three conditions: either an arrow or an O. The arrow, shown in the middle frame for the valid and invalid conditions, is an informative cue. On about 80 percent of the arrow cue trials, the arrow correctly indicates the box that will be illuminated in the Target Frame. These are called Valid Trials (or Valid cues) because the arrow correctly indicates the location of the illuminated box; this is illustrated in the leftmost panel of diagram (a) in Figure 9.23. On 20 percent of the arrow cue trials, the cued box (the one the arrow points to) will not be the one that is illuminated, as shown in the middle panel of diagram (a). These are called Invalid Trials. The Neutral cue is the "O," as shown in the middle frame of the rightmost panel of diagram (a). It is a Neutral cue because it conveys no information about the location of the target; both boxes are equally likely to be illuminated.

The data from a typical experiment of this type (Posner et al., 1978) are plotted in the graph (b) of Figure 9.23 of the event sequences. Response time is slowest on the 20 percent of cued trials that are *invalid*, fastest on the 80 percent that are *valid*, and intermediate on the *neutral* trials, where neither location is favored. These results, along with many other such demonstrations, are interpreted as arising from how attention is allocated. On cued trials, it is assumed that participants voluntarily attend to the cued location because the cue predicts the location of the target. Note that they do not move their eyes there, but adjust their processing to favor the cued location. This adjustment of processing is presumed to reflect mechanisms of visual attention. The response time on invalid trials is slowed because attention is allocated to the other location. The cueing experiment shown in Figure 9.23 is a particularly striking example of the effect of attention. The task is the simplest example of reaction time that could be imagined. Yet, attention, guided by expectations, alters the way in which information from the two locations is processed. The allocation of attention has been shown to affect the rate of processing (Carrasco & McElree, 2001), and there is evidence that more complex objects, such as words (Folk et al., 1992; Johnston, McCann, & Remington, 1995) cannot be processed without first being attended. Thus, the failure to fully encode a stimulus can arise not only from deficits in the amount of stimulus information available (i.e., data-limited processing), but also from resource limitations inherent in the allocation of attention. The allocation of attention is an example of *resource-limited* processing (Norman & Bobrow, 1975).

The distinction between data-limited and resource-limited processing has implications for the kinds of remedies that will prove effective in problem situations. When the processing of a stimulus is data limited, an effective remedy is often an augmentation of the display that reduces noise or highlights the right features. For example, sonar systems on submarines routinely amplify and attenuate sounds to present a clearer picture to the operator. People cannot overcome these kinds of data limitations by trying harder or by paying more attention.

However, data limitations can also arise from lack of knowledge. For example, if you only know the Morse code for six letters, you will not be able to effectively communicate in Morse code no matter how you try. Similarly, Navy sonar operators must train for many months to be able to distinguish the sounds made by fish, reefs, and other ships, and to accurately identify the sounds. Performance on data-limited tasks of this sort can be improved to some degree by training. When performance is affected by resource limitations, they are best dealt with by relieving the workload or attention demands on the operator. Resources are a zero-sum game where attention to one display means not attending to all the others. For this reason, training is often directed at improving the operator's control of attention, so that the allocation of attentional resources is appropriate to the situation. It is important to note, however, that in most applied situations, task performance is a function of both stimulus and resource factors. That is, to say that a task is resource limited does not necessarily imply that data limits have been reached, and a task that is data limited does not necessarily imply that resource limitations have been reached.

The Capacity of Attention

Earlier we noted that failing to attend to stimuli could lead to a failure to fully encode the stimulus. This leads to two natural questions. The first is: Just how limited is attention? That is, can only one item be attended at a time? For many practical purposes, the assumption that only one object can be attended at any given time is a good general rule. This certainly applies to identifying faces (Bindemann, Burton, & Jenkins, 2005; Boutet & Chaudhuri, 2001; Jenkins, Lavie, & Driver, 2003; Palermo & Rhodes, 2003), reading instrument gauges (Carbonell, 1966; Carbonell, Ward, & Senders, 1968; Fitts, Jones, & Milton, 1950; Senders, 1964), listening to music or conversations (Allport, Antonis, & Reynolds, 1972; Cherry, 1953), and watching video (Neisser & Becklen, 1975; Simons & Chabris, 1999).

There do seem to be specific situations, however, in which this general rule does not apply, or at least its application is more complicated. For example, research suggests that when objects can be distinguished from one another on the basis of simple perceptual features such as orientation, size, color, and the like, then multiple objects can be processed in parallel (e.g., Treisman & Gelade, 1980; see following subsection on "Visual Search"). Another factor that influences whether multiple objects can be attended in parallel is *perceptual load*, which roughly corresponds to how much perceptual processing is required to support the appropriate behavioral response. A number of studies have shown that when perceptual load is low, observers appear able to attend to multiple objects at the same time (e.g., Johnson, McGrath, & McNeil, 2002; Lavie & Tsal, 1994). For example, Lavie and Tsal (1994) found that when participants were required to identify a single letter at fixation, the identity of irrelevant letters in the periphery influenced response times, suggesting that these additional letters had also been attended. In contrast, when the letter at fixation was embedded among several other letters, thus requiring more perceptual processing to "find" the target, the identity of the peripheral letters no longer influenced response times.

The Processing of Unattended Items

The second question is: What information can be extracted from unattended stimuli and what cannot? What do we know about unattended stimuli? If it is not possible to attend to more than one object, is it still possible to derive useful information from unattended objects? Several studies have attempted to determine just how much processing gets done on unattended stimuli (Braun & Sagi, 1990; Cherry, 1953; McCann, Folk, & Johnston, 1992; Sagi & Julesz, 1985). The general conclusion from these studies is that surprisingly little information is available from stimuli that are not attended. Consider a study by Braun and Sagi (1990). Observers were presented with homogeneous textures made up of diagonal lines, and were required to focus attention on a difficult task at the center of the texture. When single horizontal and vertical lines sometimes appeared in the unattended regions of the texture, observers were able to detect the presence of these "singletons," but were unable to report their orientation. Thus, the registration of featural discontinuities (borders, edges, etc.) appears to be possible for unattended stimuli, but the derivation of the identity of those features seems to require attention. Similarly, processing the meaning of words has been shown to depend on the allocation of attention, for both visual presentations (McCann, Folk, & Johnston, 1992) and auditory presentations (Cherry, 1953).

How can it be that so little about unattended stimuli is processed when our intuition tells us otherwise? When we open our eyes, we seem aware of everything in the scene, not just the objects to which we are currently attending. Surprisingly, it is relatively easy to show that this intuition is incorrect. Imagine viewing a picture that flickers on and off once every second. It turns out that large changes can be made to the scene across presentations without observers noticing (O'Regan, Rensink, & Clark, 1999). This effect, known as *change blindness*, can be mitigated if the observer's attention is first drawn to the location of the change (Rensink, O'Regan, & Clark, 1997). What this reveals is that very little about an object in a scene is encoded in memory unless the object is attended.

An even more dramatic example of the limits on the processing of unattended information comes from a related phenomenon known as *inattentional blindness* (Mack & Rock, 1998; Simons & Chabris, 1999). In the classic study (Simons & Chabris, 1999), observers watched a short video of two groups of students, one group in white shirts and one in black shirts, each passing a ball among themselves as they moved around the room. The task was to attend to one of the teams (either the white shirts or the black shirts), and count the number of times the ball changed hands for that team. Halfway through the video, an actor in a black gorilla suit walked across the screen, turned to face the camera, beat his chest, and then walked off screen. Nearly all of the observers monitoring the team in black shirts noticed the gorilla, but only about half of those monitoring the team in white shirts noticed. In other words, selectively attending to people in the white shirts rendered the observer "blind" to the black gorilla. This provides further evidence that the processing of unattended information is severely limited, and demonstrates the importance of selective attention in determining our perception of the world.

A tragic example of the implications of inattentional blindness is the crash of an Eastern Airlines L-1011 in the Florida Everglades in 1972. On their nighttime approach to the Miami airport, the pilots noticed that a landing gear indicator was not lit and proceeded to attend to this issue until it was discovered that the lightbulb was simply burned out. With their attention focused on the gear-indicator issue, the pilots failed to notice critical changes in the altimeter (which displayed a gradual but constant descent resulting from a mistake in setting the autopilot) as well as an auditory altitude warning. By the time they realized that the aircraft had descended, it was too late to avoid an instance of "controlled flight into terrain" (Wiener, 1977).

Controlling Attention

Given that attentional capacity is limited and that the typical information content of the environment exceeds this capacity, the perceptual-cognitive system must resort to "sampling" the environment, such that, at any given point in time, attentional resources are allocated to only a subset of the available information. In the case of the visual environment, this sampling behavior typically takes one of two forms: *visual search* and *visual monitoring*.

Visual Search

In a visual search situation, the observer is typically looking for a "target" object that is important to current behavioral goals, among other "distractor" objects that are not relevant to current goals. For example, you may need to find a friend in a crowd at the train

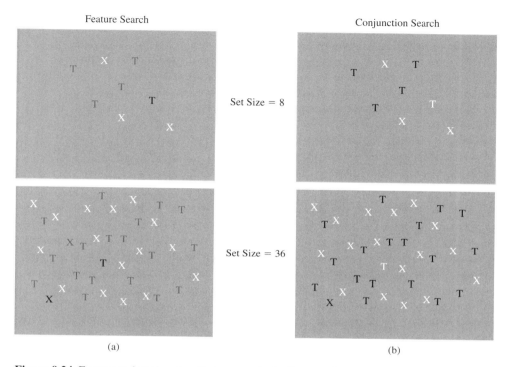

Figure 9.24 Feature and conjunction feature search. In diagram (a), targets are a black X or black T. Search is among white Xs and gray Ts. Targets are easy to find regardless of distractors, and set size has little effect. In diagram (b), targets are either a white T or a black X. Search is among black Ts and white Xs, so the target is the conjunction of color and shape. As the set size gets larger, search becomes increasingly difficult. *Source:* Treisman & Gelade, 1980; used with permission.

station, or an air traffic controller may need to find a particular aircraft on a cluttered radar display. A number of factors can influence the efficiency of visual search. For example, search is less efficient when it is difficult to discriminate targets from distractors (Geisler & Chou, 1995; Nagy & Sanchez, 1992) and when the observer must search for more than one target at a time (Craig, 1991).

One key factor that influences the efficiency with which an observer is able to find a target among distractors is target complexity. Target complexity is determined by the number of features that define the target, and the degree to which those features overlap with the features of the distractors. When a target is defined by a single feature, such as a color or shape, and appears among distractors of a different color and/or shape, search is fast and efficient. Diagram (a) of Figure 9.24 provides an example of a feature search condition. As is evident from the figure, the targets seem to "pop out" from the distractors regardless of how many distractors are present. This *popout effect* is well documented in the literature, and is consistent with the notion that simple feature discontinuities are registered without the need to allocate attention, allowing search of the display elements to

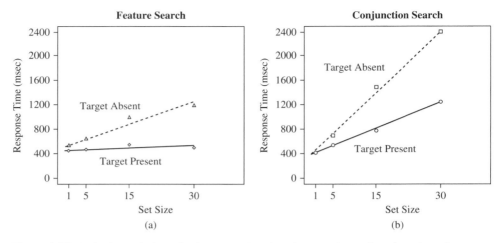

Figure 9.25 Typical search times for feature and conjunction search as a function of set size. Lines represent best fitting linear functions. Slope of "Target Absent" trials in conjunction search is twice that of "Target Present" trials, consistent with an item-by-item search that terminates when the target is found. *Source:* Data from Treisman & Gelade (1980); used with permission.

proceed in parallel (Treisman & Gelade, 1980). The diagram (a) of Figure 9.25 displays representative data from a feature search condition. Note that when the target is present, response times remain relatively constant as a function of set size (i.e., the number of items in the displays). In contrast, when a target is defined by a particular combination or "conjunction" of features, and the distractors each share one of those features, search efficiency is strongly influenced by the number of distractors. Diagram (b) of Figure 9.24 provides an example of a conjunction search condition, and graph (b) of Figure 9.25 shows representative data from a conjunction search. Under these condition, response time increases linearly with set size, and the slope of the set size-response time function for "present" trials is about one-half the slope of that obtained for absent trials. The pattern suggests that attention is serially allocated to the display elements until the particular combination of features defining the target is found, at which point a response is made. These kinds of results suggest that attention is required to identify objects in the environment, where "identification" consists of encoding the combination of features unique to a given object (Treisman & Gelade, 1980).

When serial allocation of attention to display objects is required, what determines the order in which the objects are sampled? In other words, what controls the allocation of attention? A number of computational models of serial search order have been proposed (e.g., Bundesen, 1990; Cave & Wolfe, 1990; Itti & Koch, 2000). Although these models differ in detail, they are all based on the notion that an initial, preattentive, "bottom-up" analysis of the visual field produces activity in a set of topographical feature maps across various dimensions, such as color, shape, orientation, and so on. Activity from these maps is then weighted by "top-down" biases associated with task goals (for example, looking for red circles would result in up-weighting of the activity in color and shape maps), and fed into a master "activation map" that combines the activity across dimensions for

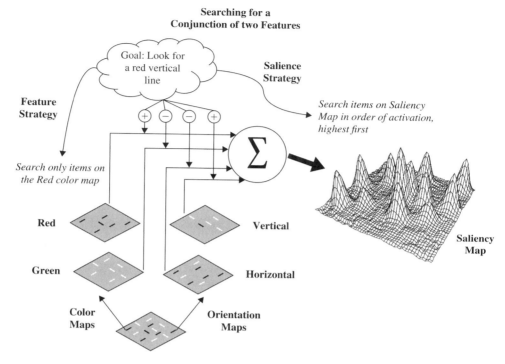

Figure 9.26 A model of attention allocation in visual search. The features of stimuli are coded in separate feature maps. Activity at each stimulus location in each feature map is weighted according to task relevance and is then combined to form an activation map. Attention can be allocated to locations and objects in order of these activation values, or by selecting a specific feature map.

each display location. Search strategies then determine how attention will be allocated. A Feature Strategy can be used, in which case attention is directed at the single feature map corresponding to the property being searched for and allocated to the location with the highest activation value. Alternatively, a Salience Strategy can be used in which attention is allocated to locations or objects in order of the magnitude of activity in the Salience Map (Cave & Wolfe, 1990). This type of model is illustrated in Figure 9.26.

There are, however, situations in which attention allocation in visual search seems to proceed against the intentions/goals of the observer. For example, we've all had the experience of having our attention "drawn" to a salient, unexpected event such as the flashing lights of a police car on the side of the road. This phenomenon is referred to as *attentional capture*. Yantis and Jonides (1984) demonstrated the ability of one particular stimulus property—abrupt onset—to produce attentional capture in visual search. Figure 9.27 illustrates the methodology and data. Participants searched for a target letter among a variable number of nontarget letters. One letter in each display appeared abruptly, whereas the other letters were revealed gradually. Critically, across trials the target was no more likely to appear as the abrupt-onset letter than one of the nontarget letters, so there was no

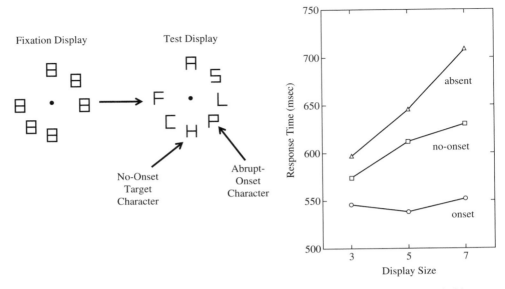

Figure 9.27 Capture by abrupt-onset characters. The fixation display consisted of placeholders that indicated where characters would appear. In addition, an abrupt-onset character was presented at a location not indicated in the fixation display. The abrupt onset could be either a target or a distractor. The right panel shows that when the abrupt onset was the target, set size had no effect on search times, consistent with the abrupt onset having captured attention. *Source:* Method and data from Yantis & Jonides (1984).

incentive to preferentially allocate attention to the onset letter. Nonetheless, when the target was abruptly onset, response times did not vary as the number of distrators increased, suggesting that attention was always first drawn to the location of the onset. Theeuwes (1992) found that attentional capture is not limited to abrupt onsets. Participants searched for a diamond among circles and then responded to the identity of a character inside the diamond. On critical trials, one of the nontarget circles was a different color from the rest of the display elements. The presence of this color "singleton" distractor produced a significant cost in response time, suggesting that it captured attention.

Subsequent studies, however, have shown that attentional capture can be modulated by the observer's top-down set. Figure 9.28 illustrates the conditions and data from a modified spatial cuing task developed by Folk, Remington, and Johnston (1992; see also Folk & Remington, 1998). Participants searched for a target defined either as an abrupt onset or a color singleton (in separate blocks of trials). The targets were preceded by peripheral spatial cues that could also be defined either by abrupt onset or by color. Critically, the location of the cues was uncorrelated with the location of the subsequent target, and thus there was no incentive to voluntarily attend to the cue location. When the defining cue property matched the defining target property (i.e., abrupt-onset cue paired with an abrupt-onset target), a spatial cuing effect was obtained, confirming that the abrupt-onset cue captured attention. However, when the cue was defined by a property different from the target (e.g., an abrupt-onset cue paired with a color target), no cuing effects were

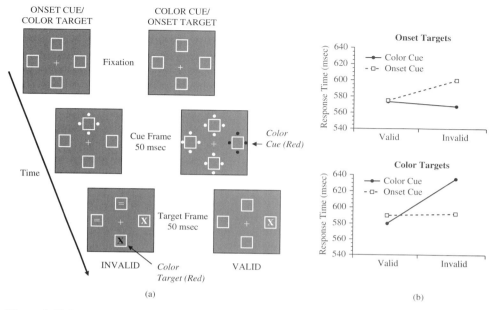

Figure 9.28 Two of the four conditions from Folk, Remington, and Johnston (1992). Each of four groups was presented with a single pairing of cue type (color, onset) and target type (color, onset). Diagram (a) shows the sequence of events for the Onset Cue/Color Target group and the Color Cue/Onset Target group. On any trial, cues could be Valid (same location as target) or Invalid (different location). Diagram (b) shows that cue validity had an effect only when the cues and targets were of the same type: Onset Cue/Onset Target and Color Cue/Color Target. When participants were looking for color, onsets would not capture attention, nor would color capture attention when they were looking for an abrupt-onset target.

obtained. This phenomenon, referred to as *contingent attentional capture*, suggests that the attention allocation system is configurable to respond to feature properties that are relevant to current behavioral goals. Once the system is configured, any stimulus carrying the relevant feature property will capture attention, whereas stimuli whose features do not match the relevant property will not capture attention. In other words, the ability of a stimulus to capture attention appears to be contingent on its match to top-down attentional control settings.

A nice demonstration of the applied significance of contingent attentional capture comes from a study by Most and Astur (2007). Using a driving simulator, participants "drove" through a city by looking for road signs of a particular color (blue or yellow) that indicated where to turn. At critical points during the drive, a motorcycle turned unexpectedly in front of the subject's car. The key manipulation was whether the color of the motorcycle matched the color of the road signs for which the participants were looking. The results showed that the percentage of collisions decreased, from 36 percent when motorcycle and sign color did not match, to 7 percent when the motorcycle and sign colors matched. When the participants were "set" for a particular road sign color, the unexpected motorcycle apparently captured their attention, resulting in fewer collisions.

Visual Monitoring

As discussed earlier, visual sampling is required when the information demands of the environment exceed the available attentional capacity. Visual search represents one form of sampling in which the observer selectively allocates attention to display information until a critical piece of information (i.e., the target) is found and processed. The second form of visual sampling, referred to as *visual monitoring*, is needed in situations where the overall state of a system can vary over time, and the operator must process information from multiple sources or "channels" in order to evaluate the state of the system and to take appropriate actions to keep the system within operational bounds. For example, the operator of the control room in a nuclear power plant must continuously monitor potentially changing information from multiple visual displays in order to assess the overall state of the system and to determine whether and when any corrective actions are needed. This typically involves scanning the available displays with eye and attention movements.

It is possible to compare the actual scanning behavior of an operator in these situations to "optimal" models of scanning, where optimal is defined in terms of maximizing the expected value of sampling (i.e., selecting the relevant displays at the appropriate time) and minimizing costs (e.g., missing a critical event). The two main factors that determine optimal scanning strategy are the frequency and regularity of critical events. Information channels (displays) that carry frequent critical events should be sampled more often, as should channels where critical events appear at unpredictable times.

Laboratory studies have shown that actual scanning behavior (as opposed to optimal scanning models) is influenced by a number of factors (Moray, 1981). One factor is the state of knowledge about the statistical properties of critical events, referred to as the operator's *mental model* of the environment. More experience leads to more accurate mental models, which, in turn, result in changes in scan patterns that improve the detection of critical signals. However, these mental models are also subject to transient biases that can produce maladaptive scanning strategies. For example, trouble detected in one channel can bias the system away from scanning other channels that might also contain critical information—a phenomenon known as *cognitive tunnelling* (Bellenkes, Wickens, & Kramer, 1997). Another factor influencing actual scan patterns is the *perceived effort* required to sample channels. Although optimal models require frequent sampling of channels with high event rates, and less frequent sampling of channels with low event rates, actual scanning behaviour shows that people don't adjust their sampling rate with event frequency as much as they should. Apparently, the subjective effort associated with taking a sample places a limit on how rapidly people are willing to scan across channels (Carbonell, Ward, & Senders, 1968). In a related study, Donk (1994) found that, all things being equal, observers prefer to scan in a horizontal direction rather than a vertical direction, suggesting that vertical switches require more effort. Finally, actual sampling behavior is influenced by limitations on *memory*, in that channels are sampled more often than predicted by optimal models. This oversampling presumably reflects the fact that people tend to forget the information processed from a previous sample, or they forget to sample a channel altogether (Moray, 1981).

Information Foraging Theory

We close this section with one other theoretical approach to modeling the sampling of information in the world. Up to this point, we've discussed the sampling of information channels that are arrayed over space, and whose values can change over time. However, it is possible to think about sampling behavior in a broader context. When writing a term paper, one needs to search for information that is relevant to the topic of the paper, among lots of information that is not relevant to the topic. The environment within which one searches consists of books, articles, magazines, and so forth, which can be found by searching in a library or on the Internet. What determines the nature of these kinds of information searches?

One influential approach to this issue, referred to as *Information Foraging Theory*, likens such searches to the behavior that animals engage in when hunting for food (Miller & Remington, 2004; Pirolli, 2007; Pirolli & Card, 1999). Ecologists have developed models of optimal foraging that are based on the notion that animals try to maximize energy intake over a given period of time. Thus, when predators decide which prey to hunt, they make decisions based on what will provide maximum energy intake with the minimum energy expenditure. Now, one can think of humans as "informavores," in that we search for and "consume" information. When searching for information on the Web, we constantly make decisions about which sites are likely to provide relevant information and whether to stay on the current site or move to a new site. By systematically analyzing search patterns on the Web, along with the "information landscape" in which those searches took place, Pirolli and Card (1999) were able to show that search strategies and decisions follow the same principles that guide animal food foraging strategies. The notion is that such principles result in optimal strategies that maximize information "consumption" and minimize energy expenditure (e.g., minimizing the amount of attention/thought required to find the relevant information).

For example, one important principle is the notion of *information scent*. Just as animals use scent to make decisions about whether to continue hunting in a particular area or move on to a new area, humans use cues to estimate the likelihood of finding relevant information on a particular path. After sampling information on the path, the user compares the actual information gained with the original estimates. When this ratio reaches some critical minimum (i.e., when the scent starts to wane), the user moves to a new path with a stronger scent. A good example of this is work by Miller and Remington (2004) on searching through websites. In deciding whether to search a website, users get a "scent" from the meaning of the website label. Miller and Remington (2004) showed that this scent interacts with the structure of the website to determine how efficiently sites can be searched. If the scent is strong (and correct), it is more efficient to stack websites in a deeper hierarchy. That way, fewer items have to be searched per page. However, when the scent is less strong and the labels are more ambiguous, deep hierarchies lead to excessive backtracking that delays search.

SUMMARY

Information comes to us through our sensory systems. This chapter focused on the visual and auditory systems, including a discussion of limits on each of these systems. The chapter then turned to a discussion of the role of attention in determining what information gets through the sensory processing system and on to central processing.

REFERENCES

Allport, D. A., Antonis, B., & Reynolds, P. (1972). On the division of attention: A disproof of the single channel hypothesis. *Quarterly Journal of Experimental Psychology, 24*(2), 225–235. doi:10.1080/00335557243000102

Andriessen, J. J., & Bouma, H. (1976). Eccentric vision: Adverse interactions between line segments. *Vision Research, 16*(1), 71–78. doi:16/0042-6989(76)90078-X

Anstis, S. (1974). Letter: A chart demonstrating variations in acuity with retinal position. *Vision Research, 14*(7), 589.

Bar, M., & Biederman, I. (1998). Subliminal visual priming. *Psychological Science, 9,* 464–469.

Bartlett, N. R., & Bartlett, S. C. (1959). Synchronization of a motor response with an anticipated sensory event. *Psychological Review, 66*(4), 203–218. doi:10.1037/h0046490

Becker, W., & Jürgens, R. (1979). An analysis of the saccadic system by means of double step stimuli. *Vision Research, 19*(9), 967–983. doi:16/0042-6989(79)90222-0

Bellenkes, A. H., Wickens, C. D., & Kramer, A. F. (1997). Visual scanning and pilot expertise: The role of attentional flexibility and mental model development. *Aviation, Space, and Environmental Medicine, 68*(7), 569–579.

Bermant, R. I., & Welch, R. B. (1976). Effect of degree of separation of visual-auditory stimulus and eye position upon spatial interaction of vision and audition. *Perceptual and Motor Skills, 43*(2), 487–493.

Bindemann, M., Burton, A. M., & Jenkins, R. (2005). Capacity limits for face processing. *Cognition, 98,* 177–197.

Bouma, H. (1970). Interaction effects in parafoveal letter recognition. *Nature, 226,* 177–178.

Boutet, I., & Chaudhuri, A. (2001). Multistability of overlapped face stimuli is dependent upon orientation. *Perception, 30*(6), 743–753. doi:10.1068/p3183

Bowmaker, J. K., & Dartnall, H. J. (1980). Visual pigments of rods and cones in a human retina. *Journal of Physiology, 298*(1), 501.

Braun, J., & Sagi, D. (1990). Vision outside the focus of attention. *Attention, Perception, & Psychophysics, 48*(1), 45–58.

Breitmeyer, B. G. (1978). Metacontrast masking as a function of mask energy. *Bulletin of the Psychonomic Society, 12*(1), 50–52.

Bundesen, C. (1990). A theory of visual-attention. *Psychological Review, 97,* 523–547.

Carbonell, J. R. (1966). A queueing model of many-instrument visual sampling. *IEEE Transactions on Human Factors in Electronics, HFE-7*(4), 157–164. doi:10.1109/THFE.1966.232984

Carbonell, J. R., Ward, J. L., & Senders, J. W. (1968). A queueing model of visual sampling experimental validation. *IEEE Transactions on Man-Machine Systems*, *9*(3), 82–87. doi:10.1109/TMMS.1968.300041

Carrasco, M., & McElree, B. (2001). Covert attention accelerates the rate of visual information processing. *Proceedings of the National Academy of Sciences*, *98*(9), 5363.

Cave, K. R., & Wolfe, J. M. (1990). Modeling the role of parallel processing in visual search. *Cognitive Psychology*, *22*(2), 225–271.

Cherry, E. C. (1953). Some experiments on the recognition of speech, with one and two ears. *Journal of the Acoustical Society of America*, *25*, 975–979.

Chittka, L., & Brockmann, A. (2005). Perception space—The final frontier. *PLoS Biol*, *3*(4), e137. doi:10.1371/journal.pbio.0030137

Craig, A. (1991). Vigilance and monitoring for multiple signals. In D. Damos (Ed.), *Multiple-Task Performance*, (pp. 153–172). Basingstoke, UK: Taylor & Francis.Dahl, J. (2008). File: Snellen chart. Retrieved from http://en.wikipedia.org/wiki/File:Snellen_chart.svg

Dahringer, F., & Gaitzsch, R. C. (n.d.). Luminosity and temperature of the sun. Retrieved from http://eaae-astronomy.org/WG3-SS/WorkShops/SunLuminosity.html

Daniel, P. M., & Whitteridge, D. (1961). The representation of the visual field on the cerebral cortex in monkeys. *Journal of Physiology*, *159*, 203–221.

Darwin, C. J., Turvey, M. T., & Crowder, R. G. (1972). An auditory analogue of the Sperling partial report procedure: Evidence for brief auditory storage. *Cognitive Psychology*, *3*(2), 255–267.

Daxx4434. (2009). File: Audio mask graph. Retrieved July 24, 2011, from http://en.wikipedia.org/wiki/File:Audio_Mask_Graph.png

De Valois, R. L. (1965). Analysis and coding of color vision in the primate visual system. *Cold Spring Harbor Symposium on Quantitative Biology*, *30*, 567–579.

De Valois, R. L., Abramov, I., & Jacobs, G. H. (1966). Analysis of response patterns of LGN cells. *Journal of the Optical Society of America*, *56*, 966–977.

Donk, M. (1994). Human monitoring behavior in a multiple-instrument setting: Independent sampling, sequential sampling or arrangement-dependent sampling. *Acta Psychologica*, *86*(1), 31–55.

Draine, S. C., & Greenwald, A. G. (1998). Replicable unconscious semantic priming. *Journal of Experimental Psychology: General*, *127*(3), 286.

Driver, J., & Spence, C. (2000). Multisensory perception: Beyond modularity and convergence. *Current Biology*, *10*(20), R731–R735. doi:16/S0960-9822(00)00740-5

Fearn, R., Cartel, P., & Wolfe, J. (1999). The perception of pitch by users of cochlear implants: Possible significance for rate and place theories of pitch. *Acoustics Australia*, *27* (2), 41–43.

Ferrand, L., Grainger, J., & Segui, J. (1994). A study of masked form priming in picture and word naming. *Memory & Cognition, 22*(4), 431–441. doi:10.3758/BF03200868

Findlay, J. M., & Harris, L. R. (1984). Small saccades to double-stepped targets moving in two dimensions. *Theoretical and Applied Aspects of Eye Movement Research, Selected/ Edited Proceedings of The Second European Conference on Eye Movements* (Vol. 22, pp. 71–78). North-Holland. Retrieved from www.sciencedirect.com/science/article/pii/ S0166411508618208

Fitts, P., Jones, R. E., & Milton, J. L. (1950). Eye movements of aircraft pilots during instrument-landing approaches. *Aeronautical Engineering Review, 9*(2), 24–29.

Fletcher, H. (1940). Auditory patterns. *Reviews of Modern Physics, 12*(1), 47. doi:10.1103/ RevModPhys.12.47

Flom, M. C., Weymouth, F. W., & Kahneman, D. (1963). Visual resolution and spatial interaction. *Journal of the Optical Society of America, 53*, 1026–1032.

Folk, C. L., & Remington, R. (1998). Selectivity in distraction by irrelevant featural singletons: Evidence for two forms of attentional capture. *Journal of Experimental Psychology—Human Perception and Performance, 24*, 847–858.

Folk, C. L., Remington, R. W., & Johnston, J. C. (1992). Involuntary covert orienting is contingent on attentional control settings. *Journal of Experimental Psychology: Human Perception and Performance, 18*(4), 1030–1044. doi:10.1037/0096-1523.18.4.1030

Forster, K. I., & Davis, C. (1984). Repetition priming and frequency attenuation in lexical access. *Journal of Experimental Psychology: Learning, Memory, and Cognition, 10*(4), 680–698. doi:10.1037/0278-7393.10.4.680

Gaugler, G. (n.d.). Color spectra and light sources. *PhotoWeb Tech*. Retrieved from http:// photoweb.gaugler.com/pw_tech/floures1.html

Gault, R. H., & Goodfellow, L. D. (1938). An empirical comparison of audition, vision, and touch in the discrimination of temporal patterns and ability to reproduce them. *Journal of General Psychology, 18*, 41–47.

Geisler, W. S., & Chou, K. L. (1995). Separation of low-level and high-level factors in complex tasks: Visual search. *Psychological Review, 102*(2), 356.

Goldstone, S., Boardman, W. K., & Lhamon, W. T. (1959). Intersensory comparisons of temporal judgments. *Journal of Experimental Psychology, 57*(4), 243–248. doi:10.1037/ h0040745

Goodfellow, L. D. (1934). An empirical comparison of audition, vision, and touch in the discrimination of short intervals of time. *American Journal of Psychology, 46*(2), 243–258. doi:10.2307/1416558

Grainger, J., & Dell'Acqua, R. (1999). Unconscious semantic priming from pictures. *Cognition, 73*(1), B1–B15.

Grondin, S., & Rousseau, R. (1991). Judging the relative duration of multimodal short empty time intervals. *Perception & Psychophysics, 49*(3), 245–256. doi:10.3758/BF03214309

Hayhoe, M. M., & Rothkopf, C. A. (2011). Vision in the natural world. *Wiley Interdisciplinary Reviews: Cognitive Science, 2*(2), 158–166. doi:10.1002/wcs.113

Hurvich, L. M., & Jameson, D. (1957). An opponent-process theory of color vision. *Psychological Rview, 64*(6p1), 384.

Itti, L., & Koch, C. (2000). A saliency-based search mechanism for overt and covert shifts of visual attention. *Vision Research, 40*, 1489–1506.

Jack, C. E., & Thurlow, W. R. (1973). Effects of degree of visual association and angle of displacement on the "ventriloquism" effect. *Perceptual and Motor Skills, 37*(3), 967–979.

Jenkins, R., Lavie, N., & Driver, J. S. (2003). Ignoring famous faces: Category-specific dilution of distractor interference. *Perception & Psychophysics, 65*, 298–309.

Johnson, D. N., McGrath, A., & McNeil, C. (2002). Cuing interacts with perceptual load in visual search. *Psychological Science, 13*(3), 284.

Johnston, J. C., McCann, R. S., & Remington, R. W. (1995). Chronometric evidence for two types of attention. *Psychological Science, 6*(6), 365–369.

Kanabus, M., Szelag, E., Rojek, E., & Poppel, E. (2002). Temporal order judgement for auditory and visual stimuli. *Acta Neurobiologiae Experimentalis, 62*, 263–270.

Lavie, N., & Tsal, Y. (1994). Perceptual load as a major determinant of the locus of selection in visual-attention. *Perception & Psychophysics, 56*, 183–197.

Lindosland. (2009). Lindos1. *Lindos1*. Retrieved July 24, 2011, from http://en.wikipedia.org/wiki/File:Lindos1.svg

Louie, E. G., Bressler, D. W., & Whitney, D. (2007). Holistic crowding: Selective interference between configural representations of faces in crowded scenes. *Journal of Vision, 7*(2):24, 1–11. doi:10.1167/7.2.24

Mack, A., & Rock, I. (1998). *Inattentional blindness*. Cambridge, MA: MIT Press.

Martelli, M., Majaj, N. J., & Pelli, D. G. (2005). Are faces processed like words? A diagnostic test for recognition by parts. *Journal of Vision, 5*(1), 58–70. doi:10.1167/5.1.6

Massaro, D. W. (1987). *Speech perception by ear and eye: A paradigm for psychological inquiry*. Hillsdale, NJ: Lawrence Erlbaum Associates.

McCann, R. S., Folk, C. L., & Johnston, J. C. (1992). The role of spatial attention in visual word processing. *Journal of Experimental Psychology: Human Perception and Performance, 18*(4), 1015–1029. doi:10.1037/0096-1523.18.4.1015

McGurk, H., & MacDonald, J. (1976). Hearing lips and seeing voices. *Nature, 264*(5588), 746–748. doi:10.1038/264746a0

Miller, C. S., & Remington, R. W. (2004). Modeling information navigation: Implications for information architecture. *Human-Computer Interaction, 19*, 225–271.

Moore, B. C. J. (1983). Suggested formulae for calculating auditory-filter bandwidths and excitation patterns. *Journal of the Acoustical Society of America, 74*(3), 750. doi:10.1121/1.389861

Moray, N. (1959). Attention in dichotic listening: Affective cues and the influence of instructions. *Quarterly Journal of Experimental Psychology, 11*(1), 56–60. doi:10.1080/17470215908416289

Moray, N. (1981). The role of attention in the detection of errors and the diagnosis of failures in man-machine systems. In J. Rasmussen & W. B. Rouse (Eds), *Human detection and diagnosis of system failures* (pp. 185–199). New York, NY: Plenum Press.

Most, S. B., & Astur, R. S. (2007). Feature-based attentional set as a cause of traffic accidents. *Visual Cognition, 15*, 125–132. doi: 10.1080/13506280600959316

Nagy, A. L., & Sanchez, R. R. (1992). Chromaticity and luminance as coding dimensions in visual search. *Human Factors: The Journal of the Human Factors and Ergonomics Society, 34*(5), 601–614.

Neely, J. H. (1991). Semantic priming effects in visual word recognition: A selective review of current findings and theories. In D. Besner & G. W. Humphreys (Eds.), *Basic processes in reading: Visual word recognition* (pp. 264–336). Hillsdale, NJ: Lawrence Erlbaum Associates.

Neisser, U., & Becklen, R. (1975). Selective looking: Attending to visually specified events. *Cognitive Psychology, 7*(4), 480–494. doi:16/0010-0285(75)90019-5

Norman, D. A., & Bobrow, D. G. (1975). On data-limited and resource-limited processes. *Cognitive Psychology, 7*(1), 44–64. doi:16/0010-0285(75)90004-3

Omegatron. (2006). Waveforms: *Triangle wave*. Retrieved July 24, 2011, from http://en.wikipedia.org/wiki/File:Waveforms.svg

O'Regan, J. K., Rensink, R. A., & Clark, J. J. (1999). Change-blindness as a result of "mudsplashes." *Nature, 398*(6722), 34–34.

Palermo, R., & Rhodes, G. (2003). Change detection in the flicker paradigm: Do faces have an advantage? *Visual Cognition, 10*(6), 683–713. doi:10.1080/13506280344000059

Palmer, S. E. (1999). *Vision science: Photons to phenomenology* (1st ed.). Cambridge, MA: MIT Press.

Pirolli, P. (2007). *Information foraging theory: Adaptive interaction with information.* New York, NY: Oxford University Press.

Pirolli, P., & Card, S. (1999). Information foraging. *Psychological Review, 106*, 643–675.

Posner, M. I. (1980). Orienting of attention. *Quarterly Journal of Experimental Psychology, 32*(1), 3–25. doi:10.1080/00335558008248231

Posner, M. I., Nissen, M. J., & Ogden, W. C. (1978). Attended and unattended processing modes: The role of set for spatial location. In H. L. Pick & I. J. Saltzman (Eds.), *Modes of perceiving and processing information* (pp. 137–158). Hillsdale, NJ: Lawrence Erlbaum Associates.

Posner, M. I., Snyder, C. R., & Davidson, B. J. (1980). Attention and the detection of signals. *Journal of Experimental Psychology: General, 109*(2), 160–174. doi:10.1037/0096-3445.109.2.160

Ray, S., Schall, J. D., & Murthy, A. (2004). Programming of double-step saccade sequences: Modulation by cognitive control. *Vision Research, 44*(23), 2707–2718. doi:16/j.visres.2004.05.029

Rayner, K. (1998). Eye movements in reading and information processing: 20 years of research. *Psychological Bulletin, 124,* 372–422.

Rayner, K., & Pollatsek, A. (1987). Eye movements in reading: A tutorial review. In M. Coltheart (Ed.), *Attention and Performance XII: The psychology of reading* (pp. 327–362). Hillsdale, NJ: Lawrence Erlbaum Associates.

Reichle, E. D., Rayner, K., & Pollatsek, A. (1999). Eye movement control in reading: Accounting for initial fixation locations and refixations within the E-Z reader model. *Vision Research, 39*(26), 4403–4411.

Reichle, E. D., Rayner, K., & Pollatsek, A. (2004). The EZ reader model of eye-movement control in reading: Comparisons to other models. *Behavioral and Brain Sciences, 26*(4), 445–476.

Remington, R., Wu, S.-C., & Pashler, H. (2011). What determines saccade timing in sequences of coordinated eye and hand movements? *Psychonomic Bulletin & Review, 18*(3), 538–543. doi:10.3758/s13423-011-0066-0

Rensink, R. A., O'Regan, J. K., & Clark, J. J. (1997). To see or not to see: The need for attention to perceive changes in scenes. *Psychological Science, 8*(5), 368.

Repp, B. H., & Penel, A. (2002). Auditory dominance in temporal processing: New evidence from synchronization with simultaneous visual and auditory sequences. *Journal of Experimental Psychology: Human Perception and Performance, 28*(5), 1085–1099. doi:10.1037/0096-1523.28.5.1085

Robinson, D. W., & Dadson, R. S. (1956). A re-determination of the equal-loudness relations for pure tones. *British Journal of Applied Physics, 7*(5), 166–181. doi:10.1088/0508-3443/7/5/302

Rovamo, J., Virsu, V., & Näsänen, R. (1978). Cortical magnification factor predicts the photopic contrast sensitivity of peripheral vision. Nature, 271, 54–56. doi: 10.1038/271054a0

Sagi, D., & Julesz, B. (1985). Detection versus discrimination of visual orientation. *Perception, 14,* 619–628.

Senders, J. W. (1964). The human operator as a monitor and controller of multidegree of freedom systems. *IEEE Transactions on Human Factors in Electronics, HFE-5*(1), 2–5. doi:10.1109/THFE.1964.231647

Shulman, G. L., Remington, R. W., & McLean, J. P. (1979). Moving attention through visual space. *Journal of Experimental Psychology: Human Perception and Performance, 5*(3), 522–526. doi:10.1037/0096-1523.5.3.522

Simons, D. J., & Chabris, C. F. (1999). Gorillas in our midst: Sustained inattentional blindness for dynamic events. *Perception, 28*(9), 1059–1074. doi:10.1068/p2952

Sperling, G. (1960). The information available in brief visual presentations. *Psychological Monographs: General and Applied, 74*(11, Whole No. 498)), 1–29.

Strasburger, H., Harvey, L. O., & Rentschler, I. (1991). Contrast thresholds for identification of numeric characters in direct and eccentric view. *Perception & Psychophysics, 49*(6), 495–508. doi:10.3758/BF03212183

Sumby, W. H., & Pollack, I. (1954). Visual contribution to speech intelligibility in noise. *Journal of the Acoustical Society of America, 26*(2), 212–215.

Taylor, A. H., & Kerr, G. P. (1941). The distribution of energy in the visible spectrum of daylight. Journal of the Optical Society of America, 31 (1), 3–8. doi:10.1364/JOSA.31.000003.

Theeuwes, J. (1992). Perceptual selectivity for color and form. *Perception & Psychophysics, 51*, 599–606.

Toet, A., & Levi, D. M. (1992). The two-dimensional shape of spatial interaction zones in the parafovea. *Vision Research, 32*(7), 1349–1357. doi:16/0042-6989(92)90227-A

Treisman, A. M. (1964). Verbal cues, language, and meaning in selective attention. *American Journal of Psychology, 77*(2), 206–219. doi:10.2307/1420127

Treisman, A. M., & Gelade, G. (1980). A feature-integration theory of attention. *Cognitive Psychology, 12*(1), 97–136. doi:16/0010-0285(80)90005-5

University of Utah. (n.d.). A drawing of a section through the human eye with a schematic enlargement of the retina. Retrieved from http://webvision.med.utah.edu/imageswv/Sagschem.jpeg

Van Nes, F. L., & Bouman, A. (1967). Spatial modulation transfer in the human eye. *Journal of the Optical Society of America, 57*, 401–406.

Wagner, A. D., Desmond, J. E., Demb, J. B., Glover, G. H., & Gabrieli, J. D. E. (1997). Semantic repetition priming for verbal and pictorial knowledge: A functional MRI study of left inferior prefrontal cortex. *Journal of Cognitive Neuroscience, 9*(6), 714–726. doi:10.1162/jocn.1997.9.6.714

Walker, J. T., & Scott, K. J. (1981). Auditory-visual conflicts in the perceived duration of lights, tones, and gaps. *Journal of Experimental Psychology: Human Perception and Performance, 7*(6), 1327–1339. doi:10.1037/0096-1523.7.6.1327

Wiener, E. L. (1977). Controlled flight into terrain accidents: System-induced errors. *Human Factors: The Journal of the Human Factors and Ergonomics Society*, *19*(2), 171–181.

Witkin, H. A., Wapner, S., & Leventhal, T. (1952). Sound localization with conflicting visual and auditory cues. *Journal of Experimental Psychology*, *43*(1), 58–67. doi:10.1037/h0055889

Wolfe, J. (n.d.). Sound. *PHYSCLIPS: A multi-level, multi-media resource*. Retrieved July 24, 2011, from www.phys.unsw.edu.au/jw/flutes.v.clarinets.html

Yantis, S., & Jonides, J. (1984). Abrupt visual onsets and selective attention: Evidence from visual-search. *Journal of Experimental Psychology—Human Perception and Performance*, *10*, 601–621.

Yarbus, A. (1967). *Eye movements and vision*. New York, NY: Plenum Press.

Zuber, B. L., Stark, L., & Cook, G. (1965). Microsaccades and the velocity-amplitude relationship for saccadic eye movements. *Science*, *150*(3702), 1459–1460. doi:10.1126/science.150.3702.1459

10

Central Processing Limitations on Multitasking

As we described in Chapter 9, capacity limits on selective attention mean that we can process only a small portion of the information available in the world at any given time. In vision, which is our primary modality, this necessitates searching the world using saccades where each fixation provides a snapshot of the information in one small region. In this chapter we show that even when there are sufficient resources to process sensory events from two or more different sources, we are limited in the amount of central processing we can do. Limited-capacity central processing produces deficits that interfere when we attempt to do two or more tasks at once. More specifically, it results in delays when the two tasks have independent goals that require different stimulus-response assignments. Multitasking, or the requirement to do two or more tasks at the same time, is more the norm than the exception in our day-to-day lives. Because of this, limitations on central processing have significant consequences for work structure, productivity, and safety. In this chapter we discuss various theoretical approaches to understanding and modeling limitations on central processing.

BOTTLENECK THEORIES

Theories of information processing assume that the brain can be described as performing a set of computations on input from the environment and that these computations determine what we see, hear, and think, and how we choose to act. In Figure 8.1, the computational entities are the boxes, such as selective attention, and central processing. This is obviously a very high-level description of the system, much like saying a traffic system consists of roads and intersections. More detailed diagrams would show intermediate computational modules for the processing of color, motion, or speech and language.

Bottleneck theories treat the modules as separate, independent computational units. Modules are connected to each other so that the output of one or more serves as the input to others. The pattern of connectivity, in terms of which modules communicate with each other, defines the architecture. In such a modular view, independence is a strong assumption. It means, for example, that in Figure 8.1 the central processor receives the output of the attended sensory buffer, but does not actively determine how that sensory buffer works. Rather, each module performs its own computation on its input and produces an output that is communicated to other modules. Further, each module is considered to be able to do only one thing at a time—or more precisely, able to process only one input at a time. This is referred to as the *single-channel* assumption. The time taken to go from stimulation of a sensory receptor to a goal-directed action would be a function of the times for each of the modules involved.

According to bottleneck theories, limitations on our ability to do two or more tasks concurrently arise when the mental processing of the two tasks make simultaneous demands on a single-channel module. When that occurs, the processing of one task is postponed until the required module has completed its computation on the other task. Postponement due to competing demands causes delays in one or both tasks. A module has no natural size or complexity, but varies considerably across theories. Some modular accounts, such as Minsky's *Society of Mind* (Minsky, 1988), posit thousands of modules interconnected in complex ways to determine our patterns of thought. Each module can perform arbitrarily complex computations, such as generating a plan for solving the Rubik's cube puzzle. Theories that attempt to simulate the neural computations of the brain, referred to as *connectionist* or *neural-net models*, model their computational units after the neuron. Each neural unit makes a simple decision about whether or not to fire. Complexity in connectionist models lies in the aggregate firing patterns of the ensemble of units. In the psychological models most used by human factors and human-system engineers, there are many fewer modules, and the computations themselves are generally not specified. Instead, as we shall see, these models treat complexity by assigning longer completion times for more difficult computations. We illustrate this in more detail by describing two bottleneck models.

Central Bottleneck Theory

One of the oldest and simplest of information-flow models is the *Central Bottleneck Model* first developed by Welford (1952, 1967). It assumes that there are only three independent processors: Perception, Cognition, and Motor (note the resemblance to Figure 8.1). These terms refer to the nature of the processing. Though they are preferred by some (e.g., Card, Moran, & Newell, 1983), more frequently the same three processes are described using functional terms associated with the functions carried out by the three processes: stimulus encoding, central processing (or response selection), and response execution. When a stimulus is attended (selected for processing), *stimulus encoding* takes the sensory information and outputs a stimulus along with all its natural associations. In short, it *encodes* the stimulus. The encoded form of a letter that has been attended might consist of the sense of familiarity, the recognition of a stimulus from the letter category. There is considerable debate over what properties automatically arise from stimulus encoding, but for a familiar letter, its name might also be part of its encoding. When Central Bottleneck Theory is used to account for dual-task performance, stimulus encoding is not treated as a single-channel process. Instead, vision and audition are assumed to consist of many computational modules. Conflicts will occur only if the stimuli are very similar, as this would produce interference during central processing. For example, if two auditory tones were within the same critical band, they could not be encoded separately. Similarly, if two letters were presented at different locations on the screen, they would compete for spatial attention. If, however, the stimuli for two tasks do not conflict in this way, it is assumed that stimulus encoding can proceed in parallel.

The encoded stimulus serves as the input to central processing. The central processor matches the encoded stimulus to the task goals and outputs the selected response. Central processing is a *single-channel processor*, capable of doing central processing for only one task at a time. According to Central Bottleneck Theory, even the simplest of tasks will interfere with each other if they make competing simultaneous demands on the central processor. As discussed in Chapter 7, central processing is chiefly concerned with selecting the action most compatible with the goal. In most laboratory tasks, this action consists of deciding which of a small number of response alternatives to select. For this reason, central processing is often referred to as performing *response selection.*

Once the response has been selected, it is then input to the response-execution module to program and turn into action. In this simple model, processing is strictly serial, so that the time taken is the sum of the times for each stage. Note how readily the Central Bottleneck Theory model could be framed in terms of queuing theory, introduced in Part II. The central processor receives information at a rate determined by stimulus encoding. Its rate of processing and the rate at which encoded stimuli arrive determine the observed delays in performance of a set of tasks.

The Psychological Refractory Period Paradigm

This simple, serial-stage arrangement of Central Bottleneck Theory makes very precise and testable predictions about what happens when you try to do two tasks at the same time. Figure 10.1 shows the sequence of events in a typical study using the *Psychological Refractory Period (PRP)* paradigm (Welford, 1952). In a PRP experiment, the participant is presented with stimuli for two distinct tasks and instructed to make two responses on each trial. One task is designated Task 1, the other Task 2. In the example shown in Figure 10.1, Task 1 requires the participant to say the word "high" or "low" to a tone, depending on its pitch. Task 2 requires the participant to press one of two keys to indicate whether the visual letter string is a word (e.g., "house") or a nonsense string (e.g., "heosu"). The stimulus for Task 2 is presented at varying durations after the presentation of Task 1, referred to as *stimulus onset asynchrony (SOA).* In trials with a short SOA, the visual letter string comes on immediately after the tone, whereas in trials with a long SOA, it comes on after a noticeable delay. At very long SOAs, the tasks can be considered as being done in isolation. Participants make a speeded response to each task as soon as they know the answer, without waiting for the processing of the other task to complete. We measure their response time to each task as a function of the time between the presentations of Task 1 (tone) and Task 2 (letters string).

The manipulation of SOA is done to vary the likelihood of competition for the single-channel central processor. As noted earlier, at a sufficiently long SOA the tasks are effectively done in isolation. The response to Task 1 is made prior to the presentation of the Task 2 stimulus. When the tone and letter string appear close together in time, the mental processing of the two tasks overlaps. The overlap creates the potential for

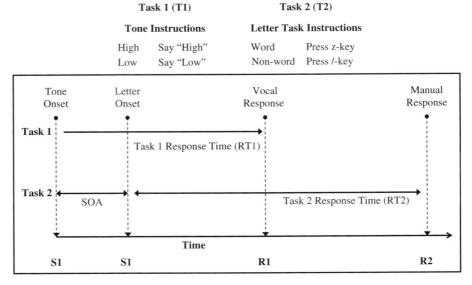

Figure 10.1 The two tasks of Figure 8.2 presented as Task 1 (T1) and Task 2 (T2) in the Psychological Refractory Period paradigm. Onset of the T2 stimulus (S2) occurs at varying times after onset of the T1 stimulus (S1), referred to as the stimulus onset asychrony (SOA). R1 and R2 refer to the responses to S1 and S2, respectively.

conflicting demands on the single-channel central processor. Central Bottleneck Theory makes strong predictions about how long response times to Task 2 should be as a function of this overlap.

The logic of these predictions is shown in graph (a) of Figure 10.2. Each of the three processing stages hypothesized by the Central Bottleneck Theory is represented by a rectangle. In Figure 10.2, the rectangle labeled SE represents the stimulus-encoding stage, RS the response-selection stage, and RE the response-execution stage. Task 1 (the tones task) is presented first, so its processing proceeds through the three stages with no interference from Task 2. Its response time is predicted to be the same at all SOAs.

Task 2 is a different story. If reasonable care is taken to avoid obvious conflicts in SE, such as asking the person to look at something on the left and right at the same time, then SE on both tasks should proceed without interference, since (as we discussed earlier) those stages have high capacity. In the preceding example, encoding the auditory tone should not conflict with reading the visual letter string. When the SOA is short, SE for Task 2 completes, but response selection (RS) is still busy with the RS mapping for Task 1, thus postponing Task 2 RS. The longer the SOA between Task 1 and Task 2, the more time Task 1 has to complete RS processing, so the less time Task 2 will be delayed.

The dashed line in graph (b) shows the predictions of Central Bottleneck Theory for Task 2 response times as a function of SOA. Because the only source of interference is waiting for Task 1 RS to complete, the theory predicts that the slope of the response time function should be −1 up until the SOA at which central processing on T1 is complete when SE on T2 completes. The connected points on the graph are data from an experiment

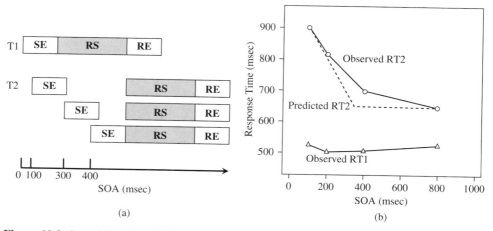

Figure 10.2 Central Bottleneck Theory account of delays in RT2 in the PRP paradigm. At short SOAs, the mental processing of T1 and T2 overlaps, creating competition for the response-selection stage (RS). This competition causes postponement of RS on T2, resulting in elevated RT2. The dotted line in graph (b) plots predicted results from Central Bottleneck Theory based on response times at the shortest and longest SOAs. *Source:* Data for RT2 and RT1 after McCann, Remington, & Van Selst (2000).

very much like the tones and letter strings described earlier (McCann, Remington, & Van Selst, 2000). In that experiment, participants said "high" or "low" to the tone, which was Task 1. In Task 2, they made a speeded response to indicate whether a visual letter string was a word or nonword (NW). Some of the words used occurred with a very high frequency in written English texts (HF), whereas others occurred with low frequency (LF). We have plotted only response times for the HF words, and response time for the tones. As predicted, tone response times do not vary much with SOA. Word response times fell with a slope of approximately –.9, very close to the –1 slope predicted. The predicted outcome is based on the observed value for the shortest SOA (100 msec) and the longest (800 msec). The discrepancy between the predicted and observed performance, at 400 msec, can be attributed to variability in the finishing times of central processing.

Central Bottleneck Theory makes several related predictions, which have been verified in numerous experiments (Pashler, 1994). Although there are data that challenge the theory (Meyer et al., 1995), it does remarkably well for such a simple conceptualization of human cognition. Perhaps it is surprising that such a strictly serial account of behavior works so well given the massively parallel connections among neurons in the brain. It attests to the fact that well-chosen abstractions can yield a model that meets three important goals for any model: (1) a good account of data, (2) generation of accurate predictions for new circumstances, and (3) insight into how and why the pattern of data emerges.

Central Bottleneck Theory and Driving

Most of the mathematical predictions of Central Bottleneck Theory for performance in the PRP paradigm have received support from experimental data. A legitimate question, though, is whether the results from such simple tasks have much relevance to our daily

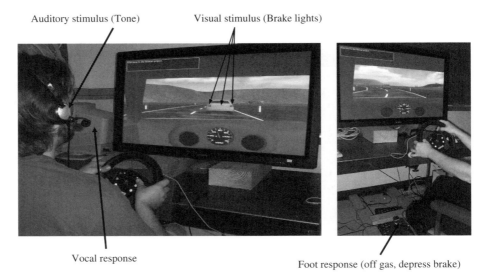

Auditory stimulus (Tone)   Visual stimulus (Brake lights)

Vocal response

Foot response (off gas, depress brake)

Figure 10.3 Stimuli and responses for dual-task driving study (Levy, Pashler, & Boer, 2006). An auditory tone was presented at varying times (SOA) prior to the illumination of brake lights of the leading car. Participants made a vocal response to the auditory stimulus. In the single-foot driving condition, the participant lifted the foot off the gas pedal and depressed the brake with the same foot as quickly as possible.

lives. We have years of practice in such tasks as driving, or the skills we exercise each day at home and at work. In most laboratory studies, participants are given only a few minutes of practice on a task they have never seen or done before. Research has shown that practice will reduce the interference seen in the PRP paradigm as long as there are no conflicts at the perceptual or motor levels (Ruthruff, Johnston, & Van Selst, 2001; Van Selst, Ruthruff, & Johnston, 1999). Perhaps in our daily lives, extensive practice on specific task pairs eliminates the bottlenecks seen in the laboratory.

A study by Levy and Pashler directly addressed this issue by embedding a PRP-like task within a simulated driving episode (Levy & Pashler, 2001). The task is shown schematically in Figure 10.3. In the one-foot driving condition, which most closely simulated normal driving, participants maneuvered a car in a driving simulator using one foot for both the accelerator and the brake. They were instructed to apply the brakes as fast as they could when the lead car's brake lights illuminated. In the single-task condition, they performed only the driving task. In the dual-task condition, a concurrent auditory task required participants to say "high" or "low" in response to auditory tones.

The results are shown in Figure 10.4. In the top portion of the graph, the filled circles plot the dual-task brake response times (BRT). Single-task BRTs were equivalent to dual-task BRTs at 350 and 1200 msec. A significant elevation in dual-task BRT was observed when the tone came on either simultaneous with the brake lights illuminating or 150 msec prior. In the bottom portion of Figure 10.4, the brake response time (BRT) is broken into

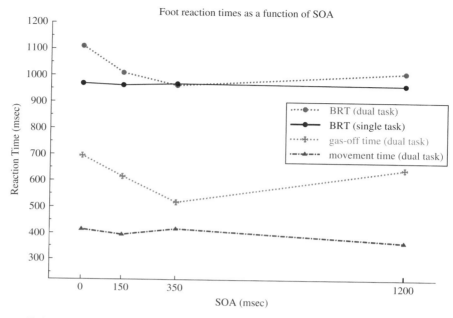

Figure 10.4 Results of the single-foot driving condition dual-task driving study (Levy, Pashler, & Boer, 2006). Brake response times (BRT) show PRP elevation similar to less familiar manual responses in laboratory. Movement time is constant across SOAs. The effect of SOA on BRT is due primarily to the time needed for participants to remove the foot from the gas pedal.

two components. The crosses plot the time to lift the foot off the gas pedal (gas-off time). The triangles plot the time to move the foot and depress the brake once the foot was off the gas pedal (movement time). Movement time remained constant across SOAs. The removal of the foot from the accelerator shows the interference from the tones task. This is evidence that it is the initiation of the separate action that is delayed by the first task. These findings are consistent with the postponement predicted by Central Bottleneck Theory. Even when the task is a familiar one, there is a cost to selecting a response when central processing on another task is still ongoing.

CENTRAL BOTTLENECK THEORY AND HUMAN–COMPUTER INTERACTION

One of the principal applications of Central Bottleneck Theory has been to the prediction of performance in computer tasks. This stems from the pioneering work of Card, Moran, and Newell (1983), who proposed a simple model of human behavior, referred to as the Model Human Processor (MHP). The MHP consists of three processors (perceptual, cognitive, and motor), two sensory memories (visual and auditory), a long-term memory, and a working memory. Figure 10.5 shows this architecture. The two sensory memories

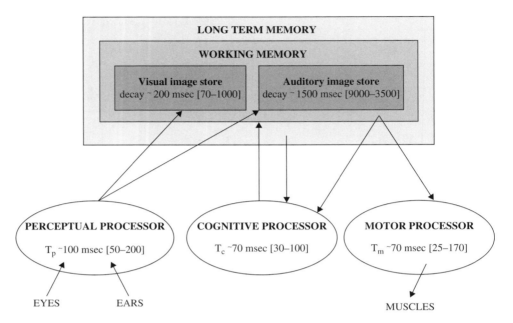

Figure 10.5 The resources of the Model Human Processor and their connections. *Source:* After Card, Moran, and Newell (1983).

correspond closely to the iconic and echoic memories discussed previously. *Long-term memory (LTM)* refers to the stored knowledge learned over experience. *Working memory (WM)* refers to the storage and manipulation of information in the current context. For example, the knowledge that the visual stimuli "25" and "32" represent numbers comes from long-term memory. In subtracting the two numbers, the intermediate products associated with the borrowing from the "3" in the subtraction of "2 – 5," the decrementing of the "3," and the storage of each component step rely on WM. The cognitive processor is an elaboration of the central stage in Central Bottleneck Theory. It consists of a "recognize-act" cycle that matches its inputs to actions through goals. The "recognize" phase is assumed to be in parallel, and corresponds roughly to the encoding phase in Central Bottleneck Theory. The "act" phase, which assigns actions to inputs, is assumed to be serial, similar to the response-selection stage.

What gives the MHP its predictive power is that each processor is assigned a *cycle time*, or the shortest unit of time required for the execution of one fundamental operation. These cycle times were estimated from numerous psychological studies and represent useful approximations. For each, an average, or "middleman" cycle time is given, along with fastest and slowest times. Added to cycle-time estimates is a statement of a clear principle of operation, which provides the framework for making calculations. To see how these two factors work together, consider the simple example of pressing a single key whenever a light appears on the computer monitor. The average (or "middleman") cycle time in milliseconds (msec) for the perceptual processor is $\tau_p \approx 100$, the fastest is $\tau_p \approx 50$, the slowest is

$\tau_p \approx 200$. The average cycle time for the cognitive processor is $\tau_c \approx 70$, with the fastest at $\tau_c \approx 30$ and the slowest $\tau_c \approx 100$. For the motor processor, average time is $\tau_m \approx 70$, with the fastest $\tau_m \approx 25$ and the slowest $\tau_m \approx 170$.

The appearance of the light causes activity in the perceptual processor, and after one perceptual cycle there is a representation of the image in visual memory (VM) and working memory (WM). This representation is purely visual, with no accompanying semantic content, but that is not relevant for this task. The cognitive processor then uses the WM representation as input and takes one cognitive cycle to generate an abstract motor command ("push key"). The motor processor then takes the abstract motor command and after one cycle generates a physical key press. The total time taken for this is the sum of these three: $\tau_p + \tau_c + \tau_m$. Thus, for the middleman values this equals $100 + 70 + 70 = 240$ msec. The fastest time would be $50 + 30 + 25 = 105$ msec, and $200 + 100 + 170 = 470$ msec for the slowest. Card, Moran, and Newell (1983) report the empirical results of laboratory studies as ranging between 100 msec and 400 msec, corresponding well to the predicted values. This is a simple example. As the tasks get more complex, more cognitive cycles are undertaken and more activity occurs in memory stores. However, this example shows the basic operation of the MHP.

Fitts' Law

It is important to emphasize that the MHP is meant to provide designers with a tool that allows them to rapidly and easily estimate the performance of users in order to make design tradeoffs. It captures many of the regularities of human behavior, but not all the nuances. One of its strengths is that it can easily incorporate known characteristics of human behavior, such as Fitts' Law (Fitts, 1954). Fitts' Law describes an important regularity of human motor behavior. In brief, it states that the time to complete a movement is proportional to both the distance moved and the size of the target. It is named for Paul Fitts, who noted the empirical regularity and developed an information-theoretic account that led to the present formulation. There are several related equations for Fitts' Law. Card, Moran, and Newell (1983) derived their formulation from considerations of the MHP. However, later in this section we present a more standard form of the law, close to that derived by Fitts from information theory. If someone moves his hand a distance D, from a starting position to a target of width W, the difficulty of that movement should be related to both the distance and the width. That is, as D gets larger, it is harder to land accurately on the same target. Likewise, if D is held constant as W decreases, it also becomes more difficult. Using information theory, Fitts developed an expression for the *Index of Difficulty (ID)* of the movement:

$$ID = \log_2(2A/W)$$

from which he derived an expression for movement time (MT):

$$MT = a + b \log_2(2A/W)$$

In this expression, "a" and "b" are constants that can change from device to device. The constant "a" represents the minimum time to initiate a movement; "b" is an expression relating to the capacity of the motor system. MT is directly proportional to b. Fitts referred to 1/b as the Index of Performance (IP) of the motor system. Since creation of the original formulation in 1954, modifications have been made to the equations that seem to give better accounts of human performance over a wider range of D and W. It is more common today to see an expression of MT closer to:

$$MT = a + b \log_2(A/W + c)$$

where c is a constant, generally 0.5 or 1 (MacKenzie, 1992).

Though there are limits to Fitts' Law, it does provide a very good approximation of human movement times for rapid, aimed movements. It is not generally applied to slower, more deliberate movements, such as those used in writing or drawing. Incorporating Fitts' Law into the MHP made it possible to predict task completion times not only for the old keystroke and command line interfaces, but also for the windowed, point-and-click interfaces to which we are now accustomed.

Project Ernestine

It is important to stress that the MHP, and associated modeling frameworks, do not just fit existing data; they can also make predictions prior to the collection of human data. The preceding example using Fitts' Law shows that accurate movement times can be estimated by knowing the parameters of the movement; human performance is well captured by a simple expression of the relationship of those parameters. In the MHP, the cycle times for each processor in combination with the principles of use also allow the human-system engineer to estimate performance from task parameters, though generally in a more complex manner.

One of the more significant and impressive applications of the MHP, and by extension Central Bottleneck Theory, came from a study by Gray, John, and Atwood (1993), which described the application of MHP to a large-scale test of new computer equipment for the company that then controlled the telephone exchange for the state of New York (NYNEX). NYNEX was engaged in testing computer equipment that it was planning to purchase to support many of the tasks performed by the human operators in directory assistance. The cost of operating the directory service would be reduced by many millions of dollars a year by cutting just a second or two from every call. Before finalizing the purchase, NYNEX was conducting a large-scale test of the system. Grey, John, and Atwood were not part of the test, but were given permission to model the task of directory assistance to see how well MHP could predict the outcome. One of the researchers (John) trained as a telephone operator, thereby gaining intimate knowledge of the task sufficient to conduct an appropriate task analysis, which resulted in accurate and complete representations of many different types of calls, the devices used, the procedures for each call, and a host of other relevant considerations. They referred to their effort as "Project Ernestine" after a popular comedy character developed by Lily Tomlin: Ernestine was a telephone operator who quickly became confused.

The surprising conclusion from the modeling effort was that the new equipment would not only *not* save time (and money), but in some cases would lead to longer call times. This prediction was in fact confirmed by the large-scale empirical test. Moreover, unlike the empirical outcomes, which just indicated that no improvement would be expected, the model actually gave some insight into why the new computer system would be no better than the existing one. To simplify greatly, automating tasks will shorten the time needed to complete a set of acts only when the automated tasks are actually a component of the completion time. For example, if you are making coffee for four people in the morning and you find you need to wash their cups because the cups are still dirty from the previous morning, it might make you angry, but would not necessarily delay coffee drinking. Why? Because you have to wait until the coffee is brewed anyway. Even though you had to do more things, those things were being absorbed into the time taken to brew the coffee. In scheduling parlance, washing the cups is off the *critical path*, in the sense that the time to wash did not contribute (add) to overall completion time.

In Project Ernestine, the new computers that NYNEX wanted to buy greatly reduced the number of keystrokes the operators needed to type; however, those tasks were not on the critical path. For the most part, they were being typed while the customer was speaking. Customer response time is much like the coffee brewing. The automation removed activities that the operators routinely carried out during the wait. Unfortunately, the new system also added a new keystroke that occurred after the customer responded and was on the critical path. The MHP-based model predicted the observed increase in time to execute the new keystroke. In response to the model, and the dismal empirical tests, NYNEX ordered revisions to the computer systems that saved millions of dollars over the life of the system.

CAPACITY THEORIES

Bottleneck theories are often referred to as *single-channel bottleneck* theories to emphasize their assumption that the central stage that creates the bottleneck can do only one thing at a time. It will come as no surprise that they are not the only account of the difficulty in doing two things at once, or more generally in how people manage multiple tasks. In fact, within experimental psychology there has been a long-standing debate over whether dual-task performance should be understood fundamentally as competition for a single-channel resource, or as part of a more flexible system of allocating limited-capacity resources to multiple tasks. Indeed, a single-channel bottleneck could, in fact, be one allocation strategy. As it turns out, the MHP and single-channel bottleneck accounts in general have had a significant impact on the study of human-computer interfaces, but have not been routinely applied more widely to the complex human-system issues that characterize other areas of human-system engineering. Before describing capacity theories in more detail, it is worth considering first why central bottleneck theories are not more often used.

Complexity in Resource Allocation

Human-system issues often arise in the context of a new design. The driving questions are generally questions of staffing (how many people are needed) and task allocation (how to divide the work among people or among people and the system). The design process is constrained by both time and money. What is often demanded of human-system engineers are concrete answers to questions in a short space of time with limited financial resources.

It took many months of dedicated effort to produce the model used for the Ernestine project. This was appropriate for a one-off exercise by academics to test their theory. However, it would not be feasible for most common design contexts. Also, the model had to be very detailed to provide the insight it did. It turns out that accurate predictions from bottleneck theories require a deep understanding of both the task and human cognitive processing, and a fine-grained analysis of tasks that are often much more complex than the simple tasks on which the theories were developed. Applying the model to these more complex tasks can be both formidable and contentious. The point to be made here is that it is often not feasible, in the design context, to analyze every task into its perceptual, cognitive, and motor components.

Another point to be made is that single-channel bottleneck theories in themselves suggest no mechanism to account for the policy that determines how operators allocate resources to multiple tasks. They only describe the throughput of the human information-processing system under a particular set of assumptions about which task gets processed first. In practice, it is relatively rare that we must make a speeded response to two closely spaced stimuli. Instead, we are more often confronted with *divided-attention tasks*, situations in which there are several concurrent ongoing activities that we must timeshare. For example, in cooking a meal, independent streams of activities for preparing a salad, the main dish, and the side dishes will require us to shift between one activity stream and another. In such cases, one is often interested in predicting the policy that determines how people will allocate their resources, or to determine what would be an optimal allocation policy given specific circumstances. Capacity theories of human information processing are well suited for these goals.

Allocation of Limited-Capacity Resources

Capacity theories take a different approach to accounting for multitasking performance than do single-channel bottleneck accounts. Capacity theories share fundamental assumptions:

1. There is a common pool of resources that can be flexibly allocated to tasks.
2. Allocating more resources to a task speeds the rate of processing of that task.
3. Processing rate can be resource limited, data limited, or both.
4. The quantity of resources can be increased or decreased.

Assumptions 1–3 provide the conceptual framework for a capacity-sharing approach to understanding human multitasking performance. Assumption 1 specifies that at any given time, only a finite amount of resource capacity is available. Assumption 2 establishes the relationship between the amount of resources allocated to a task and performance of that task, usually in terms of processing time or accuracy. The sharing is a zero-sum process, as resources given to one task are not available to others. Assumption 4 allows the pool of resources to increase or decrease, either through more effort (Kahneman, 1973), or by varying physiological states that affect alertness, as occurs with fatigue or heightened emotional state (Pribram & McGuinness, 1975). However, this does not alter the zero-sum nature of the allocation, only the total amount of resources that can be allocated.

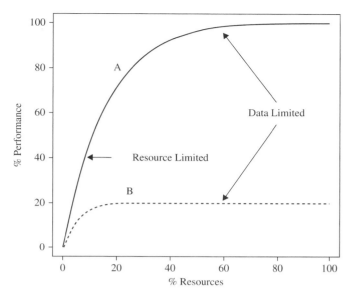

Figure 10.6 Performance-resource functions for two tasks. Task A performance peaks with 60% allocation of resources, Task B with 10%. Performance on A is resource limited up to 60%, after which it is data limited. B shows strong data limits throughout.

Assumption 3 qualifies the relationship of resources to performance in Assumption 2, by explicitly noting that *data limits* can also impair performance. Earlier we noted that data-limited processing refers to cases in which allocating more resources, or trying harder, will not improve performance, as in trying to decipher faint speech in a very noisy room. Data limits can also occur for reasons other than the signal being obscured by noise. For example, a task might be so easy that after some given point, it doesn't help to allocate more resources. In Figure 10.6 we illustrate the effect of resource allocation on two different tasks by showing two different performance-resource functions. The *x*-axis of Figure 10.6 represents the amount of resources allocated to a task and the *y*-axis the resulting task performance. Consider Task A, shown as the solid line in Figure 10.6. Performance rises steadily as more resources are allocated to it, and levels off at a value very near perfect performance at about 60 percent of total resources available. After that point, adding further resources or greater effort will not significantly improve performance, as it is at ceiling. Now consider the dashed line depicting the performance-resource function for Task B. B shows a quite different pattern, characteristic of a data-limited task. For B, rapid initial improvement quickly plateaus at a relatively low level of performance. Further allocation of resources does not improve performance. This type of pattern would be expected if, for example, one were trying to translate a language one didn't know very well (with no dictionary handy), or trying to listen in on a conversation under very high noise levels.

In Figure 10.6, A has a much higher asymptotic performance level than B. In that sense, A is easier than B. Performance-resource functions also reflect an alternative

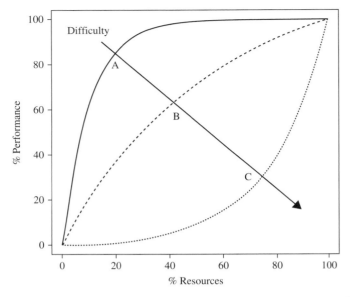

Figure 10.7 Performance-resource functions for tasks of varying difficulty. As task difficulty increases, more resources must be allocated to achieve the same level of performance. Task A is easy, reaching peak performance with about 40% allocation. Task B is more difficult, reaching peak performance only with full resource allocation. Task C is very difficult, with no performance improvements until virtually full allocation.

way in which tasks can differ in difficulty. Two tasks that have the same asymptotic performance level can also differ in the amount of resources needed to achieve a given level of performance. In the graph in Figure 10.7 we have plotted functions for three different tasks. All tasks ultimately achieve the same asymptotic performance, but differ in how they respond to intermediate levels of resource allocation. As difficulty increases, indicated by the downward-pointing arrow, it takes a greater percentage of resources to attain the same level of performance. For any given level of resource allocation short of 100 percent, performance on A will be better than B, which will be better than C. Performance on Task A, for example, peaks with only a 60-percent allocation of resources, whereas Task B does not achieve 100-percent performance until all available resources are allocated.

An example of a task such as A might be the detection of a bright light on a black background. Detection performance will likely not suffer by undertaking other tasks, so long as the eyes are not diverted from the display and minimal attention is paid to the task. The case of Task B is similar to understanding a foreign language that you know pretty well, but in which you are not completely fluent. You can pretty well follow the conversation, but will improve the more you attend. The profile shown for C is that of a task that cannot be done without nearly full commitment of resources. This is what one might expect when there was a weak signal in high noise, such that a full commitment of spatial attention to the task was required. A stimulus right at the threshold of detectability in a psychophysical experiment is one example. It might also characterize tasks such as

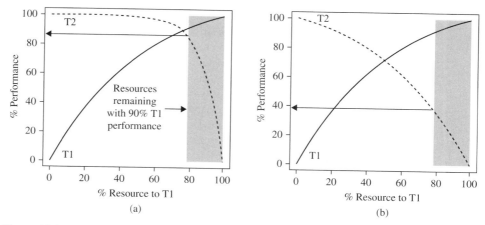

Figure 10.8 Dual-task trade-offs as depicted by the resource-performance functions. As resources are devoted to T1 (solid line), T2 performance (dashed line) declines. In graph (a), T2 is relatively easy. When performance on T1 reaches 90%, the remaining resources (shaded area) are sufficient to perform T2 at around 85%. In graph (b), T2 is more difficult. T2 performance is less than 40% when T1 is at 90%.

reading, or sight-reading music, in that these can be done at a high level, but only with a substantial allocation of resources.

How do the resource-performance profiles in Figure 10.7 relate to performing two or more tasks concurrently? In Figure 10.8 we use the resource-performance profiles to plot the performance of pairs of tasks as a function of the percentage of resources devoted to one of them. The task receiving the resources is referred to as T1 and plotted with the solid line; the one from which resources are being taken is called T2, plotted with the dashed line. As resources for T1 are increased, T2 performance drops in accordance with its resource-performance function. For a given allocation of resources on the *x*-axis, the corresponding performance on the *y*-axis is the value of the resource function for each task at that allocation.

Graph (a) shows a relatively optimistic task combination in which there are sufficient resources to maintain relatively high levels of performance on both tasks. With T1 (corresponding to B in Figure 10.7) at 90 percent performance, the remaining resources are shown in the shaded area. When T2 (corresponding to A in Figure 10.7) is easy, it can still be performed at around 85 percent. Graph (b) shows what happens when two tasks with the profile of B in Figure 10.7 are combined. Here the trade-offs are more severe. Performance on T2 is under 40 percent when T1 is at 90 percent. This combination shows that tasks need not be extremely hard before doing them together degrades performance. It should also be noted that we do not know the resource-performance functions for specific task combinations.

MULTIPLE RESOURCE THEORY

Thus far, we have discussed resource-performance profiles in the abstract. That is, we have presented notional graphs to illustrate the general principles of capacity theories. In reality, other factors must be considered to apply capacity accounts. One key omission is any discussion of resource conflicts or constraints that may emerge even for two easy tasks. For example, we noted that detecting the onset of a light was a simple task requiring few resources. The same is true of detecting an auditory tone presented at a high decibel level against a low noise background. According to our preceding notional graphs, you should do just as well with two visual or two auditory tasks, or a visual-auditory task. However, if you are required to perform two visual detection tasks concurrently (i.e., detect the onset of lights at two locations), you could do so easily—except if one light were behind your head. In that case, you would have a *structural conflict*. Both tasks would demand the eyes, but the ocular system cannot comply (unless of course it is your mother, who seems to have eyes in the back of her head). By contrast, you would have no such structural conflict if the visual task were paired with an auditory task. In general, timesharing is more efficient when the stimuli for the tasks are separated by modality (Pashler & Johnston, 1998).

The advantage of separating stimuli by modality arises not just from the lack of structural conflicts. A significant amount of sensory decoding goes on independently for audition and vision. This means that there are fewer possibilities for interference when stimuli come from separate modalities. For example, if two lights are presented close together in time and space, they can interfere with one another. Similarly, two tones can interfere if they are close together in pitch. This is called *masking*. Separating stimuli by modality avoids these and other possible sources of interference in sensory processing.

There is still another way in which stimuli can interfere, which is not captured by the preceding notional graphs. As sensory information is processed over time, stimuli are elaborated in the encoding process. Interference can occur if the resulting codes for two stimuli are very similar. This is referred to as *code interference*. For example, it is very difficult to listen to speech while reading, even though the inputs are separated by modality, thus avoiding structural conflicts, masking, or other modality-specific interference. Rather, the interference occurs because both the speech and text are developed into similar *linguistic codes*. Similarly, it is difficult if not impossible to track a visual object as it moves about the world while simultaneously tracking a sound that a different object is making as it moves about. Both of the judgments rely on similar *spatial codes* (Wickens & Liu, 1988).

Code interference can also be seen when input modalities are combined with output modalities. Even though one cannot follow two simultaneously presented melodies or read and listen to a conversation, it is possible with practice to sight-read (and play) a piece of music while repeating back a spoken passage (Allport, Antonis, & Reynolds, 1972). Because both tasks are reasonably demanding, more like C than A in our preceding examples, such timesharing would not be expected from our earlier abstract analysis. Moreover, in experiments using the Psychological Refractory Period paradigm, the typical practice is to map the visual stimulus to a manual response (VM: visual input, manual response) and the auditory stimulus to a vocal response (AV). With these VM and AV mappings, the interference seen in Task 2 performance at short SOAs (the PRP effect) is substantially diminished over time. However, the initial PRP effect is large and shows far less decrease with practice if the visual task is paired with a vocal response (VV) and the auditory task with a manual response (AM). Under VV and AM conditions, substantial interference persists even after extensive practice (Hazeltine, Ruthruff, & Remington, 2006; Levy & Pashler, 2001). The problem is likely that the auditory input and vocal response share sound-oriented code. With an AV pairing, this is an advantage because the output code for the auditory stimulus can serve as the input code for the vocal response. With VV and AM pairings, the shared code produces conflict.

Observations of such conflicts have led researchers to the conclusion that resource or capacity sharing must take place within a more complex set of structural constraints inherent in the human information-processing architecture. It is not possible to account for patterns of multitasking behavior simply by positing a single undifferentiated pool of shared resources. In fact, a number of theories have posited multiple pools of resources allocated to specific structural units in processing (Kantowitz & Knight, 1976a, 1976b; Navon & Gopher, 1979). Of these, the most widely used in applied settings is the Multiple Resource Theory (Wickens, 1980, 1984, 1991, 2002; Wickens & Liu, 1988).

Multiple Resource Theory, as its name implies, posits not one undifferentiated resource, but separate resources associated with quasi-independent processing modules. A diagram of the overall structure of processing within Multiple Resource Theory is shown in Figure 10.9. In Figure 10.9, the modules enclosed within a solid or dashed line are

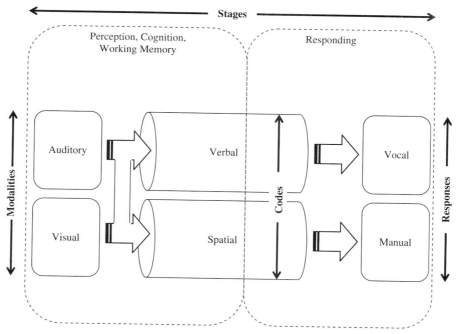

Figure 10.9 Resources and associated processing modules in Multiple Resource Theory. There are four resource dimensions associated with (1) Stages, (2) Modalities, (3) Codes, and (4) Responses. Each enclosed module has its own resources. The perceptual and response stages also have resources that limit independent internal processing. Auditory and visual outputs can lead to both verbal and spatial codes. Verbal codes are associated with vocal output, spatial codes with manual output.

meant to be independent, capable of operating in parallel with no interference from other modules, subject to resource constraints. Multiple Resource Theory characterizes resource allocation along four more or less independent dimensions: Stages, Modalities, Codes, and Responses. We discuss each of these next.

The *Stage* dimension is comprised of two resource modules, one associated with the combination of *perception, cognition*, and *working memory*, the other with *responding*. Perception, cognition, and working memory constitute a module that produces a representation of a stimulus, including identity and semantic information. This corresponds partially with the stimulus encoding stage in Central Bottleneck Theory, with additional semantic and category information. The response module selects responses intended to achieve the current goal, corresponding to the response-selection operation in Central Bottleneck Theory. The logic for the division of processing into these two stages comes from evidence that in the Psychological Refractory Period paradigm, there is a cost for the second task only when it requires a speeded response. Little or no cost is observed in accuracy of report when participants must comprehend or categorize a stimulus (Pashler, 1994; Shallice, McLeod, & Lewis, 1985). The two stage modules in Multiple Resource Theory thus reflect data showing that mapping arbitrary response for one task (response module) can occur in parallel with encoding of the stimuli for a second task (perception, cognition, and working memory module).

The *Modality* dimension is comprised of independent modules for *Vision* and *Audition* in the perception, working memory, and cognition module, as well as *Vocal* and *Manual* output in the response module. The independence of vision and audition (and presumably other sensory modalities) reflects the evidence cited earlier of greater interference from stimuli within than from stimuli between modalities. The independence of vocal and manual responses in the response module is supported by evidence from dual-task studies showing that tracking while performing a concurrent verbal task shows better timesharing when the verbal task uses a vocal output than a manual one (McLeod, 1977; Tsang & Wickens, 1988; Vidulich, 1988; Wickens, 1980; Wickens & Liu, 1988). The *Code* dimension is comprised of independent modules for verbal and spatial codes. This distinction is motivated by the evidence cited earlier that though it is not possible to follow or respond independently to two linguistic inputs, one read and the other spoken, it is possible to shadow a spoken conversation while sight-reading music (Allport, Antonis, & Reynolds, 1972).

Using Multiple Resource Theory

To illustrate how Multiple Resource Theory is applied, we consider the case in which the driver of a car (any vehicle, really) engages in a conversation with a passenger. The principal input modality for driving is vision, whereas the principal output modality is manual/pedal. The principal internal code is spatial. In short, driving can be considered to be principally a visual-spatial-manual task. One could argue that audition plays a role, as the sounds of brakes or the sound of the engine often alert one to danger. In that regard, even olfaction is useful. These are valid points, but in the main, the VSM nature of driving is illustrated by the fact that deaf people can drive and that vision is both necessary and sufficient. Talking to the passenger uses audition as the principal input modality, vocal output, and verbal codes. That is, it is primarily an auditory-verbal-vocal task. So far, this appears to be a good combination with little interference, as driving and conversing use nonintersecting sets of modality and code. In Multiple Resource Theory, the amount of interference expected is a function of the number of modules shared between the two tasks. Conversing and talking share only the resources associated with the two stages. That is, the perception, memory, and cognition resource is shared between the tasks for input, and the response resource is shared for output. According to the theory, there will be little or no interference so long as the sum of the demands for both tasks does not exceed either resource pool.

The last point is important. According to the theory, even when the inputs for two tasks are separated by modality and the internal codes are separate, they nonetheless draw on a single pool of shared perceptual resources. The same is true for the response resources. If you observe driver behavior carefully, the conversation between passenger and driver flows freely if the driving demands are light, but pauses while the driver makes a turn or responds to an unexpected traffic condition. This is fully consistent with the limit on stage resources. In making a turn, the driver must concentrate more on the position of the car and track it as it turns. This also means making decisions about the use of the steering wheel, the accelerator, and the brake. As the perceptual and response stages of the driving task demand increasing resources, these resources will be removed from the conversation (one hopes!), leaving too few resources either to understand what the passenger is saying (perceptual) or to continue speaking (responding).

If conversing and routine driving can be done concurrently without interference, why is cell-phone use while driving such an apparent danger? First, note that according to the theory, some degradation in performance of both tasks would be expected. They do compete for stage resources, so one would accept some impairment on both tasks if they were shared, much as in the left panel of Figure 10.9. Some analyses suggest that cell phones are more problematic because, unlike a passenger in the next seat, the speaker on the other end is unaware of the traffic flow, and therefore does not modulate her end of the conversation as a function of the momentary traffic demands. This could interact with our rules for conversational politeness, which dictate, in part, that we respond within a reasonable time as part of holding up our end of the conversation. If the driver felt compelled to respond, then critical stage resources could be withdrawn from the driving task. A passenger would know to pause the conversation, so there would be no conflict with such conversational conventions.

It is also possible that speaking on the cell phone places other types of demands on stage resources. Seldom is the reception as good as with a passenger, nor do speakers seem to trust the microphone to fully capture their vocal output. A common complaint is that cell-phone users speak very loudly, annoying those around them. Poor-quality sound input or a greater effort to speak loudly and clearly would also drain stage resources. As this example illustrates, it is often the competition for stage resources that causes the lengthened task completion times seen in multitasking. Indeed, when considering the kinds of tasks we do daily, it is perhaps more common to have to switch between tasks than it is to have sufficient resources to do them in parallel with no interference.

APPLICATIONS OF SINGLE-CHANNEL AND MULTIPLE RESOURCE THEORIES

Which approach to multitasking should you take: assume a single-channel central bottleneck, or a set of multiple resources as in Multiple Resource Theory? In recent years, the application of Multiple Resource Theory has steadily increased. Among university graduates from human factors programs working in complex applied military and aerospace domains, it is very likely the most common approach to estimating workload, task allocations, and staffing requirements. As we saw with the cell-phone example, the theory provides a solid framework for considering the important aspects of tasks—in particular, their input/output modalities, internal codes, and overall resource demands. The framework, by which we mean the dimensions and modules, is an elegant summary and distillation of decades of psychological research on human information processing. Moreover, the model framework corresponds quite closely to the kinds of decisions that must be made in assessing workload or staffing. The decisions in practice are often whether or which tasks should be presented using visual dials or auditory signals, whether the responses should be vocal or manual, or what form the information should take. The structure of Multiple Resource Theory closely corresponds to these questions and, in this way, supports the designers as they think through the problem. The theory is also a productive framework for research. For example, it is often difficult to know to what degree a task loads on spatial or verbal resources, or what the resource-performance profiles are for each of the modules. These are important considerations for application of the theory that will affect the accuracy of its predictions.

In contrast, mathematical and computational approaches rely more on single-channel assumptions than on Multiple Resource Theory. We mentioned earlier how research and application in computer science, notably human-computer interaction, rely to a large extent on single-channel assumptions. Central Bottleneck Theory and Multiple Resource Theory both have mechanisms to account for portions of two tasks that can be done in parallel. In Central Bottleneck Theory, parallelism occurs when stimulus encoding and response execution for one task can be overlapped with processing on another. In Multiple Resource Theory, parallelism occurs when two constraints are satisfied: (1) tasks draw on independent resources, and (2) the sum of the demand on stage resources does not exceed capacity. We saw with the Model Human Processor how the assumptions of parallelism in Central Bottleneck Theory enable very precise predictions for mouse and cursor movements in computer tasks. However, quite satisfactory answers often can be derived from simply assuming that a human can do only one task at a time. For many applications, estimates of overall completion times for a task, rather than precise calculation of individual actions within a task, are sufficient for engineering decisions. For example, in calculating how long it will take an engineer in the Launch Control Room at the Kennedy Space Center to execute a multi-item checklist on a computer, it is probably sufficient to estimate the time for each checklist item rather than compute this from the time to move a mouse to point on a display and click. At this level of analysis, single-channel assumptions are probably adequate.

TIMESHARING

Thus far, our discussion of multitasking has been devoted primarily to research documenting the limits on doing two or more things at once, and to describe how Central Bottleneck Theory, capacity theories, and Multiple Resource Theory provide frameworks for understanding the genesis of those limitations. In practice, we encounter relatively few instances at work or in daily life that test our ability to parallel processes at the millisecond level. Instead, it is much more common to switch from one task to another. Driving and talking to a passenger, for example, will require one to reason about the traffic at one instant and then transition to the topic of conversation the next. This is not to say that there isn't parallel processing of the visual driving task and the verbal conversation. It just notes the prevalence of switching tasks as a common occurrence. Switching raises interesting questions: (1) Are there costs to switching between tasks? (2) What are the cognitive mechanisms at play when switching? (3) Are there strategies that govern when and how we decide to share two tasks?

Task-Switching Costs

In what is now a landmark study, Jersild (1927) observed significant costs when people had to switch between two tasks compared to when they performed only a single task. He measured the time it took people to complete a set of problems written on sheets of paper. People took longer on average to complete a sheet that consisted of two types of problems than to complete a sheet consisting purely of one or the other problem type. The method has been improved on considerably since then, but the principal finding of a cost to switch between cognitive tasks is routinely observed (Rogers & Monsell, 1995; Ruthruff, Remington, & Johnston, 2001; Spector & Biederman, 1976; Sudevan & Taylor, 1987). The largest switch costs occur when people must perform different computations on the same type of stimulus. For example, if on one trial participants press one of two keys to indicate whether a digit presented visually is greater than or less than 5, they will be faster if the last trial asked them to make the same judgment (on a different digit) than if it asked them to judge whether the digit was odd or even (e.g., Spector & Biederman, 1976). Similarly, if people are presented with a letter-digit pair (e.g., "c 5") and asked to say whether the letter is a vowel or consonant, or whether the digit is odd or even, they will be faster if the last trial required the same judgment (e.g., Rogers & Monsell, 1995). This holds for other stimuli and judgments as well (e.g., Allport, Styles & Hsieh, 1994). In these cases, switch costs will often be on the order of 300 msec or more. It turns out that the switch cost is found only on the first trial of a new task (Altmann, 2004a, 2004b; Logan, 2003; Rogers & Monsell, 1995). It does matter, however, how long it has been since the task was last performed. Ruthruff et al. (Ruthruff, Remington, & Johnston, 2001) observed that response times for the first trial of a different task increased as a logarithmic function of the number of trials since the last time that task had been performed. The general conclusion is that there is a cost to switching between two cognitive operations.

In the preceding cases, stimuli from the same class (e.g., digits) required different judgments on successive trials. When the stimuli are not all from the same category, switch costs are still observed, though they are considerably smaller in magnitude. For example,

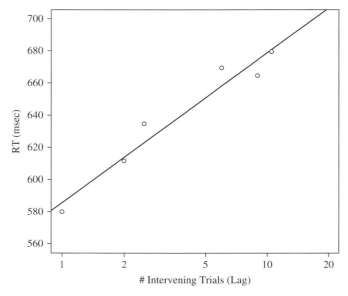

Figure 10.10 The effect of the number of intervening items on the response time to a task switch. Here the *x*-axis is in logarithmic coordinates. *Source:* Data after Ruthruff, Remington, and Johnston (2001).

Ruthruff et al. had participants press one of four keys to indicate either which of four letters (ISOX) or which of 4 colors (red, blue, green, yellow) was presented. Response times were 30 msec faster when the task (but not the stimulus) repeated than when it switched. They also looked at switching among three tasks. In addition to the color and letter task, one to four dots appeared on the screen and participants pressed the same four keys to indicate the number of dots. Switch trials were on average 55 msec slower than repeat trials. Interestingly, Ruthruff et al. found that response time on switch trials was a logarithmic function of the number of trials since the task was last presented, a measure they referred to as *lag*. Their results are shown in Figure 10.10. The longer participants were away from a task, which is a function of the number of intervening items, the longer they took to respond. These results have implications for the effect of interruptions on performance, discussed in later chapters.

Cognitive Operations in Task Switching

Because task switching seems commonplace in everyday life, its cognitive underpinnings could have significant consequences for tasks outside the laboratory. There is general agreement that switching between tasks draws on *executive control* mechanisms in human information processing. In fact, task switching is seen as the canonical demonstration of executive control. Executive control mechanisms are hypothesized to control which cognitive operations are performed on an incoming stimulus, which stimuli are selected, and which responses are selected. Task switching is seen as an important test bed for executive control, as it requires participants to directly alter their task goals from trial to trial, to select stimuli based on the new goals, to perform the cognitive operations appropriate for the current goal, and to select the correct response. In the case where the stimulus class is held constant, the cost can only arise from internal cognitive operations needed to ensure that the response reflects the goals of the immediate task. Brain-imaging studies have shown that regions in the prefrontal cortex show heightened activity on switch compared to repetition trials, consistent with the involvement of this region in the manipulation and maintenance of task goals (Yeung, Nystrom, Aronson, & Cohen, 2006).

What kinds of cognitive activities underlie task-switching costs? Allport, Styles, and Hsieh (1994) argued that the large costs seen when participants must make different judgments on stimuli from the same class arise from the need to *inhibit* the competing response selection of the previous trial. They referred to this as *task set inertia*. The central idea is that the set from the last trial is still active even though participants should have switched sets between trials. Inhibition seems particularly plausible in the case where the stimulus class remains the same, but the judgments differ from trial to trial. If, for example, you have just seen the digit "7" on the previous trial and made the "odd" judgment, it might be natural to make the same "odd" judgment on the next trial when presented with the digit "3" even though you have been told to say whether it is greater or less than five. There is evidence, however, that the costs arise not so much from the judgment as from the selection of a response. Suppose, for example, participants are told in one task to make a key press when the digit is odd, but to do nothing if it is even (a go/no-go trial), and press keys to indicate whether it is greater or less than five in the other. Magnitude judgments will show a switch cost if the previous trial was odd and required a response, but not if it was even and required no response (see, e.g., Philipp, Jolicoeur, Falkenstein, & Koch, 2007; Schuch & Koch, 2003).

Rogers and Monsell (1995) offered a somewhat different account of the source of task-switching costs. They varied the time interval between trials and found that switch costs were significantly reduced, but not eliminated, as intertrial intervals increased from 100 msec to 1200 msec. They proposed a task set reconfiguration account, which attributes a significant portion of the switch cost to the time taken to change out of the old task set and instantiate the new. Task set reconfiguration also provides an explanation of the switch costs seen when stimuli for the two tasks are from different categories (e.g., colors, digits, dots). Indeed, evidence suggests that there are two separable cognitive operations that correspond to a reconfiguration of task set. In between trials, participants are able to prepare for the upcoming task through a task set reconfiguration operation. However, response selection still retains the activation from the last selection and will produce a small residual switch cost even when the stimuli are from different classes and there is plenty of time to shift sets (see Meiran, 2000; Ruthruff, Remington, & Johnston, 2001). In short, executive control in task switching seems to be comprised of both preparatory and inhibitory operations.

TIMESHARING STRATEGIES AND THE CONTROL OF PROCESSING

Thus far, our discussion of the structural aspects of human cognition has been focused on identifying fundamental limits that constrain the flow of information processing, the acquisition of information, and our ability to timeshare two or more tasks. The data we have presented come largely from studies that by design isolate those fundamental limits, and therefore restrict the choices participants have over how they approach a task. As we noted earlier, however, when discussing how people timeshare two tasks that extend over a period of time, we must consider that people have choices to make as to when they pause one task, switch to another, return, and so forth. This choice extends to the pattern of eye fixation people make when acquiring information. People choose when to sample information from one display or another and the rate at which any particular display is sampled. When choices are stable and repeat over time, they can be said to constitute a strategy. By *strategy*, we mean behavior that reflects a performance goal. For example, when shopping, one person might have a strategy of getting the best deal. With that as a dominant strategy, he would visit a large number of stores (or online sites) and check carefully for the best deals, using coupons or special sales promotions. Another person might adopt a strategy of minimizing the time and effort spent shopping. She might visit just a single store and purchase the first acceptable item. The "best deal" strategy sacrifices time and effort for low price. The "least effort" strategy sacrifices best price for least effort.

Speed-Accuracy Trade-Off

One of the most common strategic decisions is how to trade off the desire to get things done quickly with the goal of doing them very well. This trade-off between speed and accuracy is very familiar to psychologists who measure response time. Participants can always choose to respond more quickly by making their decision based on less information, or ensure high accuracy by taking longer. The classic speed-accuracy trade-off function is plotted in Figure 10.11. Response time increases from left to right on the x-axis. Performance increases upward on the y-axis. For response times between 0–C, going faster produces more errors. For response times greater than C, waiting longer to respond has little effect on errors. One way to think about this trade-off is that information regarding a decision accumulates over time, even for the simplest of decisions. The speed-accuracy trade-off reflects the probability that, on average, at any point in time (x-axis) there is sufficient information to accurately make the decision.

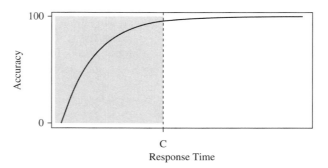

Figure 10.11 Speed-accuracy trade-off. The shaded region extending from 0–C indicates the region in which speed and accuracy show significant trade-off.

Optimal Strategies

For some tasks it is possible to derive how people should switch from one task to another to achieve optimal performance. Often, with sufficient practice and the incentive to maximize performance, people approach the predicted optimal switching. For example, eye fixation patterns when monitoring aircraft controls (Senders, 1964; Wickens, 1980) show that trained pilots sampled the instruments related to different aircraft systems in proportion to their information value for the given maneuver or regime of flight. The information value of a dial or instrument is a function of (1) how critical it is to sample that source at that moment (how rapidly the information from that source changes with time), (2) the cost of not sampling that source (the cost of failure), and (3) the cost of not sampling all the other sources. Similarly, trained air traffic controllers switch between aircraft in proportion to these three criteria (Carbonell, Ward, & Senders, 1968). Nevertheless, for human operators to learn optimal levels of performance may not be possible, or even necessary. It is often sufficient to learn effective heuristics. A *heuristic* is a strategy that more often than not produces a good outcome while minimizing the likelihood of a bad outcome. It may be less efficient in some circumstances than an optimal strategy, but usually requires less time and effort on the part of the operator.

Heuristics become increasingly important as task demands approach the limit of human information-processing capacity. Imagine, for example, that you are a doctor faced with an emergency, such as a plane crash, an earthquake or other natural disaster, a major car wreck, or a wartime battle, where too many patients are arriving too rapidly to treat them all. In this circumstance emergency doctors are instructed in the strategy of *triage*. They are taught how to tell which of the many patients to expend their limited resources on. Patients who are not seriously wounded can wait, those whose wounds are too serious are left untreated, and those who have a high likelihood of survival are given first priority. It turns out that in less dire circumstances, we all do a form of triage by *task shedding*, putting less important tasks aside to focus on more important tasks in their order of urgency. Much of the evidence on how trained people shed tasks comes from studies of pilots. In those studies, pilots and crews set priorities on tasks according to "must do," "good to do," and "could do" (Hart, 1989; Hart & Wickens, 1990; Raby & Wickens, 1994). Task shedding is a good example of how a heuristic can be usefully employed. Optimal assessment of each task (e.g., each patient in the emergency example) would require a numerical value that would be fed into an equation to compute the value of treating that person. The quick categorical assignment of patients or tasks to a limited number of treatment groups is a crude approximation, but it has the virtue of being quickly executable with little complicated overhead.

SUMMARY

We have discussed the research showing fundamental limits on people's ability to perform two or more tasks concurrently, and extended this to the discussion of task switching and to the strategies people use when there are too many tasks to perform. These limits are still those of information flow or, as we have termed it, *structure*. We now turn to the other class of human cognitive processing, which deals with how we manipulate and use the information from the environment, from our experience, and our training to select the behaviors that will achieve our immediate goals.

REFERENCES

Allport, A., Styles, E. A., & Hsieh, S. (1994). Shifting intentional set: Exploring the dynamics of tasks. In C. Umilta (Ed.), *Attention and performance XV: Conscious and nonconscious information processing* (pp. 421–452). Cambridge, MA: MIT Press.

Allport, D. A., Antonis, B., & Reynolds, P. (1972). On the division of attention: A disproof of the single channel hypothesis. *Quarterly Journal of Experimental Psychology, 24*(2), 225–235. doi:10.1080/00335557243000102

Altmann, E. M. (2004a). Advance preparation in task switching. *Psychological Science, 15*(9), 616–622. doi:10.1111/j.0956-7976.2004.00729.x

Altmann, E. M. (2004b). The preparation effect in task switching: Carryover of SOA. *Memory & Cognition, 32*(1), 153–163. doi:10.3758/BF03195828

Carbonell, J. R., Ward, J. L., & Senders, J. W. (1968). A queueing model of visual sampling experimental validation. *IEEE Transactions on Man-Machine Systems, 9*(3), 82–87. doi:10.1109/TMMS.1968.300041

Card, S. K., Moran, T. P., & Newell, A. (1983). *The psychology of human-computer interaction*. Hillsdale, NJ: Lawrence Erlbaum Associates.

Fitts, P. M. (1954). The information capacity of the human motor system in controlling the amplitude of movement. *Journal of Experimental Psychology, 47*(6), 381–391. doi:10.1037/h0055392

Gray, W. D., John, B. E., & Atwood, M. (1993). Project Ernestine: Validating a GOMS analysis for predicting and explaining real-world task performance. *Human-Computer Interaction, 8*(3), 237–309. doi:10.1207/s15327051hci0803_3

Hart, S. G. (1989). Crew workload-management strategies: A critical factor in system performance (pp. 22–27). Paper presented at the Fifth International Symposium on Aviation Psychology, Columbus, OH.

Hart, S. G., & Wickens, C. D. (1990). Workload assessment and prediction. In *MANPRINT: An approach to systems integration* (pp. 257–296). New York, NY: Van Nostrand Reinhold.

Hazeltine, E., Ruthruff, E., & Remington, R. W. (2006). The role of input and output modality pairings in dual-task performance: Evidence for content-dependent central interference. *Cognitive Psychology, 52*(4), 291–345. doi:16/j.cogpsych.2005.11.001

Jersild, A. T. (1927). Mental set and shift. *Archives of Psychology, 14*(Whole No. 89).

Kahneman, D. (1973). *Attention and effort*. Englewood Cliffs, NJ: Prentice Hall.

Kantowitz, B. H., & Knight, J. L. (1976a). On experimenter-limited processes. *Psychological Review, 83*(6), 502–507. doi:10.1037/0033-295X.83.6.502

Kantowitz, B. H., & Knight, J. L. (1976b). Testing tapping timesharing, II: Auditory secondary task. *Acta Psychologica, 40*(5), 343–362. doi:16/0001-6918(76)90016-0

Levy, J., & Pashler, H. (2001). Is dual-task slowing instruction dependent? *Journal of Experimental Psychology: Human Perception and Performance*, *27*(4), 862–869. doi:10.1037/0096-1523.27.4.862

Levy, J., Pashler, H., & Boer, E. (2006). Central interference in driving: Is there any stopping the psychological refractory period? *Psychological Science*, *17*, 228–235.

Logan, G. D. (2003). Executive control of thought and action. *Current Directions in Psychological Science*, *12*(2), 45–48. doi:10.1111/1467-8721.01223

MacKenzie, I. S. (1992). Fitts' Law as a research and design tool in human-computer interaction. *Human-Computer Interaction*, *7*(1), 91–139. doi:10.1207/s15327051hci0701_3

McCann, R. S., Remington, R. W., & Van Selst, M. (2000). A dual-task investigation of automaticity in visual word processing. *Journal of Experimental Psychology: Human Perception and Performance*, *26*(4), 1352–1370. doi:10.1037/0096-1523.26.4.1352

McLeod, P. (1977). A dual task response modality effect: Support for multiprocessor models of attention. *Quarterly Journal of Experimental Psychology*, *29*(4), 651–667. doi:10.1080/14640747708400639

Meiran, N. (2000). Modeling cognitive control in task-switching. *Psychological Research*, *63*(3–4), 234–249. doi:10.1007/s004269900004

Meyer, D. E., Kieras, D. E., Lauber, E., Schumacher, E. H., Glass, J., Zurbriggen, E., et al. (1995). Adaptive executive control: Flexible multiple-task performance without pervasive immutable response-selection bottlenecks. *Acta Psychologica*, *90*(1–3), 163–190.

Minsky, M. (1988). *The society of mind*. New York, NY: Simon and Schuster.

Navon, D., & Gopher, D. (1979). On the economy of the human-processing system. *Psychological Review*, *86*(3), 214–255. doi:10.1037/0033-295X.86.3.214

Pashler, H. (1994). Dual-task interference in simple tasks: Data and theory. *Psychological Bulletin*, *116*(2), 220–244. doi:10.1037/0033-2909.116.2.220

Pashler, H., & Johnston, J. C. (1998). Attentional limitations in dual-task performance. In H. Pashler (Ed.), *Attention*, 155–189. Hove, UK: Psychology Press.

Philipp, A. M., Jolicoeur, P., Falkenstein, M., & Koch, I. (2007). Response selection and response execution in task switching: Evidence from a go-signal paradigm. *Journal of Experimental Psychology: Learning, Memory, and Cognition*, *33*(6), 1062–1075. doi:10.1037/0278-7393.33.6.1062

Pribram, K. H., & McGuinness, D. (1975). Arousal, activation, and effort in the control of attention. *Psychological Review*, *82*(2), 116–149. doi:10.1037/h0076780

Raby, M., & Wickens, C. D. (1994). Strategic workload management and decision biases in aviation. *International Journal of Aviation Psychology*, *4*(3), 211–240. doi:10.1207/s15327108ijap0403_2

Rogers, R. D., & Monsell, S. (1995). Costs of a predictible switch between simple cognitive tasks. *Journal of Experimental Psychology: General, 124*(2), 207–231. doi:10.1037/0096-3445.124.2.207

Ruthruff, E., Johnston, J. C., & Van Selst, M. (2001). Why practice reduces dual-task interference. *Journal of Experimental Psychology: Human Perception and Performance, 27*(1), 3–21. doi:10.1037/0096-1523.27.1.3

Ruthruff, E., Remington, R. W., & Johnston, J. C. (2001). Switching between simple cognitive tasks: The interaction of top-down and bottom-up factors. *Journal of Experimental Psychology: Human Perception and Performance, 27*(6), 1404–1419. doi:10.1037/0096-1523.27.6.1404

Schuch, S., & Koch, I. (2003). The role of response selection for inhibition of task sets in task shifting. *Journal of Experimental Psychology: Human Perception and Performance, 29*(1), 92–105. doi:10.1037/0096-1523.29.1.92

Senders, J. W. (1964). The human operator as a monitor and controller of multidegree of freedom systems. *IEEE Transactions on Human Factors in Electronics, HFE-5*(1), 2–5. doi:10.1109/THFE.1964.231647

Shallice, T., McLeod, P., & Lewis, K. (1985). Isolating cognitive modules with the dual-task paradigm: Are speech perception and production separate processes? *Quarterly Journal of Experimental Psychology A: Human Experimental Psychology, 37A*(4), 507–532.

Spector, A., & Biederman, I. (1976). Mental set and mental shift revisited. *American Journal of Psychology, 89*(4), 669–679. doi:10.2307/1421465

Sudevan, P., & Taylor, D. A. (1987). The cuing and priming of cognitive operations. *Journal of Experimental Psychology: Human Perception and Performance, 13*(1), 89–103. doi:10.1037/0096-1523.13.1.89

Tsang, P., & Wickens, C. D. (1988). The structural constraints and strategic control of resource allocation. *Human Performance, 1*(1), 55–72. doi:10.1207/s15327043hup0101_3

Van Selst, M., Ruthruff, E., & Johnston, J. C. (1999). Can practice eliminate the Psychological Refractory Period effect? *Journal of Experimental Psychology: Human Perception and Performance, 25*(5), 1268–1283. doi:10.1037/0096-1523.25.5.1268

Vidulich, M. A. (1988). Speech responses and dual-task performance: Better time-sharing or asymmetric transfer? *Human Factors: The Journal of the Human Factors and Ergonomics Society, 30*(4), 517–529.

Welford, A. T. (1952). The "Psychological Refractory Period" and the timing of high-speed performance—A review and a theory. *British Journal of Psychology. General Section, 43*(1), 2–19. doi:10.1111/j.2044-8295.1952.tb00322.x

Welford, A. T. (1967). Single-channel operation in the brain. *Acta Psychologica, 27*, 5–22. doi:16/0001-6918(67)90040-6

Wickens, C. D. (1980). The structure of attentional resources. In R. Nickerson (Ed.), *Attention and performance VIII* (pp. 239–257). Hillsdale, NJ: Lawrence Erlbaum Associates.

Wickens, C. D. (1984). The Multiple Resources Model of human performance: Implications for display design. Retrieved from http://stinet.dtic.mil/oai/oai?&verb=ge tRecord&metadataPrefix=html&identifier=ADP004516

Wickens, C. D. (1991). Processing resources and attention. In D. Damos (Ed.), *Multiple-task performance* (pp. 3–34). London, UK: Taylor & Francis.

Wickens, C. D. (2002). Multiple resources and performance prediction. *Theoretical Issues in Ergonomics Science*, *3*(2), 159–177. doi:10.1080/14639220210123806

Wickens, C. D., & Liu, Y. (1988). Codes and modalities in multiple resources: A success and a qualification. *Human Factors: The Journal of the Human Factors and Ergonomics Society*, *30*(5), 599–616.

Yeung, N., Nystrom, L. E., Aronson, J. A., & Cohen, J. D. (2006). Between-task competition and cognitive control in task switching. *Journal of Neuroscience*, *26*(5), 1429.

11

Memory

The previous three chapters provided an overview of the *structure* of the mind, focusing on the characteristics of the sensory systems as well as attentional limitations on both perceptual and central processing. We now turn to a discussion of behaviors associated with the *contents* of the mind: how we store and manipulate knowledge, and how we use that knowledge to shape decisions. In this chapter we address human memory—the systems responsible for storing and retrieving information acquired through the senses. Obviously, a full description of the research on human memory is well beyond the scope of a single chapter. Therefore, we focus on fundamental characteristics in an effort to provide a basic understanding of the capabilities and limitations associated with the human memory system, and how those characteristics may play a role in systems engineering.

TYPES OF MEMORIES

Any memory system, whether in a computer, a brain, a filing cabinet, DNA, tree rings, or other, requires a means of acquiring, storing, and then retrieving information. Memory systems differ from one another with respect to the particular characteristics of these operations. Indeed, human memory itself is not a unitary construct, but instead consists of a collection of interacting subsystems, distinguished from one another in terms of the way information is acquired, stored, and retrieved. The goal of research on human memory is to determine the characteristics of these various memory components, as well as the nature of their interactions. From an applied perspective, it is particularly important to understand the limitations on memory and the implications those limitations have for operator behavior in engineered systems.

We have already discussed one form of memory system in Chapter 9, in the context of the sensory buffers (iconic and echoic memory). Recall that these buffers have relatively high capacity, but are very limited in duration (<1 second for iconic memory and <2 seconds for echoic memory), and that they code information in a very "raw" form. Perhaps the best-known set of memory subsystems, however, is *short-term/working memory* and *long-term memory*. These comprise the primary components of the *modal model* of memory, shown in Figure 11.1 (Atkinson & Shiffrin, 1968). As the names imply, the fundamental difference between these two subsystems is the duration for which information is retained.

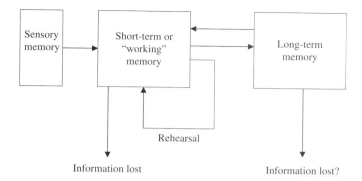

Figure 11.1 Components of the modal model of memory and their connections. *Source:* After Atkinson & Shiffrin (1968).

However, the subsystems also differ with respect to how much information they can retain (capacity) and the form of the information retained (coding).

Short-Term Memory

Much of our behavior from moment to moment is dependent on the transient maintenance of information related to current goals. The classic example is looking up a phone number and remembering it long enough to dial the phone. Note that in most situations, holding on to that information any longer would be an unnecessary waste of cognitive resources, even detrimental to many everyday functions. In his book *The Mind of a Mnemonist*, the Russian psychologist A. R. Luria describes a man with a prodigious memory, who retained the details of all that he did, saw, or heard. Because every word was associated with concrete details for all past encounters of the word, the man was unable to think metaphorically. Attempts to read poetry, for example, produced a welter of conflicting images, each associated with a concrete instance of each of the several possible meanings (Luria, 1987).

It is not surprising, then, that the human mind is equipped with a means of maintaining information for just short periods of time. This *short-term memory* system was first studied in the late 1950s using a technique known as the Brown-Peterson technique (Brown, 1958; Peterson & Peterson, 1959). In the Peterson and Peterson study (1959), participants viewed a brief presentation of three randomly selected consonants (e.g., KZQ) after which they were given a three-digit number; they were required to count backward by threes for varying durations. This "filler" task was designed to prevent rehearsal of the stimulus. They were then instructed to recall the three letters. Surprisingly, as shown in Figure 11.2, after only 15 to 20 seconds of counting backward, performance dropped to less than 10 percent, with the forgetting curve approximating a power function (i.e., the rate of forgetting leveled out with increasing time). This result provided evidence for a memory store from which information was lost over the course of 15–20 seconds, and suggested that rehearsal plays a role in maintaining information in this store. Later work, however, showed that the loss of information in the Peterson and Peterson study was likely due to

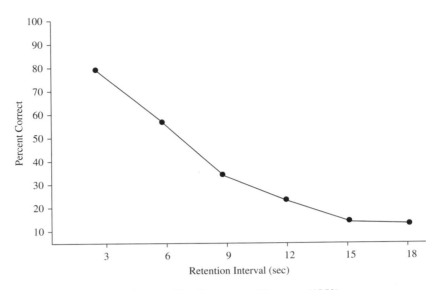

Figure 11.2 Forgetting curve. *Source:* After Peterson and Peterson (1959).

interference produced by the stimuli presented on previous trials (presumably a long-term memory effect) in the experiment (Wickens, Born, & Allen, 1963), rather than just the decay of a memory trace.

In addition to limited duration, short term memory is also limited with respect to capacity. A good example of capacity limitations on short-term memory is performance on the *digit span task*. In this task, participants are presented with an auditory list of random digits that can vary in length (usually between 3 and 15 digits), and are required to recall the list of digits in the order they were presented. Typically, there is a sharp decline in performance when the list exceeds 7 +/– 2 digits, suggesting an upper limit on how much information can be retained in short-term memory (Miller, 1956). However, these capacity limitations can be subverted by using long-term memory to group information into "chunks". For example, Ericcson, Chase, and Faloon (1980) report one participant who, after weeks of practice, was able to accurately recall lists of up to 80 random digits. It turns out that this amazing feat was made possible by an elaborate chunking scheme that took advantage of the participant's expertise with respect to running times. As digits were presented, he was able to group them based on his knowledge of running times. For example, he might label a particular sequence of digits as "one second off the world record for the 1500-meter race." Given this chunking scheme, rather than retrieving the actual digits from short-term memory, he essentially "reconstructed" the list by decoding the chunk labels based on his long-term memory knowledge. Importantly, when tested with random letters, his performance was back at 7 +/– 2, confirming that practice with digits had not increased the capacity of his short-term memory, but had instead allowed the development of the chunking scheme. Note that in applied contexts, it is not uncommon to find examples of long digit series (such as social security numbers or credit card numbers) being arranged into smaller groups to encourage chunking and improve retention.

Interestingly, the mnemonist in Luria's book may not have been relying strictly on the capacity of his memory system either. He was also a synaesthete: a person who, when presented with stimulation to one sensory modality, experiences sensations in several sensory modalities. Tones of a different frequency would appear to him as different colors. Because he retained all the concrete details of each encounter, these colors were stored, along with tastes and feelings, for each word or number he encountered. One of the problems in recall is to differentiate the item being recalled from all the other, possibly similar, events. For Luria's mnemonist, so much information was encoded for each word or number that it facilitated his discrimination between items.

With respect to the nature of the representations stored in short-term memory, early research suggested that, regardless of presentation modality, stimuli are transformed into a phonological or "sound" code (Conrad, 1964). This is certainly consistent with our intuitive experience of "saying" a phone number in our heads even when we've looked it up visually. Conrad (1964) looked at the types of errors participants made when recalling relatively short lists of letters. He found that regardless of whether the lists were presented visually or aurally, participants tended to make "sound-alike" errors, in which letters that sound alike were confused with one another in memory. However, later studies found evidence for visual and even semantic coding in short-term memory (Brooks, 1968; Phillips, 1974; Posner & Keele, 1967; Shulman, 1970; Wickens, Dalezman, & Eggemeier, 1976). Indeed, more recent treatments propose that short-term memory actually consists of a several distinct stores that vary with respect to nature of representation (Baddeley, 1986). In addition, these more recent approaches emphasize the fact that the complexity of most of the transient tasks in which we engage requires not only the temporary storage of information, but also the manipulation and integration of that information.

Working Memory

In the early studies described in the preceding section, short-term memory was conceptualized as a kind of "box" with 7 +/− "slots" that could hold chunks information. More recent work, however, has emphasized the notion that short-term memory is not simply a storage system; rather, it can be thought of as a "work area" where temporarily stored information is manipulated to accomplish goals such as doing mental calculations, comprehending sentences, and working with mental images (Baddeley, 1986). Given this emphasis on the active nature of short-term information storage and manipulation, short-term memory storage is now considered to be just one component of a memory *system* referred to as *working memory*. Figure 11.3 illustrates the functional architecture of the working memory system. The system is composed of the *central executive* and two short-term memory stores distinguished by the nature of the representations in which the information is coded: the *phonological loop*, which retains information in a verbal/phonological form, and the *visual-spatial sketch pad*, which retains information in a primarily spatial format. Associated with each of these components are rehearsal processes that refresh and maintain the information in the stores. The central executive is an attentional control system responsible for coordinating information processing in the two memory stores, including

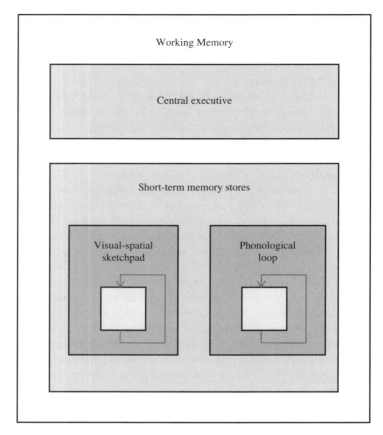

Figure 11.3 Working memory system. *Source*: After Baddeley (1986).

the retrieval of information from long-term memory and the focusing and switching of attentional resources.

It is important to note that the two storage subsystems are considered to be independent, such that processing in one of the systems should not interfere with concurrent processing in the other (Brooks, 1968). This distinction between verbal/phonological and visual/spatial working memory has a number of important applied implications. First, tasks should be designed in such a way that there is as little interference between memory codes as possible. For example, task situations that require the use of spatial working memory should not be combined with concurrent tasks that might also draw on spatial working memory. For example, Wickens, Sandry, and Vidulich (1983) looked at pilot performance in a flight simulator (a task that depends heavily on spatial processing) when holding onto verbal navigational information or when localizing a target in space. They found that the spatial localization task interfered with flying performance more than the verbal memory task.

Second, the fact that independent memory stores exist for verbal and spatial information has implications for decisions about display format. Specifically, when a task requires the maintenance and updating of spatial information (e.g., an air traffic controller maintaining a mental model of aircraft positions within her airspace), a visual-spatial display format will be the most effective means for updating memory, because very little code transformation is necessary for the update. An interesting illustration of this principle can be found in research on the best display format instructions/procedures for operating manuals. Kammann (1975) investigated instructions for operating a telephone switchboard (a primarily spatial task) and found that a spatial flowchart-type representation of the instructions produced better comprehension and retention than verbal printed instructions. However, when a task requires memory for verbal information (e.g., navigational entries presented to a pilot), a verbal display format (i.e., auditory speech) will be the most effective. Indeed, Wickens et al. (1983) found that pilots' memory for navigational information was better when the information was presented verbally rather than visually.

Long-Term Memory

Although the short-term/working memory system is important for maintaining and achieving transient behavioral goals, it is also adaptive to have a more permanent information storage system. For example, retaining information about past events can help guide current behavior. In humans, this more durable form of memory is referred to as *long-term memory*. Just how "long term" is this memory system? The duration of long-term memory is a difficult issue to address because the inability to remember information from the past could indicate that the information is no longer present in memory—but it could also mean that the information is present but inaccessible. The same difficulty surrounds the issue of the capacity of long-term memory. Thus, much of the research on long-term memory has focused instead on the nature of long-term representations and the factors that influence the probability that a particular piece of information will later be remembered.

Early models of the memory system assumed that information in long-term memory is coded in terms of *semantics* or meaning (Atkinson & Shiffrin, 1968). Evidence for this assumption comes from the kinds of errors that are made in long-term memory tasks. For example, consider a task in which participants are first asked to learn a long list of words, and are later presented with another list consisting of some of the words from the original list, as well as new "distractor" words not on the original list. For each word on the new list, the participant must say whether it was one of the original words. Participants are much more likely to falsely remember a distractor as being on the original list if that distractor is semantically related, or from the same semantic category, as one of the original words (Grossman & Eagle, 1970; Roediger & McDermott, 1995). However, there is evidence for visual representations in long-term memory as well. For example, it is well established that concrete words that are easy to visualize are remembered better than abstract words. Paivio's (1986) *dual-code hypothesis* interprets this advantage as reflecting the fact that concrete words can be coded visually as well verbally/semantically, whereas abstract words can only generate a verbal/semantic code.

A good deal of the research on long-term memory has focused on the factors that influence the probability of information being encoded into this more permanent store.

In the original modal model, it was assumed that information is first processed in short-term memory and then transferred to long-term memory by virtue of rehearsal. According to this view, the more often information is rehearsed, the higher the probability that it will be transferred to long-term memory. However, modern views of memory no longer assume that information must first reside in short-term memory before being transferred to long-term memory. In addition, in an influential series of papers, Craik and colleagues demonstrated that it is not rehearsal *per se* that increases the probability of more permanent storage, but rather the type of rehearsal in which one engages (Craik & Lockhart, 1972; Craik & Tulving, 1975). According to this *levels of processing* model of memory, we are flexible with respect to how deeply we choose to encode any given stimulus. Thus, we can choose to engage in *maintenance* rehearsal, in which information is encoded and rehearsed without any effort to process the information to a deep semantic level, such as when one simply memorizes a definition. We can also choose to engage in *elaborative* rehearsal, in which the information is processed to a deep semantic level and enriched through links with semantically related information, such as would be the case if one were studying for a written essay exam requiring the integration of concepts. Elaborative rehearsal has been found to enhance memory performance (Craik & Tulving, 1975).

Another factor associated with rehearsal that can influence the retention of information in long-term memory is the degree to which study repetitions are massed or spaced (Greene, 1989). *Massed repetition* refers to the repetition of information with little or no time between study episodes, whereas *spaced repetition* refers to the spreading-out of study episodes over time. A familiar example of massed repetition is students' frenzied cramming just before an exam. There has been much debate over the value of cramming: whether it results in learning or whether it even helps on tomorrow's exam. The bulk of the literature on memory and massed versus spaced learning episodes suggests that spaced repetition produces better memory performance than massed rehearsal, but the specific mechanisms underlying this *spacing effect* have long been the subject of debate (Greene, 1989). Some argue that spaced repetition enhances distinctiveness of the studied information and also results in a greater variety of contextual cues for retrieval. Others suggest that in spaced repetition, the later repetitions result in the retrieval of earlier study episodes, which then results in more elaboration of those episodes and a more durable memory representation.

More recently, the spacing effect has been interpreted in terms of the adaptation of our memory systems to the demands of the environment. It turns out that although most studies have found better retention with spaced repetition during learning, there is an interaction of presentation with retention interval. It is true that spaced repetition results in better recognition performance at longer retention intervals, but at short retention intervals, when the test is presented immediately following learning, massed repetition during study produces slightly better performance (Peterson, Hillner, & Saltzman, 1962; Peterson, Saltzman, Hillner, & Land, 1962). This interaction of retention interval and massed versus spaced practice reflects the need for information availability in the world. Events that occur together in time (massed) generally require one to retain information for only a short time, whereas events that recur at longer intervals (spaced) require one to retain information for longer periods. In this view, the statistics of this information need have driven our memory systems to adapt mechanisms sensitive to the frequency with which information is required.

From an applied perspective, the conclusion of the "need" function is that cramming may help on the next day's exam, but is unlikely to produce learning that endures beyond that. The practical implications of the spacing effect go far beyond performance on tomorrow's examination. The important and robust result—that long-term retention of information improves with spaced study/repetition—should inform the way curricula are structured in school and other training environments. Unfortunately, most laboratory studies have used small differences in time between massed and spaced presentation and retention intervals that seldom exceed a day (Cepeda, Vul, Rohrer, Wixted, & Pashler, 2008; Rohrer & Pashler, 2010). In contrast, learning in school takes place over a semester and is expected to produce learning that endures into the next semester. Cepeda et al. (2008) varied both study interval and retention interval over several days to determine the optimal study interval for a given retention interval (time between last study and test). They assigned university student volunteers to groups representing the combination of 6 study intervals (0, 1, 2, 7, 21, and 105 days) and 4 retention intervals (7, 35, 70, and 105 days). Participants in each of the two study groups were asked to memorize 32 obscure facts (e.g., "What European nation consumes the most spicy Mexican food?" Answer: "Norway"). As expected, the researchers found that the number of facts recalled declined as the retention interval increased: participants forgot information over time. Of particular note, however, was that the optimal study interval increased as retention interval increased. These results suggest that if one wished to achieve optimal retention of a set of facts for a year, an interval of about 23 days between study episodes was best. Longer retention would require longer study intervals. The sobering message is that this is far from the way our curricula are currently structured. In school, subjects are covered in a few days or a week, then not reintroduced when moving on to a new topic. This is in stark contrast to virtually all the psychological evidence about the retention of information over the long term, and suggests that better outcomes could be achieved by restructuring the schedule of information presentation in the classroom.

Episodic versus Semantic Memory

The research on long-term memory, as just described, involves the storage of information about events, experiences, or episodes from the past. For example, determining whether a given word was on a previously presented list involves retrieving information about the occurrence of that word at a particular time within a particular context. This type of memory, referred to as *episodic* memory, can be contrasted with memory associated with general knowledge or facts, referred to as *semantic* memory. Both involve long-term retention of information, but research suggests that the two reflect distinct forms of long-term memory (Tulving, 1972). For example, Tulving, Schacter, McLachlan, and Moscovitch (1988) report a case study of a motorcycle accident victim who suffered damage to the left frontal lobe. The patient suffered severe amnesia, but only for autobiographical events. After the accident, he was unable to remember anything he had ever done or experienced in the past (i.e., his episodic memory). However, his memory for facts, and his ability to answer questions requiring general knowledge (i.e., his semantic memory), remained reasonably intact. This pattern is an example of a *functional dissociation* in which a single variable (in this case brain damage) has different effects on two different behaviors (in this case wiping out the ability to remember personal episodes but leaving memory for facts intact). Such a dissociation supports the existence of distinct functional systems underlying the two behaviors. Thus, the case reported by Tulving et al. (1988) suggests that episodic and semantic memory are indeed two independent forms of long-term memory.

RETAINING AND FORGETTING INFORMATION

Thus far, we have described the characteristics and limitations of the various subsystems of human memory. These systems, however, are not infallible. Memory can fail in two fundamental ways: we can simply "forget" information that we've previous learned, or we can inaccurately remember information we've previously learned. The first systematic study of forgetting was conducted by Hermann Ebbinghaus in 1885, who studied lists of 13 syllables until he was able to recite the list without error twice in a row. He then tested his memory of the lists at intervals ranging from 20 minutes to 31 days (Ebbinghaus, 1885). Given that he made errors regardless of the length of the retention interval, he measured forgetting in terms of the number of repetitions of the list it took to once again achieve perfect performance (this technique of measuring forgetting is known as the *savings method*). As is evident from the graph in Figure 11.4, the *forgetting curve* for long-term memories follows the same power law as the Peterson and Peterson forgetting curve for short-term memory. This power law of learning is ubiquitous in memory research (Wixted & Ebbesen, 1991). For example, work by Bahrick and colleagues found a similar pattern for material ranging from names and faces to foreign-language vocabulary (Bahrick, Bahrick, & Wittlinger, 1975).

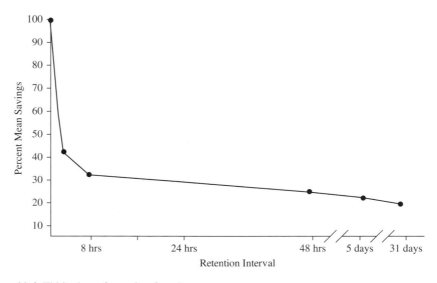

Figure 11.4 Ebbinghaus forgetting function.

There is even evidence that the learning of skills is subject to the same kind of forgetting curve. In one study with important implications for application, participants were taught the skills associated with administering cardiopulmonary resuscitation (CPR), which has been shown to significantly increase survival rates for those undergoing a heart attack (Glendon, McKenna, Blaylock, & Hunt, 1987). Memory for 4 different components of the CPR technique was tested at intervals ranging from 3 to 36 months. All four components revealed a forgetting function that again followed a power law. Remarkably, the results showed that the amount of forgetting that occurs over a one-year period reduces the survival rate of patients who could be successfully resuscitated from 100 percent to 15 percent!

Why do we forget information? One way of tackling this question is to look at the kinds of factors that influence the degree to which we forget. Suppose you put together a grocery list, and then mistakenly leave your list at home. Are there characteristics of the list that might influence memory for the items? It turns out that one important factor that influences whether a given item will be forgotten is the serial position of the item in the list. In laboratory experiments, participants are typically presented with a list of 15 or 20 items and then immediately asked to recall the items from the list in any order. Plotting memory for items as a function of list position yields a *serial position curve*. This curve is typically U-shaped, with better memory for items appearing at the beginning and end of the list than in the middle of the list. The former is referred to as the *primacy effect*, and the latter as the *recency effect* (Murdock Jr., 1962).

The primacy effect is believed to reflect the fact that items at the beginning of the list are likely to be rehearsed more often, increasing the probability that they will be transferred to long-term memory. The recency effect is believed to reflect the fact that the last few items on the list are still being maintained in short-term memory. Indeed, the serial position effect has been used to support that theory that long-term and short-term memory reflect independent memory systems. Using the functional dissociation method described earlier, it is possible to find variables that selectively eliminate the primacy effect but leave the recency effect intact (e.g., increasing the presentation rate of the list, which reduces the time available for rehearsing the first few items; Marshall & Werder, 1972). Meanwhile, there are other variables that eliminate the recency effect but leave the primacy effect intact (e.g., having participants perform a distractor task for 30 seconds before recalling the list; Bjork & Whitten, 1974).

So, what produces forgetting of items in the middle of the list? There are several possibilities. One is that because the items are not rehearsed sufficiently, they are simply not encoded as well as the items at the beginning of the list (perhaps because they do not receive as much rehearsal), resulting in a relatively feeble memory representation. Another possibility is that without rehearsal, the representations for the middle items decay such that they are no longer available at the time of recall. One other possibility is that the stronger representations for primacy and recency items interfere with the encoding and retrieval of the middle items. Note that interference by primacy items would be an example of *proactive interference*, in that information learned in the past is affecting the ability to remember information learned later. Interference by recency items would be an example of *retroactive interference*, in that more recently learned information is interfering with the ability to remember information learned previously.

From a systems engineering perspective, the serial position effect reflects a fundamental memory limitation that can have important implications in situations where the human operator is required to remember serially presented lists of items or information. Consider, for example, the presentation of a "weather briefing" to a pilot. Given the serial position effect, the weather service might do well to place the information most critical to the safety of the flight at the beginning or end of the briefing.

Interference

There is good evidence that interference plays a significant role in the loss of information from short-term memory. Waugh and Norman presented participants with lists of 16 digits, with the last digit (the "probe") being a repetition of one of the earlier digits (Waugh & Norman, 1965). The task was to report the digit that followed the first presentation of the probe. They varied the number of digits occurring between the reported digit and the end of the list, as well as the presentation rate of the list. With this design, they were able to measure the influence of decay by looking at the effect of presentation rate for a constant number of intervening items (i.e., faster presentation rates should produce less decay because less time has elapsed between the probe and the end of the list). Similarly, they were able to isolate the influence of interference by comparing conditions in which the time between the probe and the end of the list was constant, but the number of intervening items varied. The results, shown in Figure 11.5, revealed that presentation rate had very little influence on performance, whereas performance dropped substantially as the number of intervening items increased. Thus, it appears that the loss of information from short-term memory is driven primarily by interference.

Converging evidence for interference in short-term memory comes from a trial-by-trial analysis of performance using the Brown-Peterson task described earlier (Keppel & Underwood, 1962; Wickens et al., 1963). Wickens et al. (1963) presented participants with either three numbers or three common words which they were required to recall after a 20-second retention interval during which rehearsal was prevented with a filler task. The researchers found that by the third trial in the experiment, performance dropped from around 90 percent to around 40 percent (see Figure 11.6). They interpreted this effect as an example of proactive interference in which memory representations from previous trials impaired the ability to remember the stimuli from the current trial. Consistent with this interpretation, they found that if, on the fourth trial, the stimuli came from the other class (i.e., a switch from digits to words or vice versa), performance returned to the level found on the first trial. This "release from proactive interference" provided strong evidence that the similarity of codes in memory influences the degree to which they will interfere with one another.

A very nice demonstration of the applied implications of these effects comes from a study on pilots' memory for air traffic control (ATC) information (Loftus, Dark, & Williams, 1979). As an aircraft flies across the country, it sequentially travels through zones controlled by local ATC centers. As the aircraft enters a new ATC zone, the pilot is typically given multiple instructions by ground controllers that must be remembered in order to carry out the appropriate actions in the context of distracting activities, such as monitoring instrument displays. For example, ground controllers might provide "place"

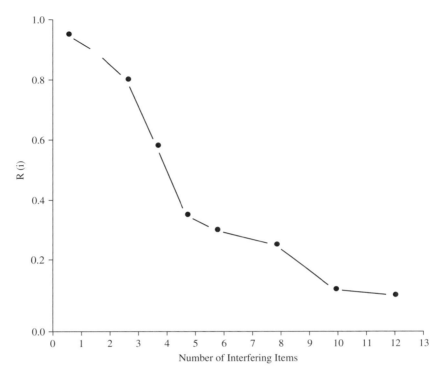

Figure 11.5 Interference effects of intervening items on short-term memory performance. *Source:* Data from Waugh and Norman (1965).

(e.g., Chicago) information about the ATC center, the radio frequency for communication (e.g., 121.3 megahertz) and transponder code (e.g., "squawk 7123"). To study memory (and forgetting!) for this type of information, Loftus, et al. (1979) presented student pilots with various combinations of place, frequency, and transponder codes in a Brown-Peterson type task. In addition, the numerical information was presented in either a chunked format (i.e., "twenty one—forty five") or in a single digit sequence ("two one four five). During a retention interval varying between 0 and 15 seconds, the pilots engaged in a distracting task consisting of repeating aloud rapidly presented random letters.

The results showed a typical forgetting function over the course of 15 seconds. However, the rate of forgetting was influenced by several factors. First, forgetting was more rapid when the memory "load" was high (i.e., when pilots had to remember two pieces of information compared to just one piece of information). In addition, under high load conditions, memory was worse when the two pieces of information were both in digit format (e.g., radio frequency and transponder code) than when one of the pieces of information was the name of the ATC center. Finally, memory for information presented in a chunked format was better than memory for unchunked information. These results

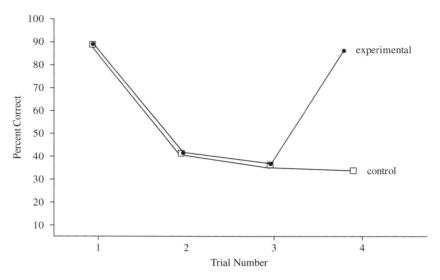

Figure 11.6 Release from Proactive Interference. *Source:* C. D. Wickens, Born, & Allen (1963).

demonstrate that issues of load, coding similarity, interference, and encoding strategies clearly play a role in memory for information in an important applied domain (see also Gronlund, Ohrt, Dougherty, Perry, & Manning, 1998).

Interference has also been found to play a significant role in performance on long-term memory tasks. Perhaps the best-known example of retroactive interference in long-term memory comes from the provocative work of Elizabeth Loftus, who was interested in the degree to which post-event experiences can actually change one's memory for the original event (Loftus, 1977). This question has important applied implications, in that demonstrating the "malleability" of memory would call into question the trustworthiness of eyewitness testimony. Indeed, Loftus's original motivation for the study came from concerns about whether misleading questions (e.g., during police investigations) might alter an eyewitness's memory for an event. Participants viewed a film of a car accident and later were asked a series of questions about the events in the film. One critical question asked how fast the cars were travelling when they hit each other. However, for different groups of participants, the word "hit" was replaced with "contacted," "bumped," "collided," or "smashed." The assumption was that these various descriptors imply different rates of speed. The results showed that even though all participants viewed the exact same film, their speed estimates varied directly with the descriptor in the sentence, with the "hit" group reporting the lowest speed and the "smashed" group reporting the highest speed. In addition, participants returned to the lab a week later and were asked whether they remembered seeing broken glass in the film (there was none). Participants who had received the "smashed" descriptor were much more likely to report that they had seen broken glass.

These results suggest that post-event experiences (e.g., a misleading question) can retroactively interfere with accuracy of the memory for the original event.

In subsequent experiments, Loftus and Palmer (1974) explored whether memory for an event is actually "overwritten" by post-event experiences. In one study, participants again viewed a presentation of a car accident where, at one point, a green car drives past the accident before the police arrive. In a subsequent questionnaire, one of the questions referred to the car that drove past the accident scene. For half the participants this question mentioned a "green car"; for the other half it mentioned a "blue car." Twenty minutes later, the participants were asked the color of the car, and those given false information were significantly more likely to describe the car as blue. These results are consistent with the notion that the original memory was replaced by the misleading information. However, subsequent research showed that memory for the original event is actually still available in memory, and that post-event experiences can "overlay" the original memories without destroying them (Bekerian & Bowers, 1983). Either way, this line of research shows that memory is indeed malleable, and can be altered through retroactive interference arising from post-event experiences.

There is also evidence that performance on long-term memory tasks can be influenced by proactive interference. For example, Underwood tested undergraduates for memory of a list of nonsense syllables (a three-letter syllable composed of a consonant-vowel-consonant that does not form a word), and was surprised by the amount of forgetting they showed after just 24 hours (Underwood, 1957). Given that he tended to use the same undergraduates for many of his memory experiments, he wondered whether participation in previous experiments might have produced proactive interference. Consistent with this hunch, he found that the amount of forgetting on the syllable task in a 24-hour period varied dramatically with the number of lists participants had previously learned (see Figure 11.7).

Forgetting to Remember to Remember: Prospective Memory

Our discussion of forgetting has thus far focused on the inability to remember information we have learned in the past. As we all know too well, there is another form of forgetting in which we fail to remember to do something we were supposed to do. This (dis)ability to remember to take some action at a specific time in the future is referred to as *prospective memory* (Dismukes, 2010; Kliegel & McDaniel, 2008; McDaniel & Einstein, 2007; Meacham & Singer, 1977). Prospective memory failure can take the form of forgetting the intended action, forgetting the relevant time frame, or both. The consequences of prospective memory failure can range from trivial (forgetting to turn the coffee maker off) to tragic (forgetting to check the status of the flaps during the take-off of a jetliner; Dismukes & Nowinski, 2007). Precisely because the intended action occurs in the future, it is not feasible to maintain a goal associated with the future action in short-term or working memory. Thus, one must rely on external environmental cues related to the action to jog memory. For example, if one has a doctor's appointment scheduled for 10:00 A.M., then either driving by the office building, or noticing the clock at 9:45 A.M. might serve as a cue for the intended action (Sellen, Louie, Harris, & Wilkins, 1997).

Research suggests that prospective memory failure is associated with the degree to which the participant engages in effortful monitoring for these environmental cues (Smith,

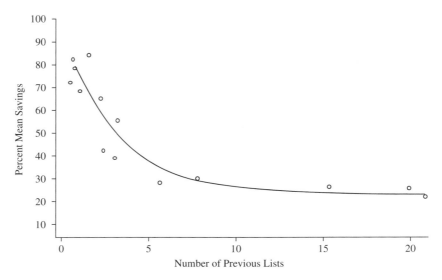

Figure 11.7 Proactive Interference and forgetting as a function of number of previous lists learned. *Source:* Data from Underwood (1957).

2003). However, there is also evidence that memories of intentions to perform an action often appear spontaneously and in the absence of active monitoring (Einstein & McDaniel, 2005). Einstein and McDaniel (2005) propose that cue processing can occur automatically (i.e., in the absence of active monitoring), but that such automatic cue processing is more likely when the cues are highly related to the target action (as in the case of seeing the doctor's office building), when cues are salient (they attract attention), or when cues are central (focal) to the processing involved for ongoing tasks (such as checking the time on a clock). For example, one study found that prospective memory errors in simulated air traffic control situations were reduced when operators were presented with external display cues indicating that an action needed to be taken (Loft, Smith, & Bhaskara, 2011). These cues were only effective, however, when they appeared at the time the action was needed.

RETRIEVING INFORMATION

Thus far we have focused our discussion of memory on factors that influence the acquisition and storage of information. It is now time to turn to characteristics of memory *retrieval*. One could argue that the reason memory systems evolve is because information learned in the past can confer a survival advantage when it comes to future actions. However, to take advantage of that learning, one must have a way of retrieving the relevant information at the appropriate time. In the following section, we discuss the characteristics of retrieval from both short-term and long-term memory.

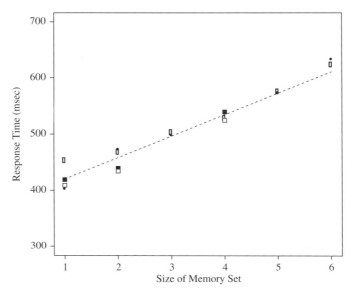

Figure 11.8 Response time in retrieval from short-term memory. *Source:* Data from Sternberg (1966).

Short-Term Memory Retrieval

Studies of the retrieval of information from short-term memory often use an experimental task known as *memory search* (Sternberg, 1966). Participants are given a set of items to "hold" in short-term memory and are then presented with a series of "probe" items. Participants are asked to respond "yes" if the probe is one of the items currently in short-term memory, or "no" if it is not. Response time is measured as a function of the number of items that are held in memory (i.e., the *memory set size*). This task clearly requires the retrieval of the items from short-term memory, so that the participant can make an appropriate response to the probe. Sternberg (1966) found that response time increased linearly with memory set size, and that the slope of the function was 38 msec (Figure 11.8). This suggests that items are retrieved from short-term memory serially, and that retrieval takes about 40 msec per item.

Interestingly, Sternberg (1966) also found that the slope of the memory set size-response time function did not vary across "yes" and "no" responses. This fact is consistent with the somewhat counterintuitive notion that retrieval from short-term memory is *exhaustive*, meaning that all the memory items must be retrieved before a response is made. To understand this interpretation, consider performance on "no" trials. If the probe does not match any of the memory set items, then all the items must be searched before a "no" response can be made. In other words, on "no" trials, search is necessarily exhaustive. On "yes" trials, however, one would expect to "find" the probe after retrieving about half of the items from memory, on average. If search were *self-terminating*, then a response would be made upon finding a match. Such a self-terminating model therefore predicts that the slope of the "yes" function should be about half the slope of the "no" function. The fact that the "yes" slope did not differ from the "no" slope therefore suggests that rather than terminating search as soon as a match was found, all the items from the memory set were retrieved before a response was made. Although this seems like an inefficient way of doing memory search, it is possible that given the relatively rapid retrieval times, the time and effort required to terminate memory search is more costly overall than engaging in a more ballistic retrieval process.

It is important to note that the memory search task provides a means of isolating the processes associated with retrieval from other processes that might contribute to response time, such as perception of the probe and the initiation and execution of the response. Although the slope of the memory set size function reflects retrieval processes, the y-intercept of the function (i.e., which technically would represent the case in which there is nothing to retrieve) reflects these other processes. Thus, the methodology allows one to determine whether variations in overall response times associated with a given variable reflect a change in memory retrieval or some other process.

For example, it is commonly believed that smoking marijuana impairs short-term memory. However, Darley, Tinklenberg, Roth, Hollister, and Atkinson (1973) administered a memory search task before and after a dose of either marijuana or placebo. As expected, response times for memory search were slower after the ingestion of marijuana, but the effect was limited to a change in the y-intercept of the memory set size function; there was no change in the slope of the function. This suggests that marijuana affects some process other than the retrieval of information from short-term memory. There are variables, however, that do influence the slope of the function. For example, relative to the "typical" adult, high school students and senior citizens produce steeper function slopes, whereas memory "professionals" (i.e., mnemonists who perform memory feats as entertainment) produce shallower function slopes (Hunt, 1978). Finally, there is evidence that the slope of the function can vary with the type of material that is being held in short-term memory (e.g., digits produce shallower slopes than nonsense syllables), which suggests that certain kinds of material require more effort to retrieve (Cavanagh, 1972). In fact, slope and intercept changes in the memory search function have been used as a means of measuring the nature of mental workload associated with work environments. For example, Wickens, Hyman, Dellinger, Taylor, and Meador (1986) had pilots in a flight simulator perform a memory search task during a simulated "holding pattern" and during a simulated landing approach. The intercept of the search function increased during approach, but the slope of the function did not change. This suggests that the landing approach is associated with increases in perceptual/motor workload, but has no effect on the cognitive workload associated with memory retrieval.

Long-Term Memory Retrieval

Logically, the apparent exhaustive nature of short-term memory retrieval is possible only because of the inherent limitations in capacity of short-term memory. As the amount of information in a memory store increases, exhaustive search simply becomes unfeasible. Thus, the retrieval processes associated with long-term memory, which is assumed to have a very large, nearly unlimited capacity, are likely to be quite a bit different from

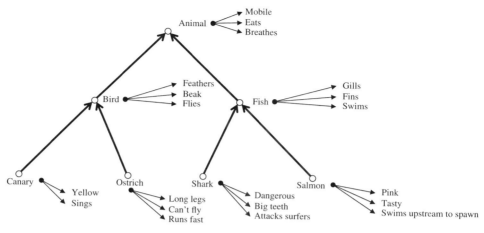

Figure 11.9 Hierarchical network model of semantic memory. Activation of one node can spread to other nodes increasing activation for related items. *Source:* Hierarchy from Collins and Quillian (1969).

those associated with short-term memory. Research on long-term memory retrieval can be organized around models of semantic memory retrieval versus models of episodic memory retrieval.

Recall that *semantic memory* refers to our memory for general knowledge about the world. For example, semantic memory would contain information about the features associated with a canary (it is a bird, it has wings, it is yellow). How is this kind of information retrieved from a "database" that is nearly limitless in capacity? To a certain extent, the nature of information retrieval will be determined by how the information in such a large system is organized. Thus, the study of the retrieval of information from semantic memory has been intimately associated with the study of the organization of semantic memory.

One of the first attempts at modeling the organization of semantic memory assumed that information is organized in a *hierarchical network* (Collins & Quillian, 1969). According to this approach, knowledge is organized with respect to levels of abstraction, such that the lowest levels represent highly concrete concepts like "canary" and higher levels represent increasingly abstract concepts, such as "bird," "animal," "living thing," and so on (see Figure 11.9). Associated with each concept at each level are a set of features that are specific to that level. Thus, the features stored with "canary" might consist of "yellow," "sings beautifully," but not "has wings" or "can fly," because those features would be more appropriately stored with the higher-level concept "bird." Notice that on the one hand, this system is very economical, in that a particular feature is stored only once in the network. On the other hand, it means that retrieving facts about a concept might require accessing concepts and features at different levels in the network. For example, retrieving a fact such as "a canary can breathe" would require establishing a pathway between the concept "canary" at one level and the feature "can breathe" at a higher level.

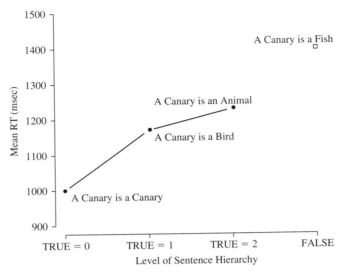

Figure 11.10 Sentence verification task results. The time to respond to TRUE questions increases with distance in the hierarchy, as measured by the number of nodes in between the exemplar and category label. *Source:* Date from Collins and Quillian (1969).

Using a *sentence verification task*, Collins and Quillian (1969) tested whether the human semantic memory system might be organized in this hierarchical fashion. In this task, a sentence is presented that states a potential "fact" about the world, and the participant responds as to whether the fact is true (e.g., A canary is a bird) or false (A canary is a fish). The critical manipulation was the number of levels or "distance" in the hypothesized network between the concept in the subject and the concept in the predicate. For example, a fact like "A canary is a bird" would require assessing concepts separated by only one level, whereas a fact like "A canary is an animal" would require assessing a concept separated by two levels. Collins and Quillian reasoned that if knowledge is stored in this hierarchical fashion, then sentence verification time should increase with the distance between concepts in the network. In general, this is precisely what they found (Figure 11.10).

There were aspect of the results, however, that didn't quite fit with the hierarchical approach. For example, verification times for "false" facts (A canary is a fish) were faster than for true facts, even though presumably the participant would have to traverse more levels to confirm that the sentence was indeed false. In addition, verification times for concepts that are more prototypical exemplars of a category were faster than for atypical exemplars. Thus, the verification time for "A robin is a bird" was faster than for "An ostrich is a bird," even though the concepts in both sentences are separated by the same number of levels in the network. This *typicality effect* led theorists to propose an alternative organizational scheme for semantic material based on the notion of *semantic relatedness* (Collins & Loftus, 1975). The idea is that the distance or length of the "pathways" between concepts in the semantic network is not a function of level of abstraction, but rather reflects the degree to which the concepts are related to one another in terms of meaning. Thus, according to this approach, retrieval times from semantic memory will depend on the length of the pathways between the relevant concepts.

One other property of semantic networks that influences retrieval times is the notion of *spreading activation*. By virtue of the connections among concepts in a network, the activation of one concept is assumed to spread to other concepts with which it is connected. Therefore, retrieval should be faster for a concept that has been partially activated by spreading activation. This prediction is confirmed in a phenomenon known as *semantic priming*. For example, Meyer and Schvaneveldt presented participants with two strings of letters, one or both of which formed a word (Meyer & Schvaneveldt, 1971). The task was to respond "yes" if both strings were words or "no" if one of the strings was a nonword. The key result was that response times on "yes" trials were faster if the two words were semantically related than if they were not related, suggesting that the activation of one word primed the retrieval of the second. Interestingly, there is evidence that the retrieval time benefits produced by spreading activation are modulated by the number of other concepts with which a given concept is associated. Specifically, as the number of associated concepts increases, the benefits produced by spreading activation decrease (Anderson, 1976). Thus, it appears that the activation spread from one concept to another is a limited resource.

The models of semantic memory just discussed emphasize the notion that related concepts are "connected" by virtue of pathways in a network, and that these connections play a role in the efficient retrieval of information. There is evidence that the retrieval of information from episodic memory is also dependent on connections or associations between representations of stored events. One of the strongest pieces of evidence for this conclusion is the fact that one memory can serve as a *retrieval cue* that enhances the probability of remembering another, associated memory. The effectiveness of a retrieval cue, however, is highly dependent on the relationship between the encoding circumstances and the retrieval circumstances (Tulving & Thomson, 1971).

Specifically, the *encoding specificity principle* states that "specific encoding operations performed on what is perceived determines what retrieval cues are effective in producing access to what is stored" (Tulving & Thomson, 1973, p. 369). Essentially, this means that memory retrieval will be enhanced to the extent that the circumstances surrounding encoding are reproduced at retrieval. For example, there is good evidence that the context in which a particular event occurs can act as a retrieval cue for the target event. Godden and Baddeley recruited scuba divers for a memory experiment in which the divers were required to learn list of words either on the beach, or beneath 15 feet of water, and then recall the lists in either the same or the opposite context (Godden & Baddeley, 1975). As shown in Figure 11.11, recall performance was best when the encoding context matched the retrieval context. This suggests that the context in which the critical information was learned can serve as a powerful retrieval cue.

Interestingly, there is evidence that a similar context effect is obtained if, at retrieval, the participants simply imagine the same context in which they actually encoded the lists (Smith, 1979). In addition, there is evidence that the "mental state" of the participant can also serve as a contextual retrieval cue. Goodwin et al. found that memory for information

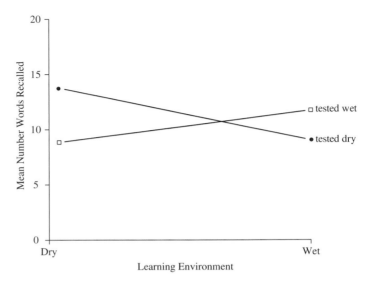

Figure 11.11 Demonstration of the encoding specificity principle. Recall is better in the same environment as learning. *Source:* Data from Godden and Baddeley (1975).

learned when under the influence of alcohol at encoding was remembered better if the participant was in the same state at retrieval (Goodwin, Powell, Bremer, Hoine, & Stern, 1969). Likewise, memory for information encoded when sober was also remembered better when sober. Finally, there is evidence that mood state can serve as a powerful contextual cue. Bower and colleagues have documented a *mood-congruent learning effect* in which retrieval is enhanced when a participant's mood state at retrieval matches the mood state at encoding (Bower, Monteiro, & Gilligan, 1978).

An extension of the encoding specificity principle is the construct known as *transfer-appropriate processing*, which refers to the fact that memory is enhanced if the nature of the processing performed on a stimulus at retrieval is similar to that performed at encoding (Morris, Bransford, & Franks, 1977; Roediger III & Blaxton, 1987). For example, Morris et al. (1977) had participants engage in a word-encoding task that required relatively shallow processing (making a rhyme judgment) or deep processing (deciding whether the word fit in a sentence). In a subsequent recognition memory task, words from the encoding phase were paired with distractor words. Recognition of words for which a rhyming judgment was made was enhanced if the distractor word also rhymed with the target word. Likewise, recognition of words for which a semantic judgment was made was enhanced when the distractor word was semantically similar to the target word.

SUMMARY

In this chapter, we described the fundamental capabilities and limitations associated with the human memory system. Human memory is not a single construct, but instead consists of a system of components that vary with respect to duration, capacity, and code and retrieval dynamics. In turn, these characteristics determine the kinds of variables that influence the probability and accuracy of memory retrieval. Thus, theories of human memory provide important information for the design and evaluation of systems in which performance is dependent, at least in part, on the human operator's ability to store and retrieve task-relevant information at the appropriate time.

REFERENCES

Anderson, J. R. (1976). *Language, memory, and* thought. Hillsdale, NJ: Lawrence Erlbaum Associates.

Atkinson, R. C., & Shiffrin, R. M. (1968). Human memory: A proposed system and its control processes. *Psychology of Learning & Motivation: Advances in Research and Theory, 2,* 89–195.

Baddeley, A. D. (1986). *Working memory.* Oxford, UK: Clarendon Press.

Bahrick, H. P., Bahrick, P., & Wittlinger, R. (1975). Fifty years of memory for names and faces: A cross-sectional approach. *Journal of Experimental Psychology: General, 104*(1), 54.

Bekerian, D., & Bowers, J. (1983). Eyewitness testimony: Were we misled? *Journal of Experimental Psychology: Learning, Memory, and Cognition, 9*(1), 139.

Bjork, R. A., & Whitten, W. B. (1974). Recency-sensitive retrieval processes in long-term free recall. *Cognitive Psychology, 6*(2), 173–189.

Bower, G. H., Monteiro, K. P., & Gilligan, S. G. (1978). Emotional mood as a context for learning and recall. *Journal of Verbal Learning and Verbal Behavior, 17*(5), 573–585.

Brooks, L. R. (1968). Spatial and verbal components of the act of recall. *Canadian Journal of Psychology/Revue canadienne de psychologie, 22*(5), 349.

Brown, J. (1958). Some tests of the decay theory of immediate memory. *Quarterly Journal of Experimental Psychology, 10*(1), 12–21.

Cavanagh, J. P. (1972). Relation between the immediate memory span and the memory search rate. *Psychological Review, 79*(6), 525.

Cepeda, N. J., Vul, E., Rohrer, D., Wixted, J. T., & Pashler, H. (2008). Spacing effects in learning. *Psychological Science, 19*(11), 1095.

Collins, A. M., & Loftus, E. F. (1975). A spreading-activation theory of semantic processing. *Psychological Review, 82*(6), 407.

Collins, A. M., & Quillian, M. R. (1969). Retrieval time from semantic memory. *Journal of Verbal Learning and Verbal Behavior, 8*(2), 240–247.

Conrad, R. (1964). Acoustic confusions in immediate memory. *British Journal of Psychology, 55*(1), 75–84.

Craik, F. I., & Lockhart, R. S. (1972). Levels of processing: A framework for memory research. *Journal of Verbal Learning and Verbal Behavior, 11*(6), 671–684.

Craik, F. I., & Tulving, E. (1975). Depth of processing and the retention of words in episodic memory. *Journal of Experimental Psychology: General, 104*(3), 268.

Darley, C., Tinklenberg, J., Roth, W., Hollister, L., & Atkinson, R. (1973). Influence of marihuana on storage and retrieval processe in memory. *Memory & Cognition, 1*(2), 196–200.

Dismukes, R. K. (2010). Remembrance of things future: Prospective memory in laboratory, workplace, and everyday settings. *Reviews of Human Factors and Ergonomics, 6*(1), 79.

Dismukes, R. K., & Nowinski, J. (2007). Prospective memory, concurrent task management, and pilot error. In A. F. Kramer, D. A. Wiegmann, & A. Kirlik (Eds.), *Attention: From theory to practice* (pp. 225–236). New York, NY: Oxford University Press.

Ebbinghaus, H. (1885). *Über das Gedächhtnis.* Leipzig: Dunker. (Reprinted: H. Ruyer and C. E. Bussenius, Trans.) (1913). *Memory.* New York, NY: Teachers College, Columbia University.

Einstein, G. O., & McDaniel, M. A. (2005). Prospective memory. *Current Directions in Psychological Science, 14*(6), 286–290. doi:10.1111/j.0963-7214.2005.00382.x

Ericcson, K., Chase, W. G., & Faloon, S. (1980). Acquisition of a memory skill. *Science, 208*(4448), 1181.

Glendon, A. I., McKenna, S. P., Blaylock, S. S., & Hunt, K. (1987). Evaluating mass training in cardiopulmonary resuscitation. *British Medical Journal (Clinical Research ed.), 294*(6581), 1182.

Godden, D. R., & Baddeley, A. D. (1975). Context-dependent memory in two natural environments: On land and underwater. *British Journal of Psychology, 66*(3), 325–331.

Goodwin, D. W., Powell, B., Bremer, D., Hoine, H., & Stern, J. (1969). Alcohol and recall: State-dependent effects in man. *Science, 163*(3873), 1358.

Greene, R. L. (1989). Spacing effects in memory: Evidence for a two-process account. *Journal of Experimental Psychology: Learning, Memory, and Cognition, 15*(3), 371.

Gronlund, S. D., Ohrt, D. D., Dougherty, M. R. P., Perry, J. L., & Manning, C. A. (1998). Role of memory in air traffic control. *Journal of Experimental Psychology: Applied, 4*(3), 263.

Grossman, L., & Eagle, M. (1970). Synonymity, antonymity, and association in false recognition responses. *Journal of Experimental Psychology, 83*, 244–248. doi:10.1037/h0028552

Hunt, E. (1978). Mechanics of verbal ability. *Psychological Review, 85*(2), 109.

Kammann, R. (1975). The comprehensibility of printed instructions and the flowchart alternative. *Human Factors: The Journal of the Human Factors and Ergonomics Society, 17*(2), 183–191.

Keppel, G., & Underwood, B. J. (1962). Proactive inhibition in short-term retention of single items. *Journal of Verbal Learning and Verbal Behavior*, *1*(3), 153–161.

Kliegel, M., & McDaniel, M. A. (2008). *Prospective memory: Cognitive, neuroscience, developmental, and applied perspectives*. New York, NY: Lawrence Erlbaum Associates.

Loft, S., Smith, R. E., & Bhaskara, A. (2011). Prospective memory in an air traffic control simulation: External aids that signal when to act. *Journal of Experimental Psychology: Applied*, *17*(1), 60.

Loftus, E. F. (1977). Shifting human color memory. *Memory & Cognition*, *5*(6), 696–699.

Loftus, E. F., & Palmer, J. C. (1974). Reconstruction of automobile destruction: An example of the interaction between language and memory. *Journal of Verbal Learning and Verbal Behavior*, *13*(5), 585–589.

Loftus, G. R., Dark, V. J., & Williams, D. (1979). Short-term memory factors in ground controller/pilot communication. *Human Factors: The Journal of the Human Factors and Ergonomics Society*, *21*(2), 169–181.

Luria, A. R. (1987). *The mind of a mnemonist: A little book about a vast memory*. Cambridge, MA: Harvard University Press.

Marshall, P. H., & Werder, P. R. (1972). The effects of the elimination of rehearsal on primacy and recency. *Journal of Verbal Learning and Verbal Behavior*, *11*(5), 649–653.

McDaniel, M. A., & Einstein, G. O. (2007). *Prospective memory: An overview and synthesis of an emerging field*. Thousand Oaks, CA: Sage Publications.

Meacham, J. A., & Singer, J. (1977). Incentive effects in prospective remembering. *Journal of Psychology: Interdisciplinary and Applied*, 97(2), 191–197.

Meyer, D. E., & Schvaneveldt, R. W. (1971). Facilitation in recognizing pairs of words: Evidence of a dependence between retrieval operations. *Journal of Experimental Psychology*, *90*(2), 227.

Miller, G. A. (1956). The magical number seven, plus or minus two: Some limits on our capacity for processing information. *Psychological Review*, *63*(2), 81.

Morris, C. D., Bransford, J. D., & Franks, J. J. (1977). Levels of processing versus transfer appropriate processing. *Journal of Verbal Learning and Verbal Behavior*, *16*(5), 519–533. doi:10.1016/S0022-5371(77)80016-9

Murdock Jr., B. B. (1962). The serial position effect of free recall. *Journal of Experimental Psychology*, *64*(5), 482.

Paivio, A. (1986). *Mental representations*. Oxford, UK: Oxford University Press.

Peterson, L., & Peterson, M. J. (1959). Short-term retention of individual verbal items. *Journal of Experimental Psychology*, *58*(3), 193.

Peterson, L. R., Hillner, K., & Saltzman, D. (1962). Supplementary report: Time between pairings and short-term retention. *Journal of Experimental Psychology*, *64*(5), 550.

Peterson, L. R., Saltzman, D., Hillner, K., & Land, V. (1962). Recency and frequency in paired-associate learning. *Journal of Experimental Psychology*, *63*(4), 396.

Phillips, W. (1974). On the distinction between sensory storage and short-term visual memory. *Attention, Perception, & Psychophysics*, *16*(2), 283–290.

Posner, M. I., & Keele, S. W. (1967). Decay of visual information from a single letter. *Science*, *158*, 137.

Roediger III, H. L., & Blaxton, T. A. (1987). Retrieval modes produce dissociations in memory for surface information. In D. S. Gorfein & R. R. Hoffman (Eds.), *Memory and learning: The Ebbinghaus Centennial Conference* (pp. 349–379). Hillsdale, NJ: Lawrence Erlbaum Associates.

Roediger III, H. L., & McDermott, K. B. (1995). Creating false memories: Remembering words not presented in lists. *Journal of Experimental Psychology: Learning, Memory, and Cognition*, *21*(4), 803.

Rohrer, D., & Pashler, H. (2010). Recent research on human learning challenges conventional instructional strategies. *Educational Researcher*, *39*(5), 406.

Sellen, A. J., Louie, G., Harris, J., & Wilkins, A. (1997). What brings intentions to mind? An in situ study of prospective memory. *Memory*, *5*(4), 483–507.

Shulman, H. G. (1970). Encoding and retention of semantic and phonemic information in short-term memory. *Journal of Verbal Learning and Verbal Behavior*, *9*(5), 499–508.

Smith, R. E. (2003). The cost of remembering to remember in event-based prospective memory: Investigating the capacity demands of delayed intention performance. *Journal of Experimental Psychology: Learning, Memory, and Cognition*, *29*(3), 347.

Smith, S. M. (1979). Remembering in and out of context. *Journal of Experimental Psychology: Human Learning and Memory*, *5*(5), 460.

Sternberg, S. (1966). High-speed scanning in human memory. *Science*, *153*(3736), 652.

Tulving, E. (1972). Episodic and semantic memory. *Organization of Memory*, 381–402.

Tulving, E., Schacter, D. L., McLachlan, D. R., & Moscovitch, M. (1988). Priming of semantic autobiographical knowledge: A case study of retrograde amnesia. *Brain and Cognition*, *8*(1), 3–20.

Tulving, E., & Thomson, D. M. (1971). Retrieval processes in recognition memory: Effects of associative context. *Journal of Experimental Psychology*, *87*(1), 116.

Tulving, E., & Thomson, D. M. (1973). Encoding specificity and retrieval processes in episodic memory. *Psychological Review*, *80*(5), 352.

Underwood, B. J. (1957). Interference and forgetting. *Psychological Review*, *64*(1), 49.

Waugh, N. C., & Norman, D. A. (1965). Primary memory. *Psychological Review*, *72*(2), 89.

Wickens, C. D., Hyman, F., Dellinger, J., Taylor, H., & Meador, M. (1986). The Sternberg memory search task as an index of pilot workload. *Ergonomics*, *29*(11), 1371–1383.

Wickens, C. D., Sandry, D. L., & Vidulich, M. (1983). Compatibility and resource competition between modalities of input, central processing, and output. *Human Factors: The Journal of the Human Factors and Ergonomics Society, 25*(2), 227–248.

Wickens, D. D., Born, D. G., & Allen, C. K. (1963). Proactive inhibition and item similarity in short-term memory. *Journal of Verbal Learning and Verbal Behavior, 2*(5–6), 440–445.

Wickens, D. D., Dalezman, R. E., & Eggemeier, F. T. (1976). Multiple encoding of word attributes in memory. *Memory & Cognition, 4*(3), 307–310.

Wixted, J. T., & Ebbesen, E. B. (1991). On the form of forgetting. *Psychological Science, 2*(6), 409.

12

Decision Making

> A young boy from southern California was scheduled for a biopsy. His X-ray showed curvilinear calcifications in the muscles of his thigh. The radiologist in charge of the case suggested three possible diseases that could have accounted for these findings. A second radiologist listening to the findings was confused about the diagnoses. In the case of the first, there were no other symptoms consistent with that diagnosis. The second two diagnoses were associated with parasites only found outside of the United States. Ultimately, the second radiologist realized that the apparent curvilinear calcifications were the result of X-ray contrast solution, which had been spilled on the X-ray machine.
>
> (Casey, 1998, pp. 152–160)

In Chapter 11 we looked at the nature of human memory storage and retrieval. In this chapter we examine how humans make decisions about what actions to take, based on information in the environment and information from memory. How do people make decisions such as those made by the radiologists in the case-study story? How is it that two trained individuals looking at the same information can come to very different decisions? Although the answers to these questions are not fully known, careful experimentation over several decades has given us important clues into how people use (and fail to use) the available information in deciding among options. To understand human decision making, it is useful to begin with the characteristics associated with any decision-making task.

ANATOMY OF A DECISION

In Figure 7.2 we presented a functional diagram of control, which included an action selection loop. That loop consisted of a sensory representation of the world, an assessment of the meaning of the sensed information with respect to immediate goals, and a plan of action designed to improve the situation by minimizing the difference between the desired goal state and the sensed state of the world. Action selection is a good starting point for understanding decision making, as it illustrates a fundamental property of decisions: Some single action must be taken with respect to one's knowledge of the world. That single action can be an overt behavior, as in the action selection example. Alternatively, it can be a covert choice, as in the categorization of a stimulus as a threat or not. Indeed, what appears to be a single decision, such as which action is selected in Figure 7.2, can be seen as a number of more specific decisions that represent choices in the decision process itself. These include choices of:

1. What decision options are under consideration
2. What criteria are relevant to the decision
3. What values are attached to good and bad outcomes
4. What information sources in the world should be sampled
5. How the sampled information should be weighted and integrated
6. How the weighted information is treated as evidence for or against an option
7. When there is sufficient evidence to select one decision option

A framework that incorporates this approach can be seen in Figure 12.1. The first three choices determine the *decision space*, by which we mean how the operator formulates the problem. The next three choices describe *evidence accumulation*, which determines how knowledge and events in the world become *evidence* for or against specific decision alternatives. The final choice refers to the *decision criterion*, which defines at what point the evidence for one specific decision alternative is sufficiently stronger than that for all

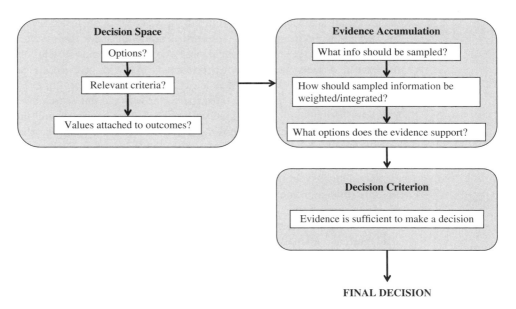

Figure 12.1 Framework for decision making.

others to declare it the decision. As this framework shows, the process of making a decision already consists of a number of decisions about how to set up the problem, what constitutes evidence, and how to reach a conclusion.

We can illustrate how these choices play out in the very simple example of buying a car. The decision space is determined first by the nature of the problem to be solved. In this case, we will assume that the decision process to be described is the choice of a specific car for purchase. This assumes that the decision has already been made that replacing the car is better than repairing it, perhaps because the existing car is getting old. Note too that there has been a decision, made either explicitly or implicitly, to buy a car rather than, say, a bicycle or scooter. As with many decisions, the problem becomes one of narrowing the possible choices, first from a large number of transportation options down to a specific car to purchase.

To perform the narrowing, a set of criteria can be established to assess the criteria by which the cars will be evaluated. For example, fuel efficiency might be one criterion, reliability another, and the list might continue with sportiness, acceleration, color, and many more. In the case of a car, a good outcome would be a car that is fun to drive; a bad outcome would be a "lemon" that is always in the shop and ends up costing a lot. The consideration of good and bad outcomes provides a means of weighting the attributes of each car. In this case, avoiding a lemon has a very high desirability and will outweigh the positive attraction of fun. If the value of reliability were high enough, it might also be the case that it would affect other attributes, so that paying more might be considered a good thing in service of higher reliability and long-term cost savings.

It would seem good, once the decision parameters have been established, to then sample all the makes of cars. This is neither practical nor really optimal, in that carefully considering clusters of features that are unlikely to be appealing (high cost plus moderate values on all attributes) would simply be a waste of time. Instead, people typically look for cues in the environment that can further prune the space of possible options. Low-cost search options would include magazines, web sites with automobile reviews, and the sites for specific models. We have noted previously that with practice, the search for information appears to be nearly optimal, at least as indicated by patterns of eye fixations. For most decisions, such as buying a car, our expertise is less and our search behavior less optimal. The information sources examined will be guided by heuristics and influenced by issues such as familiarity, previous exposure, friends, advertising, and so forth. Indeed, one of the main goals of advertising is to get you to consider the advertiser's product when you are next formulating a purchase decision. A bias that can affect which information sources are examined means that information display systems that are designed to prioritize cues may be quite influential in decision making.

In the early stages, the features of cars being weighed might include what friends say, what opinions were expressed on web sites, price, or body shape. New information becomes available once a small set of candidates has been chosen and test drives are undertaken. Each car will have a unique feel, look, color set, interior design, panel layout, and so on. The problem now becomes how to integrate all of the information. It is not sufficient to simply say that reliability, acceleration, body shape, and road feel are important. Rather, we must be able to say how they trade off: how much a pleasing body shape offsets mediocre reliability when the car has great acceleration and good handling qualities, for example. There is a large body of evidence showing that people have a great deal of difficulty integrating information about different dimensions into decision making (Dawes, 1979; Kahneman & Tversky, 1984; Kahneman, Slovic, & Tversky, 1982; Slovic, 1972; Slovic, Fischhoff, & Lichtenstein, 1977). Often a simple formula does a better job of combining all the observations and assessing how well they meet the stated characteristics than does a person.

At some point, the sampling has to stop and a decision has to be made. At what point do people stop sampling? In some cases, it turns out that we are sensitive to the rate at which new information is coming in. In other cases, people tend to be overconfident of their conclusions based on early and incomplete evidence collection (Casscells, Schoenberger, & Graboys, 1978). Information foraging theory argues that the strategies people use to search for information resemble the processes by which animals forage for food (Pirolli, 2007; Pirolli & Card, 1999); this theory provides computational approaches to determining when people are likely to stop looking for additional information.

At every stage in the process of buying a car, decisions are being influenced by other participants in the decision-making process, previous experience on the part of each individual involved in the decision-making process, cognitive biases, intuitions, and the constraints of the physical environment. Savvy car salespeople take advantage of the difficulty people have in weighing features by making the specific attributes of their products seem more appealing (higher weighting), while downplaying the importance of what they lack compared to other products.

Psychologists have tried to understand how people end up making the decisions they do. For the most part, the interest has been in understanding evidence accumulation. The reasons for this are clear. We are called on at times to sit on a jury where our ability to weigh evidence will affect the lives of others. We also elect leaders, expressing our opinion about their policy statements. This requires that we weigh the evidence for or against policies to decide which will achieve the most desirable outcome. The theories that have been put forward to account for human decision making fall generally into three categories: *normative theories*, *cognitive theories*, and *naturalistic theories*. Note that these are classes of theory, and are not mutually exclusive. For example, the cognitive biases emphasized in cognitive theories also apply in naturalistic theories.

This chapter discusses all three of these approaches taken to account for human decision-making. We will discuss both biases that influence the decision-making process, and a potential information-processing approach to describing the decision-making process. Finally, we will consider how the decision-making process and the biases that creep into human decision-making affect the development of aids designed to improve decision making.

NORMATIVE APPROACHES TO DECISION MAKING

In many situations it is possible to compute what can be considered rational behavior. Normative approaches to understanding human decision making begin with a rational analysis of the decision. They then describe systematic ways in which human decisions deviate from rationality. To understand this, we first consider the components of a rational decision.

Rational Decisions

A *decision* is a prediction about which of several options is most likely to achieve some goal. If you are on a jury, you will be presented with facts and asked to determine the degree to which those facts constitute evidence for a decision of guilt or nonguilt. If you are a doctor, you will be presented with a set of test results and asked to determine the degree to which those results constitute evidence for one of several possible underlying conditions. If you are hiring an employee, or selecting a candidate for medical school, you will have facts about that person's past performance and asked to predict the likelihood that a person will succeed given those pieces of evidence. Many times the data do not conclusively point to a single decision outcome, meaning that there can be considerable *ambiguity* and *uncertainty*. The uncertainty means that decisions will not always be correct. What is needed is a process that will guarantee that our decisions will be the best possible with respect to the uncertainty.

When the strength of the evidence for and against decision alternatives can be represented numerically and the decision process can be framed mathematically, the theory of probability allows us to combine information in a way that will lead to the best outcome in the long run. That is, probability theory provides a way of assessing the quality of a decision by asking which outcome would yield the best results overall if that decision were made over and over again. There are four components to this: (1) the prior likelihood of each decision alternative being correct; (2) the strength of the evidence for or against each of the alternatives; (3) the probability that each decision alternative is correct given the evidence; and (4) the decision rule, which specifies how these probabilities should be combined to select a single alternative. The prior likelihood is usually expressed as a probability, where $p(B)$ means the probability that B is true. The strength of evidence is given as a conditional probability, where $p(E/B)$ means the probability that E would have occurred given that B was true. In assessing the evidence, it is also important to consider the $p(E/\sim B)$, a conditional probability referring to the probability that E would have occurred given that B had not. These conditional probabilities define the evidence for each of the possible decision alternatives. The *a priori* probability and the strength of evidence are usually known beforehand. What we want to know, however, is the probability of a particular decision alternative being true given the evidence, or $p(B/E)$, referred to as the *posterior probability*. For this we need a decision rule that combines the *a priori* probability and the weight of evidence.

Bayes Theorem

The decision rule most often used to derive these probabilities is Bayes' theorem. There are several related forms of Bayes' theorem. To keep the mathematical notations relatively simple, we will use the form for deciding which of two alternatives is the most likely.

$$p(A/E) = p(E/A)p(A)/[p(E/A)p(A) + p(E/\sim A)p(\sim A)]$$

This equation says that the posterior probability that alternative A is true given the evidence (E) is a function of (1) the *a priori* likelihood of A ($p(A)$); (2) the degree to which the evidence is consistent with A ($p(E/A)$); (3) the degree to which the alternative ($\sim A$) is also consistent with the evidence (p(E/~A)); and (4) the *a priori* likelihood of the other alternative (p(~A)).

It may help to consider this in the context of a concrete example. Your friend goes to the doctor, concerned that a newly discovered and deadly type of brain tumor is causing his headaches. The doctor assures him that the tumor is rare, occurring in only 1 in 1000 people. Further, says the doctor, there is a test for this tumor. People with the tumor test positive 99 percent of the time. Those without the tumor test positive only 1 percent of the time. Your friend receives the troubling news that he tested positive. Should your friend decide that he has the deadly tumor, and proceed to get his affairs in order? We can use Bayes' theorem to tell us the probability of the tumor given the evidence.

If we let A be the alternative of having the tumor, ~A is the alternative that something else is causing the symptoms. The *a priori* probability of A is p(A) = .001, which means that the prior probability that it is something else is p(~A) = 1 − p(A) = .999. The probability of getting a positive result if he does have a tumor (A is true) is p(E/A) = .99, whereas the probability of a positive result when he doesn't have the tumor is (p(~A)) = .01. So, the probability that your friend has the tumor given the positive result is:

$$p(A/E) = (.99)(.001)/((.99)(.001) + (.01)(.999)) = .09$$

Thus, your friend should not be too worried, as there is only a 9 percent chance that he has the deadly tumor. How can it be that the probability is so low when the test is so reliable? The key is that the *base rate* of tumor occurrence is very low (.001). This is somewhat easier to see if we just use numbers. Suppose we take a population of 100,000 people. Of these, only 100 would have the tumor. Of the 100, 99 would show positive on the test. Of the 99,900 without the tumor, 999 would test positive. The total testing positive would be 99 + 999 = 1098, of which only 99 would have the tumor. This example points out the importance of base rates (a prior probability) in coming to a rational conclusion. Even expert medical professionals at high-prestige hospitals fail to use base rate information accurately when interpreting test results (Casscells et al., 1978). In one study (Eddy, 1982) 95 percent of physicians wrongly diagnosed positive test results for cancer as indicating between 70 and 80 percent likelihood of cancer, rather than true value of 7.8 percent.

Although the preceding example illustrates the importance of base rates, it does not capture the ways in which posterior probabilities change with new evidence. Suppose you are a contestant on a game show and are offered two bags. One bag contains 100 gold one-dollar coins. The other contains 50 gold coins and 50 worthless slugs. You cannot tell the worthless coins by feel, only by looking at them. You get to draw a coin to examine. How should the outcome of that draw affect your decision of which bag to choose? In this case, let A be the bag you examine and B the other bag. Your choice is to decide to if bag A is the best bag (T); that is, p(A = T). The prior probabilities are equal: p(A = T) = p(B = T) = .5. Let G be the outcome of drawing a gold coin. Because the true bag has all gold coins, p(G/A = T) = 1. The probability that you will draw a gold coin from a given B that is the true bag is p(G/B = T) = .5, as in that case A will contain 50 gold coins and 50 worthless slugs. If what you draw is a worthless slug, you know that A ≠ T, and is the wrong decision, so you choose B. If the coin from A is gold, you can't be absolutely sure. What you can do is use Bayes' theorem to compute the likelihood that A = T given the gold-coin draw, G:

$$p(A = T/G) = p(G/A = T)p(A = T)/[p(G/A = T)p(A = T) + p(G/B = T)p(B = T)]$$

$$p(A = T/G) = 1 \times .5/[1 \times .5 + .5 \times .5] = .667$$

Thus, the single draw increased the probability from .5 to .667. Let's see what happens if you put the coin back in and draw again. This time, the prior odds are .667 and, because we replaced the coin, all other quantities are equal:

$$p(A = T/G) = 1 \times .67/[1 \times .67 + .5 \times .33] = .8$$

Making the posterior probability that results from one trial the prior probability for the next provides the basis for using Bayes Theorem to learn: hence, *Bayesian learning*.

Utility and Expected Value

We still have not fully accounted for the all of the ingredients of a decision as listed earlier. In particular, we have not yet explored the way a rational model would treat the consequences of a decision. For example, would you wager money that the outcome of the roll of two dice would be an even number greater than 4 if winning yielded $1.75 per every $1 bet? Put another way, what payoff on your dollar would make it attractive? We illustrate this in Figure 12.2. In the top table we show all the possible outcomes and the payoff for each. We see more losing outcomes than winning outcomes, but the winning outcomes pay more. In reality, there are only two outcomes, winning and losing. We can get a better representation of the attractiveness of the bet by computing the probability

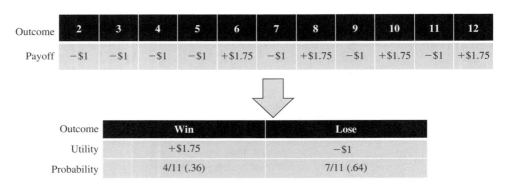

Outcome	2	3	4	5	6	7	8	9	10	11	12
Payoff	−$1	−$1	−$1	−$1	+$1.75	−$1	+$1.75	−$1	+$1.75	−$1	+$1.75

Outcome	Win	Lose
Utility	+$1.75	−$1
Probability	4/11 (.36)	7/11 (.64)

Expected value (E) is defined as the average return on the wager over the long term given the utility (U) of each outcome (i).

$$E = \Sigma U_i p(i)$$
$$= 1.75 \times 4/11 + -1 \times 7/11 = 0$$

Figure 12.2 Computation of utility and the expected value. In this example, you wager $1 on the roll of two dice and win $1.75 every time an even number greater than 4 occurs. The expected value is 0, which means that over the long run you expect to break even, neither winning nor losing. E < 0 means you expect to lose in the long run, E > 0 means you expect to win.

of winning and losing. This is shown in the lower table, along with the *utility (U)* of each win or loss. The utility of a win is $1.75, while that of a loss is $1. We can then compute the probability of winning and losing. It is not possible to predict the outcome of a single throw of the dice. Given the probabilities, however, we can calculate the *expected value (E)* of the bet over many tosses.

Expected value (E) is the sum of the utility (U) of each outcome (i) multiplied by the probability of that outcome:

$$E = \sum_i U_i p(i) = U(win) \times p(win) + U(loss) \times p(loss)$$

In the example given, the expected value is 0, meaning that in the long run you can expect to break even on this wager, neither winning nor losing money. In gambling casinos, the expected value is less than zero, meaning that in the long run you can expect to lose money. Consider roulette. A European roulette wheel has slots numbered 0–36; the American game adds a 00 slot. The payoff for a straight bet of $1 on a single slot is $35. For the American game, then, p(win) = 1/38, p(lose) = 37/38, U(win) = $35, U(lose) = −$1. This yields an expected value of –0.0526, which translates into a 5.26 percent house edge. This means that the house can expect to win and come out ahead in the long run even with perfect play (which seldom happens). Keep in mind that the expected value does not tell you what will happen on any given roll, or any small number of rolls. What expected value does tell you is that with large numbers of players over long periods of time, the outcome favors the house.

For numerical wagers with known (or calculable) probabilities of occurrence for each outcome, it is possible to predict how a rational decision maker would perform. It is not surprising, then, that much work has been done on the kinds of wagers people will accept. In normative theories of decision making, the emphasis has been on understanding how humans make decisions by looking at the systematic ways in which our decisions deviate from that of a rational decision maker.

Early theories of decision making (e.g., Edwards, 1987) focused on people making rational decisions based on careful consideration of their choices. For example, expected value theory assumes that people calculate the value associated with each possible outcome and then choose the option with the highest expected value. In this framework, people must identify the cost or benefit (value) associated with a particular outcome in some measureable unit, as well as the likelihood that the outcome will occur (probability). The product of the value and the probability provides the expected value associated with each outcome. From that calculation, people are thought to take the action associated with the highest expected value (highest expected benefit or lowest expected cost). However, research shows that people often do not select the optimal outcome (from an expected value point of view). Thus, most of the research in this area focuses on why humans depart from this optimal level of performance.

NONOPTIMALITY OF HUMAN DECISIONS

The general finding from normative approaches to decision making is that people exhibit strong nonrational tendencies in their behavior. In particular, a number of specific biases in human decision making appear over and over again. It is not just that people fail to produce the mathematically precise predictions of the Bayes Theorem, or compute the expected value correctly. Rather, there are systematic departures from rationality. We discuss a few examples in the next section. Here we focus on one particular aspect of human decision making that differs markedly from rational decisions: failure to appropriately incorporate numerical information. This failure affects the treatment of base rates as well as the appreciation of numerical quantities.

Failure to Consider Base Rate Information

As we discussed earlier, Bayes' theorem computes the posterior probability (what we usually want) by combining the evidence and prior probabilities of occurrence of the possible outcomes. These prior probabilities are often referred to as *base rates*. As a general rule, people omit these when considering a problem, or at the very least find it difficult to correctly adjust for base rates. Consider the following scenario from a study by Tversky and Kahneman (1982):

A cab was involved in a hit-and-run accident at night. Two cab companies, the Green and the Blue, operate in the city. You are given the following data:

1. 85 percent of the cabs in the city are Green and 15 percent are Blue.
2. A witness identified the cab as Blue. The court tested the reliability of the witness under the same circumstances that existed on the night of the accident and concluded that the witness was able to correctly distinguish a Blue taxi from a Green taxi 80 percent of the time.

What is the probability that the witness correctly identified the color of the cab? The answer can be solved using Bayes' theorem with the following terms: $p(\text{Blue}) = .15$, $p(\text{Green}) = .85$, $p(\text{witness says Blue/Blue}) = .8$, therefore, the $p(\text{Blue/witness says Blue}) = .8 \times .15 / (.8 \times .15 + .2 \times .85) = .41$. Instead, people tended to give a number very close to 80 percent, the accuracy of the witness (Tversky & Kahneman, 1973). This is what you would conclude if you considered only the reliability of the witness and completely ignored the base rates given, as only 15 percent of taxis are Blue. To ignore base rates is equivalent to assuming that the posterior probability, $p(\text{Blue/witness says Blue})$, equals the likelihood associated with the evidence, $p(\text{witness says Blue/Blue})$. The same is true of the brain tumor example discussed earlier. There we derived Bayes' theorem solution and found that the chance of having a fatal tumor was only 9 percent, despite the high accuracy of the test in detecting it. In that case as well, people will judge the probability of having the disease as nearly that of the test accuracy. It might be assumed that people just make mistakes in calculations, or, not being mechanical calculators, simply factor in the numerical base rates incorrectly. However, the answers given by the vast majority of people simply ignore the numerical information.

Insensitivity to base rate information is especially prevalent when it competes with descriptive information. Tversky and Kahneman (1973, 1974) had people estimate the likelihood that a given verbal description of an individual drawn randomly from a sample belonged to an engineer or a lawyer. One group was told that the sample contained 70 lawyers and 30 engineers, while another group was told the reverse, 70 engineers and 30 lawyers. The likelihoods were unaffected by the numerical information about base rates. Instead, people judged solely by the similarity of the description to their stereotype of a lawyer or engineer. Similarly, when a completely neutral description was given, participants in both groups rated the probability at 50 percent for each occupation, despite the stated differences in base rates.

Being insensitive to base rate information leads to many false impressions of the world. Television news, for instance, tends to highlight rare circumstances. After all, as the saying goes, "dog bites man is no story, man bites dog is." It would surprise many people to learn that during the Egyptian crisis of 2011, when central Cairo was teeming with protestors, the vast majority of the city was calm and peaceful. The next time you hear a report on the news reporting a threat, take a moment and ask yourself what the base rate probabilities might be.

Judging Numerical Quantities

There is some evidence that people have great difficulty judging probabilities and percentages (Gigerenzer & Hoffrage, 1995). If problems are posed using absolute numbers, they do much better. For example, when doctors are given probabilistic information about the reliability of tests and base rates of conditions (e.g., the disease occurs in 0.1 percent of the population, the test has a 5 percent false-positive rate), only about 15 percent accurately conclude that only about 2 percent of those with positive test results will have the disease. However, roughly 40 percent of doctors were able to accurately estimate the probability when the problem was described as 100 people out of 100,000 tested will have the disease, whereas 5,000 of those without the disease will test positive (Casscells et al., 1978; Dehaene, 2011; Eddy, 1982). In this case, the problem is described by concrete numbers and the numbers are chosen so that they can easily be converted to percentages. Therefore, a good rule of thumb in designing information displays is to avoid statements of probability whenever possible.

Failure to Appreciate Statistical Properties

Given the problems associated with human appreciation of probability and the failure to use base rate information, it should not be too surprising to learn that people often fail to take into account statistical properties, such as randomness, variability, and sampling. Consider the case of naval aviators learning to land a jet plane on an aircraft carrier. Instructor pilots noted that when they yelled at a trainee after making a bad landing, it improved the trainee's performance on the next landing. However, when they praised a trainee for a landing, it produced a marked deterioration in performance on the next landing. They concluded that punishment had a beneficial effect on performance whereas praise was detrimental. Statistically, because of the natural variability in performance, using the performance of the last outing to predict the next performance should lead one to estimate that the subsequent behavior will be closer to the overall long-term mean than that of the previous. This is the oft-cited *regression to the mean* phenomenon. Regression to the mean is a statistical property of noisy predictions from limited sample sizes. The optimal prediction is closer to the mean because in a probability distribution there is a very low chance of obtaining consecutive values that deviate very far from the mean. Yet, the instructor pilots attributed the good performance of a trainee to the scolding given them the previous day when their performance was under par (Kahneman & Tversky, 1973). The scolding may or may not have had the desired effect, but statistically, the optimal prediction of the next day's performance based on that of a poor day would have been closer to the overall mean performance level. Equally unwarranted was the assumption that praise was detrimental. By its nature, unusually good performance of the sort that will garner praise represents a value more extreme than mean performance. One should expect the next attempt to be poorer more often than equal or better. Likewise, when learning a sport, or a musical instrument, it seems that you might think you have mastered a skill only to have it inexplicably disappear the next day. This is likely due to the statistical properties of regression to the mean. Regression to the mean occurs in estimating the height of sons based on the father's height, the intelligence of offspring based on the parents, and scores on consecutive tests. In misunderstanding the statistics of variability and how it affects prediction, people often devise spurious explanations that attribute the change to motivation, the behavior of others, external factors, or other seemingly plausible causal factors (Kahneman & Tversky, 1973).

The effects of sample size are also often misunderstood. Statistically, one can expect small samples to vary more around the population mean than will larger samples. This makes sense, as the larger the sample size, the more representative it is of the entire population. Consider, then, the following problem posed to participants in a psychological study (Kahneman & Tversky, 1972):

"A certain town is served by two hospitals. In the larger hospital about 45 babies are born each day, and in the smaller hospital about 15 babies are born each day. As you know, about 50 percent of all babies are boys. However, the exact percentage varies from day to day. Sometimes it may be higher than 50 percent, sometimes lower.

For a period of 1 year, each hospital recorded the days on which more than 60 percent of the babies born were boys. Which hospital do you think recorded such days?

- The larger hospital (21)
- The smaller hospital (21)
- About the same (that is, within 5 percent of each other) (53)"

The numbers in parentheses are the number of participants choosing each option. The correct answer is the smaller hospital. This follows because the chances of a sample deviating from the population mean (50 percent) is greater in small samples than in larger ones.

COGNITIVE APPROACHES TO DECISION MAKING

Thus far, we have presented the ingredients of a rational decision and given evidence that human decision making deviates from rational decisions in the failure to correctly use base rates, numerical information, and statistical regularities. How serious are these deviations? After all, it could be that we are endowed with a natural ability to use efficient heuristics and that the deviations from optimality only produce a few oddities here and there when making arcane statistical judgments. Such an ability would be reasonable, as the exact base rate and strength of evidence parameters required for rational decisions are often impossible to acquire or even estimate closely in real-life situations. Unfortunately, when human decision making has been examined, it has often been found wanting. We have already seen that a failure to appreciate regression to the mean can lead to false impressions about the effects of reward and punishment. In clinical settings, failure to consider base rates is common, and doctors routinely misinterpret the outcome of clinical tests (Casscells et al., 1978). The fallibility of human judgment is further attested to by several results showing that a decision computed from a simple linear combination of evidence outperforms decisions made by highly trained, experienced clinicians (Dawes, 1976; Sawyer, 1966).

This raises the question of how we do in fact make decisions. One way to reconcile the fallibility of human judgment with normative models is to assume that decisions are arrived at by rational means insofar as is possible given the limited capacity of human cognition. This is referred to as *bounded rationality* (Simon, 1959). For example, we may ignore base rates when the task is difficult enough that computing them would be beyond the computational power of human cognition. Bounded rationality has two problems. First, it does not really say how the decisions are arrived at other than noting that there will be some constraints. Second, and more importantly, bounded rationality implies that some attempt should be made to account for the relevant factors in the decision, even if the attempt falls short of true optimality; that is, the decisions should preserve some aspects of the rational process. In contrast, the answers that people give to problems involving decisions under uncertainty deviate in fundamental ways from that of a rational decision maker.

Studies of people making decisions under uncertainty have uncovered several biases that, taken together, characterize human decision making. By *biases* we mean systematic ways in which we approach problems, reason from evidence, or are affected by the context, that predispose us to making faulty judgments. They are typically applied unintentionally and often without awareness, and are difficult to mitigate. They also occur widely and affect judgments in medicine, public policy, risk taking, and scientific inference. Here we briefly describe important biases. More exhaustive descriptions of biases and heuristics can be found in Kahneman, Slovic, and Tversky (1982) and Wickens and Hollands (2000).

Confirmation Bias

People tend to seek information that supports or conforms to their pre-established beliefs or expectations. In medical settings, politics, and other walks of life, this *confirmation bias* leads people to seek subsequent information confirming that their initial diagnosis or decision is correct (Tolcott, Marvin, & Bresnick, 1989; Woods & Cook, 1999). Conversely, people tend not to look for, and frequently fail to identify or recognize, cues that might support an alternative interpretation, or prove their interpretation incorrect. Further, if they do find disconfirming information or cues, they tend to discount them. For example, take an X-ray technician who is attempting to determine whether a child who has fallen has broken her arm. If the physician tells the technician that the child is not crying and that she is moving her arm around freely as she talks without apparent pain, the technician may go into the diagnosis with the assumption that the arm is not broken and miss, or dismiss as a shadow on the film, evidence of a small, hairline fracture. Though the confirmation bias is in direct contrast to the prevailing scientific rule that one should search for evidence to disprove a hypothesis, it is as common among scientists as in the general population.

The tendency to seek confirming rather than disconfirming evidence was first described by Wason (1960). He had people infer an underlying rule used to generate sequences. For example, he would present a sequence (e.g., 2, 4, 6) whose rule was a simple increasing magnitude, and asked participants to articulate their hypothesis and then generate sequences that tested it. Participants sought evidence that confirmed rather than tested their hypotheses. If they hypothesized even numbers, they might generate 8, 10, 12, 14. This has been termed the *positive test strategy* (Klayman & Ha, 1987). In the positive test strategy, people seek out examples having the property that is being tested. This is a robust strategy. It appears to be commonly adopted when the problem is abstract or there is no concrete instance that can easily disprove it (Klayman & Ha, 1987). Evidence suggests that people adopt this strategy as a heuristic when cognitive load is high. It will not guarantee the correct outcome, but some argue that it is optimal under the assumption that the world is deterministic to the extent that there will be only one outcome for any rule (Austerweil & Griffiths, 2011).

Framing Effects

The term *framing effects* refers to the tendency to treat equivalent decisions differently depending on how they are presented. Several examples are provided by Tversky and Kahneman (1981; see also Kahneman & Tversky, 1984). The following example shows a set of problems from Tversky and Kahneman (1981) with identical rational solutions associated with virtually opposite preferences. In the first case, the options are framed with an emphasis on the positive outcome of saving lives, where each option represents a possible gain. In the second case, the options are framed with an emphasis on the negative outcome of losing lives, where each option represents a possible loss. It is easily seen that all options, in truth, are the same: in each the same number of people live and die. Nevertheless, people treat them as markedly different. The bold numbers in parentheses beside each option represent the number of people in Tversky and Kahneman's study (1981) choosing each outcome. In the first case, the saving frame, people chose option A 72 percent of the time; in the second case, the losing frame, people chose option B 78 percent of the time.

Your state is preparing for an outbreak of an Asian disease expected to kill 600 people. The good news is that you can fund ONE of the following two vaccine plans to save lives:

If funded, 200 people will be saved *(72%)*

If funded, 1/3 chance that all 600 will be saved, 2/3 chance that 0 will be saved *(28%)*

Which plan would you choose (A or B)?

Your state is preparing for an outbreak of an Asian disease expected to kill 600 people. The good news is that you can fund ONE of the following two vaccine plans to reduce the loss of life:

If funded, 400 people will die *(22%)*

If funded, 1/3 chance that 0 will die, 2/3 chance that 600 will die *(78%)*

Which plan would you choose (A or B)?

Framing effect illustrated by examples from Tversky and Kahneman (1981). Numbers in parentheses indicate the proportion of subjects selecting A or B.

Tversky and Kahneman (1981) attribute these preferences to the tendency of people to be *risk averse*. To be risk averse is to place a higher negative utility (negative value) on a loss than positive utility on an equivalent gain. In the case of the frame, the way the question is asked draws attention differentially to the potential gains and losses. When attention is drawn to the potential of saving lives, the worst case becomes the one in which no lives are saved. People are unwilling to run the risk of the worst outcome and thus avoid option B, which has the possibility of not saving anyone. In the second case, option B is more attractive, as it holds the hope of not losing anyone. The tendency toward risk aversion is fairly strong.

Framing effects represent effects of context on decisions that a rational analysis would treat as equal. In a sense, they represent a tendency to judge the desirability of outcomes in terms of an adjustment from a baseline expectation. If that expectation is losing 600 people, then a sure bet of saving some is attractive. If the action is judged from the point of view of costing lives, people select the option with the best chance of maintaining the baseline. Ask yourself how you would feel about the following two options for buying gas with a credit card: (1) Station A, which charges $4.00 per gallon with $.20 off for cash, or (2) Station B, which charges $3.80 per gallon with a $.20 surcharge for credit card use. Framing the decision in terms of the lower baseline price makes it the more attractive option.

Related to the framing bias is the *sunk-cost* bias (Arkes & Blumer, 1985), which refers to people's tendency to continue to invest time and money in a losing endeavor. What causes the optimism that the outcome will change? In a sunk-cost situation, people tend to be focused on the loss, as in the example where the vaccine is described in terms of the percent who will die. People continue to invest on the chance that they will be able to stop or limit the loss. The same logic affects how people choose to invest in the stock market. If you have a stock that has risen from $10 per share to $100 per share, then begins to slide and is now at $80 per share, would you sell or continue to hold? If you focus on the $70 you have gained, you might be happy to sell. However, if you focus on the fact that selling will result in a sure loss of $30 per share, you might take the chance that it will turn around. If so, you have committed the sunk-cost fallacy. This is one of the reasons why modern economic theories have begun to explore the psychology of human decision making and its effects on the stock market.

Overconfidence

Having just catalogued biases that predispose human decision makers to error, it may seem paradoxical that people also appear to exhibit great confidence in their judgments, believe that their decisions are free from bias, and are more confident than would be warranted either by the outcomes or by the process of making a decision (Einhorn & Hogarth, 1978; Fischhoff & MacGregor, 1982). For example, clinicians' confidence in their judgment appears to increase with the amount of information available to them, with no corresponding increase in the accuracy of the judgment (Oskamp, 1965; Ryback, 1967). The supremacy of simple linear models over human intuitive judgment has been well documented for more than 40 years, yet clinicians, college admissions boards, and human resources departments still rely on interviews and intuitive judgments over simple formulas (see, e.g., Dawes, 1976). When people are asked to answer factual questions and then rate their confidence in their answers, they express near certainty despite error rates approaching 30 percent (Slovic et al., 1977). As we will examine further later in this chapter, people are especially confident of judgments that are based on descriptions, even when those judgments are extreme (Kahneman & Tversky, 1973).

HEURISTICS IN HUMAN DECISIONS

There have been many attempts to explain decision-making biases. One influential account is that of Kahneman and Tversky, described in several influential publications (1972, 1973; Tversky & Kahneman, 1974, 1982). They present evidence that these and other biases—indeed, much of the fallibility in human judgment—can be attributed to the use of three heuristics: availability, representativeness, and anchoring.

Availability

The *Availability heuristic* attributes many faulty judgments to people's tendency to estimate the probabilities or frequencies of events based on the ease with which instances can be retrieved from memory. In Figure 12.3, for example, data from Slovic, Fischhoff, and Lichtenstein (1976) show that people systematically overestimate or underestimate causes of death. Availability can account for this by noting that some causes of death simply "come to mind" more easily than others (e.g., flood and homicide). The media give extensive coverage to deaths due to cancer, murder, and natural disasters. In contrast, deaths due to asthma rarely make front-page news. Media exposure also interacts with Availability in other contexts. When participants are presented with lists of famous celebrities and asked to judge later whether the lists contained more men or women, their answers were biased by whether the women or men were relatively more famous. If the men were more famous, respondents tended to say men, even when the number of men was numerically less than the number of women, and vice versa. According to the Availability

---

Causes of Death

Subject estimates of the frequency of various causes of death per year (per 100 million U.S. residents)

Cause	Estimate	Truth
Tornado	282	44
Fireworks	80	3
Asthma	253	920
Drowning	842	3600

Figure 12.3 Estimated and true rates of death from various causes. Pattern illustrates the Availability heuristic, according to which people estimate the frequency of occurrence (base rate) by how accessible their memories are for the last incident. High estimated rates for low-occurrence events are influenced by news reports. *Source:* Data from Slovic, Fischoff, and Lichtenstein (1976), Lichtenstein, et al. (1978).

heuristic, these false judgments arise because the more famous names are more easily recalled and, hence, seem more plentiful. Similarly, use of the Availability heuristic can account for the observation that more salient cues in the environment tend to receive more weight than perhaps they should (Wickens & Hollands, 2000).

Availability will also be influenced by how we have stored or represented information. The fact that our internal lexicon appears to be indexed by the initial letter of the word should make it easier to recall words given their initial letter. For example, does the letter "k" occur more frequently at the beginning of a word or in the third letter position? Most people will say at the beginning because they can access words that begin with "k" more easily than words with "k" in the third position. In reality, however, there are more words with "k" in the third position.

Another example of the Availability heuristic comes from a study by Ross and Sicoly (1979). They asked 37 married couples how responsible they were for specific household chores (shopping, cleaning, preparing meals, child care, etc.). For 16 out of 20 activities, both husbands and wives thought they contributed more than their spouse, and were able to back this up by giving more examples of their own contributions than their spouses' contributions. This seeming conflict—how both can provide evidence of doing more—has a simple explanation when considered in the light of Availability. Couples judged their relative contributions based on the ease with which examples came to mind (Availability), and they recalled their own efforts more easily than their spouse's.

Because the availability of instances can be influenced by factors other than the true rate of occurrence—media exposure, memory storage, or ease of imagination—it is easy to see that use of the Availability heuristic will distort perception of risk. After an automobile accident, or when seeing one, the perceived risk of driving is raised somewhat. That risk is reduced after a few weeks because now memory holds mostly instances of accident-free driving episodes. At the same time, a trip to the wilderness will seem inherently dangerous, as attention while planning the trip will be focused on all the things that could go wrong. Yet, it is very likely much safer than driving the car on the routine trip to work. Likewise, the apparent health threat of pesticide spraying is both easy to imagine and widely talked about in the media. Because of this availability, there is every chance that its true risk is much less than commonly assumed.

Representativeness

Representativeness describes the tendency to judge the relation between object A (e.g., "Steven is quiet and introverted") and category B (e.g., "Steven is a programmer") based on the match between the attributes of A and the *perceived* characteristics of the category. Most of us have ideas, impressions, or intuitions, for example, about the kind of person who typifies an engineer or an actor, or about what constitutes a random string of numbers (i.e., no perceptible pattern), and we often judge or predict based on how well the evidence conforms to our intuitive notions. For example, which of these two number sequences has a better chance of winning the lottery: (A) 1, 2, 3, 4, 5, 6, or (B) 3, 11, 17, 22, 24, 41? Most people choose (B) because it seems more representative of a random number sequence. In fact, both are equally likely (or equally unlikely). Think of a random number between 1 and 100. Was your choice an odd number? Most people choose odd numbers because odd numbers seem more representative of random numbers. In both examples, the choice is based on the degree to which the instance matches the perceived characteristic of the category in question. The use of representativeness can lead to false judgments that produce bad outcomes. For example, people often trust individuals who impress them with good manners and an apparently friendly disposition, never suspecting that they might be villains underneath. When judging companies to invest in, people mistakenly rely on favorable descriptions of the company without regard to the reliability of those descriptions (Kahneman & Tversky, 1984). The latter two examples show how use of the Representativeness heuristic can lead us to make false assumptions. Our conception of a good person includes friendliness and good manners, so we tend to assume that someone with good manners is a good person.

Notice that this leads to confusion of the posterior probabilities with the strength of evidence; it also ignores base rates. The probability that a person is good given a warm disposition, p(good/warm friendly disposition), is not the same as the probability that a good person will have a warm and friendly disposition, p(warm friendly disposition/good). As we discussed in our treatment of Bayes' theorem, these will be conditioned on the prior probability of good people, p(good), and the prior probability of a warm and friendly disposition, p(warm friendly disposition).

Indeed, use of the Representativeness heuristic can account for a wide range of cases in which people ignore base rate information. For example, when given a description of a person that matches our intuitions about an actor—extroverted, good looking, charming, dynamic—we tend to put weight on that evidence, as it provides a positive example of the category. We discussed earlier how our natural tendency to seek positive information could itself lead to a confirmation bias.

Use of the Representativeness heuristic has also been argued to give rise to the overconfidence we exhibit about our decisions (Einhorn & Hogarth, 1978; Tversky & Kahneman, 1974). When evidence strongly conforms to our internal representation of a category (e.g., the personality associated with an engineer), it is hard not to feel confident about our judgment (also known as the *illusion of validity*). It has been shown that trained psychologists, who understand the vast research on the fallibility of human judgment, are nonetheless confident of their judgments or assessments of candidates based on a single selection interview.

Still another cognitive illusion stems from the Representativeness heuristic: the *conjunction fallacy*. Consider the following example:

Steven is smart and educated. He likes computer games, health food, and exercise, but is quiet and reserved. What is the probability that Steven

A. is a computer programmer?

B. runs marathons?

C. is a computer programmer and runs marathons?

In judging questions such as these based on verbal descriptions, the vast majority of participants rated option C as more likely than either A or B (Tversky & Kahneman, 1983). However, according to probability theory, the probability of the conjunction of two events must be equal to or less than the probability of the least probable of the individual events. In short, the laws of probability dictate that C can never be more likely than A or B. These participants' rating can easily be understood in light of the Representativeness heuristic. Option C has two positive attributes that match the description of Steve, whereas A and B have only one each.

Use of the Representative heuristic can also explain why people fail to appreciate regression to the mean. Whenever there is an outcome, people assume it is indicative of an internal state without adjusting for its extreme value. Poor performance fits the internal model of either a poorly skilled person or someone not trying hard enough, whereas good performance typifies a highly skilled and motivated person.

Anchoring

The Anchoring heuristic, like the framing effect, demonstrates the ability of context to affect decisions. *Anchoring* refers to the tendency to assume a perceived state as baseline and weigh evidence by adjusting from that base state. Anchoring as a decision heuristic becomes problematic because the adjustment from the baseline is usually inadequate. One concrete example of how anchoring affects judgment is provided by a study in which participants were asked to estimate various quantities. For example, one question asked them to estimate the percentage of African countries in the United Nations (Tversky & Kahneman, 1974). After receiving the quantity to estimate, a large, clearly visible wheel was spun to yield a value between 0—100. Participants first decided whether they thought that value was higher or lower than the quantity to be estimated, then made a numerical estimate of the actual number of African countries in the UN. For the percentage of African countries in the UN, the estimate was 25 percent for the group whose wheel number was 10, and 45 percent for the group whose wheel value was 65. Thus, their numerical estimates were systematically related to the number on the wheel, even though they knew that this was randomly determined and unrelated to the quantity they were to estimate. Participants apparently began with the number they saw and adjusted it in the right direction, but insufficiently.

Use of the Anchoring heuristic has consequences for how we integrate evidence over time. It is an inescapable fact of life that evidence is evaluated sequentially. As evidence accumulates, the early information gives rise to a set of beliefs about the world, which form the basis, or anchor. Additional evidence is then assessed with respect to that state. Such a strategy results in a *primacy effect*, where early information has more weight than later-acquired information (Hogarth & Einhorn, 1992; Tversky & Kahneman, 1974). This has practical implications. When, for example, does an operator (e.g., a pilot) determine that the evidence is sufficient to overturn the belief that the controlled system is functioning normally? In the Chernobyl nuclear accident, there were several indications that the core temperature had continued to rise, much to the concern of junior team members. However, the supervisor did not flag the situation as serious until very late. Similar failures to detect deviations from normal behavior are seen in aircraft accidents. One passenger airliner made a belly landing at the Dallas-Fort Worth Airport, having failed to deploy the landing gear. The first officer had made several comments about the speed being higher than normal, all of which were ignored by the captain, who continued to believe that the flight parameters were just a little outside normal (National Transportation Safety Board,

1978). Apparently, the captain made an insufficient adjustment of his belief concerning the state of the aircraft, despite the evidence that something was wrong.

Other, subtler aspects of the use of anchoring can also have practical consequences. People often *overestimate the probability of the conjunction of events*. In a complex sequential plan, success depends on all of the many stages being completed successfully. In building a house, all the component stages must be completed, usually with a time deadline. It is common to have only the probability of each elementary stage from which to judge the likelihood of success. But the actual likelihood is the conjunction of the probabilities of each stage, computed as the product of the individual probabilities. The true probability of success of a conjunctive event is less than the probability of success of any given stage. An intuitive adjustment using the probabilities of the component stages will overestimate the chances of success. Conversely, reliance on the Adjustment heuristic will *underestimate the probability of a disjunctive event*. Disjunctive events are characteristic of assessing the risk of a complex system, such as the space shuttle. An accident can be caused by failure of any of several systems. Thus, the true probability of failure is higher than the probability of any one component system failing. If one starts with the failure probability of a single component system as the anchor, insufficient adjustment will lead to an underestimate of failure.

The Use of Heuristics

It must be noted that the use of heuristics is not inherently bad. Indeed, it is often difficult to come by the frequency statistics that would allow us to behave optimally. In courtroom situations, we are in fact instructed to use only the strength of the evidence, not the prior probability of criminal behavior, to determine guilt or innocence. The key is to be aware of the pitfalls of these heuristics, temper one's confidence in one's own intuitions, and at least consider that base rate information might be a critical factor.

OTHER INFLUENCES ON DECISION MAKING

We are often called on to make decisions in competitive situations. Success in competition often requires an understanding of how the other player(s) will react to your action. In poker, for example, the person with the best hand at cards does not always win, as opponents can bluff. In chess, you might consider a certain move, but decide against it after reflecting on your opponent's possible countermoves. Even in nominally cooperative situations, such as when on the same sports team or working for the same company, individual goals can conflict with the goals of the other individual or even the larger entity. Consider a baseball player who is asked to bunt or make a sacrifice play to advance the runner. Baseball statistics will not penalize him for doing this successfully, but his individual reward will be less than if he were to get a hit and drive in the run. In short, decisions become more complex as the space of possible outcomes comes to include the decisions of competitors. Such competitive situations gave rise to the field of game theory. Game theory has wide application in economics, evolutionary biology, and social sciences, as its ability to express cooperation and competition provides insights into why we behave as we do.

		Suspect A	
		Silent	Testifies
Suspect B	Silent	0, 0	0, 1
	Testifies	1, 0	.25, .25

Figure 12.4 Payoff matrix for the Prisoner's Dilemma. Each cell represents the utility of the strategy for both participants (Suspect A, Suspect B). Staying silent yields the best outcome only if the other stays silent as well. The tendency is to take the suboptimal alternative of testifying, as it yields the minimax solution.

The classic game-theory problem, the Prisoner's Dilemma, illustrates how this is so. There are many versions of this game and many lengthy discussions. Here we present a simple case. Imagine that two burglary suspects have been arrested. The police need testimony from one or both to get a conviction. They separate the two suspects and offer each the same deal. If one testifies against the other and the other remains silent, the one who testified goes free and the other serves, say, one year in jail. If both testify against each other, both get a reduced sentence, say, three months. If both remain silent, both go free. It is easy to see that the best outcome is for both to remain silent. This, however, requires strong trust, as the utility of remaining silent depends on the behavior of the other. The table in Figure 12.4 illustrates the payoff matrix associated with each outcome. Each column represents the strategy adopted by Suspect A, each row that of Suspect B. If A chooses to remain silent, he will benefit only if B also so chooses. Otherwise, A will pay a stiff penalty. The mirror is true for B. The tendency is for players to adopt the "testify" strategy, as it guarantees a minimum penalty. The strategy to minimize the maximum loss is referred to as a *minimax* strategy.

A version of the Prisoner's Dilemma applied to social psychology is the Commons Dilemma. The "Dilemma of the Commons" was first described in medieval England where common land was used for grazing cattle and sheep of all the local farmers. Each farmer was supposed to restrict the grazing of his or her own cattle to preserve the grazing for all. Some would defect by allowing their cattle to graze more than allowed. Defection yields a large advantage for the individual defector at cost for those who cooperate, whereas cooperation yields a modest gain for all. The structure of the payoff matrix is the same as for the Prisoner's Dilemma. With two farmers, each can raise 10 head of cattle on the commons (payoff = 10, 10) if both cooperate. If both defect, and graze all the cattle they have, few of them will get enough to eat, so each may only raise the equivalent of 5 head (payoff = 5, 5). However, if one cooperates while the other defects, the defector will get 20 head raised, the cooperating farmer none (payoff = 20, 0). Clearly, according to game theory, farmers should defect, as such a minimax solution guards against a much worse outcome.

According to game theory, then, defection (testifying) is the rational choice. Indeed, defection appears to be the dominant strategy when people play the game once, or for the first time. There is evidence, however, that the choices made by individuals change with repeated playing even when confronted by games with the same payoff matrix as the Prisoner's Dilemma. This is the so-called Iterated Prisoner's Dilemma (see Axelrod, 1984). As people begin to see the advantage of cooperation, they more frequently choose the optimal strategy, which is to cooperate. In fact, in simulated games, the most successful strategy is "tit-for-tat." In a tit-for-tat strategy, the player begins by cooperating (e.g., staying silent in Figure 12.4), defects if the opponent defected on the previous trial, and cooperates if the opponent cooperated on the previous trial.

PROCESS MODELS OF HUMAN DECISION MAKING

Heuristics and biases describe the information and representations on which people base decisions. It is also of interest to understand how such biases interact with other cognitive mechanisms to arrive at a decision. Wickens, Keller, and Shaw (in press) offer a three-stage model of decision making that attempts to capture the decision-making process. This model is based primarily on an information-processing approach that incorporates the classic "biases and heuristics" analyses work (Kahneman, 2003; Kahneman et al., 1982; Tversky & Kahneman, 1974) and related work by others (Gigerenzer & Todd, 1999; Einhorn & Hogarth, 1981; Payne, Bettman, & Johnson, 1993). In the three-stage model, the operator first selects and pays attention to environmental cues that the operator feels are relevant to the question at hand. Next, the operator uses these cues as well as prior knowledge to form an assessment of the current or predicted state of the world. Finally, the operator chooses a course of action. This choice is informed by a number of factors, including the likelihood of different environmental states and the values and costs associated with different outcomes.

To illustrate the model (see Figure 12.5), consider, for example, a physician who needs to decide on a treatment for a particular patient. Let's further assume that the patient presented himself to this physician, stating that he is concerned that he may have cancer. The physician will have a number of cues (*Stage 1*) available to help her assess the current or predicted state of the patient, including, for example, data arising from her physical examination of the patient, imaging data from tests that were ordered, and results from physical testing, such as a biopsy. The physician will use these cues to make an initial assessment about whether she believes the patient has cancer (*Stage 2*). Based on that assessment, the physician will choose one of two actions—surgery or no surgery (*Stage 3*). The decision will be influenced by a number of factors. First, each decision will be associated with a set of outcomes. For simplicity, let's assume that there are only two outcomes associated with each decision. If the physician chooses to operate, two potential outcomes for the patient are that the patient is cured, or that the patient is left impaired. If the physician chooses not to operate, two potential outcomes for the patient are that the patient is impaired, or that the patient dies.

For each of these decisions (surgery/no surgery), and each situation (patient has cancer/patient does not have cancer), one can calculate the value and probability associated with that outcome. For example, the negative value associated with dying will be quite high, whether or not the patient actually has cancer. The probability of this occurring will be much higher, though, if the patient has cancer than if the patient does not (although we must recognize that there is a chance that the patient might die even if he does not have

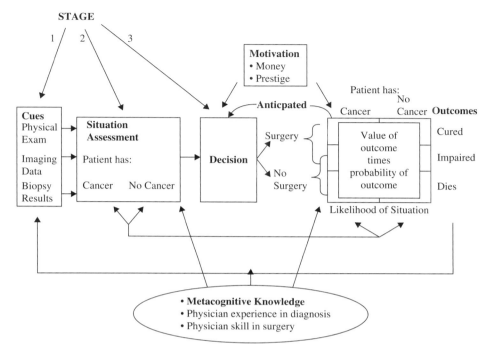

Figure 12.5 A cognitive model of decision making illustrating stages and mental operations in arriving at a decision. *Source:* Reprinted with permission from Wickens, Keller, and Shaw (in press).

cancer and does not have surgery). Whether the patient has cancer or not, there will be a risk of impairment if the physician decides that the patient should have surgery. This is likely to have a negative value associated with it as well (although perhaps not as high as that associated with dying). If the patient does not have surgery, there is no risk of impairment arising from that procedure, whether or not the patient has cancer. Thus, the value associated with each decision and the likelihood of each outcome will influence the decision maker.

Second, the decision will be influenced by the physician's motivation. For example, if she is currently having money issues, she may be more inclined to recommend surgery so that she can generate some income. If she is motivated by prestige factors, she will be motivated to make a decision that is later validated by a successful patient outcome. Third, the physician will be influenced by her metacognitive knowledge; that is, she will be influenced by her knowledge of her expertise. For example, she may be influenced by the amount of experience that she has had in diagnosing patients with this type of cancer; she may also be influenced by her personal assessment of her expertise in the operating room.

Finally, this model allows feedback from prior outcomes to influence the physician's likelihood of looking for particular types of cues. Thus, if this physician has had success in using biopsies in previous cases, she may be more likely to order them, and use the data arising from them, in future cases. In contrast, if she has found biopsies unreliable in past cases, she may be more likely to look for or rely on other sources of data.

It should be noted that the decision-making process is affected by external events that create "stress" on the system. Brunswik (1952, 1956) talked about "correspondence constancy," the tendency to maintain a constant level of performance as the difficulty of the task changes. He argued that people try to maintain a stable level of performance even when the environment and context change. This can be done through a process of "satis-ficing," as suggested by Simon and Hogarth (Hogarth, 1987; Simon, 1955), and reflected in the naturalistic decision-making approach, in which people make a decision after a minimally acceptable solution is identified rather than evaluating all of the alternatives. It has also been suggested that this can occur through a process of "cognitive acceleration" (Adelman, Miller, Henderson, & Schoelles, 2003), in which people increase the rate at which they process information in each unit of time or filter their processing of stimuli.

The model in Figure 12.5 is a qualitative description of the high-level, deliberate cog-nitive processing that might underlie a decision. Quantitative models have been developed that attempt to investigate how evidence accumulates over time by modeling the decision processes using random walks (Brown & Heathcote, 2005; Busemeyer & Townsend, 1993; Dror, Basola, & Busemeyer, 1999; Goldstein & Busemeyer, 1992; Ratcliff & Smith, 2004). In a random-walk model, information accumulates until there is sufficient evidence to choose one of several hypotheses (decision alternatives). There are many varieties of random-walk models, which vary in how the information accumulates, where randomness affects the behavior of the model, and whether evidence for one option must be evidence against the others, as well as other details. Nevertheless, all share the common assump-tion that the initial starting point for evidence accumulation can be biased in favor of a specific outcome or class of outcomes. Essentially, this is a way of implementing *a priori* probabilities. All also share the assumption that evidence is sequentially sampled until a criterion has been reached.

An example of such a model is Decision Field Theory (e.g., Busemeyer & Townsend, 1993; Dror et al., 1999; Goldstein & Busemeyer, 1992). In Decision Field Theory, the decision maker considers the consequences of all possible outcomes for all possible deci-sions. Assume that you are a doctor trying to diagnose a patient who reports persistent fever, sweats, and swelling of lymph nodes. You must decide whether the patient has leukemia (L) or a simple but persistent flu (F). You can prescribe two treatments, chemo-therapy (C) or aspirin (A). It is apparent that the consequences of the wrong treatment are severe in both cases. This creates the utility of each outcome: F $\rightarrow$ A = cheap, effective pain relief; L $\rightarrow$ C = expensive, painful, but life-saving treatment; F $\rightarrow$ C = expensive, painful treatment for no gain; L $\rightarrow$ A = death. Each of these disease $\rightarrow$ treatment out-comes has an *attention weight* representing the retrieval of an association between an action and a consequence. The sum of all these for each action (C, A) gives a valence to the action. These valences are momentary and yield a momentary preference for one action over another. You begin a series of tests to help decide. As you collect information from the tests, the evidence for one or the other grows until the difference in preferences is large enough to select one action.

Decision Field Theory has been widely applied to laboratory and real-world prob-lems, as have other quantitative decision models. Qualitative models, like the one shown in Figure 12.5, provide a framework for organizing one's thinking about any given decision problem. The added strength of quantitative models is their ability to make precise predictions about the numerical preferences of people across tasks. The problem with quantitative models, however, is similar to that with rational models: It can be difficult to identify the numerical parameters needed for the model to compute. As with Model Human Processor models (see Chapter 10), the time and detail required for these models limit their applicability to system development.

NATURALISTIC DECISION MAKING

The problems associated with estimating the parameters for quantitative or rational decision approaches have been a barrier to their application in complex domains. Although it is important to point to the faulty decisions and cognitive illusions that result from a reliance on heuristics such as Representativeness, Availability, and Anchoring, it is difficult to see how we could hope to specify costs, values, and probabilities for most of the decisions we make in daily life (Zsambok & Klein, 1996). One could even argue that a reliance on Availability as a measure of the base rates is the best we could do, at least before extensive records of outcomes were commonplace. In this respect, it is probably not surprising that we are subject to cognitive illusions or rely on the representativeness of the evidence. Perhaps it was the best choice open to evolution.

Moreover, studies of expert decision making, notably that of master chess champions (Chase & Simon, 1973), reveal that experts are able to select the most promising moves from the generally wide range of possible moves, and focus detailed analysis on this small subset. In contrast, mediocre chess players often do not even consider the more promising moves, focusing attention instead on inferior moves that were rejected by experts without apparent deliberate consideration. Experts were not performing an explicit computation of utility or factoring of base rates, but recognizing patterns and matching those patterns to stored patterns accumulated in the development of their skill. Subsequent investigations of other skilled domains (Klein, 1989) reinforced the hypothesis that behind expert decision making lies a wealth of patterns learned from experience, with decisions reflecting a reliance on pattern recognition and matching.

Such observations formed the basis for a new movement referred to as Naturalistic Decision Making (NDM). Naturalistic Decision Making emphasizes the point that in daily life, we make many routine decisions, mostly in situations in which we have extensive practice or are well trained. Air traffic controllers, pilots, firefighters, and business executives all undergo extensive training or apprenticeships, and have immediate feedback on the correctness of their decisions. Expertise endows us with a store of patterns against which we match incoming information to decide which of the alternative actions has most often led to the desired outcome. These considerations have led to a new model of human decision making called *recognition-primed decision making* (Klein, 1993, 1997). According to recognition-primed decision making (RPDM), pattern recognition forms the basis of situation assessment. When a firefighter sees a fire, her perceptual processing includes activation of long-term memory representations that immediately tell her that this is a fire of type "X," which requires a specific kind of solution, as well as the dangers that must be considered in approaching it. According to RPDM, these factors simply come to mind without any explicit decisions about base rates, strength of evidence, or questions of how to combine evidence. Instead, it is assumed that a user will know "X" when he or she sees it and choose the action that has been most successful in the past. In situations where the experts may not be able to immediately choose a course of action, RPDM posits that they will use mental simulation. The mental simulation will use stored knowledge to evaluate the consequences of different courses of action. The expert then selects an action that leads to a satisfactory outcome. In these situations, the first option found that satisfies the constraints is the one selected.

The model in Figure 12.6 illustrates the basic structure and information flow proposed by RPDM. No problem solving is required at those times the world conforms to our expectations. Once we encounter a violation of those expectations, RPDM assumes that we begin a process of selecting cues from the environment and matching them to stored patterns. This matching process forms the basis for our assessment of the situation we are in and possible courses of action. We continue to sample cues until we recognize the situation as a familiar one. We then begin an assessment of possible courses of action, estimating the effectiveness of each by mentally simulating the possible consequences. In this context, mental simulation draws on the same patterns used for recognition. Note how readily this process can lead to some of the biases discussed earlier. For example, we discussed how the confirmation bias reflects a preference for positive exemplars. The pattern-matching process in RPDM is based on finding positive exemplars for stored patterns. The reliance on descriptive information, apparent in the use of the Representativeness heuristic, can be directly related to the matching process, because the descriptive information forms the cues that are used to match stored patterns.

Figure 12.7 shows an example of how RPDM might affect a decision. Imagine that you are the commander of the naval squadron shown in the bottom of each picture in Figure 12.7, and you are presented with the following radar display of the arrangement of enemy ships. Recognition-primed decision making would suggest that you are likely to identify the leftmost configuration of ships as one in which the enemy squadron forms a barrier to your forward progress. Your prior experience has taught you that the number and spacing of ships will not allow some straightforward maneuvers to succeed in breaking through the line, and instead will suggest others. Now, consider the second example shown in the middle of Figure 12.7. Here your prior training would flag this as a poor representation of a barrier, with an obvious opening to maneuver through. Finally, consider the rightmost picture in Figure 12.7. In this scenario, a number of ships have been replaced with the representation of an island. Although you may never have been faced with this particular configuration of ships and land, it is likely that, because of your training and perceptual system, you will recognize that this configuration provides as effective a barrier as the leftmost row of ships shown in Figure 12.7. Recognition and training will allow you as a commander to navigate successfully through this scenario without needing to compute individual costs, probabilities, or values.

In contrast to the laboratory methods used by researchers to identify heuristics and biases (discussed earlier), researchers in Naturalistic Decision Making rely more heavily on field studies or high-fidelity simulations of operators in complex environments. Researchers elicit the "patterns" that experts use to make judgments through structured

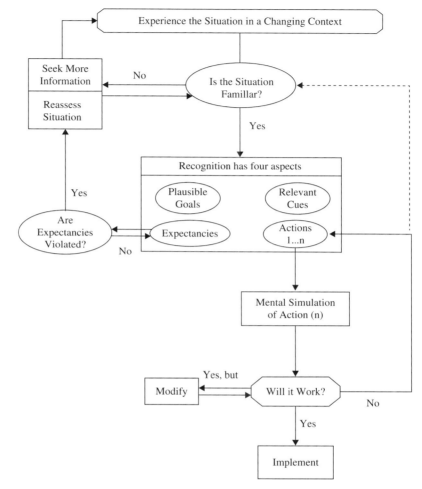

Figure 12.6 The process of selecting appropriate action according to Recognition-Primed Decision-Making (RPDM). *Source:* Reprinted with permission from Klein (2008).

interviews in which they present complex problems from the expert's domain and record the thought processes as the expert solves the problem.

The rise of NDM and RPDM in no way invalidates the lessons from laboratory studies or the reliance on heuristics and presence of biases in human judgment. Indeed, traditional rational and cognitive approaches to decision making were concerned with the nature of "intuitive" judgments and the effects of a reliance on them. NDM and RPDM are also concerned with intuitive judgments, in the sense that they ask how expert intuition differs from that of naïve operators and how intuition improves with experience. The answer appears to be that when people get immediate feedback regarding their decisions over a long period

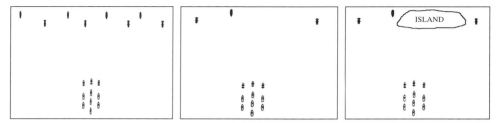

Figure 12.7 Example of recognition and pattern matching as the basis for decision making. The possible solutions are heavily influenced by the decider's perceptual structure of the world and experience with similar situations. *Source:* Adapted from Noble, Boehm-Davis, and Grosz (1986).

of time, their stored patterns come to closely reflect the regularities in the domain. In a sense, they still rely on Availability and Representativeness, but the correct patterns are readily available and the cues used by experienced operators are more representative of the true state. In short, the patterns contain the information about successes and failures that approximates true base rates.

RELATIONSHIP BETWEEN DECISION-MAKING MODELS AND SYSTEMS ENGINEERING

Understanding the ways in which people make decisions has broad implications for systems engineering. The models described in this chapter can help in the analysis of the requirements of a system by specifying the perceptual and memory supports the human operator may need for decision tasks associated with the system. They can also guide the design phase of a system by providing principles for information display that are consistent with the model. Wickens and Hollands (2000) suggest a number of such principles that derive directly from knowledge about decision-making processes. For example, display technology could be used to make all cues equally available from a perceptual point of view. This technology could also be used to make more diagnostic cues more salient to the user. Of course, this requires that the designers be certain that the cues they choose to highlight are indeed the most relevant and/or diagnostic cues for all decisions to be made within this domain.

Another application is training for decision makers. Within this application area, one approach would be to develop instruction describing the biases or heuristics that users are likely to bring to the table. This "de-biasing" is thought to have the potential to improve the quality of decision making (Larrick, 2004). A second approach within this area is to instruct decision makers to explicitly entertain reasons why their hypothesis (that is, their assessment of the situation) might be wrong.

Finally, a third approach is to develop automation that can either take the decision out of the hands of the human decision maker entirely, or provide a ranked set of alternatives to the decision maker based on algorithms put in place by the developer.

SUMMARY

This chapter focused on how people make decisions. We presented three approaches taken to account for human decision making: normative theories, cognitive theories, and naturalistic theories. Biases that influence the decision-making process and a potential information-processing approach to describing the decision-making process were also described. Finally, we considered how best to aid the decision-making process given the biases that creep into human decision making and the processes by which decisions are made.

REFERENCES

Adelman, L., Miller, S. L., Henderson, D. V., & Schoelles, M. (2003). Using Brunswikian theory and a longitudinal design to study how hierarchical teams adapt to increasing levels of time pressure. *Acta Psychologica, 112*(2), 181–206.

Arkes, H. R., & Blumer, C. (1985). The psychology of sunk cost. *Organizational Behavior and Human Decision Processes, 35*(1), 124–140. doi:16/0749-5978(85)90049-4

Austerweil, J. L., & Griffiths, T. L. (2011). Seeking confirmation is rational for deterministic hypotheses. *Cognitive Science*, 35(3), 499–526.

Axelrod, R. M. (1984). *The evolution of cooperation*. New York, New York: Basic Books.

Brown, S., & Heathcote, A. (2005). A ballistic model of choice response time. *Psychological Review, 112*(1), 117–128. doi:10.1037/0033-295X.112.1.117

Brunswik, E. (1952). *The conceptual framework of psychology* (Vol. 1). Chicago, IL: University of Chicago Press.

Brunswik, E. (1956). *Perception and the representative design of psychological experiments* (2d ed.). Berkeley, CA: University of California Press.

Busemeyer, J. R, & Townsend, J. T. (1993). Decision field theory: A dynamic-cognitive approach to decision making in an uncertain environment. *Psychological Review, 100*(3), 432.

Casey, S. M. (1998). *Set phasers on stun: And other true tales of design, technology, and human error* (2nd ed.). Santa Barbara: Aegean.

Casscells, W., Schoenberger, A., & Graboys, T. B. (1978). Interpretation by physicians of clinical laboratory results. *New England Journal of Medicine, 299*(18), 999–1001.

Chase, W. G., & Simon, H. A. (1973). Perception in chess. *Cognitive Psychology, 4*(1), 55–81. doi:16/0010-0285(73)90004-2

Dawes, R. M. (1976). Shallow psychology. In J. S. Carroll & J. W. Payne (Eds.), *Cognition and social behavior*. Hillsdale, NJ: Lawrence Erlbaum Associates.

Dawes, R. M. (1979). The robust beauty of improper linear models in decision making. *American Psychologist, 34*(7), 571.

Dehaene, S. (2011). *The number sense: How the mind creates mathematics*. New York, NY: Oxford University Press.

Dror, I. E., Basola, B., & Busemeyer, J. R. (1999). Decision making under time pressure: An independent test of sequential sampling models. *Memory & Cognition, 27*(4), 713–725.

Eddy, D. M. (1982). Probabilistic reasoning in clinical medicine: Problems and opportunities. In D. Kahneman, P. Slovic, & A. Tversky (Eds.), *Judgment under uncertainty: Heuristics and biases* (pp. 249–267). Cambridge, UK: Cambridge University Press.

Edwards, W. (1987). Decision making. In G. Salvendy (Ed.), *Handbook of human factors & ergonomics* (pp. 1061–1104). New York, NY: Wiley.

Einhorn, H. J., & Hogarth, R. M. (1978). Confidence in judgment: Persistence of the illusion of validity. *Psychological Review, 85*(5), 395–416. doi:10.1037/0033-295X.85.5.395

Einhorn, H. J., & Hogarth, R. M. (1981). Behavioral decision theory: Processes of judgment and choice. *Annual Review of Psychology, 32*, 53–88.

Fischhoff, B., & MacGregor, D. (1982). Subjective confidence in forecasts. *Journal of Forecasting, 1*(2), 155–172.

Gigerenzer, G., & Hoffrage, U. (1995). How to improve Bayesian reasoning without instruction: Frequency formats. *Psychological Review, 102*(4), 684.

Gigerenzer, G., & Todd, P. M. (1999). *Simple heuristics that make us smart*. New York, NY: Oxford University Press.

Goldstein, W. M., & Busemeyer, J. R. (1992). The effect of "irrelevant" variables on decision making: Criterion shifts in preferential choice? *Organizational Behavior and Human Decision Processes, 52*(3), 425–454. doi:16/0749-5978(92)90028-6

Hogarth, R. M. (1987). *Judgement and choice: The psychology of decision*. Oxford, UK: John Wiley & Sons.

Hogarth, R. M., & Einhorn, H. J. (1992). Order effects in belief updating: The belief-adjustment model,. *Cognitive Psychology, 24*(1), 1–55. doi:16/0010-0285(92)90002-J

Kahneman, D. (2003). A perspective on judgment and choice: Mapping bounded rationality. *American Psychologist, 58*(9), 697–720. doi:10.1037/0003-066X.58.9.697

Kahneman, D., Slovic, P., & Tversky, A. (1982). *Judgment under uncertainty: Heuristics and biases*. Cambridge, UK: Cambridge University Press.

Kahneman, D., & Tversky, A. (1972). Subjective probability: A judgment of representativeness. *Cognitive Psychology, 3*(3), 430–454.

Kahneman, D., & Tversky, A. (1973). On the psychology of prediction. *Psychological Review, 80*(4), 237.

Kahneman, D., & Tversky, A. (1984). Choices, values, and frames. *American Psychologist, 39*(4), 341–350. doi:10.1037/0003-066X.39.4.341

Klayman, J., & Ha, Y. W. (1987). Confirmation, disconfirmation, and information in hypothesis testing. *Psychological Review, 94*(2), 211.

Klein, G. (2008). Naturalistic decision making. *Human Factors, 50*(3), 456–460. doi:10.1518/001872008X288385

Klein, G. A. (1989). Recognition-primed decisions. *Advances in Man-Machine Systems Research, 5,* 47–92.

Klein, G. A. (1993). A recognition-primed decision (RPD) model of rapid decision making. *Decision Making in Action: Models and Methods,* 138–147.

Klein, G. A. (1997). The recognition-primed decision (RPD) model: Looking back, looking forward. In C. E. Zsambok & G. A. Klein (Eds.). *Naturalistic decision making* (pp. 285–292). Mahwah, NJ: Lawrence Erlbaum Associates.

Larrick, R. P. (2004). Debiasing. In D. J. Koehler & N. Harvey (Eds.), *Blackwell handbook of judgment and decision making* (pp. 316–338). Malden, MA: Blackwell Publishing.

Lichtenstein, S., Slovic, P., Fischhoff, B., Layman, M. Combs, B. (1978). Judged frequency of lethal events. *Journal of Experimental Psychology: Human Learning and Memory,* 4(6), 551-578. doi: 10.1037/0278-7393.4.6.551

National Transportation Safety Board. (1978). *Aircraft accident report: National Airlines, Inc., Escambia Bay Pensacola, Florida, May 8, 1978* (No. AAR78-13.pdf). Washington, DC: National Transportation and Safety Board.

Noble, D. F., Boehm-Davis, D. A., & Grosz, C. (1986). *Schema-based model of information processing for situation assessment* (No. N00014 84 C 0484). Vienna, VA: Engineering Research Associates.

Oskamp, S. (1965). Overconfidence in case-study judgments. *Journal of Consulting Psychology,* 29(3), 261.

Payne, J. W., Bettman, J. R., & Johnson, E. J. (1993). *The adaptive decision maker.* Cambridge, UK; New York, NY: Cambridge University Press.

Pirolli, P. (2007). *Information foraging theory: Adaptive interaction with information.* New York, NY: Oxford University Press.

Pirolli, P., & Card, S. (1999). Information foraging. *Psychological Review, 106*(4), 643.

Ratcliff, R., & Smith, P. L. (2004). A comparison of sequential sampling models for two-choice reaction time. *Psychological Review, 111*(2), 333–367. doi:10.1037/0033-295X.111.2.333

Ross, M., & Sicoly, F. (1979). Egocentric biases in availability and attribution. *Journal of Personality and Social Psychology, 37*(3), 322.

Ryback, D. (1967). Confidence and accuracy as a function of experience in judgment-making in the absence of systematic feedback. Perceptual and Motor Skills, 24(1), 331-334. doi: 10.2466/pms.1967.24.1.331.

Sawyer, J. (1966). Measurement and prediction, clinical and statistical. *Psychological Bulletin,* 66(3), 178.

Simon, H. A. (1955). A behavioral model of rational choice. *Quarterly Journal of Economics,* 69(1), 99.

Simon, H. A. (1959). Theories of decision-making in economics and behavioral science. *American Economic Review,* 49(3), 253–283.

Slovic, P. (1972). Psychological study of human judgment: Implications for investment decision making. *Journal of Finance, 27*(4), 779–799.

Slovic, P., Fischhoff, B., & Lichtenstein, S. (1976). Cognitive processes and societal risk taking. In J. S. Carroll and J. W. Payne (Eds.). *Cognition and social behavior* (pp. 165–184). Potomac, MD: Lawrence Erlbaum Associates.

Slovic, P., Fischhoff, B., & Lichtenstein, S. (1977). Behavioral decision theory. *Annual Review of Psychology, 28*(1), 1–39. doi:10.1146/annurev.ps.28.020177.000245

Tolcott, M. A., Marvin, F., & Bresnick, T. A. (1989). The confirmation bias in military situation assessment. *Proceedings of the 57th MORS symposium.* Reston, VA: Decision Science Consortium.

Tversky, A., & Kahneman, D. (1973). Availability: A heuristic for judging frequency and probability. *Cognitive Psychology, 5*(2), 207–232.

Tversky, A., & Kahneman, D. (1974). Judgment under uncertainty: Heuristics and biases. *Science, 185*(4157), 1124–1131. doi:10.1126/science.185.4157.1124

Tversky, A., & Kahneman, D. (1981). The framing of decisions and the psychology of choice. *Science, 211*(4481), 453–458. doi:10.1126/science.7455683

Tversky, A., & Kahneman, D. (1982). Evidential impact of base rates. In D. Kahneman, P. Slovic, & A. Tversky (Eds.), *Judgment under uncertainty: Heuristics and biases* (pp. 153–160). Cambridge, UK: Cambridge University Press.

Tversky, A., & Kahneman, D. (1983). Extensional versus intuitive reasoning: The conjunction fallacy in probability judgment. Psychological Review, 90(4), 293.

Wason, P. C. (1960). On the failure to eliminate hypotheses in a conceptual task. The Quarterly Journal of Experimental Psychology, 12, 129–140. doi:10.1080/17470216008416717

Wickens, C. D., & Hollands, J. G. (2000). *Engineering psychology and human performance* (3rd ed.). Upper Saddle River, NJ: Prentice Hall.

Wickens, C. D., Keller, J., & Shaw, C. (in press). Human factors of high altitude mountaineering. In J. Kring (Ed.), *Human performance in extreme environments.* Boca Raton, FL: CRC Press.

Woods, D. D., & Cook, R. I. (1999). Perspectives on human error: Hindsight biases and local rationality. In F. Durso (Ed.). *Handbook of applied cognition* (pp. 141–171). West Sussex, UK: Cambridge University Press.

Zsambok, C. E., & Klein, G. A. (1996). Naturalistic decision making. Mahwah, NJ: Lawrence Erlbaum Associates.

Part IV

Human-System Integration

"About 0009, on March 24, 1989, the U.S. tankship *EXXON VALDEZ*, loaded with about 1,263,000 barrels of crude oil, grounded on Bligh Reef in Prince William Sound, near Valdez, Alaska. At the time of the grounding, the vessel was under the navigational control of the third mate. There were no injuries, but about 258,000 barrels of cargo were spilled when eight cargo tanks ruptured, resulting in catastrophic damage to the environment. Damage to the vessel was estimated at $25 million, the cost of the lost cargo was estimated at $3.4 million, and the cost of the cleanup of the spilled oil during 1989 was about $1.85 billion.

Probable Cause. The National Transportation Safety Board determined that the probable cause of the grounding of the *EXXON VALDEZ* was the failure of the third mate to properly maneuver the vessel because of fatigue and excessive workload; the failure of the master to provide a proper navigation watch because of impairment from alcohol; the failure of Exxon Shipping Company to provide a fit master and a rested and sufficient crew for the *EXXON VALDEZ*; the lack of an effective Vessel Traffic Service because of inadequate equipment and manning levels, inadequate personnel training, and deficient management oversight; and the lack of effective pilotage services."

(National Transportation Safety Board, 1990)

The grounding of the tanker ship *Exxon Valdez* on the pristine shores of Alaska was a national tragedy and, until the blowout of the BP deep-drilling rig Horizon in 2011, the largest oil spill and cleanup in U.S. history. The safety issues and probable causes raised in the NTSB's executive summary seem far removed from the research on human decision making, perception, memory, and attention that we have been describing. We hardly need a book on humans in engineered systems to conclude that a drunken captain and incompetent crew working for a lax company constitute a recipe for disaster. Indeed, this was the perception created in the wake of the accident, as newspapers and magazine articles reported the findings of the NTSB. It probably remains the popular explanation among those who remember the accident.

However, the full 255-page NTSB report contains much more information about the circumstances leading up to the grounding that would make such a conclusion seem too limited. It would miss the fact that there was no evidence before the incident that the captain, crew, or company were an accident waiting to happen. Tankers had been safely navigating in Prince William Sound for 12 years, more than 8,700 trips, without incident (State of Alaska, 1990). Within the larger NTSB report is testimony from numerous witnesses who testified that the captain exhibited no visible signs of drunkenness. Although it is true that the captain did drink earlier, his blood and urine tests came up with only very small traces of alcohol, and a lengthy argument was needed to show that there could have been some impairment at the time of the accident. Moreover, as documented in the NTSB report, the third mate in command was not incompetent, but a highly trained and seasoned sailor. Nevertheless, he failed to properly navigate the vessel. In previous sections, we have talked about how the environment and human capabilities limit human-system performance. In this section, we focus on how interactions between the human and the system within a particular environment affect the likelihood of error and system safety. We begin with a case study of the *Exxon Valdez*. In Chapter 14, we define what we mean by human versus system error and then talk about the likelihood of error increasing as the human operator's understanding of the situation becomes less complete. Chapter 15 revisits the role of context by showing how the demands placed on the human by the context can influence the likelihood of error. In Chapter 16, we focus on human interactions with automated devices to show how the demands of those devices interact with human information processing. Finally, in Chapter 17, we show how an understanding of the nature of human information processing can be used to better design systems such that they support human-system performance.

REFERENCES

National Transportation Safety Board. (1990). *Executive summary: Grounding of the U.S. Tankship Exxon Valdez on Bligh Reef, Prince William Sound near Valdez, Alaska March 24, 1989* (No. National Transportation and Safety Board Marine Accident PB90-916405, NTSB/MAR90/04). Washington, DC: National Transportation Safety Board.

State of Alaska. (1990). *SPILL: The wreck of the Exxon Valdez* (Final Report). Retrieved from www.evostc.state.ak.us/facts/details.cfm

13

A Case Study in Human-System Performance: The *Exxon Valdez*

We begin this section with an extended description of the incident described in the preface: the oil spill created by the grounding of the *Exxon Valdez*. The accident illustrates the myriad ways in which the environment, constraints on human information processing, the task the human is trying to accomplish, and the tools available to do so interact and create opportunities for error. The official NTSB report on the *Exxon Valdez* disaster identified a range of contributing factors:

1. The adequacy of the navigation watch on the *Exxon Valdez* on the night of the grounding;
2. The role of human factors, including fatigue and alcohol abuse, in this accident;
3. Coast Guard and Exxon Shipping Company manning standards and Exxon's procedures for determining manning levels for tankships;
4. Exxon Shipping Company's drug/alcohol testing and rehabilitation program;
5. Coast Guard regulations and procedures for drug/alcohol testing aboard commercial vessels;
6. The role of the Coast Guard Vessel Traffic Service at Valdez; and
7. Oil spill contingency planning and initial response to this accident (National Transportation Safety Board, 1990).

Nonetheless, it attributes the proximal cause of the accident to human error: specifically, the failure of the third mate to navigate the vessel properly. How could the third mate, an experienced seaman, make such a grievous error? The details leading up to the *Exxon Valdez* disaster highlight how circumstances interact with human capabilities and limitations to determine outcomes in real-world contexts. This chapter first describes the event, as reconstructed from testimony to the National Transportation Safety Board and other accounts of the accident, and then discusses factors that may have contributed to causing the accident.

AN ACCOUNT OF THE GROUNDING OF THE TANKSHIP *EXXON VALDEZ*

The ship had left Berth 5 at the Alyeska Marine Terminal shortly after 9:00 P.M. on March 23, 1989. She was scheduled to leave at 10:00 P.M., but her departure time was advanced because loading had completed well before the master, chief mate, and radio officer returned from a day ashore at 8:34 P.M. As a consequence, the master had not completed all the required paperwork and had not fully recovered from several alcoholic drinks consumed during the afternoon. Because of this, he left the bridge during a difficult maneuver, leaving control solely to the third mate. According to one recent critical account of the accident (Palast, 2009), the master was asleep when the accident occurred. It also meant that the third officer, whose duty schedule went from 5:50 P.M. til 11:50 P.M., was on duty despite reports that he had not slept much previously. "Testimony before the NTSB suggests that Cousins [first mate] may have been awake and generally at work for up to 18 hours preceding the accident" (State of Alaska, 1990).

The ship's transit through the Valdez Narrows was guided by the harbor pilot and was completed without incident. The master (captain), who had retired to his quarters, returned to the bridge at 11:10 P.M. This was during the exit of the harbor pilot, who had guided the ship through the narrows. Figure 13.1 shows the track of the *Exxon Valdez* from the clearing of the narrows to the grounding on Bligh Reef, including a depiction of the ice floe and sea lanes. Following the transit of the narrows, the *Exxon Valdez* was in the outbound shipping lane on a course of 219°. At 11:30, the master informed the Valdez traffic center that the *Exxon Valdez* would exit the outbound transit lane to avoid a large ice floe that straddled both outbound and inbound shipping lanes, and set a course of 200°. At 11:39 he altered the course to 180°, a track roughly between Bligh Reef and Bligh Island. He also ordered the ship set to autopilot. This course would move the ship to the south to allow a sweeping right turn once the ship cleared the ice floe. This would cause the ship to pass between the ice floe and Bligh Reef, a channel about 1 mile wide.

At 11:52, the master ordered the ship's engine to be put on a program that would increase speed to full ahead sea speed. The master and third mate conferred on the point at which the turn would be executed. The master indicated that the third mate should begin turning the ship back toward the ice floe when Busby Island (see Figure 13.1) was on the port beam—off the middle of the left side of the ship. At approximately 11:53 P.M., the master exited the bridge, leaving the third mate and two able seamen (a helmsman and lookout) to man the bridge. However, the planned maneuver clearly fell into a category of difficulty that company policy had deemed to require the presence of two experienced officers. Thus, the NTSB report concluded that the master was remiss in leaving the bridge at this point.

When the master left the bridge, the ship was on a course that would exit the safe transit lanes. It was then accelerating toward a point between Bligh Reef and Reef Island (see Figure 13.1). Independently, the third mate and the helmsman each stated that they pushed the button that would disengage the autopilot and return the ship to manual steering. At 11:55, the third mate checked the radar display and observed Busby Island off the port beam. He then went outside and took a compass bearing on the island to confirm its location. Following that, he went inside to the chart room to plot the position of the ship. While plotting the fix, the third mate received a report from the lookout that confirmed

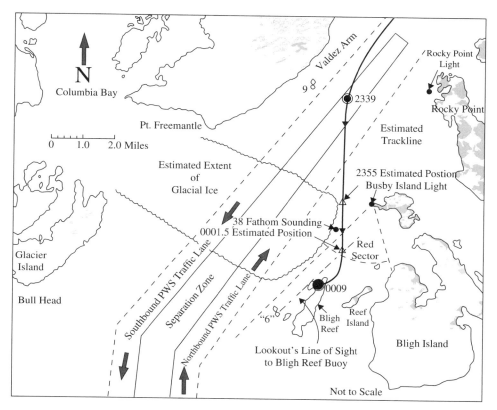

Figure 13.1 The geography of Prince William Sound and track of the *Exxon Valdez* leading up to the grounding on Bligh Reef. *Source:* Taken from the NTSB report of the accident (National Transportation Safety Board, 1990).

Busby Island off the port beam and the Bligh Reef buoy (see Figure 13.1) broad on the starboard beam—45° off the right side of the ship. At about 11:56, the third mate ordered 10° right rudder to swing the tanker to the right around the ice and through the 1-mile-wide passage. No speed change was ordered. He notified the master of the course change in a phone conversation that he later estimated to have taken 1 to 1.5 minutes.

At this point, the third mate began to monitor the location of Busby Island and the Bligh Reef buoy on the port radar to look for evidence of the commanded course change. He received a report from the lookout that the Bligh Reef buoy was off the starboard beam and confirmed this visually. The lookout testified later that at the time, she noticed the ship slowly turning to the right. However, the third mate was unable to detect any visible change in course on the radar and, 1 to 2 minutes after giving the 10° command, issued a command for 20° right rudder. An estimated two minutes later, the Third Mate ordered a "hard right rudder." From radar observations, he later testified that the heading of the ship was turning right, but the ship's track remained 180°. He called the master and told him, 'I think we are in serious trouble' (NTSB, 1990, p. 11). Shortly thereafter, the ship struck the reef.

THE NATURE OF THE ERROR

The sequence of events described in the preceding section is taken largely from the testimony of the various participants during subsequent hearings, which form a large portion of the NTSB report. The report contains additional simulation results and track data that paint a somewhat different picture. Apparently, there is an ambiguity as to whether the helm was ever taken off autopilot. In autopilot, the helm will turn in response to input, but the ship will not. According to NTSB simulations, there was no evidence that the ship began the turn at the commanded 10° right rudder, or even the 20° command. The maximum rudder estimated from the simulations never exceeded 5° until the hard right rudder command. The track of the vessel is consistent with the autopilot not having been disengaged until immediately prior to the emergency hard right rudder command.

The NTSB report makes several findings related to the cause of the accident. It also lists how each participant and organization contributed to the grounding that led to the disastrous oil spill. Ultimately, it attributes the proximal cause of the accident to faulty navigation of the vessel, in particular the third mate's "failure to turn the vessel at the proper time and with sufficient rudder" (1990, p. 166). Our goal here is not to challenge or otherwise reinterpret the conclusions of the NTSB report, but rather to examine how it is possible to use our earlier characterization of environments, control theory, or human perceptual and cognitive factors to gain insight into how this accident happened.

The NTSB report is concerned with the cause of the accident from the point of view of the responsibilities of the individual operators, the company, and the supporting environment. It further elaborates its finding by noting that the failure of the third mate to turn the vessel with sufficient rudder "probably was the result of his excessive workload and fatigued condition, which caused him to lose awareness of the location of Bligh Reef" (p. 166). Workload, fatigue, and loss of situation awareness are topics we will treat in depth in later chapters. Our goal here is to probe a little further into the specific decisions and conditions that may have affected the third mate's performance that night. Our account is speculative and we do not present it as a definitive account of the cognitive state of the third mate. Rather, our goal is to illustrate how knowledge of environments and people can focus attention on key questions.

Mode Errors

The NTSB report spends several pages developing the theory that, contrary to the testimony of the third mate and helmsman, the helm autopilot was never disengaged until the hard right rudder command that came too late. The report includes a possible alternative scenario in which the autopilot was set to intercept a course of 247° using a rudder limit setting of 7–10°. It concludes that the truth may never be known. Accepting that it may not be possible to ascertain the true sequence of events, nor the intentions of the third mate and helmsman, it is possible to draw parallels between the conditions on the bridge and known conditions that promote certain kinds of errors in systems with discrete modes, as discussed earlier in Part II.

The autopilot was one of several elements of the sophisticated helm control system on the *Exxon Valdez*. Once an automated system, like the helm autopilot, is engaged, it must be instructed as to the control criterion it is to meet (e.g., hold course, hold speed, hold rudder setting), as well as how it should respond to manual inputs while engaged. The human operator must remember not only which system mode is active at any one time, but also understand how the system will behave if the operator makes an input while it is engaged. Failure to remember or consider the operating mode of equipment is a common ingredient in accidents involving *automation*.

To illustrate the kinds of mishaps that can occur, the cruise control on a car is a piece of automation designed to maintain speed. All cruise-control systems disengage whenever the brake is depressed, but the behavior from one car to another is less predictable when the accelerator is depressed. In the case where depressing the accelerator disengages cruise control, the consequence of forgetting the effect is that the car will slow down when the driver eases off the accelerator. In the case where the accelerator does not disengage the cruise control, the consequences of forgetting that information can be more dramatic. The following incident is described in Andre and Degani (1997):

> The incident occurred while the second author [Degani] was driving on a highway during a rainy night. The traffic was slow at about 40 miles per hour. Bored and tired, the driver engaged the cruise control by turning it ON and pressing the "set-speed" button. The cruise control engaged, and the car cruised at 40 mph. Several minutes later the rain stopped and the traffic speed increased; subsequently, the driver depressed the gas pedal to manually override the cruise control and increase the speed to 60 mph. He drove in this configuration for some 10 miles until coming to his planned exit from the highway. At this point he had completely forgotten that the cruise control was previously engaged (there was no indication in this type of car that the cruise control was on and engaged).
>
> The exit ramp was initially sloped downhill and then extended uphill ending with a curve into a busy intersection. Aware of this landscape, the driver planned to release the gas pedal and let the car glide downhill (lifting the foot from the gas pedal) and maintain a slow speed during the turn into the intersection. Initially it all worked as planned. However, once the car reached a speed of just below 40 mph the cruise control "kicked in." Not expecting such a jolt, the driver lost control of the car as it sped into the intersection. Luckily, no other cars were present at this late-night hour.
>
> *(Andre & Degani, 1997)*

The autopilot on the helm of the *Exxon Valdez* did not disengage when manual inputs were made. Moreover, it allowed the helmsman to make inputs without providing any warning or other indicator that those helm commands would not be executed. The helm of the *Exxon Valdez* did contain a rudder angle indicator that should have alerted the third mate or the helmsman to the true setting of the rudder. That is, it would not have indicated a 10° right rudder if the autopilot had still been engaged. Neither, however, recalls looking at the rudder indicator prior to the 20° command. We discuss possible reasons for this later.

If the third mate and helmsman did fail to disengage the autopilot, they committed a common error known as a *postcompletion error*. Blandford (2000) gives a cogent description of them. "[T]he phenomenon can be described simply: the user of some device achieves the purpose of the interaction and goes away, or continues with other (unrelated) activity, leaving loose ends. This is possible because achieving the main goal requires the user to set up some initial condition, which then has to be reset before the total task goal can be considered achieved." Such errors were frequent in older automated teller machines (ATMs). Older ATMs would dish out the money and then, with the ATM card still inserted, ask if further transactions were desired. Users would frequently take the money and walk away, forgetting to retrieve the card once the primary goal of withdrawing cash had been achieved. Byrne and Bovair studied postcompletion errors experimentally, investigating the role of memory load (Byrne & Bovair, 1997). They engaged each participant in a video game as commander of a starship. Participants could shoot enemies either with a phaser or photon torpedos. In separate conditions, participants had to hold differing numbers of items in working memory as a secondary task. The key element was that the phasers had to be recharged after firing a set number of times. Like the autopilot on the *Exxon Valdez*, trying to work the phaser without recharging would not produce a warning, but no phaser fire would follow. Participants made a significant number of postcompletion errors, attempting to fire the phasers without recharging them. Error rates increased as memory load increased.

According to Byrne and Bovair's (1997) analysis, postcompletion errors occur when the working memory activation of the resetting operation is too low. In their model, each working memory item receives a share of activation and also gets a boost in activation if that item is attached to an active goal. When working memory load is high, there are insufficient working memory resources to fully activate all items in working memory. If a step in a procedure is to be recalled, it must receive the boost in activation associated with being attached to an active goal. Recharging the phaser (or resetting the autopilot control), however, is not part of the goal of shooting (or steering) and therefore receives no goal activation. This highlights the fact that operators will occasionally forget actions that are not strongly attached to primary goals, even when procedure manuals specify resetting a mode. Such errors do not necessarily reflect neglect, but can arise because the mental representation of tasks may not include resetting as part of the goal. Presumably, in Byrne and Boviar's study (1997), the goal was interpreted as shooting, not recharging; thus, when the goal of shooting was accomplished, the participants thought they were finished and forgot to recharge. It is likely that on the bridge of a vessel, the primary goal is maneuvering, not resetting the state of a subsystem from autopilot to manual. Thus, despite procedures and training, it would not be surprising to find that operators set the controls for the next planned maneuver, but forgot to reset the system from one mode to another.

Control Dynamics and Detection Times

One of the key conclusions of the NTSB report was that the third mate waited too long before turning the vessel. According to the NTSB report, it should have taken only 10 to

20 seconds to note the failure of a course change (1990, p. 118). We will not assert that we know for certain the cognitive factors that contributed to the third mate's failure to detect that the ship had not turned. However, it is possible to see how a combination of situation and human characteristics would promote such a failure.

We noted in Part II that certain systems have control dynamics that are inherently difficult for human operators to understand and control. This is especially true for systems whose behavior is sluggish due to long lags in responding to inputs. The supertanker is one such system. Determining that the ship was responding to the command to turn the vessel would have required the third mate to watch for signs that the commands were taking effect over at least a 10- to 20-second interval. Because the turn was gradual, the actual displacement of the symbol for the ship on the radar screen would have been small. It is not possible to tell from the report how much the ship would have deviated in 10–20 seconds, and therefore not possible to tell how difficult a visual discrimination would have been to detect a change on the radar; however, it is likely safe to say that it would have been at least a somewhat difficult visual discrimination.

While he was monitoring the radar to detect the change of course, the third mate took a reading on one of the buoy lights off Busby Island and determined that his position was safe. The lookout also reported a sighting that could be interpreted as safe. At some point, the lookout testified that she saw the ship change heading (turn). Thus, even though the radar indicated that the ship was not turning, the position indications were still giving evidence of a safe position.

It is worth noting that the third mate was looking for positive evidence that the ship was turning (confirmatory evidence). However, he would have had to interpret the negative evidence (absence of positive evidence) to conclude that further action was necessary. We have discussed how visual search times are typically longer for negative cases in which targets are absent. In a sense, detecting a failure to change course involves detection of a nontarget, which would be expected to take longer. Thus, the sluggish response of the system, coupled with the need to search for negative evidence in an environment where the discrimination cues were potentially difficult, may have combined to create a climate in which error was likely.

Time Estimation

Monitoring the radar to ensure that the course change had taken effect would have required keeping mental track of time; that is, it would involve estimating how much time had elapsed and the expected course change given the amount of time that had elapsed. Mental timekeeping is a difficult task that is subject to many influences, including the level of activity within a given time period (Baldauf, Burgard, & Wittmann, 2009; Block, Hancock, & Zakay, 2010; Hart, 1975). A meta-analysis of 119 studies of time perception (Block, Hancock, & Zakay, 2010) found that there was a systematic effect of task difficulty on time estimation. In busy environments when participants were explicitly trying to judge temporal intervals, they tended to give estimates that were on average 80 percent of the true duration of the interval. This bias in temporal estimation can help account for some discrepancies in the testimony regarding the *Exxon Valdez* compared to actual track data.

According to the NTSB, the *Exxon Valdez* maintained a course of 180° for a full 6 minutes before turning. During testimony, the third mate estimated the time to be less than

4 minutes, closer to 3.5 minutes. He testified that about 1.5 minutes after the 10° rudder command, he issued the 20° command, and about 2 minutes later issued the hard right rudder command. Given that the NTSB estimated that it would have taken 10 to 20 seconds to determine that the course had not changed, it is not clear why the third mate waited so long to issue the 20° command. However, it does call attention to the fact that such a detection would have involved: (1) the detection of a negative outcome, (2) uncertainty about the elapsed time, (3) a small expected deviation of the radar symbol as the target, and (4) ambiguous information as to the safe location of the vessel.

Decision Biases

In this incident, information that would have served to correct the incorrect conclusion that the ship was changing course was absent or ambiguous. As a result, a human factors specialist would suspect that one or more biases were at work, including anchoring, overconfidence, and confirmation. In Chapter 12, we discussed how an *Anchoring heuristic* could preclude timely detection of off-nominal system states. The third mate's delay in detecting the change in state is consistent with an anchoring bias, in that the presumption of normality or safe operation persisted until the evidence became overwhelming, at which point it was too late. *Overconfidence bias* in a judgment made under uncertainty could also have played a part. Given that the third mate had commanded the rudder to be shifted, he may have placed excessive weight on his expectation that the rudder was in the correct position, and insufficient weight on the radar indications. His confidence in the belief that the rudder was correctly positioned would also have affected his perception of the state of the situation, delaying the detection of no change in course. A *confirmation bias* would have had the effect of giving more weight to the evidence that the ship was in a safe operating state, and reduced the weight given to information that it was not; it may also have resulted in him missing the conflicting evidence entirely.

One might question why the situation did not trigger the kind of recognition of trouble expected of an expert, according to *recognition-primed decision making* (Klein, 1993) or the common reliance on the *Representativeness heuristic* (Kahneman & Tversky, 1984). In this respect, the NTSB notes that although the third mate had much experience as a seaman, he had been an officer for only one year and had little experience in navigating a vessel in congested waterways. Recall that according to Recognition-Primed Decision Making (Klein, 1993), situations are understood and actions selected by matching features of the situation to stored representations built by past experience. The much more experienced master might have detected the danger lurking more easily, as experience would have given him representations more sensitive to the right clues in the environment.

In general, the situation that confronted the third mate on that evening is not unusual for demanding environments—complex environments are often high in ambiguity and uncertainty. Further, when actions are undertaken, people tend to look for information that confirms their expectation of the impact of their actions on the environment. In many instances, there may be only one key instrument that provides the critical piece of information that things are amiss. Finally, all this often takes place when the individual in charge is dealing with multiple tasks.

Multitasking

In this incident, a major consequence of the master leaving the bridge was that all of these tasks were left to the third mate, increasing his multitasking load. In this case, the difficult navigation required frequent visual fixes to be taken and plotted to provide more precise information on the ship's position, heading, and track. Typically, a bridge officer verifies the actions of the helmsman. Instead, the third mate was focused on monitoring the radar display; this prevented him from carrying out frequent compass fixes that would have given better position information, or from observing the rudder angle indicator, which would have shown whether the rudder commands had been implemented. With two bridge officers, one would have taken closely spaced visual bearings on all buoys and taken charge of giving orders to the helm (conning the ship). The other would have monitored the radar and supervised the helmsman, verifying the rudder setting (NTSB, 1990).

In response to the increased multitasking demands, the third mate responded by strategically shedding tasks. *Task shedding* is a common strategy in multitasking, where operators under pressure devote all their resources to the most critical tasks and let less critical ones go undone (Hart, 1989; Raby & Wickens, 1994). Raby and Wickens (1994) examined task shedding by pilots in a simulated flight regime as a function of workload, which was manipulated by varying the number of tasks (multitasking demand). They reasoned that high multitasking demands would deplete available processing resources and that, in response, pilots might alter when they began a task, shorten the time on task, or simply shed less important tasks. They found that workload did not affect when a task was undertaken or the time spent on a task once undertaken. However, as multitasking demands increased, the time spent on the most critical tasks increased, while the time spent on less critical tasks decreased. Moreover, they calculated that the distribution of time devoted to each task was roughly optimal, indicating that task shedding was being done in a way that preserved the essential tasks. Several other previous observations of monitoring multiple displays (Carbonell, Ward, & Senders, 1968; Moray, 1984; Senders, 1964) and multitask performance (Moray, Dessouky, Kijowski, & Adapathya, 1991) suggest that with practice (or expertise), operators adapt their resource allocation according to the incentives in the environment.

When task shedding is strategic, it retains those essential functions that can be done with existing resources. A degenerate form of task shedding, referred to as *tunnel vision*, or *cognitive tunneling*, occurs when attention becomes fixated on a single task or goal. Cognitive tunneling is a general phenomenon, strongly driven by the symbology and design of visual displays (Foyle, Sanford, & McCann, 1991; McCann, Foyle, & Johnston, 1993; McLeod, Driver, Dienes, & Crisp, 1991; Wickens & Long, 1995). In the context of multitasking, it refers to a form of task management in which an operator or entire crew devotes resources exclusively to a single task. It is often driven by interruptions, faults, or excessive concern.

Cognitive tunneling reflects a specific response to task management, one that takes task shedding to a potentially hazardous extreme. There have been several accidents in which the cause can be attributed to an operator or entire crew attending solely to an interrupting event and failing to manage other tasks (Degani & Wiener, 1993; Dismukes & Nowinski, 2007; Funk, 1990). In the case of the *Exxon Valdez*, the third mate was fixated on the radar screen, watching for an indication that the ship was turning. In doing so, he neglected the rudder angle indicator and failed to take an adequate number of observations that would have given him a more precise location, heading, and track for the tanker. His strategy of shedding tasks led to a tunneling of his attention to a single display.

Strategic task shedding represents a kind of triage on existing tasks, undertaking tasks on a priority basis to optimize the limited cognitive resources by ensuring that critical system functioning is maintained. Yet, successful application of strategic task shedding itself imposes an additional task load. The determination of a task's priority and the decision about which tasks to undertake and which to shed requires cognitive resources that would otherwise be applied to executing one of the tasks. Is there a point at which the operator becomes so overloaded that strategic task shedding becomes infeasible, and tasks are undertaken randomly or otherwise uncorrelated with their priority or criticality?

Hollnagel developed a framework for human control called the Contextual Control Model (CCM), shown schematically in Figure 13.2 (Hollnagel, 1993). According to the CCM, human control during multitasking shifts dynamically between four states as a function of multitasking load. One way to estimate multitasking load is to consider the number of active goals the operator must satisfy and the time frame in which they must be satisfied. As the time grows shorter, or the number of goals increases, multitasking becomes more difficult given that the length of time available for each task is reduced.

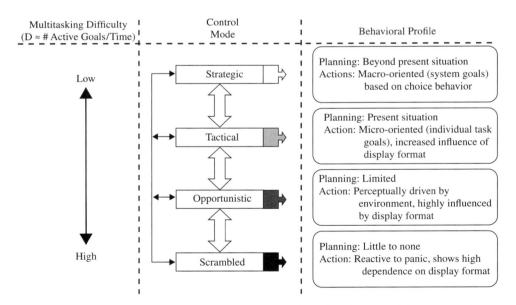

Figure 13.2 Contextual Control Model. Multitasking difficulty is a function of the number of concurrently active goals the operator must satisfy and the time interval within which they must be done. As multitasking difficulty increases, control becomes less proactive, less responsive to future system states, and more reactive, increasingly focused on managing immediate demands. *Source:* After Hollnagel (1993).

The highest control state is strategic control. In *strategic control mode*, the operator has time to plan with the global view in mind, and choose actions with respect to the future efficiency and safety of the system. Such strategic control requires time and cognitive resources and is thus characteristic of behavior only when multitasking demands are low. As the index of multitasking difficulty increases, operators are presumed to shift into tactical control mode. In *tactical control mode*, the operator maintains a shortened planning horizon, but is driven more by the immediate demands of individual tasks. In this mode, actions are generally routine or preprogrammed. Because of the increased time demands, less time is available for mental computation. Thus, displays and controls will have a bigger role in shaping performance than in low-demand situations. That is, operators will be more influenced by what they see.

According to CCM, as multitasking load is further increased, control becomes opportunistic. In *opportunistic control mode*, the next action derives solely from the immediate context. The operator will be driven more by perceptual events and less by cognitive processing, and thus will be more influenced by the format of visual displays. One way to think of it is to imagine that you could do only the shallowest of cognitive processing: What you see is what you do. Finally, the situation can become so hectic that control becomes scrambled. In *scrambled control mode*, planning is impossible, priority is not assessed, and the operator simply does whatever task is most readily at hand; the choice of what task to undertake next may be random. In some cases, the operator may freeze, unable to do anything.

The theory of CCM is meant to be dynamic, in that operators switch control modes back and forth as task loading changes. The black lines connecting all four modes in Figure 13.2 are meant to indicate that control modes do not necessarily progress in sequence. It is not necessary to go from strategic to tactical control mode in order to get to scrambled mode. If alarms suddenly start going off, the operator may transition directly from strategic mode to scrambled mode. Some empirical support for the CCM framework comes from studies showing the existence of the four modes of control and a correlation between performance and subjective rating of CCM modes. Stanton and colleagues showed that it was possible to categorize the performance of teams of naïve participants in a simulated gas distribution task into the four modes of control in CCM (Stanton, Ashleigh, Roberts, & Xu, 2001). Feigh and colleagues (Feigh, Pritchett, Jacko, & Denq, 2005) found significant positive correlations between rated CCM and performance using naïve participants in a simulated airline management task.

SUMMARY

The NTSB report attributes the *Exxon Valdez* accident to human error. With no evidence of equipment or systems failures and no adverse weather, there is no reason to doubt their conclusion that the third mate failed to properly maneuver the vessel. There also was no reason to believe that he deliberately grounded the vessel; thus, at some point he must have lost awareness of where the ship was, where it would be in a few moments, and what its current commanded state actually was. At the very least, he was wrong about one of those, or he would have acted sooner to avert the disaster. In short, he made an error. In Chapter 14, we will discuss the nature of error, theories of error, and factors that contribute to a loss of situation awareness.

REFERENCES

Andre, A., & Degani, A. (1997). Do you know what mode you're in? An analysis of mode error in everyday things. In M. Mouloua & J. M. Koonce (Eds.) *Human-automation interaction: Research & practice* (pp. 19–28). Mahwah, NJ: Lawrence Erlbaum.

Baldauf, D., Burgard, E., & Wittmann, M. (2009). Time perception as a workload measure in simulated car driving. *Applied Ergonomics, 40*(5), 929–935.

Blandford, A. (2000). *Designing to avoid postcompletion errors* (Working Paper No. WP33). London, UK: Middlesex University.

Block, R. A., Hancock, P. A., & Zakay, D. (2010). How cognitive load affects duration judgments: A meta-analytic review. *Acta Psychologica, 134*(3), 330–343.

Byrne, M. D., & Bovair, S. (1997). A working memory model of a common procedural error. *Cognitive Science, 21*(1), 31–61. doi:10.1207/s15516709cog2101_2

Carbonell, J. R., Ward, J., & Senders, J. W. (1968). A queueing model of visual sampling experimental validation. *IEEE Transactions on Man-Machine Systems, 9*(3), 82–87.

Degani, A., & Wiener, E. L. (1993). Cockpit checklists: Concepts, design, and use. *Human Factors: The Journal of the Human Factors and Ergonomics Society, 35*(2), 345–359.

Dismukes, R. K., & Nowinski, J. (2007). Prospective memory, concurrent task management, and pilot error. In A. F. Kramer, D. A.Wiegmann, & A. Kirlik (Eds.), *Attention: From Theory to Practice* (pp. 225–238). New York, NY: Oxford University Press.

Feigh, K. M., Pritchett, A. R., Jacko, J. A., & Denq, T. (2005). *Decision making during an airline rescheduling task: A contextual control model description.* Presented at the 13th Annual Symposium on Aviation Psychology, Oklahoma City, Oklahoma.

Foyle, D., Sanford, B., & McCann, R. S. (1991). Attentional issues in superimposed flight symbology. *Sixth International Symposium on Aviation Psychology* (proceedings) (pp. 577–582). Columbus, OH: Ohio State University.

Funk, K. (1990). Cockpit task management. IEEE International Conference on Systems, Man and Cybernetics. Conference Proceedings (pp. 466–469). Piscataway, NJ: IEEE.

Hart, S. G. (1975). Time estimation as a secondary task to measure workload. *Proceedings of the 11th Annual Conference on Manual Control* (pp. 64–77). Washington, DC: NASA.

Hart, S. G. (1989). *Crew workload-management strategies—A critical factor in system performance* (pp. 22–27). Presented at the Fifth International Symposium on Aviation Psychology, Columbus, OH.

Hollnagel, E. (1993). *Human reliability analysis: Context and control.* London, UK: Academic Press.

Kahneman, D., & Tversky, A. (1984). Choices, values, and frames. *American Psychologist, 39*(4), 341.

Klein, G. A. (1993). A recognition-primed decision (RPD) model of rapid decision making. *Decision Making in Action: Models and Methods,* 138–147.

McCann, R. S., Foyle, D., & Johnston, J. C. (1993). Attentional limitations with head-up displays. In R. S. Jenson (Ed) *Proceedings of the Seventh International Symposium on Aviation Psychology* (pp. 70–75).Columbus, Ohio: Ohio State University.

McLeod, P., Driver, J., Dienes, Z., & Crisp, J. (1991). Filtering by movement in visual search. *Journal of Experimental Psychology: Human Perception and Performance, 17*(1), 55.

Moray, N. (1984). Attention to dynamic visual displays in man-machine systems. In R. Parasuraman (Ed.) *Varieties of attention* (pp. 485–513). Orlando, FL: Academic Press.

Moray, N., Dessouky, M. I., Kijowski, B. A., & Adapathya, R. (1991). Strategic behavior, workload, and performance in task-scheduling. *Human Factors, 33,* 607–629.

National Transportation Safety Board (NTSB). (1990). *Grounding of the U.S. Tankship Exxon Valdez on Bligh Reef, Prince William Sound near Valdez, Alaska March 24, 1989* (No. National Transportation and Safety Board Marine Accident PB90-916405, NTSB/MAR90/04). Washington, DC: National Transportation Safety Board.

Palast, G. (2009, March 23). Stick your damn hand in it: 20th birthday of the *Exxon Valdez* lie. *Greg Palast: Journalism and Film.* Retrieved from www.gregpalast.com/stick-your-damn-hand-in-it-20th-birthday-of-the-exxon-valdez-lie/

Raby, M., & Wickens, C. D. (1994). Strategic workload management and decision biases in aviation. *International Journal of Aviation Psychology, 4*(3), 211–240. doi:10.1207/s15327108ijap0403_2

Senders, J. W. (1964). The human operator as a monitor and controller of multidegree of freedom systems. *IEEE Transactions on Human Factors in Electronics, HFE-5*(1), 2–5. doi:10.1109/THFE.1964.231647

Stanton, N. A., Ashleigh, M. J., Roberts, A. D., & Xu, F. (2001). Testing Hollnagel's Contextual Control Model: Assessing team behavior in a human supervisory control task. *International Journal of Cognitive Ergonomics, 5*(2), 111–123.

State of Alaska. (1990). *SPILL: The wreck of the Exxon Valdez* (Final Report). Retrieved from www.evostc.state.ak.us/facts/details.cfm

Wickens, C. D., & Long, J. (1995). Object versus space-based models of visual attention: Implications for the design of head-up displays. *Journal of Experimental Psychology: Applied, 1*(3), 179.

14

Human Error

The role of operator error in the *Exxon Valdez* incident is hardly unique. The National Aeronautics and Space Administration (NASA) established and maintains the Aviation Safety Reporting System (ASRS), which accepts anonymous reports of incidents of error in commercial flight operations. The ASRS Web page (http://asrs.arc.nasa.gov/) indicates that, as of 2011, the system contains roughly 975,000 reports, consisting of cases of system failure, difficult situations, or human error that did not result in an accident. An analysis of the reports conducted as part of the 25th anniversary of its establishment suggested that 80 percent of the reports involved the "human factor" (NASA, 2001). This is in keeping with other investigations into the causes of accidents, which estimate that anywhere between 45 percent and 85 percent of all accidents can be attributed to errors on the part of human operators (Allnutt, 1987; Barach & Small, 2000; Endsley, 1997; Nagel, 1989; Shappell & Wiegmann, 2003, 2004; Sumwalt, Morrison, Watson, & Taube, 1997; Treat, 1980; Williamson, Webb, Sellen, Runciman, & Van der Walt, 1993; Zapf & Reason, 1994).

Estimates of human error might be even higher if one considered poor choices in the design of human interfaces, maintenance errors, or errors in manufacturing. Humans are involved in all aspects of engineered systems, from conception, operating concept, design, and construction through operation and maintenance. Human error at any of these stages can lead to system failures. If we want to understand how to make engineered systems safer, we must begin analyzing patterns of human error. These considerations will, in turn, lead to a kind of philosophy for human-centered design of systems that enhances safety. We begin with a discussion of what is known about human error. We then describe a primary contributor to human error: lack of a full understanding of the situation in which an operation is taking place.

HUMAN ERROR AND SYSTEM ERROR

In understanding the nature of human error in engineered systems, it is important to distinguish human error from system error. Although human operators are frequently mentioned as the source of system errors, the attribution of human error, or even the claim of a causal role of the human operator in accidents, is not without problems. The first question that comes to mind is the basis for saying that human error caused the accident. Some of the variability in estimates of the human operator's contribution to accidents comes from differences in what Rasmussen, Nixon, and Warner (1990) refer to as the "stop rule"—the depth to which an investigator goes in attributing the cause of the accident. Any violation of procedure can legitimately be deemed human error, as could bad judgment or a bad outcome that has no mechanical failure or other obvious source. It was once common to consider operator error as the cause of an accident when there was no apparent mechanical failure or extreme conditions. Colloquially, it still remains common to attribute bad outcomes to bad judgment. Yet not all bad outcomes, certainly in complex engineered systems, can be said to derive from human error.

Decisions made under uncertainty with only partial information can lead to bad outcomes with no apparent human error. This is especially the case in competitive situations, such as sports or military confrontations, in which the behavior of the opponent cannot be fully known. Take, for instance, the 1988 downing of an Iranian airliner by the USS *Vincennes*. After repeated failed attempts to contact it, the captain of the USS *Vincennes* ordered a missile to be fired at an unidentified aircraft (which happened to be a civilian passenger airliner). The failure to respond to radio calls increased the captain's suspicion that the aircraft was purposely trying to conceal its identity, as it would if it were attacking. The captain had also received word from the radar officer that the aircraft was descending. With this information he concluded, incorrectly, that it was indeed attacking and ordered a missile strike that killed more than 200 innocent civilians. The radar operator had incorrectly reported the aircraft as descending when it was actually climbing. Furthermore, the reason the aircraft was not responding was because the radio calls were going out only over military frequencies, so the pilot of the aircraft never heard the calls. Applying the stop rule here, and calling a bad outcome an error, we would conclude that the captain erred.

Though the captain was cleared of wrongdoing, controversy still remains over his decision to launch (Cannon-Bowers & Salas, 1998). If you concluded that his decision to launch was an error, is it of the same magnitude as that made by the radar operator, who reported that the plane was descending when it was in fact climbing? Did the radar operator commit an error? Clearly yes. But should the stop rule end with that observation, or should we look deeper for an underlying cause? Climbing and descending aircraft on many radar screens (we do not know if this is true of the screens on the *Vincennes*) are differentiated by a small upward- or downward-pointing caret next to the numeric altitude. This might not be a sufficiently salient or unambiguous clue in very stressful situations where operators must make rapid decisions in stressful multitasking environments. In cases such as this, it might be more appropriate to indicate that the error was caused by the system rather than faulting the operator.

THE NATURE OF HUMAN ERROR

Human error may be inescapable; it can certainly seem so. Anyone who has tried to learn a skill or perform under pressure can attest to that. Yet, as ubiquitous as human error may seem, it is not in reality that frequent (Reason, 1990b). If you consider how many words we speak each day, the average number of syllables and phonemes we produce (individual unit sounds like "s," "sh," "t," and so forth) is quite large. Given that errors could and do occur at the syllable and phoneme level, the potential for error is substantial, especially considering that errors could occur not only in articulation, but also in grammar and semantics. Viewed in this light, then, the number of speech errors we actually make seems modest. The same is true for most other tasks in which we have sufficient expertise. Indeed, the problem with studying errors, as with studying accidents, is often their scarcity, not their abundance. However, due to the time and intensity of human-system interaction, errors remain a problem for human-system design. Even when error rates are at only one in a million actions, totalling these actions across all operators over many years, errors accumulate to cause significant system problems.

Consider first all the drivers on the road at any given time in a major city. Now multiply that by the number of decisions and actions each driver makes in a small period of time; there are bound to be many errors occurring across all automobiles at any given time. Indeed, a central concern of human factors engineering is to guard against small-probability events that can propagate into major accidents due to the sheer frequency of behavior.

If errors were random, this would be a real problem, as no systematic understanding would be possible. Fortunately, though it is not yet possible (and may never be so) to predict exactly when an error will occur, most are not random. Rather, errors tend to exhibit regular patterns that emerge from how we process information, represent situations, or decide on actions. This regularity in errors has provided insights into how our actions are structured. For example, as we speak we sometimes stumble over words, swap syllables in words (e.g., "cuff of coppee" for "cup of coffee"; see Fromkin, 1971, for examples), or forget entirely what we meant to say. Still, the errors preserve the underlying structure of the language. The most common errors involve substituting one sound for another in words; thus, "also share" can become "alsho share" where the "sh" of the next word gets inserted into the current word, or "fish grotto" becomes "frish gotto," where the future sound is bound mistakenly to the current word.

Semantic errors also occur, such as spoonerisms, named for the Reverend Archibald Spooner who regularly produced them. Classic spoonerisms include such phrases as (examples taken from Fromkin, 1971): "you have hissed all my mystery lectures" instead of "missed all my history lectures"; "I saw you fight a liar in the back quad" instead of "light a fire"; "tasted a whole worm" instead of "wasted a whole term"; and the unforgettable "three cheers for our queer old dean" instead of "dear old queen [Victoria]."

Whether in articulation or semantics, all errors preserve the rules of the English language. In speech errors, the transpositions and substitutions follow rules of phonology, which describes how sounds in a given language are permitted to go together. Spoonerisms are particularly interesting because the utterance remains meaningful, although perhaps with a different meaning than was intended. Similarly, in sentence-planning errors, people substitute words from the same grammatical category (i.e., noun, verb), preserving syntactic rules on sentence construction (see, e.g., Fromkin, 1971; Motley, 1985). In this sense, errors are not random but constrained by the underlying process. Speech errors are helpful because they provide us with a better understanding of the underlying processing of speech; unfortunately, they do not explain how errors arise.

Cognitive psychology provides a framework for understanding behavior and offers more mechanistic accounts. Given our previous discussion of limited-capacity resources, it might be supposed that errors arise when demands exceed available resources. For example, insufficient activation due to limited memory resources has been hypothesized to underlie postcompletion errors (Byrne & Bovair, 1997; Byrne & Davis, 2006; Chung & Byrne, 2008). As described earlier, *postcompletion errors* refer to errors in which one forgets to perform a "cleanup" activity after the main goal has been completed, such as removing the original document from a copier after making the copy.

Postcompletion errors are similar to the *prospective memory* errors described earlier, in that the operator, who must defer an intended action until later, forgets to do so at the appropriate time. In accounting for prospective memory errors, theories emphasize the activation produced from the visual environment. If the visual or auditory stimulation produces strong activation of the memory representation for the prospective memory task, it will serve as a strong reminder, reducing the incidence of error (Einstein & McDaniel, 2005; Einstein et al., 2005; McDaniel, Guynn, Einstein, & Breneiser, 2004). However, the salience of the prospective memory stimulus is not the only determinant of performance on the prospective memory task. Other evidence suggests that it is necessary to devote cognitive resources to the prospective memory task to increase its activation even further (Smith, 2003; Smith & Bayen, 2004). The prospective memory theories developed from laboratory studies have provided good accounts of the conditions that either promote or discourage prospective memory errors in the more complex domains of air traffic control (Loft & Remington, 2010; Loft, Smith, & Bhaskara, 2011) and medicine (Grundgeiger, Sanderson, MacDougall, & Venkatesh, 2010), as well as in demanding multitasking environments (Einstein, McDaniel, Williford, Pagan, & Dismukes, 2003).

Noise in the information-processing system, a modern cognitive concept, has also been seen as a cause of errors. As discussed earlier, studies of cognitive processing frequently test hypotheses about the underlying mechanisms of attention and memory by measuring the response time to make simple choice decisions. Computational accounts of these choice response times posit that they are determined by two factors: the rate at which information accrues and the amount of information required. These theories assume that people set a threshold that determines how much information is needed and that they will not respond until the accumulated information exceeds that threshold. These models provide good fits to response times of errors in simple speeded tasks by assuming that errors arise from noise in setting the thresholds for responses or in the rate at which evidence accumulates (Smith & Ratcliff, 2004).

It is also possible that momentary fluctuations in activation levels, due to noise, could cause some items to rise above threshold and be retrieved in error. In this way, these two factors (rate at which information accrues and the amount of information required) can be seen to underlie some of the decision biases noted earlier, chiefly availability and representativeness. Note that the models based on information accumulation plus threshold do not preclude factors other than noise. Thresholds may be lowered if the operator is in a hurry or believes less information is needed to make a decision. Likewise, thresholds will be raised when the operator wants to be cautious, reducing the chances of an error. Fluctuations in activation levels, information accrual rates, or response thresholds arising from noise seem plausible as fundamental error-generating mechanisms. However, these accounts of error are extensions of a theory of processing, not explicit theories of errors themselves. We now turn our attention to explicit theories of error that have been influential in complex domains.

THEORIES OF HUMAN ERROR

Theories of human error have as their goal an account of the range of errors people make in terms of the underlying cognitive mechanisms and, derived from this, the environmental factors that predispose people to commit errors. The first step in creating such a model is to develop a scheme for classifying errors that describes the regularity in error patterns. Rasmussen (1983) developed an error taxonomy based on levels of human information processing, which could be applied to complex domains, as seen in Table 14.1. He postulates three levels of behavior: skill-based, rule-based, and knowledge-based. *Skill-based* behavior deals with sensory-motor performance, an action level concerned with the execution of a chosen behavior or the processing of sensory stimulation. Given that the behaviors have been highly practiced, processing and execution of actions are fairly automated. Thus, the units of skill-based processing are *signals* at the level of sensory or motor activation.

Rule-based behavior, in contrast, deals with routine procedures for accomplishing goals in familiar situations. In this regard, rule-based processing is similar to the "Methods" part of the GOMS (*G*oals, *O*perators, *M*ethods, *S*election rules) analysis described earlier. That is, it represents routine strategies for selecting actions that advance one toward the goal. A concrete example might be the formation of syntactically correct utterances in speech. The words to express a meaning have been chosen and must be assembled into a grammatical sentence. The task is familiar, relying on ingrained rules of grammar for determining the final form of the utterance. Rasmussen considers the units of rule-based processing to be signs. *Signs* are signals that have been transformed into units so that they can activate predetermined patterns, analogous to a key unlocking a door. In contrast, *knowledge-based* behavior deals with the selection of behaviors to accomplish intended goals. The functional units for knowledge-based processing are *symbols*, which are units that activate internal concepts, not simply previously stored procedures.

In Rasmussen's account (also see Norman, 1981), the nature of the error will differ considerably depending on whether it occurs at the level of skill-based, rule-based, or knowledge-based behavior. Errors at the skill level represent cases in which the action did not correspond to the intent, typically referred to as a *slip* (Rasmussen, 1983). Typing errors are examples of slips. Errors at the rule-based or knowledge-based levels reflect cases in which the wrong procedure was executed or the intent itself was wrong, which Rasmussen considers a *mistake* (Rasmussen, 1983). One of the contributing factors to the nuclear disaster at Chernobyl was the fact that the engineering team decided to go ahead with the planned test of the reactor despite the reactor pressure being below normal due to a previous operator error. This can be classified as a mistake because the test procedure was incorrect given the state of the reactor (see Reason, 1990a).

Table 14.1 Types of behavior proposed by Rasmussen (1983) and the types of errors associated with those behavior levels.

TYPE OF BEHAVIOR	CHARACTERIZATION OF BEHAVIOR	TYPE OF ERROR
Skill-based	Sensory-motor performance	Slip
Rule-based	Execution of routines	Mistake
Knowledge-based	Selection of behaviors to accomplish goals	Mistake

Error Types

Perhaps the most influential and systematic work on the general subject of human error is that of Reason (1990b, 2000). Reason largely adopts the skill-based, rule-based, and knowledge-based distinctions of Rasmussen, while extending the categories of error. Reason draws the important distinction between the *error type* and the *error form*. The error type is a product of the level of processing at which the error occurred, and corresponds to the slips and mistakes described by Rasmussen (1983). Reason elaborates the error types to distinguish between skill-based mistakes and knowledge-based mistakes. Three examples taken from Reason (1990b) illustrate the three error types using incidents in nuclear power plants:

1. In a 1985 incident at Davis-Besse, "[a]n operator, wishing to initiate the steam and feedwater rupture control system manually, inadvertently pressed the wrong two buttons on the control panel, and failed to realise the error."

2. In a 1982 incident at Ginna, "[t]he operators, intending to depressurise the reactor coolant system, used the wrong strategy with respect to the pressure operated relief valve (PORV). They cycled it open and shut, and the valve stuck open on the fourth occasion."

3. In a 1979 incident at Three Mile Island, "[t]he operators did not recognize that the relief valve on the pressurizer was stuck open. The panel display indicated that the relief valve switch was selected closed. They took this to indicate that the valve was shut, even though this switch only activated the opening and shutting mechanism. They did not consider the possibility that this mechanism could have (and actually had) failed independently and that a stuck-open valve could not be revealed by the selector display on the control panel."

In case 1, the error type is at the skill-based level. The intended action was correct to meet the goal of initiating the control system, and the procedure was correct, but the execution was flawed. In case 2, the error type is at the rule-based level, similar to the Chernobyl example cited earlier. The strategy of cycling open and shut is an appropriate one for some valves under some circumstances, but not this valve. In case 3, Reason argues that the error type cannot be attributed to either skill-based or rule-based processing. Instead, it exemplifies a deeper problem in which the operators exhibited an incomplete understanding of the meaning of the displayed information. They failed to achieve a deep understanding of the meaning of the gauge, and the possibility of how it could signal one state while in another. They substituted the more common assumption that the indicator always represented the true state of the system, an assumption that had worked perfectly for them in the past.

In Reason's theory, errors at the skill-based level arise either from inattention in the monitoring of dials or action; or overattention, which can result in missing cues coming from other sources. Errors at the rule-based level arise from either the misapplication of a good rule (one that has proven useful before but is not appropriate to the present circumstance), or the application of a bad rule (one that is not permissible). Errors at the knowledge-based level arise from a number of sources, including those associated with decision biases (e.g., availability, representativeness, anchoring, overconfidence, and confirmation) and inadequate encoding of information. Reason also cites complexity, system design, information selection, and issues with ascribing causality as sources of error at this level. Errors at the knowledge-based level often involve substituting a reliance on familiar past events for thorough analysis of the current system.

In this light, we can speculate that the error type of the third mate of the *Exxon Valdez* was at the knowledge-based level. The incident was not triggered by an obvious slip or selection of the wrong procedure. The NTSB agreed that the plan to gradually swing the ship around the ice floe was appropriate. Rather, the third mate displayed an inadequate awareness of the current state of the ship, and failed to track its progress accurately—and did not appreciate the consequences of the current state on the future state until it was too late.

Error Forms

Error forms are "pervasive varieties of fallibility that are evident at all performance levels." Reason is not unique in positing a common form as the basis of errors. Earlier we discussed the activation and noise accounts, and Norman (1981) proposes that observed error patterns can be accounted for by assuming *slips* at all levels. Reason departs from his predecessors in arguing that errors occur at all levels because the operator relies on an incomplete representation of the action or decision—what he labels *cognitive underspecification*. To make this concrete, consider a rule of the form: if A & B & C are true, then select action Y (e.g., if an applicant to graduate school has a grade point average above 3.5, test scores over 2000, and strong letters of recommendation, then select that student for admission). Underspecification would refer to an action that is selected based on fewer than all three criteria (e.g., using only grade point average and test scores).

We can see evidence of underspecification in the incidents described previously. In case 1, the operator committed a skill-based error because he failed to attend to the relevant information on the buttons. The plan to push a button was appropriate, but the action was underspecified because it did not include evaluating information about the buttons that were being pressed. In case 2, the operator committed a rule-based error because the selection of plans was underspecified; it did not fully consider the conditions that had to be satisfied before the plan could be correctly invoked. In case 3, the operators acted without fully considering the meaning of the label on the switch.

In Reason's theory, underspecification fosters errors through the influence of two factors: *similarity* and *frequency*. If we are trying to retrieve the right course of action from memory, a cluster of similar items will come to mind. A complete specification of the criteria for selection will yield the right answer, but an underspecification allows similar items to match, leading to the possibility of selecting the incorrect procedure. Reason refers to this as *similarity-matching*. Likewise, the baseline memory activation of a habitual routine procedure will be higher than less routine actions. Underspecifiying the retrieval will favor the incorrect selection of the more habitual routine. Reason refers to this as *frequency-gambling*.

It is easy to see how both of these two factors, combined with underspecification, can lead to a range of errors. Suppose, for example, that you intend to go to the store on the way home, requiring you to take an unusual off ramp from the freeway. In this prospective memory task, you might erroneously select the more habitual action (staying on the freeway) over the rarely performed one (exiting at the unusual off ramp). The selection of the appropriate action would be underspecified, in the sense that a full specification would have included the instruction to deviate from routine, and the nature of the deviation. Similarity-matching might also have played a role, as the habitual action shares much in common with the exception, or at least provides a satisfactory choice given an underspecified retrieval. Thus, this ensemble of overspecification, similarity-matching, and frequency-gambling can provide a theoretical underpinning for decision biases such as availability and representativeness.

Why might underspecification occur? The logical reason is that it takes cognitive resources to perform the matches. If there were no cost to the complexity of the criteria (all the AND and OR conditions), there would be no incentive to underspecify the memory search or the action. One kind of cost in complex criteria lies in acquiring all the parameters for the decision. Consider a case in which the procedure for clearing an aircraft to make a landing approach requires checking six conditions: aircraft altitude, speed, descent rate, runway clear, cross traffic, and wind speed. Each one of these may be displayed in different spatial locations and in different ways: numeric visual information, auditory alerts, out-the-window views. It would take time and effort to check each one every time. If one of the variables, say wind speed, changed more slowly than the others, operators might be tempted to use the last value rather than check for the most current one, especially if this works in almost all situations. This is the frequency-gambling to which Reason refers.

A second kind of cost in complex criteria arises if there is an additional cost associated with retrieving items from memory using a compound criterion. Although data are not available to support this interpretation clearly, anecdotally there do seem to be cases in which retrieval is iterative. That is, items are recalled from memory using a more simplistic criterion, and then rejected after conscious examination, such as when searching for the name that goes with a face. As a general rule, there is a human tendency to skip steps or ignore factors (e.g., Degani & Wiener, 1993), especially when they have not proven reliably informative.

Reason's theory provides a very constructive approach to understanding errors in context and, for this reason, has been very influential. It is not without problem, however. One issue is that it lends itself more to post-hoc explanations than to the identification of error potential in a system. There is also the problem that the concept of underspecification can be both too broad and too narrow. It is potentially too broad in the sense that all errors are perforce examples of mis-specification. That seems to be the common ingredient in an error at all levels. If underspecification is the only kind of mis-specification that people make, then it adds less to our understanding than it might otherwise. However, it is possible to conceive of errors that result from overspecification. We know of no direct data on this, but anecdotally, student errors in mathematics often seem to involve bringing in extra assumptions that do not apply to the problem at hand and that artificially constrain a problem. Nonetheless, Reason provides a well-articulated theory of the cognitive factors in errors. Its acceptance in operational environments is evidence that it has bridged the gap between the science of cognitive psychology and its application.

SITUATION AWARENESS

Theories of human error (Byrne & Bovair, 1997; Norman, 1981; Rasmussen, 1982; Reason, 1990b) all share the assumption that error emerges from the natural processes of human cognition that are involved in the control of complex systems. The likelihood of an error increases as the human operator's understanding of the situation becomes more incomplete. In our earlier discussion of control theory, we indicated that in controlling a system, the sensed data from displays had to be integrated into a representation of the situation from which the operator could predict the near future and anticipate the consequences of an intended action. Such a representation of the situation is a process that unfolds over a period of time and involves sequential sampling of multiple information sources through a series of eye fixations on instruments, or by shifting attention. As noted in the preceding error examples, the data must be combined with knowledge of the system, learned criteria for action selection, and recent history to achieve a clear awareness of the current state of the controlled system. The more completely the state is specified, the more likely it is that the right action will be selected.

This can be seen clearly in the discussion of the nature of the errors made by the third mate on the *Exxon Valdez* and those on board the USS *Vincennes*. In each of these situations, at some point, the operators lost awareness of the true situation. This loss of awareness led to the failure to select actions that would have led to a safe outcome. In truth, most of us, most of the time, are aware of only a small portion of the actual state of the devices we use, or the environments in which we find ourselves. In large part then, it was the failure to maintain the appropriate level of awareness that led to the grounding of the *Exxon Valdez* and the downing of the Iranian passenger airplane.

Situation Awareness in Individuals

Had the *Exxon Valdez* accident happened more recently than it did, it is almost certain that the NTSB report would have cited a loss of *situation awareness* as a principal cause. In a now-classic series of papers, Endsley (1988a, 1988b, 1995a, 1995b, 2000) developed the theory of situation awareness and described its application to problems of system design, accident investigation, and system safety. Up until that time, the term had been used to denote a rather loose collection of cognitive operations associated with attention, working memory, and mental models, any or all of which could be said to constitute situation awareness (Sarter & Woods, 1995; Wiener, 1985; Wiener & Curry, 1980). Endsley (1995a) distinguished the state of situation awareness (SA), which is the basis of action selection, from the psychological processes (attention, working memory, mental representations) involved in establishing SA.

Endsley (1988a, 1999) defined *situation awareness* as "the perception of the elements in the environment within a volume of time and space, the comprehension of their meaning, and the projection of their status in the near future." She then described three taxonomic levels of situation awareness in the context of pilot performance, which described increasing levels of awareness (taken verbatim from Endsley, 1999, p. 259):

Level 1 SA—Perception of the elements in the environment—The first step in achieving SA involves perceiving the status, attributes, and dynamics of relevant elements in the environment. For example, pilots need to perceive other aircraft, terrain, system status and warning lights in their environment. In the cockpit, keeping up with all of the relevant system and flight data and other aircraft and navigational data can be quite taxing.

Level 2 SA—Comprehension of the current situation—Comprehension of the situation is based on a synthesis of disjointed Level 1 elements. Level 2 SA goes beyond simply being aware of the elements that are present, to include an understanding of the significance of those elements in light of the pilot's goals. The aircrew puts together Level 1 data to form a holistic picture of the environment, including a comprehension of the significance of objects and events. For example, upon seeing warning lights indicating a problem during take-off, the pilot must quickly determine the seriousness of the problem in terms of the immediate air worthiness of the aircraft and combine this with knowledge on the amount of runway remaining in order to know whether it is an abort situation or not. A novice pilot might be capable of achieving the same Level 1 SA as a more experienced one, but may fall far short of being able to integrate various data elements, along with pertinent goals to comprehend the situation as well.

Level 3 SA—Projection of future status—It is the ability to project the future actions of the elements in the environment, at least in the near term, that forms the third and highest level of situation awareness. This is achieved through knowledge of the status and dynamics of the elements and a comprehension of the situation (both Level 1 and Level 2 SA).

Thus, Level 1 SA is the apprehension of individual pieces of information; Level 2 SA is their integration into a representation of the state of the system and its environment; Level 3 SA is the ability to project this understanding to anticipate the consequences of intended actions. Level 1 SA corresponds well to the skill-based error type of Reason (1990a), discussed earlier. Levels 2 and 3 SA both appear to correspond to Reason's knowledge-based error type, in that they involve an understanding of the situation. The taxonomy of SA does not have a level that corresponds to the rule-based level of Reason (see also Rasmussen, 1982, 1983). This reflects the difference in goals between the two approaches. Whereas the goal for Reason was to systematize the range of errors people make, the goal for Endsley was to provide a typology of the nature of momentary awareness relevant to control in a dynamic system. The fuller theory of SA (e.g., Endsley, 1995b, 2000) does incorporate procedures as an element of the processing that establishes SA, but not as a part of the formal structure of SA as a construct.

The division of SA into Levels 1, 2, and 3 also offers a deepening hierarchy for the taxonomy of errors. It follows from the definitions of each level that errors at Level 1 SA will reflect misapprehension of specific instruments, errors at Level 2 SA will reflect mistaken assessments of the situation, and errors at Level 3 SA will reflect incorrect anticipation of future states of the system given some course of action.

For SA to be a useful concept, it must be bounded. After all, none of us is fully aware of all that is happening around us or of the devices we use. Few of us understand the software and computer networks that we use daily. Cognitive limitations, as discussed earlier, place limits on the amount of information we can process in a given time span, as well as the amount we can retain. Endsley (1995a) bounds the concept by restricting its application to information directly pertaining to the state of a dynamic environment. She excludes what she refers to as "static knowledge," such as doctrine, rules, procedures, and checklists. In driving a car, to give a concrete example, your situation awareness would reflect your knowledge of the speed of your car, the immediate and near-term trajectories of the cars around you, your perception that the patterns are normal or becoming dangerous, and the consequences of actions such as maneuvering into the next lane to avoid an object in your lane. Objects not a property of your situation awareness would include your knowledge of the local traffic rules, the details of the conversation with your passenger, the song playing on the radio, and so forth. Situation awareness is a construct closely tied to the goals one is trying to accomplish with respect to a dynamic environment.

Situation Awareness of Teams

It is also possible to apply the construct of situation awareness to teams. In an earlier chapter, we described how we often work in groups, and that groups can vary considerably in the degree to which individuals interact and the overlap of their responsibilities. These differences contribute to differences in the SA of individuals within the group. In a soccer team, for example, there must be much overlap of the SA of each of the offensive players. They must work as a unit, coordinating their actions with their fellow team members on the run. As the game unfolds dynamically, each offensive player needs to be aware of the position and intent of the other offensive players (as well as of the opposing defenders). Similarly, the SA of the defensive players has to overlap considerably. However, the offensive players do not interact in close coordination with the defensive players on their own team, so their need to share a common SA is diminished.

In complex operations, the division of responsibility leads to an organizational structure that affects the degree to which SA for any operator will overlap with that of another. In Figure 14.1 we use Venn diagrams to depict a simplified parcelling of SA for the Launch Control Center at Kennedy Space Center. The space shuttle was perhaps the most complex system ever to fly and required expertise in several distinct subsystems. During launch, subsystem preparation and monitoring were organized hierarchically. In Figure 14.1 we show only the highest level of four subsystems; each of the listed subsystems could be decomposed further into smaller units. Notice how each subsystem needs very little awareness of the state of the other subsystems. The goal of each subsystem manager is to conduct all the necessary checks for her subsystem and to deal with any problems that arise. She needs to be aware of the state of other subsystems only to the extent that they bear on her goal. The entire launch is coordinated through the NASA Test Director. He needs to

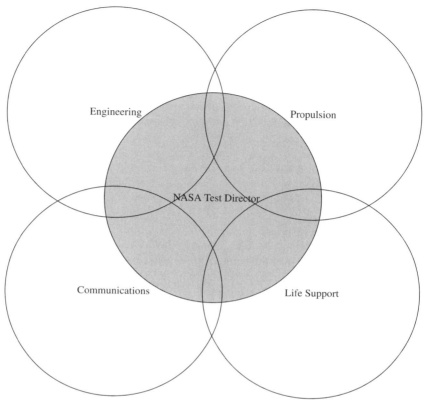

Figure 14.1 Overlap in situation awareness for different subsystems of the shuttle Launch Control Center. The NASA Test Director coordinates all subsystems, but does not maintain complete situation awareness of the state of each system.

have some awareness of the state of each subsystem, but not a complete awareness. The fact that SA is driven by goals in a dynamically evolving environment means that it is not a fixed, static property of the operator, but will change depending on circumstances. If the NASA Test Director is satisfied that Propulsion and Life Support are progressing normally, but Communications is having difficulty, his goal would change to reflect the importance of solving the problem in the communication subsystem.

Cognitive Processing in Establishing Situation Awareness

Endsley distinguished the state of situation awareness (SA) from its component elements and the mental processes used to establish it. This distinction is central to differentiating SA from purely cognitive descriptions of mental processing. SA is not simply perception, attention, working memory, long-term memory, or any other specific mental process.

It is instead the product of a number of these fundamental mental processes in service of a goal. In short, SA represents the state of the human controller at any given time: it is a construct that derives from the combined activity of one or more elementary mental operations. Situation awareness can be driven by both top-down and bottom-up mechanisms (Endsley & Garland, 2000). In ordinary operations, top-down mechanisms determine SA (Endsley & Garland, 2000). As described in Chapter 8, executive control over cognitive processing allows task goals to specify which information is needed from the environment. From here, visual attention (along with eye movements) is deployed to successively acquire the needed information (see, e.g., Yarbus, 1967). The integration of information makes use of mental representations that combine elements in working memory with knowledge from long-term memory to build a meaningful picture of the world. Central attention is involved in selecting and evaluating possible actions. Executive control is required to maintain the alignment of information acquisition and action selection with task goals. As described in Chapter 9, attention can also be driven by bottom-up mechanisms in response to alarms or other stimuli that capture attention (see, e.g., Theeuwes, 1992; Yantis & Jonides, 1984). When attention is captured by an alarm or other salient event, it will initially interrupt cognitive activity to determine the meaning of the event (see Boehm-Davis & Remington, 2009). Goals can thus change in response to an event, in which case a new instantiation of SA will ensue.

Measuring Situation Awareness

A construct such as SA is useful to the extent that its presence or completeness can be quantified in any given setting. Because SA refers to the current state of knowledge of the controlled system, the methods of assessing SA have relied on probes that test the operator's ability to identify or respond to state information. Endsley (Endsley, 1988a, 1988b, 1995a, 1995b; Endsley & Garland, 2000) developed a technique for assessing the degree of SA, called SAGAT (Situation Awareness Global Assessment Technique), which provides an objective measure of current system knowledge suitable for use in a simulator or laboratory setting. SAGAT measures SA by freezing the simulation, or laboratory experiment, and asking a series of questions about the system state that test all three levels of SA. Because it requires stopping the system, it is not suitable for use in operational settings. The questions asked are developed from an extensive cognitive task analysis, described in Chapter 15. A task analysis alone would provide the goals, but a deeper analysis of operator cognition is needed to establish the necessary knowledge and then probe at the different levels. Level 1 SAGAT questions probe knowledge of instrument readings or of relevant objects external to the controlled system. In driving, for example, a Level 1 SAGAT question might ask for the last speed, or whether there was a car immediately to the side of your car in the left lane. Level 2 SAGAT questions probe the understanding of the situation. Questions at this level might ask whether your car was accelerating or decelerating, whether there was merging traffic that might cause you to brake, or whether there was a car that appeared to be changing lanes. Level 3 SAGAT questions probe the ability to anticipate the consequences of various actions. Questions at this level might probe what you would need to do to change lanes safely, or what maneuver you would make to avoid a ball or person who suddenly appeared in your lane. Answers to SAGAT questions are scored against preferred answers and an objective score is computed for each level.

There are limitations associated with this method. Answering SAGAT questions relies on the operator both noticing and processing the information requested as well as remembering the information. In some situations, an operator may check on the value of a parameter (e.g., oil pressure in an aircraft) to ensure that it is within normal operating limits; although the operator may have noticed and processed the actual value of the oil pressure, he may not be able to remember it when asked during the pause. The pauses themselves can be problematic. That is, they do not reflect what would happen in the real world; they also may change the dynamics of the situation.

Other methods have attempted to address these issues by inserting probe questions during operations without having to freeze the environment. In SPAM (Situation Present Assessment Method), for example, SA probe questions are presented while the operator actively controls the task (Durso & Dattel, 2004; Durso & Sethumadhavan, 2008; Durso, Bleckley, & Dattel, 2006; Durso, Truitt, Hackworth, Crutchfield, & Manning, 1998). With this method, the same questions that might be used following the SAGAT technique are used; however, performance of the task is not interrupted. Rather, an indication that a question is available to be answered is provided and operators are asked to answer the question as soon as they are able after receiving the alert. SPAM then records both the accuracy of the response and the time the operator took to respond to the question.

If SA is necessary for performance, then it should follow that measures of SA predict or correlate with performance. Surprisingly little work has directly compared measured SA to performance. The work that has been done suggests that although good situation awareness is related to good operator performance, the relationship is noisy. This may be due to operators with poor SA getting lucky (that is, they make a mistake, but the system "catches" the error), while operators with good SA can get unlucky (for a discussion, see Durso et al., 2006).

Some evidence that measured SA does correlate with performance comes from a study of air traffic control operations. Investigations of air traffic control errors suggests that controllers who made more errors also showed signs that they would have had lower SA scores (Durso et al., 1998). Additionally, a study by Durso et al. (2006) used SPAM to record air traffic controller response time and accuracy to online questions about past, present, and future airspace states during an air traffic control simulation. They also collected data on a battery of personal factors and cognitive tests for each controller and entered it into a stepwise regression to determine the proportion of variance accounted for in predicting three observed measures of air traffic control performance: handoff delays (the time to clear the aircraft to the next sector once its icon began flashing), air traffic control errors (e.g., landing a plane at the wrong altitude or allowing an airspace violation), and total time taken to traverse the sector. They followed this by adding the SPAM results to the regression to determine if SPAM scores contributed to the proportion of variance accounted for. Adding in the SPAM results for accuracy on past, present, and future state yielded a 9 percent improvement in proportion of variance accounted for in predicting handoff delays, and a 15 percent improvement in predicting air traffic control errors, but had no effect on total time to transit the sector. These results suggest that SPAM, and by extension other probe measures, can capture an independent source of variance underlying actual performance.

Other questions remain regarding the use of query-based assessments of SA. Although SAGAT, SPAM, and other online probes provide an objective score with respect to the questions asked, there is no alternative independent measure of the "true" SA against which to assess the scores from these measures. This puts a great burden on the specific questions asked to be truly representative of the knowledge that operators need to have in mind and ready for explicit report. Human-system engineers, not expert operators, determine the SA probes using cognitive task analysis methods. One can question how well this approach elicits the knowledge that must be in the mind of the operator.

In Klein's studies of decisions made by firefighters, soldiers, and other experts (Klein, 1989; Klein & Calderwood, 1991; Klein, Calderwood, & Clinton-Cirocco, 1986), for example, he observed that experts often select their action based on the match of the current experience to their stored experiences. This matching is essential to his model of Recognition-Primed Decision Making, as we discussed earlier. Such matching is not inherently contradictory to a theory of SA (see, e.g., Endsley, 2000). Nevertheless, it is hard to see how explicit questioning of the expert will yield a good sense of SA if the process is largely unconscious, as it is well recognized that experts have difficulty articulating the mental components that comprise their superior performance.

This raises questions about whether all of the features of the fire that primed a firefighter's decision would be available for verbal report on demand. Moreover, if the firefighter has selected an action approach by a rapid, intuitive internal match, then she might not have explicitly thought through all the alternatives or all the possible outcomes for this or alternative actions. Thus, there remains a question as to whether scores on the probe tests reflect what experts need to know or what human-system specialists think they need to know.

There is also the related issue of how one acquires the expert knowledge that would yield appropriate queries. Were SPAM, SAGAT, or similar query-based probes to be administered to firefighters, or experts in other domains, all of the extensive knowledge that makes a firefighter an expert would somehow have to be elicited from expert firefighters by nonexperts through a series of questions. Without this knowledge, it would not be possible to say what the right answers to the questions would be at that instant in time. The process would then have to distill the exact knowledge needed and ensure that that knowledge was contextualized to exactly the right moments in time. In the absence of a benchmark of "true" SA against which to refine the method, questions will remain as to whether the ability or inability to answer the questions used as probes really does measure what is important to know at that moment.

Level 1 SA seems particularly susceptible to these problems. In the cockpit, at an air traffic control station, in the control room of a nuclear power plant, or at one's desk, many clearly visible indicators of state are arrayed around the operator. If the displays are designed well and arranged well, then it may be preferable for the operator to acquire exact state parameters at the exact time needed rather than store them for a few minutes in her memory. A similar criticism could be applied to Levels 2 and 3 SA. Frequent monitoring of the situation may yield the assessment needed without much explicit mental integration or representation. Despite such lingering issues, SAGAT and SPAM have proven useful in diagnosing operator SA in a range of aviation and military applications, including team performance (Durso & Sethumadhavan, 2008; Durso et al., 2006; Endsley, 1988b, 1995b, 1996; Endsley & Kaber, 1999; Leiden, Keller, & French, 2001; Salas, Prince,

Baker, & Shrestha, 1995). Assessment techniques can be useful if they provide a reasonable indication of a construct that both operators and researchers agree is valuable, even if questions remain about the true underlying state being assessed.

An operator's awareness can be reflected in measures other than direct questioning about system state. In SART (Situational Awareness Rating Technique), operators are asked to give their subjective judgment of their SA on 14 dimensions divided into 3 groups (Taylor, 1990), including factors that affect the demand for attentional resources (e.g., instability, variability, complexity of the situation), the supply of attentional resources (e.g., arousal, spare mental capacity), and understanding (e.g., information quality, quantity, familiarity). The SART scale was developed through interviews of experienced aircrew who identified factors that they felt affected their SA, and it has been shown to be correlated with performance (Prinzel et al., 2009). In this regard, it represents an operator's view of the important underlying dimensions, not the human-system engineer's view derived from a cognitive task analysis. Though it was developed specifically for aviation, SART asks general questions related to the environment, the operator, and the state of the dynamic system that have wide applicability.

Unlike SAGAT and SPAM, SART yields no objective measures of SA. In this respect, it resembles the NASA-TLX or SWAT workload scales (described in Chapter 15) in eliciting the postexperience impressions of the operators rather than being a real-time performance-based measure. It shares with NASA-TLX and SWAT the fact that it is easy to apply and can be inserted as a separate measure in the context of an existing experiment (e.g., See & Vidulich, 1997). It also shares with those two workload scales some of the criticisms of subjective measures, chiefly that operators are asked to rate their mental activity along an unfamiliar dimension. While controlling a system, or responding to a fire, skilled operators attend to the problem at hand and not to their SA per se. Questioning them later about a construct such as their spare mental capacity or level of arousal is asking them to reflect on something they had not been attending to. It invites answers based on general knowledge rather than momentary on-the-fly knowledge. Ratings can also be skewed by recall or performance—and, in the case of SA, operators cannot be expected to know what they don't know (Endsley, 1995a, 1995b; Endsley, Selcon, Hardiman, & Croft, 1998).

Inferring Situation Awareness from Eye Fixation Patterns

Although SAGAT, SPAM, and SART have been the primary vehicles for assessing SA in complex systems, it is worth noting that there are other, less intrusive, measures that can be taken from the operator as she controls the system, which could be closely related to her SA. In particular, we have noted the role of attention in the sequential monitoring of displays as an important component of establishing SA. These shifts of attention are usually done with a sequence of observable eye fixations, which can be recorded. As we discussed in earlier chapters, a number of studies have noted that eye fixation patterns are not random, but dictated to a large extent by the information-seeking goals of the observer (Card, 1983; Kinsler & Carpenter, 1995; Weiss, Remington, & Ellis, 1989; Wickens, Goh, Helleberg, Horrey, & Talleur, 2003). If eye fixation patterns derive from the underlying goals and information seeking establishes the elements of situation awareness that derive from those same goals, then eye fixation patterns might provide a way to infer the operator's situation awareness. If so, this measure would circumvent some of the issues regarding probe questions or subjective reports. Because eye fixations can be measured with little interference during operation, it would provide a practical way of gaining an objective measure of SA.

The relationship between eye fixation pattern and goals has been formalized in a theory of SA called the Attention-Situation Awareness (A-SA) model (Wickens et al., 2003, 2008). In the model, the probability that attention will be directed toward a particular element in the visual world is a function of four factors: the *salience* of the object, the *effort* required to attend to it, its *expectancy*, and its *value*. *Salience* refers to the visual contrast with other items in the environment. The higher the salience, the more likely the object is to be attended (fixated). *Effort* refers to the difficulty of attending, which generally includes the distance the object is away from the current fixation and, hence, whether the eyes, head, body, or all must be moved to view it. Effort is also affected by concurrent workload. The less effort required, the greater the chance of being fixated. *Expectancy* refers to whether the event or object was expected; this might happen, for example, when an event is cued by the occurrence of another event. *Value* refers roughly to the importance of the event. The greater an object's value, the higher the probability is of it being fixated. The probability of attending to any object in the environment, then, can be described by a simple equation, with α, β, χ, and δ as constants:

$$P(\text{attend}) = \alpha \text{ Salience} - \beta \text{ Effort} + \chi \text{ Expectancy} + \delta \text{ Value}$$

The eye fixation component of the A-SA model is referred to as SEEV, from the four factors that determine how attention is allocated. The contribution of salience to the fixation probability provides SEEV with a bottom-up mechanism that will allow it to model the capture of attention by salient events. The contribution of expectancy and value provide SEEV with the elements that translate goals into actions, giving it the ability to model top-down guidance by task goals. SEEV thus contains the same top-down and bottom-up capability of Guided Search (Wolfe, 1994; Wolfe, Cave, & Franzel, 1989), discussed in Chapter 9. SEEV differs from Guided Search in containing a finer-grained analysis of top-down factors, as well as including the role of effort. SEEV also approaches the problem of determining a fixation from consideration of the optimal fixation. In this regard it is similar to other optimal approaches to monitoring (Carbonell, 1966; Carbonell, Ward, & Senders, 1968; Senders, 1964). A-SA has been applied primarily in aviation domains (Wickens et al., 2008; Wickens et al., 2003), though there has been no rigorous test of its predictions against data from pilots or air traffic controllers. Indeed, it would be difficult to estimate the four principal parameters with any accuracy if the task were too complex, and there would be no standard way of doing so. It remains to be seen whether the model can make useful predictions from fairly straightforward estimates of its parameters. Model parameters can be estimated from data and used to fit a set of observations.

Summary of Situation Awareness

The operator's situation awareness is an important component in the control of a dynamic system. This is a point on which virtually all agree. Several theories of SA have been put forward, all of which draw heavily on constructs from cognitive psychology. Attempts to measure SA are based on one of three general approaches: SAGAT and SPAM probe the operator with specific questions related to the state of the controlled system during ongoing control; SART elicits subjective judgments from operators along several dimensions; A-SA and its component SEEV infer SA from patterns of eye fixations, presumed to reflect the importance of objects and events. All methods have strengths and weaknesses that ultimately derive from trying to assess the internal state of the operator, which cannot be directly observed. Nonetheless, the value of all these attempts is that their measures of SA constitute a formal system for bridging the gap between laboratory research on cognitive processing and the realities of the applications domain. The theories of SA provide a principled way to relate these two disparate endeavours, one that can foster productive interchanges between researchers and operators.

SUMMARY

If we want to make engineered systems safer, we must understand human error. This chapter distinguished between human error and system error, describing the nature and theories of human error. The chapter also described the concept of situation awareness—the operator's perception, comprehension, and projection of the status of the environment—as human error has been shown to arise from an incomplete understanding of the situation.

REFERENCES

Allnutt, M. F. (1987). Human factors in accidents. *British Journal of Anaesthesia, 59*(7), 856.

Barach, P., & Small, S. D. (2000). Reporting and preventing medical mishaps: Lessons from non-medical near miss reporting systems. *BMJ, 320*(7237), 759.

Boehm-Davis, D. A., & Remington, R. (2009). Reducing the disruptive effects of interruption: A cognitive framework for analysing the costs and benefits of intervention strategies. *Accident Analysis and Prevention, 41*, 1124–1129. doi:10.1016/J.Aap.2009.06.029

Byrne, M. D., & Bovair, S. (1997). A working memory model of a common procedural error. *Cognitive Science, 21*(1), 31–61. doi:10.1207/s15516709cog2101_2

Byrne, M. D., & Davis, E. M. (2006). Task structure and postcompletion error in the execution of a routine procedure. *Human Factors: The Journal of the Human Factors and Ergonomics Society, 48*(4), 627–638. doi:10.1518/001872006779166398

Cannon-Bowers, J. A., & Salas, E. E. (Eds.). (1998). *Making decisions under stress: Implications for individual and team training.* Washington, DC: American Psychological Association.

Carbonell, J. R. (1966). A queueing model of many-instrument visual sampling. *IEEE Transactions on Human Factors in Electronics, HFE-7*(4), 157–164. doi:10.1109/THFE.1966.232984

Carbonell, J. R., Ward, J. L., & Senders, J. W. (1968). A queueing model of visual sampling: Experimental validation. *IEEE Transactions on Man-Machine Systems, 9*(3), 82–87. doi:10.1109/TMMS.1968.300041

Card, S. K. (1983). Visual search of computer command menus. In H. Bouma & W. Bouwhuis (Eds.), *Attention and performance X*. Hillsdale, NJ: Lawrence Erlbaum Associates.

Chung, P. H., & Byrne, M. D. (2008). Cue effectiveness in mitigating postcompletion errors in a routine procedural task. *International Journal of Human-Computer Studies, 66*(4), 217–232. doi:16/j.ijhcs.2007.09.001

Degani, A., & Wiener, E. L. (1993). Cockpit checklists: Concepts, design, and use. *Human Factors: The Journal of the Human Factors and Ergonomics Society, 35*(2), 345–359.

Durso, F. T., Bleckley, M. K., & Dattel, A. R. (2006). Does situation awareness add to the validity of cognitive tests? *Human Factors: The Journal of the Human Factors and Ergonomics Society, 48*(4), 721–733. doi:10.1518/001872006779166316

Durso, F. T., & Dattel, A. R. (2004). SPAM: The real-time assessment of SA. In S. Banbury & S. Tremblay (Eds.), *A cognitive approach to situation awareness* (pp. 137–154). Aldershot, UK: Ashgate.

Durso, F. T., & Sethumadhavan, A. (2008). Situation awareness: Understanding dynamic environments. *Human Factors: The Journal of the Human Factors and Ergonomics Society, 50*(3), 442–448. doi:10.1518/001872008X288448

Durso, F. T., Truitt, T., Hackworth, C., Crutchfield, J., & Manning, C. (1998). En route operational errors and situational awareness. *International Journal of Aviation Psychology, 8*(2), 177–194. doi:10.1207/s15327108ijap0802_6

Einstein, G. O., & McDaniel, M. A. (2005). Prospective memory. *Current Directions in Psychological Science, 14*(6), 286–290. doi:10.1111/j.0963-7214.2005.00382.x

Einstein, G. O., McDaniel, M. A., Thomas, R., Mayfield, S., Shank, H., Morrisette, N., & Breneiser, J. (2005). Multiple processes in prospective memory retrieval: Factors determining monitoring versus spontaneous retrieval. *Journal of Experimental Psychology: General, 134*(3), 327.

Einstein, G. O., McDaniel, M. A., Williford, C. L., Pagan, J. L., & Dismukes, R. K. (2003). Forgetting of intentions in demanding situations is rapid. *Journal of Experimental Psychology: Applied, 9*(3), 147.

Endsley, M. R. (1988a). Design and evaluation for situation awareness enhancement. *Proceedings of the Human Factors Society Annual Meeting, 32*, 97–101.

Endsley, M. R. (1988b). Situation awareness global assessment technique (SAGAT). *Proceedings of the IEEE National Aerospace and Electronics Conference* (pp. 789–795). Dayton, Ohio: IEEE.

Endsley, M. R. (1995a). Measurement of situation awareness in dynamic systems. *Human Factors: The Journal of the Human Factors and Ergonomics Society, 37*(1), 65–84.

Endsley, M. R. (1995b). Toward a theory of situation awareness in dynamic systems. *Human Factors: The Journal of the Human Factors and Ergonomics Society*, *37*(1), 32–64.

Endsley, M. R. (1996). Automation and situation awareness. In R. Parasuraman & M. Mouloua (Eds.), *Automation and HumanaPerformance: Theory and Applications* (pp. 163–181), Mahwah, New Jersey: Lawrence Erlbaum Associates. Inc.

Endsley, M. R. (1997). The role of situation awareness in naturalistic decision making. *Naturalistic Decision Making*, *269*, 284.

Endsley, M. R. (1999). Situation awareness in aviation systems. In D. J. Garland, J. A. Wise, & V. D. Hopkin (Eds.), *Handbook of aviation human factors*. Mahwah, NJ: Lawrence Erlbaum Associates.

Endsley, M. R. (2000). Theoretical underpinnings of situation awareness: A critical review. In M. R. Endsley & D. J. Garland (Eds.), *Situation awareness analysis and measurement* (pp. 3–32). Mahwah, NJ: Lawrence Erlbaum Associates.

Endsley, M. R., & Garland, D. J. (2000). *Situation awareness: Analysis and measurement*. Mahwah, New Jersey: Lawrence Erlbaum Associates, Inc..

Endsley, M. R., & Kaber, D. B. (1999). Level of automation effects on performance, situation awareness and workload in a dynamic control task. *Ergonomics*, *42*(3), 462–492.

Endsley, M. R., Selcon, S. J., Hardiman, T. D., & Croft, D. G. (1998). *A comparative analysis of SAGAT and SART for evaluations of situation awareness*. Presented at the 42nd Annual Meeting of the Human Factors & Ergonomics Society, Santa Monica, CA.

Fromkin, V. A. (1971). The non-anomalous nature of anomalous utterances. *Language*, *47*(1), 27–52. doi:10.2307/412187

Grundgeiger, T., Sanderson, P. M., MacDougall, H. G., & Venkatesh, B. (2010). Interruption management in the intensive care unit: Predicting resumption times and assessing distributed support. *Journal of Experimental Psychology: Applied*, *16*(4), 317.

Kinsler, V., & Carpenter, R. H. S. (1995). Saccadic eye-movements while reading music. *Vision Research*, *35*, 1447–1458.

Klein, G. A. (1989). Recognition-primed decisions. In W. B. Rouse (Ed.), *Advances in man-Machine Systems Research* (pp. 47–92). Greenwich, CT: JAI Press.

Klein, G. A., & Calderwood, R. (1991). Decision models: Some lessons from the field. *IEEE Transactions on Systems, Man and Cybernetics*, *21*(5), 1018–1026. doi:10.1109/21.120054

Klein, G. A., Calderwood, R., & Clinton-Cirocco, A. (1986). Rapid fire decision making on the fire ground. *Human Factors and Ergonomics Society Annual Meeting Proceedings*, *30*(6), 576–580.

Leiden, K., Keller, J. W., & French, J. W. (2001). *Context of human error in commercial aviation*. (Technical Report). Boulder, Colorado: Micro Analysis & Design, Inc.

Loft, S., & Remington, R. W. (2010). Prospective memory and task interference in a continuous monitoring dynamic display task. *Journal of Experimental Psychology: Applied*, *16*(2), 145.

Loft, S., Smith, R. E., & Bhaskara, A. (2011). Prospective memory in an air traffic control simulation: External aids that signal when to act. *Journal of Experimental Psychology: Applied*, *17*(1), 60.

McDaniel, M. A., Guynn, M. J., Einstein, G. O., & Breneiser, J. (2004). Cue-focused and reflexive-associative processes in prospective memory retrieval. *Journal of Experimental Psychology: Learning, Memory, and Cognition*, *30*(3), 605.

Motley, M. T. (1985). Slips of the tongue. *Scientific American, 253*, 116-127.

Nagel, D. C. (1988). Human error in aviation operations. In E. L. Wiener (Ed.), *Human Factors in Aviation* (pp. 263–301), San Diego, California: Academic Press.

NASA. (n.d.). Aviation safety reporting system: About ASRS data. *Aviation Safety Reporting System*. Retrieved October 25, 2011, from http://asrs.arc.nasa.gov/search/dbol/aboutdata.html

NASA. (2001). The case for confidential incident reporting systems. NASA ASRS (Pub. 60). Retrieved from http://asrs.arc.nasa.gov/publications/research.html

Norman, D. A. (1981). Categorization of action slips. *Psychological Review*, *88*(1), 1.

Prinzel, L. J. I., Shelton, K. J., Jones, D. R., Allamandola, A. S., Arthur, J. J. I., & Bailey, R. E. (2009). *Evaluation of mixed-mode data-link communications for NextGen 4DT and equivalent visual surface operations*. Hampton, VA: NASA Langley Research Center.

Rasmussen, J. (1982). Human errors: A taxonomy for describing human malfunction in industrial installations. *Journal of Occupational Accidents*, *4*(2–4), 311–333. doi:10.1016/0376-6349(82)90041-4

Rasmussen, J. (1983). Skills, rules, and knowledge: Signals, signs and symbols, and other distinctions in human performance models. *IEEE Transactions on Systems, Man and Cybernetics*, *13*(3), 257–266.

Rasmussen, J., Nixon, P., & Warner, F. (1990). Human error and the problem of causality in analysis of accidents [and discussion]. *Philosophical Transactions of the Royal Society of London, Series B, Biological Sciences*, *327*(1241), 449–462.

Reason, J. (1990a). The contribution of latent human failures to the breakdown of complex systems. *Philosophical Transactions of the Royal Society of London, Series B, Biological Sciences*, *327*(1241), 475–484.

Reason, J. (1990b). *Human error*. New York, NY: Cambridge University Press.

Reason, J. (2000). Human error: Models and management. *BMJ*, *320*(7237), 768–770. doi:10.1136/bmj.320.7237.768

Salas, E., Prince, C., Baker, D. P., & Shrestha, L. (1995). Situation awareness in team performance: Implications for measurement and training. *Human Factors:*

The Journal of the Human Factors and Ergonomics Society, *37*(1), 123–136. doi:10.1518/001872095779049525

Sarter, N. B., & Woods, D. D. (1995). How in the world did we ever get into that mode: Mode error and awareness in supervisory control. *Human Factors*, *37*, 5–19.

See, J. E., & Vidulich, M. A. (1997). *Computer modeling of operator mental workload during target acquisition: An assessment of predictive validity* (Interim No. AL/CF-TR-1997-0018) (pp. 1–45). Dayton, OH: United States Air Force Armstrong Laboratory, Wright-Patterson AFB.

Senders, J. W. (1964). The human operator as a monitor and controller of multidegree of freedom systems. *IEEE Transactions on Human Factors in Electronics*, *HFE-5*(1), 2–5. doi:10.1109/THFE.1964.231647

Shappell, S. & Wiegmann, D. (2003). A human error analysis of general aviation controlled flight into terrain (CFIT) accidents occurring between 1990–1998. Federal Aviation Administration, Office of Aerospace Medicine Technical Report N. DOT/FAA/AM-03/4. Office of Aerospace Medicine: Washington, DC.

Shappell, S., & Wiegmann, D. (2004). HFACS analysis of military and civilian aviation accidents: A North American comparison. Proceedings of the Twelfth International Symposium on Aviation Psychology, Columbus, Ohio: The Ohio State University.

Smith, P. L., & Ratcliff, R. (2004). Psychology and neurobiology of simple decisions. *Trends in Neurosciences*, *27*(3), 161–168. doi:10.1016/j.tins.2004.01.006

Smith, R. E. (2003). The cost of remembering to remember in event-based prospective memory: Investigating the capacity demands of delayed intention performance. *Journal of Experimental Psychology: Learning, Memory, and Cognition*, *29*(3), 347.

Smith, R. E., & Bayen, U. J. (2004). A multinomial model of event-based prospective memory. *Journal of Experimental Psychology: Learning, Memory, and Cognition*, *30*(4), 756.

Sumwalt, R. L., Morrison, R., Watson, A., & Taube, E. (1997). What ASRS data tell about inadequate flight crew monitoring. In R. S. Jensen & L. Rakovan (Eds.) *Proceedings of the Ninth International Symposium on Aviation Psychology*, Columbus, Ohio: The Ohio State University.

Taylor, R. M. (1990). *Situational awareness rating technique (SART): The development of a tool for aircrew systems design* (pp. 3/1–3/7). Presented at the AGARD-CP-478, Neuilly Sur Seine, FR: NATO-AGARD.

Theeuwes, J. (1992). Perceptual selectivity for color and form. *Perception & Psychophysics*, *51*, 599–606.

Treat, J. R. (1980). A study of precrash factors involved in traffic accidents. *HSRI Research Review*, *10*, 1–35.

Weiss, R. S., Remington, R. W., & Ellis, S. R. (1989). Sampling distributions of the entropy in visual scanning. *Behavior Research Methods Instruments & Computers*, *21*, 348–352.

Wickens, C. D., Goh, J., Helleberg, J., Horrey, W. J., & Talleur, D. A. (2003). Attentional models of multitask pilot performance using advanced display technology. *Human Factors: The Journal of the Human Factors and Ergonomics Society*, *45*(3), 360–380. doi:10.1518/hfes.45.3.360.27250

Wickens, C. D., McCarley, J. S., Alexander, A. L., Thomas, L. C., Ambinder, M., & Zheng, S. (2008). Attention-situation awareness (A-SA) model of pilot error. *Human Performance Modeling in Aviation*, 213–239.

Wiener, E. L. (1985). Beyond the sterile cockpit. *Human Factors: The Journal of the Human Factors and Ergonomics Society*, *27*(1), 75–90.

Wiener, E. L., & Curry, R. (1980). Flight-deck automation: Promises and problems. *Ergonomics*, *23*(10), 995–1011. doi:10.1080/00140138008924809

Williamson, J. A., Webb, R. K., Sellen, A., Runciman, W. B., & Van der Walt, J. H. (1993). The Australian Incident Monitoring Study. Human failure: An analysis of 2000 incident reports. *Anaesthesia and Intensive Care*, *21*(5), 678.

Wolfe, J. M. (1994). Guided search 2.0: A revised model of visual search. *Psychonomic Bulletin & Review*, *1*(2), 202–238.

Wolfe, J. M., Cave, K. R., & Franzel, S. L. (1989). Guided search: An alternative to the feature integration model for visual search. *Journal of Experimental Psychology: Human Perception and Performance*, *15*(3), 419.

Yantis, S., & Jonides, J. (1984). Abrupt visual onsets and selective attention: Evidence from visual-search. *Journal of Experimental Psychology–Human Perception and Performance*, *10*, 601–621.

Yarbus, A. (1967). *Eye movements and vision*. New York, NY: Plenum Press.

Zapf, D., & Reason, J. T. (1994). Introduction: Human errors and error handling. *Applied Psychology*, *43*(4), 427–432.

15

Contextual Factors Affecting Human-System Performance

As operators interact with systems, certain features of the task, the situation, and the operator affect overall system safety and performance. These include workload, interruptions during task execution, and the physical state of the operator. This chapter discusses the impact of each of these factors on system safety.

WORKLOAD

Accident reports involving human error routinely find that workload contributes to error. In aviation, for example, where reporting systems are available to track accidents and incidents (NASA, 2001), estimates are that 80 percent of aircraft accidents and incidents have high workload as a contributing factor (Airbus, 2004). Workload is thus one of the chief concerns in the workplace, especially those domains with a high concern for safety.

Procedures and institutional practices are designed to keep an operator's workload as high as feasible without either endangering system safety or putting the operator at risk of stress-related health issues. As a result, one of the first questions to be addressed whenever a new technology is introduced into the workplace is whether it will increase or decrease workload, or how workload will change with its implementation. In aviation, for example, the introduction of sophisticated automation reduced the degree to which the crew needed to actively fly the aircraft. However, it created the demand to monitor the automation to determine whether it was working correctly and how it would behave in upcoming circumstances (Boehm-Davis, Curry, Wiener, & Harrison, 1983; Wiener, 1985). Because high levels of automation reduced the number of tasks assigned to the crew, there was pressure to reduce the mandated size of aircrews from three (captain, first officer, flight engineer) to two (captain, first officer). The driving question in that debate was whether the reduction in crew size would increase workload to the extent that safety would be endangered (McLucas, Drinkwater III, & Leaf, 1981).

Workload is a concern in system development as well as operations. Because workload levels are often key to the acceptance and safe functioning of new systems, developers attempt to predict the level of workload associated with equipment at various stages of its development. It is very costly to field a new system only to realize that workload levels are too high and then be forced to rework an already completed design. Instead, workload concerns are best dealt with during design and testing. For example, the U.S. Navy undertook a radical redesign of its destroyers. The DD21 project, as it was originally named, sought to build a multi-mission warship. Moreover, the crew size was slated to be decreased from something on the order of 350–400 officers and enlisted personnel to less than 100. These requirements initiated a long process of task analysis to determine all the tasks that would have to be done and the steps required to complete them. The design team used this analysis to estimate the new levels of workload for a system whose hardware had yet to be built (Wetteland, Bowen, & French, 2002; Wetteland, Miller, French, O'Brien, & Spooner, 2000).

In commercial enterprises, workload assessment is important not just for safety, but also for labor-management relations. Inherent in the consideration of workload is a trade-off that often surfaces as labor-management disputes. From the point of view of management, high productivity is key to profit. This often manifests as a desire to maintain fewer employees at higher activity levels. From the point of view of workers, high activity levels lead to stress, fatigue, and ultimately burnout. Their concern is often to reduce the amount they are required to do. We will not pass judgment on how such opposing concerns should be resolved. Rather, we will present what is known about the chief causes of workload, how it is measured, and how performance is affected by varying levels of workload.

Defining and Measuring Workload

What constitutes excessive workload? Despite the fact that everyone seems to understand intuitively what workload is, it has proven difficult to arrive at a consensus of just what exactly *workload* means. Lack of a clear construct has contributed to the difficulty of measuring it. In many ways the debate over different approaches to measuring workload reflects competing views on its essential nature. On the one hand, workload is about how much we must do in a defined time window. Because we seldom do just one thing, workload is most often about our ability to multitask, to service a number of concurrent goals that compete for limited-capacity cognitive resources. On the other hand, workload can be seen as a state of the operator that is influenced by how much must be done, but also by emotional factors, such as stress. These emotional states arise because of time demands or the consequences of failure. Finally, workload can be seen as the experience of the operator, not simply as a measure of state or task demand. In this view, workload is what the operator says it is, and cannot be deduced from observational data or objective measurement. These three conceptualizations underlie the three predominant methods of assessing workload.

Performance-Based Metrics

In *performance-based* approaches to workload assessment, the emphasis is on the task demands and how those demands drive limited-capacity cognitive processing. It seems intuitively obvious that the complexity and pace of events should drive workload, as there is a sense that workload would increase as we expend more effort. In queuing-theory terms, the workload of an individual server should have an obvious relation to the number of events it must process and the rate at which those events occur.

The assumption that workload closely tracks the demands of multitasking and resource usage suggests that it should be possible to directly measure the spare capacity of the operator at given points in time within a context that matches a domain of interest. The most common approach has been to insert a secondary task into the primary task context and measure response time changes to either the secondary task or the primary task. For example, in driving simulations, it is possible to track how well the driver performs the primary task of keeping the car in the center of the lane in single-task compared to dual-task conditions. The secondary task could be a speeded response to the onset of a tone or light, or a more demanding task, such as counting backward by seven. The results from several simulation studies seem to show a decrement in primary task performance with the addition of a secondary task (Casali & Wierwille, 1984; Hicks & Wierwille, 1979; Verwey, 2000; Verwey & Veltman, 1996). Although such realistic simulation techniques are useful, they can be difficult and expensive to conduct, a problem that limits their widespread utility. Moreover, as would be expected, the demands of one domain usually do not generalize to a different domain, and the level of interference produced by the secondary task can depend not just on workload, but also on factors such as task similarity or use of specific modalities. That is, the secondary task will produce more interference if it taps the same resources as the primary task. However, patterns of interference between secondary and primary tasks can be difficult to identify and quantify. In short, the secondary task introduces its own level of workload that is difficult to quantify or anticipate in advance.

A more fundamental issue with secondary task techniques is that the relevant environment must already exist, and that simulations of those domains must be available for testing. These conditions are met only for large-scale manufacturing companies that devote resources to research departments. This is the case for the military, NASA, aircraft manufacturers, automobile manufacturers, and major computer makers, but is not typical of medium or small companies. In response, researchers have sought to develop techniques for assessing workload from task analyses that can be used during development, before the system is actually built.

To this end, researchers have worked toward developing a metric of workload that would compute or estimate it directly from a characterization of the environment. The question is what features of the environment must or should be included. The ideal metric would simply compute workload from the task load. By *task load*, we mean some objective, observable characteristics of the task, such as the number of aircraft in a sector, the number of cars merging at some point in the roadway, or the limited time required to complete a surgical procedure. If task load determined workload, then it should be possible in principle to automate the computation of workload by deriving an algorithm that computes workload directly from the task, or from a task analysis. Certain cases seem to lend themselves to this approach. Researchers in air traffic control have defined a number of measures of *dynamic density* to provide an index of difficulty for a sector controller at any instant in time. Dynamic density refers to a changing pattern of aircraft transiting a given sector, where the features of that flow are thought to drive the workload of the controller. The goal has been to describe the airspace as a linear combination of the observable characteristics that would correlate with controllers' subjective ratings of their workload (Grossberg, 1989; Kirwan, Scaife, & Kennedy, 2001; Manning, Mills, Fox, Pfleiderer, & Mogilka, 2002). Simulation studies have found that a combination of number of aircraft, number of aircraft changing altitude, and number of aircraft on potential conflict routes can account for about 50 percent of the variance in controllers' estimates of workload (Kopardekar & Magyarits, 2003; Laudeman, Shelden, Branstrom, & Brasil, 1998; Loft, Sanderson, Neal, & Mooij, 2007). Similarly, a driving simulation study by Verwey (2000) found that driver workload was driven strongly by the difficulty of the road, as indexed by the angle of the turns required and the speed of the car. Approached this way, a measure of task load provides a convenient and justifiable way to regulate work so that operators avoid becoming overloaded and possibly endangering system safety. The FAA, for example, has mandated that no more than a certain number of aircraft can be under the control of a single air traffic controller at any given time.

A problem with the task-load approach is that workload is intuitively about what the operator must do, not simply about how complex a situation is by some information theoretic measure. If one wants to stick closely to observable features, it will be necessary to have identified characteristics of the task structure that can serve as a proxy for some output of the operator, such as effort, resource competition, or cognitive processing. The dynamic density metrics just discussed do this by including not simply the count of all traffic, but the number of planes changing altitude and the number on possible conflicting trajectories. These work because they identify situations that will require extra effort and cognitive resources from the controller. If you are a controller responsible for some number of aircraft on the screen, it makes a big difference if those aircraft are all converging on one point in space, as opposed to moving rapidly away from each other. In the latter case, nothing need be done, and most of us would agree that the workload is low. In the former case, you would be scurrying to maneuver all the aircraft safely in the short time remaining before they collided, and most would judge the workload as very high if time was very short or there were many aircraft to maneuver.

If the success of task load depends on the degree to which the measured quantities reflect operator activity, we should be able to improve on the measurement of workload if we replace the count of events with the count of activities over some time interval. As we saw in Chapter 13, the Contextual Control Model (Hollnagel, 1993) uses a metric for multitasking load that divides the number of concurrently active goals by the time available to do them. This treats goals as the unit of activity and gives a density of goals per unit time. Though useful, such an index assumes that each goal (activity) would take about the same amount of time. We might do even better if we could estimate the time for each activity (or goal) and compare this to the time limits placed on the operator. Each goal would be given a typical execution time and the total time needed to service all the goals would be the sum across all active goals. Intuitively, this seems much closer to the heart of our common sense understanding of workload.

Counting current and pending activities relates to methods used to calculate the time it will take to complete a series of actions. One of the earliest examples of this is the time-motion methodology widely used in manufacturing to analyze worker activity with the goal of increasing productivity (Barnes, 1963). In a time-motion study, individual actions are timed and these actions are summed to get the total time for an entire set of actions.

Consider an assembly-line worker whose job is to use a press to shape metal sheets. As a rectangular sheet of metal arrives, she first grabs the sheet, positions it on the press, making sure that it is properly aligned, then presses a button that causes the stamping machine to press the metal into shape and release. She then takes the formed sheet, discards the bits that were cut off and puts the shaped portion on the belt to the next station. Originally, an observer would use a stopwatch to time each individual operator action as the operator performed a task. We now have much more sophisticated techniques, such as laser timers or keystroke timers for computer tasks. These times are compiled into tables of means and standard deviations for each act. The tables can be used in the redesign of workspaces or when new equipment or procedures must be implemented.

The assembly-line example is a very simple case. The worker executes the same actions in the same order time after time. Not only that, but the pieces are located in roughly the same spot each time the worker reaches for them. Time-motion studies of the kind just described work best when the tasks are repetitive. When we consider more representative tasks, like cooking or using a computer, people have choices about which actions to perform in what order and show greater flexibility in choosing one of several ways to accomplish the same task. Consider the task of editing a document in a modern word processor. It is possible to cut and paste using the mouse and menus or by using a keyboard shortcut, such as Ctrl-X followed by Ctrl-V. In essence, there are decision points at which behavior could branch off into one or another direction. A simple time-motion summation cannot easily accommodate this flexibility. More sophisticated modeling frameworks are able to represent these options, generally as branches in an activity network. In finite-state modeling, graph theory, Markov models, or Petri Nets, for example, each act can be entered as a node in a network with branches between nodes weighted by the probability of going down that path.

In Figure 15.1 we present a simple finite-state graph for moving text from one place to another in a sentence. The purpose of the graph is primarily to show how branching is represented in networks. Each box represents a state and each arc between boxes an action that takes the user from one state in the space to another. In short, the states represent the result of actions and from any given state there can be more than one action that terminates on another state. One of the advantages to a model such as Figure 15.1 is its ability to highlight the fact that the internal state of the machine may be hidden from the user. When an item has been selected, the user can delete it by cutting it with Ctrl-X or using the mouse and menus. It can also be deleted by backspacing. In both cases the item disappears, but the internal states differ. With the cut the text is stored in an internal buffer, but with the backspace it is not. As a performance model, this graph would have to be augmented with transition probabilities and durations for each step in the process. Each node would be given a representative duration and weights on the paths connecting it to other nodes corresponding to the frequency with which people have been observed using a given method. The time to complete a task can be calculated by multiplying the time for each operation by the probability of each path. This provides an average across all the choices that could be made weighted by their likelihood. In this way, it is possible to use these approaches to better capture the full set of actions that characterize a set of activities.

This technique has been extensively used in analyses of human-computer interaction to examine the workload associated with various computer interface options

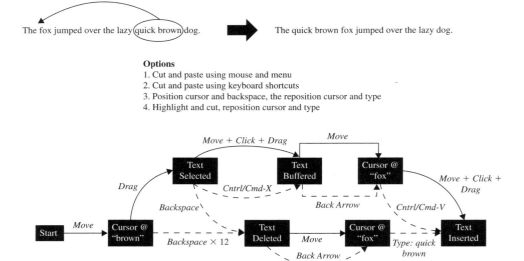

Figure 15.1 Simplified activity network for moving text showing how state networks can represent options. Boxes correspond to states in the process, arrows to operators that transition between states. Dotted arrows represent keyboard inputs, solid arrows mouse actions. The "Move + Click + Drag" represents mouse actions in selecting from a menu.

(Wu, Tsimhoni, & Liu, 2008). The sensible idea is that if common activities, such as opening a file or finding a file, require many actions, their workload will be unacceptably high and users will opt for a different operating system or software package. One such approach is the Goals, Operators, Methods, and Selection (GOMS) approach described by Card, Moran, and Newell (1983; see also John, 1990; John & Kieras, 1996a, 1996b; Kieras, 1996). The nodes in Figure 15.1 would correspond to goals in a GOMS analysis that featured a hierarchical decomposition of the task. The arcs would represent operators that transitioned between goals. An analysis in GOMS would also include rules for selecting which of the operators to employ under specific conditions. For example, if you just want to get rid of text, you might backspace after selecting, but if you thought you might need it later you would choose to cut. Further, given the decision to cut some text, the user would have a choice of using the pull-down menus or Ctrl-X to actually cut the text. Finally, there can be methods in GOMS that describe stable strategies users have of selecting operators. In this way, GOMS can represent different strategies for achieving the same goals.

The level of the task analysis at which one "bottoms out" into primitive operations can vary depending on the goals. If we were researching movement dynamics, it would be necessary to further decompose mouse actions into movement starts, travel times, and corrective adjustments. We could go even further and look for initial signs of muscle or brain activation. In contrast, for an analysis of an entire software package for editing text, it might be sufficient to bottom out at a much coarser level, omitting many of the detailed states. In those circumstances it might be sufficient to model a single "move text" link.

Estimates of the time to move text could be taken from observations, as in time-motion studies, or computed as the average from the network in Figure 15.1.

Finite-state representations are not confined to simple examples such as that shown in Figure 15.1. They have been used as general models of human performance (e.g., Liu, 1996) as well as to predict workload in applied settings (see, e.g., Wetteland et al., 2002, 2000; Wu & Liu, 2007; Wu et al., 2008). As noted earlier, the level of granularity in the model (the level of detail) can be adapted to suit the need. Finite-state network models have also been used to estimate workload and task scheduling in multiperson teams (e.g., Sierhuis et al., 2003), in very large-scale simulations of future space systems (Clancey, Sachs, Sierhuis, & Van Hoof, 1998; Sierhuis et al., 2003), and in military systems (Wetteland et al., 2002, 2000).

Cognitive Task Analysis

Estimating workload, or task times, from a sum of the actions has been a useful technique. However, it is limited in that it neglects some of the important properties of human information processing covered in Part III. In particular, activities differ not only in the time needed to complete them, but also in the cognitive processing that they require. A distinction has been made, for example, between two types of effort: *computational effort*, which is required for appropriate executive control over cognitive processing; and *compensatory effort*, which is required to overcome deficits in resource levels due to fatigue or stress, with the claim that these represent distinct mental processes (Brookhuis & de Waard, 2001; Mulder, 1980, 1986).

Moreover, several experiments have found that perceptual, cognitive, and motor actions have separate effects on the perception of workload, and thus their individual contributions should be assessed separately (see, e.g., Verwey, 2000; Verwey & Veltman, 1996; Wickens, 1984; see Wierwille & Eggemeier, 1993, for a review). Evidence for these distinctions comes from experiments that add an external secondary task that is not part of the primary task goal. The effect of a secondary task on primary task performance depends on whether the secondary task loads vision, audition, or cognition, and the degree to which the primary task relies on the loaded stage of processing. Secondary task probes that manipulate *visual load* might require the operator (e.g., driver, pilot) to respond to light or detect changes in the rate of a blinking light. Similarly, secondary tasks to produce *auditory load* might introduce a tone-detection task or have operators repeat a continuous spoken message (shadowing). Cognitive load has been varied by having operators hold a number of items in working memory, perform mental mathematical calculations, or estimate temporal intervals.

Performance on the primary task under secondary task conditions would be compared to control conditions to see which aspects of primary task performance were affected or how rated workload varied. For example, a difficult *visual* secondary task has been shown to impair the frequency of corrective vehicle control actions, whereas a difficult *cognitive* secondary task did not affect vehicle control, but did produce changes in galvanic skin response (Verwey & Veltman, 1996). That the three stages of information processing represent separable contributions can help us understand why it is that tracking targets moving on a screen is much more difficult when they move randomly than when they follow a pattern. When random, the observer has to be vigilant to detect the next move or increase the number of active items in working memory to include each additional target. When there is a pattern, the observer needs only a short glance to identify changes, and the tracking task devolves into a perceptual-motor loop. The same perceptual-motor loop enables us to drive in light traffic on undemanding roads and carry on a conversation at the same time.

The observation that perceptual, cognitive, and motor processing each contributes separately to workload in driving or piloting is consistent with the Multiple Resource Theory (MRT) of Wickens (1984). As discussed earlier, MRT posits separate resource pools associated with each of these three stages of processing. Thus, in theory, it is possible to overload one stage without necessarily overloading another. The theory accounts for a range of laboratory findings in dual-task experiments supporting the observation that the results observed by manipulating visual difficulty can be distinguished from those manipulating cognitive (response selection) difficulty. As we show later, subjective ratings of workload also differ depending on whether the load is primarily visual or primarily cognitive (see, e.g., Hart & Staveland, 1988; Hart & Wickens, 1990).

The application of MRT to understanding workload requires an augmentation of the normal task analysis to include the perceptual, cognitive, and motor demands of the task. The general term for this process is *cognitive task analysis*. There are several methods of carrying out a cognitive task analysis. For the most part, they involve first doing a *task analysis* as described in Chapter 6, which terminates in primitive actions in the domain. In the text-editing example in Figure 15.2, these primitives would be mouse movement (e.g., move, drag, click) and typing actions. In the driving domain, task primitives might be steering wheel, brake, and accelerator actions. These primitives are overt, observable actions in the task domain. Cognitive task analyses extend this by assigning to these primitive actions the covert mental actions involved in their execution. These mental actions often cannot be directly observed, but must be inferred from theory.

In MRT, each primitive task operation is assigned to one or more of the multiple resource pools—visual, auditory, cognitive, motor, and general resources—along with a percentage estimating the amount of each resource needed to carry it out. In Figure 15.2, each mouse movement may be estimated to take 100 percent of the right-hand resource for the duration of the movement, 30 percent of the total motor resources, 20 percent of cognitive resources at the beginning and 20 percent at the end, 90 percent visual at the beginning and end of the task, and 50 percent during the actual movement. MRT could thus specify a resource loading for the entire analysis shown in Figure 15.2. Note that just as the task analysis can end in coarser primitives than in Figure 15.2, the mental resources associated with tasks in MRT can be allocated to entire actions.

The resources required by a task can also be calculated at a much higher (coarser) level using IMPRINT (Improved Performance Research Integration Tool), which is used heavily within the Department of Defense (U.S. Army Research Laboratory, 2010) to model both individual and crew performance. This discrete event simulation tool used Micro Saint Sharp, a discrete event task network modeling language.

Because the mental operations associated with a primitive task operation are not directly observable, but inferred, a cognitive task analysis is by its nature theory specific. Each theory will establish its own set of resources, its own way in which those resources interact, and its own way of assigning resources to task primitives. It is becoming common to embed the resource theory in a larger computational modeling framework that

Description	Operator	Duration (sec)
Mentally prepare	M	1.35
Move cursor to "quick"	P	1.10
Double-click mouse button	K	0.40
Move cursor to "brown"	P	1.10
Shift-click mouse button	K	0.40
Mentally prepare	M	1.35
Move cursor to Edit menu	P	1.10
Click mouse button	K	0.20
Move cursor to Cut menu item	P	1.10
Click mouse button	K	0.20
Mentally prepare	M	1.35
Move cursor to before "fox"	P	1.10
Click mouse button	K	0.20
Mentally prepare	M	1.35
Move cursor to Edit menu	P	1.10
Click mouse button	K	0.20
Move cursor to Paste menu item	P	1.10
Click mouse button	K	0.20
TOTAL PREDICTED TIME		**14.90**

Figure 15.2 Analysis of cut-and-paste text editing using a mouse and menu. Example uses the Keystroke-Level Model (KLM) from Card, Moran, and Newell (1983). *Source:* Adapted from John, Vera, Matessa, Freed, and Remington (2002).

will support computer simulations of human performance and workload calculations (e.g., OMAR—Pew & Deutsch, 2007; ACT-R—Anderson & Lebiere, 1998; Soar—Newell, 1990; CPM-GOMS—John, 1990; MIDAS—Corker, Gore, Fleming, & Lane, 2000; EPIC—Kieras & Meyer, 1997). For example, Multiple Resource Theory (Wickens, 1984) has been incorporated into MIDAS, a large-scale computational model used to simulate helicopter and fixed-wing pilots as well as air traffic controllers. MIDAS has been used to evaluate the impact of new operational concepts for air traffic control, including the impact on controller workload (Corker et al., 2000; Gore & Corker, 2000). The Model Human Processor (Card et al., 1983), discussed in Chapter 10, has been developed into a computational method for assessing usability in human-computer interface (John, 1990; John & Kieras, 1996a, 1996b). It assigns cognitive, perceptual, and motor operations to the task primitives of a GOMS analysis (see preceding discussion)—hence the term *CPM-GOMS* (John, 1990). The CPM-GOMS architecture has been used successfully to predict usability in both small-scale (Gray & Boehm-Davis, 2000) and large-scale systems (Gray, John, & Atwood, 1993).

One of the benefits of a cognitive task analysis is that it can highlight conflicts that may cause two tasks to be done inefficiently, and suggest ways to improve the presentation of information or collection of responses. It also provides performance-based approaches to workload assessment; it provides a way of anticipating workload before a system is constructed. The method does, however, have drawbacks. The assignment of resources to primitive task operations tends to be underconstrained, in that there are often no reliable data or other means of determining the assignment. This leads to some "art" in the analysis. The computational models help by providing a theoretical basis for assignment, and make it possible to rigorously compute the resulting workload or task completion times for very complex tasks. The computational architectures themselves suffer from being difficult and time-consuming to build. Some progress toward simplifying the modeling process has been successful using the CPM-GOMS method (Gray & Boehm-Davis, 2000; Vera, John, Remington, Matessa, & Freed, 2005), but large-scale applications and human-computer interface evaluation still require significant development time and resources.

A different approach to cognitive task analysis has been taken in a method known as a *cognitive walkthrough* (Lewis & Rieman, 1993; Wharton, Rieman, Lewis, & Polson, 1994), which was developed to support human-computer interface evaluations. Its goal is not to predict workload or task completion times, but to assess the degree to which the interface supports the decisions users must make. It is possible to perform a cognitive walkthrough using the device, a prototype of the device, or a storyboard; thus, this technique can be used in early phases of interface development. The technique does not rest on fixed assumptions of resource pools or stages of processing. Rather, the evaluator, or evaluation team, performs a structured mental simulation of using a proposed device focused on answering basic questions for each possible state of the system (see Wharton et al., 1994).

These questions deal with whether users will know what goal they are to achieve, how easily they can detect the correct action and associate it with their goal, and how easily they can detect that they are making progress toward achieving the goal. It is based on a functional model of human-computer interaction that views user cognition as setting goals, searching the interface for suitable actions to achieve those goals, selecting actions, and verifying the results of those actions with respect to goals. Thus, instead of focusing on the demands on attention and resource loading, a cognitive walkthrough tries to infer the state of the operator (user) with respect to the decision that must be made and to evaluate how well the physical environment (visual display of information) guides users to the right choice. Although it does not directly capture the contribution of busyness to workload, it does capture the contribution of decision difficulty.

Physiological Indices of Workload
Performance-based metrics of workload attempt to assess the nature of the load placed on the human by the volume of activities that must be completed. There is another sense, though, in which workload seems more related to the *internal state* of the operator than any pure performance metric. We can imagine circumstances in which resource allocation would be increased or decreased without adding tasks or even speeding them up. For example, you would probably find it quite easy to walk across a 4-inch board placed a few inches off the ground, and would likely be able to converse while doing so. It would be very different if that same board were placed 30 feet above the ground. You would no doubt allocate many more resources to the task, probably avoiding conversation, even though the task imposes no extra actions. Yet, our intuition is that we would perceive

workload to be higher because of the consequences of potential outcomes—the stress associated with the fear of falling. Similarly, workload can be increased by reducing the time needed to perform the same number of events at the same overall level of complexity (Hendy, Liao, & Milgram, 1997).

Emotional states, such as anxiety or stress, arise from activity in the *autonomic nervous system* (ANS). The ANS regulates levels of arousal and is the predominant system in the human "fight or flight" response to potentially dangerous situations. Activation of the sympathetic branch of the autonomic nervous system gives rise to internal states of alertness, arousal, and stress, and induces physiological reactions that can be measured to assess the degree of arousal or stress. This underlying logic has led to the use of *physiological measures* of workload. A constellation of physiological measures has been shown to reliably correlate with task difficulty, including increases in heart rate along with decreases in the variability of the heart rate (more regular beat) (see, e.g., Backs, 1995; Berntson, Cacioppo, & Quigley, 1991; Brookhuis & de Waard, 2001; Gopher & Donchin, 1986), as well as increases in pupil diameter and the conductivity of the skin, referred to as the galvanic skin response or GSR (Kramer & Weber, 2000; Wierwille, 1979; Wierwille & Eggemeier, 1993; Wilson, 2002). The pitch of the voice also tends to rise when under stress (e.g., Hansen, 1995; Protopapas & Lieberman, 1995, 1997).

A question to be addressed is the relationship between physiological and performance measures. Studies have examined the correlation between individual physiological measures and the demand characteristics that drive performance. For example, heart rate has been shown to correlate with the difficulty of a turn in driving simulations (see, e.g., Backs, Lenneman, Wetzel, & Green, 2003). There is also a link between performance and levels of arousal. Well before the scientific study of arousal, drill sergeants in military boot camp knew how to induce fear and stress with a few words and a look, causing recruits to fail to be able even to speak their own names.

The first attempt to systematize this relationship led to the well-known Yerkes-Dodson law, a hypothetical function relating level of arousal or stress to performance (Yerkes & Dodson, 1908). When performance is plotted as a function of arousal level, the hypothesized curve is an inverted U-shape. At low levels of arousal, performance increases as arousal levels increase. Maximum performance is achieved with moderate levels of arousal. After that, increased arousal causes performance to deteriorate. The Yerkes-Dodson law has provided a basis for associating the high levels of arousal seen in stress and fear with a depletion of limited-capacity resources that leads to impaired performance. At least one of the reasons for drill instructors to stress recruits is to prepare them for the high stress of combat by recalibrating their response to environmental stressors; levels of stress that would seem excessive before training will seem only moderately high afterward. Still, the actual mechanisms by which task difficulty induces changes in heart rate, pupil size, voice pitch, or other measures of internal emotional state remains unresolved (see, e.g., Mulder, 1980, 1986).

A major advantage of these physiological (and vocal) measurements of internal state over the performance-based secondary task method is that they can be recorded in the operating environment with minimal intrusion or change in the way operators work. Passive sensing devices can detect changes in heart rate and its variability, skin conductivity, or voice pitch. Moreover, they can be informative as to the operator's state even under low workload conditions. Operators are frequently asked to maintain high levels of performance even when task demands are low or events very infrequent. Studies of these conditions, referred to as *vigilance*, find that operator performance at target detection is very poor when the targets are infrequent. The inability to sustain attention and, in turn, performance, over a prolonged period of time suggests that monitoring, especially for low-probability events, is a poor task to assign to human operators (Kahneman, 1973; Mackworth, 1948). Research suggests that this poor performance degrades even further as cognitive load increases (Parasuraman & Davies, 1977; Warm, Parasuraman, & Matthews, 2008).

Vigilance has great practical importance. A sentry on duty or a night watchman for a company rarely encounters events that require taking action. They are nonetheless expected to maintain high levels of alertness. For example, a baggage screener at the airport may inspect hundreds of bags an hour for many hours or even days without noticing an event that requires action. Vigilance poses problems that are best viewed as problems of internal state, not of a heavy task demand to which a performance measure would be sensitive. Passive measures of internal state can serve as an index of alertness that researchers can use to test ways of improving performance under vigilance conditions.

Subjective Ratings of Workload

Physiological and performance indices of workload are based on objective measurements of operator state or behavior, respectively. In both cases, the underlying assumption is that workload is driven by both internal and external factors that can be objectively assessed. However, collecting either of these measures is sometimes difficult. One alternative is to collect subjective ratings from users. Studies of operator workload in several complex domains, such as air traffic control, driving, and piloting, have found that subjective estimates of workload are sensitive to variations in task demand (e.g., Hart & Staveland, 1988; Hart & Wickens, 1990; see Wierwille & Eggemeier, 1993, for a review). Some subjective ratings are taken very informally; operators are asked to rate their workload during or after a portion of a mission or simulated mission. At the other extreme, there are formal test batteries for eliciting subjective estimates that use a very structured approach (SWAT—Reid & Nygren, 1988; NASA-TLX—Hart & Staveland, 1988; Modified Cooper Harper (MCH)—Casali & Wierwille, 1983). Figure 15.3 shows the questions used by the NASA Task Load Index (NASA-TLX). Note that the NASA-TLX implicitly uses the Multiple Resource Theory in its requirement that operators rate visual, auditory, cognitive, and motor workload separately. It also includes a question that addresses the emotional internal state of the operator. In this sense, the NASA-TLX, and other rating systems, try to incorporate a broad sense of workload as comprised of both task load and the operator state.

Subjective workload assessments, typically used on complex systems such as those mentioned earlier, comprise by far the bulk of workload assessments done in practice. They are easy to administer and score and do not require more than a paper and pencil, meaning that they can be administered even under the most trying of circumstances. They can thus be viewed as a convenient and practical way of acquiring information about workload. Subjective ratings can also be seen to embody a somewhat different view of workload than either performance or state measures. Rather than seeing workload as a

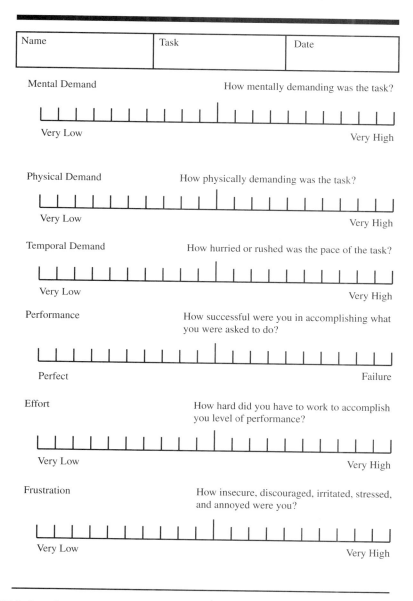

Figure 15.3 Questions used by the NASA Task Load Index (NASA-TLX).

combination of external and internal influences that can be objectively measured, subjective approaches claim that workload is the experience of the operator, which cannot be measured directly from internal or external factors (Hart & Staveland, 1988; Hart & Wickens, 1990). However, it is not necessary to subscribe to this view to use subjective ratings effectively.

Workload Summary

Workload is a complex conceptual construct that embodies at least a combination of external factors, internal state, and quite possibly the experience of the operator. The assessment of workload can be done through physiological or performance metrics. In practice, most assessments of workload rest principally on the subjective estimates of operators, based either on informal questioning or structured interviews. Research on the mental operations involved in primitive task operations hold promise for the assessment of performance under moderate to high workload. Using computational models and cognitive task analyses, performance-based approaches promise to provide insight into human-system interaction even during the design phase. Passive measures of operator state are useful in assessing a larger view of workload and human performance that incorporates the importance of outcomes and is applicable to periods of very low workload.

INTERRUPTION

Interruption is one of the seemingly inescapable features of life and an inherent consequence of having to perform multiple tasks concurrently. The structure and responsibilities of workplaces and home life make interruption inevitable. Jobs arrive without regard for our progress on existing jobs, colleagues need to consult and cannot be expected to know when we are busy without asking, and the jobs themselves cause interruption, as work is halted while awaiting signatures or the arrival of necessary documents. It should be noted that although interruptions share features with prospective memory (described in Chapter 11), there are features that distinguish them from each other. In prospective memory, the individual has to interrupt an ongoing primary task (typically well practiced) to perform a secondary task. The interruptions literature, though, focuses on situations in which a primary task (which may or may not be well practiced) is prevented from being completed by the intrusion of a secondary task. The other differentiating feature is that in the case of an interruption, the operator's desire is to complete the primary task without interruption; in prospective memory, the goal is to remember to perform the secondary task prior to completing the primary task. Nonetheless, both interruptions and prospective memory share the need to maintain operator intent and take action without prompting; thus, they are both subject to factors such as delay and degree of cueing available in the environment.

Interruptions, while mostly an annoyance, do have significant impacts on productivity and system safety. In aviation, reports have linked interruption and distraction to problems in the cockpit (Latorella, 1999; Loukopoulos, Dismukes, & Barshi, 2003) as well as in maintenance (Latorella & Prabhu, 2000). A review of incidents in the NASA Aviation Safety Reporting System (ASRS) found that nearly half the reports surveyed list lapses of attention associated with interruptions and/or distractions as having contributed to the incident (Dismukes, Loukopoulos, & Jobe, 2001; Dismukes, Young, & Sumwalt, 1998). Simulation studies have shown that commercial pilots who were interrupted made significantly more errors than those who were not (Latorella, 1999; Latorella & Prabhu, 2000). In the crash of Northwest Airlines Flight 255 on takeoff from Detroit in 1987, the NTSB report noted that the preflight checklist procedure had been interrupted to deal with a missed runway (National Transportation Safety Board, 1988). In medicine, there have been a number of articles and reports on the problems associated with interruption and distraction in critical care wards (Ash, Berg, & Coiera, 2004; Beyea, 2007; Brixey et al., 2005; Grundgeiger, Liu, Sanderson, Jenkins, & Leane, 2008; Grundgeiger, Sanderson, Orihuela, et al., 2010; Grundgeiger, Sanderson, MacDougall, & Venkatesh, 2010), primary care offices (Rhoades, McFarland, Finch, & Johnson, 2001), and teaching (Volpp & Grande, 2003). One study of medication errors in U.S. hospitals attributes 43 percent of the errors to interruption or distraction (Santell, 2005). Studies of software engineering have routinely shown that distraction and interruption can reduce productivity and lower job satisfaction (Barber & Lucas Jr., 1983; Czerwinski, Cutrell, & Horvitz, 2000; Czerwinski, Horvitz, & Wilhite, 2004; Doherty & Thedani, 1982). Surprisingly, it turns out that an interruption duration as short as a quarter of a second can adversely affect performance (Monk & Kidd, 2008).

What makes interruption so disruptive to performance? A simple cognitive task analysis of a generic interruption gives us some insight into the underlying processing issues (for a detailed analysis, see Boehm-Davis & Remington, 2009). An interruption entails first a disengagement from the origin task, which reorients attention to the interrupt task. Thus, the first step is a task switch, which also requires leaving the origin task in a state in which it can be resumed. Disengagement from the origin task occurs upon a triggering event, which can be external, such as an alarm or a person walking into the office, or internal, as when we voluntarily switch from one activity to another when completing simultaneous tasks. Of course, one of the issues with an external trigger is that not all such events should distract us. There are a number of times when calls, computer alerts, or people drop by whose presence interrupts a task more urgent or important. Attempts have been made to develop intelligent filtering agents that can learn our patterns, infer the importance of ongoing tasks relative to the interrupting task, and intercede to stop a low-priority event from causing an interruption (e.g., Cutrell, Czerwinski, & Horvitz, 2001; Horvitz & Apacible, 2003; Horvitz, Breese, Heckerman, Hovel, & Rommelse, 1998; Horvitz, Kadie, Paek, & Hovel, 2003; Iqbal & Horvitz, 2007). Though they show promise, these approaches rely on Bayesian techniques and are heavily dependent on learned associations, making them error prone for situations they have not previously encountered. It is also inherently difficult to track the user's goals in a dynamic environment where priorities can shift over time.

After disengaging from the origin task, the operator engages attention in the interrupt task for some period of time, and then disengages from that task to resume the origin task. The resumption following the interruption is by far the most problematic issue with interruption. Operators either fail to resume the origin task, or its resumption takes time and cognitive effort that impairs performance (see, e.g., Boehm-Davis & Remington, 2009; Dismukes et al., 2001; Monk, Boehm-Davis, Mason, & Trafton, 2004). One of the key factors affecting resumption is the time spent on the interrupting task. A study of simulated driving by Monk, Boehm-Davis, Mason, and Trafton (2004) found that the longer people spent on the interrupting task, the more frequent the errors in resumption. This is consistent with task-switching research showing that switch costs are greater as the time since last performing the task increases (Ruthruff, Remington, & Johnston, 2001). As mentioned earlier, the interruption duration need not be very long; deficits in resumption can be seen with interruptions as brief as 250 msec (Monk & Kidd, 2008).

Studies of the effect of time on interrupting tasks have been able to model the effect on performance by assuming that the duration spent on the interrupting task causes decay in the memory activation for state information on the origin task (Altmann & Trafton, 2002, 2007; Trafton, Altmann, & Ratwani, 2011). A study by Altman and Trafton (2007) interrupted undergraduates as they played a video game. The game was a demanding military strategy game that required subjects to store state information and required frequent manual responses to events. The interrupting task lasted from 35 to 45 seconds before the main game was restored. Upon resumption, response time was initially elevated, decreased over the first three events, and thereafter stabilized. The data were fit well by a model which assumed that resumption is characterized by a recovery of the memory based on the strength of activation of state information. These findings are consistent with the theoretical predictions from computational models of human memory (Altmann & Gray, 2008; Altmann & Trafton, 2002; Fu & Gray, 2004; Salvucci & Taatgen, 2008; Trafton et al., 2011).

Monk et al. (2004) found that resumption was impaired if the interruption occurred when subjects were in the midst of an ongoing task. In Chapter 6, we discussed how task analysis decomposes activities into goals and subgoals in a hierarchical manner. Monk et al.'s data indicate that subgoal boundaries are psychologically important in task switching. One reason for this may be that achieving a subgoal allows the operator to release from working memory state information that is important only to achieving that subgoal.

How can the disruptive effects of interruption be curtailed? Several proposals for dealing with interruptions have been made. They can be roughly divided into three approaches: strategies, perceptual support, and training. Strategic approaches focus on ways the user can control the situation to avoid the worst of the disruptive effects. One suggestion has been to allow operators to negotiate when they will accept an interruption (McFarlane, 2002). Another has been to make operators aware of their vulnerability to interruption (Beyea, 2007; Loukopoulos et al., 2003), for example, by teaching them the warning signs of impending interruption (Loukopoulos et al., 2003). Though these approaches may have merit, the remedies involve a resource-demanding activity that itself represents an additional task. It is not clear that operators will remember to do that when they are busy.

The approach of providing perceptual support may be more successful, as it does not require cognitive resources on the part of the operator. Researchers have suggested providing bookkeeping aids (e.g., a slider that points to the last step completed or a computerized checklist) to avoid skipping or repeating steps (LeGoullon, 2008). Others have suggested providing "traps" to catch items that have not been done as intended (Loukopoulos, Dismukes, & Barshi, 2003). This could take the form of "prevention" systems that do not allow you to continue with a task unless the previous steps have been completed (Ash et al., 2004). Other proposed remedies are concerned with supporting the retrieval of information about what users were doing when they left the primary task (Ash et al., 2004). The value of such an approach was shown in a computer-based task, where a physical cue was provided when the number and duration of the participant's fixations (based on eye-tracking data) indicated that the individual was not attending to the appropriate location on the screen (Ratwani, 2008).

A third approach is training. Research has shown that practicing with interruptions can reduce their disruptiveness (Cades, Boehm-Davis, Trafton, & Monk, 2011; Detweiler,

Hess, & Phelps, 1994). However, it should be noted that this training may have to be at the level of specific pairs of primary and interruption tasks.

In summary, interruptions occur in almost all work settings, and they typically increase the time to complete the original task. They also can contribute to errors in which operators forget to resume or resume at the wrong point in the task. Thus, interruptions can contribute to decreasing system safety and performance. However, research is starting to identify strategies for reducing the disruptive effects caused by interruptions.

OPERATOR STATE

In the preceding sections, we have discussed how environmental factors, such as workload or interruptions, can increase the potential for human error. We are also intuitively aware that our mental states fluctuate in level of preparedness, readiness to undertake work, clarity of thought, and the effort we are willing to expend. In short, the mental and physiological state of the operator plays a role in determining performance, mood, and motivation, as well as our subjective experience. There are a number of potentially dissociable operator states that can impair performance. A short list would include fatigue, loss of sleep, anxiety, stress, depression, and illness. Here we briefly discuss performance changes that occur as a function of fatigue and sleep loss. We will try to separate the effects of fatigue resulting from prolonged, continuous effort from those associated with sleep loss and jetlag (circadian desynchronosis). In reality, these factors are often combined when considering real-world scenarios. As an example, the NTSB report on the *Exxon Valdez* went to great lengths to document the role fatigue played in the errors made by the third mate. It notes that he had not slept much in the past 48 hours and had spent a number of hours in the previous days assisting with the provisioning of the ship and loading of cargo. A similar emphasis on fatigue and sleep loss can be observed in many safety-conscious applications, including aviation, medicine, long-distance truck driving, and manufacturing, to name just a few (Caldwell Jr., 1997; Hanowski, Wierwille, & Dingus, 2003; Owens, Veasey, & Rosen, 2001).

However, the causal linkage of fatigue per se to human error can be more indirect or circumspect than one might suppose. The 1984 death of 18-year-old college freshman Libby Zion within 24 hours of being admitted to a New York hospital illustrates the ongoing debate over the causal role of fatigue. She came to the emergency room complaining of fever and agitation, accompanied by shaking. Her records showed that she was on antidepressant medication to treat recurrent bouts of depression. Her main physician was a resident who was 8 months out of her internship, had been continuously on duty for 36 hours, and had 41 other patients. After phone consultations with the chief physician, the attending resident diagnosed Ms. Zion with a viral infection. Because Ms. Zion remained agitated and visibly shaking, she was given a sedative. When this did not sufficiently calm her, she was placed in restraints. Sometime later, a nurse noticed that her fever had spiked alarmingly and she had lapsed into unconsciousness. Attempts to bring the fever down and revive her were unsuccessful and she died shortly thereafter. In the subsequent lawsuit brought by her father, it was argued that the hospital was negligent for leaving Ms. Zion in the care of a resident with 41 other patients.

Based on this event, a campaign ensued to reduce the work hours for medical residents. The Libby Zion Law was passed by the state of New York in 1989, effectively limiting residents to 80 hours of work in a given week (Lerner, 2006). In 2003, the largest medical accreditation agency, the Accreditation Council for Graduate Medical Education (ACGME), revised its standards, limiting shifts for residents to 80 hours per week (Philibert, Friedmann, & Williams, 2002).

Was fatigue a contributing or even causal factor in either the *Exxon Valdez* disaster or the Libby Zion case? That can be difficult to establish. In the Libby Zion case, subsequent medical inquiry identified the probable cause of death as a drug reaction referred to as the serotonin syndrome (an excess of the neurotransmitter serotonin), likely brought on by her antidepressant medication. Diagnosis of the serotonin syndrome can be quite difficult, and it is unclear whether a rested and calm physician would have been able to diagnose it (see, e.g., Boyer & Shannon, 2005). Does this mean that concern over fatigue is overstated? That is hard to say for certain, as the details of individual circumstances make it difficult to confidently attribute a causal effect to the operator state per se. What has been demonstrated is a pattern of perceptual, motor, and cognitive impairment with fatigue and loss of sleep. We shall briefly touch on this large body of research. We deal with issues of fatigue separately from sleep-related disorders, although the reader should be aware that, as noted, they are often coupled in applied environments.

Fatigue

We use the term *fatigue* to refer to the internal mental state arising as a result of prolonged and taxing activity, not as the result of sleep deprivation. Used in this way, fatigue has been associated with measurable performance decrements along a range of mental tasks (e.g.,Boksem & Tops, 2008; Boksem, Meijman, & Lorist, 2005; Hamilton, Vohs, Sellier, & Meyvis, 2011; Hancock & Verwey, 1997; Persson, Welsh, Jonides, & Reuter-Lorenz, 2007; Rauch & Schmitt, 2009), as well as changes in levels of motivation and willingness to engage in tasks (Boksem & Tops, 2008; Boksem, Meijman, & Lorist, 2006; Desmond & Matthews, 1997; Mital, Foononi-Fard, & Brown, 1994; Vohs et al., 2008).

How much prior activity does it take to induce fatigue? This is difficult to say with confidence. In driving simulations, impairments in performance on straight segments of the road have been shown to occur after a taxing 30-minute driving episode (Desmond & Matthews, 1997). In laboratory tests, increases in mean response time and errors on standard attention tasks have been found with times ranging between 20 minutes (Persson et al., 2007) and 2–3 hours (Boksem et al., 2005, 2006; van der Linden, Frese, & Meijman, 2003). It has also been shown that short periods of continuous activity can alter judicial sentencing (Danziger, Levav, & Avnaim-Pesso, 2011) and purchasing decisions (Hamilton et al., 2011; Vohs et al., 2008).

What cognitive processes are impaired by fatigue? Most accounts of the effects of fatigue, separate from sleep deprivation, posit some kind of global deficit in cognitive processing. Vohs and colleagues (Baumeister, Vohs, & Tice, 2007; Hamilton et al., 2011; Vohs & Heatherton, 2000; Vohs et al., 2008) have studied the effects of fatigue on self-regulation: the ability to exert control over our momentary desires. Numerous results have shown that self-regulatory behavior is reduced following episodes in which individuals exercised control for some period of time. Vohs and colleagues advocate a strength model of self-control in which self-control draws on a single bodily energy resource associated with glucose, which also underlies the executive functions that control processing. A similar global perspective underlies accounts in which fatigue depletes a unitary attention resource, thereby reducing the resources available to undertake additional tasks (e.g., Brown, 1994; Sarter, Gehring, & Kozak, 2006; van der Linden et al., 2003).

An analysis of electrical activity in the brain as a function of sustained performance of a simple key task show changes in brain activity associated with attention and target detection that mirror the behavioral findings of longer response times and decreased accuracy (Trejo et al., 2011, 2005). Boksem and colleagues (Boksem & Tops, 2008; Boksem et al., 2005, 2006) also found changes in the electrical activity of the brain after prolonged practice. They do not attribute these changes to depletion of a unitary attention resource, but instead propose a motivational account in which fatigue affects neural systems associated with the evaluation of reward and effort. Similar motivational accounts have been proposed to underlie the effects of fatigue on driving performance (Desmond & Matthews, 1997; Desmond, Hancock, & Monette, 1998; Hancock & Verwey, 1997).

Desmond and Matthews (1997) observed that a taxing 30-minute driving episode in a driving simulator led to impairments on the easier task of maintaining lane position in easy straightaway sections of the road, but not the more difficult sections with curves. They argue against a global resource-based account on the ground that depleted resources should have affected the more difficult, not the easier, condition. Although these results are consistent with lower motivation after prolonged practice, it is also known that more difficult tasks can at times overcome low levels of alertness by recruiting extra resources (see, e.g., Kahneman, 1973). Indeed, it has been difficult to tease apart the effect of motivation from specific cognitive impairments to processing. Regardless of interpretation, the findings of Desmond and Matthews have practical implications. They suggest that the effects of fatigue will show up more on repetitive or monotonous tasks that do not, in themselves, provide sufficient arousal, conditions which are similar to those of vigilance tasks. Such a position is consistent with the results from application domains showing that fatigue impairs performance on routine tasks (Baker, Olson, & Morisseau, 1994; Mital et al., 1994; Rosekind et al., 1994; Summala & Mikkola, 1994).

A study of judicial decision making by Danziger, Levav, and Avnaim-Pesso (2011) provides further evidence for an interaction of fatigue and motivation. They recorded the sentences given out by judges as a function of the duration of continuous performance. Judges were observed to provide progressively harsher sentences the longer they persisted prior to a break. Favorable rulings declined from approximately 65 percent at the beginning of a session to near zero at the end. After a break that included food, favorable sentences rose again to about 65 percent. The lesson in this for offenders is self-evident.

The same evidence that supports claims of a global impairment of executive control or motivation also supports a more local explanation of fatigue. It is well known that sensory processing is subject to fatigue from prolonged stimulation of specific receptors. The visual system, for example, will adapt to a constant stimulus presented over a period of time, such that when that stimulus is removed, the opposite "after image" is perceived. An example is continuous motion in one direction (e.g., watching the garage door close), which when removed is perceived as motion in the opposite direction (e.g., the garage door appears to have an upward motion though it remains fixed down). Likewise, continuous exertion of a specific muscle group can fatigue that muscle, causing problems. Thus, the effect of repeated exposure to stimulation or exertion is to fatigue a specific receptor, muscle, or functional process. Could the same be true for cognitive fatigue?

Evidence for specific functional cognitive impairment associated with prolonged task activity has been observed in a study of cognitive control. Persson et al. (2007) found evidence of impaired executive control after extensive, continuous practice. They divided participants into two groups, high interference and low interference. The high-interference group was asked to generate words from a base word that had several associates and no clear dominant response (e.g., ball -> throw, kick, bounce). The low-interference group generated words with few competing associates (e.g., scissors -> cut). After a baseline performance task, the groups were engaged in a demanding secondary task for approximately 20 minutes. Then they were retested on the interference task. Performance for the high-interference group was impaired when the secondary task was a working memory task that required resolution of interference, but not for the low-interference group. When the fatiguing task was a demanding response-inhibition task, no impairment was found. The authors concluded that sustained performance on the working memory tasks reduced the efficiency of specific brain regions associated with filtering unwanted information. These results are also consistent with the finding that making decisions leads to fatigue on subsequent decision tasks (Hamilton et al., 2011; Vohs et al., 2008).

There is no requirement that prolonged performance on a demanding task should have a single explanation, or a single site for its effect. Indeed, it is likely that as we tire, our brains function less efficiently and we find it harder to make good decisions or sustain attention. Our subjective experience reflects this and colors our judgment. It does appear, though, that short breaks can counteract these effects (Rosekind et al., 1995).

Sleep Deprivation and Circadian Rhythms

The causal link between sleep deprivation and cognitive impairment has long been recognized (Dement, 1960; Dinges et al., 1997; Durmer & Dinges, 2005; Fisher & Dement, 1963). There are two interrelated factors here that complicate the picture. Sleep itself is governed by homeostatic mechanisms that regulate the drive for sleep. The longer we are awake, the greater the drive to sleep. Sleep serves important cognitive restorative functions, especially associated with the consolidation of learning and memory (Walker & Stickgold, 2004; Walker, Brakefield, Allan Hobson, & Stickgold, 2003; Walker, Brakefield, Morgan, Hobson, & Stickgold, 2002). If we are deprived of sleep for even a single night, there is evidence of cognitive impairment (Dinges et al., 1997). The second sleep-related component is a circadian pacemaker. It generates a 24-hour rhythm, synchronizing our cognitive function roughly to the day–night cycle. When that rhythm is disturbed, as it is in jetlag, performance on a number of tasks has been shown to suffer (e.g., Folkard & Rosen, 1990; Rosekind et al., 1994).

A series of studies of airline pilots was the first to clearly dissociate the effects of sleep loss and the disruption of circadian rhythms from the subjective reports of sleepiness (Rosekind & Gander, 1996; Rosekind et al., 1994). The reports documented biological effects associated with disrupted circadian rhythms even for crew members who had ample preflight sleep (Rosekind & Gander, 1996; Rosekind et al., 1994). The consensus from that research is that on long flights, crews report fewer sleep-related problems when able to take short naps (Rosekind & Gander, 1996; Rosekind et al., 1995), a finding also supported by research in other domains (e.g., Purnell, Feyer, & Herbison, 2002).

What cognitive impairments are associated with sleep deprivation? In general, sleep deprivation has been associated with impairments in working memory tasks and sustained attention, as well as decisions and judgment (see Durmer & Dinges, 2005, for a review). In contrast to the Persson et al. results discussed earlier, the deficits with sleep deprivation appear to be systemic and not confined to specific cognitive operations. One piece of evidence for this comes from a study of visual search by Horowitz, Cade, Wolfe, and Czeisler (2003). They had participants perform difficult search tasks continuously for 38 hours. The testing schedule was conducted to compare the effects of sleep deprivation at different points on the circadian cycle. If sleep deprivation affected a specific cognitive process associated with search, such as visual attention or object identification, that deficit should have added to the time for each item, increasing the slope of the search function with set size. Instead, they found that sleep deprivation had an equal effect on both small and large set sizes. They concluded that sleep deprivation affected either perceptual encoding or response initiation.

Another alternative has been advanced (Durmer & Dinges, 2005) to explain these search results. The claim is that the increased drive to sleep has a physiological basis in midbrain structures. These structures become more active in insisting on sleep, resulting in micro-sleep episodes. Essentially, the midbrain tells the cortex to cease functioning. Evidence for this comes from a low event-rate vigilance task, referred to as the psycho-motor vigilance task (PVT). In this task, participants have only to indicate the presence of a randomly occurring stimulus (Dinges & Powell, 1985). As the period without sleep increases, the participant misses more and more. This can be traced to micro-sleep events that effectively shut down the cortex. A practical application of this is the development of sleepiness detecting systems for use in driving and other critical situations. Most of these systems detect eyelid droops, which are one of the first signs of the onset of micro-sleep episodes.

SUMMARY

This chapter focused on features of the task, the situation, and the operator that affect overall system safety and performance. These include workload, interruptions during task execution, and the physical state of the operator. We saw that each of these factors can have deleterious effects on human and system performance. None of these features occur in isolation; rather, they occur as an interaction of the human with the environment. Thus, they provide unique challenges in supporting system safety.

REFERENCES

Airbus. (2004). Human performance: Human factors aspects in incidents/accidents. In *Flight operations briefing notes*. Retrieved from http://www.airbus.com/fileadmin/media_gallery/files/safety_library_items/AirbusSafetyLib_-FLT_OPS-HUM_PER-SEQ01.pdf

Altmann, E. M., & Gray, W. D. (2008). An integrated model of cognitive control in task switching. *Psychological Review, 115*(3), 602–639. doi:10.1037/0033-295X.115.3.602

Altmann, E. M., & Trafton, J. G. (2002). Memory for goals: An activation-based model. *Cognitive Science, 26*, 39–83. doi:10.1207/s15516709cog2601_2

Altmann, E. M., & Trafton, J. G. (2007). Timecourse of recovery from task interruption: Data and a model. *Psychonomic Bulletin & Review, 14*(6), 1079–1084.

Anderson, J. R., & Lebiere, C. (1998). *The atomic components of thought*. Mahwah, NJ: Lawrence Erlbaum Associates, Inc.

Ash, J. S., Berg, M., & Coiera, E. (2004). Some unintended consequences of information technology in health care: The nature of patient care information system-related errors. *Journal of the American Medical Informatics Association, 11*(2), 104–112.

Backs, R. W. (1995). Going beyond heart rate: Autonomic space and cardiovascular assessment of mental workload. *International Journal of Aviation Psychology, 5*(1), 25.

Backs, R. W., Lenneman, J. K., Wetzel, J. M., & Green, P. (2003). Cardiac measures of driver workload during simulated driving with and without visual occlusion. *Human Factors: The Journal of the Human Factors and Ergonomics Society, 45*(4), 525.

Baker, K., Olson, J., & Morisseau, D. (1994). Work practices, fatigue, and nuclear power plant safety performance. *Human Factors: The Journal of the Human Factors and Ergonomics Society, 36*(2), 244–257. doi:10.1177/001872089403600206

Barber, R. E., & Lucas Jr., H. C. (1983). System response time operator productivity, and job satisfaction. *Communications of the ACM, 26*(11), 972–986.

Barnes, R. M. (1963). *Motion and time study*. New York, NY: John Wiley & Sons.

Baumeister, R. F., Vohs, K. D., & Tice, D. M. (2007). The strength model of self-control. *Current Directions in Psychological Science, 16*(6), 351–355. doi:10.1111/j.1467-8721.2007.00534.x

Berntson, G. G., Cacioppo, J. T., & Quigley, K. S. (1991). Autonomic determinism: The modes of autonomic control, the doctrine of autonomic space, and the laws of autonomic constraint. *Psychological Review, 98*(4), 459.

Beyea, S. C. (2007). Distractions, interruptions, and patient safety. *AORN Journal, 86*(1), 109–111.

Boehm-Davis, D. A., Curry, R. E., Wiener, E. L., & Harrison, R. L. (1983). Human factors of flight-deck automation: Report on a NASA-industry workshop. *Ergonomics, 26*(10), 953–961.

Boehm-Davis, D. A., & Remington, R. (2009). Reducing the disruptive effects of interruption: A cognitive framework for analysing the costs and benefits of intervention strategies. *Accident Analysis and Prevention, 41*, 1124–1129. doi:10.1016/J.Aap.2009.06.029

Boksem, M. A. S., Meijman, T. F., & Lorist, M. M. (2005). Effects of mental fatigue on attention: An ERP study. *Cognitive Brain Research, 25*(1), 107–116. doi:10.1016/j.cogbrainres.2005.04.011

Boksem, M. A. S., Meijman, T. F., & Lorist, M. M. (2006). Mental fatigue, motivation and action monitoring. *Biological Psychology, 72*(2), 123–132. doi:10.1016/j .biopsycho.2005.08.007

Boksem, M. A. S., & Tops, M. (2008). Mental fatigue: Costs and benefits. *Brain Research Reviews, 59*(1), 125–139. doi:10.1016/j.brainresrev.2008.07.001

Boyer, E. W., & Shannon, M. (2005). The serotonin syndrome. *New England Journal of Medicine, 352*, 1112–1120. doi:10.1056/NEJMra041867

Brixey, J. J., Robinson, D. J., Tang, Z., Johnson, T. R., Zhang, J., & Turley, J. P. (2005). Interruptions in workflow for RNs in a level one trauma center. *Proceedings of the American Medical Informatics Association Symposium* (pp. 86–90). Washington, DC: American Medical Informatics Association..

Brookhuis, K. A., & de Waard, D. (2001). Assessment of drivers' workload: Performance and subjective and physiological indexes. *Stress, Workload, and Fatigue*, 321–333.

Brown, I. D. (1994). Driver fatigue. *Human Factors: The Journal of the Human Factors and Ergonomics Society, 36*(2), 298–314. doi:10.1177/001872089403600210

Cades, D. M., Boehm-Davis, D. A., Trafton, J. G., & Monk, C. A. (2011). Mitigating disruptive effects of interruptions through training: What needs to be practiced? *Journal of Experimental Psychology: Applied, 17*(2), 97.

Caldwell Jr., J. (1997). Fatigue in the aviation environment: An overview of the causes and effects as well as recommended countermeasures. *Aviation, Space, and Environmental Medicine, 68*(10), 932.

Card, S. K., Moran, T. P., & Newell, A. (1983). *The psychology of human-computer interaction*. Hillsdale, N J: Lawrence Erlbaum Associates, Inc.

Casali, J. G., & Wierwille, W. W. (1983). A comparison of rating scale, secondary-task, physiological, and primary-task workload estimation techniques in a simulated flight task emphasizing communications load. *Human Factors: The Journal of the Human Factors and Ergonomics Society, 25*(6), 623–641. doi:10.1177/001872088302500602

Casali, J. G., & Wierwille, W. W. (1984). On the measurement of pilot perceptual workload: A comparison of assessment techniques addressing sensitivity and intrusion issues. *Ergonomics, 27*, 1033–1050.

Clancey, W. J., Sachs, P., Sierhuis, M., & Van Hoof, R. (1998). Brahms: Simulating practice for work systems design. *International Journal of Human Computer Studies, 49*(6), 831–866.

Corker, K. M., Gore, B. F., Fleming, K., & Lane, J. (2000). Free flight and the context of control: Experiments and modeling to determine the impact of distributed air-ground air traffic management on safety and procedures. *Proceedings of Third USA/Europe Air Traffic Management R&D Seminar (pp. 13–16)*. Napoli, Italy.

Cutrell, E., Czerwinski, M., & Horvits, E. (2001). Notification, disruption, and memory: Effects of messaging interruptions on memory and performance. In *Proceedings of*

Interact 2001. IFIP. Conference3 on Human-Computer Interaction (pp. 263–269). Tokyo, Japan.

Czerwinski, M., Cutrell, E., & Horvitz, E. (2000). Instant messaging and interruption: Influence of task type on performance. *Proceedings of OZCHI 2000* (pp. 356–361). Sydney, Australia..

Czerwinski, M., Horvitz, E., & Wilhite, S. (2004). A diary study of task switching and interruptions. Proceedings of HCI 2002 (pp. 230–245). Vienna, Austria.

Danziger, S., Levav, J., & Avnaim-Pesso, L. (2011). Extraneous factors in judicial decisions. *Proceedings of the National Academy of Sciences, 108*(17), 6889–6892. doi:10.1073/pnas.1018033108

Dement, W. (1960). The effect of dream deprivation. *Science, 131*, 1705–1707.

Desmond, P. A., Hancock, P. A., & Monette, J. L. (1998). Fatigue and automation-induced impairments in simulated driving performance. *Transportation Research Record: Journal of the Transportation Research Board, 1628*(1), 8–14.

Desmond, P. A., & Matthews, G. (1997). Implications of task-induced fatigue effects for in-vehicle countermeasures to driver fatigue. *Accident Analysis & Prevention, 29*(4), 515–523.

Detweiler, M., Hess, S., & Phelps, M. (1994). *Interruptions and working memory* (Unpublished technical report). University Park: The Pennsylvania State University.

Dinges, D. F., Pack, F., Williams, K., Gillen, K. A., Powell, J. W., Ott, G. E., Aptowicz, C., et al. (1997). Cumulative sleepiness, mood disturbance, and psychomotor vigilance performance decrements during a week of sleep restricted to 4–5 hours per night. *Sleep, 20*(4), 267–277.

Dinges, D. F., & Powell, J. W. (1985). Microcomputer analyses of performance on a portable, simple visual RT task during sustained operations. *Behavior Research Methods, 17*(6), 652–655.

Dismukes, R. K., Loukopoulos, L., & Jobe, K. K. (2001). The challenges of managing concurrent and deferred tasks. In R. Jensen (Ed.) Proceedings of the 11th International Symposium on Aviation Psychology. Columbus, OH: Ohio State University.

Dismukes, R. K., Young, K., & Sumwalt, R. L. (1998). *Cockpit interruptions and distractions: Effective management requires a careful balancing act* (ASRS Directline). Moffett Field, CA: NASA Ames Research Center.

Doherty, W. J., & Thedani, A. J. (1982). *The economic value of rapid response time.* IBM Technical Report Publication #GE20-0752-0. Yorktown Heights, NY: Watson Research Center.

Durmer, J. S., & Dinges, D. F. (2005). Neurocognitive consequences of sleep deprivation. *Seminars in Neurology, 25*, 117–129.

Fisher, C., & Dement, W. C. (1963). Studies on the psychopathology of sleep and dreams. *American Journal of Psychiatry, 119*(12), 1160.

Folkard, S., & Rosen, S. D. (1990). Circadian performance rhythms: Some practical and theoretical implications [and discussion]. *Philosophical Transactions of the Royal Society of London. Series B, Biological Sciences, 327*(1241), 543–553.

Fu, W. T., & Gray, W. D. (2004). Resolving the paradox of the active user: Stable suboptimal performance in interactive tasks. *Cognitive Science, 28*, 901–935.

Gopher, D., & Donchin, E. (1986). Workload: An examination of the concept. In K. R. Boff, L. Kaufman, & J. P. Thomas (Eds.) *Handbook of perception and human performance: Vol. 2 Cognitive Processes and performance* (pp. 41.1–41.49). New York: Wiley.

Gore, B. F., & Corker, K. M. (2000). A systems engineering approach to behavioral predictions of an advanced air traffic management concept. *Proceedings of the 20ᵗʰ Digital Avionics Systems Conference* (pp. 4.B.3.1–4.B.3.8). Philadephia, PA.

Gray, W. D., & Boehm-Davis, D. A. (2000). Milliseconds matter: An introduction to microstrategies and to their use in describing and predicting interactive behavior. *Journal of Experimental Psychology Applied, 6*(4), 322–335.

Gray, W. D., John, B. E., & Atwood, M. (1993). Project Ernestine: Validating a GOMS analysis for predicting and explaining real-world task performance. *Human-Computer Interaction, 8*(3), 237–309. doi:10.1207/s15327051hci0803_3

Grossberg, M. (1989). Relation of sector complexity to operational errors. *Quarterly Report of the Federal Aviation Administration's Office of Air Traffic Evaluations and Analysis*. Washington, DC: Federal Aviation Administration.

Grundgeiger, T., Liu, D., Sanderson, P. M., Jenkins, S., & Leane, T. (2008). *Effects of interruptions on prospective memory performance in anesthesiology*. Presented at the Proceedings of the 52ⁿᵈ Annual Meeting of the Human Factors and Ergonomics Society, September 22–26, New York, NY.

Grundgeiger, T., Sanderson, P. M., MacDougall, H. G., & Venkatesh, B. (2010). Interruption management in the intensive care unit: Predicting resumption times and assessing distributed support. *Journal of Experimental Psychology: Applied, 16*(4), 317.

Grundgeiger, T., Sanderson, P. M., Orihuela, C. B., Thompson, A., MacDougall, H. G., Nunnink, L., & Venkatesh, B. (2010). Distractions and interruptions in the intensive care unit: A field observation and a simulator experiment. Proceedings of the Human Factors and Ergonomics Society 54ᵗʰ Annual Meeting (pp. 835–839). San Francisco, CA: Human Factors and Ergonomics Society.

Hamilton, R., Vohs, K. D., Sellier, A.-L., & Meyvis, T. (2011). Being of two minds: Switching mindsets exhausts self-regulatory resources. *Organizational Behavior and Human Decision Processes, 115*(1), 13–24. doi:10.1016/j.obhdp.2010.11.005

Hancock, P. A., & Verwey, W. B. (1997). Fatigue, workload and adaptive driver systems. *Accident Analysis & Prevention, 29*, 495–506.

Hanowski, R. J., Wierwille, W. W., & Dingus, T. A. (2003). An on-road study to investigate fatigue in local/short haul trucking. *Accident Analysis & Prevention, 35*(2), 153–160.

Hansen, J. P. (1995). An experimental investigation of configural, digital, and temporal information on process displays. *Human Factors: The Journal of the Human Factors and Ergonomics Society, 37*(3), 539–552. doi:10.1518/001872095779049345

Hart, S. G., & Staveland, L. E. (1988). Development of NASA-TLX (Task Load Index): Results of empirical and theoretical research. *Human Mental Workload, 1,* 139–183.

Hart, S. G., & Wickens, C. D. (1990). *Workload assessment and prediction. MANPRINT, an approach to systems integration* (pp. 257–296). New York, NY: Van Nostrand Reinhold.

Hendy, K. C., Liao, J., & Milgram, P. (1997). Combining time and intensity effects in assessing operator information-processing load. *Human Factors: The Journal of the Human Factors and Ergonomics Society, 39*(1), 30–47.

Hicks, T. G., & Wierwille, W. W. (1979). Comparison of five mental workload assessment procedures in a moving-base driving simulator. *Human Factors: The Journal of the Human Factors and Ergonomics Society, 21*(2), 129–143.

Hollnagel, E. (1993). *Human reliability analysis: Context and control.* London, UK: Academic Press.

Horowitz, T. S., Cade, B. E., Wolfe, J. M., & Czeisler, C. A. (2003). Searching night and day: A dissociation of effects of circadian phase and time awake on visual selective attention and vigilance. *Psychological Science, 14,* 549–557. doi:10.1046/j.0956-7976.2003.psci_1464.x

Horvitz, E., & Apacible, J. (2003). Learning and reasoning about interruption. In *Proceedings of the 5th International Conference on Mulitmodal Interfaces* (pp. 20–27). New York, NY: ACM.

Horvitz, E., Breese, J., Heckerman, D., Hovel, D., & Rommelse, K. (1998). The Lumiere project: Bayesian user modeling for inferring the goals and needs of software users. In *UAI'98 Proceedings of the 14th Conference on Uncertainty in Artificial Intelliegence* (pp. 256–265) San Francisco, CA: Morgan Kaufmann Publishers, Inc.

Horvitz, E., Kadie, C., Paek, T., & Hovel, D. (2003). Models of attention in computing and communication: From principles to applications. *Communications of the ACM, 46*(3), 52–59.

Iqbal, S. T., & Horvitz, E. (2007). Disruption and recovery of computing tasks: Field study, analysis, and directions. In *CHI '07 Proceedings of the SIGCHI Conference on Human Factors in Computing Systems* (pp. 677–686). New York, NY: ACM.

John, B. E. (1990). Extensions of GOMS analyses to expert performance requiring perception of dynamic visual and auditory information. *Proceedings of the SIGCHI Conference on Human Factors in Computing Systems: Empowering people* (pp. 107–116). New York, NY: ACM.

John, B. E., & Kieras, D. E. (1996a). The GOMS family of user interface analysis techniques: Comparison and contrast. *ACM Transactions on Computer-Human Interaction, 3,* 320–351. doi:http://doi.acm.org/10.1145/235833.236054

John, B. E., & Kieras, D. E. (1996b). Using GOMS for user interface design and evaluation: Which technique? *ACM Transactions on Computer-Human Interaction (TOCHI), 3*(4), 287–319.

John, B. E., Vera, A., Matessa, M., Freed, M., & Remington, R. (2002). Automating CPM-GOMS. *Proceedings of CHI*, April 20–25. Minneapolis, MN: ACM.

Kahneman, D. (1973). *Attention and effort*. Englewood Cliffs, NJ: Prentice Hall.

Kieras, D. E. (1996). Guide to GOMS model usability evaluations using NGOMSL. In M. Helander & T. Landauer (Eds), *Handbook of human-computer interaction* (2nd ed.). Amsterdam: North-Holland.

Kieras, D. E., & Meyer, D. E. (1997). An overview of the EPIC architecture for cognition and performance with application to human-computer interaction. *Human-Computer Interaction, 12*, 391–438.

Kirwan, B., Scaife, R., & Kennedy, R. (2001). Investigating complexity factors in UK air traffic management. *Human Factors and Aerospace Safety, 1*(2), 125–144.

Kopardekar, P., & Magyarits, S. (2003). Measurement and prediction of dynamic density. *Proceedings of the 5ᵗʰ USA/Europe Air Traffic Management R & D Seminar*. Budapest, Hungary.

Kramer, A., & Weber, T. (2000). Applications of psychophysiology to human factors. In J. T. Cacioppo, L. G. Tassinary, & G. G. Berntson (Eds.), *Handbook of Psychophysiology* 2ⁿᵈ ed. (pp. 794–814). New York: Cambridge University Press.

Latorella, K. A. (1999). *Investigating interruptions: Implications for flightdeck performance* (NASA Technical Memorandum No. NASA/TM-1999-209707). Hampton, VA: National Aeronautics and Space Administration, Langley Research Center.

Latorella, K. A., & Prabhu, P. V. (2000). A review of human error in aviation maintenance and inspection. *International Journal of Industrial Ergonomics, 26*(2), 133–161.

Laudeman, I., Shelden, S., Branstrom, R., & Brasil, C. (1998). Dynamic density: An air traffic management metric. NASA Technical Report # NAS 1.15:112226, NSA/TM-1998-11226, A-98-10366. Moffett Field, CA: Ames Research Center.

LeGoullon, M. D. (2008). *Where do people resume interrupted tasks?* (Doctoral Dissertation). Fairfax, VA: George Mason University.

Lerner, B. H. (2006, November 28). A case that shook medicine. Retrieved October 3, 2011, from www.washingtonpost.com/wp-dyn/content/article/2006/11/24/AR2006112400985.html

Lewis, C., & Rieman, J. (1993). *Task centered user interface design: A practical introduction* [shareware book]. University of Colorado, Boulder. Available at ftp://ftp.cs.colorado.edu/pub/cs/distribs/clewis/HCI-Design-Book

Liu, Y. (1996). Queueing network modeling of elementary mental processes. *Psychological Review, 103*(1), 116.

Loft, S., Sanderson, P. M., Neal, A., & Mooij, M. (2007). Modeling and predicting mental workload in en route air traffic control: Critical review and broader implications. *Human Factors: The Journal of the Human Factors and Ergonomics Society, 49*(3), 376–399. doi:10.1518/001872007X197017

Loukopoulos, L. D., Dismukes, R. K., & Barshi, I. (2003). Cockpit interruptions and distractions: A line observation study. In R. Jensen (Ed.), Proceedings of the 11th International Symposium on Aviation Psychology. Columbus, OH: Ohio State University.

Mackworth, N. (1948). The breakdown of vigilance during prolonged visual search. *Quarterly Journal of Experimental Psychology, 1*, 6–21

Manning, C. A., Mills, S. H., Fox, C. M., Pfleiderer, E. M., & Mogilka, H. J. (2002). Using air traffic control taskload measures and communication events to predict subjective workload. Retrieved from http://stinet.dtic.mil/oai/oai?&verb=getRecord&metadataPrefix=html&identifier=ADA401923

McFarlane, D. (2002). Comparison of four primary methods for coordinating the interruption of people in human-computer interaction. *Human-Computer Interaction, 17*, 63–139. doi:10.1207/S15327051HCI1701_2

McLucas, J. L., Drinkwater III, F. J., & Leaf, H. W. (1981). *Report of the president's task force on aircraft crew complement* (No. A988601). Washington, DC: US State Department.

Mital, A., Foononi-Fard, H., & Brown, M. L. (1994). Physical fatigue in high and very high frequency manual materials handling: Perceived exertion and physiological indicators. *Human Factors: The Journal of the Human Factors and Ergonomics Society, 36*(2), 219–231. doi:10.1177/001872089403600204

Monk, C. A., Boehm-Davis, D. A., Mason, G., & Trafton, J. G. (2004). Recovering from interruptions: Implications for driver distraction research. *Human Factors, 46*(4), 650.

Monk, C. A., & Kidd, D. G. (2008). The effects of brief interruptions on task resumption. *Proceedings of the Human Factors and Ergonomics Society Annual Meeting, 52*, 403–407.

Mulder, G. (1980). The heart of mental effort. Unpublished Doctoral Dissertation. University of Groningen, The Netherlands: University of Groningen.

Mulder, G. (1986). The concept and measurement of mental effort. In G. R. J. Hockey et al. (Eds.), *Energetics and human information processing* (pp. 175–199). Dordrecht, Netherlands: Martinus Nijhoff.

NASA. (2001). The case for confidential incident reporting systems. NASA ASRS (Pub. 60). Retrieved from http://asrs.arc.nasa.gov/publications/research.html

National Transportation Safety Board (NTSB). (1988). *Aircraft accident report: Northwest Airlines, Inc., McDonnell Douglas DC-9-82, N312RC, Detroit Metropolitan Wayne County Airport, Romulus, Michigan, August 16, 1987* (National Transportation Safety Board No. NTSB/AAR-88/05). Washington, DC: NTSB.

Newell, A. (1990). *Unified theories of cognition*. Cambridge, MA: Harvard University Press.

Owens, J. A., Veasey, S. C., & Rosen, R. (2001). Physician, heal thyself: Sleep, fatigue, and medical education. *Sleep-New York, 24*(5), 493–498.

Parasuraman, R., & Davies, D. (1977). A taxonomic analysis of vigilance performance. In R. Mackie (Ed.), *Vigilance: Theory, operational performance, and physiological correlates* (pp. 559–574). New York, NY: Plenum Press.

Persson, J., Welsh, K. M., Jonides, J., & Reuter-Lorenz, P. A. (2007). Cognitive fatigue of executive processes: Interaction between interference resolution tasks. *Neuropsychologia, 45*(7), 1571–1579. doi:10.1016/j.neuropsychologia.2006.12.007

Pew, R. & Deutsch, S. (2007). D-OMAR: An architecture for modeling multi-task behaviors. In D. Foyle & B. L. Hooey (Eds.), *Human performance modeling in aviation* (pp. 183–212). Boca Raton, FL: CRC Press/Francis & Taylor.Philibert, I., Friedmann, P., & Williams, W. T. (2002). New requirements for resident duty hours. *JAMA: The Journal of the American Medical Association, 288*(9), 1112.

Protopapas, A., & Lieberman, P. (1995). Effects of vocal F0 manipulations on perceived emotional stress. In SUS-1995 ESCA/NATO Tutorial and Research Workshop on *Speech under Stress* (pp. 1–4). Lisbon, Portugal.

Protopapas, A., & Lieberman, P. (1997). Fundamental frequency of phonation and perceived emotional stress. *Journal of the Acoustical Society of America, 101*, 2267–2277.

Purnell, M., Feyer, A. M., & Herbison, G. (2002). The impact of a nap opportunity during the night shift on the performance and alertness of 12-h shift workers. *Journal of Sleep Research, 11*(3), 219–227.

Ratwani, R. M. (2008). *A spatial memory mechanism for guiding primary task resumption* (Doctoral dissertation). Fairfax, VA: George Mason University.

Rauch, W. A., & Schmitt, K. (2009). Fatigue of cognitive control in the Stroop-Task. In N. A. Taatgen & H. van Rijn (Eds.), *Proceedings of the 31ˢᵗ Annual Conference of the Cognitive Science Society* (pp. 750–755). Austin, TX: Cognitve Science Society, Inc.

Reid, G. B. & Nygren, T. E. (1988). The Subjective Workload Assessment Technique: A scaling procedure for measuring mental workload. In P. A. Hancock & N. Meshkati (Eds.) Human Mental Workload (pp. 185–218), Elsevier Science Publishers, North Holland.

Rhoades, D. R., McFarland, K. F., Finch, W. H., & Johnson, A. O. (2001). Speaking and interruptions during primary care office visits. *Family Medicine, 33*(7), 528–532.

Rosekind, M. R., & Gander, P. H. (1996). Managing fatigue in operational settings: Physiological considerations and countermeasures. *Behavioral Medicine, 21*(4), 157.

Rosekind, M. R., Gander, P. H., Miller, D. L., Gregory, K. B., Smith, R. M., Weldon, K. J., Co, E. L., et al. (1994). Fatigue in operational settings: Examples from the aviation environment. *Human Factors: The Journal of the Human Factors and Ergonomics Society, 36*(2), 327–338. doi:10.1177/001872089403600212

Rosekind, M. R., Smith, R. M., Miller, D. L., Co, E. L., Gregory, K. B., Webbon, L. L., Gander, P. H., et al. (1995). Alertness management: Strategic naps in operational settings. *Journal of Sleep Research, 4*(2), 62–66.

Ruthruff, E., Remington, R. W., & Johnston, J. C. (2001). Switching between simple cognitive tasks: The interaction of top-down and bottom-up factors. *Journal of Experimental Psychology—Human Perception and Performance, 27*, 1404–1419.

Salvucci, D. D., & Taatgen, N. A. (2008). Threaded cognition: An integrated theory of concurrent multitasking. *Psychological Review, 115*(1), 101.

Santell, J. P. (2005). Medication errors: Experience of the United States Pharmacopeia (USP). *Journal of Quality and Patient Safety, 31*(2), 114–119.

Sarter, M., Gehring, W. J., & Kozak, R. (2006). More attention must be paid: The neurobiology of attentional effort. *Brain Research Reviews, 51*(2), 145–160. doi:10.1016/j.brainresrev.2005.11.002

Sierhuis, M., Bradshaw, J. M., Acquisti, A., Van Hoof, R., Jeffers, R., & Uszok, A. (2003). Human-agent teamwork and adjustable autonomy in practice. *Proceedings of the Seventh International Symposium on Artificial Intelligence, Robotics and Automation in Space* (i-SAIRAS). Nara, Japan.

Summala, H., & Mikkola, T. (1994). Fatal accidents among car and truck drivers: Effects of fatigue, age, and alcohol consumption. *Human Factors: The Journal of the Human Factors and Ergonomics Society, 36*(2), 315–326. doi:10.1177/001872089403600211

Trafton, J. G., Altmann, E. M., & Ratwani, R. M. (2011). A memory for goals model of sequence errors. *Cognitive Systems Research, 12*(2), 134–143. doi:10.1016/j.cogsys.2010.07.010

Trejo, L. J., Knuth, K., Prado, R., Rosipal, R., Kubitz, K., Kochavi, R., Matthews, B., et al. (2011). EEG-based estimation of mental fatigue: Convergent evidence for a three-state model. In D. D. Schmorrow & L. M. Reeves (Eds.), *Foundations of augmented cognition* (Vol. 4565, pp. 201–211). Berlin, Heidelberg: Springer Berlin Heidelberg. Retrieved from www.springerlink.com/content/11422082x1t43577/

Trejo, L. J., Kochavi, R., Kubitz, K., Montgomery, L., Rosipal, R., & Matthews, B. (2005). EEG-based estimation of cognitive fatigue. In D. D. Schmorrow & L. M. Reeves (Eds.) *Augmented Cognition* (pp. 201–211). Heidelberg, Germany: Springer-Verlag.

U.S. Army Research Laboratory. (2010, September 1). Improved performance research integration tool. Retrieved October 29, 2011, from www.arl.army.mil/www/default.cfm?page=445

van der Linden, D., Frese, M., & Meijman, T. F. (2003). Mental fatigue and the control of cognitive processes: Effects on perseveration and planning. *Acta Psychologica, 113*(1), 45–65. doi:10.1016/S0001-6918(02)00150-6

Vera, A. H., John, B. E., Remington, R., Matessa, M., & Freed, M. A. (2005). Automating human-performance modeling at the millisecond level. *Human-Computer Interaction, 20*, 225–265.

Verwey, W. B. (2000). On-line driver workload estimation. Effects of road situation and age on secondary task measures. *Ergonomics, 43*, 187–209.

Verwey, W. B., & Veltman, H. A. (1996). Detecting short periods of elevated workload: A comparison of nine workload assessment techniques. *Journal of Experimental Psychology—Applied, 2*, 270–285.

Vohs, K. D., Baumeister, R. F., Schmeichel, B. J., Twenge, J. M., Nelson, N. M., & Tice, D. M. (2008). Making choices impairs subsequent self-control: A limited-resource account of decision making, self-regulation, and active initiative. *Journal of Personality and Social Psychology, 94*, 883–898. doi:10.1037/0022-3514.94.5.883

Vohs, K. D., & Heatherton, T. F. (2000). Self-regulatory failure: A resource-depletion approach. *Psychological Science (Wiley-Blackwell), 11*(3), 249.

Volpp, K. G. M., & Grande, D. (2003). Residents' suggestions for reducing errors in teaching hospitals. *New England Journal of Medicine, 348*(9), 851–855.

Walker, M. P., Brakefield, T., Allan Hobson, J., & Stickgold, R. (2003). Dissociable stages of human memory consolidation and reconsolidation. *Nature, 425*(6958), 616–620. doi:10.1038/nature01930

Walker, M. P., Brakefield, T., Morgan, A., Hobson, J. A., & Stickgold, R. (2002). Practice with sleep makes perfect: Sleep-dependent motor skill learning. *Neuron, 35*(1), 205–211. doi:10.1016/S0896-6273(02)00746-8

Walker, M. P., & Stickgold, R. (2004). Sleep-dependent learning and memory consolidation. *Neuron, 44*(1), 121–133. doi:10.1016/j.neuron.2004.08.031

Warm, J. S., Parasuraman, R., & Matthews, G. (2008). Vigilance requires hard mental work and is stressful. *Human Factors, 50*, 433–441.

Wetteland, C. R., Bowen, S., & French, J. (2002). Task network modeling: Resolving manning issues in complex environments. *Proceedings of the 2002 IEEE 7th Conference on Human Factors and Power Plants, 2002* (pp. 4–1 to 4–5). Presented at the Proceedings of the 2002 IEEE 7th Conference on Human Factors and Power Plants. doi:10.1109/HFPP.2002.1042838

Wetteland, C. R., Miller, J. L., French, J., O'Brien, K., & Spooner, D. J. (2000). Simulation in shipbuilding: The human simulation: Resolving manning issues onboard DD21. *Proceedings of the Winter SimulationConference 2000* (pp. 1402–1406). Orlando, FL.

Wharton, C., Rieman, J., Lewis, C., & Polson, P. (1994). The cognitive walkthrough method: A practitioner's guide. *Usability Inspection Methods*, 105–140.

Wickens, C. D. (1984). The Multiple Resources Model of human performance: Implications for display design. Retrieved from http://stinet.dtic.mil/oai/oai?&verb=getRecord&metadataPrefix=html&identifier=ADP004516

Wiener, E. L. (1985). Beyond the sterile cockpit. *Human Factors: The Journal of the Human Factors and Ergonomics Society, 27*(1), 75–90.

Wierwille, W. W. (1979). Physiological measures of aircrew mental workload. *Human Factors: The Journal of the Human Factors and Ergonomics Society, 21*(5), 575–593.

Wierwille, W. W., & Eggemeier, F. T. (1993). Recommendations for mental workload measurement in a test and evaluation environment. *Human Factors: The Journal of the Human Factors and Ergonomics Society, 35*(2), 263–281.

Wilson, G. F. (2002). Psychophysiological test methods and procedures. In S. G. Charlton & T. G. O'Brien (Eds.) *Handbook of Human Factors Testing and Evaluation* (pp. 127–156). Mahwah, NJ: Lawrence Erlbaum Associates.

Wu, C., & Liu, Y. (2007). Queuing network modeling of driver workload and performance. *IEEE Transactions on Intelligent Transportation Systems, 8*(3), 528–537.

Wu, C., Tsimhoni, O., & Liu, Y. (2008). Development of an adaptive workload management system using the queueing network-model human processor (QN-MHP). *IEEE Transactions on Intelligent Transportation Systems, 9*(3), 463–475.

Yerkes, R. M., & Dodson, J. D. (1908). The relation of strength of stimulus to rapidity of habit-formation. *Journal of Comparative Neurology and Psychology, 18*(5), 459–482.

16

The Role of Automation in Human-System Performance

In Parts I–III, we have described human error tendencies and the relationship between situation awareness (SA) and problems of control. Given the propensities for human error and the difficulties that operators experience in maintaining SA in high-workload environments, it would seem natural to try to automate functions where necessary to relieve them of some of the tasks. Because a large number of accidents have been attributed to human error, or labeled human-caused, automation of system functions—thus relieving the human operator from entire tasks—should result in fewer accidents, as well as lower workload for the operators. In large part, the introduction of automation has in fact yielded many benefits. Nowhere is this more evident than in aviation, where the widespread adoption of high levels of cockpit automation was driven by the desire to increase system safety and reduce flight costs (see, e.g., Parasuraman & Riley, 1997; Parasuraman & Wickens, 2008; Sarter, Woods, & Billings, 1997; Wiener, 1985; Wiener & Curry, 1980). Flight crews can program the flight management system to fly precise routes between chosen points in space, climb and descend with precision at prespecified intervals, and choose routes that optimize fuel usage. With the new technology of Data Link, it is possible for ground computers, either from air traffic control or airline control centers, to uplink new flight trajectories or commands automatically. Few would question that the introduction of automated systems in aircraft has made flying much safer. In a 2011 report, the Federal Aviation Administration calls the period from 2001 to 2009 the safest in commercial aviation history (Charette, 2011; Reuters, 2009; Takemoto & Jones, 2011).

Automation has also reduced the operating costs of airlines by introducing efficiencies into operations, as in flying more fuel-efficient routes. Though aviation in many ways was a leader in the introduction of automation, and provided the principal test bed for research, automation is beginning to have significant impact on our everyday lives as well. Computers can control many household functions, from security, to lighting, to climate control. Consumers often demand systems that have more "bells and whistles" or that relieve them of tedious portions of a job, as with cruise control in automobiles; or of difficult tasks, as with the automated parallel-parking feature currently being offered in luxury automobiles. The design of advanced driver assistance systems is a major component of automotive design in response to consumer demand (Risto, Martens, & Wilschut, 2010; Strandberg, 1983; van Waterschoot & van der Voort, 2009).

Although automation has largely accomplished both the goals of improved safety and reduced workload, it has also introduced its own new challenges for operators. In the NTSB report of the *Exxon Valdez* accident, for example, there is much discussion of the role the helm autopilot might have played. In particular, the report develops the premise that the third mate and helmsman failed to realize that the autopilot was engaged. As we discussed in Chapter 13, the helm autopilot would have allowed the helmsman to make manual inputs, but would not have responded to them. Instead, it would have kept to the course originally assigned to it. This is one example of what has been a set of long-standing concerns with automation in commercial transport aircraft since the rapid adoption of advanced systems beginning in the 1970s. The foreword to a 1996 report by the Federal Aviation Administration (FAA Human Factors Team, 1996) reads:

> On April 26, 1994, an Airbus A300-600 operated by China Airlines crashed at Nagoya, Japan, killing 264 passengers and flightcrew members. Contributing to the accident were conflicting actions taken by the flightcrew and the airplane's autopilot. The crash provided a stark example of how a breakdown in the flightcrew/automation interface can affect flight safety. Although this particular accident involved an A300-600, other accidents, incidents, and safety indicators demonstrate that this problem is not confined to any one airplane type, airplane manufacturer, operator, or geographical region. This point was tragically demonstrated by the crash of a Boeing 757 operated by American Airlines near Cali, Columbia on December 20, 1995, and a November 12, 1995 incident (very nearly a fatal accident) in which an American Airlines Douglas MD-80 descended below the minimum descent altitude on approach to Bradley International Airport, CT, clipped the tops of trees, and landed short of the runway.

Concerns over the effect of the highly sophisticated automated cockpits of modern transport aircraft are at the core of several news articles reporting on a 2011 draft report from the FAA. According to these news articles, the FAA notes that in the five years from 2006 through 2010, there had been 51 "loss of control" accidents worldwide in which failure to properly interact with the automation or inability to manually fly the aircraft were contributing factors. According to Rory Kay, an airline captain and co-chairman of the FAA committee on pilot training, "We're seeing a new breed of accident with these state-of-the-art planes . . . We're forgetting how to fly" (Charette, 2011; Dolak, 2011; Lowy, 2011).

How is it that even while automation is making the skies safer, and we are poised for similar benefits from the introduction of automation into automobiles, people remain concerned over the potential problems of automation? One reason is that two decades of intense study of automation in the cockpit of modern aircraft has documented a class of errors associated with highly automated systems (Parasuraman & Wickens, 2008; Sarter & Woods, 1995; Sarter et al., 1997; Wiener, 1985; Wiener & Curry, 1980). These include:

1. Forgetting the state of the automated device (on/off, mode)
2. Improper setting of the device
3. Failing to understand how the device will respond under various conditions given its current mode
4. Loss of situation awareness
5. Erosion of basic skills

The first three of these deal with difficulties encountered in interacting with the automated system itself. For example, in Chapter 13, we provided the example of failing to recall that the cruise control was active when exiting the freeway (Andre & Degani, 1997). The last two issues concern the more general question of whether the use of automation produces changes in operator behavior that will degrade performance in the short or long term. Loss of situation awareness becomes an issue because the operator is no longer in direct control of the system and may therefore not be fully aware of relevant state information (Endsley, 1996; Sarter & Woods, 1997; Sarter et al., 1997; Wiener, 1985; Wiener & Curry, 1980). Concerns over loss of skill, consistent with the comments of Captain Kay quoted earlier, arise because of the reduced opportunity to practice.

USING AUTOMATED DEVICES

There are numerous documented cases in which failures to correctly use an automated device have led to frustration or errors (Andre & Degani, 1997; FAA Human Factors Team, 1996; Nagel, 1989; Parasuraman & Riley, 1997; Sarter & Woods, 1994, 1995; Sarter et al., 1997; Wiener, 1985; Wiener & Curry, 1980). In some cases these errors arise because the design of the automation puts the operator into conditions conducive to known error patterns. Consider the first issue, failure to recall the state of the automated system. It can be understood in terms of two concepts described earlier: attentional tunneling and postcompletion (or prospective memory) errors. An example of this is the China Air Flight 006 accident in 1985 (National Transportation Safety Board, 1986). The Boeing 747 aircraft was flying at 41,000 ft with the autopilot set in altitude hold mode when it lost an engine. The crew attempted to restart the engine with the autopilot engaged. Repeated attempts to restart the engine failed. During this time the autopilot remained in altitude hold mode and continued to attempt to maintain the 41,000-ft altitude. The three remaining engines were producing insufficient thrust for this. The autopilot attempted to compensate by raising the nose of the aircraft until it eventually stalled (lost lift across the wing surfaces) and entered an "uncontrolled descent." The crew restored control at 9,500 ft, after falling 31,500 ft and injuring several passengers. The crew became engrossed in restarting the engine, tunneling their attention to a task that was not immediately critical. Had they turned the autopilot off and descended to a lower altitude, the aircraft could have safely flown on three engines while they sorted out the problem. The failure to consider the autopilot in the first place closely resembles the postcompletion error discussed previously. The goal of the crew became focused on the engine. Once that happened, turning the autopilot off became a "cleanup" task, much like taking the card out of the ATM, exactly the kind of error that people make commonly. Checklists provide a barrier against such errors. Had the crew followed instructions to invoke the engine-out checklist correctly, the accident would have been prevented.

We have discussed how postcompletion and prospective memory errors have been shown to increase with increases in multitasking demands that reduce available resources for the cleanup tasks. This tendency is evident in another airline accident, the crash of Air Inter Flight 148 while on hold to land at Strasbourg, France. The report of the crash (Aviation Safety Network, 1992) listed the likely cause of the accident as a failure of the crew to properly configure the sophisticated flight management system (FMS) of their Airbus A320. They typed in "–3.3" to the FMS. This would have been the correct input for a glide slope of –3.3°, which was what they probably intended. They had failed, however, to reset the FMS to Flight Path Angle mode, leaving it instead set to Vertical Speed mode, which caused the aircraft to descend at a rate of 3,300 ft/minute. The incorrect use of automated equipment often involves a failure to consider the mode of the system or the consequences of the mode with respect to other system changes, such as the engine performance in China Air 006. It seems somewhat perverse that in both cases the automation would lack the information about the consequences of its own behavior on the controlled system. It is likely that operators fail to deal with the automation correctly in part because they fail to consider that it would fly the aircraft into a dangerous situation without at least warning them. No human co-pilot would do this. To some extent, then, we may bring faulty assumptions into play when dealing with automation, thinking it will behave reasonably as would be expected from a human assistant (Wiener, 1985).

Perhaps the most frequently written about problem with automation is operators' lack of understanding of the automation, the confusion that this produces, and the lack of trust in automation that ensues (Adams, Tenney, & Pew, 1995; Barach & Small, 2000; Dolak, 2011; Endsley, 1996; Green, 1990; Lowy, 2011; Miller & Parasuraman, 2007; Nagel, 1989; Parasuraman & Riley, 1997; Parasuraman & Wickens, 2008; Sarter & Woods, 1995, 1997; Wiener, 1985; Wiener & Curry, 1980). From observations of flight crews over several months, Wiener and Curry distilled their comments into three questions that summarized their problems with automated systems (Wiener, 1989; Wiener & Curry, 1980):

1. What is it doing?
2. Why is it doing that?
3. What will it do next?

It is not difficult to see that unfamiliar and sophisticated systems place additional burdens of understanding on operators. They must understand the input-output relations that govern the automated devices' response to their inputs. This understanding is hampered by the complexity of the devices, a complete treatment of which is beyond most training courses (Wiener, 1985, 1989; Wiener & Curry, 1980). As a result, operators often understand only portions of the many functions and modes. In many cases, operators even lack awareness of how the device works, relying on memorized sequences of inputs in frequently used situations (Sarter & Woods, 1994). Added to this is that, as evidenced by the China Air and Air Inter accidents cited earlier, the automation receives a limited amount of information about the entire system and its behavior must be comprehended in light of what it knows. This means that the operator must be aware of what the automated device knows separate from what the operator knows. This knowledge is not likely to be available without conscious attention being directed toward its realization. Thus, the operator cannot benefit from the kind of recognition-primed decision making that characterizes expert behavior, but must deliberately apply limited cognitive resources to the problem. Indeed, it has been noted that automation often relieves the operator of tasks that were not very demanding in the first place, and replaces them with tasks that produce a greater burden on the operator's limited cognitive resources (Sarter & Woods, 1994, 1995; Woods, Johannesen, Cook, & Sarter, 1994).

Issues in comprehending sophisticated automated devices are made more difficult because the automation does not solve problems in the same way as humans do. People often rely on their perceptual systems to provide insight into problems. For example, we can "see" the trajectories of moving objects; we do not need to compute them. However, computer algorithms have only the most rudimentary ways of defining objects in the visual scene; they do not have access to the structured scene that our visual system provides. Thus, computers must use other sources of information, or computational algorithms, which are opaque to all except for the engineers who developed them. This makes it difficult for the human operator to intuit what the system "knows" and how it chooses its actions.

These examples illustrate the kinds of problems that people have in dealing with automation, and some insight into to the cognitive difficulties that automation poses. They do not, though, say much about which particular aspects of automation are problematic. Once we begin to examine automation in detail, it turns out to be a very complex issue. The term is applied, or can be applied, to the automatic focus and light settings of many small cameras, to the sophisticated algorithms that alert air traffic controllers to potential conflicts, to the robot vacuum cleaner that navigates around the room, to medical systems that attempt to diagnose diseases, or to the advanced research cars that drive themselves. Some of these automated systems seem to work fine and have become standard, if not essential, features of our technological lives. Others remain problematic for people to interact with, and cause errors. A fuller understanding of the issue of automation and human error requires a more detailed treatment of the way automation is implemented.

LEVELS OF AUTOMATION

Automation seldom fails at the task for which it was designed. Engineers develop requirement documents that detail a set of specifications for what the automation should do, specify the conditions under which it will function, and set criteria to be met during testing. For most commercial systems where safety is a consideration, there has been considerable testing to ensure that the automation performs to its specified requirements. In the preceding accident examples, the automation performed exactly as designed; in no case was there a failure of the automation itself. The problem is in the interface of the automation with the human operator and, in some cases, with the other systems of the aircraft. It has even been claimed that automation has been most successful in producing dramatic increases in productivity when it completely removes the human operator from any role other than turning it on (Landauer, 1996). If true, then the introduction of systems that automatically parallel-park an automobile will be a resounding success, as many people find this a daunting problem and are happy to be rid of it.

Automation of a function is intended to reduce the role of the human. However, the functions that are automated often are a subset of those originally carried out by the user. The term *partial automation* is used in this case. The term *full automation* is used in cases where the automation replaces a large functional unit that the operator would consider a complete task. Cruise control is a partial automation of the function of speed control. Speed control requires the maintenance of the desired speed, the detection of when that speed is no longer appropriate, and the adjustment of speed to the appropriate level. Cruise control automates only the maintenance of speed, leaving the rest to the driver.

Partial automation is problematic for two reasons. First, it leaves a remnant of an integrated task as the responsibility of the human operator, creating the need for the operator to redefine a formerly well-understood function, and to remember where the responsibility of the automation ends. Second, partial automation by its nature is piecemeal; it automates a subset of function but does not integrate its control into the larger set of functions needed to meet overall system goals. The result is that while the operator has been relieved of active control, a simple repetitive perceptual-manual task, the automation has created the new need to explicitly consider the state of the automated subsystem when deciding on action, a resource-demanding task. Too often, there are few salient visual reminders of state on which to rely.

Issues with the changed operator role created by partial automation have arisen in part because the decisions of what to automate have been driven largely by what *can* be automated (Parasuraman & Wickens, 2008; Sarter & Woods, 1995; Sarter et al., 1997; Wiener, 1985; Wiener & Curry, 1980). This is almost inevitable given the complexity of systems and how their components interrelate. We can illustrate how automation is introduced, progresses, and creates difficulties for the operator by returning to the cruise-control incident. Recall that in that incident, one of the authors (Degani) depressed the accelerator while in cruise control and maintained speed control manually until departing the freeway. An accident nearly ensued when the car did not slow as expected entering the curve, but reasserted the speed for which the cruise control had been previously set.

Speed control represents one small component of the driving task. The automobile is typical of complex systems in that it is a collection of physical devices with differing degrees of linkage or coupling between them serving different system functions. Tightly coupled physical devices are often thought of as a separate mechanical subsystem associated with a single function. For example, the steering wheel serves the function of altering the angle of the tires acting through connections with the steering column, which in turn connects to the axle through a differential gear. The accelerator controls the speed of the car by determining the rate at which the tires rotate. Altering pressure on the accelerator alters the fuel flow into the engine, causing it to change its power output, which in turn is translated into rotation rate of the tires through linkages that involve the transmission, driveshaft, and axle. At the physical level, then, steering and propulsion constitute largely independent systems that serve distinct functions. As we have discussed in the treatment of task analysis methods, these functions can be expressed as a nested hierarchy. Driving, for example, can be decomposed into subtasks, one of which would be vehicle maneuvering (navigation might be another). Maneuvering might consist of subtasks for keeping within the lateral bounds of the lane, maintaining desired speed, avoiding contact with the car in front, and safely executing turns. In this context, current cruise-control devices are examples of partial automation of a low-level subtask: they automate speed maintenance, but leave all other functions to the driver.

Speed maintenance was one of the first automobile functions to be computer controlled. It provides a clear benefit to the driver. By restricting control to speed maintenance, the cruise control system requires inputs from the driver only for setting the speed, and it uses the same information as the driver to maintain the setting (the speedometer). The formal relationship between accelerator depression and speed change is more complicated, but mathematically tractable. The upshot is a system that replaces a psychomotor action (foot depression on the accelerator), relieving the operator of the tiring constant physical exertion. But notice how, as revealed by the incident, it is necessary for the driver now to remember what state the cruise control is in: active or inactive. Unless there is a highly salient visual cue to this, it can easily be overlooked.

Automation of subsystem functions often results in control that is independent of other subsystems. While at the physical level the systems have a great many independent linkages, couplings emerge at the functional level in carrying out tasks. In the car, as an example, the mechanical elements of the steering subsystem are independent of those for the velocity subsystem. There is a functional coupling that emerges when making a turn. The car will only be stable at some speeds given the angle of the tires. Because it has no information on the state of sharp turns or systems in the car, the cruise control will attempt to maintain its speed setting even in conditions where it would constitute a danger. The China Air 006 accident is an example of this type of system behavior.

With improvements in computers and algorithms, automation naturally extends to larger task units. The introduction of laser-guided ranging for automobiles now makes it possible to automate distance keeping, changing the automation of speed maintenance into partial automated control of automobile separation. Such systems are collectively known as Adaptive Cruise Control (ACC; Stanton, Young, & McCaulder, 1997). Now, notice that ACC is qualitatively different from the simple computerization of a low-level function. The automation is now making real-time decisions about what the speed of the car should be and adjusting the speed without asking or informing the driver. In a small but tangible way, the driver's role has changed from direct control of the car to *supervisory control*. In supervisory control, the operator relinquishes direct control authority to automated equipment and takes the role of manager of the automated system(s). Supervisory control, like automation, can be implemented fully or partially. Thus, operators may have direct control of some subsystems and supervisory control of others. In the cockpit, the introduction of automation has dramatically increased the supervisory control role for the crew. The flight management systems in modern aircraft can control not only the propulsion system and control surfaces (the horizontal stabilizer, ailerons, and rudder that determine pitch, roll, and yaw, respectively), but can also automatically initiate course changes in response to the programmed flight plan. The crew in modern transport aircraft takes direct control of the aircraft predominantly during takeoff, landing, and emergency conditions.

A TAXONOMY OF AUTOMATION LEVELS

Direct control over physical subsystems is only one level of control, that is associated with the execution of an action plan. Recall from our discussion of control theory that control operates in a continuous loop: The controller sets a goal, processes sensory information regarding the state of the system with respect to that goal, decides on a plan of action with respect to that goal, executes that action, and begins the loop again by perceiving the effect of that action. A higher level of control is associated with the selection of the immediate plan of action. At that level, the controller determines what the current rate of speed of rotation and angle of the tires should be; that is, to determine how fast the car should be going and how much it should be turning. Note that these levels of control are still associated with the immediate state of the system. A higher level of control is concerned with the state of the automobile in the near future, determining which of several paths the automobile should take to reach its destination (goal). At the highest level of control is the determination of what that destination should be.

The scope and nature of automation vary with the level of control. Current cruise control automates at the lowest level, action execution. Adaptive cruise control systems that adjust speed to keep a safe distance behind the leading car demonstrate partial automation at the level of immediate state. It determines what speed the car should be going regardless of the driver's desired speed. The flight management system used in aircraft partially automates at an even higher level, making decisions about the route the aircraft will take next, based on the way in which it has been programmed. In this progression from lower to higher levels of automation, more decision-making responsibility is being given to the automated system.

The fact that automation has been introduced at multiple levels of control has given rise to concern over the desirability and consequences of various *levels of automation*. Level of control should not be confused with level of automation. *Level of control* refers to the hierarchy of tasks the operator must perform. The level of automation, as typically used, corresponds more to the *control authority* discussed in conjunction with the cruise-control example. *Authority* refers to the power to control the future state of the system. Thus, the level of automation refers to the level of control authority, not to the level of system function.

The discussion of levels of automation typically includes a treatment not just of control authority, but also of how the automation communicates its intent or action to the human operator. Table 16.1 illustrates the concept of level of automation by depicting a range from low to high. We have indicated four distinct levels, but this is arbitrary, and more extensive treatments use ten or more (Parasuraman, Sheridan, & Wickens, 2000; for related discussions, see also Kantowitz & Sorkin, 1983; Parasuraman & Riley, 1997; Parasuraman, Mouloua, & Hilburn, 1999). In one column we list the authority, which indicates the degree to which the automation has the ability to take action without consulting the human operator. In the next column we list the communication, which indicates the degree to which the automation informs the human operator as to its intent or its action. The two bottom levels—Complete Manual, Automation Suggests Alternatives—correspond to cases in which the human operator is still in direct control and may be assisted by the automation in some way. The upper two—Automation Consults, Automation Acts—represent cases in which the human operator exercises supervisory control.

A complete taxonomy must also indicate the nature of the function the automation is replacing. We refer to this as the *stage of automation* in reference to the kinds of human information processing it replaces. In terms of the structure of human information processing, automation can replace functions previously done by human perception, encoding, attention, response selection, response execution, and working memory (goals).

Table 16.1 Levels of Automation.

LEVEL OF AUTOMATION	CONTROL AUTHORITY	OPERATOR-AUTOMATION COMMUNICATION
High	**Automation Acts:** Operator not informed prior to system action by automation	Operator can request information from automation, but automation does not routinely inform operator
	Automation Consults: Automation selects action, presents it to human operator, may act if urgency dictates	Automation presents planned action to operator; will respond to user inquiries if capable
	Automation Suggests Alternatives: Automation has no authority to act, only to supply information or actions for consideration	Automation detects system state and presents information and action options to operator
Low	**Complete Manual:** Automation plays no role, or can be used if explicitly initiated by operator	Automation does not initiate communication, but will supply information requested by operator (if capable)

Source: Abbreviated scheme based on Parasuraman et al. (2000).

These mental stages have been grouped into four functional *stages of automation*: information acquisition, information analysis, decision selection, and action implementation (Parasuraman et al., 2000). These correspond to the functional stages in control theory that turn incoming sensory signals into executable actions.

Automation at the level of *action implementation* replaces motor activity associated with response execution in the structure of human information processing. The cruise control is a good example of this. On modern military jet fighter aircraft, as well as the former space shuttle, sophisticated computer control at this level—referred to as fly-by-wire—actually determines the instantaneous position of the control surfaces of the aircraft. In these cases the control surfaces must be moved more rapidly than a human pilot could possibly achieve. In such cases, there is no need to inform the pilot every time a control action is taken.

Automation of *information acquisition* is meant to replace higher-order perceptual processing, and can reduce demands on sensory attention. This level of automation involves directing the user's attention to important information by various highlighting techniques, with the raw data being preserved.

Automation of the *information analysis* stage tries to relieve the operator of the resource-demanding central processing operations associated with working memory operations and decision making, as well as to ease demands on visual attention (for example, by replacing raw data with highly encoded data representations). An example of this is the heat map that shows temperature across a surface by color, or the views of stars and galaxies that use color to represent the frequencies of light emitted. High levels of automation at this stage can help ease the workload on operators and improve their efficiency by replacing resource-demanding central processing with less demanding and more robust perceptual processing. For example, it would be more efficient to automate the integration of information from several different sources, turning a resource-demanding task into a perceptual task. Highway-in-the-Sky prototypes exemplify this (Beringer, 2000). They help pilots determine if they are on the correct flight path, or descent path for landing, by presenting a visual tunnel for the aircraft to fly through. The tunnel is computed by combining the desired heading, airspeed, and descent rate. Visualizations produced by automation at the information-analysis level can provide good support for recognition-primed decision making.

Automation at the level of *decision selection* tries to relieve the operator of the resource-demanding stages of processing associated with response selection and decision making. One way in which this could benefit operator decision making is for the computer to calculate the numerical costs and benefits associated with various outcomes. By presenting this information to the operator, we may reduce the impact of human decision biases and heuristics, such as not making use of base rate information or being influenced by the verbal descriptions.

AUTOMATION AS A DECISION SUPPORT AID

In the preceding discussion, we focused on the role of the automated device in the active control of a dynamic system, such as a car or airplane. More typically, automation is being used as a support for what people do, providing information or guidance rather than taking active control. We tend not to think of the modern Internet search engines as automation, but they implement highly sophisticated inference algorithms that attempt to relate your interest, as stated in the search query, to items in their enormous databases. They then collate these, select the most relevant, and present it as a list that you can scroll through. This corresponds roughly to Level 2, in which the automation presents options to the user from which to select. The search engine does not decide what you should look for or which of the returned options you should pursue. It does not automatically open documents that it thinks are valuable or divert you to pages. It does the low-level work of intelligently sifting through massive databases, freeing you of routine tedious activity but leaving the decisions to you.

A similar support role for automation is present in aviation. Air traffic controllers are frequently put in high-workload situations in which they must take various actions regarding multiple aircraft. They clear aircraft to enter their sectors, hand aircraft off to downstream sectors, maintain separation between aircraft, intervene when conflicts arise, communicate with aircraft about weather or other relevant airspace properties, respond to the requests of flight crews, and respond to emergency situations. Automated systems are slowly being introduced that relieve the controllers of the most routine tasks. There are now automated handoff systems that reduce the actions the controller must perform on departing aircraft. Data Link capabilities (sending clearances to the aircraft by computer rather than over the voice channel) will provide automated upload of new heading, airspeed, and altitude commands.

When used to support operator decisions, what features characterize automated systems that operators find useful and beneficial, and distinguish them from those that are problematic? Some insight into this question can be achieved by examining the use of conflict detection probes in air traffic control. Conflict detection and resolution present a particularly time-consuming task in which controllers must reason in four-dimensional space, taking account of altitude, latitude, longitude, and time to determine which aircraft are likely to violate required separation distance and which solutions are to be used to solve the potential conflict without creating other problems (Loft, Bolland, Humphreys, & Neal, 2009). It is an inherently difficult problem, and automated conflict probes to support air traffic controllers in the detection and resolution of conflicts have been under development in many laboratories over many years. One such device, the User Request Evaluation Tool (URET) is now in operational use in the U.S. airspace (Kerns, 2001; Kerns & McFarland, 1998). URET aids air traffic controllers by implementing algorithms that will automatically detect aircraft predicted to violate minimum separation and determine efficient maneuvers to avoid the conflict.

At present, URET functions at Level 2 in the levels-of-automation scale in Table 16.1. It detects conflicts automatically and places the target aircraft in a conflict list on the screen along with relevant flight data. URET maintains a list of active conflict pairs. Controllers can request solutions or explore their own solutions. The flexibility of the option to query the system means that authority and control continue to reside with the human controller. This perhaps accounts for its success in receiving favorable ratings from controllers on acceptability, benefit to safety in the airspace, and workload management (Kerns, 2001; Kerns & McFarland, 1998). The URET example also shows how automation can function at multiple stages and why the classification of stages should be a dimension separate from the automation level. With respect to its detection of potential conflicts, URET functions as an aid to information analysis. It integrates data on wind, aircraft trajectory (heading, altitude, speed, climb/descent rate), and airspace conditions into a projection of the probability of conflict within the next 20 minutes. It then presents that information to the controller. With respect to its ability to select routes that will resolve the potential conflict, URET functions as an aid at the decision-selection stage. It can assess the cost (e.g., fuel, time) of various maneuvers and the likelihood that a maneuver will produce a later conflict that will need further controller action, relieving the controller of the burden of using that central processing resources that would be needed for these determinations (for a detailed discussion of conflict probes, see Kuchar & Yang, 2000). In both of these capacities, URET remains an advisory tool at Level 2.

The interactive flexibility provided by URET appears to be an important ingredient in the success of an automated decision aid. Evidence for this can be seen in attempts to provide automated aids to doctors for diagnosing and treating patients. These systems are referred to variously as computer-based decision support systems, computerized clinical decision support systems, or clinical decision support systems, all abbreviated CDSS. Many different kinds of CDSS systems are employed for a variety of medical purposes. Reviews of a range of systems (e.g., Fieschi, Dufour, Staccini, Gouvernet, & Bouhaddou, 2003; Garg et al., 2005; Hajioff, 1998; Kaplan, 2001) contain listings of the features and general characteristics that doctors find helpful, have proven beneficial to patient care, and have gained acceptance. Many CDSS systems function at Level 2 automation, aiding in information acquisition by searching multiple databases for responses matching a doctor's query. Such systems have come into widespread use, but are limited in that the information they provide is not specific to an individual patient. There is as yet no documented proof of direct improvements to patient care (Hajioff, 1998). Other systems provide online support to aid the doctor in diagnosing a condition and selecting treatment options for a specific patient. The most common mode is to provide information or recommendations for action when queried, conforming to Level 2. There are alerting systems in wide use that automatically generate and send reports when they detect specific conditions in a patient's records related to laboratory test results, drug therapy, or other medical data stored in computerized databases, or to remind doctors that a patient should be seen (Garg et al., 2005; Hajioff, 1998; Kaplan, 2001; Shortliffe, 1987).

It can be difficult to determine the direct benefit of these systems. Several reports cite a reduction in drug dosage errors and closer adherence to standard procedure (see Hajioff, 1998). Subjective scoring of doctor performance shows that use of CDSSs yielded improvements of 60–70 percent, depending on the specific application (Garg et al., 2005; Hajioff, 1998). Doctor satisfaction with advisory systems, however, is seldom addressed; concern over patient outcomes is more often used as the primary measure of success. When doctors have been asked what kind of support they would find useful (Hajioff, 1998), the highest scores went to a comprehensive database of drug information (95 percent) and automatic monitoring of patient records (93 percent), both of which now exist as Level 2 systems. Early systems met with resistance because the manual data entry required that a doctor interrupt the normal pattern of patient interaction, were too slow, and made errors hard to correct (see, e.g., Shortliffe, 1987). In general, acceptance of systems depends in large part on those systems not producing extra activities that interfere with normal duties, or are not seen as necessary to achieving the goal (patient care in this instance).

It is interesting that in all the studies reviewing evaluations of CDSS systems, the poorest ratings go to automatic aids to diagnosis. There has been success with CDSS systems that aid in comprehending medical images (e.g., Doi, 2007) and automate the search through patient medical records to detect illness patterns (e.g., Lazarus, Kleinman, Dashevsky, DeMaria, & Platt, 2001). Automated biopsy, in the absence of an attending pathologist, has also been shown to have success rates comparable to those of human physicians (Tsukada, Satou, Iwashima, & Souma, 2000). These success stories are cases in which the aid is really in interpreting a diagnostic test. CDSS systems have been less successful at the task facing most doctors: inferring and identifying the underlying disease from a set of observations. According to one survey (Hajioff, 1998), doctors rated the desirability of an aid to diagnosis relatively high (81 percent). Diagnosis is difficult and misdiagnosis is a common medical error.

The reasons for the low ratings are complex, but may relate in part to the poor performance of such systems (Hajioff, 1998; Kaplan, 2001; Wickens & Dixon, 2007). Aids to diagnosis take input from the doctor about symptoms, preexisting conditions, laboratory test results, and other medical data as input into a computer algorithm that attempts to infer the underlying condition giving rise to these observations. In the *expert-system* approach, a set of if-then rules manipulates knowledge in a large database of medical conditions and their associated symptoms, frequency of occurrence, at-risk populations, and other information. In *probabilistic systems*, the weight of evidence of each piece of information for each possible disease is assessed, typically using the Bayes Theorem to optimally combine the evidence. In both cases, the CDSS returns a diagnosis or set of possible diagnoses. Unlike the Level 2 systems that respond to user queries, the attending physician cannot query the system about the reasons for its choices. In the probabilistic systems, for example, the "reason" for the outcome is just the calculation of likelihood from a set of weights linking symptom to disease.

In a sense, these CDSS systems try to implement a kind of *collaborative decision making* in which the doctor and the CDSS both have hypotheses. This resembles the situation in which peers collaborate at the decision selection stage, in contrast to the information-analysis support provided by the more highly rated CDSS systems. In Level 2 or Level 3 advisory systems, the user remains in control. The automated system provides assistance by performing an integration of information that is highly accurate and reliable. In contrast, there is often much more uncertainty in medical inference, going from symptoms to diagnosis. For the expert system or Bayesian CDSS to be useful, it would have to be much more flexible in communication and able to "discuss" the situation with the physician. Without that ability, the physician will have difficulty knowing what to do with a diagnosis from the CDSS that differs from her own.

The accuracy of the automation appears to play a central role in whether the human operator (doctor, pilot, nuclear plant operator) will use the automation. Lee and Moray (1992, 1994) had subjects learn to control a simulated juice pasteurization plant. The plant was complex, consisting of three dynamic component systems, which were independent with couplings in the outcome. Subjects could control the entire plant or any of the three subsystems manually or automatically. In automatic mode they switched on an automated system that kept production at a high level. The interest was in how subjects would allocate functions to their own manual control or the automated system, and what effect the introduction of faults to one or more systems would have on this allocation policy. The results showed that when faults occurred in manual mode, subjects allocated function to the automation, and when faults occurred in the automated operation they tended to take control manually.

The results also suggest that multiple components affect when operators will use automation. If their own self-confidence is high, participants tend to assume manual control. As faults occur (even when those faults are not the result of their own errors), they begin to lose self-confidence and rely more on automation. The converse is also true. If the faults occur while in automated mode, trust in automation is reduced and participants are more likely to take manual control. The relationship of *self-confidence* to *trust in automation* appears to influence the use of automation. This conclusion is supported by a review of 20 previous studies assessing the costs and benefits of automation to support medical diagnosis (Wickens & Dixon, 2007). They observed that across the 20 studies, there was a correlation of 0.7 between the benefit and the reported reliability of the automation; doctors tended to use and to trust the diagnostic CDSS as it became more reliable. One study found that the introduction of an automated aid to conflict detection in simulated air traffic control operations reduced workload and improved conflict detection performance when reliable, but manual detection was better when the automation was unreliable (Metzger & Parasuraman, 2005).

In summary, automation has shown to be of benefit when it provides accurate integration of information or when it aids in the computationally demanding analysis of costs and benefits. Successful systems combine high accuracy with flexible interactive interfaces that allow the user access to information that would otherwise be time-consuming to acquire. Ratings appear to be very sensitive to accuracy. The systems rated lowest in studies of medical CDSSs were those for diagnosis and treatment guidelines, which also had the lowest validity.

AUTOMATION AND SYSTEM SAFETY

In the preceding section we discussed issues regarding the ability of human operators to work effectively with automated devices. We now turn our attention to the question of whether automation has the potential to jeopardize system safety in either the short term or the long term. In addition to the safety benefits of automation, which are well documented and acknowledged even by its critics (e.g., Charette, 2011; FAA Human Factors Team, 1996; Garg et al., 2005; Hajioff, 1998; Parasuraman & Riley, 1997; Parasuraman & Wickens, 2008; Sarter & Woods et al., 1994; Stanton et al., 1997; Wiener, 1985; Wiener & Curry, 1980), the nature of automated systems can increase the potential for certain kinds of errors. Earlier we discussed the potential of automated systems to induce postcompletion and prospective memory errors. It can also amplify the consequences of small slips, or mistakes.

In automated systems, errors in input can lead to disproportionate errors in the output. In a continuous system, errors tend to cluster near the norm. When you throw darts, shoot arrows, or tune radios, errors are usually clustered around the intended goal in a normal distribution. This is not the case when programming a digital device. If I intend to type the sentence "He languished in port" to describe a sailor waiting in a harbor, but instead mistakenly type "He languished in porn," the simple substitution of one letter makes a vast difference in the outcome. In fact, the intended meaning cannot easily be inferred given the mistake, whereas the intended target can often be inferred from a regular pattern of errors. A more serious example concerns the 1984 downing of Korean Airlines (KAL) Flight 007 over Soviet airspace. A number of conspiracy theories exist in which KAL 007 was actually on a spy mission, which is the official Russian version. There is no doubt that the aircraft was 300 miles or more off course, well within Soviet airspace. However, a strong case can be made that the cause was an error in programming or use of the Inertial Navigation System, a computer tool for flying precise routes between selected waypoints. It could have been as simple as incorrectly keying in the initial position of the aircraft before take-off, or incorrectly keying in an intended waypoint along the route (Wiener, 1985).

Note that the KAL 007 accident was also associated with a failure to adequately monitor the situation. The crew failed to monitor not only the automation, but the aircraft's flight path as well. Such behavior highlights two other issues with highly automated systems: *complacency* and *lack of situation awareness*. The introduction of automation by its nature removes the human operator from direct interactive control, and more often than not leaves her to monitor the automation in supervisory control mode. *Complacency* refers to the reliance on the assumption that the automation was correctly set and that its actions will not endanger the system. Such attitudes lead to an overreliance on automation that underlies the concept of complacency (Parasuraman & Riley, 1997; Sarter & Woods, 1994; Wiener, 1985; Wiener & Curry, 1980). The potential for complacency is increased as the reliability of the automation increases—the very property that encourages its use.

The high reliability of automated systems itself creates difficulties when human operators are in the mode of supervisory control. In Chapter 15 we described the poor performance of human subjects in vigilance conditions—conditions in which target stimuli occurred very infrequently. In those experiments, subjects may receive 3–10 targets per hour out of perhaps 1,000 trials, or a rate of about 0.3–1 percent. In the cockpit, failures or even errors are much less frequent. Given that the automation itself is highly reliable, failures are most often complex interactions between the automation, human expectations, and other system components. This complexity is more troublesome because the automation often does not provide useful or detectable feedback about important aspects of its state. In 1972, an Eastern Airlines L-1011 aircraft was on approach to Miami. When the crew put the landing gear down, the light indicating that the gear was down-and-locked failed to illuminate. The crew was directed to a holding pattern to work on the problem and set the aircraft to autopilot while they concentrated on the landing gear. At one point they attempted to manually deploy and lock the landing gear, which required access via a panel in the floor of the cockpit. It is speculated that in doing so, one of the crew must have bumped the control yoke, causing the autopilot to turn off. Under the assumption that the autopilot was in control, the three crewmembers continued to diagnose the landing-gear problem. With the autopilot off, the aircraft began a slow descent, eventually crashing in the Everglades with significant loss of life. The problem with the landing gear was a faulty light. The highly reliable past performance of the autopilot had led the crew to become complacent about its performance; it led them to become overconfident in their expectation that they would not have to monitor the autopilot too closely (Wiener, 1985; Wiener & Curry, 1980).

This example also highlights the way in which complacency and overconfidence in the automation can lead to loss of situation awareness (SA), through operators' failure to monitor the automation when in supervisory control mode. It is well known that vigilance tasks lead to changes in detection performance. In signal detection terms, the criteria for detecting a signal shifts rightward toward the signal distribution, causing an increase in misses with a decrease in false alarms. If the operator and the automation are both "in control" of some function, then the strong tendency will be for the operator to reduce the rate at which that function is sampled when the automation is highly reliable (Sorkin & Woods, 1985). This can be seen in a simulation study by Sarter, Mumaw, and Wickens (2007), who recorded the eye fixation pattern of experienced Boeing 747 pilots as they flew a demanding simulated mission within a highly automated cockpit. They found that pilots fixated primary flight indicators to a far greater extent than they fixated the mode indicators of the automated system. Errors can often be traced to a failure to fixate specific equipment (for an example using automation, see Metzger & Parasuraman, 2001a). Interestingly, in these examples, and others in which automation reliability has been manipulated, high levels of automation lead to fewer errors, faster decisions, and lower workload when the automation is highly reliable. Wickens and Dixon (2007) observed that a reliability of 0.7 was a crossover point after which automated medical diagnosis aids began to show benefit.

Decreased monitoring of automation in supervisory control mode is one factor contributing to decreased situation awareness. Overreliance on automation can also lead to failures to attend to other systems. This is evident in the crash of Northwest Flight 255, a DC-9, on takeoff from Detroit in 1987. Typically, the crew executes a checklist prior to takeoff to see that the aircraft is properly configured for takeoff. There is also an automated warning system that alerts the crew when it detects an initiation of takeoff without the aircraft having been properly configured, including having the flaps down in the appropriate position. In the case of Northwest 255, an electrical failure disabled the automated system, while confusion over a missed taxiway distracted the crew from setting the flaps appropriately. The airplane crashed on takeoff because it could not generate enough lift without the flaps being down. The NTSB report (National Transportation Safety Board, 1988) found that a reliance on the automated alerting system contributed to a lack of awareness of the configuration of the aircraft.

Loss of SA, complacency, and human failures in vigilance tasks that require monitoring for infrequent events will always be threats to safety, with or without automation. Although automation by its nature puts the human operator in a vulnerable position with respect to these tendencies, the most important factor is the design of the automation and its integration with information displays. Nevertheless, direct comparisons of manual and automated operations show that reliable automation leads to improvements in SA (Endsley, 1999) and other measures of performance (Galster, Duley, Masalonis, & Parasuraman, 2001; Ganster et al., 2001; Garg et al., 2005; Metzger & Parasuraman, 2001a, 2001b; Parasuraman & Wickens, 2008; Parasuraman et al., 2000; Sarter et al., 2007; Sheridan & Parasuraman, 2005; Wickens & Dixon, 2007; Wiener, 1985; Wiener & Curry, 1980). The common theme expressed in a range of studies is that high reliability must be coupled with salient indicators of the state of the automation (FAA Human Factors Team, 1996; Parasuraman & Riley, 1997).

SUMMARY

Automation has found its way into most systems with which humans interact. In large part, the introduction of automation has in fact led to many benefits. However, although the goal in implementing automation is typically to reduce accidents and lower workload for human operators, it often does not meet that goal. Although automation has largely accomplished both the goals of improved safety and reduced workload, it has also introduced its own new challenges for operators. This chapter described some of the problems that users encounter when interacting with automation, discussed a taxonomy of levels of automation, and described the impact that full versus partial automation is likely to have on performance. We gave examples of how automation can be used to support decision making, along with examples of some of the problems that have arisen from the use of automation in complex systems.

REFERENCES

Adams, M. J., Tenney, Y. J., & Pew, R. W. (1995). Situation awareness and the cognitive management of complex systems. *Human Factors: The Journal of the Human Factors and Ergonomics Society*, *37*(1), 85–104. doi:10.1518/001872095779049462

Andre, A., & Degani, A. (1997). Do you know what mode you're in? An analysis of mode error in everyday things. *Human-automation interaction: Research & practice* (pp. 19–28). Mahwah, NJ: Lawrence Erlbaum.

Aviation Safety Network. (1992). *ASN aircraft accident Airbus A320-111 F-GGED Strasbourg-Entzheim Airport (SXB)*. Retrieved September 12, 2011, from http://aviation-safety.net/database/record.php?id=19920120-0

Barach, P., & Small, S. D. (2000). Reporting and preventing medical mishaps: Lessons from non-medical near miss reporting systems. *British Medical Journal, 320*(7237), 759.

Beringer, D. B. (2000). Development of highway-in-the-sky displays for flight path guidance: History, performance results, guidelines. *Human Factors and Ergonomics Society Annual Meeting Proceedings, 44*, 21–24.

Charette, R. (2011, September 6). How serious are the air safety concerns being raised in the press? *IEEE Spectrum*. Retrieved September 12, 2011, from http://spectrum.ieee.org/riskfactor/aerospace/aviation/how-serious-are-the-air-safety-concerns-being-raised

Doi, K. (2007). Computer-aided diagnosis in medical imaging: Historical review, current status and future potential. *Computerized Medical Imaging and Graphics, 31*(4–5), 198–211.

Dolak, K. (2011, August 31). "Automation addiction": Are pilots forgetting how to fly?—ABC News. Retrieved September 12, 2011, from http://abcnews.go.com/Technology/automation-addiction-pilots-forgetting-fly/story?id=14417730

Endsley, M. R. (1996). Automation and situation awareness. In R. Parasuraman & M. Mouloua (Eds.), *Automation and human performance: Theory and applications* (pp. 163–181). Mahwah, NJ: Lawrence Erlbaum Associates.

Endsley, M. R. (1999). Situation awareness in aviation systems. In D. J. Garland, J. A. Wise, & V. D. Hopkin (Eds.), *Handbook of aviation human factors*. Mahwah, NJ: Lawrence Erlbaum Associates.

FAA Human Factors Team. (1996). *Report on the interfaces between flightcrews and modern flight deck systems*. Washington, DC: Federal Aviation Administration.

Fieschi, M., Dufour, J. C., Staccini, P., Gouvernet, J., & Bouhaddou, O. (2003). Medical decision support systems: Old dilemmas and new paradigms. *Methods of Information in Medicine, 42*(3), 190–198.

Galster, S. M., Duley, J. A., Masalonis, A. J., & Parasuraman, R. (2001). Air traffic controller performance and workload under mature free flight: Conflict detection and resolution of aircraft self-separation. *International Journal of Aviation Psychology, 11*(1), 71–93.

Ganster, H., Pinz, P., Rohrer, R., Wildling, E., Binder, M., & Kittler, H. (2001). Automated melanoma recognition. *IEEE Transactions on Medical Imaging, 20*(3), 233–239.

Garg, A. X., Adhikari, N. K., McDonald, H., Rosas-Arellano, M. P., Devereaux, P. J., Beyene, J., Sam, J., et al. (2005). Effects of computerized clinical decision support systems on practitioner performance and patient outcomes. *JAMA: The Journal of the American Medical Association, 293*(10), 1223.

Green, R. (1990). Human error on the flight deck. *Philosophical Transactions of the Royal Society of London. Series B, Biological Sciences, 327*(1241), 503–511.

Hajioff, S. (1998). Computerized decision support systems: An overview. *Health Informatics Journal, 4*(1), 23–28. doi:10.1177/146045829800400104

Kantowitz, B. H., & Sorkin, R. D. (1983). *Human factors: Understanding people-system relationships*. New York, NY: Wiley.

Kaplan, B. (2001). Evaluating informatics applications: Clinical decision support systems literature review. *International Journal of Medical Informatics, 64*(1), 15–37.

Kerns, K. (2001). An experimental approach to measuring the effects of a controller conflict probe in a free routing environment. *IEEE Transactions on Intelligent Transportation Systems, 2*(2), 81–91.

Kerns, K., & McFarland, A. L. (1998). Conflict probe operational evaluation and benefits assessment. *MITRE Technical Report Number MP 98W0000239*. McLean, VA: The MITRE Corporation. Retrieved from http://atmseminar.eurocontrol.fr/past-seminars/2nd-seminar-orlando-fl-usa-december-1998/papers/paper_027

Kuchar, J. K., & Yang, L. C. (2000). A review of conflict detection and resolution modeling methods. *IEEE Transactions on Intelligent Transportation Systems, 1*(4), 179–189.

Landauer, T. K. (1996). *The trouble with computers: Usefulness, usability, and productivity*. Cambridge, MA: MIT Press.

Lazarus, R., Kleinman, K., Dashevsky, I., DeMaria, A., & Platt, R. (2001). Using automated medical records for rapid identification of illness syndromes (syndromic surveillance): The example of lower respiratory infection. *BMC Public Health, 1*(1), 9.

Lee, J. D., & Moray, N. (1992). Trust, control strategies and allocation of function in human-machine systems. *Ergonomics, 35*(10), 1243–1270. doi:10.1080/00140139208967392

Lee, J. D., & Moray, N. (1994). Trust, self-confidence, and operators' adaptation to automation. *International Journal of Human-Computer Studies, 40*, 153–184.

Loft, S., Bolland, S., Humphreys, M. S., & Neal, A. (2009). A theory and model of conflict detection in air traffic control: Incorporating environmental constraints. *Journal of Experimental Psychology: Applied, 15*(2), 106.

Lowy, J. (2011, August 30). AP IMPACT: Automation in the air dulls pilot skill. Retrieved September 12, 2011, from www.google.com/hostednews/ap/article/ALeqM5gdmYSGPD7TdQa-QsiKHXDoTd_uaA?docId=a4e56bdd941949d9b5f711277b56bdf5

Metzger, U., & Parasuraman, R. (2001a). Conflict detection aids for air traffic controllers in free flight: Effect of reliable and failure modes on performance and eye movements. *Proceedings of the 11th International Symposium on Aviation Psychology*. Columbus, OH: The Ohio State University.

Metzger, U., & Parasuraman, R. (2001b). The role of the air traffic controller in future air traffic management: An empirical study of active control versus passive monitoring. *Human Factors, 43*, 519–528.

Metzger, U., & Parasuraman, R. (2005). Automation in future air traffic management: Effects of decision aid reliability on controller performance and mental workload. *Human Factors, 47*, 35–49.

Miller, C. A., & Parasuraman, R. (2007). Designing for flexible interaction between humans and automation: Delegation interfaces for supervisory control. *Human Factors: The Journal of the Human Factors and Ergonomics Society, 49*(1), 57.

Nagel, D. C. (1989). Human error in aviation operations. In E. L. Wiener & D. Nagel (Eds.) *Human Factors in Aviation* (pp. 263–304). New York, NY: Academic Press.

National Transportation Safety Board. (1986). *Aircraft accident report—China Airlines Boeing 747-SP, N4522V, 300 Nautical Miles Northwest of San Francisco, California, February 19. 1985* (No. NTSB/AAR-86/03). Retrieved from www.rvs.uni-bielefeld.de/publications/Incidents/DOCS/ComAndRep/ChinaAir/AAR8603.html

National Transportation Safety Board. (1988). *Aircraft accident report: Northwest Airlines, Inc., McDonnell Douglas DC-9-82, N312RC, Detroit Metropolitan Wayne County Airport, Romulus, Michigan, August 16, 1987* (National Transportation Safety Board No. NTSB/AAR-88/05). Washington, DC: NTSB.

Parasuraman, R., Mouloua, M., & Hilburn, B. (1999). Adaptive aiding and adaptive task allocation enhance human-machine interaction. *Automation Technology and Human Performance: Current Research and Trends*, 119–123.

Parasuraman, R., & Riley, V. (1997). Humans and automation: Use, misuse, disuse, abuse. *Human Factors: The Journal of the Human Factors and Ergonomics Society, 39*(2), 230–253.

Parasuraman, R., Sheridan, T. B., & Wickens, C. D. (2000). A model for types and levels of human interaction with automation. *IEEE Transactions on Systems, Man and Cybernetics, Part A: Systems and Humans, 30*(3), 286–297.

Parasuraman, R., & Wickens, C. D. (2008). Humans: Still vital after all these years of automation. *Human Factors: The Journal of the Human Factors and Ergonomics Society, 50*(3), 511.

Reuters. (2009, February 13). FACTBOX—Recent fatal airplane crashes in United States. Retrieved September 12, 2011, from http://uk.reuters.com/article/2009/02/13/uk-crash-plane-incidents-sb-idUKTRE51C4HL20090213

Risto, M., Martens, M., & Wilschut, E. (2010). Introduction to the connected cruise control and related human factors considerations. 23–24 November, Delft. In T. P. Alkim & T. Arentze e.a. (Eds.), 11th Trail Congress Connecting People - Integrating Expertise, 23 and 24 November 2010. (on CD-ROM). Delft: TRAIL (ISBN 978-90-5584-139-4).

Sarter, N. B., Mumaw, R. J., & Wickens, C. D. (2007). Pilots' monitoring strategies and performance on automated flight decks: An empirical study combining behavioral and eye-tracking data. *Human Factors: The Journal of the Human Factors and Ergonomics Society, 49*(3), 347.

Sarter, N. B., & Woods, D. D. (1994). Pilot interaction with cockpit automation II: An experimental study of pilots' model and awareness of the flight management system. *International Journal of Aviation Psychology*, *4*(1), 1–28. doi:10.1207/s15327108ijap0401_1

Sarter, N. B., & Woods, D. D. (1995). How in the world did we ever get into that mode: Mode error and awareness in supervisory control. *Human Factors*, *37*, 5–19.

Sarter, N. B., & Woods, D. D. (1997). Team play with a powerful and independent agent: Operational experiences and automation surprises on the Airbus A-320. *Human Factors*, *39*, 553–569.

Sarter, N. B., Woods, D. D., & Billings, C. E. (1997). Automation surprises. *Handbook of Human Factors and Ergonomics*, *2*, 1926–1943.

Sheridan, T. B., & Parasuraman, R. (2005). Human-automation interaction. *Reviews of Human Factors and Ergonomics*, *1*(1), 89–129. doi:10.1518/155723405783703082

Shortliffe, E. H. (1987). Computer programs to support clinical decision making. *JAMA: The Journal of the American Medical Association*, *258*(1), 61–66. doi:10.1001/jama.1987.03400010065029

Sorkin, R. D., & Woods, D. D. (1985). Systems with human monitors: A signal detection analysis. *Human-Computer Interaction*, *1*(1), 49–75.

Stanton, N. A., Young, M., & McCaulder, B. (1997). Drive-by-wire: The case of driver workload and reclaiming control with adaptive cruise control. *Safety Science*, *27*(2–3), 149–159.

Strandberg, L. (1983). On accident analysis and slip-resistance measurement. *Ergonomics*, *26*(1), 11–32.

Takemoto, P., & Jones, T. (2011, July 6). Press release—FAA celebrates 75th anniversary of air traffic control. Retrieved September 12, 2011, from www.faa.gov/news/press_releases/news_story.cfm?newsId=12903&omniRss=press_releasesAoc&cid=102_P_R

Tsukada, H., Satou, T., Iwashima, A., & Souma, T. (2000). Diagnostic accuracy of CT-guided automated needle biopsy of lung nodules. *American Journal of Roentgenology*, *175*(1), 239.

van Waterschoot, B., & van der Voort, M. (2009). Implementing human factors within the design process of Advanced Driver Assistance Systems (ADAS). *Engineering Psychology and Cognitive Ergonomics*, 461–470.

Wickens, C. D., & Dixon, S. R. (2007). The benefits of imperfect diagnostic automation: A synthesis of the literature. *Theoretical Issues in Ergonomics Science*, *8*(3), 201.

Wiener, E. L. (1985). Beyond the sterile cockpit. *Human Factors: The Journal of the Human Factors and Ergonomics Society*, *27*(1), 75–90.

Wiener, E. L. (1989). *Human factors of advanced technology ("glass cockpit") transport aircraft* (NASA Contractor Report No. NASA Contractor Report 177528). Moffett Field, CA: NASA Ames Research Center.

Wiener, E. L., & Curry, R. (1980). Flight-deck automation: Promises and problems. *Ergonomics, 23*(10), 995–1011. doi:10.1080/00140138008924809

Woods, D. D., Johannesen, L. J., Cook, R. I., & Sarter, N. (1994). *Behind human error: Cognitive systems, computers and hindsight.* Technical Report CSERIAC SOAR 94-01 Dayton, OH: University of Dayton Research Institute. Retrieved from http://www.dtic.mil/cgi-bin/GetTRDoc?Location=U2&doc=GetTRDoc.pdf&AD=ADA492127

17

Supporting Human-System Performance

In its analysis of the *Exxon Valdez* accident, the National Transportation Safety Board (NTSB) does not specifically call attention to inadequacies of the information display. It does, however, criticize the third mate for not taking more visual fixes to more accurately compute the vessel's position, and does criticize the Valdez Terminal Control for not monitoring the position of vessels more precisely. It is possible that the entire accident could have been avoided had better information been available to the third mate about the true position of the *Exxon Valdez* and, particularly, predictor information about the near future course of the vessel. In aviation, where time-critical decisions must be made rapidly, a great deal of attention has been devoted to reducing pilot and air traffic control error by means of visual, auditory, and tactile displays. Displays are the primary means of developing and maintaining situation awareness. Research programs within the military, FAA, and NASA have been directed at ways to provide information displays that take advantage of how the operator processes information, avoiding the bottlenecks in information acquisition discussed in Chapter 10. The volume of literature on the topic of information display is vast and we can do no more than provide a glimpse into the lessons learned through research and trial and error. Our discussion will be structured around two different kinds of information required: alerts and alarms, which direct the operator's attention to a new or emerging condition, and displays of state information, which provide the knowledge on which to form awareness of a situation and plan action.

ALARMS AND ALERTS

Alarms and *alerts*, as their names imply, are displays whose primary goal is to capture the operator's attention and divert it from an ongoing task to deal with a new goal that the system has determined to be urgent. The two are distinguished principally by the degree of urgency implied. An *alert* is meant to call attention to a developing situation that the operator should factor into plans for the near future, while an alarm generally requires a more immediate response. A common alert in the car is a light that comes on to remind the driver that the gas tank is low; another is the familiar sound that occurs when email arrives. In the cockpit, there are a number of auditory, visual, and tactile alerts; in the car this is usually done via red lights on the dashboard; in the operating room or critical care units, there are a number of auditory alerts and flashing lights. The principal design issue for a given context is to identify a sensory signal that will be both distinct from other sensory signals in the ongoing environment and of a nature that will automatically capture attention and interrupt the operator (e.g., pilot, driver, doctor, or anesthesiologist), causing the operator to suspend ongoing task processing for the new goal of evaluating the alert. Alarm and alert displays are often designed so that the alerting signal provides some information on the system involved or the nature of the problem, although such information is secondary. For example, the auditory signal for a stall in an aircraft is a unique sound whose occurrence should immediately tell the pilot that the aircraft is in danger of stalling (losing lift on the wings and falling from the sky). Through training, pilots can come to recognize the stall warning almost as soon as they become aware there is a problem.

Sensory Characteristics of Good Alerts and Alarms

By definition, if an alarm or alert is to interrupt an operator, whose attention is directed elsewhere in service of a different goal, the sensory signal must be physically salient. Generally, high-intensity signals (bright, loud) whose frequency is in regions distinct from that of the background noise have been typical choices. A baby's cry is a good example. It has been shown that a cry from a normal baby elicits a heart-rate response from adults; a cry from a high-risk baby elicits a greater change in heart rate from baseline (Zeskind, 1987). As the baby becomes more agitated and desires more immediate attention, it conveys this by crying louder. Fire alarms; emergency police, fire, or ambulance sirens; and other public warning systems create their unique distinguishing sound by varying pitch and amplitude over time, creating "wavering" or oscillating sounds that are not part of the typical background.

Even though high-intensity signals are by far the most typical alarm or alert signals, this is not always the case, nor always the most effective. Work in intensive care facilities has found that doctors and nurses can be quite sensitive to changes in background sounds if those sounds are carefully matched to the physical systems they are monitoring (Sanderson et al., 2008; Watson & Sanderson, 2004). A simulation study by Watson and Sanderson (2004) tested the ability of an auditory representation of breathing (sonification) to alert the doctor to changes in patient respiration. Their studies compared the ability of doctors to respond to faults introduced in the patient's respiration presented either using standard displays or using the sonified display. Their sonified display represented breathing using pitches that rose and fell in proportion to the rate of breathing, while the amplitude profile of the pitches conveyed the strength of the breathing, becoming softer as the breathing became weaker. The standard intensive care displays visually depict the amplitude and frequency of respiration using lines above the visual display of heartbeat. The doctor must physically orient toward the display and visually inspect each of the lines. In all conditions, trained anesthesiologists sustained very high levels of patient monitoring. However, in one study they found that performance on a secondary, arithmetic judgment, task was performed better with the sonified display of respiration than with the standard displays alone. This suggests that the sonified displays were effective alerting displays, allowing doctors to monitor for exceptions using fewer cognitive resources.

Thus far, we have concentrated principally on auditory alerts and alarms. In general, emergency alarms contain both visual and auditory components. Which is more effective will likely depend on the environment in which the alarm is being delivered. There are both practical and empirical reasons for thinking that auditory signals are the most effective. Because vision is our primary sensory modality, most displays of information tend to be visual displays. For complex domains, such as nuclear power plants, aircraft cockpits, or intensive care units, this means that there are many visual displays and display clutter is a problem. Thus, there is simply less competition for attention when using an auditory signal.

Auditory signals may be more effective for other reasons as well. When spatial attention is focused at a specific location or instrument, we are less sensitive to visual signals at other locations (Posner, 1980; Remington, 1980; Sperling & Reeves, 1976). In contrast, auditory signals can be processed regardless of where the user is looking (Baldwin, in press; Baldwin & Garcia, in press). Moreover, after detecting the alert, it may be desirable to complete the ongoing task before handling the alert. A visual alert that is effective in capturing attention may make it more difficult to focus attention elsewhere, reducing the operator's efficiency. It is also the case that the most effective visual alerts involve both color (usually red) and blinking. Because most modern computer-based displays contain many colors, blinking helps to physically separate the alert signal. However, blinking reduces the readability of text. Thus, if the information needed to process the fault is blinking, people may find it distracting (van Orden, Divita, & Shim, 1993). Auditory alerts have fewer of these issues. Although the noise can be bothersome, it does not direct spatial attention, as would a localized visual signal. Thus, it is likely to interfere less with the encoding of visual information; further, it will not degrade the processing of visual information as blinking does. Finally, there is evidence to suggest that people may respond more quickly to auditory alerts (Liu, 2001) than to visual alerts, although this result has been questioned (see, e.g., Kohfeld, 1971; Niemi & Näätänen, 1981).

Design Considerations in Alerts and Alarms

In addition to the ability of the physical signal to capture the operator's attention, other characteristics of the situation will determine whether the alert or alarm allows the operator to deal efficiently with the problem. One issue to consider is how much of the operator's attention should immediately be devoted to the condition causing the alert or alarm. In the case of alerts, where a timely, but not necessarily immediate, response is required, the continued presence of the alert may interfere with other ongoing tasks (Woods, 1995). In situations in which an immediate response is required, it has proven critical to provide operators with exact information as to the response they should make. This frees them from the cognitively demanding tasks of assessing the situation, selecting courses of actions, and evaluating prospective courses of action. An example of this is the Traffic Alerting and Collision Avoidance System (TCAS), which is now mandatory equipment on all aircraft flying into major U.S. airports. Unlike the conflict probes currently installed in air traffic control, which detect potential conflicts 20 minutes in the future, TCAS is designed to provide emergency collision avoidance in the one- to five-minute time frame.

It is often the final barrier to a conflict. When the system recognizes an imminent collision, it is not possible for the crew members of the respective aircraft to locate each other and execute a maneuver that will be sure to avoid the conflict (i.e., the maneuvers would have to be coordinated to be effective, which would require communication). Instead, TCAS issues commands to the pilot to, for example, "Climb, Climb, Climb" or "Bank Right, Bank Right, Bank Right." The voice for the TCAS commands is loud and distinct in timbre. Pilots have been taught not to question the commands, but simply to execute them.

A similar "directive" alarm has been implemented for stall warnings on some types of commercial aircraft. A stall warning alerts the pilot to a configuration of the aircraft in which it will lose lift on the wings, causing it to fall. The aircraft orientation has to be stabilized so that air flows more smoothly across the wings. Often, the proper response is counterintuitive: pitch the nose down so that the plane descends nose first. Most stall warning systems include vibrating the control column (stick shaker) to encourage the pilot to take immediate action.

Human Factors Issues with Alerts and Alarms

A number of problems have been documented with alerts and alarms, chiefly in aviation and nuclear power plant operation and, more recently, intensive care units (Sanderson, Crawford, Savill, Watson, & Russell, 2004; Sarter, 2000; Seagull & Sanderson, 2001; Seagull, Wickens, & Loeb, 2001; Watson, Sanderson, & John Russell, 2004; Watson, Sanderson, & Russell, 2000; Woods, 1995; Xiao, Mackenzie, Seagull, & Jaberi, 2000). One issue, often referred to as the "alarm problem" (Sarter, 2000; Woods, 1995), occurs when there is a failure in a system that triggers multiple alarms. In a complex system with multiple coupled systems, each system will generally be associated with an alarm to alert the operator of a fault or abnormal condition in that system. The problem is that a failure in one system can lead to a failure in any or all of the coupled systems. The accident at the Three Mile Island nuclear plant typifies this problem (Office of Inspection and Enforcement, 1979). The original coolant temperature problem spawned multiple alarms as it spread to other plant systems. Operators complained that the difficulty of diagnosing the problem was exacerbated by the presence of loud continuous alarms.

The alarm problem is related to another well-documented issue with alarms and alerts: Operators turn them off. Whereas the alarm problem just described relates to excessive and interfering noise from cascading alarms, turning alarms off is generally associated with unacceptable false alarm rates; that is, the alarms regularly trigger in the absence of a fault. It is, of course, illegal to disable alarms on commercial aircraft. Nevertheless, even safety-conscious and responsible crews have been known to disable alarms that frequently trigger under other-than-fault situations (i.e., false alarm) because the alarm is a nuisance that interferes with performance under both normal and abnormal situations. An example of this is the Ground Proximity Warning System (GPWS) found on all commercial aircraft. The purpose of the GPWS is to alert the crew when they are too close to terrain or are approaching terrain at an unacceptable rate. Early versions of the GPWS frequently sounded false alarms on standard approaches to many airports. Pilots and crew would routinely disable the circuit breaker associated with them. Such behavior contributed to an accident in Escambia Bay, Florida, in 1972. The aircraft was too low on approach (because of other faults) and crashed into the bay. The GPWS had sounded, only to be disabled 9 seconds later by the flight engineer. Several accidents on takeoff have occurred because of faulty configuration of flaps or slats without the standard configuration warning alert sounding. It has not been determined whether the alarms failed to sound because of a failure in electrical power, the alarm itself, or the crew having disabled it (National Transportation Safety Board, 1978). As might be suspected, excessive false-alarm rates also give rise to ignored warnings even if the alarms are not turned off (for an analysis, see Sorkin & Woods, 1985).

In part, the alarm problem and the response of operators to false alarms are related to the ability of the alarm signal to capture attention. The signal is designed to be distracting. There is also a question of whether such a signal effectively orients the operator to the emergency, or instead produces first a sense of startle and confusion. Issues of interpreting alarms have been documented in aviation (Sarter, 2000; Woods, 1995) and emergency intensive care units (Sanderson, Liu, & Jenkins, 2009; Seagull & Sanderson, 2001). Part of the problem is the nature of the interruption itself. As we discussed in Chapter 10, it takes time and cognitive effort to switch tasks. Because most alarms do not have special signatures that can be distinguished without attention, the occurrence of an alarm imposes an additional task on the operator: that of interpreting the sensory signal and formulating a new interpretation of the scene.

There have been a number of suggestions that presenting trend information would be more useful than simply sounding an alarm. The success of the respiration sonification in intensive care (Sanderson et al., 2004; Seagull & Sanderson, 2001; Watson & Sanderson, 2004) is an example of this. By providing continual background information as to the patient's respiration, the display can alert the operator to an impending situation before it becomes critical. Future research will be required to determine how well continual-trend information would work across a range of environments.

INFORMATION DISPLAYS

In contrast to alarms and alerts, the goal of information displays is to provide the data needed to efficiently and safely control a situation. In the critical care ward, this can be patient parameters, including heart rate, respiration, and other vital signs; in the car this can be the speed, engine temperature, and other information on the dash; for the aircraft cockpit, there are a tremendous number of systems whose state must be monitored. The amount of information to be monitored in modern commercial airliners or high-performance military aircraft is too large to devote a single dial at a specific location to each piece. Instead, there are *multifunction displays* that allow the pilot or crew to flip through a number of separate information screens, each displaying data on some specific system or function. The principal design challenge for information displays is how to organize information presentation so that operators can easily acquire and interpret it. The layout of information can also facilitate or inhibit efficient orienting of attention. For example, in a car, the primary displays for speed, rpm, fuel, and engine temperature are located in the driver's line of sight, whereas the heating/air conditioning is generally located off center. This allows the driver to easily monitor the road and check system state. In the cockpit this has been further advanced by the use of heads-up displays (HUDs). A HUD projects flight (and, for military, weapons) information onto the windscreen, or in some cases to a head-mounted display (HMD), allowing the pilot to monitor system state without having to look away from the outside view. This illustrates one way the design of the display can foster an efficient allocation of attention: by placing important information to facilitate access. Other ways of directing attention include using color to highlight important information, grouping information by function (or other metrics of relatedness), and where possible assigning specific pieces of information to specific spatial locations. The spacing of information on the display will also affect how easily it will be to attend to that information. If too many data pieces are packed into too little space, crowding can occur and it will take longer to select any individual piece of data (Pelli, 2008; Pelli, Palomares, & Majaj, 2004). If, however, information that is often acquired together is placed too far apart, excessive effort will be required to acquire it and generate the possibility that operators will rely on memory rather than search for the entire set of data.

The ability of an information display to direct attention efficiently will aid the primary goal of clear presentation of state information. That said, factors other than the distribution of attention will affect how easily information is comprehended. As a general principle, *the less mental effort required for comprehension, the better the display*. This principle is often given as advice to *minimize the number of mental operations* needed to acquire, comprehend, and respond to the information. How this is instantiated in practice will depend on the details of the task, the environment, and the user goals. A few examples will give a more concrete idea of what this principle means. We present these not as design guidelines, per se, but rather as examples of characteristics that, if followed, should improve the ability of a display to convey information.

Transform Information to Take Advantage of Human Perceptual Systems

The images of distant galaxies made so clear by the Hubbell Space Telescope are received on Earth as digital images. That means that every picture element (pixel) is described completely by a number specifying its luminance and color. All the information we have about that image is contained in the numbers. Yet, unless we wanted to know the value of a single pixel, that numeric information would not be very enlightening. Instead, the numbers are assigned colors according to a formula. By using color we see patterns that connect similar numbers into regions of similar color, and our visual systems see patterns that would be much more difficult to discern using only numbers. This is an example of transforming information to take advantage of humans' perceptual systems. With the numbers alone, the perceptual system shows us a fragmented display; the information that we really want is contained in the value of the numbers, not their physical appearance. The use of color transforms the image so that the relevant information is incorporated into the physical appearance.

Match Perceptual Cues to the Nature of the Judgment

The practice of transforming information that is conceptual into a representation that is perceptual reduces the demands placed on central processing operation and replaces them with those on visual or auditory processing. Consider another example. Assume that you are flying an aircraft during a refueling operation, which entails connecting a hose and nozzle on your aircraft with the hose and matching nozzle from the aircraft in front. The maneuver requires your aircraft to slowly catch up to the leading aircraft, which must fly at a fixed speed. Your task requires you to assess the rate of change of your position relative to that of the leading aircraft. This is an example of a dynamic judgment in an analog frame of reference. The judgment is dynamic because you need to monitor the rate at which the distance is changing, and analog because the space is a continuous space. A digital representation of distance from the leading aircraft would require you to read the numbers as they scrolled by to determine if you were moving toward or away from the lead aircraft. That is, the digital display conveys the relevant information (rate of change of distance) conceptually, requiring you to read and decode it. Moreover, in this example you, as the pilot, would need not only distance information and rate of change of distance, but also horizontal and vertical alignment. These are inherently analog spatial judgments that would be most compatible with an equivalent analog representation that integrated the disparate sources into a single picture. Yet, just prior to contact, you would need very precise information about distance and closing rates. This precise information is best supplied by digital readings.

A more familiar example of matching the perceptual cues to the nature of the judgment can be seen in reading dials and data graphs. The top panel of Figure 17.1 shows four dials that display the state of a part of a larger system. For our purposes, they could be pressure, fluid level, temperature, and output power. Each dial has a normal range in which it should operate, as well as a larger range of values below and above that range, which indicate an out-of-tolerance reading. One way to align the dials for operator examination would be to put them in a row, as in the top panel of Figure 17.1, with the zero values aligned on the left. Note, however, that the judgment the operator would normally make is whether all three dials are reading normally. With the dials aligned as in the top row, she would have to inspect each individually to determine if the needle were in the gray (normal) zone. The alternative arrangement in the bottom row orients the dials so that the normal ranges are aligned. Now when the operator checks, she can easily detect that the four are normal by the perceptual alignment of the needles. Notice that this makes use of the powerful orientation-detection capabilities of the visual system, which automatically detects line orientation and deviations from a common orientation, and requires little direct comparison, which would involve more resource-driven limited-capacity processing. Also note that this would not necessarily be the optimal way to orient any individual display. We have a natural tendency to represent numbers on a left-to-right number line with the lowest on the left. This suggests that any individual dial would benefit from having the smallest numbers on the left, or, in the case of quantities like altitude, on the bottom.

The bottom row of Figure 17.1 takes advantage of an *emergent property* of visual processing. At a local-detail level, each dial can be examined against its own normal state. The alignment of the needles, however, creates a new, more global perceptual property that can also convey useful information. The effect of emergent properties can also be seen in data graphs. In Figure 17.2, we have plotted the same data in two formats. Graph (a) is a bar graph and graph (b) is a connected line graph. Notice how the bar graph invites one to attend to the individual comparisons, whereas the line graph invites one to attend to the

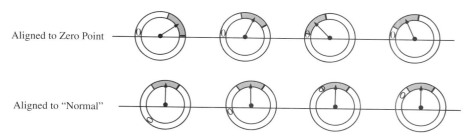

Figure 17.1 Emergent properties in human vision. Each "gauge" has a zero point and a normal operating range, indicated by the shaded portion.

pattern of each variable over the conditions on the abscissa. Indeed, an important property that separates graphs from tables is that graphs make use of preattentive visual processing to provide information without resource-demanding activities such as reading or comparing two values (Cleveland, 1993; Cleveland & McGill, 1985, 1987).

Choose Perceptual Depictions Compatible with Internal Representations

Earlier we discussed how stimulus compatibility can affect response time. People are faster and more accurate when the display is compatible with the response. Examples of this are

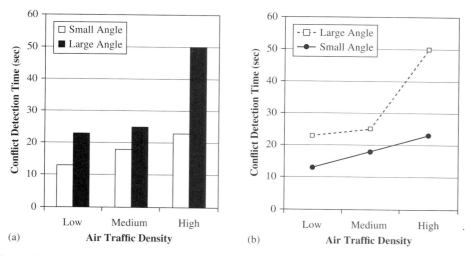

Figure 17.2 Conflict detection times as a function of the size of the angle formed by a conflict pair and the density (number) of aircraft in a sector. In graph (a), data are plotted as a column bar graph; in graph (b) the same data are plotted as connected lines. In graph (a), attention is drawn to the comparison at each density level; in graph (b) the lines draw attention to the relationship of each angle to the density. *Source:* Data from Remington, Johnston, Ruthruff, Gold, and Romera (2000).

numerous, but a study by Duncan (1977, 1978) shows how the spatial correspondence of the arrangement of items on the screen can interact with the spatial layout of the fingers. Duncan had participants respond to the onset of one of four lights arrayed in a row on a monitor. In the *compatible* condition, subjects responded to the lights from left to right by pressing the forefinger, middle finger, ring finger, and little finger, respectively, of the right hand. The response in that condition corresponded in a natural way to the spatial configuration of the fingers. There were three incompatible conditions in which the responses were not mapped in such a straightforward correspondence. In *consistent* conditions, a single rule was applied to generate the mapping, but all responses were noncorresponding. In the *inconsistent* conditions some fingers were mapped in a corresponding way, others in a noncorresponding way. Response times to press the correct key in the compatible corresponding conditions were between 400–500 msec depending on the experiment. They were between 500–600 msec in the consistent conditions, and between 600–700 msec in the inconsistent conditions. This highlights two important compatibility considerations. First, spatial compatibility leads to faster and more accurate responses. Second, consistency also promotes faster and more accurate responding. Research on helicopter displays confirmed this, showing that when the displays were arranged in a compatible arrangement, there were significant savings in both time and workload (Hartzell, Dunbar, Beveridge, & Cortilla, 1983).

Even when responses are not spatially compatible, performance can be improved if people can apply a single rule to generate the response (Newell, 1990). This result is consistent with our earlier analysis of information theory, in that a situation with a different rule for different fingers generates more uncertainty than does a simple rule that applies to all fingers. The compatibility principle applies not just to response format, but also to the match between the information presentation and the internal mental representations that govern our analysis of the world. For example, people have a strong tendency to represent numbers on a mental number line running from low on the left to high on the right, a characteristic that can be seen in response times to low and high numbers (Fias, 1996). Consequently, it would be counter to this internal representation to indicate a high on the left.

The match to internal representations can be subtler with complex data. Figure 17.3 shows four aircraft displays of attitude, which indicates how the aircraft is oriented relative to the ground (i.e., banking left or right, pitched up or down). The top-left dial shows a basic display similar to that found in most modern aircraft. The horizon is indicated as the straight edge separating the "sky" (white in this depiction) from the "ground" (gray). In this simple display, the aircraft is indicated by the shorter horizontal line with the vertical line running through it. In level flight the horizontal aircraft line is superimposed on the edge representing the horizon. When the pilot pitches the nose up to climb, the angle of the climb is indicated by the widening gap between the horizontal aircraft line and the edge of the horizon. Similarly, when the pilot pitches the nose down to descend, the angle of descent is indicated by the distance of the aircraft line below the horizon edge. In Figure 17.3 (a), then, the aircraft is in a shallow climb and a roll to the right (30° bank angle). What is the best way to indicate a change in the attitude of the aircraft? The standard display, shown in Figure 17.3 (a), keeps the aircraft symbol constant and orients the horizon line to correspond to what the pilot would see looking outside the windscreen. This is referred to as an *inside-out* representation as it corresponds to the pilot's view from inside the

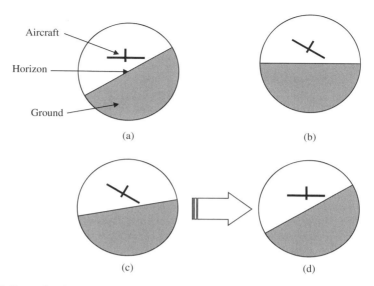

Figure 17.3 Example of (a) standard inside-out attitude display showing a 30° bank to the right and (b) an outside-in display of the same bank angle. Diagrams (c) and (d) show how this would be represented on a frequency-separated display. The representation in (c) shows the initial response to the bank command. The aircraft symbol rotates as it would in the outside-in display in (b) as the horizon begins to rotate toward its final position. In (d) the aircraft symbol has rotated back to its horizontal orientation while the horizon line now reflects the inside-out orientation of (a). By "quickening" the display with the initial rotation of the aircraft, the pilot gets immediate feedback as to the control action and predictive information about the future state of the aircraft.

cockpit. An alternate way to display the same bank and climb information is to keep the horizon fixed and change the angle of the aircraft symbol. This is shown in the upper-right dial in Figure 17.3 (b) for the same bank to the right. This is referred to as an *outside-in* representation, as it gives a view as if looking at the aircraft from the outside. The outside-in representation is compatible with the spatial movement of the control stick. As the stick is moved to the right, the aircraft symbol changes correspondingly. However, the outside-in view is incompatible with what the pilot sees looking outside the aircraft. When looking out the windscreen, the pilot sees the world as tilted, not the aircraft she is in. Thus, the outside-in representation is not compatible with the pilot's *frame of reference*.

To increase the compatibility of the display with the pilot's frame of reference, most modern attitude displays keep the aircraft symbol fixed and move the horizon. This way, a pilot who looks at the display and then looks out the window can directly compare the two without having to perform mental transformations, which would be needed with the outside-in display. When pilots in training initially encounter the inside-out attitude display, it seems counterintuitive for a couple of reasons. First, it is not compatible with the spatial movement of the control stick. As the pilot moves the stick to the right, the aircraft symbol remains stationary and the horizon tilts to the left, in the opposite direction. This means that when the pilot wants to change the attitude, say to straighten the aircraft after banking, she must move the stick in a direction opposite to her natural inclination when looking at the display. The motion of the display after making the correction is also in the direction opposite the pilot's natural inclination. In emergency situations, under high stress, this could lead to errors when rapid action is required and the only information is the attitude display (as would be the case under instrument flying). Second, the control stick should affect the aircraft, not the world. Yet, the aircraft indicator doesn't change, but the world does, a counterintuitive outcome. In the same vein, the inside-out display represents the *result* of the control input, but does not reflect the actual control *input*. It gives no immediate feedback to indicate what the "commanded" state of the aircraft is. Only after the control surfaces have overcome the inertia inherent in the physical system does the attitude actually begin to change.

Studies by Roscoe and colleagues (Beringer, Williges, & Roscoe, 1975; Johnson & Roscoe, 1972; Roscoe, 1997; Roscoe & Williges, 1975; Roscoe, Corl, & Jensen, 1981) have found a pattern of errors with inside-out attitude displays consistent with the noted incompatibility between pilot expectations and the depiction and motion of the display. They attribute the cause of several accidents, including the fatal flight of John F. Kennedy, Jr., to a misperception of the attitude information that occurs most frequently in the dark or fog, where there is no visible ground reference. Flying in low-visibility conditions—through fog, clouds, or in darkness—deprives the pilot of a familiar, stable frame of reference. Because of the unusual vestibular inputs common in flying, pilots sometimes think they are flying straight and level when in fact they are banking or descending. If the pilot in such a state looks at the attitude display and sees the horizon tilted to the left, for example, the natural response is to move the stick to the right to rotate it in the clockwise direction. Of course, when the horizon is tilted to the left the aircraft is in a right bank, so moving the stick to the right actually increases the bank angle. This can lead to a "graveyard spiral" in which the aircraft loses lift and plummets uncontrollably.

Roscoe and colleagues (Beringer et al., 1975; Johnson & Roscoe, 1972; Roscoe, 1997; Roscoe & Williges, 1975; Roscoe et al., 1981) have suggested a modification of the attitude display, which they refer to as the *frequency-separated* display (sometimes also referred to as a *quickened display*) in which both the horizon and aircraft symbol move in response to a stick input, but at different frequencies. When the pilot moves the control stick to the right, the display immediately shows the aircraft banking to the right, as it would in an outside-in display. Then, more gradually the horizon tilts leftward, and the aircraft symbol rotates back to its original horizontal position. *Frequency separation* refers to this timing difference and to the fact that the aircraft symbol returns to horizontal more rapidly than the horizon. Note how this simple change increases the overall compatibility of the display. The pilot gets immediate feedback on the control input from a change in the aircraft symbol that corresponds in a natural way to the movement of the stick. An incorrect input will be immediately recognized as such because the aircraft—the system controlled by the stick—will show its commanded state clearly. The frequency-separated display actually incorporates the immediate feedback and direct control of an outside-in display with the perceptual compatibility of the inside-out display. Research has suggested that this display does improve performance (Beringer et al., 1975; Roscoe, 1997; Roscoe & Williges, 1975).

Issues with an inside-out display versus an outside-in display have also arisen in areas more familiar to all of us: the GPS map displays now common in cars and cell phones.

Should the map be oriented so that north is up or the direction of travel is up? The student is encouraged to think about this in the context of the previous discussion before proceeding. A north-up orientation is inherently an outside-in configuration; it displays the car in its surroundings as it would appear if viewed from above (a God's-eye perspective). Having such a vantage point is very helpful in calculating alternate routes to a known destination. The global view, with a fixed perspective, makes it easy to choose streets that will take you in the direction you want to travel. The downside is that the steering-wheel inputs will be compatible with the observed path of the car only when the car is headed north. If the car is headed south, moving the wheel to the right will make the car symbol go left. This adds mental calculations to the task of determining which way to turn, as the driver now must rotate the frame of reference to correspond with that of the map display. These days, GPS maps in cars mostly use the inside-out representation that rotates the map to keep the path-up orientation. Now, movements of the steering wheel produce corresponding movements of the car symbol on the map. This makes it easy to follow directions, but difficult to use the map in calculating a route from one place to the next. The location of the destination is always changing, so it is hard to see if you are making progress in that direction with each turn. Nonetheless, the inside-out representation fits well with the instruction—following nature of such maps. The driver is not expected to discover the path, just to follow the path given. The compatibility is then a necessary condition for effective use. The example does illustrate how the goals of a task can determine which format is preferable. It points to the necessity of a careful cognitive task analysis that can determine the goals of the operator, choose the information most critical to those goals, and help guide the selection of an appropriate representation (see also Olmos, Wickens, & Chudy, 2000).

Provide Feedback

It is worth calling attention to the role of feedback in the preceding example. The lack of adequate feedback can make it difficult to maintain awareness of the situation. Indeed, a problem with sophisticated automation, as discussed earlier, is that it often does not provide feedback as to its state. Further, devices such as the autopilot and flight management systems on modern aircraft change internal modes without alerting the operator. Recall that the autopilot on the *Exxon Valdez* gave no indication of its state, a fact that could have led to the accident. Without feedback, operators have no perceptual event telling them that an action has been completed successfully. In 1995, American Airlines Flight 965 crashed into a mountain (controlled flight into terrain) while on approach to Cali, Columbia. The crew had inadvertently set the wrong waypoint into the flight management system. The waypoint they entered was very similar to the one for Cali. The investigative report of the accident (Aeronautica Civil of The Republic of Colombia, 1995) concludes that the flight management system provided inadequate feedback to alert the crew that the wrong waypoint had been entered.

In addition to the importance of timely feedback in maintaining situation awareness, delays in feedback can also affect productivity. In early computer systems, the response time of the computer to keyboard inputs could be slow, with consequent delays in seeing the letter that was typed. Research on programmer productivity showed that delays as short as a quarter of a second could slow the completion of programming tasks, impairing productivity and reducing job satisfaction (Barber & Lucas Jr., 1983; Brady, 1986; Butler,

1983; Doherty & Thedani, 1982). The relationship of productivity and creativity to the timeliness of feedback has been related to the benefit of keeping neural circuits active (see Brady, 1986). Delays of as little as a quarter to half a second allow for decay of the complex patterns of neural activation that hold together the elements of a thought.

Use Presentation Techniques That Minimize Demand for Focal Visual Attention

Because so much of our information comes from visual displays that require focal attention to read or interpret, the operator is often visually overloaded, compared with auditory or tactile information. This has led to several calls to develop auditory displays that can offload or augment the visual information. As we discussed in our treatment of information flow, perceptual processing can be done in parallel for visual and auditory information, making it possible to timeshare the two more effectively than with two or more visual displays (see, e.g., Sanderson et al., 2009; Sanderson et al., 2008; Sarter, 2000). We presented the sonified displays of respiration in the section on alerts and alarms, but it is important to note that these displays cross a somewhat artificial boundary in that they present continuous information about the state of the patient's respiratory function (Sanderson et al., 2009; Watson & Sanderson, 2004).

According to the model of information flow presented earlier, it should be possible to make use of both visual and tactile information if the judgments can be made perceptually, without resource-demanding central processing. In aviation, for example, peripheral visual information appears to play an important role in maneuvering the aircraft when close to the ground. The absence of peripheral information has been shown to degrade the quality of the landing (Roscoe, 1948; Roscoe & Williges, 1975; Roscoe et al., 1981). The effectiveness of peripheral visual input is apparent once it is understood that motion through the world creates visual flow fields (Gibson, 1958). The rate at which objects move by us is inversely related to their distance: closer objects move faster than objects further away. The visual system naturally processes these differences in motion without the need for us to reason about them (Gibson, 1958).

Similarly, experiments have shown that tactile displays can provide spatial information to allow the blind to navigate (Brabyn, 1982; Gemperle, Ota, & Siewiorek, 2001; Hui Tang & Beebe, 2006). These devices couple a camera, generally worn on the forehead or head, to a bank of vibrating rods. The camera image is transformed into a vibrotactile pattern. It appears that blind individuals can use such devices not only to navigate, but also to read or interpret pictures and sound (Brewster & Brown, 2004; Gemperle et al., 2001; Kamel & Landay, 2002; Wall & Brewster, 2006). There is also emerging evidence that tactile information would improve performance when coupled with visual information. A study of driving (Van Erp & Van Veen, 2004) shows that vibrotactile feedback delivered through the steering wheel reduced the driver's measured perceptual and cognitive load and reduced navigation errors.

Use Perceptual Distinctions That Match Visual and Auditory Capabilities

In the preceding sections we commented on the benefits of taking advantage of perceptual processing, especially over resource-demanding limited-capacity processing. In doing so, it is important to consider characteristics of the visual system (and auditory system)

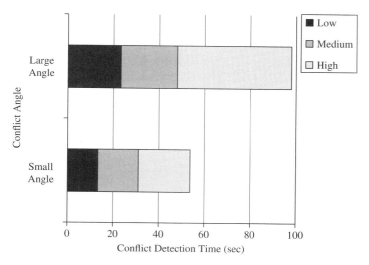

Figure 17.4 Data from Figure 17.2 plotted as a stacked bar graph. Note how the relationships in each stack can be judged roughly against one another by inspecting the size of the rectangles. Exact comparisons require estimation of starting and ending points. Comparisons of the middle and end components of different stacks require adjustment based on the starting points, which are a function of earlier stack elements. *Source:* Data from Remington et al. (2000).

that may bias or distort accurate perception. A number of these have been documented in graphing scientific and statistical data (see Cleveland, 1993; Cleveland & McGill, 1985, 1987). For example, it is common to display data in stacked graphs, with the values of several quantities forming a single column or bar. This can create a problem in estimating the relative extent of the stacked quantities. The visual system is good at judging extent if the quantities being judged are aligned to the same baseline, but not in judging absolute length per se. In Figure 17.4, for example, judging the relative magnitude of the black rectangles yields much more accurate judgments than either of the gray rectangles. Because the gray rectangles start from different baselines (determined by the magnitude of the black), it is necessary to judge the actual length of each, a task that humans cannot do as accurately (Cleveland & McGill, 1985).

The visual system also tends to judge the slant of lines in reference to the angle with the horizontal, not by reference to the slope of the line itself (Cleveland & McGill, 1985, 1987; see also Marr, 1982; Stevens, 1981). This has consequences when judging the relative slope of lines. Two lines with the same relative slope will be judged differently depending on whether the ratio of the angles is different. In Figure 17.5 we illustrate this by showing the same graph at three different aspect ratios. Experiments on graph perception show that subjects judge the ratio of the slope of line segment A to line segment B to be different in each of the three cases. In the tall and flat graphs, the slope ratio is the same as in the square graph. What is different is that the ratio of the angles has changed and is much smaller in the tall and flat graphs. This is one illustration of how the frame of a graph can visually distort the perception.

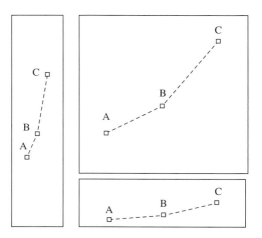

Figure 17.5 Frame effects in graph perception. The apparent slope of the line from A to B and B to C looks larger inside a tall narrow frame than a wider frame, and smallest inside the short and wide rectangle.

Apply the Proximity Compatibility Principle

We have organized the presentation of display characteristics around specific design features that have known interactions with human visual and cognitive processing. Wickens and colleagues (e.g., Carswell & Wickens, 1996; Wickens & Carswell, 1995) have proposed and tested a unified theoretical framework relating many of these characteristics, from which they have developed a set of general display guidelines. The *proximity* component says that separate displays representing data from similar systems or displays that are often scanned together should be located in close proximity to each other. The *compatibility* component of the theory reflects the concerns with compatibility expressed earlier in this chapter. One of the consequences of this theory is its suggestion that integrating multiple displays into a single display will yield processing advantages. The single displays are referred to as *object displays*. How the information is integrated will depend on the information requirements of the operator. Investigations into the utility of the integrated displays support our earlier observations that both emergent visual properties and specific information are often required to perform the task.

CREATE BARRIERS

Many reports, from both the National Transportation Safety Board (NTSB) and the Aviation Safety Reporting System (ASRS), look for factors that contribute to failures of human performance. In these reports, it is common to note that other individuals, organizations, training, or the environment contribute to human error. These reports highlight the fact that human error is affected by context. The observation that human error is both conditioned by context and, as widely acknowledged, inescapable (Reason, 1990a, 1990b,

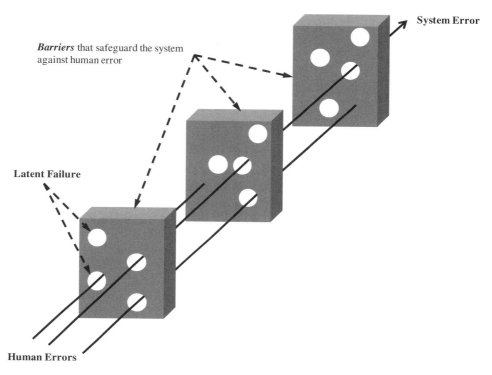

Barriers that safeguard the system
against human error

Latent Failure

System Error

Human Errors

Figure 17.6 Swiss cheese model showing how human error leads to system error. Barriers prevent latent failures that promote human error at a given layer from leading to system-wide error. Only a few errors that manage to interact with failures in all barriers will lead to system error.

2000) has led some to argue that perhaps trying to eliminate human error is not the right approach (as it is impossible). Rather, they argue that systems should be designed to erect barriers against error (Rasmussen, 1982; Rasmussen, Nixon, & Warner, 1990; Reason, 1990b). Figure 17.6 schematically depicts the idea behind barriers to system error. Figure 17.6 shows the "Swiss cheese" model (Reason, 2000) to illustrate how system safety can be achieved in the face of human error. In that model, each of the barriers (the rectangular blocks of "cheese") represents a set of system-level protections against error. The barriers are porous (the "holes"), meaning that they protect against some error types, but not all. The holes are thought to be created by *latent failures* (Reason, 1990a)—that is, decisions or actions that do not cause an error unless they occur in combination with triggering factors. Human error can lead to system error if the holes in all the layers are aligned, which would indicate that decisions made or actions taken at individual layers interacted with those at other layers to create a vulnerability to a system error.

A concrete example may make this clearer. A word processor has a spell checker that can match any typed letter string against its internal dictionary to see if it is a legitimate word. By turning on the feature that highlights a string each time a letter sequence doesn't match a dictionary entry, the user invokes one barrier against misspellings. However, the spell checkers are not good at distinguishing between legitimate words used inappropriately, such as substituting "their" for "there," or a poor choice of words. By proofreading the document, the author provides a second barrier that will catch many of these errors. Still, it is hard to read for spelling rather than meaning, and the authors are already very familiar with what they have written, making them susceptible to mistaking what they meant to say with what they actually wrote. For these reasons, it is useful to have a third reader, or a copyeditor assigned by the publisher, to serve as a check on the author. Nevertheless, some misspellings or bad word choices will still get through, because the copyeditor, like the authors, is subject to the same kind of biases toward reading for content. In the Swiss cheese model of Figure 17.6, this is depicted by the arrow through the holes, which are aligned in each layer of protection.

In more complicated systems, such as nuclear power plants, airline cockpits, or air traffic control, the barriers can consist of alarms, automatic shutdown procedures, other people, or procedures that are closely followed. An example of the latter is the checklist that an aircrew performs prior to takeoff, on landing, and in an emergency. Each aircraft has a checklist that prescribes a step-by-step sequence of actions to be performed in specific circumstances. There is a preflight checklist, a landing checklist, a checklist for emergency procedures to accommodate an individual system failure, and many more. These checklists provide barriers against errors that would happen by forgetting or not fully understanding how to configure the aircraft in all circumstances.

Accidents generally happen when several failures or exceptional circumstances occur such that the barriers are either peeled away or were not designed sufficiently to prevent a particular problem. There have, indeed, been cases in which a single error has caused a major problem. A well-known incident occurred in 1999 when NASA lost the Mars Climate Orbiter because the orbital parameters transmitted to NASA mission control were in English standard units, when the spacecraft was set to accept metric units. More generally, a single error rarely causes an accident because systems are designed with buffers that prevent single small errors from producing catastrophic results. In a sense, the Mars Climate Orbiter accentuates this point; the accident might well have been prevented had there been a barrier in place that explicitly called for all parties to agree that the measurements were in metric units.

One approach to making systems safer, then, is to add more barriers. As more layers of buffering are added, it becomes less likely that any single error will "line up" in all layers, or more formally, less likely that errors will propagate to system failures. As you might suspect, though, there is a cost in efficiency to doing so. Adding more people to check on existing operators is expensive. Even if this is done, unless errors are quite frequent, the operators monitoring the system may be faced with a vigilance problem. That is, research suggests that people are not good at detecting infrequent events, and that their performance degrades significantly as time on task increases (for one of the early descriptions of this issue, see Mackworth, 1948). Adding more alarms or high-tech system management software imposes its own load on operators and has its own failure modes. Further, adding more alarms also increases the expense of the system, sometimes at a cost in effectiveness.

Another approach to making systems safer is to decrease the number of latent conditions ("holes" in each layer). That is, we could strive to design systems that better match human capabilities, are easier to use, and in which there is a decreased likelihood of human error. It is not possible to eliminate errors entirely, but good design can minimize the propensity for errors by designing for human use. To do that, we need to understand a bit more about human error, and how error is affected by the environmental factors that shape human performance.

SUMMARY

Human error is inevitable, but there are ways in which error can be reduced. This chapter discussed ways to develop alarms, alerts, and improved displays that support the human in making decisions while operating in a complex environment. Even when errors are made, though, the error does not always lead to a poor outcome or a potentially dangerous system state. Human errors that get "caught" by the operator, the system, or colleagues do not propagate into this sort of system error. This calls attention to the importance of *barriers to system error* that prevent human error from developing into system error. This chapter described a model of how human error propagates into a system failure, and suggested ways to design barriers that can reduce system error.

REFERENCES

Aeronautica Civil of The Republic of Colombia. (1995). *Aircraft accident report: Controlled flight into terrain, American Airlines Flight 965, Boeing 757-223, N651AA, near Cali, Colombia, December 20, 1995.* Retrieved September 28, 2011, from http://sunnyday.mit.edu/accidents/calirep.html

Baldwin, C. L. (in press). *Auditory cognition and human performance: Research and applications.* Clermont, FL: CRC Press/Taylor & Francis.

Baldwin, C. L., & Garcia, A. (in press). Multi-modal and cross-modal perception: Audition. In R. R. Hoffman, P. A. Hancock, R. Parasuraman, J. R. Szalma, & M. Scerbo (Eds.), *Handbook of applied perception.* New York, NY: Cambridge University Press.

Barber, R. E., & Lucas Jr., H. C. (1983). System response time operator productivity, and job satisfaction. *Communications of the ACM, 26*(11), 972–986.

Beringer, D. B., Williges, R. C., & Roscoe, S. N. (1975). The transition of experienced pilots to a frequency-separated aircraft attitude display. *Human Factors: The Journal of the Human Factors and Ergonomics Society, 17*(4), 401–414.

Brabyn, J. A. (1982). New developments in mobility and orientation aids for the blind. *IEEE Transactions on Biomedical Engineering, BME-29*(4), 285–289. doi:10.1109/TBME.1982.324945

Brady, J. T. (1986). A theory of productivity in the creative process. *Computer Graphics and Applications, IEEE, 6*(5), 25–34.

Brewster, S., & Brown, L. M. (2004). Tactons: Structured tactile messages for non-visual information display. In A. Cockburn (Ed.) Proceedings of the 5th Australasian User Interface Conference (28), Dunedin, AU: Australian Computer Society. (pp. 15–23).

Butler, T. W. (1983). Computer response time and user performance. *Proceedings of the SIGCHI conference on human factors in computing systems* (pp. 58–62). Presented at the CHI'83, ACM. doi:10.1145/800045.801581

Carswell, C. M., & Wickens, C. D. (1996). Mixing and matching lower-level codes for object displays: Evidence for two sources of proximity compatibility. *Human Factors: The Journal of the Human Factors and Ergonomics Society*, *38*(1), 1–22. doi:10.1518/001872096778940750

Cleveland, W. S. (1993). A model for studying display methods of statistical graphics. *Journal of Computational and Graphical Statistics*, 323–343.

Cleveland, W. S., & McGill, R. (1985). Graphical perception and graphical methods for analyzing scientific data. *Science*, *229*(4716), 828–833.

Cleveland, W. S., & McGill, R. (1987). Graphical perception: The visual decoding of quantitative information on graphical displays of data. *Journal of the Royal Statistical Society. Series A (General)*, 192–229.

Doherty, W. J., & Thedani, A. J. (1982). *The economic value of rapid response time* (IBM Technical Report). Yorktown Heights, NY: IBM. Retrieved from http://www.vm.ibm.com/devpages/jelliott/evrrt.html

Duncan, J. (1977). Response selection errors in spatial choice reaction tasks. Quarterly *Journal of Experimental Psychology*, *29*(3), 415–423.

Duncan, J. (1978). Response selection in spatial choice reaction: Further evidence against associative models. *Quarterly Journal of Experimental Psychology, 30*(3), 429–440.

Fias, W. (1996). The importance of magnitude information in numerical processing: Evidence from the SNARC effect. *Mathematical Cognition*, *2*(1), 95–110.

Gemperle, F., Ota, N., & Siewiorek, D. (2001). *Design of a wearable tactile display* (pp. 5–12). Presented at the Fifth International Symposium on Wearable Computers, 2001 (IEEE Proceedings). doi:10.1109/ISWC.2001.962082

Gibson, J. J. (1958). Visually controlled locomotion and visual orientation in animals. *British Journal of Psychology*, *49*(3), 182–194. doi:10.1111/j.2044-8295.1958.tb00656.x

Hartzell, E. J., Dunbar, S. L., Beveridge, R., & Cortilla, R. (1983). *Helicopter pilot response latency as a function of the spatial arrangement of instruments and controls*. Retrieved from http://stinet.dtic.mil/oai/oai?&verb=getRecord&metadataPrefix=html&identifier=ADP001636

Hui Tang, & Beebe, D. J. (2006). An oral tactile interface for blind navigation. *IEEE Transactions on Neural Systems and Rehabilitation Engineering*, *14*(1), 116–123. doi:10.1109/TNSRE.2005.862696

Johnson, S. L., & Roscoe, S. N. (1972). What moves, the airplane or the world? *Human Factors: The Journal of the Human Factors and Ergonomics Society*, *14*(2), 107–129.

Kamel, H. M., & Landay, J. A. (2002). *Sketching images eyes-free*. In *Assets '02 Proceedings of the fifth international ACM conference on Assistive technologies* (pp. 33–40). New York, NY: ACM Press. doi:10.1145/638249.638258

Kohfeld, D. L. (1971). Simple reaction time as a function of stimulus intensity in decibels of light and sound. *Journal of Experimental Psychology*, *88*(2), 251.

Liu, Y. C. (2001). Comparative study of the effects of auditory, visual and multimodality displays on drivers' performance in advanced traveller information systems. *Ergonomics*, *44*(4), 425–442.

Mackworth, N. (1948). The breakdown of vigilance during prolonged visual search. *Quarterly Journal of Experimental Psychology*, 1, 6–21.

Marr, D. (1982). *Vision: A computational investigation into the human representation and processing of visual information*. San Francisco, CA: W. H. Freeman.

National Transportation Safety Board. (1978). *Aircraft accident report: National Airlines, Inc., Escambia Bay Pensacola, Florida, May 8, 1978* (No. AAR78-13.pdf). Washington, DC: Author.

Newell, A. (1990). *Unified theories of cognition*. Cambridge, MA: Harvard University Press.

Niemi, P., & Näätänen, R. (1981). Foreperiod and simple reaction time. *Psychological Bulletin*, *89*(1), 133.

Office of Inspection and Enforcement. (1979). *Investigation into the March 28, 1979, Three Mile Island accident* (No. NUREG-0600 (no. 50-320/79-10)). Washington, DC: U.S. Nuclear Regulatory Commission.

Olmos, O., Wickens, C. D., & Chudy, A. (2000). Tactical displays for combat awareness: An examination of dimensionality and frame of reference concepts and the application of cognitive engineering. *International Journal of Aviation Psychology*, *10*, 247–271. doi:10.1207/S15327108IJAP1003_03

Pelli, D. G. (2008). Crowding: A cortical constraint on object recognition. *Current Opinion in Neurobiology*, *18*(4), 445–451.

Pelli, D. G., Palomares, M., & Majaj, N. J. (2004). Crowding is unlike ordinary masking: Distinguishing feature integration from detection. *Journal of Vision*, *4*(12), 1136–1169.

Posner, M. I. (1980). Orienting of attention. *Quarterly Journal of Experimental Psychology*, *32*, 3–25.

Rasmussen, J. (1982). Human errors. A taxonomy for describing human malfunction in industrial installations. *Journal of Occupational Accidents*, *4*(2–4), 311–333. doi:10.1016/0376-6349(82)90041-4

Rasmussen, J., Nixon, P., & Warner, F. (1990). Human error and the problem of causality in analysis of accidents [and discussion]. *Philosophical Transactions of the Royal Society of London. Series B, Biological Sciences*, *327*(1241), 449–462.

Reason, J. (1990a). The contribution of latent human failures to the breakdown of complex systems. *Philosophical Transactions of the Royal Society of London. Series B, Biological Sciences, 327*(1241), 475–484.

Reason, J. (1990b). *Human error.* New York, NY: Cambridge University Press.

Reason, J. (2000). Human error: Models and management. *British Medical Journal, 320*(7237), 768–770. doi:10.1136/bmj.320.7237.768

Remington, R. W. (1980). Attention and saccadic eye-movements. *Journal of Experimental Psychology—Human Perception and Performance, 6,* 726–744.

Remington, R. W., Johnston, J. C., Ruthruff, E., Gold, M., & Romera, M. (2000). Visual search in complex displays: Factors affecting conflict detection by air traffic controllers. *Human Factors, 42,* 349–366.

Roscoe, S. N. (1948). The effect of eliminating binocular and peripheral monocular visual cues upon airplane pilot performance in landing. *Journal of Applied Psychology, 32*(6), 649.

Roscoe, S. N. (1997). Horizontal control reversals and the graveyard spiral. *Gateway,* 7(3) (DTIC document). 1–4.

Roscoe, S. N., Corl, L., & Jensen, R. S. (1981). Flight display dynamics revisited. *Human Factors: The Journal of the Human Factors and Ergonomics Society, 23*(3), 341–353.

Roscoe, S. N., & Williges, R. C. (1975). Motion relationships in aircraft attitude and guidance displays: A flight experiment. *Human Factors: The Journal of the Human Factors and Ergonomics Society, 17*(4), 374–387.

Sanderson, P. M., Crawford, J., Savill, A., Watson, M., & Russell, W. J. (2004). Visual and auditory attention in patient monitoring: A formative analysis. *Cognition, Technology & Work, 6*(3), 172–185.

Sanderson, P. M., Liu, D., & Jenkins, S. A. (2009). Auditory displays in anesthesiology. *Current Opinion in Anaesthesiology, 22,* 788–795.

Sanderson, P. M., Watson, M., Russell, W. J., Jenkins, S., Liu, D., Green, N., Llewelyn, K., et al. (2008). Advanced auditory displays and head-mounted displays: Advantages and disadvantages for monitoring by the distracted anesthesiologist. *Anesthesia & Analgesia, 106*(6), 1787.

Sarter, N. B. (2000). The need for multisensory interfaces in support of effective attention allocation in highly dynamic event-driven domains: The case of cockpit automation. *International Journal of Aviation Psychology, 10,* 231–245.

Seagull, F. J., & Sanderson, P. M. (2001). Anesthesia alarms in context: An observational study. *Human Factors: The Journal of the Human Factors and Ergonomics Society, 43*(1), 66.

Seagull, F. J., Wickens, C. D., & Loeb, R. G. (2001). When is less more? Attention and workload in auditory, visual, and redundant patient-monitoring conditions. *Human Factors and Ergonomics Society Annual Meeting Proceedings, 45,* 1395–1399.

Sorkin, R. D., & Woods, D. D. (1985). Systems with human monitors: A signal detection analysis. *Human-Computer Interaction, 1*(1), 49–75.

Sperling, G., & Reeves, A. (1976). Reaction-time of an unobservable response. *Bulletin of the Psychonomic Society, 8*, 247.

Stevens, K. A. (1981). The visual interpretation of surface contours. *Artificial Intelligence, 17*(1–3), 47–73. doi:10.1016/0004-3702(81)90020-5

Van Erp, J. B. F., & Van Veen, H. A. H. C. (2004). Vibrotactile in-vehicle navigation system. *Transportation Research Part F: Traffic Psychology and Behaviour, 7*(4–5), 247–256. doi:10.1016/j.trf.2004.09.003

van Orden, K. F., Divita, J., & Shim, M. J. (1993). Redundant use of luminance and flashing with shape and color as highlighting codes in symbolic displays. *Human Factors: The Journal of the Human Factors and Ergonomics Society, 35*(2), 195–204. doi:10.1177/001872089303500201

Wall, S., & Brewster, S. (2006). *Feeling what you hear: Tactile feedback for navigation of audio graphs.* ACM In Proceedings of the SIGCHI Conference on Human Factors in Computing Systems (pp. 1123–1132). New York, NY: ACM Press. doi:10.1145/1124772.1124941

Watson, M., & Sanderson, P. M. (2004). Sonification supports eyes-free respiratory monitoring and task time-sharing. *Human Factors: The Journal of the Human Factors and Ergonomics Society, 46*(3), 497.

Watson, M., Sanderson, P. M., & Russell, W. (2000). Alarm noise and end-user tailoring: The case for continuous auditory displays. *Proceedings of the 5th International Conference on Human Interaction with Complex Systems,* 75–70.

Watson, M., Sanderson, P. M., & John Russell, W. (2004). Tailoring reveals information requirements: The case of anaesthesia alarms. *Interacting with Computers, 16*(2), 271–293.

Wickens, C. D., & Carswell, C. M. (1995). The proximity compatibility principle: Its psychological foundation and relevance to display design. *Human Factors: The Journal of the Human Factors and Ergonomics Society, 37*(3), 473–494. doi:10.1518/001872095779049408

Woods, D. D. (1995). The alarm problem and directed attention in dynamic fault management. *Ergonomics, 38*(11), 2371–2393.

Xiao, Y., Mackenzie, C. F., Seagull, F. J., & Jaberi, M. (2000). Managing the monitors: An analysis of alarm silencing activities during an anesthetic procedure. *Human Factors and Ergonomics Society Annual Meeting Proceedings, 44*, 250–253.

Zeskind, P. S. (1987). Adult heart-rate responses to infant cry sounds. *British Journal of Developmental Psychology, 5*(1), 73–79.

Index